Routledge Revivals

From Mathem

CW01083555

First published in 1974. Despite the tendency of contemporary analytic philosophy to put logic and mathematics at a central position, the author argues it failed to appreciate or account for their rich content. Through discussions of such mathematical concepts as number, the continuum, set, proof and mechanical procedure, the author provides an introduction to the philosophy of mathematics and an internal criticism of the then current academic philosophy. The material presented is also an illustration of a new, more general method of approach called substantial factualism which the author asserts allows for the development of a more comprehensive philosophical position by not trivialising or distorting substantial facts of human knowledge.

From Mathematics to Philosophy

Hao Wang

Routledge
Taylor & Francis Group

First published in 1974
by Routledge & Kegan Paul

This edition first published in 2016 by Routledge
2 Park Square, Milton Park, Abingdon, Oxon, OX14 4RN
and by Routledge
711 Third Avenue, New York, NY 10017

Routledge is an imprint of the Taylor & Francis Group, an informa business

© 1974 Hao Wang

Publisher's Note
The publisher has gone to great lengths to ensure the quality of this reprint but
points out that some imperfections in the original copies may be apparent.

Disclaimer
The publisher has made every effort to trace copyright holders and welcomes
correspondence from those they have been unable to contact.

A Library of Congress record exists under LC control number: 74158590

ISBN 13: 978-1-138-68773-8 (hbk)
ISBN 13: 978-1-315-54216-4 (ebk)
ISBN 13: 978-1-138-68779-0 (pbk)

From Mathematics
to Philosophy

Hao Wang

王
浩

从 数学到哲学

London
ROUTLEDGE & KEGAN PAUL
New York Humanities Press

First published in 1974
by Routledge & Kegan Paul Ltd
Broadway House, 68–74 Carter Lane,
London EC4V 5EL
Printed in Great Britain by
Butler & Tanner Ltd, Frome and London
Copyright © Hao Wang 1974
ISBN 0 7100 7689 4

CONTENTS

v

Contents

Contents

Contents

PREFACE

Directly and indirectly logic plays an important part in much of contemporary Anglo-American academic philosophy. Sociologically, this is comfortable for those of us who are interested in both logic and philosophy. But I have for years had two interrelated misgivings. The way logic is commonly used in philosophy seems to me to do less than justice to the full richness of logic as a study of the foundations of mathematics; and the excessive emphasis on the importance of logic for philosophy, combined usually with a misapplication of logic, seems to me to have led to a far from balanced view of philosophy, especially as it is understood in the traditional sense. Moreover, the much publicized juxtaposition of logic with positivism (or empiricism or 'analytic' philosophy) has burdened logic with a guilt by association, resulting in a surprising ignorance of logic on the part of philosophers of other persuasions. This has the unfortunate consequence that not only is logic misused by those who are guided by misplaced precision, but the other philosophers also are not making what is a proper and fruitful use of logic, namely, to use it not so much explicitly but more as a way of acquiring the habit of precise thinking.

I attempt to express these misgivings in this book by putting forward an alternative view. The chapters dealing with concepts in logic and mathematics attempt to bring out what I consider to be the philosophically more interesting aspects of these concepts. The chapters on more general issues try to discuss the general nature of philosophy. And the two parts are loosely linked together by an emphasis on gross facts. The emphasis on mathematics (rather than, for example, physics or biology or history) is partly due to my lack of knowledge in the other fields, and partly due to a belief that, at the present stage of our knowledge, mathematics is specially suited to the type of general discussion of conceptual thinking which I wish to encourage. It is thought that mathematics is sufficiently rich and central to illustrate most of the basic issues in the philosophy of knowledge.

This book certainly makes no claim to a philosophical theory or a system of philosophy. In fact, for those who are convinced that philosophy should yield a theory, they may find here merely data for philosophy. However, I believe, in spite of my reservations about the possibility of philosophy as a rigorous science, that philosophy can be relevant, serious, and stable. Philosophy should try to achieve some reasonable overview. There is more philosophical value in placing things in their right perspective than in solving specific problems. Both hasty speculations and piecemeal persistence on artificial issues tend to hamper a cumulative progress in philosophy. Given the basically unsatisfactory condition of philosophy today, the line between philosophy and data for philosophy is not easily drawn. We are generally able to see whether certain statements are true and significant and of more than technical interest. There is a temptation to believe that a concentrated body of such statements on a basic concept comes close to exhausting the noncontroversial philosophical elucidations of the given concept. At any rate, this book will, it is thought, serve as an antidote to the prevailing trends in Anglo-American philosophy, and possibly help in a small way to hasten bringing about the much-needed change into more appealing directions.

An earlier draft of this book was completed about a year ago, and, during the last few months, expansions have been made in several parts, mostly as a result of discussions with Professor Kurt Gödel. I am grateful to Professor Gödel for consenting to discuss some of the topics dealt with in the following four parts: the introduction; the section on mechanical procedures (in chapter II); the chapter on the concept of set (chapter VI); and the section on mathematical arguments about minds and machines (in chapter X). Beginning from October, 1971, I have had the privilege of enjoying a number of meetings with Professor Gödel to talk about these and related matters. As a result, I have made revisions and additions in the first three parts listed above and added a new section 7 to chapter X. However, in consequence of certain basic differences in our approach to philosophy, these expanded parts generally should not be interpreted as representing Professor Gödel's views. Exceptions are the additions which have been revised and approved by him, and they are the following: section 3.1 of chapter II, section 7 of chapter X, and the attributions to him in section 2 of the introduction and in section 1 of chapter VI, namely, the paragraph on the axiom of replacement and the summary of the five principles by which we set up axioms of set theory.

HAO WANG

June, 1972

A NOTE ON THE TEXT

About three-quarters of this book consists of material previously unpublished. The remaining quarter has been published before and is now organized into broader contexts. Continuous efforts have been devoted to the writing of new chapters and the revision of old drafts since September, 1970. The actual writing and revising done during this period probably account for over a third of the book.

I and II are a quite extensively revised version of the John Locke lectures given at Oxford in the spring of 1955. The series of six lectures was under the general title 'On formalizing mathematical concepts.' The individual lectures were: 1 the relevance of logic to philosophy; 2 natural numbers; 3 the continuum; 4 consistency and reducibility; 5 the concept of computability; 6 the business of mathematical logic.

III is, with slight revisions, from 'Russell and his logic,' *Ratio*, vol. 7, 1965, pp. 1–34. IV has been largely written recently, although a small part came from a lecture of the same title given in 1955 at an Oxford colloquium. V is based on an article prepared in 1970 for the *Encyclopaedia Britannica*.

VI was written largely during the academic year 1969–70. Parts of VII are drawn from 'Process and existence in mathematics,' *Essays on the foundations of mathematics*, 1961, pp. 328–51 and 'Logic, computation and philosophy,' *L'âge de la science*, vol. 3, 1970, pp. 101–15. VIII is in part based on 'Notes on the analytic-synthetic distinction,' *Theoria*, vol. 21, 1955, pp. 158–78.

A small part of IX has been included in 'Remarks on mathematics and computers,' *Theoretical approaches to nonnumerical problem solving*, 1970, pp. 152–60. Section 6 has been published as 'Logic

xiii

and computers' in *American mathematical monthly*, vol. 72, 1965, pp. 135–40.

Parts of X were read as an Isenberg Lecture at Michigan State University on April 18, 1969; parts of X were presented on August 25, 1969, at Berkeley to a conference on 'Concepts of mind' organized by the study group on the unity of knowledge.

XI and XII have mostly been written recently except for section 4 of XI (based on 'Russell and his logic' mentioned above) and some scattered remarks (drawn from 'Russell and philosophy,' *Journal of philosophy*, vol. 63, 1966, pp. 670–3).

The Appendix consists of five previously published papers. The sources are indicated at the end. In this same category of early philosophical writings, there are left out here two papers published in Chinese, one on synthetic a priori propositions and one on language and metaphysics (in *Philosophical review* of the Chinese Philosophical Society, vol. 9, 1944, pp. 39–62, and vol. 10, 1945, pp. 35–8), as well as an uninhibited sizable master's dissertation (in Chinese) at Tsing Hua University written in 1943–5 with the title *Essays on the foundations of empirical knowledge* (1 induction; 2 truth; 3 sense data; 4 verifiability).

In recent years, I have had the opportunity of discussing many of the issues considered in this book with L. H. Tharp, D. A. Martin, and S. A. Kripke, as well as the opportunity of looking into published works by various philosophers for suggestions. Often I have, without specific explicit acknowledgments, made indirect use of oral and published observations from these sources to state what I take to be sound views shared by a number of individuals. S. Weinstein has carefully read a major portion of the manuscripts and made many helpful suggestions to improve the presentation.

May 20, 1971

INTRODUCTION

1 SUBSTANTIAL FACTUALISM AS A METHOD AND AN ANTIDOTE

The different chapters of this book are only loosely interconnected and can all be read more or less independently of one another. A number of basic concepts from the areas of logic and mathematics are selected for closer examination. But the discussions are meant to illustrate a general position on the philosophy of knowledge. The unifying theme is to take each of these basic concepts and aspects seriously and study it on its own level. The goal is to confine oneself to what is fundamental and at the same time to check the general considerations constantly against solid facts, including the facts of introspection and conceptual thinking.

The central bias (or dogma) is what might vaguely be called 'substantial factualism' or perhaps 'anthropocentric magnifactualism.' The underlying belief is in the overwhelming importance of existing knowledge for philosophy. We know more about what we know than how we know what we know. We know relatively better what we believe than what the ultimate justifications of our beliefs are. That we know what we know is an amazing brute fact, and, of all possible knowledge, what is known is the most easily accessible and it is rich enough to fertilize the most interesting philosophy of knowledge at each historical period. For example, it is surprising that man has discovered classical physics with its wide range of successful descriptive and engineering applications, Mendelian genetics with its curious simplicity and power, calculus with its coherence and applicability, and set theory with its elegance and stability. That this was possible depends on the fact that the world is the way it is, and we are the way we are. We do not possess ready-made first principles

1

which enable us to see that the world and we must be such that knowledge so impressively stable and comprehensive must arise. That classical physics and genetics are true to the extent they are suggests an orderliness of the way the world is which we had no good reasons to expect before we acquired the knowledge.

It is necessary to point out at the outset certain ambiguities and the consequent limitations of the vague position of substantial factualism. In its general conception it is not intended to apply exclusively to knowledge in the exact sciences. We are also interested in less exact knowledge and less clearly separated-out gross facts. The phenomenon of language is undoubtedly an impressive pervasive fact about human beings. Marxist philosophy and Freudian psychology are thought to reveal certain gross facts about human nature. It is an important (historical) fact that these doctrines play an important part in the contemporary human conditions, so that there is a question of how certain doctrines influence human actions extensively. More relevantly, we recognize in these doctrines a large amount of basic truth so that they provide, at least, a source of valuable suggestions for locating certain gross facts about man. Although many people are not able to embrace Marxism (say) in its full comprehensiveness, one feels that we do get a good deal of knowledge (in a broader sense than knowledge in the mathematical sciences) from its development and application. In another direction, history and fiction also tell us many general facts about the human experience. In particular, the history of philosophy is of course specially relevant to philosophy. All these areas are thought to contain rich data for the philosophical study of gross facts.

It is then difficult to separate out the truly stable and central facts and to make proper use of them in the development of philosophy. While there is a natural desire to have philosophy bear significantly on all important areas of the human experience and we are believed to be able to cultivate our intuition to reach a pretty good agreement on what the important areas are, such a desire and such a belief are not sufficient to give much definite positive content to substantial factualism as a method. It seems that a general clarification of the general position would have to depend to a considerable extent on the end results of applying the vaguely felt 'method' or attitude in large areas. In any case, it seems desirable, in the present book, to confine our attention to a narrower and more definite notion of substantial factualism that deals only with the philosophical study of knowledge in the exact sciences. And this book is meant to be a preliminary attempt to carry out such a study in some parts of the general areas of logic and mathematics.

Given this restriction to the exact sciences (and, in particular, to

2

logic and mathematics), we are able to say a few more definite things by contrasting the present position with several dominant trends in contemporary philosophy, which, moreover, are, in their foundations, largely concerned with data that fall within the range of concepts considered in this restricted domain. These trends are positivism and empiricism (particularly the two different directions of R. Carnap and W. V. Quine), and linguistic philosophy. It is thought that substantial factualism is a useful antidote to these fashionable trends. To what extent this present position is compatible with other larger views which are also against these current trends will not be considered extensively in this book.

It is thought that positivism does not have enough respect for gross scientific facts. In particular, Carnap's position often lays too much emphasis on empty artificial structures to the neglect of the serious factual (or rather conceptual) content. A more extensive discussion of Carnap is contained in chapter XII, section 3. While Quine seems to speak in favor of some sort of factualism, there appears to be a partiality towards reductionism and inadequately justified general (often negative) conclusions. I would like to suggest that a comparison of the discussions of the concept of set by Quine with the chapter on sets in this book will provide a striking (though perhaps not completely fair) illustration of the difference between the two approaches. Linguistic philosophy on the whole tends to be piecemeal (lacking in substance) and pays little attention to facts (except detailed linguistic facts). The notion of gross facts is considered more extensively in chapter XII, section 4.

In contrast with positivism and linguistic philosophy, the present position puts more trust in intuition, not in the sense of what comes at first to one's mind, but in the sense of extended reflective thinking which leads to an agreement on what is not immediately obvious. The emphasis on gross facts is meant to be an antidote not only to the anarchy of philosophical systems, but also to the anarchy of philosophical problems.

Substantial factualism is opposed to reductionist positions as they are commonly understood. To begin with, there is little sympathy with phenomenalism, be it epistemological or metaphysical or linguistic; physical objects are favored over sense data on the ground that the former are closer to the facts of knowledge. A more congenial reductionism is embodied in the familiar hierarchy which ranks knowledge according to the degrees of priority (though by no means coinciding with the degrees of importance): physics, chemistry, biology, physiology, psychology, sociology. Related to this hierarchy is the desire to view mind as a black box interacting with the environment, and even to guess what is in the black box. Conceptually this picture can be helpful. But clearly we do not have enough physiological knowledge about such mechanisms as are presumed to be in the black box to be able to say much that is substantial. Kant and Husserl may be thought of as trying to determine the content of the black box by reflecting on how the mind functions while disregarding physiology.

Even if this familiar hierarchical reductionism is the correct position in some absolute sense, it may still be the case that we can and should pursue biology and psychology as independent subjects, not for the practical reason that we do not know enough of the physics and chemistry of life and mind, but for the deeper reason that higher forms of being come into existence only because they are sufficiently stable and even self-contained. For example, higher level machine languages are independent of the particular computers on which they are realized. It has been suggested that the stabilization on various levels of being enables us to disregard the details as to how these beings are made up from simpler elements. In particular, the human mind has its own sphere of operation and can be investigated fruitfully independently of the physical and biological details of the functioning of the brain.

In any case, there is for the current state of knowledge room for another kind of work. While suspending judgment on the methodological value of the reductionist picture for specific scientific researches and the likelihood of its eventual confirmation, we can regard the examination of the foundations of each basic branch of knowledge on its own level as a major philosophical task for each historical period. Instead of adhering to an uncritical imitation of physical methods and techniques, philosophers are to find different ways of thinking and communication which are appropriate to foundational studies. In this regard, we may think of Kant's work on the foundations of what he takes to be the a priori knowledge as an illustration of the kind of thing which could be done.

There are two presuppositions in the position of (restricted) substantial factualism which call for elaborations and clarifications. The first is the emphasis on the basics of scientific knowledge, which is not acceptable to, for example, common sense and ordinary language philosophers. The second is the denial of the existence of sufficient evidence to believe in the feasibility of philosophy as a superscience for the foreseeable future; this is contrary to, for example, Husserl's views.[1] Both presuppositions are recommendations based on some vague general empirical evidence as to what philosophical efforts are likely to be fruitful. Both could be viewed as judgments on priority: if it turns out that the more fruitful approach is to begin with everyday knowledge and to work toward

4

philosophy as a rigorous science, results obtained from the alternative approach proposed here will, one hopes, yet have contributed, at an intermediate stage, to the general advance of philosophy nonetheless. Whatever the eventual outcome, we would like to offer some inconclusive defense of the two presuppositions.

One aspect of substantial factualism is to take the idea of reflection seriously. It seems to follow that we should pay sufficient attention to the data on which we are to reflect and not to philosophize over thin air. This belief seems to be shared widely among people who otherwise hold rather diverse views. For example, Blanshard states:[2] 'But while rational practice may be developed independently of theory, the theory of reason does depend on a developed practice; it is only with instances of an accomplished use of reason before them that philsophers have ever succeeded in giving an account of that use.'

In philosophy one would, moreover, like to reflect on important data, if we can find a clue to select what is important. We can agree that moral, political, and esthetic problems and, more generally, emotional problems connected with how to live one's life all are important. If, however, we wish to confine ourselves, initially at least, to sharper, more stable and better organized data, we are often led to knowledge. There is then the contrast between everyday knowledge and scientific knowledge. Since everyday knowledge is more basic, it appears to be a primary candidate for a philosophical study. On the other hand, scientific knowledge is more developed and more structured. In view of the great difficulty of philosophy, it seems reasonable to begin with magnified and streamlined data, especially if we are impressed by the fact of the accumulation of knowledge. Moreover, we have in scientific knowledge a fairly stable and elaborate sense of what is central and important, which provides a guide in the search for a relevant notion of importance. History of philosophy is another valuable source of data but has to be used with even more care.

It should be emphasized that no recommendation of encyclopedic knowledge of the sciences is intended. Rather the suggestion is somewhat in the spirit of Plato's requirement: let no one who is ignorant of geometry enter the academy. Knowledge of the fundamentals of science (or at least some central branch of science) is thought to help clear thinking and improve one's understanding of what knowledge is. More generally, philosophy is too abstract and at the same time inexact to be a natural starting point for developing a good taste for intellectual matters. A more special subject such as perhaps mathematics or history is more likely to produce an initial taste for judging what is more interesting work.

We cannot expect to transcend existing knowledge and, so to speak, to think on a higher level so as to see a more general truth that includes the existing knowledge as a special case. Many people have paid lip service to this denial of a superreason, but often they seem unwilling to face its consequences. They continue to look for and find special keys such as psychology, or logic, or language, or history, or art, or economics, or anthropology which are supposed to be capable of unlocking most or all of the mysteries of human knowledge. It is not denied that some area of study is more relevant to a philosophy of knowledge than some other. The plea is merely to look more closely at the facts of human knowledge and refrain from rushing to oversimplifications. And this is in a vague way based in part on the empirical evidence that attempts at simple keys have not led to any truly promising line of approach. It may of course be argued that if in physics and genetics we have had such amazing successes, what is to prevent us from expecting and looking for similar surprises in philosophy? The answer can only be that in one sense we have no method of finding such surprises and, insofar as we can look for any breakthrough, we have no evidence which promises a quick solution. In any case, we do feel there should be some difference between science and philosophy such as is embodied in the familiar saying that philosophy is reflective.

This position may be contrasted with Husserl's program of establishing philosophy as a rigorous universal science by the method of phenomenology. According to Husserl, the difference between science and philosophy is that science as it is is not sufficiently scientific and can only become truly scientific after we have developed a scientific philosophy and reconstructed ordinary sciences on such a basis. We cannot deny the great intellectual appeal of such a program. Nor can I give an informed evaluation of the prospects and promises of the project. The contrary opinion is in part based on a skepticism toward the feasibility of such a project with a view to steady accumulations of results and in part based on an unwillingness to wait patiently for the eventual success of the program before dealing with urgent and immediate philosophical problems. It is felt that actual knowledge in its fundamentals on the whole acts more to control our study of basic categories and correct the all too human tendency to assimilate differences, rather than to mislead and prejudice us in our pursuit of general philosophy. In fact, Husserl himself puts great value on the achievements of the exact sciences, and is acutely concerned with the importance of rich and central data for philosophy. One would like to believe that a more developed substantial factualism will remove an ambiguity in its formulation so as to accommodate some austere form of phenomenology. It cannot,

6

however, be denied that factualism suggests a different ordering of priorities and is ambivalent towards absolutism.

2 AGAINST POSITIVISM

There are two related but different criticisms of positivism. One is that it arrives at a general position by looking at science and then unjustifiably applies it to other things. The other is that it is a sterile and inadequate position even for science. The second fault may be explained either by saying that in order to understand science it is not enough to look only at science or by saying that the positivists have not looked at science in its full richness.

It is notoriously difficult to define positions such as positivism sufficiently exactly so that one's vaguely felt objections could be turned into forceful and convincing arguments. Let us begin with the general objections. First, positivism seems to be strangely detached from actual knowledge, especially in the unrealistic central program of reconstructing empirical knowledge on the basis of sense data and simple empirical induction. Second, positivism denies the possibility of any serious conceptual knowledge, thereby failing to give an adequate account of the basic stability of the exact sciences; in particular, the positivistic account of mathematics is disappointingly unsatisfactory. Third, positivism as empiricism is also self-contradictory in rejecting the rich experience from introspection and confining itself to sense experience (derived from sense perceptions). The three objections have a common basis in the fact that empiricism uses too narrow a notion of experience.

Instead of trying to elaborate these inexactly stated general objections to positivism, we invite the reader to infer the differences between positivism and the present approach by comparing the treatment of mathematical concepts in this book with the treatment of mathematics by Carnap and A. J. Ayer.[3] For concentrated arguments against positivism, we shall limit ourselves in the present context to quotations of certain of Gödel's views.

In the history of science, there are certain well-known examples of philosophical disagreements which greatly influence each scientist's judgment of the value and the correctness of his opponent's scientific work. There are the controversies between Cantor and Kronecker,[4] between Hilbert and Brouwer,[5] and the friendly exchange of views between Einstein and N. Bohr.[6] I have not studied closely any of these cases and cannot give any adequate account of how their different philosophical views influence their scientific work.

Introduction

We do have the striking example of Gödel who possesses firmly held philosophical views which played an essential role in making his fundamental new scientific discoveries, and who is well aware of the importance of his philosophical views for his scientific work. A paper of Skolem in 1922 contains the mathematical core of the proof of the completeness of pure logic. In commenting on the puzzling fact that Skolem failed to draw the interesting conclusion of completeness from his work, Gödel wrote the following paragraphs about the role which his philosophical views played in his work in mathematical logic:[7]

The completeness theorem, mathematically, is indeed an almost trivial consequence of Skolem 1922. However, the fact is that, at that time, nobody (including Skolem himself) drew this conclusion (neither from Skolem 1922 nor, as I did, from similar considerations of his own).

As you mention yourself, Hilbert and Ackermann, in the 1928 edition of their book on p. 68, state the completeness question explicitly as an unsolved problem. As far as Skolem is concerned, although in 1922 he proved the required lemma, nevertheless, when in his 1928 paper (at the bottom of p. 134) he stated a completeness theorem (about refutation), *he did not use his lemma of 1922 for the proof. Rather he gave an entirely inconclusive argument.* (See p. 134, line 10 from below to p. 135, line 3.)

This blindness (or prejudice, or whatever you may call it) of logicians is indeed surprising. But I think the explanation is not hard to find. It lies in a widespread lack, at that time, of the required epistemological attitude toward metamathematics and toward non-finitary reasoning.

Non-finitary reasoning in mathematics was widely considered to be meaningful only to the extent to which it can be 'interpreted' or 'justified' in terms of a finitary metamathematics. (Note that this, for the most part, has turned out to be impossible in consequence of my results and subsequent work.) This view, almost unavoidably, leads to an exclusion of non-finitary reasoning from metamathematics. For, such reasoning, in order to be permissible, would require a finitary metamathematics. But this seems to be a confusing and unnecessary duplication. Moreover, admitting 'meaningless' transfinite elements into metamathematics is inconsistent with the very idea of this science prevalent at that time. For according to this idea metamathematics is *the* meaningful part of mathematics, through which the mathematical symbols (meaningless in

8

themselves) acquire some substitute of meaning, namely rules of use. Of course, the essence of this viewpoint is a rejection of all kinds of abstract or infinite objects, of which the prima facie meanings of mathematical symbols are instances. I.e. meaning is attributed solely to propositions which speak of *concrete and finite objects*, such as combinations of symbols.

But now the aforementioned easy inference from Skolem 1922 is definitely non-finitary, and so is any other completeness proof for the predicate calculus. Therefore these things escaped notice or were disregarded.

I may add that my objectivistic conception of mathematics and metamathematics in general, and of transfinite reasoning in particular, was fundamental also to my other work in logic.

How indeed could one think of *expressing* metamathematics *in* the mathematical systems themselves, if the latter are considered to consist of meaningless symbols which acquire some substitute of meaning only *through* metamathematics? Or how could one give a consistency proof for the continuum hypothesis by means of my transfinite model Δ if consistency proofs have to be finitary? (Not to mention that from the finitary point of view an interpretation of set theory in terms of Δ seems preposterous from the beginning, because it is an 'interpretation' in terms of something which itself has no meaning). The fact that such an interpretation (as well as any non-finitary consistency proof) yields a finitary *relative* consistency proof apparently escaped notice.

Finally it should be noted that the heuristic principle of my construction of undecidable number theoretical propositions in the formal systems of mathematics is the highly transfinite concept of 'objective mathematical truth', as *opposed* to that of 'demonstrability' (Cnf. M. Davis, *The Undecidable*, New York 1965, p. 64, where I explain the heuristic argument by which I arrived at the incompleteness results), with which it was generally confused before my own and Tarski's work. Again the use of this transfinite concept eventually leads to finitarily provable results, e.g., the general theorems about the existence of undecidable propositions in consistent formal systems.

Further elaborations are included in a letter of March 7, 1968:

On rereading my letter of December 7, I find that the phrasing of the last but one paragraph [as just quoted] is perhaps a little too drastic. It must be understood cum grano salis. Of course, the formalistic point of view did not make *impossible* consistency proofs by means of transfinite models. It only made them much harder to discover, because they are somehow not congenial to this attitude of mind. However, as far as, in particular, the continuum hypothesis is concerned, there was a special obstacle which *really* made it *practically impossible* for constructivists to discover my consistency proof. It is the fact that the ramified hierarchy, which had been invented *expressly for constructivistic purposes*, has to be used in an *entirely nonconstructive way*. A similar remark applies to the concept of mathematical truth, where formalists considered formal demonstrability to be an *analysis* of the concept of mathematical truth and, therefore, were of course not in a position to *distinguish* the two.

I would like to add that there was another reason which hampered logicians in the application to metamathematics, not only of transfinite reasoning, but of mathematical reasoning in general [and, most of all, in expressing metamathematics in mathematics itself – added April, 1972]. It consists in the fact that, largely, metamathematics was not considered as a science describing objective mathematical states of affairs, but rather as a theory of the human activity of handling symbols.

Gödel's letter of March 7 contains also replies to several questions I raised in correspondence. 1 Professor P. Bernays has observed that Skolem did not think of the theorems of elementary logic as given in a formal system and, therefore, that the question of full completeness had no meaning for Skolem. 2 Skolem did use nonfinitary reasoning in his earlier proof of Löwenheim's Theorem. 3 Von Neumann used a transfinite model to prove the relative consistency of his axiom of regularity. Gödel's replies are, with minor omissions, as follows:

> I am still *perfectly convinced* that reluctance to use non-finitary concepts and arguments in metamathematics was the primary reason why the completeness proof was not given by Skolem or anybody else before my work. It may be true that Skolem had little interest in the formalization of logic, but this does not in the least explain why he did not give a correct proof of *that* completeness theorem *which he explicitly stated* (op. cit., p. 134), namely that there is a contradiction at some level *n* if there is an informal disproof of the formula. On the basis of his lemma of 1922 this would have been quite easy, since evidently a correct informal disproof implies the nonexistence of a model.
> Moreover, what he tried to accomplish on page 29 of his paper of 1929 *evidently was* to eliminate transfinite arguments from metamathematics (in a manner quite similar to Herbrand's).
> That he used non-finitary reasoning for Löwenheim's Theorem proves nothing, because pure model theory, where the concept

Introduction

of proof does not come in, lies on the borderline between mathematics and metamathematics, and its applications to special systems with a finite number of axioms actually belong to mathematics, at least for the most part. This also explains von Neumann's use of a transfinite model of set theory, which, by the way, is rather trivial.

Gödel observes that it is possible to get, without his objectivism, different proofs of his incompleteness results, by using, for example, the analysis of formal systems in terms of Turing machines. But the proofs are much harder to discover.[8]

With regard to the consistency of the continuum hypothesis, Gödel attributes to a philosophical error Hilbert's failure to attain a definite result from his approach to the continuum problem.[9] The approaches of Gödel and Hilbert are similar in that they both define, in terms of ordinal numbers, a system of functions (or sets) for which the continuum hypothesis is true. The differences are 1 Gödel takes all ordinal numbers as given, while Hilbert attempts to construct them; 2 Hilbert considers only recursively defined functions or sets, while Gödel admits also nonconstructive definitions (by quantification).

Of course, Hilbert's error is not that he was a constructivist in the sense of total rejection of nonconstructive proofs. As is well known, he had no reluctance in using nonconstructive proofs to get theorems. His error rather consists in his view (agreeing with Skolem's, criticized by Gödel in the two letters just quoted) that nonconstructive *metamathematics* is of no use. Hence he expected that his constructive metamathematics would lead to the solution of the problem and thereby yield a 'last trump' for his proof theory. 'The final test of every new theory,' he says, 'is its success in answering preexistent questions that the theory was not specifically created to answer' (p. 384).

According to Gödel, Hilbert's claim that his proof really *solves* the problem, i.e. yields the *truth* of the continuum hypothesis, is due to his belief that 1 the continuum hypothesis is true (and provable by his outline) in constructive mathematics (see his Lemma II, p. 391); 2 nothing true in constructive mathematics can ever be wrong in classical mathematics, since the role of the latter is solely to *supplement* the former (so as to obtain a complete system in which every proposition is decided). Of course Hilbert deemed it necessary to prove 2 *mathematically* in its application to specific questions. This, in our case, was to be done with respect to the axioms of classical mathematics known at that time and omitting the part in parentheses by Lemma I on p. 385. In Gödel's opinion the assertion 2 is another

11

philosophical error (stemming from the same quasi-positivistic attitude), and will be disproved by the continuum hypothesis. If the term 'constructive' is (as Hilbert had in mind) identified with 'finitary,' Hilbert's proof scheme is not feasible. Otherwise it might be. But it would at any rate be an enormous detour if one only aims at a consistency proof for the continuum hypothesis. On the other hand, it would solve the much deeper, but entirely different, problem of a constructive consistency proof for Zermelo's axioms of set theory.

It must be admitted that the positivistic position also has turned out to be fruitful on certain occasions. An example often mentioned as in favor of the positivist position is the special theory of relativity. The rough idea is that asking the operational meaning of simultaneity is a crucial step in the discovery of the special theory. Einstein himself speaks of:[10]

A paradox upon which I had already hit at the age of sixteen: If I pursue a beam of light with the velocity *c* (velocity of light in a vacuum), I should observe such a beam of light as a spatially oscillatory electro-magnetic field at rest. . . . Today everybody knows, of course, that all attempts to clarify this paradox satisfactorily were condemned to failure as long as the axiom of the absolute character of time, viz., of simultaneity, unrecognizedly was anchored in the unconscious. Clearly to recognize this axiom and its arbitrary character really implies already the solution of the problem. The type of critical reasoning which was required for the discovery of this central point was decisively furnished, in my case, especially by the reading of David Hume's and Ernst Mach's philosophical writings.

On the other hand, Einstein also says:

In order to be able to consider a logical system as physical theory it is not necessary to demand that all of its assertions can be independently interpreted and 'tested' 'operationally'; *de facto* this has never yet been achieved by any theory and cannot at all be achieved. In order to be able to consider a theory as a *physical* theory it is only necessary that it implies empirically testable assertions in general.

Gödel points out that the fruitfulness of the positivistic point of view in this case is due to a very exceptional circumstance, namely the fact that the basic concept to be clarified, i.e. simultaneity, is directly observable, while generally basic entities (such as elementary particles, the forces between them, etc.) are not. Hence the positivistic requirement that everything has to be reduced to observations is justified in this case. That, generally speaking, positivism is not fruitful even in physics seems to follow from the fact that, since it has been more or less adopted in quantum physics (i.e. about 40 years ago) no substantial progress has been achieved in the basic laws of physics, even though the present 'two-level' theory (with its 'quantization' of a 'classical system,' and its divergent series) is admittedly very unsatisfactory. Perhaps, what ought to be done is to separate the subjective and objective elements in Schrödinger's wave function, which so far has by no means been proved impossible. But exactly this question is 'meaningless' from the positivistic point of view.

3 AGAINST LINGUISTIC PHILOSOPHY

Language plays an especially prominent role in contemporary philosophy. Wittgenstein's two philosophies (or antiphilosophies) have been said[11] to be similar to Kant's critical philosophy on the ground that they attempt to demarcate the limits of language while Kant attempts to demarcate the limits of thought. But the similarity has drastic limitations as is seen from the fact that Kant's two leading questions concerning the conditions which make mathematics and physics possible recede pretty much to remote corners in the linguistic philosophies. It is in this central respect that the goals of factualism are more akin to Kant's approach than to linguistic philosophies which are generally more concerned with logic than with mathematics and physics.

It seems at first sight surprising that language should be looked upon with so much favor in philosophy. There is undoubtedly the crude sociological factor that every educated man has a pretty good command of his native language and that even if the concern with language has contacts with linguistics, linguistics as a discipline is more easily accessible. But the more official reasons are the feeling that language is clearer than thought and yet reveals its most basic features. The clarity aspect came initially in part from the preoccupation with syntactical considerations in logic, where there is the natural feeling that symbols or sentences are more concrete and more tangible than ideas or propositions. This was combined with the oversimplified view of factual knowledge in the *Tractatus*, which proposes to provide not only an adequate explanation of logical necessity but also a theory of language and reality according to which fairly simple linguistic forms are sufficient to represent all factual knowledge and reality. When this idea is applied to combine force with the extensive concern over the meaning and analysis of concepts by G. E. Moore, there results a profession occupied primarily with the meaning and analysis of words, as well as the stress on the analytic (or verbal meaning) component of language.

When both syntax and the *Tractatus* were found to be inadequate, instead of retreating from or going beyond logic and language, attempts were made to amplify logical constructions and refine linguistic analysis. As a result, we drift into opaque discourses on semantics and empirical piecemeal considerations of pragmatics and linguistics. Some are pleased that philosophy is now tied up to a science, viz. linguistics, and sometimes refute competing philosophical views by an appeal to the relevance to linguistics. Others are hard at work arguing that linguistic philosophy is like a science but not a science and, therefore, different from linguistics. For a number of people, the simultaneous interest in logic and language leads to a gratifying field of operation on account of the many points of contact between the foundations of linguistics and the philosophy of logic. But if one recalls that the initial infatuation with language was occasioned by false promises, then it is no longer necessary to regard as sacred the philosopher's preoccupation with language. A plausible conclusion is that while language may be more basic, it need not be the most appropriate primary concern of philosophy if only because a preoccupation with it fails to take sufficient advantage of actual human knowledge.

It cannot be denied that attention to language, and in particular its syntactical aspect, has rendered many results in mathematical logic sharper than they would otherwise be. But unless there are special reasons for bringing language in, it would appear more efficient to deal directly with reality. For example, in studying set theory, it seems generally more effective to think in terms of intuitive models rather than formally in terms of specific axioms and explicit defining properties. As a result of the emphasis on syntactical concepts, in discussing the foundations of set theory, there is often a tendency to confuse language, theory, axiom systems and their theorems, truth and intended models. Actually for many of these considerations, it is less cumbersome if we leave out the language aspect. For example, the concern with language makes it seem attractive to define a deterministic world in terms of deterministic theories but the result seems to multiply difficulties instead of gaining the anticipated clarity. In insisting on defining properties and sentences, one also runs into obstacles with regard to uncountably many sets and propositions.[12] There are indications that some philosophers are, when appropriate, beginning to face reality directly rather than by way of language.

4 EXPLANATORY REMARKS ON
SUBSTANTIAL FACTUALISM

Substantial factualism as an approach to philosophy presupposes a distinction between fundamental and technical knowledge, which reminds one of the traditional contrast between essential and accidental properties. Thus, philosophy is concerned only with fundamental knowledge, while science is also, and one might say most of the time, interested in technical knowledge. It is not necessary that we can state a clear distinction to begin with. In practice, there is little danger of mistaking special technical details in science for philosophical material. In fact, normally one accepts the current standards of a given subject and does not spend much time in reflecting on the nature of the subject. It is only because one feels unhappy over the current state of philosophy that an attempt is made to redefine the task of philosophy. And the sermon is to take actual knowledge more seriously in order to correct a fashionable tendency toward a form of neoscholasticism. There is presently no likelihood of overcorrecting the tendency in the direction of confusing technical scientific details with philosophical issues, especially if we exclude the peculiarly favored subject of linguistics.

We do have a fairly definite idea of the distinction between more fundamental subjects such as physics and more technical ones such as engineering, as well as one between first principles and derived consequences. For example, the initial definitions of points, lines and planes in Euclid are more fundamental than the definitions of other figures in terms of them. The distinction between subatomic and molecular forces is fundamental and the linking of biology to chemistry in molecular biology is of philosophical interest, while most results in synthesizing new drugs and new fibres are clearly of a technical nature only. General considerations on concepts such as proof, set, mechanical procedure are no doubt fundamental.

Another troublesome aspect of factualism is the implied respect for science and scientists. One is bothered by the danger of appealing to authorities. Clearly we do not wish to be at the mercy of the caprices of individual successful scientists, or even those of the fashions of a particular historical period. But there is no reason why this is necessary since we respect only the current scientific beliefs and not temperamental misinterpretations of them, and we are supposed to acquire a historical understanding of the basic issues. In fact, what is deplorable is a more superficial respect for science which tends to value the more mechanical in philosophy. The underlying idea is apparently that since science is more mechanical than philosophy, making philosophical work more mechanical makes it more like science and therefore more respectable. Of course, even within science, the better scientists are generally supposed to be the more imaginative ones.

The preference for the more mechanical in philosophy is related to the idolatry of 'clarity.' What is meant is local clarity comparable to the listing of historical dates rather than global clarity as one would speak of a clear overview of history. Many of us have been brought up to think of such clarity as a minor virtue which becomes a primary concern only after we have given up looking for the important, either because we are in despair or because we have succeeded and are currently engaged in a careful exposition of what we have. To elevate local clarity to the status of the dominating goal of philosophy can appeal only to those who have been successfully indoctrinated.

When philosophy is closely attached to actual knowledge, there is the natural question that if knowledge changes quickly, philosophy becomes a very unstable subject, trying to keep up with the newest advance every day. In this regard we accept as an empirical fact that fundamental knowledge does not change quickly and that even when there is a basic advance, the old knowledge such as Newtonian physics contains a good deal that is stable and well worth reflecting on.

Factualism suggests immediately philosophies of special subjects such as the philosophy of mathematics, of physics, of biology, or of history. What happens then to the general philosophy of knowledge? There are problems envisaged by factualism which seem to transcend individual disciplines, for example, minds and machines. There are problems which are common to all disciplines, for example, the phenomenon of accepting something as knowledge, and that of regarding some contribution as important in the particular field. More sweepingly, we would like eventually to combine results from the philosophies of separate disciplines into a sort of organic whole. In this respect, one might say that the long range goal of factualism is to achieve with regard to current knowledge something like what Aristotle did with regard to the existing knowledge of his time. It is empirically certain that no single individual can achieve such a goal at the present stage. But it is hoped that philosophy will also acquire to some extent the capacity of science to be cumulative.

There are some philosophers who are capable of discoursing after dinner on various results in modern science and their philosophical significance, but manage to preserve a basic opacity while creating an illusion of understanding and not committing factual mistakes. Since substantial factualism is not after such sophisticated popularization, one is inclined to ask for a deeper understanding and a

16

better taste which, with most people seem to come only after an actual experience of doing a subject. One is tempted to be pompous and require that nobody is permitted to enter the academy of philosophy without a practicing knowledge of logic or physics or mathematics or biology or history or art or some combination of several subjects.

It would help to explain the vague conception of factualism, if one could give appropriate illustrative examples. The difficulty is not only that only one-sided examples can be given, but also that an attempt to hint at unexamined illustrations is inevitably superficial, misleading, and probably missing the mark. With these reservations, we proceed to list a number of gross phenomena which seem to promise some reward to further explorations.

There is the phenomenon of the interplay of concepts and experiences (in a broad sense) in the progress of knowledge. The search for new axioms in current set theory seems to provide us with a clear and yet sufficiently complex situation for a case study of this. There is a feeling that in contemporary philosophy we do not pay enough attention to the actual scientific practice; a closer look at theory and practice in mathematics might serve to bring out some of the relevant points and to illustrate partially more general problems. The area of mathematical logic yields fairly definitive analyses of general concepts such as logical validity, number, set, and mechanical procedure. These may be thought as providing paradigms for philosophical analysis.

The development of large computers gives new impetus to the study of tacit knowledge or the contrast between the intuitive and the formal, of the differences between minds and machines, of the question whether mathematical reasoning is or is not mechanical.

Of more traditional topics, the foundations of classical physics, the relation of Euclidean geometry to intuition and to the nature of the continuum, the place of logic and geometry in mathematics as complementary aspects, and the theory of evolution continue to be of contemporary interest. In particular, the idea of progress in the evolution theory is of course quite difficult. But methodologically, the more significant aspect of evolution is perhaps the idea that all living things are connected. It is on account of this idea that we have developed the practice of studying lower animals for the purpose of medicine and the understanding of human physiology. The general theory of relativity is a paradigm of a theory that outsiders find practically impossible to understand; an account which is understandable to some qualified outsiders may also be regarded as a sort of philosophical task.

The majority of physicists seem to regard quantum theory as a more or less finished product, while many philosophers and a minority of physicists feel uncomfortable about the foundations of quantum theory. It seems to be an attractive philosophical project to make clear in terms not too technical the different overall viewpoints which yield the feeling of comfort in one case and that of discomfort in the other.

A sort of minor paradox is the fact that physicists generally show no interest in formal axiomatization and even disregard attempts at clarifying the mathematical foundations of physics. At first, one is inclined to think that such attempts are of foundational interest and therefore should be quite helpful conceptually. One can speculate on the reasons why physicists do not think so. Perhaps they find that these are irrelevant as far as the main task of making new discoveries is concerned. Perhaps these do not help clarify the basic concepts. Perhaps in physics assumptions have neither sharp ranges nor inviolability, and you modify and adjust them as you go along. It has been suggested that in physics the authentic and more rewarding attitude is like that of the Babylonians (in contrast to the Greeks) toward geometry. One is tempted to compare these attempts with cleaning up somebody's office which, for some curious reason, was more conducive to his efficiency in its natural state of mess. The essential point of the comparison must be that neither kind of service is of crucial importance for the central pursuit in view.

There is a justifiable concern that the type of work we have thus hinted at will more likely yield data for philosophy than philosophy proper, as it has been said of G. H. Hardy's views in the philosophy of mathematics. The dividing line may not be easy to draw, and even in cases where a natural distinction can plausibly be made, what are considered mere data for philosophy may be more interesting, not only intrinsically but even also for the overall development of philosophy. In this regard, one might wish to contrast A. N. Whitehead's *Science and the modern world* with his *Process and reality*. Many philosophers are inclined to consider the latter book to be philosophy and the former book to be mere data for philosophy. But it is highly debatable whether the latter is a more valuable work than the former. A more striking example is Gödel's four famous philosophical papers[13] which are respected but disregarded by the majority of professional philosophers as not really philosophical papers. According to the viewpoint of factualism, these papers are thought to be of more philosophical interest than most of Carnap's books. This comparison serves to bring out a preference implicit in factualism, viz. the preference to find stable and naked truths which are, as far as possible, independent of the vicissitudes of exuberant current fashions in philosophy. Within the framework of professional

Introduction

philosophy as a going concern, there is a tendency to pay attention
more to context-dependent debating points than to less controversial
observations which are pertinent to the long range philosophical
problems. Traditionally epistemology as the philosophy of knowledge is said
to be the theory or science of the method and grounds of knowledge,
especially with reference to its limits and validity. The central bias
of factualism implies a dissatisfaction with epistemology as it is
commonly pursued on the ground that it is too abstract and too
detached from actual knowledge, often too one-sided to take into
consideration the anthropic element in the pursuit of knowledge,
often too piecemeal to permit the emergence of any larger connected
and coherent outlook. To emphasize this divergence of emphasis
from traditional epistemology, we would like to speak of epistemo-
graphy which, roughly speaking, is supposed to treat of actual
knowledge as phenomenology proposes to deal with actual phenomena. What is wanted should be, among other things, more
structured and more confined to essentials than an encyclopedia.

To repeat, we know more about what we know than how we know
what we know. This means that, as a matter of fact, there is more
interesting material in the domain of what we know, which is, therefore, a more promising area according to factualism. One might say
that epistemology is more interested in how we know, while episte-
mography is more concerned with what we know. It seems that the
former is, therefore, more properly philosophy since reporting what
we know appears to be a matter for the individual disciplines of
knowledge, while how we know has more the flavor of foundational
questions. Of course, the philosophical interest in what we know is
inevitably concerned with what is more basic such as number,
proof, space, time, matter, life, mind, society, nation, and economic
class. Actual knowledge has the highly attractive property of
uniqueness which is not shared by free speculations. And there is the
belief that by looking closely at actual knowledge, we can reach,
with effort, a better understanding of what it is that we know which
in turn will reveal, as far as is humanly possible at each historical
period, aspects of what we are and what the world is.

While we are skeptical of oversimplified accounts of the foundations of human knowledge, factualism is much interested in how we
know in the sense of desiring to consider the basic aspects of the
factual process of knowing. An attention to these not only helps to
uncover shortcomings of oversimplified pictures, but also promises
to lead to a balanced and appropriately anthropocentric overview
of how stable and how structured actual knowledge is. The most
important single aspect is the process by which a proposition or a

MP—B   19

theory becomes accepted as part of human knowledge or a particular individual's knowledge. This factor of acceptance is the central anthropocentric component of factualism which is related to intellectual comfort, understanding, coherence, and perspicuity. It introduces a theoretically practical component that is to prevent us from going astray into excessive unprincipled tolerance and idle intellectual gymnastics.

We are naturally interested in the world and in our mind; it is not intended to deny that physics and psychology can give us knowledge of them. But a philosophically more interesting line of approach is Kant's ambitious transcendental method. By applying the method, we are expected to find out what the world and our mind must be like in order that the impressive actual knowledge we do possess could be possible. In the abstract, it would appear that we can at most hope to determine some sufficient but not necessary conditions, since different sufficient conditions might produce the same effect. In practice, even Kant's derivation of Newtonian physics from first principles is far from conclusive. However, the feeling that Kant has done something impressive in his study of pure reason is based on better evidence than merely a respect for authority.

5 LOGIC, MATHEMATICS, AND THE SCOPE OF THIS BOOK

In this book, we are interested in examining the relations between logic and knowledge. The general viewpoint implies a dissatisfaction with the dominance of mathematical logic in current academic philosophy: with both its improper use in philosophy and its intrinsic potential limitations for a foundation of philosophy. The considerations are centered around logic, treating of its achievements to combat the misuse and its inadequacies in connection with the study of the philosophy of knowledge to invite a broader outlook. At any rate, it is utterly erroneous to identify positivism with mathematical logic.

The term 'logic' has been used in various different ways. For our present purpose, we may conveniently distinguish three. In one sense (pure or formal) logic is concerned with sentences which are valid, i.e. hold independently of any special subject matter or are true in all possible worlds. There is an ambiguity in this conception which turns on a confusing question which boils down to whether pure sets are to be regarded as forming a special subject matter. It seems clear that a sufficiently important concept of logic does result by excluding sets which inevitably involve concepts such as infinity, uncountability. Since we intend to disregard modal logic altogether, we thus arrive at the first and narrowest sense of logic: (elementary or pure) logic is nothing but quantification theory or (first order) predicate calculus, with or without equality.

A second sense corresponds roughly to what is commonly known as mathematical logic which includes, besides pure logic, also model theory, recursion theory, the axiomatic treatment of integers, reals, and sets. In either case, logic is closely mixed up with metalogic or metamathematics.

The third and broadest sense is far less definite. It is the study of pure reason or the treatment of what is rational. In this broad sense, it could include a logic of discovery, a logic of development, some form of inductive logic, or some form of dialectic logic. Even though we are interested in some of these aspects, we shall not speak of logic in this broad sense, but rather confine ourselves to the first two more definite and narrower senses.

We are not only interested in the applications of mathematical logic to problems of the foundations of mathematics and to philosophy in general, but are also concerned with ideas which transcend mathematical logic and would remedy its limitations with regard to a general study of human knowledge. Thus, logic is generally contrasted with intuition or tacit knowledge, and logic in its present state at any rate fails to deal with the activity of thinking (in contrast with the idealized end results), in particular its efficiency aspect. A more basic but related limitation of approaching the phenomenon of knowledge from logic or from any abstract viewpoint is the danger of missing the fundamental basic concerns of each individual branch of knowledge. It is for the purpose of remedying this defect of the emphasis on logic that we attempt to look at mathematics in terms of the practice and the activity from several angles.

In a formal sense, mathematical logic includes mathematics because it includes axiomatic set theory to which all mathematics is formally reducible. On the other hand, we know very well that, as practiced, mathematical logic is but a special branch of mathematics and, in fact, it is not often regarded as a very central branch. This 'paradox' renders highly plausible the conclusion that the concentration in the study of the philosophy of mathematics on mathematical logic is one-sided and inadequate.

A major preoccupation of mathematical logic is to characterize exactly basic mathematical concepts such as natural numbers, real numbers, sets, and (logically correct) proofs. A basic tool for this purpose is axiom systems and the axiomatic method. Reflection on the axiom systems leads to metamathematics which is largely concerned with a general study of symbol manipulations (syntax) and to model theory which studies interpretations of axiom systems (semantics). Syntactical considerations are closely related to the interest in constructive methods and a surprisingly elegant characterization of the concept of a mechanical procedure or of being strictly formal. And this happens to supply an abstract theory of computers. Computers in turn suggest the practical possibility of carrying out tedious formal proofs as envisaged by the logicians. This provides an incentive for looking in more exact terms at the roles of logic and intuition in the activity of pursuing mathematics. Hence, it is not unnatural that a study on knowledge and logic should include considerations on minds and machines, computers and mathematical activities.

The interest in models and interpretations naturally leads to the central concept of set. In fact, the pivotal position of sets reveals itself in many different ways. That we have an adequate formal system of pure logic (the completeness problem of the first order logic) depends for its very formulation on the concept of arbitrary sets. And we have unique (categorical) characterizations of natural numbers and real numbers by axiom systems only if we use second order theories, i.e. presuppose a fixed comprehensive concept of arbitrary sets of these numbers. Thus we see again and again that we appeal to a concept of set in order to justify absolute results in other areas. On the other hand, we do not have a similarly adequate characterization of sets. Even if we enrich each type or rank (increase the density) of sets by using a second order theory and appealing to a higher level concept of class, we have no way of freezing also the open extension of sets (in length) to higher and higher ranks. Another fascinating feature about set theory is the apparent paradox that doubts about its foundations are widespread yet we are capable of acquiring very strong intuitions to arrive informally at correct, interesting, and coherent concepts and theorems. More, philosophical problems on mathematical objects and on the inner resources of a given branch of knowledge come to a specially conspicuous focus in the examination of set theory. For all these reasons, the concept of set deserves some attention in considering knowledge and logic.

It makes a difference whether we take logic or take mathematics as central to the philosophy of knowledge. When logic is taken to be central, a primary epistemological position is generally given to pure logic (logic in the first and narrowest sense), and the emphasis is on the concepts and judgments which arise from the general forms and conditions of the discourse. Mathematics, on the other hand, stresses numbers and spaces, or more generally idealized structures which supply simplified but manageable models in different sciences. Mathematics is a more substantial subject than logic in that we think of mathematical objects such as numbers and functions and spaces. Admittedly these are not like physical objects and in fact there are many reasons for regarding mathematical objects as determined only by mathematical structures. Nonetheless, these shadowy objects are particularly helpful in applying mathematics to capture the theoretically exact components in our knowledge of natural processes.

At first sight, it is not easy to understand why so much attention is paid to the thesis that mathematics is reducible to logic. One important reason is undoubtedly its relation to the contention of logical empiricists that all a priori propositions are analytic, since it is relatively easy to concede that logic is analytic and since mathematics is conspicuously a priori but not easily seen to be analytic. The reducibility thesis is open to different interpretations. Frege did not include geometry in the reduction.[14]

Empirical propositions hold good of what is physically or psychologically existent, the truths of geometry govern all that is spatially intuitable, whether existent or product of our fancy. ... For the purpose of conceptual thought we can always postulate the contrary of one or other of the geometrical axioms, without involving ourselves in any self-contradiction when we proceed to our deductions, despite the conflict between our postulates and our intuition. The fact that this is possible shows that the axioms of geometry are independent of one another and of the primitive laws of logic, and consequently are synthetic.

Russell at one time drew from the reducibility thesis the complementary conclusion that logic is synthetic.[15]

Kant never doubted for a moment that the propositions of mathematics are synthetic. It has since appeared that logic is just as synthetic as all other kinds of truth; but this is a purely philosophical question, which I shall here pass by. ... But now, thanks mainly to the mathematical logicians, formal logic is enriched by several forms of reasoning not reducible to the syllogism, and by means of these all mathematics can be, and large parts of mathematics actually have been, developed strictly according to these rules.

Russell has since changed this view; for instance,[16] 'Thus mathematical knowledge ceases to be mysterious. It is all the same nature as the "great truth" that there are three feet in a yard.'

Of course, the terms 'logic' and 'analytic' are highly ambiguous, and it does not follow from the reducibility thesis that all a priori knowledge is analytic. But once mathematics, which has been traditionally the main stumbling block to empiricism, has been taken care of by reducibility, it becomes easier for ardent empiricists to stipulate that no nonanalytic knowledge can be a priori. Now why is this analyticity thesis of all a priori knowledge regarded as so important by philosophers? The reason is that for a long time the majority of philosophers had regarded the chief concern of philosophy as the study of a priori knowledge about the world. From this point of view, the analytic or verbal doctrine of the a priori, if true, would trivialize or wipe out philosophy as a profession. To quote Blanshard[17]:

> This account of a priori knowledge is ingenious, plausible, and extremely important. It is important because, if true, it effectively discredits the main instrument of speculative philosophy and theology, and also many of what were supposed to be their self-evident conclusions. . . . In the positivist conception of reason, the necessity of an insight is no guarantee that it applies to nature or reveals anything outside the confines of meaning. . . . That a new theory would find us with our occupation gone is no argument against it.

It seems dogmatic to stipulate that philosophy only looks for a priori or analytic propositions. We are more ready to assert that philosophy is after what is important and fundamental and general. It is natural to shift from the fundamental to the ultimate and to feel that unless the ultimate truths are a priori, we have not found a solid foundation. But when a priori propositions are identified with analytic ones and analytic propositions are said to be characterized by verbal conventions, we seem to have accomplished a *reductio*. Either there are more important a priori propositions, or philosophy is not just after a priori propositions.

With regard to the reducibility thesis, we have four alternatives: to deny that mathematics is reducible to logic, to conclude that mathematics is analytic, to conclude that logic is synthetic, to examine more closely the concepts involved such as logic and analytic. Similarly with regard to the analyticity thesis, we may either follow Blanshard in denying the thesis, or conclude with many analytic philosophers[18] that philosophy indeed has no pretensions of going beyond the confines of meanings, or conclude that there is no reason for philosophy to confine itself to the search for a priori knowledge, or lastly examine closely the concepts of analytic, a priori, self-evident, and necessary. These alternatives need not be mutually exclusive. For example, we may find it necessary to make more distinctions so that different alternatives become compatible after distinguishing a broader and a narrower sense of logic or analytic.

The reducibility thesis also seems to make it easier to distinguish between physics and mathematics insofar as we feel that it is relatively easy to see a distinction between physics and logic. But conversely, the recognition of a distinction between mathematics and physics does not yield the reducibility thesis. We do feel there is a distinction between the ways in which mathematical and physical propositions are established. One also has the feeling that while objects are basic in physics, relations and structures are more basic than objects in mathematics.

The relation of the axiom of measurable cardinals to the usual axioms of set theory is in one way comparable to that between the law of gravitation and the laws of classical mechanics: in both cases the axiom and law are not derivable from the other principles but extend them without contradicting them. However, while measurable cardinals might be implicit in the concept of set codified in *ZF*, the law of gravitation requires new considerations. An analog perhaps erring in the opposite direction is to compare the addition of measurable cardinals to *ZF* with the extension of the law of gravitation from the planetary system to fixed stars. If one says that truth or falsity of this proposition or the continuum hypothesis is contained in our concept of set, then the sense of containing is somewhat complex. One is reminded of the extension of a novel, but the crucial difference is that in extending set theory, one feels there is less arbitrariness. It is not denied that alternative extensions of the current axioms of set theory may be experimented with, and in fact one does study mutually incompatible axioms such as the axiom of choice and the axiom of determinateness, or the existence of measurable cardinals and the axiom of constructibility. What the objectivists would like to say is that we have in our intention an equally fixed model of sets as with natural numbers. Only we do not perceive it as clearly. Consequently, when the dust settles down, one expects to recognize only one of the incompatible alternatives as conforming to the intended concept of set. Others find this belief too optimistic since they deny that we have such a fixed intended model of sets and they point out that we do not have any explicit description of the circumstances under which we would, for example, say that the continuum hypothesis has been proved or disproved.

In any case, clearly there are many obvious differences between such propositions and the statement that there are three feet in a yard. On the other hand, these differences do not seem to affect the belief that mathematics and physics are different. One might even imagine that general relativity or some other conceptually satisfying theory yielded no observable differences from classical physics. Even in such a case, one would still like to say that the new theory is different as physics because its acceptance would depend on its fitting physical observations, even though it differs from classical physics only conceptually.

Sometimes computers can be used to assist the study of pure mathematics (e.g. number theory) by verifying special cases or perhaps by checking the correctness of calculations and proofs. Since the computers employed are part of the physical world, we seem to be appealing to physical phenomena in justifying mathematical results. But here of course we are interested primarily in certain abstract properties of the actual computers we use and our conclusions do not depend essentially on which particular physical object the computer is or on all its detailed physical properties.

A more serious example may be the idea that Newtonian physics is true of Newtonian worlds. Even though we all believe now that Newtonian physics is not strictly true of the actual world, we may still claim that it is true and even a priori when correctly applied. One might feel that this is no different from $2 + 2 = 4$ which is not falsified by misapplications to pieces of cloud or to fertile rabbits. There remains, however, the vague feeling that $2 + 2 = 4$ is more abstract and has a wide range of examples, while Newtonian physics deals once and for all with a more or less unique thing, viz. the actual physical world or parts thereof. We also feel that Newtonian physics is meant to describe the world as it is, while $2 + 2 = 4$ contains more of a conceptual element; we seem to have a clearer idea of its range of application than that of Newtonian physics. It would be difficult to carry out the idea of a Newtonian world, because certain natural requirements would rule out the possibility that the physical world is Newtonian. The situation is very different with $2 + 2 = 4$.

There is a natural inclination to be impatient with the concern over whether mathematics and physics are different. Those who wish to emphasize a difference tend to view it as the kernel of a distinction between the a priori and the a posteriori, or one between the analytic and the synthetic. But it is not clear what work such a difference would do. If one believes that philosophy is after a priori propositions, then the conclusion may be drawn that philosophy is more like mathematics than physics. But we may also be led to doubt the assumption through questioning the conclusion. After all, physics deals with the fundamental aspects of this unique physical world, while mathematics seems much more diversified, treating of various abstract possibilities. If, as we believe, the actual is more central and important than the possibles, then it would appear more reasonable to expect philosophy to be concerned with basic features of the actual physical and mental worlds, or more accessibly with the actual knowledge mankind possesses.

In everyday life, physics is regarded as more closely connected with mathematics than with other natural sciences. It is, therefore, of interest to examine the interconnections and the similarities between physics and mathematics. Kant's theory of the synthetic a priori has the advantage of not only distinguishing physics (as connected with the understanding) from mathematics (as connected with the forms of intuition) but also emphasizing their similarities by the thesis that they are both intimately related to the way the human mind works.

The development of mathematical logic is associated with the idea of formality or formalization. Logicians have sometimes been accused of believing that to be is to be formal. In the field of elementary education, there has recently been an unhappy emphasis on the formal aspect of mathematics. Within advanced mathematics, there is also a controversy over the issue of traditions against the modern trend of piling up definitions. There seem to be four distinct elements in the idea of the mathematical tradition. First, it seems to be believed that traditional mathematics has been generally closer to applications in the physical sciences. Second, traditionalists consider older mathematical problems to be at the heart of mathematics because they are more natural, involve fewer structures, and are easier to state. Third, there is the feeling that traditional mathematics is more interested in the numerical contents of mathematical results and is, therefore, if often unconsciously, constructively oriented. Hence, according to this view, the logician's practice of contrasting classical with constructive mathematics (in particular, analysis) is based on a misunderstanding. But the notion of constructivity was intended in idealized senses and not clearly investigated. Fourth, traditional mathematics pays more attention to intuition and, for example, the attempt to make Euclidean geometry more formal is, at least pedagogically, a mistake. The basic (the underlying) difference is that traditional mathematics is less abstract.

While there is much substance in these points and in the implied traditionalist criticisms of a good deal of contemporary practice, the issues involved are by no means of the kind which admit simple sharp answers. For example, we might say that set theorists appeal to their intuition to find new axioms but use formal deductions to see whether the new axioms will decide the cardinality of the continuum. The concepts of groups and fields are undoubtedly of mathematical interest, yet one might legitimately claim that they have been singled out by the formal method. Even in studying the very formal question of the independence of axioms and hypotheses, the best results have been obtained by extensive appeals to the mathematical intuitions. There is the difficult question of perspicuity: sometimes the formal method helps to gain perspicuity and sometimes it hinders. In fact, the very concept of formal method is highly ambiguous when it is taken to be dealing with the mathematical activity rather than the end results.

A striking phenomenon about mathematical logic is its development into a more and more mathematical discipline. As it becomes ever more interesting mathematically, the logicians find themselves attracted into the whirl of mathematical activity. At the same time, its contribution to the philosophical understanding of the foundations of human knowledge (and mathematics in particular) appears to decrease rather than increase. This appearance can partly be accounted for by the clarification of a mistaken belief: as we understand the nature of mathematical logic better, we find that the early belief in its philosophical relevance was largely an illusion. But another reason may be the sociopsychological pull toward more definite results. This has produced the effect that the philosophically more relevant aspects of logic are left underdeveloped and consequently driven underground by the less relevant but more impressive mathematical advances.

The central place of logic is rather detached from actual knowledge. If we distinguish the three main aspects of knowledge of end results, activities, and progress, logic as a tool for formalizing all scientific knowledge seems to be concerned only with end results. Even in this one aspect, an unrealistic assumption is made that scientific theories are taken to have been formulated and formalized within the framework of mathematical logic or pure logic. Since these are not as a matter of fact so formulated and generally not presently suited to such formulations, much discussion on questions such as ontological assumptions and formal truth definitions of theories takes on a hypothetical and unreal air. One might wish to compare this type of hypothetical investigation to mathematics, but it is not clear how it naturally fits into the framework of human knowledge.

There are branches of knowledge, notably mathematics and the study of computers, which in a number of basic aspects do seem closer to logic and therefore are more likely to derive some benefit from sharp general results in mathematical logic. In any case, in view of the central place which logic occupies currently with regard to the philosophy of knowledge, it seems reasonable to use logic as a starting point even though serious misgivings are felt about the overemphasis on logic.

Introduction

NOTES

1 Compare, in particular, E. Husserl, 'Philosophie als strenge Wissenschaft,' *Logos*, vol. 1, 1910–11, pp. 289–341; English translation in Quentin Lauer, *Edmund Husserl: phenomenology and the crisis of philosophy*, 1965.

2 B. Blanshard, *Reason and analysis*, 1962, p. 52.

3 Compare, in particular, R. Carnap, *Logical syntax of language*, 1934 and 1937, and A. J. Ayer, *Language, truth and logic*, 1936 and 1946, chapter IV.

4 See G. Cantor, *Gesammelte Abhandlungen*, 1932, pp. 458–61, 465–6; and A. Schoenflies, 'Der Krisis in Cantors mathematischen Schaffen,' *Acta Math.*, vol. 50, 1928, pp. 1–23.

5 See D. Hilbert, *Gesammelte Abhandlungen*, vol. 3, 1935, pp. 202, 403.

6 See, e.g., their exchange in *Albert Einstein – philosopher-scientist*, ed. P. A. Schilpp, 1949.

7 In a letter to the author dated December 7, 1967. For exact references to Skolem's papers and some more historical details about the completeness theorem, compare 'A survey of Skolem's work in logic' in T. Skolem, *Selected works in logic*, ed. J. E. Fenstad, 1970, pp. 22–6.

8 In this connection, the reader may wish to consult the rather discursive considerations in section 10 of E. Post, 'Absolutely unsolvable problems and relatively undecidable propositions,' *The undecidable*, ed. M. Davis, 1965, pp. 414–17.

9 D. Hilbert, 'Über das Unendliche,' *Math. Annalen*, vol. 95, 1926, pp. 161–90. Page references are to the English translation in *From Frege to Gödel*, ed. J. V. Heijenoort, 1967.

10 *Albert Einstein – philosopher-scientist*, op. cit., pp. 53, 679. In a recent lecture entitled 'Poincaré on hypotheses, electrodynamics, and relativity,' Howard Stein argues that Poincaré missed discovering the special theory on account of a philosophical error. While it is inadequate to characterize the error in terms of positivism, the drift of Stein's argument seems to imply that Poincaré's fault was being too positivistic rather than not sufficiently positivistic.

11 David Pears, *Ludwig Wittgenstein*, 1971.

12 There is also a genuine sense in which language is inadequate to the expression and the communication of complicated thoughts or feelings. Hence, we have the saying that the best poets do not write. Those who possess a more delicate sense of what is appropriate will generally find it harder to write, because they cannot satisfy themselves as easily as their colleagues.

13 K. Gödel, 'Russell's mathematical logic,' 1944, 'What is Cantor's continuum problem?' 1947 and 1964 (all included in a collection entitled *Philosophy of mathematics*, ed. P. Benacerraf and H. Putnam), a paper on finitism and its extensions in *Dialectica*, 1958, and 'A remark about the relationship between relativity theory and idealistic philosophy,' *Albert Einstein – philosopher-scientist*, op. cit., pp. 555–62.

14 G. Frege, *Foundations of arithmetic*, § 14.

15 B. Russell, *Principles of mathematics*, p. 457.

16 B. Russell, *History of western philosophy*, p. 860.

17 B. Blanshard, op. cit., p. 259.

18 According to A. J. Ayer, 'philosophical propositions, if they are true, are usually analytic. (I have put in the qualifying word 'usually' because I think some empirical propositions, such as those that occur in histories of philosophy, may be counted philosophical. And philosophers use empirical propositions as examples, to serve philosophical ends.)' *Language, truth and logic*, 2nd edition, 1946, p. 26.

I

MATHEMATICAL LOGIC
AND PHILOSOPHY
OF MATHEMATICS

1 TOPICS IN THE PHILOSOPHY
OF MATHEMATICS

There has been much interaction between the philosophy of mathematics and the development of mathematical logic. In this regard, the central figure was Frege. He formalized pure logic, proposed a reduction of arithmetic to logic (or rather set theory) thereby inviting the broader thesis of the reducibility of all mathematics to logic, and broadened Kant's concept of analytic propositions. Frege's inclination to include set theory under logic was in part responsible for the interest of mathematical logicians in Cantor's intuitive and mathematical set theory. Frege's extension of the domain of analytic propositions and Hilbert's emphasis on implicit definitions have influenced the trend of magnifying the importance of analytic propositions for philosophy.

The achievements of Frege have led gradually to a formal and rigid trend not only in the philosophy of mathematics but also, notably through the work of the earlier Wittgenstein and Carnap, in general philosophy. On the more mathematical side, the influences of Cantor and Hilbert culminated in the works of Gödel. He is the central figure in the discipline of mathematical logic, which has more recently evolved into a technical branch of mathematics. Gradually the inadequacies of mathematical logic as the basic tool for the philosophy of mathematics and for general philosophy have come to be felt. On the one hand, as mathematical logic develops into a substantial subject, the appeal of bold simplicity both inside the subject and as projected on mathematics and on knowledge is lost. On the other hand, the disregard by mathematical logic of actual mathematical activity and practice is seen to yield a one-sided approach to the philosophy of mathematics and knowledge in general.

A partial list of overlapping basic issues commonly discussed in the philosophy of mathematics is the following.

1 The nature of pure logic and its place in human knowledge.
2 The characterization of mathematical concepts.
3 The place of intuition and formalization in mathematics.
4 The relation between logic and mathematics.
5 The nature of mathematics and its relation to concepts such as necessity, analyticity, certainty, the a priori, and self-evidence.
6 The place of mathematics in human knowledge.
7 Mathematical activity and practice.

It is widely accepted that first order predicate calculus (with or without equality) gives a fairly definitive characterization of pure logic. A task of much philosophical interest is to give reasons to justify (or refute) such a belief and to argue against (or for) other candidates such as modal logic, intuitionistic logic, and logic with additional primitives such as 'for uncountably many x.' Given the belief in the identity of logic with the predicate calculus, one is inclined to think of every scientific theory as formulated within the framework of the predicate calculus. And we have positive attempts so to formulate scientific theories and to claim, by way of concepts and results in pure logic, hypothetical generalities about scientific theories thus formulated such as definability, eliminability of intermediate terms, and ontological assumptions. There are also projects to extend the domain of pure logic to deal with causality, time, truth and meaning in natural languages.

Mathematical logic is perhaps most successful in the exact characterization of mathematical concepts. The central examples are (natural) number, the continuum, set. The formalization of pure logic may also be viewed as an exact characterization of the concept of logical proof or logical validity. On a different level, which might be called metalogical, the intuitive concept of adequacy of a theory is rendered more exact by the concepts of completeness and categoricity; the intuitive concepts of consistency and model are sharpened in mathematical logic. The most surprising and interesting example is perhaps the exact definition of the concept of formality or mechanical procedure which yields mathematical treatments of decidable theories, computability, and general impossibility results. Whether all these characterizations are illuminating or even correct is not beyond debate. For example, intuitionists would prefer a different and less formal characterization of number theory; there are many interesting questions about the continuum (such as its applications in physics and the geometrical intuition) which remain untouched by an axiomatic characterization and the issue of constructivism against objectivism appears in an acute form with regard to the continuum.

The two components of intuition and formalization get some clarification from the exact definition of mechanical procedure. While mathematical logic has little to say about heuristic procedures, it offers a sharp distinction between strict demonstrations, which are extensively investigated in mathematical logic, and heuristic procedures, which are closely related to questions of pedagogy and the psychology of mathematical innovation. A related question is the possibilities and limitations of mechanized thinking. These questions are considered under the headings 'mathematics and computers' and 'minds and machines.' The contrast of intuition with formalization also cuts across the issue of constructivism against objectivism, both of which are, as coherent positions, denied the power of looking from outside. In other words, both positions are open ended so that, for example, there can be no constructive characterization of all constructive methods, and whether a procedure is constructive is to be decided by an appeal to intuition. An objectivist is inclined to take an exactly delineated area such as recursive or hyperarithmetic as the domain of constructive methods and then the domain often invites further extensions.

The moot question of whether mathematics is reducible to logic can also be formulated in a different way. While the reductionist agrees that Aristotle's theory does not provide a complete analysis of mathematical reasoning, he contends that with an enlarged logical theory having a character similar to the theory of syllogism, such an analysis is possible. The opponent would argue that mathematical reasoning requires procedures which are essentially different from syllogisms. Intuitively we are inclined to say that infinity is a mathematical but not a logical concept. For example, Poincaré regards each use of mathematical induction as an infinite sequence of syllogisms. It follows that mathematics cannot be reduced to pure logic. Or, if logic is to include set theory, we might include number theory as well and dispense with the reduction. Moreover, it is natural and advantageous to separate out the interesting domain of pure logic, given its current sharp delineation.

There is another position which may be called hypothetical or if-then reductionism. According to this view, the business of mathematics is to show that if there is a structure satisfying such and such axioms, then the structure satisfies such and such further statements. Even though neither the axioms nor the theorems are generally theorems of pure logic, each statement 'if A, then p,' where p is a theorem and A is the conjunction of axioms applied in deriving p, is a theorem of pure logic. Note first that since the axioms need not be concerned with any mathematical subject matter, this is too broad as a definition of mathematics. We may yet uphold hypothetical reductionism which says merely that all of mathematics is reducible to pure logic in the above sense. This thesis is not much different from the belief that all mathematical arguments can be formalized (in the framework of logic).

Since we would like to leave out the practical question of actually formalizing complicated intuitive proofs, we may easily dispense with the question of incomplete or inadequate sets of axioms. Given a proof of a theorem p, we collect together all the extralogical axioms we have used. For example, we may include among these not only axioms of any familiar system S, but also a proposition Con(S) that expresses the consistency of S and thus defeat Gödel incompleteness. Often we would have neglected to make explicit additional assumptions such as that the field or the group is finite, and we proceed to formulate and add these axioms in set theoretical terms. It is true that 'If A, then p' can only establish those true theorems p which are not only true in the intended model of A but also true in all models of A. But this does not entail a necessary limitation since we are not confined to a fixed recursive set A of axioms given in advance, and different theorems p_t often require different combinations A_t of axioms. Incidentally, if we use Frege's definition of natural numbers, we can also, with some care, derive in pure logic the applied conclusion 'there are altogether 12 coins in my pockets' from the general principle '$7 + 5 = 12$' in combination with empirical premises such as 'there are 7 coins in my lefthand pocket and 5 in my righthand pocket.'

This familiar sense of 'hypothetical logicism' is undoubtedly what was implicit in the reducibility thesis of all mathematical problems to the Entscheidungsproblem (for pure logic), emphasized by the Hilbert school in the twenties. It says very little to distinguish mathematics from empirical knowledge, and it would be circular to require that the axioms and the conclusions contain only mathematical terms. To require that they contain only variables and logical constants (i.e. constants of pure logic plus the membership relation of set theory) would be more informative but merely transform the definition to the other familiar thesis that mathematics is (reducible to) set theory. The burden of characterizing mathematics is shifted to the problem of characterizing the extralogical axioms.

The hackneyed motto is that we require consistency and only consistency of these axioms. Even if we assume, as we reasonably can, that we are able to rule out empirical terms, the requirement is of little value. Of course, if the axioms are inconsistent, most of us would like to revise them. But we operate constantly with axioms (of set theory, for instance) which are not proven to be consistent. On the other hand, there are many consistent systems which are of no interest. In fact, since we all have some experience playing with permutations and combinations, it is clear that most possible consistent systems are uninteresting. The special intuitive features of the axioms of (say) arithmetic, geometry, and set theory which make them so central to mathematics remain untouched by the doctrine of hypothetical logicism. Actually, there is also implicit in this doctrine the feeling that in mathematics we are mainly interested in abstract structures such as groups, rings, and fields which are powerful because they are realized in diverse ways. Here again, we are not interested in just any possible abstract structure (i.e. combination of properties) but rather in only a very few of them.

Frege's extension of Kant's concept of analytic proposition has gradually assimilated all of mathematics and led to arresting views such as: all mathematical propositions are analytic (true in virtue of the meanings of the concepts involved), true by convention (of the same kind as the proposition there are three feet in a yard), 'tautologous' (true in all possible worlds). If 'father of' and 'to the left of' are relations in the natural sense, while 'a thousand miles away from' is a relation in the philosophical sense, we might claim that Kant attempts to use 'analytic' in the natural sense and Frege introduces the philosophical sense. Even if we agree that there is a seductive sense of 'analytic' such that all mathematical propositions are analytic, the sweeping generalization does not seem to offer very much concerning the nature of mathematics, and it seems to obliterate many conceptually important distinctions. This and related questions will be considered under the heading 'necessity, apriority, and analyticity.'

The place of mathematics in human knowledge seems to be more interesting than that of pure logic. The overemphasis on logic and the ambiguous identification of logic with mathematics in contemporary philosophy tend to evade many substantial philosophical issues such as the relation between mathematics and physics. While many are tempted to identify the theoretical component with the mathematical component of a science, the two do not coincide in practice. For example, there is an established usage among physicists which distinguishes theoretical from mathematical physics, and theoretical physicists seem to enjoy a greater prestige among physicists.

With regard to biology, there is a small number of people called mathematical biologists but one rarely speaks of theoretical biology. The majority of biologists do not seem to take mathematical biology seriously, perhaps because mathematical considerations do not promise central contributions to biology in the near future. Among biologists there is a certain reluctance in speaking of theoretical biology, and if asked about theoretical biology, there is a surprising tendency to equate it with mathematical biology. There is undoubtedly a distinction between actually performing experiments and reflecting on known results so as to predict future developments (in particular, to suggest lines of approach and even specific new experiments to be carried out). The latter sort of activity would seem to be of a more theoretical character, and hypotheses can be and are tested by experiments in biology. Perhaps the reason why it is unnatural to distinguish experimental from theoretical biology is because experiments and reflections are so closely intermixed that it is impossible to isolate any reasonably long chains of theoretical deliberation. At any rate, the center of gravity of an empirical science cannot lie in its mathematical part but must be at a point that is concerned with an intercourse of the science in its current state with brute empirical facts.

With regard to activity and practice in mathematics, it is desirable to consider an abstract history of mathematics, the phenomena of understanding a proof and accepting a theorem as established, as well as the interaction of the intuitive and the mechanical. Some of these issues are considered under the headings 'theory and practice in mathematics' and 'mathematics and computers.'

2 THE AXIOMATIC METHOD AND ABSTRACT STRUCTURES

The use of formal axiomatic systems is a familiar feature of mathematical logic. Each scientific theory involves a body of concepts and a collection of assertions. When questioned about the meaning of a concept, we often explain it or define it in terms of other concepts. Similarly, when questioned about the truth or the reason for believing the truth of an assertion, we usually justify our belief by indicating that it follows from or can be deduced from certain other assertions which we accept. If somebody, as many children do, continues indefinitely to ask for definitions or deductions, it is obvious that sooner or later one of two things will happen. Either we find ourselves traveling in a circle, making use, in our answers, of concepts and assertions whose meaning and justification we originally set out to explain; or, at some stage, we refuse to supply any more definitions and deductions, and reply bluntly that the concepts and assertions we employ in our answer are already the most basic which we take for granted.

When the problem is to understand the meaning of a concept or to see that a proposition is true, there is no basic objection to circular procedures, and indeed, mutual support may in many cases prove to be the best sort of evidence we can ever obtain. But, when we are able to start merely with a small number of primitive ideas and propositions, the linear mode of appoach does have a special appeal and fascination in that questions of meaning and truth become concentrated in these few initial primitives plus certain typical ways of definition and deduction.

Usually the primitive propositions are called axioms or postulates. When the concepts and propositions of a theory are thus arranged according to the connections of definability and deducibility, we have an axiomatic system for the theory.

The formal axiomatic approach makes general considerations about whole disciplines possible, and often produces a feeling of increased control and understanding of the subject matter.

The best known axiom system is undoubtedly Euclid's for geometry. His *Elements* is said to have had a wide circulation next only to the Bible. Admiration for its rigor and thoroughness has been expressed frequently. Spinoza, for example, attempted to attain the same formal perfection in his *Ethics*.

While Euclid's unification of masses of more or less isolated discoveries was undoubtedly an impressive success in the program of systematizing mathematics, his actual axiom system is, according to the standard generally accepted now, far from formally perfect.

The discovery of non-Euclidean geometries around 1830 led to a desire to separate abstract mathematics from spatial intuition. For example, Grassmann stressed in his *Ausdehnungslehre* (1844) the distinction between a purely mathematical discipline and its application to nature. Since the axioms are no longer necessarily true in the physical world, there arises a desire to make deductions independent of spatial intuition, and to avoid reliance on diagrams and the meaning of geometrical concepts.

Meanwhile, there were also other forces at work such as the impossibility proofs in algebra and geometry, and the widespread discomfort over concepts and proofs in higher analysis. All these converged to the same ideals: explicit enunciation of presuppositions, rigor of proof, and sharp definition of concepts. There was the demand that in mathematics everything capable of proof should be proved. It was appreciated that proofs not only establish truth but reveal interconnections between different theorems. Often the exact limit of validity of a theorem was determined only after a rigorous proof had been given. In general, there are different degrees of formalization. If Euclid thought wrongly that his axiom system was completely, formal, how do we know that a system considered formal now will not be seen to be imperfectly formalized in the future? In the evolution of axiom systems there has emerged a sharp criterion of formalization in terms, not of meaning and concepts, but of notational features of terms and formulas. The criterion goes like this: There is a mechanical procedure to determine whether a given notational pattern is a symbol occurring in the system, whether a combination of these symbols is a meaningful formula (a sentence), or an axiom or a proof of the system. Thus, the formation rules, i.e. rules for specifying sentences, are entirely explicit in the sense that theoretically a machine can be constructed to pick out all sentences of the system if we use suitable physical representation of the basic symbols. The axioms and rules of inference are also entirely explicit. Every proof in each of these systems, when written out completely, consists of a finite sequence of lines such that each line is either an axiom or follows from some previous lines in the sequence by a definite rule of inference. Therefore, given any proposed proof, presented in conformity with the formal requirements for proofs in these systems, we can check its correctness mechanically. Theoretically, for each such formal system, we can also construct a machine which continues to print all the different proofs of the system from the simpler ones to the more complex, until the machine finally breaks down through wear and tear. If we suppose that the machine will never break down, then every proof of the system can be printed by the machine. Moreover, since a sentence is a theorem if and only if it is the last line of a proof, the machine will also, sooner or later, print every theorem of the system.

There are two different directions of development of the axiomatic method. On the one hand, we have formal systems such as those of arithmetic and Euclidean geometry, each with one intended model. These are categorical (but no longer completely formal) systems if we think of them as the second order theories which presuppose an intended informal concept of sets (of integers and of points or real numbers). On the other hand, we have abstract structures whose strength is derived from the fact that each of them (groups, field, topological spaces) permits varied and diverse realizations.

The influential Bourbaki group proposes to unify mathematics by means of abstract structures.[1] Their purpose is not to unify mathematics in connection with a more or less ambitious philosophical system in the sense of Plato, or Descartes, or Leibniz, or arthmeticism, or logicism. The goal is more modest and more restricted. There is no attempt to examine the relation of mathematics to physical reality or to the major conceptual categories. The intention is to remain inside mathematics and to analyze its internal workings, in order to refute the impression that mathematics is in the process of becoming a motley of autonomous disciplines which are isolated from one another, in their goals, as well as in their methods and their language. It is believed that today the internal evolution of mathematics has, despite appearances to the contrary, reasserted more than ever the unity of the diverse parts and created a sort of central kernel more coherent than ever, viz. the hierarchy of structures.

The axiomatic method is to reveal the essence of a proof by singling out the most general natural structure in which the proof is valid. In this way, one is taught to look for deeper reasons why exceptional mathematicians can unexpectedly bring apparently unrelated theories to bear on one another, to find common ideas hidden under the external details of each theory, and to extract these ideas and to bring them in relief. From this approach, we seem to acquire a new dimension of depth in mathematics which increases with universality rather than specificity. Abstract structures enable us to prove once and for all different theorems in different theories which share the same structure.

One thinks of a hierarchy of structures, from simple to complex, from general to particular. At the center are mother structures such as groups and ordered sets. These lead directly to finite groups, Abelian finite groups, linearly ordered sets, well-ordered sets. We have also multiple structures obtained from diverse mother structures not by mere juxtaposition but organically by one or more connecting axioms; for example, we get various structures studied in algebraic topology. Gradually we reach particular theories by iterating such organic combinations and then we recover the particular theories of classical mathematics.

Several limitations of this general viewpoint are recognized. For example, the completely particular theory of real numbers is indispensable for developing general theories such as topology and integration. There are numerous isolated results in many theories (in particular, the theory of numbers) which we cannot today classify and relate satisfactorily to known structures. Also the structures are not unchangeable; it is very likely that we shall find new fundamental structures, new axioms, and new combinations of them.

This view is contrasted with the harmless but uninformative thesis that mathematics is unified by the use of deductive reasoning (or pure logic), which is similar to a proposal to unite physics and biology in one science by the observation that both use the experimental method. Codifying the language by listing the vocabulary and clarifying the syntax is the least interesting aspect of the axiomatic method; this aspect is identified with logistic formalism and probably a criticism of mathematical logic is implied. Logistic formalism is contrasted with a good formalism in the sense of emphasizing structures, i.e. forms of theories. The good formalism stresses the important or essential aspect of the axiomatic method and begins with the assumption that mathematics is more than a chain of syllogisms discovered at random, more than a mere collection of more or less cunning artifices contrived accidentally by pure technical competence. It is capable of furnishing an account of the profound intelligibility of mathematics.

A familiar objection to this structuralism is that it fails to take into account the important relations between the world of mathematics and the world of natural sciences. Even though one may quote unexpected applications of pure mathematics and speak of finding that certain aspects of the experimental reality realize these abstract structures by a sort of preadaptation, it cannot be denied that this structuralism is a plea for a very special kind of autonomy of pure mathematics. One of its main appeals is its isolation of mathematics from its applications. An additional appeal is its aim at a neatly structured grand edifice and its avoidance, as far as possible, of isolated brute facts about numbers and geometrical figures. Both appeals have their prices. Those who find applications the heart and soul of mathematics (as distinct from intellectual games) would prefer to return frequently to the empirical sciences to look for new suggestions. Those who think of numbers and figures as the ultimate subject matter of mathematics would consider structuralism a systematic attempt to evade tough genuine mathematical problems. Of course, there is also the reply that in the long run structuralism will fare better even for applications and the solution of tough concrete problems. But then, the strength of the position would depend on a prediction and such predictions are notoriously hard to evaluate. They often serve to rationalize doing what one would prefer to do for quite other reasons.

It often happens that when we cannot solve a given problem, we try to transform it into more abstract ones which become more manageable. Ideally these would eventually lead us back to a solution of the original problem. Natural or mathematical reality sometimes seems too vague, too fragmentary, or too recalcitrant to be sucessfully handled by our abstract thoughts. We have a choice of trying harder or just doing what we can at the moment with the hope of coming back to the old problem later. Structuralism appears to make the gap between concrete reality and abstract thought a virtue, recommending that the best way is first to clean the inside of the house of mathematics by emphasizing abstract structures. It is postulated that eventually structures and reality will converge.

According to Bourbaki, a 'mathematical structure' is by nature abstract. 'The common character of the different concepts designated by this generic name, is that they can be applied to sets of elements whose nature has not been specified.' The central dogma of structuralism is that all particularities in mathematics can be analyzed without residue into abstract structures. A more drastic thesis dealing with all scientific knowledge was at one time put forward by Carnap:[2]

> Thus, our thesis, namely that scientific statements relate only to structural properties, amounts to the assertion that scientific statements speak only of forms without stating what the elements and the relations of these forms are. . . . Thus, the result is that a definite description through pure structure statements is generally possible to the extent in which scientific discrimination is possible at all; such a description is unsuccessful for two objects only if these objects are not distinguishable at all by scientific methods.

This general structuralism shows much less respect for actual knowledge than Bourbaki's mathematical structuralism. It presupposes a logicist view of mathematics which is in part based on a confusion between Frege's and Cantor's different concepts of set. There is also an unwarranted emphasis on the syntactic aspect of theories and 'constructions.' The general tendency to avoid intended meaning and to claim the thesis *T*, that what can be said scientifically can be said structurally, completely overlooks the rich complexities of successful scientific practice. If we take existing science as brute data to be accounted for, it is abundantly clear that the thesis *T* is not proven and the program suggested by it is misguided.

It seems clear that Carnap's structural description of the given in experience does not and cannot capture the given. There is the problem whether the given is the same for everybody. And the structure of the given cannot be communicated between subjects, unless a certain common intended interpretation of the axioms is postulated; yet the given is supposed to be identified with its structural description. As 'empiricism,' we have a difficulty in understanding how according to this view experience controls the formation of scientific concepts, since such control can occur only at the beginning of the whole conceptual system. Some intuitive element is necessary in order to induce a revision of a given structural description, but it is something scientifically unknowable according to the thesis *T*. The position is perhaps amusing in that it proposes a radical empiricism which seems to dispense with experience and empirical data altogether.

3 QUESTIONS OF CONSISTENCY

In discussing modern foundational researches, it is customary to exaggerate the importance of the discovery of paradoxes around 1900. Actually, present day mathematical logic is derived from a number of different sources, none of which dominates the whole outlook.

Reacting against the prevalence of nonconstructive proofs in analysis, Kronecker emphasized the desirability of using constructive methods of proof long before the discovery of paradoxes in set theory. The problem of constructive proofs continues today to enjoy a fair amount of attention. Not only can Brouwer's position be regarded as a call to banish nonconstructive proofs but even Hilbert's approach can also be regarded as a request to justify nonconstructive proofs by constructive methods. And there are recent attempts to develop constructive mathematics. In mathematical logic we have quite a bit of work on the nature and peculiarities of constructive proofs. For example, working mathematicians often have a pretty good idea how certain nonconstructive proofs can be transformed into constructive ones. Mathematical logic makes possible a more explicit and more systematic treatment of large classes of proofs on which such transformations can be made.

Another remote source is the negative answers obtained in the nineteenth century to questions such as that of solving quintic equations or trisecting angles by elementary methods, and, to some extent, that of deriving the parallel postulate from other axioms of Euclidean geometry. These impossibility proofs required the sharp delineation of all constructions or all proofs of some branch of mathematics. The phrases 'all algebraic proofs' and 'all geometrical methods of construction' sound hopelessly vague, and it was a remarkable achievement to have succeeded in replacing these by precise concepts. A powerful tool along the same line is the diagonal method, commonly credited to Cantor. Impossibility proofs, in particular undecidability proofs, occupy an important place in present day mathematical logic. Variants of the diagonal method are frequently applied in such proofs.

The construction of formal systems for various branches of logic and mathematics also preceded the discovery of paradoxes in set theory. Some people, for example E. V. Huntington, had been led to take an interest in building formal systems for their own sake. Although there is sometimes the impression that logicians are largely concerned with the game of adding or taking away a few slightly different axioms to make new formal systems, I think it is fair to say that such activities are neither the more important nor the more interesting business of logicians.

Even when Hilbert raised in 1900 the question of the consistency of arithmetic, he did not do so because he was concerned over the paradoxes in set theory. (He was aware of the paradoxes.) Rather the question of the consistency of formal systems seems inevitable when we wish to formalize and avoid appeal to intuition. If we no longer require that the axioms of a formal system be intuitively obvious, we have no assurance that no contradictions will arise. It is not sufficient to say that the axioms correspond pretty closely to our intuition, for it may happen that contradictions come in exactly through the slight discrepancy between intuition and formalization.

In order to prove the consistency of a formal system, we have to have a pretty thorough understanding of the proofs in the system. The question of consistency provides one sharp criterion for deciding how well we know a system. It also supplies a channel to help concentrate our efforts to improve understanding. Consistency alone does not make a system interesting, but the absence of a consistency proof for an interesting system is often thought to be an indication that we are not yet at home with the system.

A formal system is consistent if there is no theorem whose negation is also a theorem. This is equivalent to saying that some proposition of the system is not a theorem, because in an inconsistent system every proposition is a theorem. In each of certain systems a proposition *p* can be found and interpreted as saying that *p* itself is not a theorem. It can also be proved that the proposition *p* cannot be proved in the system (if the system is consistent). Some people think[3] that this already establishes the unprovability of consistency in the same system. This involves a misunderstanding because, although if *p* is not provable, then the system is consistent, it remains to be demonstrated that if there is any proposition not derivable, *p* is also not derivable. It is not sufficient to say that *p* is intuitively equivalent to the proposition expressing consistency: 1 the question whether the natural proposition expressing consistency is provable remains to be decided; 2 there are propositions which intuitively also express consistency of the system but are provable.

As we know, a natural proposition which expresses consistency is not provable in the system. This result of Gödel led many to the conclusion that no significant consistency proofs are possible, in particular that the highly informative consistency proofs for number theory are not interesting. The reasoning seems to proceed as follows. Gödel's theorem shows that a proof of consistency must use means not formalizable in the given system. Therefore, the proof is less elementary (less indubitable) than any proof in the system. Therefore, the proof cannot improve our psychological state of belief in the trustworthiness of the system. Therefore, the proof is not interesting. I am inclined to question all three steps. We can find more difficult proofs in number theory than proofs of its consistency. There is no reason to suppose that current formalizations of number theory must correspond so closely to the degree of reliability of proofs, that every proof in the system is more dependable than one outside it. Rather, there are certain intuitive modes of reasoning about natural numbers whose transparent character has evaded our usual formalizations.

It might seem puzzling that, e.g. the Peano axioms, in particular, an alternative explicit formulation with only a finite number of axioms should contain so many surprises. The essential thing is, of course, the possibility of iterated applications of the same old rules in an unbounded number of combinations. This is also why proving the consistency of such a system is no easy matter.

There is a great difference between understanding a single proof and seeing that none of a whole infinite collection of proofs would lead to a contradiction. For example, in proving the consistency of number theory, a principle of transfinite induction is applied and one is inclined to consider the rule in its full generality as in no way more transparent than the ordinary rule of mathematical induction, thus proved consistent. We must, however, remember that in the consistency proof we are called upon to grasp a *single application* of the rule of transfinite induction in order to see the truth of the more difficult conclusion that the rule of mathematical induction in all its applications never can lead to contradictions. Perhaps a more convincing method of argument in this connection would be obtained only by actual examination of a given proof of consistency.

The situation with regard to number theory is obscured by the fact that we are usually convinced of its consistency, and that even when we try to practice deliberate skepticism we have no idea where we are to look for contradictions. And in other areas, such as set theory, we do not have serious consistency proofs. It seems, therefore, natural to doubt whether a proof of consistency makes any difference so far as reliability of the system is concerned. We cannot, however, deny that it does improve our understanding of the general nature of proofs in the system. For instance, we are led to interpretations of quantifiers by computable functions and classification of proofs according to several natural measures of complexity.

Insofar as a formal system is to represent an intuitive theory, we expect that theorems of the system represent intuitively true propositions. To assure this, consistency is necessary but not sufficient. All theorems of an inconsistent system cannot be true. But all theorems of a consistent system need not be true. Indeed, it is possible to build up consistent systems whose theorems cannot all be true. For example, we can find a calculus and a formula $F(a)$ such that $F(n)$ is a theorem for each given number n and at the same time 'there exists some number y, not-$F(y)$' is also a theorem. We are, however, inclined to think that, if $F(n)$ is true for every n, then '$\exists y$ not $F(y)$' must be false.

Wittgenstein sometimes[4] identifies true in a system with provable in a system. If we assume that the meaning of basic terms of a calculus is completely determined by the rules of proof, then the identification seems inescapable. How, then, can a theorem be false, or even a nontheorem be true? It becomes necessary to introduce another system in which the false theorem of the original system is refutable or the true nontheorem is provable. This way of speaking is not very convenient. Moreover, if, for example, all cases of $F(n)$ are theorems of a system but '$\forall x\, F(x)$' is neither provable nor refutable, is there any question that adding '$\forall x\, F(x)$' as an axiom is a more natural extension than adding its negation?

Consider the following situation. Nobody has proved or disproved Fermat's conjecture. Imagine that somehow it has been proved to be undecidable by elementary methods. Then it would follow that Fermat's conjecture is true. For suppose it were false. There would be positive integers m, n, k, $j > 2$ such that $m^j + n^j = k^j$. But such an equation can be established by elementary methods, m, n, k, j being constants. Since these elementary methods can be got from the current system of number theory, the argument also proves that if Fermat's conjecture is undecidable in that system, then it is true. If one identifies true with provable, to ask whether an undecidable sentence is true or false is meaningless. Here we have an example where not only is the question meaningful but the answer is determined provided the sentence is indeed undecidable. If one finds the example unrealistic because Fermat's conjecture has not been shown to be undecidable, we can take the sentence p which can be interpreted as saying p is unprovable in a given system. p is actually known to be undecidable in the system and therefore true. The proof of p is of course no longer a proof in the given system. It is, nonetheless, hard to deny that it does establish the truth of p. If, by some method, we see that all instances of a general proposition about numbers are true, we cannot help concluding that the general proposition itself is also true.

Assuming again that Fermat's conjecture is undecidable in the system of current number theory, then we can add the conjecture or its negation as a new axiom and get two consistent systems; say, a Fermat arithmetic, and a non-Fermat arithmetic. Both of them are consistent. Yet the non-Fermat arithmetic admits only of very strange interpretations because it would be, in technical terms, ω-inconsistent.

Both Gödel and Hardy speak of a mathematical reality. For example, Hardy says,[5] 'I believe that mathematical reality lies outside us, that our function is to discover or *observe* it.' This sounds obscure. It may be suggested that the Fermat arithmetic and the non-Fermat arithmetic define two concepts of number, and that it is meaningless to ask whether Fermat's conjecture is true or false, because a mathematical formula has no well-determined meaning independently of any calculus to which it belongs. If Hardy's remark is meant to refute this suggestion, then it is right, at least insofar as natural numbers are concerned.

On the other hand, the question whether the parallel postulate is true may seem to depend on the particular kind of geometry we wish to use. Here we seem to have a case where our meaning is not entirely determinate (to imagine lines meeting at infinity, etc.) so that it may be possible to have different determinations. In other words, when pressed, we are not able to say whether the parallel postulate is true or false. Indeed, this example probably led people to refuse to speak of truth outside a calculus. But there is no reason to suppose that this is the general rule.

It is remarkable that the Russell-Zermelo contradiction led Frege to doubt whether arithmetic can be given a reliable foundation at all. Actually the contradictions in no way make it necessary to abandon all definitions of number in terms of sets. What is affected is only the project of formalizing a general theory of sets, and that only according to the Fregean conception which seems to make sets a part of logic. We were at first struck by the fact that natural numbers, real numbers, and many other things can all be gotten out of sets. Then we found that contradictions can be gotten out of sets too. Many people conclude, therefore, that we are now to design a calculus which includes as much of the other things as possible but not the contradictions.

If we do not think in terms of a system, why can we not treat a proof of contradiction as just another piece of mathematics which could be judged interesting or uninteresting more or less in the same manner as other mathematical proofs? True, the conclusion, being a contradiction, cannot be significant in the same way as an ordinary theorem is. The proof establishes either more or less than usual. It either shows 'the unreliability of our basic logical intuition,' or reveals some confusion on the part of the owner of the proof. Dividing both sides of the correct equation $3 \cdot 0 = 2 \cdot 0$ or $3(2 - 2) = 2(2 - 2)$ by 0, we easily get the contradiction: $3 = 2$. Such a discovery does not excite us because it is well established that the restriction $c \neq 0$ is essential in inferring $a = b$ from $ac = bc$. Why can one not discard the contradictions in set theory as easily? The reason, on the surface, is the lack of any comparably simple and natural restriction which would do the job. This is, it is sometimes said, an indication of the more basic fact that our concept of set is not sufficiently clear.

Formal systems are to suit the actual proofs in living mathematics, not the other way about. If a formal system adequate for analysis yields a contradiction, we say that we no longer trust the formal system. How would this affect the many mathematical results in analysis, accumulated through the centuries? It is hard to speculate on the basis of such an indeterminate hypothesis. We may, however, remind ourselves that practically no significant mathematical theorems or proofs have been given up because of the contradictions of set theory, which have, according to some people, discredited the fundamental methods of argumentation in set theory.

The emphasis on a consistent adherence to the rules we use in mathematical reasoning has generated a sharper distinction between confusion and contradiction. To treat an infinitesimal sometimes as zero and sometimes as a positive quantity in the same proof is a confusing and inconsistent procedure, but does not yet yield an explicit contradiction. The criticism of a proof using infinitesimals is ambiguity and not that a contradiction follows.

Why should contradictions worry anybody? Imagine a mathematician who is pleased with the discovery of a group of new theorems and publishes a book. A rival studies the proofs and comes along with the challenge, 'Using your kind of argument, I can prove even contradictions.' Could he then reply, 'Well, how nice! My methods have interesting applications of which I was not aware. Let me add another chapter entitled "Further Applications of the Above Methods" '? Even though contradictions are often interesting and new methods are often recommended by the interesting theorems which they enable us to prove, nobody, unless his purpose were to experiment with contradictions, has recommended a method on the ground that it is powerful enough to yield contradictions. One possible reaction to the discovery of a contradiction is to analyze the moves involved in the derivation and pronounce some of the moves unwarranted. It is more desirable to reflect on the basic concepts involved. The repercussions of a contradiction include the rejection of all proofs which involve similar moves. In this sense, contradictions are contagious. Proofs which were otherwise considered healthy are put into concentrated isolation on account of their contact with contradictions.

There is the idea of using formal systems as a tool for separating desirable from undesirable arguments. Formal systems are constructed under the guiding principle that when an argument is found to be faulty, all arguments of the same *kind* are to be excluded. This gives the impression of being less arbitrary in our exclusion of certain arguments because we are rejecting not only one particular argument but all arguments of its kind. Given any argument, there is, however, inevitably an element of arbitrariness in any attempt to determine the kind to which it belongs. Indeed, there are so many different ways by which we can determine the underlying category of an argument, that we do not even have to use formal systems for this particular purpose.

Suppose we are given a group of theorems and a formal system in which proofs for these theorems can be carried out. Suppose that a contradiction is discovered in the formal system. The system is thereby discredited. What about those theorems which were originally discovered with no regard to this formal system? True, there is now a uniform method of proving all these theorems *in the formal system* because there is a generally accepted principle that a contradiction implies everything. We may yet distinguish proofs of the system which go through contradictions from those which do not. Every proposition of the system has a proof of the first kind but not necessarily one of the second kind.

Does the inconsistency of a formal system destroy the value of those proofs which do not go through contradictions? The first question is, of course, what values we attached to the proofs to begin with. Were we originally interested in the proofs on account of their beauty, or the truth of the conclusions they established, or their utility? Proofs in an inconsistent system or a system not known to be consistent can often have heuristic value: for instance, divergent series have often led to interesting results and there are theorems of number theory which were at first proved by methods of analysis and later on received more elementary proofs.

It is known that we can derive the differential and integral calculus in some system of set theory which is not known to be consistent. Suppose the system is found to be inconsistent. It follows that we can derive all sorts of false and absurd consequences in this system, some of them having to do with the differential and integral calculus.

Since the calculus can be applied in constructing bridges, we may be able to prove that a pillar whose diameter is three feet is strong enough although actually we need a pillar whose diameter is seven feet. Hence, it might be argued, bridges may collapse because of the inconsistency of the particular system in which we can develop the calculus.

Actually no such thing can happen. For one thing, those who construct and develop axiomatic foundations of the calculus are usually not the same people as those who apply the calculus in the construction of bridges. It is not impossible that, by accident, the same person may be engaged in both kinds of activity. Even then, he is not going to do his calculations by going all the way back to his favorite axiomatic set theory. Moreover, even if he does take the trouble to justify his calculation, after it is done, by citing explicitly the axioms and theorems of the set theory, he is still in no danger of getting the wrong result because he does not use all the complicated apparatus that is available in the system but makes only such turns as could also be justified in consistent systems.

It is not necessary to formalize mathematics nor to prove consistency of formal systems if the problem is to avoid bridges collapsing unexpectedly. There are many things which are much more pertinent insofar as bridges are concerned.

So far as the present state of mathematics is concerned, speculations on inconsistent systems are rather idle. No formal system which is widely used today is under very serious suspicion of inconsistency. The importance of set-theoretical contradictions has been greatly exaggerated in some quarters. When the non-Euclidean geometries were discovered and found to be unintuitive, it was natural to look for consistency proofs by modeling considerations. And then it was a short step before one asked for the basis on which the model itself is founded. When Kronecker thought of classical analysis as a game with words, it was again natural that he raised the question whether such a game was even consistent. But the more modern search for consistency proofs is differently motivated and has a more serious purpose than avoiding contradictions: it seeks for a better understanding of the concepts and methods.

'The superstitious fear and awe of mathematicians in face of the contradiction.' But Frege was a logician and Cantor was a mathematician. Cantor was not a bit worried about the contradictions. In fact, he said: 'What Burali-Forti has produced is thoroughly foolish. If you go back to his articles in *Circolo Matematico*, you will remark that he has not even understood properly the concept of a well-ordered set.' Admittedly Cantor's well-known definition of the term 'set' is difficult, yet it cannot be denied that the definition does exclude, through the mildly 'genetic' element, the familiar derivation of contradictions.

The explanation of mathematical existence in terms of consistency appears to be an evasive twist; since we cannot give a suitable positive characterization of all mathematical objects, let us say that in mathematics all that is not impossible is real. On the one hand, constructivity seems to leave out some desirable mathematical objects and faces us with the question of explaining the existence of a construction. On the other hand, a Platonic world of ideas, unlike material things in space and time which form the basis of the physical sciences, seems to have very little explanatory power in mathematics.

The classical definition of the existential quantifier in terms of the universal quantifier has the flavor of identifying existence with consistency, while our experience with the physical world suggests that although the actual is not impossible, the possible does not always exist. While in physics there is a natural distinction between things and laws, laws and constructions seem to be all-pervading in mathematics. Radical phenomenalism is idle and futile as far as the foundations of empirical knowledge are concerned, but even there the basic distinction is hesitantly preserved in the dubious entities called sense data. Yet mathematical objects are primarily connections, relations, and structures.

In doing mathematics, it might even increase some people's power of penetration to think of mathematics as a study of the natural history of numbers and classes. As a philosophical position, such a view would lead too quickly to mysticism and make an articulate philosophy of mathematics well nigh impossible, except perhaps as a sort of metaphysical poetry.

If, e.g., numerals are treated as proper names, there is no point in asking whether positive integers exist, since otherwise numerals would not be proper names. The question of existence has to be directed to the satisfiability of a property, a relation, a condition, a theory: is there some object or some set of objects with a suitable structure that satisfies a given condition? There exist non-Euclidean spaces since axioms of non-Euclidean geometries have models in the Euclidean. There exist complex numbers since axioms for them can be satisfied by pairs of real numbers. Each particular complex number, e.g., i, has a derived existence as a constituent of the whole structure of complex numbers, satisfying certain relations to other complex numbers.

It is familiar that such modeling considerations generally come to an end with positive integers and the continuum: there is in any case a sort of circularity in the explanation of existence by consistency and consistency by satisfiability. We need some basic stuff to begin with: in what sense does it exist?

It seems reasonable to suppose that if a theory is consistent, it must have some interpretation. It may be very difficult to fabricate a model, but how can a theory be consistent and yet be satisfied by no model whatsoever? The fundamental theorem of logic gives a sharper answer for theories formulated as formal systems within the framework of pure logic, i.e. the theory of quantifiers: any such theory, if consistent, has a relatively simple model in the theory of positive integers, simple in the sense that rather low level predicates in the arithmetic hierarchy would suffice. Hence, we may feel that the basic question is the sense in which positive integers exist. More exactly, we are concerned with the existence of a structure or a relation that would satisfy the axioms of arithmetic; the individual positive integers would enjoy a derived existence in such a structure.

It appears at first sight that the proof-theoretical consistency proofs of the axioms of arithmetic provide a (modified) finitist solution to this question, and that the translation into the intuitionistic system of arithmetic gives an intuitionistic solution of the problem. If this were indeed so, we could at least concentrate on what Hilbert calls the combinatorial hard-core of mathematical thinking or what Brouwer calls the basic intuition of two-in-one. There are, however, a number of difficulties accompanying the incompletability of the axioms of arithmetic.

The arithmetic translations of theorems in the usual systems of set theory are often no longer theorems of the usual system of arithmetic. As a result, a consistency proof of the axioms of arithmetic does not settle the consistency question for classical analysis or set theory. Even in the consistency proof of arithmetic, there appears to be an indeterminacy in the notion of finitist proofs.

Moreover, there is a choice between different axiom systems of arithmetic not only in the simple sense that alternative equivalent formulations of, say, the Euclidean geometry are familiar, but in the deeper sense that extensions of the usual set of arithmetic axioms seem to be just as natural, e.g. the addition of transfinite induction to the first epsilon number. This tends to indicate that there is something absolute in the concept of number and we only gradually approximate it through mental experimentations. Or, at least, we have no full control over our intentions and mental constructions which, once in existence, tend to live a life of their own.

In a different direction, the existence of consistent systems which have no standard models (e.g. are omega inconsistent) points to a certain discrepancy between existence and consistency. The usual axioms require that certain sets or numbers exist but remain mum on what things to exclude. On account of this, we can add unnatural numbers to the natural numbers without violating the axioms, and, indeed, consistently add new axioms to require that there must be unnatural numbers too. One might argue with reason that although these unnatural numbers are required by the axioms of a consistent system, they should not be said to exist. Such a position would foil the unqualified identification of consistency with existence.

There is a temptation to cut through the foundational problems by using the nonconstructive rule of induction (the omega rule) and similar semantic concepts to characterize all true propositions in arithmetic, classical analysis, and set theory. In this way, of course, e.g. unnatural numbers are excluded by the basic principles. However, there is not much explaining left to be done, since what is to be explained is simply taken for granted. With the infinite rule, more is accepted which is a projection by analogy of the finite into the infinite. We can never go through infinitely many steps in a calculation or use infinitely many premises in a proof unless we have somehow succeeded in summarizing the infinitely many with a finite schema in an informative way. Both mathematical induction and transfinite induction are principles by which we make inferences after we have found by mental experimentations two suitable premises which summarize together the infinitely many premisses needed. A very essential purpose of the mathematical activity is to devise methods by which infinity can be handled by a finite intellect. The postulation of an infinite intellect has little positive content except perhaps that it would make the whole mathematical activity unnecessary.

4 THE DECEPTIVE APPEAL OF MATHEMATICAL LOGIC TO PHILOSOPHERS

In some lectures at Oxford in 1955, I attempted to plead the case of mathematical logic to a group of philosophers. I have since then come to doubt many of my enthusiastic assertions, not only because mathematical logic has become a more technical subject but also for the reason that, insofar as it has been influential in philosophy, I am not sure the influences have been good ones. Since, however, similar views seem still to be held in some quarters, I propose to reproduce these pleas (headed by A's) and add some comments (headed by B's).

A Mathematical logic is a meeting ground of mathematics and philosophy. To an outsider, pure mathematics seems piecemeal, highly technical, at best an esoteric game; philosophy seems shifty, slippery, full of misplaced exactness and platitudes repeated interminably. Now mathematical logic promises to be systematic, accumulative, and confined to fundamentals. It is a relatively simple branch of mathematics with a wealth of new *methods* of proof; in it philosophers can learn the greatest number of methods for a given amount of effort.

The principal task of mathematical logic is, of course, the study of basic concepts and methods of proof in mathematics, or, as it is often briefly expressed, the study of the foundations of mathematics. In discussing foundational questions, it is customary to speak in terms of three schools of thought: the intuitionists, the formalists, and the logicists. Their differences are stressed. This procedure is not satisfactory because points on which they disagree are far less important than those on which they do or would agree. Disputes may stimulate and refresh. It is, however, the gradual emergence of larger and larger areas of universal acceptability which saves foundational studies once and for all from dangers of laziness, woolliness, or scholasticism.

The labels are also unfortunate in giving the impression that every logician belongs to one and only one of the three schools. This is far from true. Indeed, it would be nearer the truth to say that no active logician represents faithfully any of the so-called schools. To play up too much the differences can therefore be misleading. To fight a straw man is bad enough. It is far worse to have several straw men fight one another.

I think that instead of distributing people into schools according to idealized personal convictions, a more profitable approach is to divide methods and matter into regions according to the nature of their supporting evidence. This is, by the way, very different from the patronizing view which recommends that everyone is free to build up formal systems to express his own logic, however fanciful it may be. In fact, the several regions are determined by principles derived from certain basic insights into our mathematical thinking. While formal systems can be constructed according to the principles and then be used as indispensable tools for investigating the different regions, they are neither prior to the initial intuitions nor even entirely adequate to expressing them.

The most fundamental division is between objectivistic mathematics and constructive mathematics. The former includes all number theory, classical analysis, and Cantor's higher infinities. The latter can be delineated in three somewhat different ways. The first position deals only with natural numbers, using just computable functions and quantifier-free methods of proof. The second is intuitionism which admits quantifiers but denies the law of excluded middle. The third is predicative set theory which permits quantifiers and the general law of excluded middle, but rejects impredicative definitions on the ground that they violate the vicious-circle principle.

We have, therefore, four domains: 1 finitism (computable quantifier-free methods), 2 intuitionism, 3 predicative set theory, 4 objectivistic mathematics. The characteristics of the four regions and their interrelations seem to me to constitute a central problem of foundational studies. A middle position is contemplated between the extreme conventionalists and the absolute realists on the nature of logical truth. On the one hand, it is thought that, for example, a case can be made in general terms both for the rejection and for the retention of impredicative definitions. On the other hand, it is believed that such a matter is to be decided not by an arbitrary choice, but by further investigations into the relative merits of the two positions and into the nature of impredicative definitions. In other words, I feel that better understanding can lead either to a natural, rather than arbitrary, choice between alternative positions, or to some way of seeing impredicative definitions as natural limits of predicative definitions so that a sort of continuous extension from the latter to the former can be established.

B Elsewhere[6] I have further elaborated the four domains mentioned above, adding a fifth which is the most restrictive position and might be called ultrafinitism. It distinguishes even finite numbers into manageable and unmanageable ones and urges that only the manageable ones are intuitively evident. Roughly speaking, finitism and intuitism accept only the potentially infinite, predicativism accepts the set of natural numbers as actual but not the higher infinities, while objectivism accepts the actual infinities.

It is true that there has been much activity during the period since 1955 on the characteristics of the four regions and their interconnections. But no clear conceptual picture has emerged and most of the results thus obtained are esthetically unappealing. The mathematical problems which at first appeared philosophically natural have turned out to be rather artificial and piecemeal as mathematics. At any rate, the more interesting advances in mathematical logic during this period came from work pursued with little philosophical concern. It seems that mathematical logic has matured as a mathematical discipline so that direct connections with philosphy have become less and less strong. Substantial progress in set theory, model theory, and mechanically unsolvable problems came largely as the result of internal considerations in these developing areas of mathematics which have become cumulatively more technical.

A In the domain of mathematical logic, speculative freedom on basic problems remains respectable and is indeed a most attractive right of everyone. Only there is a strong demand to extract quickly from philosophical opinions more precise and perhaps drier questions which are capable of exact treatment. If the adventurous philosopher finds the emergence of programs of scientific research distasteful, he could at least remind himself that the work of transforming philosophical views into science is no less philosophical than mathematical.

Mathematical logic and philosophy of mathematics are closely related, even though their emphases are different. Formal or axiomatic systems are constructed and studied in mathematical logic, while philosophical views give directions to technical researches and provide justification for formal systems already in existence. Here we have at the same time a branch of philosophy whose problems can be studied by the sharp tool of formal systems, and a branch of mathematics which keeps constantly in touch with our desire to understand fundamentals.

I venture to use Brouwer and Wittgenstein as examples to illustrate how interaction between mathematics and philosophy takes place in the study of foundations. Brouwer, who knew a good deal of mathematics, reached certain basic convictions on the nature of mathematics. These he expressed in a rather special language of his own which is only imperfectly understood by others. Formal systems have been constructed to represent Brouwer's views as faithfully as possible. The interconnection between these systems and those formalizing classical concepts of mathematics has been investigated. Such formal investigations, motivated by Brouwer's philosophical ideas, can in turn render these ideas clearer and more easily understandable to a larger circle of people. There is some hope that formal treatment of divergent philosophical positions will not only bring out sharply the differences but in so doing also dissolve them rather completely. Thus philosophy determines the directions of technical research which in turn clarifies and elucidates the initial motives.

In contrast with Brouwer, Wittgenstein, who was very much less a mathematician, was also able to do interesting philosophy of mathematics. It seems to me that much of Wittgenstein's *Tractatus* could be viewed as an attempt to explain the necessity of the logical propositions of the first half of the first volume of *Principia mathematica*. The *Tractatus* provided a justification, if not correct at least of the right sort, of the sloppy formal system in *Principia*, and influenced more technical works such as those of Ramsey. On the other hand, the *Tractatus* could also be regarded as a powerful channel through which mathematical logic made philosophy change its course.

B In view of the recent extensive and depressingly nondefinitive formal treatments of Brouwer's ideas, I doubt that such work is of great philosophical or mathematical interest. Brouwer himself certainly did not much favor either logic as a subject or extensive formal studies of his ideas.

While the influences of the *Tractatus* have been great, it is highly debatable whether these were on the whole positive or negative. Of course, Wittgenstein came to see the work as a result of gross over-simplifications. And it is reasonable to suppose that had mathematical logic been less primitive and murky when the *Tractatus* was being prepared, the sweeping picture of knowledge and reality would not have been painted, if at all, in the same way.

A After Ramsey's death at the age of 26, Keynes wrote to say:[7]

> If he had followed the easier path of mere inclination, I am not sure that he would not have exchanged the tormenting exercises of the foundations of thought and of psychology, where the mind tries to catch its own tail, for the delightful paths of our own most agreeable branch of the moral sciences (viz. economics), in which theory and fact, intuitive imagination and practical judgment, are blended in a manner comfortable to the human intellect.

It seems to me that the use of formal systems as a tool has made the exercises of the foundations of thought less tormenting. One might regard formal systems as the telescopes or microscopes in studying the philosophy of mathematics. Or one might compare them to the laboratories where philosophical ideas, instead of scientific theories, can be tested. Instead of trying to catch its own tail, mind now uses formal systems to do the catching. Rigor and speculation, formal and informal, get blended in a most satisfying manner.

The function of formal systems resembles that of language games. Both are more or less simplified models of the actual situation which assist us in our attempts to disentangle the foundations of thought. Language games have a wider range of application in the study of philosophical problems, while formal systems, when they are rightly applicable, are more powerful as tools and often yield more lasting, more profound results.

A language game is a formal system in this sense: though one does not enumerate the words to be used, one describes such a well-defined concrete situation that the words and inferences used in connection with this situation are, in fact, essentially determined. A typical use of such a construction is this: a person *A* says that a concept *X* must be so; some suitable language game gives a counter-example. Formal systems can often serve the same kind of purpose.

Consider for example Kant's view that the necessity of Euclidean geometry is a philosophical matter. The construction of a non-Euclidean geometry and the exhibition of a model of it in the

Euclidean geometry is a more effective counterexample than language games depending (say) on considerations of our visual space. Or, the construction of a formal system in which it is meaningful to ask whether certain sets belong to themselves is an effective counterexample to the view that the theory of types *must* be obeyed.

Formal systems are more suitable than language games when a concept has wide application. The contrast between a single concept and a family of concepts comes in here. The error of excessive use of formal systems consists in treating a family of concepts as a single concept. The error of unrestricted repugnance against formal systems consists in treating every concept of wide application as a family of concepts. Mathematical concepts are at the same time widely applicable and yet need not be treated as families of concepts. That is why in the study of mathematical concepts formal systems are most suitable, while simpler language games are less effective.

One must not forget that formal systems are tools and *only* tools in the study of philosophy. Like other tools, they are useful only for certain purposes. They are not the philosopher's stone which can solve all problems for us. When applied indiscriminately to all questions, they cause at best waste and at worst disaster. The use of formal systems in studying the philosophy of mathematics has proved to be successful, so much so that nowadays nobody can hope to become a serious mathematical philosopher unless he possesses considerable skill in the manipulation of formal systems. On the other hand, the application of these tools to the treatment of problems of inductive logic, meaning, time, causality, has met with little success. It is indeed hard to estimate whether these commendable efforts to expand the sphere of influence of mathematical logic have done more good or more harm to philosophy. One is tempted to wonder whether these applied logicians have not committed the 'fallacy of too many digits': viz. the fallacy, emphasized by Ramsey, of working out to (say) seven places of decimals a result only valid to two.

The 'machine without a heart view' of mathematical logic arose largely as a reaction against the widespread misapplication of formal systems in philosophy. The unjustifiable belief that what is good for philosophy of mathematics is good for all philosophy has led to the equally unjustifiable conception that mathematical logic has no relevance to philosophy. My own position is that through the central position which philosophy of logic and mathematics occupies in the theory of knowledge, mathematical logic and views on it can indirectly shape one's whole philosophy. I have no wish to tie mathematical logic to the coat tail of big names, but I think it is not just unfair propaganda to mention Frege, Russell, Wittgenstein, and

Mathematical Logic and Philosophy of Mathematics

Ramsey. I do not believe that it was entirely an accident that they are all among the most interesting of recent philosophers and that they were all deeply interested in the foundations of mathematical logic.

B The excessive emphasis on formal systems seems unwarranted. The prize example of formalizing the intuitive concept of a mathematical procedure is not accomplished by using formal systems. In recent times, mathematical results and popular philosophical applications have more to do with thinking in general terms about existing and nonexisting formal systems than actually constructing formal systems. In the mathematical direction, independence results and experimentations with new axioms in set theory, which all the time appeal to our rich mathematical intuitions, come closest to the project of playing with formal systems. In the philosophical direction, there are not many recent examples of successful considerations by constructing formal systems. For example, if one wishes to study the nature of constructive mathematics, it is not at all clear that the 'dinky formal systems' are in the long run of more interest than actual efforts to develop mathematics constructively.

As to the more general impact of mathematical logic on philosophy, even if we leave out the question whether the impact was good, the fact that Frege, Russell, and early Wittgenstein did have great influence may reasonably be accounted for by the particular historical context they were in. There is no good reason to infer that at the present stage mathematical logic will, except through inertia, continue to be central to philosophy. It is hard to predict how Ramsey might have developed, had he lived longer. Certainly the later Wittgenstein thought that mathematical logic was a bad influence both in philosophy and in mathematics.

NOTES

1 Nicolas Bourbaki, 'L'architecture des mathématiques,' *Les grands courants de la pensée mathématique*, 1948, pp. 33–47.
2 R. Carnap, *The logical structure of the world* (English translation of *Der logische Aufbau der Welt*, 1928), § 15, p. 27. 'Thepurely structural definitions which I have here discussed are closely related to the *implicit definition* which Hilbert has used for his axiomatic geometry. . . . Strictly speaking, it is not a definite object (concept) which is implicitly defined through the axioms, but a class of them. A structural definite description, in contradistinction to an implicit definition, characterizes (or defines) only a single object, to wit, an object belonging to an empirical, extralogical domain' (§ 15, p. 28). Implicit definitions were first considered by J. D. Gergonne, *Ann. de math. pures et appl.*, vol. 9, 1818–19, pp. 1–35 and emphasized in D. Hilbert's famous *Foundations of geometry*, 1899. G. Frege has commented extensively on these questions in *Jahresber. d. deuts. Math.-Verein.*, vol. 12, 1903, pp. 319–24,

Mathematical Logic and Philosophy of Mathematics

368–75, vol. 15, 1906, pp. 293–309, 377–403, 423–30. There were also correspondences between Hilbert and Frege on this matter. Frege argued that the implicit definitions are not definitions because they do not determine the concept or concepts completely. In this connection, it is natural to say that categorical systems would do so. There is first the question that in order to get categorical systems of, for example, arithmetic or geometry, we need to assume an informal concept of set which has no categorical axiomatization. Moreover, even if we relax our requirements and permit such informal categorical systems, there is a serious problem whether, in applying such systems or structural descriptions to empirical concepts (or objects) we would capture what we want, especially since it is highly implausible that experience can be analyzed completely into structures. Carnap's concept of structure goes back to B. Russell (e.g. *Introduction to mathematical philosophy*, p. 53, also called relation numbers): 'We now can give an exact definition of the structure or relation number of a relation extension P: it is the class of relation extensions which are isomorphic to P' (§ 34, p. 60). This does not give a definition of the structure of a theory or a system, but presumably he meant to confine himself to categorical systems so that the relations are determined up to isomorphism. In a similar manner, in category theory, the category of (say) groups would be the collection of all groups or rather their morphisms. In model theory, a structure is often used in a different way to mean a model unattached to a theory. The usage reflects the ambiguity in phrases such as 'the organization of an organization' so that the structure of a given structure S is what is common to all structures isomorphic to S.

3 See, for example, S. C. Kleene, *Introduction to metamathematics*, 1952, p. 211, where there is unjustifiable criticism of the work of D. Hilbert and P. Bernays.

4 *Remarks on foundations of mathematics*, pp. 49–54.

5 G. H. Hardy, *A mathematician's apology*, 1940, end of § 22.

6 'Eighty years of foundational studies,' *Dialectica*, vol. 12, 1958, pp. 466–97.

7 F. P. Ramsey, *Foundations of mathematics*, 1931, p. x.

II

CHARACTERIZATION OF GENERAL MATHEMATICAL CONCEPTS

1 NATURAL NUMBERS

We successfully learn the use of the natural numbers 1, 2, 3, etc. at an early age. It does not seem possible to reduce our knowledge of the sequence of natural numbers to anything intuitively more basic. It is hard to imagine how a normal person can fail to use small natural numbers correctly.

A natural number can be used both as an ordinal and a cardinal number. Thus, take the process of counting

$$\triangle \qquad \square \qquad \bigcirc$$

We point to one figure and say 1, another and say 2, a third and say 3; then we conclude that there are 3 figures. The square is not 2 but rather the second in our counting. Only the last, 3, is used as a cardinal number. We can count in different orders and yet get the same final result: this seems so obvious that it is hard to imagine how it could be different. It also seems evident that the last ordinal used in counting gives the cardinal number of the collection. We can use different symbols for cardinals and ordinals. We can also, as we often do with natural numbers, use the same set of symbols to stand for both ordinals and cardinals. Such a practice is no longer feasible when we come to infinite cardinals and ordinals. Thus, if we view cardinal numbers as obtained by counting, the concept of ordinal number seems more basic.

Often we can compare the cardinal numbers of two collections without counting; for example, to determine whether there are enough chairs in a room, for people present, or whether there are more males or females at a dance. In such cases, it is true that the acts of matching off must be carried out one by one in temporal succession, even if it is simply the process of looking to see that each chair is occupied.

Nonetheless, the ordinal *numbers* are not involved because we do not have to keep track of the relative order of which of two chairs was first checked: we need only distinguish checked from non-checked. The concept of more or equal is prior to both cardinals and ordinals. Matching off is sufficient for arranging different heaps of pebbles in order of more and less. But in order to get representations of the natural numbers, we need the concepts of one and one more. Given these concepts, both cardinals and ordinals can be gotten. It seems reasonable to say that both ordinals and cardinals presuppose the concept of a unit and the concept of adding one more, but neither is more primary than the other. We should distinguish all sets with 3 members from a particularly simple set with 3 members. A model set is enough to give us the concept 3 even though once given it is to apply to all sets with 3 members. When we are fortunate, we may be able, as a matter of fact, to get representative groups of physical objects for all natural numbers up to 1000, say, even though, without the notion of one more, we are not able to know that this is actually so.

If we represent natural numbers by strings of strokes, the role of natural numbers can be played by such strings of strokes, actual or imagined. '2 plus 2 is 4' means, if we write down two strokes, and two strokes again, we get four strokes. This cannot mean that actually in writing, such a state of affairs must always happen, but rather that if it does not happen, we are inclined to search for other explanations in order to uphold the conclusion that without inter-ference, such would happen. We can avoid all such imaginary diffi-culties if we avoid them in going to the next stroke. It seems there are still questions in conceiving of arithmetic as concerned with concrete numerical symbols such as strings of strokes whose shape is recognizable by us independently of time and space, and of minor differences in their occurrences. They are, however, useful because we know that as a matter of fact we can use their concrete occur-rences, and in theory we can depend on their abstract form. There is no possibility of error with type, and no actual error even with token. To talk about strings of strokes is one way of communicating our thoughts on the justification of arithmetic. It is useful even though inadequate.

The continuing philosophical interest in natural numbers and the continuum may be contrasted with the situation of negative and complex numbers. Historically these numbers appeared to be puzzling at first and there is some resistance to absorbing them when first exposed to them in schools. But they are 'reducible' to simpler con-cepts and do not create serious conceptual problems. When one was accustomed to think only of real numbers, one was puzzled by the question: how could there be any number which, when mutiplied by itself, yields minus 1? what sort of things are the complex numbers? or, more simply, what are complex numbers? There were, therefore, speculative discourses on the true metaphysic of complex numbers. Around 1800, Gauss and C. Wessel supplied interesting and definite answers to this question which are still preserved in mathematics textbooks. Nobody would now regard their representations of complex numbers by pairs of real numbers and by diagrams as philosophy. In fact, as their replies gradually got accepted by everyone, the original question ceased to be of philosophical interest, and speculative doctrines on the topic have been quickly forgotten. Thus, we have a clear case where a philosophical question got solved and immigrated into mathematics.

The question about natural numbers could be, what is a natural number? Or how do we characterize the concept of natural number? What do we mean by the term 'natural number'? At first, we may try to answer the question by giving typical examples such as 25, 61, 1000. Or, we may say that natural numbers are 1, 2, 3, and so on. To explain the phrase 'and so on' in this particular context can without exaggeration be said to be one of the central problems of mathematical logic. If we say that a natural number is either 1 or the successor of another natural number, then we have made no sufficient restriction as to what is not a natural number. We can for example also take an arbitrary additional thing ω as a natural number so that we have besides 1, 2, 3, and so on, also ω, $\omega + 1$, $\omega - 1$, $\omega + 2$, $\omega - 2$, and so on; although this sequence contains more things than what we would like to call natural numbers, it satisfies the condition that a natural number is either 1 or a successor. A next attempt is to require further that natural numbers must satisfy the principle of mathematical induction; in other words, every set which contains 1 and contains the successor of every member of it must contain all natural numbers. It was thought that if we take the common part of all such sets, it must contain exactly the desired natural numbers and no more, since otherwise there would be a smaller set which contains 1 and the successor of every member of it. This, however, leads immediately to the question of characterizing the concept of an arbitrary set of natural numbers, and also the question of reducing arithmetic to logic.

There are interesting philosophical views on the nature of arithmetic which have little to do with mathematical logic. A famous example is Kant's theory in terms of the form of the pure intuition of time. Brouwer argues[1] that the position of intuitionism:

Has recovered by abandoning Kant's apriority of space but adhering the more resolutely to the apriority of time. This neo-intuitionism considers the falling apart of moments of life into qualitatively different parts, to be reunited only while remaining separated by time, as the fundamental phenomenon of the human intellect, passing by abstracting from its emotional content into the fundamental phenomenon of mathematical thinking, the intuition of the bare two-oneness. This intuition of two-oneness, the basal intuition of mathematics, creates not only the numbers one and two, but also all finite ordinal numbers, inasmuch as one of the elements of the two-oneness may be thought of as a new two-oneness, which process may be repeated indefinitely.

This oft-quoted passage is singularly attractive, capturing or at least hinting at a familiar basic vague thought about the foundation of arithmetic and its place in human thought. It is, unlike additional ideas of Brouwer's intuitionism, rather neutral to different approaches to the foundation of arithmetic and can even serve to enrich the logic-oriented views we are about to consider.

Leibniz proposes to prove numerical truths such as $2 + 2 = 4$ by definitions (of 2 and 4) and axioms only. Frege points out[2] that the associative law is implicitly assumed in moving from $2 + (1 + 1)$ to $(2 + 1) + 1$. The crucial missing step is that in addition to the definitions of each number, $2 = 1 + 1$, $3 = 2 + 1$, etc., we need also the recursive definition of addition which says in general $a + (b + 1) = (a + b) + 1$. This is indeed how Grassmann[3] corrects the proposed proof of Leibniz. In fact, Grassmann introduces recursive definitions of addition and multiplication, and proves ordinary laws of arithmetic by mathematical induction. He offers a development which amounts to characterizing all integers (positive, negative, and 0) as an ordered integral domain in which each set of positive members contains a smallest element. A formal imperfection of his calculus is the omission of the principle that distinct numerals denote distinct numbers. As a result, his whole system would be satisfied if all integers are taken to be identical with one another.

The nature of recursive definitions presents some complication. Frege feels that they are not proper definitions. Both he and Dedekind prefer to use more complex and essentially set-theoretic explicit definitions which yield the recursive definitions as consequences. Today we generally agree that it is all right to begin with recursive definitions and justify them directly by a sort of combinatorial intuition.

The omission in Grassmann's calculus gets corrected by Dedekind,[4] and we arrive at what are commonly known as Peano's axioms:

Characterization of General Mathematical Concepts

P1 1 is a number.

P2 The successor of any number is a number.

P3 No two numbers have the same successor.

P4 1 is not the successor of any number.

P5 Any set K contains all numbers, if 1 belongs to K and the successor of any member of K also belongs to K.

In a private letter,[5] Dedekind gives an account of how he arrived at the above five axioms by analyzing the concept of number. Dedekind poses the question rather exactly:

> Which are the mutually independent fundamental properties of the number-sequence N, i.e. those properties which are not deducible from one another and from which all others follow? How should we divest these properties of their specifically arithmetical character so that they are subsumed under more general concepts and such activities of the understanding, which are *necessary* for all thinking, but at the same time *sufficient*, to secure reliability and completeness of the proofs, and to permit the construction of consistent concepts and definitions?

According to Dedekind, one is then forced to accept the following facts. 1 N is a set of elements which are called numbers. 2 The elements of N stand in a certain relation to one another, they are in a certain order determined, in the first place, by the fact that to each definite number n, belongs again a definite number n' or $\phi(n)$, the successor of n. The mapping ϕ maps N into itself and $\phi(N)$ is a part of N. 3 Distinct numbers have distinct successors, i.e., the mapping ϕ is one-one. 4 Not every number is a successor, i.e. $\phi(N)$ is a proper part of N. More precisely, 1 is the only number not in $\phi(N)$. 5 One might think that these facts are sufficient to determine N. But they also apply to every set S, which, in addition to N, contains also a set T of arbitrary elements t. One can always extend the one-one mapping ϕ so that $\phi(T) = T$. In particular, we may use the example mentioned before, where $T = \{. . ., \omega - 1, \omega, \omega + 1, . . .\}$. According to Dedekind, one of the most difficult points of his analysis is to find what to add to the above facts in order to cleanse our set S from such alien intruders t which disturb every vestige of order, and restrict ourselves to the set N.

If one assumes knowledge of the sequence N of natural numbers to begin with and accordingly permits himself an arithmetic terminology, then he has of course an easy time of it. He needs only to say: an element n belongs to the sequence N if and only if by starting with the element 1, and going on counting, i.e., by a finite number of iterations of the mapping ϕ, I eventually reach the element n; on the other hand, I never reach an element t outside the sequence N by means of this process. But it is quite useless for our purpose to adopt this manner of distinguishing those elements t which are to be ejected from S, and those elements n which alone are to remain in S. Such a procedure would surely involve the most pernicious and obvious kind of *circulus vitiosus*.

The solution is provided by P5. Or stated as a definition, 'an element n of S satisfying P1 to P4 belongs to the sequence N if and only if n is an element of *every such* part K of S which possesses the two properties i. that the element 1 belongs to K and ii. that the image $\phi(K)$ is part of K.'

In order to characterize the concept of natural number, we might consider the question of organizing the mathematical theory of natural numbers into a formal system. There is a more or less determined body of theorems and concepts relating to natural numbers. How can we find the basic concepts and axioms from which the whole theory can be developed? One possible approach which suggests itself is to take typical theorems and proofs and examine what assumptions and concepts are needed. It is remarkable that Dedekind obtained the Peano axioms entirely by analyzing the sequence of natural numbers. What is more remarkable is, once he had completed his analysis, he believed that properties of and theorems about natural numbers could all be derived from his characterization. This belief has, to a large extent, been confirmed by later developments. Clearly, Dedekind did not look at a great number of theorems and proofs about natural numbers to see that no other characteristics are needed. Rather, he just verified to his own satisfaction that the sequence of natural numbers is completely determined by his axioms, and then concluded that the axioms are adequate to the derivation of theorems as well. Now this can be made plausible in the following manner. If a theorem is independent of the axioms, then there are two possible interpretations (or models) of the axioms according to one of which the theorem is true and according to the other the theorem is false. If the axioms determine a unique model of the theory, such a situation cannot arise. Therefore, all theorems about natural numbers must be derivable. This argument is plausible but not entirely rigorous because, among other things, the notion of interpretation has not been made sufficiently explicit.

While it is easy to see that the natural numbers do satisfy P1 to P5, one might wonder how we can be sure that they determine all the properties of the natural numbers. Dedekind's conclusion that these determine adequately the sequence of natural numbers is often expressed by saying that the axioms are categorical or have no essentially different models. As we know, the axioms do admit different models such as taking 100 as 1 or taking the square of a number as the successor of a number. But they are all essentially the same in the technical sense of being isomorphic. Thus, given two models of these axioms, let 1_a, S_a, N_a stand for 1, successor, number in one model, and 1_b, S_b, N_b in the other model. Correlate 1_a with 1_b. In general if m is correlated with n, correlate $S_a m$ with $S_b n$. Our purpose is to prove that in this way we get a correct one-one correspondence between members of N_a and those of N_b. To accomplish this, we have to make use of the fact that there exists a set which contains exactly 1, 2, 3, . . . and no other things. Since we permit arbitrary sets, it seems reasonable to suppose that there exists such a set. If there is such a set, then by P5 this should be identical with the set N of numbers in each model. Consequently, N_a contains exactly 1_a, $S_a 1_a$, etc., N_b contains exactly 1_b, $S_b 1_b$, etc. The proof that there is a one-one correspondence between objects in the two interpretations which preserves 1 and the transition from a number to its successsor is, therefore, complete. And this is the sense in which we say that Peano's axioms possess no essentially different models.

The idea of Dedekind seems to be this: the set N of natural numbers obviously satisfies the conditions i. and ii. If we consider all sets which satisfy the two conditions, their common part or intersection must be exactly the desired set: it cannot contain less members because every number must be in every one of them; it cannot contain more because then there would be a smaller set which again satisfies the conditions. Now there is, however, the question of specifying the arbitrary sets. How do we know whether a given specification of sets will include the set N of numbers as desired?

Intuitively it seems obvious that N is a possible set. But Gödel's incompleteness result shows that no completely formal system can force on us a sufficiently rich domain of sets so that the intended set N must be in it. This puzzling state of affairs can be clarified by reflecting that in a formal system we specify sets by defining properties all given in advance. It is not at all obvious that all sets and, in particular N, which is infinite, will be thus specified. Consider a simple example.[6] In P5 we might happen to express only certain simple defining properties so that every K thus specified is either finite or cofinite (i.e. containing all except finitely many numbers). It is then easy to find a model of P1 to P5 which contains certain 'alien intruders.' In fact, $T = \{(2b + 1)/2\}$, where b is any integer, will do.

According to current usage, what is known to be categorical and complete is the second order (quasiformal) system of arithmetic which uses an informal notion of set as in P5, while the first order system of arithmetic is incompletable when we make it reasonably rich (say) by including simple recursive functions. Even though it is customary to belittle second order characterizations because they only shift the difficulties in formalization from numbers to sets, we should consider Dedekind's acute analysis as a remarkable success. In fact, second order categoricity is an interesting phenomenon which occurs with natural numbers and real numbers but not with the theory of sets.

It is necessary to add a few technical remarks in order to bring out another distinction. Traditionally, P1-P5 as stated above are said to give an axiom system A. The natural way to make it into a formal system in the strict sense mentioned before is to confine the classes K in P5 to ones which are expressible in the given notation and adjoin the underlying apparatus of pure logic (first order logic) with equality. The resulting system B is formal because the axioms and the proofs can be checked mechanically, and the theorems form a recursively enumerable set. For the system A, on the other hand, even though the axioms are mechanically checkable, we need a second order logic to bring out the underlying assumptions. But it is impossible to get a complete (i.e. adequate to the intended purpose) formal system for the second order logic. Hence, we cannot in this way make A into a categorical formal system. Since we cannot fully capture formally the additional strength of A over B due to the set variable K, we are led to strengthening B by other means.

The standard way is to extend the language of B by adding addition and multiplication (which are explicitly definable in A and in formal set theory) and also their recursive definitions as axioms. In this way, we arrive at a formal system C which again contains pure logic (the complete system of the first order logic with equality). Gödel's theorem establishes that C, or any system 'like' it (in a very loose sense of 'like'), is incomplete. Hence, C is not categorical and, also, B is not categorical since the nonisomorphic models of C contain nonisomorphic models of B.

We can also generalize formal systems such as B and C to (first order) 'theories' in a technical sense of theory. In a theory, we may choose more complex sets of theorems than in a formal system so that, e.g., we may consider all true sentences in C as theorems. In this way, we arrive at a complete (first order) theory D of the language of C. A natural question to ask is whether D is categorical. A result of Skolem establishes that even D is not categorical.[7] Here, we have a stronger sense of the noncategoricity of the domain of natural numbers. Not only can we not capture all true sentences by a formal system (and therefore cannot have a categorical formal system of number theory) but also we cannot obtain categoricity with (first order) complete theories which preserve some of the sharpness of formal systems because the language (the symbols and the sentences) is effective even though the proofs can no longer be checked effectively (and the theorems or true sentences are not recursively enumerable).

The contrast between the (categorical) axiom system A and the formal systems B and C can also be described in another way. The theorems of A can be approximated by using stronger and stronger formal systems of 'logic', but there exists no formal system which gives a complete characterization of the intended strong (second order) logic. In this way, we are faced with the question whether pure logic (first order logic) is indeed the whole of logic as intended. It is not sufficient to exclude extensions of logic merely on the ground that there are no complete formal systems for them. For example, there is a complete formal system for the extension obtained by adding the quantifier 'for uncountably many x.' This area of questions will be discussed under 'logical truth.'

With regard to the thesis that arithmetic is reducible to logic, it may be of interest to compare the views of Dedekind and Frege. According to Dedekind,[8] 'In speaking of arithmetic (algebra, analysis) as a part of logic I mean to imply that I consider the number-concept entirely independent of notions of space and time, that I consider it an immediate result from the laws of thought.' According to Frege,[9] 'Dedekind also is of the opinion that the theory of numbers is a part of logic; but his work hardly goes to strengthen this opinion, because the expression "system" ["set"] and "a thing belongs to a thing" used by him are not usual in logic and are not reduced to accepted logical notions.' Here we have two different notions of 'logic.' From the present point of view, we would say that arithmetic is reducible to logic in Dedekind's sense but not in Frege's. It is perhaps amusing to see that the familiar disagreement owing to the ambiguity of the term 'logic' goes so far back.

Formal systems help to get a systematic survey of the relation between existence theorems and computable functions. The connection between computable functions and existence theorems in mathematics can best be illustrated by considering an existence assertion of the form 'for every natural number m, there exists a natural number n, such that the relation R holds between m and n.' The meaning of the statement depends pretty much on the method by which we can get, for every given natural number m, a corresponding natural number n satisfying together the relation R; or, in other words, on the function which yields, for each m, its corresponding n. In general, this function may be computable or not computable. It is always computable if R is computable or decidable. The exact nature of the function can be determined through an examination of a given proof which leads to the existence assertion. In this sense, we can say that the meaning of an existence statement depends on the method by which it is proved. Or, if one is impressed by the fact that there may be different methods for proving the same conclusion, we can perhaps say that the meaning of an existence statement is determined by all its possible proofs.

The interrelationship between proofs of an existence theorem and functions which give explicitly the correlation leads to the possibility of classifying proofs according to their corresponding functions, as well as classifying computable functions according to the proofs which establish their computability.

Since computable functions form only a proper subcollection of arbitrary functions, there is a lack of symmetry between the existence of a computable function and the nonexistence of an arbitrary function. This asymmetry can be employed to get an outsider's understanding of Brouwer's rejection of the law of excluded middle.

The concepts of mathematical proof and mathematical truth are closely related; both acquire sharper shape with regard to formal systems. One motive for organizing proofs of a given branch of mathematics in a formal system may be explained in the following manner. It has been several hundred years since Fermat first asserted that for all n greater than 2, there exist no natural numbers a, b, c such that the n-th power of a plus the n-th power of b is equal to the n-th power of c. Nobody has so far either proved or disproved this conjecture. Since there are a small number of typical methods of proof in number theory, one may wonder whether the prolonged failure to decide the truth or falsity of Fermat's conjecture could not be explained by the possibility that none of the typical methods of proof is adequate to establish it. In order to determine whether this is the case, a preliminary step is to delineate sharply the range of applicability of the methods of proof. Clearly to prove that a conclusion cannot be proved by a given method requires more knowledge of the method than to use the method to prove a conclusion. Formalization is an efficient way of delineating given methods of proof. A concept is often made especially clear by considering its limits.

There have been attempts, unsuccessful so far, to show open problems of number theory such as Fermat's conjecture undecidable in current formal systems of number theory. The difference between such goals and the known existence of independent propositions from Gödel's theorem is analogous to the contrast between the proofs of transcendence of e and π and Cantor's general diagonal proof that there must be transcendental numbers.

2 THE CONTINUUM

There are two different types of question which are both regarded as having to do with the continuum. The first type includes Zeno's paradox and, to a considerable extent, the notion of infinitesimals. These problems are concerned more with infinity as a general concept and would arise even if we were not dealing with the continuum but just with the rational numbers. The second type of question, e.g. the definition of continuity of a set of points or the concept of uncountable sets, is concerned exclusively with the continuum.

The use of infinitesimals in the calculus is a rather technical question which has been solved completely through the advance of mathematics. In contrast, the situation with Achilles and the tortoise is less determinate, as is evidenced by the fact that philosophical discussions about the paradox continue to appear and flourish.

In the Chinese classic *Chuang-tse*, there is the following assertion: 'If a rod one foot in length is cut short every day by one half of its length, it will still have something left even after ten thousand generations.' This can hardly be regarded as a paradox, because we are inclined to take it as true, even though there are practical difficulties in the way of actually cutting a physical rod into too many parts. If we now assume the first cut is made in one minute, the second cut in half a minute, and so on, then we may be inclined to say that two minutes after we begin to cut, nothing of the rod will be left. Or we may feel there is something odd. Now compare this with drawing a line along the rod. If we draw the first half in one minute, half of the remainder in half a minute, half the remainder in a quarter of a minute, and so on, then we seem to be in a similar situation. Yet we can draw the whole line all at one stroke. Indeed, it may be said that the complicated manner of drawing the line thus described is but a peculiar way of saying that a line is drawn along the rod in two minutes with uniform speed. To say so is to say that we can in the specified sense conceive of a completed infinite process. We certainly can conceive of half the rod, one fourth the rod, one eighth the rod, $1/16$ of the rod, etc. For each n, we can think of $1/2^n$. When we think of the totality of all points $1/2, 1/4, \ldots$, we certainly cannot give each as much attention as when we are thinking just of a single number. Sense experience does not give us infinity. In measuring parts of a rod, we quickly reach parts which are too small for our eyes and for scientific instruments. In thinking of parts, we can think of arbitrarily small parts, but we do not think of infinitely many parts in the same way as we think of an arbitrary finite number of parts. It is not easy to say what it is in thinking of infinitely many parts that is beyond the thinking of arbitrary finite numbers of parts.

There is an easier and perhaps less essential moment in the story of Achilles and the tortoise. Bolzano[10] considered the equation $5y$ equals $12x$ and observed that to every quantity x between 0 and 5, there corresponds one and only one quantity y between 0 and 12, and conversely. In other words, the equation gives a one-to-one correspondence between one collection and a bigger one containing it as part. Bolzano draws the conclusion that the existence of a one-to-one correspondence between two infinite sets A and B does not justify us in inferring the equality of A and B, with respect to the multiplicity of their members. Cantor, on the other hand, defined two sets as having the same number of members when there is a one-to-one correspondence between the members of the two sets. Then the conclusion drawn was that one set and a proper subset of it can have the same number of members. The reason why Cantor's definition and its consequences have been accepted is certainly not that it is closer to common usage but rather that it is more useful in mathematics. Even today we tend naturally to think that there are more natural numbers than even natural numbers.

Russell argues[11] that once we reject the assumption that a whole must have more members than a part of it, we no longer feel that Achilles cannot catch the tortoise. Thus, according to Russell, the paradox arises because Achilles has to cover more ground and yet there is a one-to-one correspondence between positions occupied by the tortoise and those by Achilles. There is at first sight some difficulty in believing that as x goes from 0 to 1, there is a one-to-one correspondence between values of $2x$ and those of 1 plus x, since the values of the former contain the values of the latter as a part. Once it is realized that a whole and a part can have the same members, it is no longer difficult to believe this, as well as that Achilles did cover more ground than the tortoise.

What Russell does seems to be this. We know that one premiss (viz. whole has always more members than part) is sufficient to give the paradox, therefore we shall not get the paradox if we are able to reject the premiss. There remains the possibility that some other premiss is also sufficient to produce the paradox. Or, one might wish to say that Russell gave a mathematical solution to a problem which can only be solved by combining mathematics with philosophy. It seems of interest to contrast the unsettled state of the paradox with that of the use of infinitesimals in the calculus which has been more completely dealt with by a mathematical solution.

Consider one example treated by Berkeley.[12] We wish to find the derivative of x^2. Take the ratio $((x + d)^2 - x^2)/d$, where d is an infinitesimal. We get $(2dx + d^2)/d$. Since d is an infinitesimal, but not zero, we can cancel the factor d and get $2x + d$. Since d is so small we can neglect it, and we get $2x$ as the derivative of x^2. But notice we are doing exact mathematics and not just to get approximate results. Hence, we cannot omit d unless it is zero. But if it is zero, we can neither cancel the factor d nor have division by d. Hence, in proving that $2x$ is the derivative of x^2, we seem to be following a highly inconsistent procedure: treat d as zero or not to suit our pleasure and convenience. In the words of Berkeley: 'by virtue of a twofold mistake, you arrive, though not at science, yet at truth.'

Now the difficulty has been dissolved through the advance of mathematics. But it took a long time, more than one hundred years. The final result depends on a new definition of the whole sentence 'the derivative of x^2 is $2x$': viz., given any positive number e, there exists a positive number d such that for all t, $0 < |t| < d$, $|((x + t)^2 - x^2)/t - 2x| < e$. In this statement, e and d are ordinary (rational, if we wish) numbers and no longer infinitesimals. In order to prove this, we proceed to find a d for each e. We need only take e as d, then we see that $|2x + t - 2x| = |t| < e$. This simple example of a contextual definition of the derivatives is of philosophical interest. It may be compared with Russell's use of what he calls 'incomplete symbols' in his theory of descriptions.

There are also other temptations for introducing infinitesimals. If points have no length, how can we put points together to get a line which has length? But a point cannot have a positive number as length, for it must be smaller than any given number. Hence, the simplest way out is to say that a point has infinitesimal length. Or, it seems natural to think that on a line each point has two immediately neighbouring points, the distance between a point and its immediate neighbors must be infinitesimal. Or, take the following argument of Bernoulli: 'If 10 members are present (in the sequence $1/2$, $1/2^2$, $1/2^3$, . . .), the 10th must necessarily exist, if 100 then necessarily the 100th, . . . if therefore their number is ∞, then the ∞-th member must exist.' This ∞-th is then the infinitesimal. All these arguments can be elucidated by results achieved in the actual progress of mathematics. It is out of the question to enter upon a detailed exposition here.

It should be pointed out that the image of infinitesimal segments, areas, or volumes continues to be useful as a heuristic aid in differentiations and integrations. Moreover, in recent years there has been an amusing discovery in mathematical logic in connection with nonstandard models, according to which it is possible to give a coherent system of 'nonstandard analysis' in which infinitesimals can be manipulated unambiguously.

The contextual definition of the derivative of x^2 mentioned above is an example of the elucidation of the limit concept, which is also applied in giving a technical definition of continuity. The general question as to when limits exist is closely related to the problem of continuity and the characterization of the continuum.

What is the essence of continuity? Take a line segment. What do we mean when we say it is continuous? At least this much: if we make an arbitrary cut of the segment into two parts, the cut must hit a point which is between the two parts; we must never encounter a gap which would break the continuity. The problem is, what methods or principles are to be used in making the cuts?

At first it must have appeared natural to the Greeks to assume that all magnitudes of the same kind are commensurable, and that, for example, any two lengths are multiples of the same unit. It follows from this assumption that all points on a line can be represented by rational numbers. The discovery that the square root of 2 is not rational, or in geometrical terms, that the diagonal of a square is not commensurable with its sides, made it clear that there are points on a line which are not represented by rational numbers. It remains an unsettled historical question whether the irrationality of $\sqrt{2}$ was discovered by Pythagoras or his immediate pupils, or not long before 400 B.C. In any case, consequences of this discovery were drawn only at the beginning of the fourth century B.C. Eudoxus constructed a general theory of proportion which was adopted by Euclid and further developed by Archimedes. The theory of Eudoxus may be regarded as the beginning of a rigorous theory of irrational numbers. It leads to the question of determining all irrational numbers or all ratios of line segments which are not represented by fractions. Hardy considers[13] the proof of the irrationality of $\sqrt{2}$ as one of two examples of beautiful and significant mathematics. Indeed, the proof is so simple and pure, and the theorem is so full of deep consequences, that it cannot fail to satisfy the desire to find simple keys to bodies of science.

If we examine the irrational or real numbers actually used in mathematics, we easily see that the domain has gradually expanded. $\sqrt{2}$ belongs to the kind of numbers which correspond to segments constructible from unity by ruler and compass. It seems natural to consider not only the particular number $\sqrt{2}$, but all numbers of this type. The Greeks did consider many irrational numbers of this type, but seem not to have realized the possibility that there are irrational numbers of any other type. As we know, these numbers are special cases of algebraic numbers, i.e. real roots of arbitrary equations with integral coefficients. Hence, the next natural extension is to include all algebraic numbers since there are such numbers which cannot be obtained by ruler and compass construction from unity. The proof that e and π are not roots of any algebraic equations tells us that the domain of real numbers is even broader than algebraic numbers.

How are we to determine the domain of real numbers so that it includes not only real numbers which have actually been discovered and used in mathematics, but also real numbers which will be found in the future?

This question is of philosophical interest because it asks for all possible methods of defining real numbers, a general question about different modes of abstract thought. To get a rough idea of the nature of the question, let us look briefly at the representation of real numbers by infinite decimals. What are the possible laws or definitions for determining these decimals?

We can contrast 'natural' with 'artificial' definitions. The natural ones arise out of the actual development of mathematics and usually have organic connections with our main body of knowledge so that we have, about real numbers defined by them, information which is not directly implied by the definitions. On the other hand, artificial definitions can be manufactured by playing with accidental features of notation or actuality. As a result, we know practically nothing about these real numbers apart from what is obviously contained in the definitions.

Thus, e, π, $e\pi$, $e^{\sqrt{2}}$, π^e, etc. all are natural reals, while a decimal expansion which is defined in terms of Fermat's conjecture or the time when it will be solved or the presence or absence of eclipses at different times, etc. would be an artificial real. We may wish to confine our attention only to reals which we have occasion to consider in mathematics. This would determine a minimum requirement that a general theory of real numbers is to satisfy.

The question of devising an adequate theory of the continuum can also be viewed from a different angle. According to Dedekind, in science nothing capable of proof ought to be accepted without proof. But it is not always clear whether or not a proposition is capable of proof, and what exactly constitutes an acceptable proof. For example, in 1799 Gauss employed without proof the proposition which says that if we draw a continuous curve from one side of a straight line to the other, the continuous curve must cross the line somewhere. Intuitively, this is obvious. In 1817, Bolzano[14] attempted to give a rigorous 'arithmetic' proof of this proposition. In his proof, he uses an auxiliary proposition which says that every set of real numbers bounded above has a least upper bound. In other words, among all the numbers which are greater than every number of the given set, there is a smallest. It is easy to prove that there cannot be more than one such. But it is more complex to prove that there actually exists one such. Indeed Bolzano proves merely that it is not impossible that there exists such a bound, i.e. that existence of such a bound is not self-contradictory. It seems rather curious that he should draw the conclusion of actual existence merely from a proof of possibility.

If we look at the matter more closely, we can see that this is not just a careless slip, but a serious difficulty which could only be removed by a general theory that tells us positively what kind of real numbers exist. In order to know whether a particular definition determines a real number, we should know what kinds of definition can in general determine real numbers.

The Greeks, and apparently also Cauchy, appeal to our geometrical intuition as assurance that such bounds or limits do exist. In contrast with the Greeks who wished to base real numbers on geometry, Weierstrass, Dedekind, and Cantor were interested in the arithmetization of analysis and geometry. These exact theories boil down essentially to the position that the existence of a least upper bound of a bounded set of rational numbers is taken as a postulate or axiom. It then follows that every bounded set of real numbers also has a least upper bound. If we call such sets exhaustive when every rational number less than a member of the set also belongs to it, then there is a one-to-one correspondence between real numbers and exhaustive bounded sets of rational numbers (if we adopt the convention that they contain no greatest number).

It is convenient to identify a real number with its corresponding bounded set of rational numbers. One advantage of this identification is, according to Russell,[15] that it leaves no doubt as to the existence of real numbers, since sets obviously exist. This is questionable even if we leave aside any thorough skepticism toward sets. If we want to be sure that these sets of rational numbers exist, we have to use a theory of sets in which they are assumed to exist. Assuming the existence of these sets is in many ways just as much a postulation as assuming the existence of their corresponding real numbers. Hence, the identification does not make the existence of real numbers more certain. The main recommendation for the identification is rather, that in order to develop the theory, or if we are interested in developing mathematics in a comprehensive theory of sets, we would probably need sets of rational numbers even apart from the question of defining real numbers. Hence, the identification ensures economy.

Obviously such theories involve a very high degree of abstraction, since no restrictions whatsoever are made on the nature of the method or law which defines the exhaustive bounded sets of rational numbers. As a result, it is neither possible to define a real number

Characterization of General Mathematical Concepts

which is not one of these sets, nor to develop a formal system which captures categorically all such sets. Whether or not we identify a real number with its corresponding bounded set of rational numbers, there remains the problem of the existence of real numbers. According to Dedekind, a cut is a division of all rational (or real) numbers into two sets A and B such that every member of A is smaller than every member of B. The formal development proceeds by assuming that every cut of rationals determines a unique real. The justification seems to go in the opposite direction. What is taken as an axiom or a definition of continuity is the principle that every cut on the straight line determines a unique point.[16] 'I am utterly unable to adduce any proof of its correctness, nor has anyone the power. The assumption of this property of the line is nothing else than an axiom by which we attribute to the line its continuity, by which we find continuity in the line.' By correlating reals with points on the line, each cut of reals determines a real. Hence, if we delete all irrational numbers in the cut, we can get all cuts of rationals too and each such cut determines a unique real (recalling that rationals are dense in the reals). The formal move to return then to cuts of rationals has the advantage that we obtain the reals from rationals and their sets.

Dedekind did not give an explicit axiomatic characterization of the real numbers although he remarks that the rationals form a field and implies that we need only to add the axioms for ordering and the cut principle. His idea is very close to the current characterization[17] that the reals form a continuously ordered field F. Since the axioms of an ordered field are not problematic, we consider only the *axiom for continuity* which is basically the cut principle, but can also conveniently be stated in terms of upper bounds.

Every bounded (from above) set K of reals (i.e. a subset of F) has a least upper bound.

It is worth remarking that this is, again, a second order system, because the above axiom deals not only with reals but also with arbitrary sets K of reals. This feature makes the axiom system strong enough to be categorical, and the usual proof of categoricity depends heavily on this informal aspect. If we use a first order system, i.e. consider instead of arbitrary sets K in the above axiom, only sets expressible by the notation of the system (0, 1, $+$, $\cdot$, $<$, variables and the notations of logic), then it is known that the resulting elementary theory is complete and decidable[18] but of course no longer categorical. The situation is quite similar to that with the Peano axioms of natural numbers. While the second order system for reals is as strong as we could wish, but not entirely formal, the elementary theory of reals is as transparent as we could wish, but does

75

not even give us a close approximation to the richness we want, since, for example, we cannot even single out the subset of natural numbers within the system. What is usually considered as analysis or the theory of real numbers is better approximated by a formal system treating of natural numbers as well as sets of them which can be identified with the reals, or by taking the current formal system of set theory (commonly known as *ZF*) and deleting the power set axiom. The first order axioms for a continuously ordered field delimit the area of elementary algebra or geometry, rather than the area of analysis.

If we identify real numbers with arbitrary sets of natural numbers or arbitrary exhaustive bounded sets of rational numbers, the problem of characterizing the continuum is shifted to that of characterizing arbitrary sets of natural numbers. The well-known theories of real numbers by Dedekind, Cantor, and others are insufficiently explicit because they presuppose but do not include a theory as to how sets are to be introduced. In this connection it is of interest to recall Cantor's proof that given any enumeration of real numbers, we can find a real number which does not occur in the enumeration. The wider implication of this proof is that no completely explicit characterization can exhaust all real numbers. In particular, no formal system can contain all the real numbers. Nonetheless, there is a counterpart of Cantor's theorem in certain formal systems. Here we have a case where by one interpretation the real numbers of a formal system are countable and by another interpretation they are uncountable.

Since Cantor's proof establishes that given any enumeration of real numbers, there is a real number not in it, it seems possible to infer that the totality of all real numbers is not countable. However, does the second sentence mean exactly the same as the first sentence? The situation resembles pretty much the argument that since for each time we can always imagine a time before it and a time after it, time is therefore infinite. But it is not easy to understand what is meant by saying that time is infinite: does this merely mean that for each moment we can always think of a before and an after, or does this mean something more? This question has been treated by Kant, among others.

With regard to the meaning of uncountability of the totality of real numbers, we encounter a rather subtle and more exact situation. If we say merely that given any sequence of real numbers, we can find one not in it, then everything is entirely straightforward. Thus, given any definition or law for generating a sequence, just apply the diagonal procedure and define a real number which is not in the sequence. By this interpretation, what is proven is not a single theorem but rather a schema which yields a definite theorem for each given enumeration. On the other hand, it is not clear to everybody what is meant by calling a collection absolutely uncountable. For one not comfortable with the classical concept of sets, the situation resembles the question whether space or time is bounded. To parrot Kant's remarks on his first antinomy: Now if I inquire after the quantity of the collection of all sets of natural numbers, it is equally impossible, as regards all my notions to declare it countable or to declare it uncountable. For neither assertion can be contained in mental construction, because construction of an absolutely uncountable collection or a closed countable collection incapable of further expansion, is impossible; these are mere ideas.

More specifically, if we try to extract more from the diagonal argument to get a single theorem, we have to use an indirect argument and also impredicative definitions. It goes like this. Assume there were an enumeration of *all* real numbers, then we can define in terms of the totality a real number which cannot possibly occur in the enumeration. In this argument, since we assume, contrary to fact, that all real numbers are in the sequence, we have to use an impredicative definition to get a real number not in the sequence. The definition of the number is impredicative because in defining it we refer to all real numbers among which it is one. In general, a definition is impredicative if it contains reference to a totality which contains the object thus defined as member.

A similar thing occurs with regard to the construction of the least upper bound of a bounded set of real numbers. Taking again real numbers as sets of rational numbers, the least upper bound of a set K of real numbers is the set of all rational numbers r such that there exists some real number s in K, such that r belongs to s. In this definition we refer to the totality of all real numbers in asserting the existence of some real number in K. To avoid the impredicative definition, we can distinguish real numbers and sets of different orders. For example, given a set of real numbers of order n, its least upper bound is of order n plus 1. In this way, we avoid the use of impredicative definitions because the newly defined real number falls outside the given totality of real numbers. There appears then, however, the difficulty of referring to all real numbers at the same time. One can only refer to all real numbers of a given order. This simple obstacle seems to be the least fictitious of all the difficulties which Russell repeatedly announced in his attempt to adhere to the vicious-circle principle. This can also be viewed as the most substantial reason for Russell's introduction of the axiom of reducibility, even though at first he did not seem to be aware of this particular difficulty but was preoccupied with easily resolvable pseudo obstacles. There is no need to go into details about the axiom of reducibility except to say merely that it serves the purpose of double negation by rejecting completely the rejection of impredicative definitions which the vicious-circle principle was supposed to accomplish. As a result, so far as the original constructive approach is concerned, the axiom of reducibility is completely useless.

What Russell did not realize was the fact that one could accomplish the purpose of talking about real numbers of all orders at once without using the axiom of reducibility. Simply by this method: introduce a new kind of variable to range over sets and real numbers of all and only the finite orders. Since each general set of real numbers must be of some finite order n, its least upper bound is of order n plus 1, which is again of finite order and therefore a real number falling within the range of the general variable for real numbers. In this way, we can state and prove the general theorem that every bounded set of real numbers has a least upper bound, without using impredicative definitions.

The complication with impredicative definitions is that we lose track of how new sets are introduced. To justify them we have to assume that sets are more or less already there so that the definition merely serves to describe certain properties of pre existing things rather than to bring the set defined into being. Or, in more technical terms, it is often hard to see whether or how an impredicative definition is satisfied. When we have already defined a domain of sets, the introduction of a new set by an impredicative definition would disturb the size and arrangement of the original domain, while a predicative definition would not.

Let me illustrate what I mean by a very simple example. Suppose first that we wish to define a single set of natural numbers m satisfying the condition that m belongs to the set if and only if there exists a set to which m does not belong. Since this states the existence of a single set, it is natural to try to give a single set which satisfies this condition. Let the set be K. Does 1 belong to K or not? If it does not, then by definition it belongs to every set and in particular to K, a contradiction. Hence, it does. If it does, then, by definition, there exists some set to which 1 does not belong, hence there must be some other set besides K. Hence, even though the proposition asserts explicitly only the existence of a single set, it can hold only if there exist other sets in addition to fill the gaps.

A more complex example is the following. Suppose a domain $\{a_1, a_2, \ldots\}$ of sets of natural numbers is already given. We now define a new set K satisfying the condition that a natural number m

belongs to *K* if and only if there exists a set *a*, such that a given relation *R* holds between *m* and *a*:

$$m \; \varepsilon \; K \equiv (\exists \, a) \, R \, a \, m$$

If one asks whether 1 belongs to *K*, one has to decide whether *R a* 1 holds for some a_i in the domain originally given. If the answer is no, then 1 ε *K* if the relation *R* holds between 1 and *K*. But the relation *R K*1 can easily contain a phrase 1 ε *K* in such a manner that *R K*1 is true only if 1 ε *K* is false. As a result, in order that *K* could satisfy the condition specified, we must introduce some other auxiliary set. It is quite easy to find cases which are more complex.

It is this kind of difficulty in finding intuitively clear interpretations of impredicative definitions which has thus far prevented us from getting any informative proof of the consistency of impredicative definitions.

A fairly natural mathematical example of impredicative definitions mentioned in the literature is the following. A natural number *n* belongs to *K* if there is a partition of the set *N* of natural numbers into *n* disjoint sets none of which contains arithmetic progressions of arbitrary length. In order to determine, e.g., whether 3 ε *K*, we have to consider all partitions of *N* into 3 sets including possibly partitions defined in terms of *K* itself.

From the classical point of view, the impredicative formulation of classical analysis can be justified by what is called the quasi-combinatorial principle. This depends on a natural but uncontrolled generalization of a situation with finite sets to infinite sets. There are 8 or 2^3 subsets of $\{1, 2, 3\}$, since the set either contains 1 or not, 2 or not, 3 or not. Similarly, a set of natural numbers either contains 1 or not, either contains 2 or not, etc., hence there must be $2^{\aleph_0}$ possible sets which include all the number sets definable in any formal set theory. While this supplies a sort of inaccessible model for the continuum, it says nothing about how reals (or number sets) are to be specified explicitly.

The desire to avoid impredicative definitions suggests the possibility of developing some form of predicative analysis (or set theory), one candidate being hyperarithmetic set theory. This differs from strict constructive approaches which uphold the thesis that existence requires a method of construction. According to this thesis, it would seem natural to require that each real number be given constructively by a sequence of rational or natural numbers. Brouwer, however, has a more subtle theory which includes as reals also free choice sequences for the purpose of preserving our intuition of the continuum as a sort of infinite binary tree. The more simple minded (or the 'non-idealistic') constructive interpretation of the real numbers has recently been developed extensively by Bishop.[19] There have also been various attempts to develop recursive analysis.

In the programs of developing constructive or predicative analysis, there is also a contrast between those who prefer formal systems and those who reject them. When a formal system is chosen, there is often an unpleasant dilemma. Either the system is too strong and therefore cannot be fully justified on the given point of view (say a particular form of constructivism). Or, the system can indeed be so justified, but by a sort of diagonal argument it invites further extensions which will not violate the given viewpoint. This dilemma seems to be of an intrinsic nature because our natural conception of constructive methods is not sharply defined, certainly not in constructive terms. One could still argue that even though we cannot expect a satisfactory constructive characterization of all constructive methods, it is desirable to give a formal system which would contain all the constructive methods we actually use (e.g. by using the restricted domain of primitive recursive functionals[20] or the non-constructively characterized broad domain of all recursive functions). Whether one chooses to give a formal system would seem to depend to a considerable extent on each individual's esthetic sense.

In the cases of classical number theory and analysis, we have seen that second order systems give us more adequate characterizations of the natural numbers and the continuum. This suggests the concept of quasiformal systems which are almost like formal systems but at one point or another leave room for a freer play of our intuition. In the two examples mentioned, we allow informal considerations about arbitrary sets of natural and real numbers. There are also other possibilities such as extending elementary number theory (the first order system) by permitting transfinite induction over any (say) primitive recursive well-ordering of the natural numbers, any time we happen to know informally that the relation in question is indeed a well-ordering. Or one may leave open the infinite ordinals to be used as indices for keeping account of the complexity of (predicative say) definitions so that given any fixed ordinal number a definite formal system can be set up relative to that ordinal, but the discovery and introduction of the ordinal is left to luck and ingenuity.

There is also the possibility of a more schematic approach to mathematics of the continuum which avoids the commitment to particular viewpoints and formal or quasiformal systems. It is a striking fact that in diverse systems of different strength, we can prove counterparts of all ordinary theorems about real numbers. This suggests that no proof in any system formalizes faithfully the true mathematical result. Our intuition of the real numbers is not captured in any of the particular systems. A closer approximation could be obtained if we looked instead for the class of proofs (and therewith the underlying systems) which can all represent a given intuitive proof. In this way, each intuitive proof would correspond to a class of proofs, or rather partial interpretations, and we could classify intuitive theorems according to the classes of systems in which they can be represented naturally. This approach would avoid the dispute as to which viewpoint is the correct one. Also it would reveal more fully the intuitive content of ordinary informal mathematical proofs.

3 MECHANICAL PROCEDURES

The definition of mechanical procedures in terms of general recursiveness or Turing computability in mathematical logic is generally regarded as of great importance. In the words of Gödel:[21]

It seems to me that this importance is largely due to the fact that with this concept one has for the first time succeeded in giving an absolute definition of an interesting epistemological notion, i.e., one not depending on the formalism chosen. In all other cases treated previously, such as demonstrability or definability, one has been able to define them only relative to a given language, and for each individual language it is clear that the one thus obtained is not the one looked for. For the concept of computability, however, although it is merely a special kind of demonstrability or definability, the situation is different. By a kind of miracle, it is not necessary to distinguish orders, and the diagonal procedure does not lead outside the defined notion. This, I think, should encourage one to expect the same thing to be possible also in other cases (such as demonstrability or definability).

There are systematic procedures or mechanical routines for treating certain questions. For example, is a given natural number the square of some natural number? We have a systematic procedure by which we can decide, for every natural number n, whether n is a square. How can we formalize, i.e. bring into a sharper form, the notion of a systematic procedure? If we begin with a vague intuitive concept, how can we find a sharper concept to correspond to it faithfully?

It is often not necessary to be entirely faithful. So long as a hard core is preserved, trimming on the margin is quite acceptable. Rigidity of the formalized concept leads to decisions in cases where mere use of the intuitive notion was insufficient. For instance, the existence of a space-filling curve can only be established after the exact definition of curve is introduced. This kind of thing is at the same time an advance and a distortion. To eliminate borderline cases may be useful for certain purposes, while to get answers to questions which initially required no answer is hardly desirable in general.

Another way of sharpening a concept is by reducing more components to less or by simplifying each separate aspect. For instance, if certain properties follow from others, then we need only study the latter and neglect the former in a definition of the concept.

It happens fairly frequently that we are able to concentrate all the indeterminateness in one corner so that we no longer have to be concerned with the vagueness in every respect. Conceptually this could be a great gain. It is probably the most important function of formalizations of intuitive concepts.

What are the advantages of formalizing a concept? How do we know whether or not a formalization corresponds exactly to the intuitive concept? It may be thought that the safest method to decide the value of a formalization is by the degree of acceptance it receives. (This may be a tautology according to some use of the word 'value.') But as Gödel points out, this 'democratic' criterion depends on the times one is living in. A period may be dominated by prejudices. Gödel thinks that the present period is not *so* bad that this criterion becomes completely unreliable.

In practical applications, we often find it easier to use the intuitive notion; for example, when we are confronted with the question whether a certain not very peculiar curve is continuous. Once the formalization of a concept is accepted, we usually find it easier to be articulate about what we have to say on the concept. When we are pressed, we feel better able to defend our answers. Formalization of a concept enables us to prove things which otherwise we could only hint at.

It is too simple to say that a formalization is acceptable if and only if it agrees with our intuitive notion in all cases. It would be more correct to speak of all interesting known cases instead. It is, however, hard to decide what is known and what is not. It is harder to decide what is interesting or significant. We may have to require just the preservation of basic characteristics. What the basic or essential characteristics of a concept are depends very much on the use which we put the concept to.

Historically, many interesting questions were answered, or at least clarified, only after the crucial concepts (such as 'continuity', 'area', 'construction by ruler and compass', 'theorem', 'set', etc.) had been formalized. For example, there are continuous functions which have no derivatives. It is impossible to trisect an arbitrary angle by ruler and compass. In every fairly rich formal system there are sentences such that neither they nor their contradictions are provable. This last result clarifies the concept of (absolute) provability, at least to the extent that provability in any given formal system cannot capture fully the intuitive concept. The independence results (e.g. on the continuum hypothesis) with regard to familiar formal systems of set theory improve our understanding of the assertions shown to be independent and invite the search for new axioms of set theory.

The concept of a mechanical procedure is involved in the characterization of formal systems. It seems natural to ask what mechanically solvable problems or computable functions are. This is related to the rather popular question: can machines think? can machines imitate the human mind? One often hears that in mathematical logic a sharp concept has been developed which corresponds exactly to our vague intuitive notion of computability. But how could a sharp concept correspond exactly to a vague notion? A closer look reveals that the sharp notion, often referred to as recursiveness or Turing computability, is actually not as sharp as it appears at first sight. Roughly speaking, in the definition of the sharp concept, one makes use of a condition 'for every natural number m, there exists a natural number n, such that a definite relation R holds between m and n.' It is only required that this condition be true, the method to be used in establishing its truth is left open, and, therefore, the method of finding a number n corresponding to a given number m is also left open.

On the general question of sharpening and formalizing an intuitive concept, I have in the few preceding pages discussed matters in a noncommittal way. I have left much room for indeterminateness. I have not excluded intrinsically vague concepts such as perhaps the concept of poverty. I have not excluded relatively new concepts such as perhaps the concepts of groups and fields which we do not seem to recognize as old friends in new dresses when they first appear. I have left room for diverse ways of clarifying a concept. I have not ruled out the vague idea of a concept evolving into a clear and interesting one on account of, e.g., intrinsic stability and extensive applications. I have not ruled out the possibility of some overabundant platonism which allows for good and bad concepts, to be separated only by certain extraneous relative criteria. I have evaded the question with regard to the 'existence' of concepts and offered no theory either to defend a position that the question can be consistently evaded or even to give a satisfactory meaning to the question. It is for these reasons that I have resolved to retain the few previous pages and just quote, in the following few pages, Gödel's comments and criticisms, rather than attempting to revise my few preceding pages in the light of Gödel's views of which I have so far only a very partial knowledge.

3.1 Gödel on mechanical procedures and the perception of concepts

Gödel points out that the precise notion of mechanical procedures is brought out clearly by Turing machines producing partial rather than general recursive functions. In other words, the intuitive notion does not require that a mechanical procedure should always terminate or succeed. A sometimes unsuccessful procedure, if sharply defined, still is a procedure, i.e. a well determined manner of proceeding. Hence we have an excellent example here of a concept which did not appear sharp to us but has become so as a result of a careful reflection. The resulting definition of the concept of mechanical by the sharp concept of 'performable by a Turing machine' is both correct and unique. Unlike the more complex concept of always-terminating mechanical procedures, the unqualified concept, seen clearly now, has the same meaning for the intuitionists as for the classicists. Moreover it is absolutely impossible that anybody who understands the question and knows Turing's definition should decide for a different concept.

It may be argued that the procedures not requiring general success are mathematically uninteresting and therefore artificial. Gödel emphasizes that there is at least one highly interesting concept which is made precise by the unqualified notion of a Turing machine. Namely a formal system is nothing but a mechanical procedure for producing theorems. The concept of formal system requires that reasoning be completely replaced by 'mechanical operations' on formulas in just the sense made clear by Turing machines. More exactly, a formal system is nothing but a many valued Turing machine which permits a predetermined range of choices at certain steps. The one who works the Turing machine can, by his choice, set a lever at certain stages. This is precisely what one does in proving theorems within a formal system. In fact, the concept of formal systems was not clear at all in 1931. Otherwise Gödel would have then proved his incompleteness results in a more general form. Note that the introduction of many valued Turing machines is necessary only for establishing agreement with what mathematicians in fact do. Single valued Turing machines yield an exactly equivalent concept of formal system.

'If we begin with a vague intuitive concept, how can we find a sharp concept to correspond to it faithfully?' The answer Gödel gives is that the sharp concept is there all along, only we did not perceive it clearly at first. This is similar to our perception of an animal first far away and then nearby. We had not perceived the sharp concept of mechanical procedures sharply before Turing, who brought us to the right perspective. And then we do perceive clearly the sharp concept. There are more similarities than differences between sense perceptions and the perceptions of concepts. In fact, physical objects are perceived more indirectly than concepts. The analog of perceiving sense objects from different angles is the perception of different logically equivalent concepts. If there is nothing sharp to begin with, it is hard to understand how, in many cases, a vague concept can uniquely determine a sharp one without even the *slightest* freedom of choice. 'Trying to see (i.e. understand) a concept more clearly' is the correct way of expressing the phenomenon vaguely described as 'examining what we mean by a word.' Gödel conjectures that some physical organ is necessary to make the handling of abstract impressions (as opposed to sense impressions) possible, because we have some weakness in the handling of abstract impressions which is remedied by viewing them in comparison with or on the occasion of sense impressions. Such a sensory organ must be closely related to the neural center for language. But we simply do not know enough now, and the primitive theory on such questions at the present stage is likely to be comparable to the atomic theory as formulated by Democritus. Philosophy as an exact theory should do to metaphysics as much as Newton did to physics. Gödel thinks it is perfectly possible that the development of such a philosophical theory will take place within the next hundred years or even sooner.

Gödel mentions that the precise concept meant by the intuitive idea of velocity clearly is ds/dt, and the precise concept meant by 'size' (as opposed to 'shape'), e.g. of a lot, clearly is equivalent with Peano measure in the cases where either concept is applicable. In these cases the solutions again are *unquestionably* unique, which here is due to the fact that only they satisfy certain axioms which, on closer inspection, we find to be undeniably implied in the concept we had. For example, congruent figures have the same area, a part has no larger size than the whole, etc.

There are cases where we mix two or more exact concepts in one intuitive concept and then we seem to arrive at paradoxical results. One example is the concept of continuity. Our prior intuition contains an ambiguity between smooth curves and continuous movements. We are not committed to the one or the other in our prior intuition. In the sense of continuous movements a curve remains continuous when it includes vibrations in every interval of time, however small, provided only that their amplitudes tend toward 0 if the time interval does. But such a curve is no longer smooth. The concept of smooth curves is seen sharply through the exact concept of differentiability. We find the example of space-filling continuous curves disturbing because we feel intuitively that a continuous curve, in the sense of being a smooth one, cannot fill the space. When we realize that there are two different sharp concepts mixed together in the intuitive concept, the paradox disappears. Here the analogy with sense perception is close. We cannot distinguish two neighboring stars a long distance away. But by using a telescope we can see that there are indeed two stars.

Another example along the same line is our intuitive concept of points. In set theory we think of points as parts of the continuum in the sense that the line is the set of the points on it (call this the 'set-theoretical concept'). In space intuition we think of space as a fine matter so that each point has zero weight and is not part of matter (but only a limit between parts). Note that it is not possible to cut a material line segment or a rod in two ways at the same point or surface P, once with P on the left part, once on the right, because there is nothing in between the two completely symmetrical parts. According to this intuitive concept, summing up all the points, we still do not get the line, rather the points form some kind of scaffold on the line. We can easily think of intervals as parts of the line and assign lengths to them, and, by combining intervals, to measurable sets, where we have to consider two measurable sets which differ only by sets of measure zero as representing the same part of the continuum. But when we use the set-theoretical concept and try to assign a length to any arbitrary set of points on the line, we lose touch with the intuitive concept. This also solves the paradox that set theoretically one can decompose a globe into a finite number of parts and fit them together to form exactly a smaller globe. In the light of what has been said this only means that one can split the scaffold consisting of the points into several parts and then shift these parts together so that they will all be within a smaller space without overlapping. The result holds only for the set-theoretical concept, while it is counterintuitive only for the intuitive concept.

3.2 General recursive functions

To come back to the consideration of mechanical procedures, I shall mostly pay no special attention to partial recursive functions and confine myself to aspects which are neutral to the problem of termination and aspects which are special to the equally interesting and mathematically more familiar concept of always-terminating procedures, explained in terms of general recursiveness or Turing computability. Precisely because, as Gödel observes, the concept of mechanical procedures without the requirement of termination is a perfect example of seeing an intuitive concept sharply, there are no essential ambiguities in the concept which call for extensive special elaborations.

While the most convincing definition of mechanical procedures is by means of Turing's concept of abstract machines, the equivalent concept of recursive functions appeared first historically as more or less a culmination of extensions of the simple recursive definitions of addition and multiplication. For example, it is natural to iterate the process of compressing additions into multiplications so that we can have: $f_1(m, n) = m + n$, $f_2(m, n) = mn$, $f_3(m, 1) = m$, $f_3(m, n + 1) = f_2(f_3(m, n), n)$, and in general, for each $k, f_{k+1}(m, 1) = m, f_{k+1}(m, n + 1) + f_k(f_{k+1}(m, n), n)$. This suggests the class of primitive recursive functions.[22] It is easy to agree that all these functions are computable mechanically. By combining the sequence $f_1, f_2, \ldots$ into a single function with three arguments, we get another computable function which Ackermann shows, by a sort of diagonal argument, to be no longer primitive recursive.[23] This proves not only that we cannot say all computable functions are primitive recursive but also that any fairly simple class is likely to be inadequate on account of the possibility of finding a new computable function by way of diagonalization.

The earliest proposal for a general definition of recursive functions seems to be Herbrand's private communication quoted by Gödel[24] in 1934. 'If ϕ denotes an unknown function, and $\psi_1, \ldots, \psi_k$ are known functions, and if the ψ's and the ϕ are substituted in one another in most general fashions and certain pairs of the resulting expressions are equated, then if the resulting set of functional equations has one and only one solution for ϕ, ϕ is a recursive function.' It should be emphasized that the existence of a solution for ϕ is here intended in an intuitionistic sense. If it is taken in the classical sense, then it is known that the definition determines a much broader class than general recursive functions. For example, if g is a given function, $f(m, n) = g(m, n, f(m, n + 1))$ satisfies the classical interpretation but can produce a nonrecursive f, for a suitably recursive g.[25] Observe that as a computational procedure, the above equation involves an infinite regress since the value of $f(m, n)$ depends on the value of $f(m, n + 1)$.

A related concept is given by Herbrand in his last publication.[26] 'We can also introduce any number of functions $f_i(x_1, x_2, \ldots, x_{n_i})$ together with hypotheses such that (a) the hypotheses contain no apparent variables; (b) considered intuitionistically, they make the actual computation of the $f_i(x_1, \ldots, x_{n_i})$ possible for every given set of numbers, and it is possible to prove intuitionistically that we

Characterization of General Mathematical Concepts

obtain a well-determined result.' Elsewhere, Herbrand says that intuitionism in its extreme form 'allows only arguments dealing with the integers (or with objects that can actually be numbered by means of integers) and satisfying the following conditions: all the functions that are introduced must be actually computable for all values of their arguments, by means of operations that are completely described in advance.' To connect the two definitions, Gödel suggests that as an intuitionist Herbrand requires a constructive proof of the existence and uniqueness of ϕ in the first definition and that probably he believed that such a proof can be given only by exhibiting a computational procedure. It remains, however, true that Herbrand did not exhibit explicitly any such procedure, and that, without explicit rules of computation, the definition is circular and not useful. Gödel's modification by bringing in derived equations stipulates that the computation, for all computable functions, proceeds by exactly the same simple rules.

According to Gödel,[27] 'In intuitionistic mathematics the two Herbrand definitions are trivially equivalent.... Whether Herbrand's second concept is equivalent with general recursiveness is a largely epistemological question which has not yet been answered.' Evidently Gödel means here by 'general recursiveness' intuitionistically demonstrable general recursiveness.

Sharpening Herbrand's first definition, Gödel introduced the first definition of general recursive functions. Kleene simplified the definition by bringing in the general concept of derived equations, thereby producing the definition, now in common use, of general recursive functions. Roughly speaking,[28] derived equations are obtained by substituting numerals for variables and function values for function expressions, and a set of equations defines a general recursive function, if and only if for every fixed argument values $m_1, \ldots, m_n$, there is exactly one numeral k such that $\phi(m_1, \ldots, m_n) = k$ is a derived equation. This requirement is equivalent to the condition that all possible sets of arguments $(m_1, \ldots, m_n)$ of ϕ can be so arranged that the computation of the value of ϕ for any given set of arguments $(m_1, \ldots, m_n)$ by means of the given equations requires a knowledge of the values of ϕ only for sets of arguments which precede $(m_1, \ldots, m_n)$, and that in whatever way this is done the same values for ϕ are obtained. It gives a more explicit form to Herbrand's requirement of a unique solution, and defines classically a much more restricted class than Herbrand's definition.

If we look at familiar recursive definitions by primitive recursion, multiple recursion, etc. and try to find a suitable general concept, we find two striking features. a They are all given by (finite sets of) equations of the general form specified above under note 28. b There is an inductive or recursive direction of computation so that evaluation of a function for given argument values can be reduced to evaluating it for 'earlier' argument values in such a way that the process always terminates (i.e. there is no infinite regress). The most surprising feature of the definition of general recursiveness is the replacement of *b* by what appears at first sight to be a totally different kind of requirement, viz. that there be exactly one derived equation $\phi(m_1, \ldots, m_n) = k$, for each fixed $(m_1, \ldots, m_n)$. This 'external' condition makes it possible for us to allow feature *a* to stand in its utmost generality which no longer invites any immediate further extension. The requirement of existence and uniqueness on derived equations has the effect that we forgo all attempts to characterize in advance in what form the intuitive principle of induction would manifest itself in each general recursive definition. It should be noted that, for this reason, the diagonal argument fails to yield a new computable function which goes beyond all general recursive functions. Thus, even though we can enumerate effectively all finite sets of equations, we cannot single out from these the ones which do define general recursive functions. Hence, a function introduced by the diagonal procedure would no longer be computable in the intuitive sense.

The fact that general recursiveness yields an adequate definition of mechanical procedure depends essentially on the fact that it is equivalent to Turing computability, motivations of which are generally thought to provide the most convincing argument for identifying our intuitive notion with the mathematical one. It is, therefore, appropriate to take for granted the simple technical result of the equivalence of general recursiveness with Turing computability, and concentrate our attention on Turing's concept and the arguments for it.[29] We note at this stage a distinction which is often overlooked. What is adequately explicated is the intuitive concept of mechanical procedures or algorithms or computation procedures of finite combinatorial procedures. The related concept of effective procedures or constructive procedures, meaning procedures which can in the most general sense be carried out, suggests somewhat different elements which are related to the difference between mental and mechanical procedures and the question as to the method by which a Turing machine or a set of equations is seen to be one which defines a Turing computable or general recursive function. In other words, what is established is that from a classical point of view Turing computability gives an adequate analysis of mechanical procedures. From a constructive point of view, the concept is not entirely determinate and, indeed, is circular as a way of making explicit what a constructive method is, since the definition again involves an existential quantifier which is to be interpreted by a function. Another different question is that of practical feasibility. We shall return to these two questions later. First, we proceed to consider Turing's concept.

3.3 Turing machines

An algorithm is a finite set of rules which tell us, from moment to moment, precisely what to do with regard to a given class of problems. Given an algorithm for solving a class K of problems and a problem belonging to K, anybody can solve the problem provided he is able to perform the operations required by the algorithm and to follow exactly the rules as given. For example, a schoolboy can learn the Euclidean algorithm correctly without knowing why it gives the desired answers. In practice, when a man calculates, he also designs small algorithms on the way. But to simplify matters, we may say that the designing activity is no longer a part of his calculating activity.

Thus, in following an algorithm, a human calculator uses certain data, including the instructions of the algorithm, which he remembers in part but are mostly written down on sheets of paper or printed in reference tables or charts. In short, there is a some storage device to store initial data and intermediate results. In addition, he performs b certain elementary operations such as multiplication or integration. Moreover, he exercises c control of the sequencing of steps by consulting the instructions to determine what step is to be performed next.

Of these three components, b is the easiest to mechanize, at least when operations are sufficiently elementary. The introduction of desk calculators delegates a considerable portion of this part to machines. What the automatic (sequencing) computer does is to add 1 a memory unit to store information, and 3 a control unit to carry out the instructions according to a program which embodies the algorithm. In addition, the desk calculator is replaced by 2 an arithmetic unit, which is integrated with 1 and 3. At first the program was given externally (by plugboards) so that the machine could not be instructed to modify the program to add flexibility. But soon machines began to include 'stored programs' in such a way that the program is treated as part of the initial data and, with ingenuity, one program can be written to instruct the machine to do automatically the work of a bundle of programs.

This sketch emphasizes numerical calculations. But it is known that nonnumerical algorithms can often be realized on existing machines since, for example, letters of the English alphabet can be represented by numbers.

The above description gives, in the roughest terms, an outline of the concepts behind existing computers. It leaves out on the one hand the enormous engineering research and development needed in building and improving the actual computer, and on the other hand a careful analysis of the basic notion of computations and algorithms.

The intuitive notion of an algorithm is rather vague. For example, what is a rule? We would like the rules to be mechanically interpretable, i.e. such that a machine can understand the rule (instruction) and carry it out. In other words, we need to specify a language for describing algorithms which is general enough to describe all mechanical procedures and yet simple enough to be interpreted by a machine. Thus, instead of the one problem of defining an algorithm, we are led to two equally difficult problems of defining a mechanical language and a machine. We seem to be moving in circles. One might suggest that we should collect a large sample of algorithms and analyze them to find out their common feature. But it is hard to see how such an inductive approach in the manner of J. S. Mill can, without some appropriate powerful ideas, produce a satisfactory abstraction.

What Turing did was to analyze the human calculating act and arrive at a number of simple operations which are obviously mechanical in nature and yet can be shown to be capable of being combined to perform arbitrarily complex mechanical operations. Qualitative increase in the complexity of an algorithm is replaced by quantitative increase in memory size and time needed for carrying out the algorithm. Moreover, once such a simple conception of a machine is given, the problem of designing a mechanical language also gets solved easily.

If we think of a man computing on a piece of paper, which we may suppose is divided into squares, we find that the following things are all involved in the process. 1 a storage medium, viz. the piece of paper; 2 a language, with symbols to represent numbers and directions which, for simplicity, we may assume are written down on the piece of paper; 3 scanned regions, i.e. certain squares are observed at each moment; 4 'states of mind', viz. at each stage the man keeps track of the stage of computation and decides what step is to be taken next; 5 the act of taking the next step of computation which may involve *a* a change in the symbols by writing or erasing (crossing out) certain symbols, *b* a change of the scanned region, *c* a change of the 'state of mind.'

What makes the process mechanical, i.e. capable of being performed by a machine, or by a man in a mechanical (noncreative) way, can be summarized in the following two principles.

A The principle of determinacy.
B The principle of finiteness.

According to the first principle, the only relevant information in deciding what act is to be performed next is the symbols currently observed in the region under scan and the present 'state of mind.' Now in computing according to an explicit algorithm, the algorithm is supposed to specify what is to be done under all possible circumstances arising from the computation. But the only way the present circumstances at each moment can be delineated for the man doing the computation is through his present experience, viz. the symbols (on the paper) currently observed plus his present 'state of mind.'

The rather vague notion 'state of mind' calls for some further examination. In a way, the symbols currently observed, as observed, are part of the man's present experience, but isolating them as a separate unit makes the situation more precise. The present 'state of mind' may contain many irrelevant factors, human nature being what it is. The relevant factors which need to be taken into consideration are primarily the mind's response to the symbols currently observed in the light of the instructions of the algorithm and the process of computation as carried out thus far. Now, in the normal course of a human computation, the memory of what one has done thus far may help to decide the next step to be taken. However, we believe that if one is sufficiently careful, this indeterminate element can be made exact and written down on the piece of paper. In this way we may think of the present 'state of mind' as an exact conditional attitude of being ready to perform certain specific acts depending only on what the currently observed symbols on the piece of paper are. And this agrees with our concept of a precise algorithm which specifies that at each stage different specific acts are to be performed according to the data currently available. The 'state of mind' is merely to keep track of what the present stage is in the whole process of computation.

According to the principle of finiteness, the mind is only capable of storing and perceiving a finite number of different items at each moment; in fact, there is some fixed finite upper bound on the number of such items. The upper bound on the number of items perceived at each moment is rather small, while the bound on those stored is quite large, although it still seems reasonable to agree that there is some such upper bound. From this principle, it follows immediately that at each moment only finitely many squares can be scanned. If the computing individual wishes to observe more, he must make successive observations.

Moreover, the number of states of mind which need be taken into account is also finite, because these states must be somehow stored in the mind, in order that they can all be ready to be entered upon. An alternative way of defending this application of the principle of finiteness is to remark that since the brain as a physical object is finite, to store infinitely many different states, some of the physical phenomena which represent them must be 'arbitrarily' close to each other and similar to each other in structure. These items would require an infinite discerning power, contrary to the fundamental physical principles of today. A closely related fact is that there is a limit to the amount of information that can be recovered from any physical system of finite size.[30]

As a third application of B, we may assume that the number of symbols which can be printed is finite. An infinity of different symbols cannot be stored in the human mind, even though we seem to feel we can, in theory, make arbitrarily long combinations of a certain small number of given symbols. We distinguish single symbols from compound symbols by the criterion that we must be able to observe a single symbol at one glance. Given a finite bound to the area we can observe at a glance, an infinity of symbols must include ones which differ to an arbitrarily small extent, and to recognize them as different would require capacity to make arbitrarily minute distinctions. In any case, to make proper use of an infinity of symbols would require states of mind which are infinitely complex. We can argue against the assumption of a single state of mind which is infinitely complex, with much the same arguments as those used against the supposition of an infinite number of states of mind.

The fourth application of B is to the operations performed at each step of the computation. As we noted before, the operations involve three types of change: the state of mind, the symbols as written on the working sheet, and the region under observation. It may seem rather idle and frivolous to introduce a state and then change it without changing the written symbols or the region under observation. But, since the operation is determined by the state and the symbols observed, the same state may cause other changes when other symbols are observed. In fact, even a state which always causes only changes of states is useful because the difference in the symbols observed may effect a conditional transfer to different states. For much the same reason, it is possible to keep the state unchanged while making a change of another type. We may, therefore, think of each operation as either a change of just one of the three types, or a change of both the state and one of the two other factors, or a change of all three items. Depending on which alternative is chosen, one obtains different but equivalent formulations of the abstract machines. The choice, however, makes no difference for our immediate purpose here, and we shall for the moment assume that each operation makes only one of the three types of change.

Since there are only a fixed finite number N of states in each problem of computation, there are no more than $N(N - 1)$ possible changes of states. Similarly, since there is a fixed finite bound B to the number of squares scanned at each moment and there are only finitely many different symbols, there are a finite number of distinct observable regions, and finitely many possible changes of such regions. In view of this fact, we could either represent each possible region (e.g., n^2 connected squares on the piece of paper with 'blank' counted as a symbol) by a single symbol so that each time only a single symbol is observed and changed; or else, we may avoid the increase of the total number of available symbols but observe or change only a single symbol at a time. Other observations and changes can be split into simple ones of this kind. This simplification would, in general, entail an increase in the number of states. But that is all right.

It remains to consider the change from observing one region on the piece of paper to observing another. The new region must be immediately recognizable by the computing individual. It would seem reasonable to suppose that the distance between the two successively observed regions does not exceed a fixed amount, say L units. If we assume, as we just defended, that each time a single square is scanned, then the situation is slightly simplified since we can easily delineate the possible units next to be observed in a region of $(2L + 1)^2$ squares with the currently scanned square at the center. As before, we may reduce L to 1 by splitting a move to unit steps, possibly at the cost of increasing the number of states.

One relatively minor point is the tacit assumption of the two-dimensional nature of the storage (and working) space, viz. the piece of paper. Using a one-dimensional medium would simplify somewhat the description of the abstract machines and make no theoretical difference. As we grow up, we tend to abandon the two-dimensional computation we did in our childhood, and we are convinced that a one-dimensional paper or tape, when long enough, is adequate. Moreover, as the one-dimensional model is developed further, it will be clear that a higher dimensional medium does not increase the range of what is computable in theory, because any computation with that medium can be simulated by one on a one-dimensional tape.

We may now construct a mechanical model of the computation with a given algorithm. Each state of mind corresponds to a 'configuration' or state of the machine. The machine scans B squares at each moment. In any operation, the machine can change its configuration, can change a symbol on a second square, or can change the scanned region to another region no more than L squares away. As we have observed, there is no loss of generality if we restrict both B and L to be unity and let the machine work on a linear tape. Hence, the only variable elements are the number of available distinct symbols (the size of the alphabet) and the number of states. Since with a larger alphabet we can embody more information in a given state, it is possible to reduce the number of states by enlarging the alphabet and reduce the size of the alphabet by increasing the number of states.

This completes our review of the arguments for the conclusion that Turing machines, and therewith general recursive functions, provide classically an adequate analysis of mechanical procedures. We turn now to questions of constructivity and practical feasibility.

3.4 Constructivity and practical feasibility

We refer to the exact description of Turing machines given under footnote 29 and recall in addition that a function ϕ of natural numbers is Turing computable if and only if it is computable by a Turing machine. And the function ϕ is computable by a Turing machine if and only if beginning with a representation of any given argument values $(m_1, \ldots, m_n)$ on the initial tape the machine will eventually stop with the representation of a numeral k which is the value of $\phi(m_1, \ldots, m_n)$. In this definition, as well as in the definition of general recursive functions, there are two assertions of existence: the existence of a Turing machine or a set of equations, and the existence of a final (output) tape with the representation of a numeral or a derived equation, for each given set of argument values. If we assume a Turing machine or a set E of equations given and ask whether it defines a function of natural numbers, we have to face merely the second existence assertion. Since the situations are completely analogous, we may conveniently consider just one of the two concepts.

For our present purpose, we shall confine our attention to the question whether a given E defines a general recursive function and in particular to the existence condition that for any numerals $m_1, \ldots, m_n$, there exists a (unique) derived equation of E which has the form $\phi(m_1, \ldots, m_n) = k$. In arithmetic form, we may briefly summarize the condition by $\forall m \, \exists n (g_E(m, n) = 0)$, where n is the (Gödel number of the) shortest derivation from E of an equation of the required form with m as the argument value, for a suitable primitive recursive function g_E. One of the reasons that we get a sharp definition of mechanical procedures is our willingness to disregard the question how this condition is to be established. This is justifiable from a classical point of view since we feel we know the meaning of saying that the condition is true. Thus, $\forall m \exists n(g_E(m, n) = 0)$ is true if and only if for every numeral m there exits a numeral n such that $g_E(m, n) = 0$ is verifiable (i.e. can be proved by numerical calculations alone). But if we accept a constructive position, we have a different interpretation of the condition and get into a sort of circularity if general recursiveness is viewed as an analysis of constructivity, since the meaning of the condition requires the existence of a constructive function f with $g_E(m, f(m)) = 0$, for all m.

There seems to be a widespread equivocation over these two distinct issues. The official statement of Church's thesis proposes to identify general recursive functions with effectively calculable functions. In fact, Church[31] seems to be concerned with the question of how the existence condition is established.

The reader may object that this algorithm cannot be held to provide an effective calculation of the required particular value of ϕ unless the proof is constructive that the required equation $\phi(m_1, \ldots, m_n) = k$ will ultimately be found. But if so this merely means that he should take the existential quantifier which appears in our definition of a set of recursive equations in a constructive sense. What the criterion of constructiveness shall be is left to the reader.

We are faced with two nonexclusive alternatives of a disregarding the apparent semantic difference between effective procedures (or effectively calculable functions) and mechanical procedures (or algorithms) and b considering Church to be concerned with analyzing a basically different intuitive concept than that of mechanical procedures. The above quotation seems to suggest that alternative b is the case, because otherwise it would be irrelevant to bring in the question of constructive proofs. On the other hand, Church also argues that a function is effectively calculable in his proposed sense if and only if there exists an algorithm for the calculation of its values. Hence, alternative a seems also to hold. A more congenial interpretation would be that Church deliberately permits both a classical and a constructive reading of his thesis. In any case, there is a natural inclination to ask questions about the existence condition, and we shall in the present context distinguish mechanical from effective procedures with the understanding that such questions are, for most of us, only directed appropriately to effective procedures.

If the existence condition is taken in a constructive sense, we have to presuppose a meaning of constructive proofs. If we try to explain the notion of constructive proofs in the familiar manner by saying that a proof of an existence statement $\forall m \exists n \ Rmn$ should give a method by which one could in principle find for each m an example n such that Rmn, we seem to involve ourselves in a circle. We do not know exactly what kind of method is acceptable. With regard to the case which concerns us, we do have a method of finding the corresponding equation for given $m_1, \ldots, m_n$. The method consists in enumerating all the derived equations of E until we come upon one with $\phi(m_1, \ldots, m_n)$ as left member and a numeral as right member. Indeed, no matter how we have reached the existence assertion, this method is always applicable in the sense that we shall sooner or later arrive at the equation, since it does exist in the infinite sequence of derived equations. If we find such methods acceptable, then the question whether the existence assertion is proved constructively makes no more difference. Or alternatively and what is more likely, we find the methods unacceptable because we want to have effective methods, and we feel that the method of enumerating derivative equations is not always an effective one for finding the desired equations. To decide between the two alternatives, we need a more exact explanation of the notion of effectiveness.

If we leave aside all concerns with constructivity, there remains a desire to have a pretty good idea of how soon an effective procedure terminates in each case. Precisely where general recursive functions get their greatest strength in having strong closure properties by a big sweep, there we tend to ask for a more orderly structure which offers some hierarchical classification of these functions. This is related to but distinct from the interest in practical feasibility. In both cases, we are interested in finding some measure of the complexity of different computations. But, for example, unbounded iterations of exponentiation are for all practical purposes no longer feasible, yet in the sense of getting an orderly structure, we can easily understand such a simple primitive recursive function. There are attempts to get some natural notion of practical decidability by counting, for example, the number of additions and multiplications needed, so that, for example, 'the travelling salesman problem' could be shown to be practically undecidable. We shall refrain from discussing this vast problem of practical feasibility and confine our attention to the less practical question of an orderly structure.

That we do have a natural urge to look for a more effective process than general recursiveness can be illustrated by some familiar examples. One is the result of Turing that every complete formal system (in the sense that every sentence or its negation is a theorem) is decidable. Since complete, we can enumerate all theorems by a general recursive function and all nontheorems (viz. negations of theorems because of completeness) in the same way. Hence, every sentence appears in one of the two general recursive enumerations and we can find out in finite time which is the case. When formalized, this gives a general recursive procedure for deciding whether any sentence is a theorem. But very often when the argument is presented, we find the vague feeling that the procedure is not sufficiently effective. Another example is Péter's objection to the use of the operator 'the smallest number such that.' Thus, she assumes that there exists some number which has a given recursive property and continues to say,[32] 'One cannot effectively search from all natural numbers for the smallest number with a given property.' This contradicts the identification of effectiveness with general recursiveness, but seems to conform pretty well to common sense.

We note that not all existence conditions $\forall x \, \exists y (g_E(x, y) = 0)$ for general recursive definitions can be proved in a single formal system. The functions which are provably general recursive in any given formal system can be enumerated in a general recursive way and the diagonal argument can be applied to get a new general recursive function. Moreover, for each formal system S, the arithmetic statement Con (S) is equivalent to the existence condition of some general recursive function.[33] Hence, by Gödel's theorem the existence condition is not provable in S. This suggests the idea of imposing an orderly structure on general recursive functions by finding a hierarchy of stronger and stronger formal systems. But the idea seems unpromising.

Another idea is to use 'speed functions.' Corresponding to each set E of equations which defines a general recursive function $f(m)$, choose some speed function $f_s(n)$ which, for each constant n_o, gives an upper bound to the number of steps needed for getting the value of $f(n_o)$ from E. This would be useful, if the speed functions f_s are in general simpler in some sense than f, but the obvious ways of defining speed functions do not give this desired property.[34] Something of mathematical interest for practical feasibility has been obtained in the literature by refining the considerations to include notational features of the representation of the numbers. Thus, for example, the representation of n in the binary notation has length much shorter than n. But this type of consideration does not go very far in moving from simpler recursive functions to more complex ones, since, for example, the binary or decimal notation is tied up with exponentiation and has little effect on much faster increasing functions.

The most popular approach toward getting an orderly structure is by considering 'ordinal recursions.' In the case of primitive recursive functions, we take the usual ordering of natural numbers and move from each number to its successor. It is natural to generalize this so that we reduce the calculation of $f(n)$ not just to $f(n-1)$, but directly to the calculation of $f(k)$ for any number k smaller than n. And it is known that this generalization gives no new functions. But there is a wider generalization. We may rearrange the natural numbers in some other ordering (for example, odd ones before even ones) and consider definitions which obey the principle of reducing to smaller (in the new ordering) argument values. Now we can get well-orderings of natural numbers which have different order types (correspond to different ordinal numbers of Cantor's second number class) and also widely different ones which correspond to the same ordinal number. For each well-ordering $<$, we can introduce the scheme of ordinal recursion $f(m, n) = g(m, f(h(m), n), n)$ with the restriction that $h(m) < m$, where g and h are given functions.

The idea is that by classifying the well-ordering, we might be able to get an orderly structure of all general recursive functions. It is easy to show that if $<$ is general recursive, then all functions thus definable are general recursive. In fact, it is familiar that if we start from a given ordinal and proceed to smaller and smaller ordinals, we must come to a stop in a finite number of steps. Conversely, it is also known that any general recursive function can be so defined even if we restrict $<$ to be primitive recursive ones or to be[35] of order type ω, and so on. The problem now is to classify well-orderings by some appropriate standard. And the known results just mentioned show that 'extensional' properties such as order type or primitive recursiveness of the orderings are not sufficient in themselves to give an informative classification. We may have to consider how they are proven to be well-orderings. We seem to be led back to the question of classifying proofs, only this time the proofs are concerned with establishing that certain given recursive relations are well-orderings. This may be a gain, but the prospect of finding an informative orderly structure over all general recursive functions seems remote.

Mathematically the classical thesis of identifying mechanical procedures with Turing computability or general recursiveness has been fruitful in making possible a number of diverse mechanical unsolvability results. In contrast, the concern with getting an orderly structure for effective procedures has not been nearly as rewarding in terms of significant mathematical results.

NOTES

1 L. E. J. Brouwer, 'Intuitionism and formalism,' *Bull. Am. Math. Soc.*, vol. 20, 1913, pp. 81–96.
2 *Foundations of arithmetic*, § 6.
3 Hermann Grassmann, *Lehrbuch der Arithmetik*, 1861.

Characterization of General Mathematical Concepts

4 R. Dedekind, *Was sind und was sollen die Zahlen?*, 1888. There is also a letter by Dedekind quoted at length in 'The axiomatization of arithmetic,' *J. symbolic logic*, vol. 22, 1957, pp. 145–57, which contains more historical details on the contributions of Grassmann and Dedekind.

5 Reproduced in the paper listed in note 4.

6 For more details, see the paper cited in note 4.

7 See Th. Skolem, *Selected works in logic*, 1970. The paper itself dates back to 1933. The result has been generalized to the conclusion that no first order theory with infinite models is categorical. The theory *D* has both countable and uncountable nonstandard models. An interesting special case is the theory of the ordering relation of rational numbers (dense linear ordering with no first or last element). It is decidable and categorical in a restricted sense, viz. that any two countable models are isomorphic.
   The first order Peano axioms, i.e. P1 to P5 with *K* in P5 confined to sets definable with the successor function and notations of logic only, determine the weak system *B* and are actually complete in the sense that every statement expressed in terms of the primitives of the system is either provable or refutable. Only when we add the notations and axioms for addition and multiplication do we get a system which is incomplete. This is of interest in that a richer system is incomplete while a poorer is complete. What happens is that the expressive power of a system increases so much faster than the proving power that even though there are more axioms, they are not adequate to the treatment of the wealth of new problems arising out of the increased expressive power of the new symbols for addition and multiplication.

8 See the preface to Dedekind's monograph listed under note 4.

9 *Grundgesetze der Arithmetik*, vol. 2, 1893, p. viii.

10 Bernard Bolzano, *Paradoxien des Unendlichen*, 1851, § 19.

11 *Principles of mathematics*, 1903, § 331.

12 *The analyst*, 1734.

13 *A mathematician's apology*

14 *Rein analytischer Beweis des Lehrsatzes, dass zwischen je zwei Werten, die ein entgegengesetztes Resultat gewahren, wenigstens eine reelle Wurzel der Gleichung liege*, Prague, 1817.

15 *Principles of mathematics*, op. cit., last page of the preface.

16 *Stetigkeit und irrationale Zahlen*, Braunschweig, 1872. See the last paragraph of section III. The point might be the least in *B* or the greatest in *A*. We shall not distinguish two cuts which are so related and determine the same point, or we can stipulate that the point in question is always considered to be in *B*.

17 Another familiar characterization is that the reals are a simply ordered set which has the cut property, contains a countable subset dense in it, and has no first or less element. The first axiomatic characterization of the reals seems to go back to D. Hilbert, 'Ueber den Zahlbegriff,' *Jahresber. deuts. Math.-Verein*, vol. 8, 1900, pp. 180–4. Extensive discussions are contained in E. V. Huntington, *The fundamental propositions of algebra*, 1911, and Alfred Tarski, *Introduction to logic*, 1941.

18 See Alfred Tarski, *A decision method for elementary algebra and geometry*, 1948.

19 Erret Bishop, *Foundations of constructive analysis*, 1967.

20 Kurt Gödel, 'Ueber eine bisher noch nicht benutzte Erweiterung des finites Standpunktes,' *Dialectica*, vol. 12, 1958, pp. 280–7.

21 Kurt Gödel, 'Remarks before the Princeton Bicentennial Conference, 1946,' *The undecidable*, ed. Martin Davis, 1965, p. 84. With regard to the independence from the formalism chosen, Gödel adds a footnote: 'To be more precise: a function of integers is computable in any formal system containing arith-

metic, if and only if it is computable in arithmetic, where a function f is called computable in S if there is in S a computable term representing f.'

22 The first systematic use of primitive recursive functions is in Th. Skolem, 'Begrundung der elementaren Arithmetik durch die rekurrierende Denkweise,' *Videnskap. skr. I. Mat. Nat. Kl.*, vol. 6, 1923, pp. 3–38. A more exact characterization of the class of primitive recursive functions was given by Gödel in 1931 in his famous paper on undecidable propositions where extensive use of primitive recursive functions is made. Roughly, these are functions definable by substitution (composition) and the scheme $f(0, x, \ldots, y) = g(x, \ldots, y)$, $f(n + 1, x, \ldots, y) = h(n, x, \ldots, y, f(n, x, \ldots, y))$, with g and h given.

23 See W. Ackermann, 'Zum Hilberstchen Aufbau der reellen Zahlen,' *Math. Annalen*, vol. 99, 1928, pp. 118–33. The example has been simplified to a function of two arguments. $f(0, n) = n + 1$, $f(m + 1, 0) = f(m, 1)$, $f(m + 1, n + 1) = f(m, f(m + 1, n))$. For this and related matter on primitive recursive functions and their extensions, see R. Péter, *Rekursive Funktionen*, 1951 and 1957.

24 See *The undecidable*, op. cit., pp. 70–3.

25 In fact, the class thus determined classically coincides with that of hyperarithmetical functions and could be called effectively definable (rather than computable) functions. See e.g., *J. symbolic logic*, vol. 23, 1958, pp. 199–201. For the function g, let $g(m, n, k)$ be 1 or $2k$ according as whether there is a number $x < n$, such that $T(m, n, x)$, T being the familiar predicate for calculating all recursive functions.

26 See axiom C in § 2 of J. Herbrand, 'Sur la non-contradiction de l'arithmétique,' *J. reine u. angew. Math.*, vol. 166, 1931, pp. 1–8. This is reprinted in English in *From Frege to Gödel*, ed. J. van Heijenoort, 1967, where we find also on p. 619 an additional reference to Herbrand and a quotation from Gödel which are used below in this paragraph.

27 *The undecidable*, op cit., pp. 70, 72–3. It may be noted that intuitionistically there is a broader question of the relation between computability (not necessarily described by equations as in Herbrand's definitions) and general recursiveness.

28 There are various problems of detail with regard to the exact formulation. The exact form of the definition of general recursiveness used today is due to S. C. Kleene who has introduced equivalent variant forms of Gödel's definition which are, if somewhat less intuitive, simpler to state and easier to use than Gödel's. See Kleene's two papers reprinted in *The undecidable*, and, in particular, § 1 of the first paper (originally in *Math. Annalen*, vol. 112, 1936) and § 8 of the second paper (originally in *Trans. Am. Math. Soc.*, vol. 53, 1943). Generally, each equation is of the form $s = t$, where s and t are terms, and terms are defined recursively as follows. Thus, 0 is a term; a variable is a term; if t is a term, t' is a term (successor of t); and if $s, \ldots, t$ are terms and f is a function symbol, $f(s, \ldots, t)$ is a term. For the discussion in this and the next paragraph, compare also S. C. Kleene, *Introduction to metamathematics*, 1952, § 54 and § 55 (especially p. 274). We note that Kleene has an alternative (derived) definition of general recursive functions in terms of special definitional schemes (those for primitive recursion plus one for the smallest number operator), which is simpler to describe and often convenient to use (see his book, pp. 279, 289).

29 A. M. Turing, 'On computable numbers,' *Proc. London Math. Soc.*, vol. 42, 1936, pp. 230–65; reprinted in *The undecidable*.

A Turing machine is defined as follows. Each machine is capable of being in any one of a fixed finite list of states. It is supplied with a linear tape, (potentially) infinite in both directions. The tape is divided into squares each capable of bearing a symbol, which, without loss of generality, could be taken as either the blank or a mark (fixed once for all). The tape will pass through the machine so that at each moment the machine scans only one square, and is in one of the given states. The content of the square under scan (either blank or marked) and the state at each moment determines the current configuration of the machine. The current configuration determines the move (or atomic act) which the machine is to make (or perform): either change the content of the scanned square, or change the scanned square to the neighboring square on the left or on the right (by shifting the tape or shifting the machine), or change the current state to another state, or stop. The machine starts with any initial state and any initially scanned square; the initial tape (the input) may contain any combination of marked and blank squares, although normally we assume that the initial tape contains only finitely many marked squares. Once started, the machine is supposed to make moves according to the current configuration at each stage. If it never gets to make the 'move' of stopping, it will go on forever. If the machine does stop, the content of the tape at that stage is often called the output.

30 Gödel points out that the argument in this paragraph, like the related arguments of Turing, depends on certain assumptions which bear directly on the broader question as to whether minds can do more than machines. The assumptions are: 1 there is no mind or spirit separate from matter; 2 physics will always remain of the same kind in that it will always be one of limited precision. For a more detailed report on Gödel's views about this and related issues, compare the last section of the chapter on minds and machines in this book.

31 See footnote 10 and § 7 of Alonzo Church, 'An unsolvable problem of elementary number theory,' *Am. j. math.*, vol. 58, 1936, pp. 345–63. By the way, under footnote 18, Church states: 'The question of the relationship between effective calculability and recursiveness (which it is here proposed to answer by identifying the two notions) was raised by Gödel in conversation with the author.' It seems likely, in view of Gödel's repeated emphasis of Turing's work (see *The undecidable*, pp. 71–2 and *From Frege to Gödel*, p. 616) that Gödel does not regard Church's argument for his thesis as sufficiently convincing.

32 R. Péter, *Rekursive Funktionen*, 1951, foot of p. 9.

33 Let $B(m, n)$ be the primitive recursive predicate expressing that m is the Gödel number of a proof of S whose last line has the Gödel number n, and Con(S) be the statement expressing that for no m, $B(m, n_o)$ where n_o is the Gödel number of the sentence 'p and not p.' Let $g(m, n)$ be the Gödel number of the sequence of lines obtained from the proof whose Gödel number is m by adding two lines 'if p and not p, then q_n' and 'q_n,' where q_n is the formula having the Gödel number n. Let neg(k) be the Gödel number of the negation of the sentence whose Gödel number is k and $G(m, n)$ be the primitive recursive predicate: $B[g(m, n), n]$ and $B\{g[m, \text{neg}(n)], \text{neg}(n)\}$.

Then Con(S) is equivalent to: 1 $\forall m \exists n[\text{not } G(m, n)]$. Thus, if Con($S$), take q_n as '$o = 1$.' If not Con(S), then there is m_1 such that $B(m_1, m_o)$ and we have: $\neg \forall n G(m_1, n)$.

34 See 'A variant of Turing's theory,' *J. Assoc. Computing Machinery*, vol. 4, 1957, pp. 63–92, end of § 3.

35 See John Myhill, 'A stumbling block in constructive mathematics,' *J. symbolic logic*, vol. 18, 1953, pp. 190–1; and N. A. Routledge, 'Ordinal recursion,' *Proc. Cambridge Philos. Soc.*, vol. 49, 1953, pp. 175–82.

III

RUSSELL'S LOGIC AND SOME GENERAL ISSUES

1 *PRINCIPLES* (1903)

Russell's first major work in logic and foundations was undoubtedly his *Principles*, of which part I and appendix B are probably the most interesting. Furthermore, the Introduction to the second edition (1937) gave a summary and evaluation of works related to his original interests, done by himself and others during the thirty-four intervening years. Since he did nothing in this area after 1937, it seems reasonable to use this book as a preliminary guide to a discussion of his work in logic.[1]

The book begins with a bold definition of pure mathematics as the class of all propositions of the form '*p* implies *q*,' where *p* and *q* are propositions containing one or more variables, the same in the two propositions, and neither *p* nor *q* contains any constants except logical constants. In 1937, this was modified to include other truth functions besides implication. It could, however, be argued that even though the conditional is indeed only one among the truth functions and no more important than others, implication occupies a special place as is seen, e.g. from the importance of *modus ponens* and the deduction theorems. This is a question which Russell does not consider. But the logical constants are a topic to which he frequently returns.

The fundamental thesis of the book is that mathematics and logic are identical (reducibility of mathematics to logic). This is a position to which Russell adhered until his death. A third global issue is the question of realism and constructivism with regard to classes. In *Principles*, the realistic position is conspicuous, e.g. it is said in the preface that defining different types of numbers as classes leaves no doubt as to the existence theorems, i.e. that there are entities of the kind in question. This is quite the opposite of his later emphasis on logical constructions. Another favorite question of the philosophers, the analytic-synthetic distinction, did not interest Russell as much, although he has a singular remark buried in a chapter on Kant (p. 457) to the effect that since mathematics is obviously synthetic, the reduction shows that logic is also synthetic. Finally, continuing on the same high level of philosophical generality, we include a quotation which points to an interest in language and grammar (p. 42): 'On the whole, grammar seems to me to bring us much nearer to a correct logic than the current opinions of philosophers; and, in what follows, grammar, though not our master, will yet be taken as our guide.'

On a more manageable level, Russell outlines a system of symbolic logic and hints at a type theory as a way of resolving the set-theoretic paradoxes. The system contains three parts with seven indefinables and nineteen premisses.[2]

It appears that formal implication and propositional function are related and both are quite complex. In analyzing them, Russell comes across new indefinables such as *every term* (p. 40) and *variable*, which in turn lead to *denoting*, and *any term* (p. 80), as well as the class of propositions defined by a propositional function (p. 93). Moreover, in the chapter on denoting we encounter *all, every, any, a, some, the*: 'Concepts of this kind, we found, are fundamental in mathematics, and enable us to deal with infinite classes by means of propositions of finite complexity' (p. 106).

It goes without saying that logicians today would not be happy with the inaccurate way in which the constructions are carried out. What is less clear is whether these primitive attempts might contain germs for fruitful developments which have been left out of the clearer logical systems we possess nowadays.

In discussing classes and the paradoxes, Russell first proves that for all R, there can be no a such that, for all w, $wRa \equiv \neg\, wRw$. Hence, we have to drop either the axiom $x \in \hat{x}\phi x \equiv \phi x$, or the principle that every class can be taken as one term. At this juncture, a distinction is suggested between a class as many and a class as one (pp. 104–5 and p. 76):

A class as one, we shall say, is an object of the same *type* as its terms; i.e. any propositional function ϕx which is significant when one of the terms is substituted for x is also significant when the class as one is substituted. But the class as one does not always exist, and the class as many is of a different type from the terms of the class. . . . In this view, a class as many may be a logical subject, but in propositions of a different kind from those in which its terms are subjects.

Russell's Logic and Some General Issues

In what sounds like a change of topic, Russell throws in a contrast between all and any: 'Thus the correct statement of formal truths requires the notion of *any* term or *every* term, but not the collective notion of *all* terms.'

Although the distinction of class as one and class as many sounds superficially like Cantor's and von Neumann's separation of sets and classes, Russell does not adopt the decisive criterion that a class as many is also a class as one only when it is not too large. The general point suggested is rather that $a \in \hat{x}\phi x$ is sometimes meaningless although $a \in \hat{x}\phi x \equiv \phi a$ is always true if $a \in \hat{x}\,\phi x$ is meaningful. This doctrine is elaborated further in appendix B. It should be noted that Russell speaks of 'the true solution' (p. 522) and 'a first step towards the truth' (p. 523) in connection with the resolution of the paradoxes. He apparently does not envisage the possibility that there are alternative solutions, none of which is a unified theory that is superior in every way. This reminds one of the debate between Einstein and Bohr on the foundations of physics.

In appendix B, the doctrine of types is set out in greater detail. It contains essentially the simple theory of types, although some of the difficulties discussed here do not seem to have been faced squarely even in the more definitive versions. The idea is not unnatural when we recall the familiar example that 'virtue is triangular' is neither true nor false, but meaningless. The two basic postulates are stated explicitly (p. 523):

T1 Every propositional function ϕx has, in addition to its range of truth, a range of significance, i.e. a range within which x must lie if ϕx is to be a proposition at all, whether true or false.

T2 Ranges of significance form *types*, i.e. if x belongs to the range of significance of ϕx, then there is a class of objects, the *type* of x, all of which must also belong to the range of ϕx, however ϕ may be varied.

On the basis of these two postulates, types are discussed for classes, relations, propositions, and numbers. At the bottom are the individuals: an individual is any object which is not a range; this is the lowest type of object. There is a basic difficulty with numbers and propositions, because all numbers are regarded as a type and all propositions are regarded as a type (because they can all be, significantly, said to be true or false). The type of all numbers requires a consideration of the totality of types and ranges since all ranges have numbers. The type of all propositions yields a contradiction by considering all classes of propositions and the class K of all propositions, one proposition p_m for each class m of propositions, viz. 'every proposition in the class m is true,' which, according to the type structure, does not belong to the class m. Therefore, p_k belongs to and does not belong to k.

105

In the more definitive version of *Principia*, these difficulties are avoided by taking each number as realized on different levels with infinitely many different copies, and by applying the vicious-circle principle to get different orders of the concept of truth. The semantic concepts such as truth present other questions to which we shall return later on.

There are other difficulties which seem to have been more or less bypassed in Russell's later writings. Russell does not consider anywhere the possibility of keeping T1 but dropping T2, thereby permitting overlapping types. Although T2 excludes overlapping types, Russell does suggest that 'the sum of any number of minimum types is a type, i.e. is a range of significance for certain propositional functions' (p. 525). This would seem to permit a less rigid type theory, although it is not clear how such a scheme is to be carried out. Moreover, the question whether there are types of infinite order is also raised: 'All ranges certainly form a type, since every range has a number; and so do all objects, since every object is identical with itself . . . but the range of all ranges is of course a type of infinite order' (p. 525).

2 PRELUDES TO *PRINCIPIA* (1903-10)

In 1902, Frege discussed the paradoxes and considered the possibility that there might be concepts with no corresponding classes.[3] But he decided on a mild remedy which excludes only a few 'singular points.' The modified system has since been shown to be inconsistent by various people. In fact, during his later years, Frege abandoned the belief that mathematics is reducible to logic and took up, among other things, an investigation of our geometric intuition of the continuum.

Meanwhile, Russell was concentrating on finding a solution to the paradoxes. In his own words,[4] 'Throughout 1903 and 1904, my work was almost wholly devoted to this matter, but without any vestige of success. My first success was the theory of descriptions, in the Spring of 1905 . . . It was afterwards generally accepted, and came to be thought my most important contribution to logic.' Although the analysis does some violence to ordinary usage (e.g. as G. E. Moore points out,[5] it does not apply to 'the whale is a mammal'), it has become a standard paragraph in logic books. In fact, Ayer, following Ramsey, once called it the paradigm of philosophical analysis.[6] In form it is similar to the more ancient example of getting rid of infinitesimals by means of the limit concept. In any case, the theory of descriptions has got more than its share of publicity and need not be elaborated here.

In 1906, Russell used a reply to a paper by E. W. Hobson as an occasion to set forth his thoughts on the paradoxes.[7] There were, he thought, some propositional functions (norms, properties) which did not determine classes, and the problem was to give rules by which these non-predicative norms could be separated from the others. He discussed three alternative courses: A, the zigzag theory; B, the theory of limitation of size; C, the no-classes theory (p. 37). The paper was received on November 24, 1905, and in a note added February 5, 1906, we have: 'From further investigation I now feel hardly any doubt that the no-classes theory affords the complete solution of all the difficulties stated in the first section of the paper.'

In the zigzag theory, 'we start from the suggestion that propositional functions determine classes when they are fairly simple, and only fail to do so when they are complicated and recondite . . . in the zigzag theory the negation of a predicative function is always a predicative function.' Quine's stratification[8] seems to fulfill quite well the requirements laid down, although it is doubtful that Russell would have been happy to present a system with so little conceptual motivation. There is an incidental remark which seems hardly compatible with the no-classes theory: 'When a new entity is introduced, Dr. Hobson regards the entity as *created* by the activity of the mind, while I regard it as merely *discerned*' (p. 41).

Russell pointed out that in the theory of limitation of size, no set can have a complement. Furthermore, he gave a generalization of the Burali-Forti paradox[9] and continued as follows:

It is probable, in view of the above general form of all known contradictions, that if ϕ is any demonstrably non-predicative property, we can actually construct a series, ordinally similar to the series of all ordinals, composed entirely of terms having the property ϕ. Hence, if the terms satisfying ϕ can be arranged in a series ordinally similar to a segment of the series of ordinals, it follows that no contradiction results from assuming that ϕ is a predicative property. But this proposition is of very little use, until we know how far the series of ordinals goes (p. 36).

The axiom of replacement and von Neumann's axiom excluding classes as large as the universal class seem to carry out these ideas quite literally.

Russell's remarks on the no-classes theory in this paper are very cryptic, but he hinted at treating classes as 'incomplete symbols' and correlated a class u with an open sentence Fx so that 'u has only one member' becomes $(\exists b)(x)(x = b \equiv Fx)$.

At this stage, there came an intervention from Poincaré. In 1905, Richard initiated the consideration of semantic paradoxes by considering the set of all decimal fractions definable in a finite number of words.[10] Richard resolved the paradox by suggesting that the set of decimals definable in a finite number of words could not properly be understood to include any decimal definable only by reference to the whole set. This was taken over by Poincaré in 1906 while commenting on the Russell paper just considered.[11] Poincaré proposed to identify non-predicative norms with those which contain a vicious circle as evidenced in Richard's paradox. This has come to be regarded as an established concept under the term 'impredicative definitions.' It is quite clear from the context that Poincaré's main objection was against higher infinities and he had no wish to submit basic principles such as mathematical induction to the test of predicativity.

In a prompt reply,[12] Russell agreed to the suggestion, laid down the vicious circle principle, pointed out the similarity to the old paradox of Epimenides, and defended Cantor's doctrine of infinity. Russell also pointed out that it remained a major task to construct a theory on the basis of the vicious circle principle, because what was needed was to build up a positive structure and not merely to say negatively what was not permitted. Russell's reluctance to treat finite classes and infinite classes in basically different manners is closely tied up with the wish to identify logic with mathematics. Since infinity is central to mathematics, a theory which blames the paradoxes on the peculiarities of infinite classes would cast doubt on the claim that logic contains the full richness of mathematics.

The first full account of Russell's type theory appeared in 1908, the year when Zermelo's paper on the foundations of set theory and Brouwer's paper on the unreliability of the principles of logic also were published.[13] The type theory paper contains essentially the basic framework of *Principia* as elaborated in the first 200 pages of Volume 1 (1910). It seems best to consider the two works together. In fact, since the latter treatment largely superseded the former, we shall be mainly concerned with the book.

In 1909 Poincaré commented on Russell's 1908 paper, pointing out that ordinals were presupposed in the description of type theory.[14] In reply, Russell published a French translation[15] of pp. 37–60 of *Principia* with an added note arguing that one could pedantically avoid speaking of the order of a type by speaking of $\phi! x$, $f! (\phi! x)$, 'and so on.' Since the general theory mentions every finite order, the defense seems hardly acceptable.

One small matter is the distinction between *any* and real variables on the one hand, and *all* and apparent variables on the other, in part credited to Peano. This undoubtedly corresponds to the contrast of free against bound variables. In the second edition of *Principia* (1925), this distinction was abolished altogether. In the informal discussion, free variables and schematic letters (communication symbols) seem to be thrown together. Thus, e.g. by Gödel's construction, there is in the usual system a predicate *Px* such that for any *m*, *Pm* is a theorem, but (*x*)*Px* or *Pa* (with free variable *a*) is not a theorem. Hence, there is certainly a distinction between *all* and *any* taken in the schematic sense. As to the distinction between free and bound variables, the German school continues to use different letters for them. In one sense, the free variables seem to correspond to the parameters which remain unchanged through the course of a proof so that e.g. the induction variable cannot be viewed as a free variable. In another sense, the free variables are the universally quantified variables which are not governed by any existential quantifiers and they do behave like constants in considering validity of quantificational schemata. As Skolem observed,[16] free variable systems are specially transparent, at least when one uses only decidable predicates and effective functions.

Although formal implication does not figure as prominently in *Principia*, it is pointed out (p. 21) that implications between closed sentences:

> do not serve the purpose for which implications are chiefly useful, namely that of making us know, by deduction, conclusions of which we were previously ignorant. *Formal* implications, on the contrary, do serve the purpose, owing to the psychological fact that we often know '(*x*) ($\phi x \supset \psi x$)' and ϕy, in cases where ψy (which follows from these premisses) cannot easily be known directly.

This distinction is not very sharp; in particular, Quine was able to derive the *modus ponens* for formal implication from the special case with closed sentences only.[17]

3 PRINCIPIA

To avoid extraneous complexities, we shall confine our attention to classes, leaving out relations which could be added with the help of ordered pairs either as another primitive as in Peano or as defined in some suitable manner. Also, we shall, for the moment, stay away from semantic notions such as truth and denotation.

On the bottom type, there are the individuals and certain predicates applicable to individuals. In this way, we get a class of atomic propositions from which we get other propositions by truth functional connectives. There are variables *x*, etc., ranging over individuals. By quantification over these variables, we obtain first-order propositional functions. Variables ϕ, etc. (preferably ϕ_1, etc.)

are introduced to range over these functions, which are construed as an open sentence Px or the abstractive expression $P\hat{x}$ or the property denoted by it. Using the variables, we get from $\ldots Px \ldots$ results such as $(\phi_1) \ldots \phi_1 x \ldots, (\phi_1) \ldots \phi_1 \hat{x} \ldots, (x) \ldots \phi_1 x \ldots, (x) \ldots \phi_1 x \ldots$ which are all (except the third) of order 2. The order of a propositional function is taken as the least integer exceeding the order of all bound variables therein, i.e. all quantified variables and all circumflexed ones as well. Thus, the order of an open sentence $F\phi$ is determined by the orders of the bound variables in it, the order of an abstract $F\hat{\phi}$ (the expression) and the property named by it is determined by the order of the open sentence $F\phi$ and that of the variable of abstraction ϕ. The order of a variable (an expression) is in turn determined by the unique order of all the properties which the variable takes as values.

A property must be of higher order than the things having the property, e.g. $\phi_1 x$ is a property of order 1 of individuals (things of order 0) while $(\phi_1) \ldots \phi_1 x \ldots$ is of order 2. Properties which are of just next higher order than things having them (their arguments in terms of propositional functions) are called *predicative* by Russell (p. 53), a usage which harks back to the discussions with Poincaré; but introduces differences through the axiom of reducibility (see below). It might be thought that we need to introduce variables for the properties of, say, individuals of each order m and use variables of order m and level n for every pair (m, n) of positive integers. This was, according to Russell, unnecessary (p. 54). In fact, he only introduced variables for predicative functions and, hence, if we disregard relations, the variables needed form a simple infinite hierarchy; x, y, etc.; ϕ_1, etc; ϕ_2, etc.; and so on.

On account of the axiom of reducibility, this simpler procedure actually accomplishes the same purpose as the alternative approach of using two hierarchies. Thus, the axiom states that, for every open sentence $F\phi_n$, we have:

$$(\exists \phi_{n+1})(\phi_n)(\phi_{n+1}\phi_n \equiv F\phi_n)$$

This means that even if we had included infinitely many kinds of variables for properties of objects of a given level and order, they could have been replaced by the variables from the smaller class used by Russell, with the help of the axiom.

Once, however, this is realized, the difference between Russell's theory and the modern version of simple type theory is essentially reduced to a matter of properties versus classes for which the axiom of extensionality is true. In fact, the concealed formal system can be brought out without too much difficulty. In particular, each variable or abstract may be spoken of as of some type $_i (i = 0, 1, \ldots)$.

110

3.1 The formal system *PM*

P1 The alphabet includes variables over individuals x, y, etc. (or rather ϕ_o, etc.), variables over propositional functions of individuals ϕ_1, etc., and in general, variables ϕ_n, etc., for each positive integer n; $\vee$, $\neg$; symbol for universal quantification; possibly certain constant names for individuals and properties of fixed types which we shall disregard. An atomic formula is any expression of the form $\phi_{n+1}\phi_n$, for some n; formulas in general are obtained from given ones by $\neg$, $\vee$, and universal quantification in the usual manner. The constants $\supset$, $\equiv$, $\vee$, $(\exists)$, are defined from $\neg$, $\vee$, $(\#)$ in the usual manner. In what follows, it is most natural to construe p, q, F, etc. as schematic letters.

P2 The propositional calculus
     *1.1 If p and $p \supset q$, then q
     *1.2 $(p \vee p) \supset p$
     *1.3 $q \supset (p \vee q)$
     *1.4 $(p \vee q) \supset (q \vee p)$
     *1.5 $(p \vee (q \vee r)) \supset (q \vee (p \vee r))$ (redundant, as shown by Bernays)[18]
     *1.6 $(q \supset r) \supset ((p \vee q) \supset (p \vee r))$

P3 The quantification theory In each of the following, x, y, are any variables of the same type, and x is not free in p.
     *10.1 $(x)Fx \supset Fy$
     *10.11 If Fy, then $(x)Fx$
     *10.12 $(x)(p \vee Fx) \supset (p \vee (x)Fx)$

P4 The axiom of reducibility
     *12.1 $(\exists\phi_{n+1})(\phi_n)(F\phi_n \equiv \phi_{n+1}\phi_n)$

P5 Identity
     *13.01 $(\phi_n = \psi_n) = (\phi_{n+1})(\phi_{n+1}\phi_n \supset \phi_{n+1}\psi_n)D_J$

P6 The axiom of infinity

P7 The axiom of choice

As an integral part of the system *PM*, classes are introduced as 'incomplete symbols.' The cumbersome notation $\phi\hat{x}$ of local circumflexes for properties is now replaced by a related but more convenient notation $\hat{x}\phi x$ for class abstraction. In *20, we find:

> propositions in which a function ϕ occurs may depend, for their truth value, upon the particular function ϕ, or they may depend only upon the *extension* of ϕ. In the former case, we will call the proposition concerned an *intensional* function of ϕ; in the

latter case, an *extensional* function of ϕ. . . . The functions of functions with which mathematics is specially concerned are all extensional. When a function $\phi! z$ is extensional, it may be regarded as being about the class determined by $\phi! z$, since its truth value remains unchanged as long as the class is unchanged.

The contextual definition of classes is:

$$20.01 \quad G(\hat{\phi}_n F\phi_n) = (\exists \phi_{n+1})((\phi_n)(\phi_{n+1}\phi_n \equiv F\phi_n) \wedge G\phi_{n+1})Df$$

Variables α, etc. ranging over classes are introduced again in context:

$$*20.07 \quad (\alpha_{n+1})F\alpha_{n+1} = (\phi_{n+1})F(\hat{\phi}_n(\phi_{n+1}\phi_n))Df$$
$$*20.071 \quad (\exists \alpha_{n+1})F\alpha_{n+1} = (\exists \phi_{n+1})F(\hat{\phi}_n(\phi_{n+1}\phi_n))Df$$

On the basis of these definitions, the axiom of extensionality is derived as a theorem:

$$*20.43 \quad (\phi_n)(\phi_n \varepsilon \alpha_{n+1} \equiv \phi_n \in \beta_{n+1}) \supset \alpha_{n+1} = \beta_{n+1}$$

For $n > 0$, we can also derive:

$$(\gamma_n)(\gamma_n \in \alpha_{n+1} \equiv \gamma_n \in \beta_{n+1}) \supset \alpha_{n+1} = \beta_{n+1}$$

From the above discussion, it should be clear that all that the no-classes theory accomplished is the reduction of classes to properties. This is much less of a reduction than Russell undoubtedly intended originally: the axiom of reducibility makes much more difference than the distinction between properties and classes. In fact, in the introduction to the second edition to *Principia* (1925), the distinction between propositional functions and classes is abandoned on the ground that we are only interested in extensional functions. The axiom of reducibility is also dropped, and classes of different orders composed of members of the same order are distinguished so that variables get both superscripts and subscripts.

To continue with our consideration of the first edition, we come back to several peculiar features we deliberately left out.

In practice, type indices are suppressed altogether by a convention of *systematic ambiguity*. The convention is, in effect, that indices are to be imagined supplied in any way conformable to the restriction that a class gets a type index one higher than its members ('stratification'). This makes the resulting development quite similar to Quine's *New Foundations* except that *PM* remains weaker in its quantification theory because in Quine's system[19] no requirement of stratification is imposed on the quantificational part.

Something like the system *PM* with the axiom of extensionality added as applying directly to the variables for propositional functions is preserved through Hilbert and Ackermann,[20] and is known in the literature as higher order predicate or functional calculi.

The mixture of semantic with mathematical paradoxes creates more serious difficulties. It is not unreasonable to wish to develop a more comprehensive logic in which semantic notions appear directly. In fact, such a development seems highly attractive and appears to await a satisfactory execution even today. But in order to develop such a theory we are forced to face the distinction between use and mention, symbols and their meaning. Thus, in *Principia*, there is also a hierarchy of propositions (closed sentences). However, the great complexities resulting from the interactions of propositions and propositional functions are not at all seriously treated. For example, if A means 'asserted by Epimenides' and T means true, although we have $(p_n)(Ap_n \supset \neg T_n p_n)$, briefly q, and Aq, we cannot derive $\neg T_n q$ because q is of order $n + 1$. In order to develop such a theory explicitly, we would, among other things, have to include axioms like $p_n \equiv T_n p_n$, and allow propositional variables to play a double role, as standing in place of nouns and of sentences. We need, of course, rules to permit substitution of propositions for propositional variables, which may be supposed to be implicit in *10.1.

While it seems quite possible to develop some such unified theory, this was apparently not central to Russell's purpose. At various places in more recent years Russell agrees to cut off the part having to do with semantic notions from his theory.

There is a philosophical idea about the development of quantification theory which is of considerable technical interest. This is the idea that truth functions governing quantified expressions must be explained in terms of propositions in which truth functions do not govern quantified expressions. In *9 and in the second edition (*8 and the new introduction), where alternative developments to replace *10 are described, it is elaborated at great length that the truth function theory is assumed only for quantifier-free sentences at first, together with quantifiers occurring in formulas in the prenex normal form. Quantifiers occurring otherwise are introduced by definitions.

The system hinted at in *9 is essentially the following:

*1.1–*1.6 Quantifier-free theorems of truth functions
*9.01–*9.06 For example, $\neg (\exists x)Fx = (x) \neg Fx Df$.
  $(x)Fx \lor p = (x)(Fx \lor p)Df$
*9.1 $Fx \supset (\exists y)Fy$
*9.2 $Fx \lor Fy \supset (\exists z)Fz$
*9.12 If p and $p \supset q$, then q (p, q may contain quantifiers)
*9.13 If Fx then $(y)Fy$

The primitive concepts are $\lor$, $\neg$, (x), $(\exists y)$. This is practically

113

the same as the system in Herbrand's dissertation,[21] except that here the system is assumed simultaneously for all the different types while Herbrand's system is just for one type. The definitions *9.01 to *9.06 are properly construed as permitting reiterated applications so that Fx and p may contain quantifiers. This was not appreciated by Russell because the distinction between theorems and metatheorems was not familiar: 'Mathematical induction is a method of proof which is not yet applicable, and is (as will appear) incapable of being used freely until the theory of propositions containing apparent variables has been established' (p. 130).

In connection with the idea of isolating the rules for shifting quantifiers, it is also, for certain purposes, convenient to use mini-scope forms (with quantifiers as far inward as possible) rather than prenex forms, or even proceed without any extensive shifting of quantifiers. In that case, it is natural to have rules for introducing quantifiers inside a formula rather than at the beginning only. A simple example that several people have found convenient to use is to take $\wedge$, $\vee$, $\neg$, (x), $(\exists y)$ as primitive and consider only formulas in the positive form, viz. in a form in which the negation sign governs only atomic formulas. We obtain then a formally simple system with three rules only:

Q1 Any truth-functional tautology (possibly with quantifiers) is a theorem.

Q2 If . . . Fx . . . is a theorem and x is not free elsewhere, . . . $(x)Fx$ . . . is a theorem.

Q3 If . . . $((\exists x)Fxy \vee Fyy)$ . . . is a theorem, then . . . $(\exists x)Fxy$ . . . is one.

To extend the system to include formulas not in the positive forms, we have to add:

Q4 In any context, $\neg (\exists x)Fx$ and $\neg (x)Gx$ can be replaced respectively by $(x) \neg Fx$ and $(\exists x) \neg Gx$; $\neg (p \wedge q)$, $\neg (p \vee q)$, $\neg \neg p$ by $(\neg p \vee \neg q)$, $(\neg p \wedge \neg q)$, p; and conversely.

If we use Herbrand's concepts of general and restricted quantifiers in place of (x) and $(\exists x)$ in Q2 and Q3, we can dispense with Q4 altogether.

4 WITTGENSTEIN AND RAMSEY

So far we have largely refrained from discussing the philosophical passages in *Principia*, especially pp. 37–59. The writer can still remember puzzling over these pages as a freshman in 1940, hour

Russell's Logic and Some General Issues

after hour, with little success. Particularly relevant to Russell's philosophy of logic are some works of Wittgenstein, Ramsey and Gödel.[22]

In section 1 above, we have mentioned the principles T1 and T2. From 1908 on, a third principle has been particularly conspicuous, viz. T3. The vicious-circle principle.

The principle T2 excludes the possibility of mixed types. This principle is stated fairly explicitly as *1.11 (p. 95). The three principles together determine essentially some form of the ramified type theory although there remains the question of what ordinals are permitted as order indices. In particular, we can infer from these principles:

T3a No class and its members can be of the same type.

From T1, T2, T3a, we arrive at the simple type theory.

The derivation of T3a from T3 is given explicitly (p. 40):

Now given a function $\phi\hat{x}$, the values for the function are all propositions of the form ϕx. It follows that there must be no proposition, of the form ϕx, in which x has a value which involves $\phi\hat{x}$. (If this were the case, the values of the function would not all be determinate until the function was determinate, whereas we found that the function is not determinate unless its values are previously determinate.) . . . In fact, $\phi(\phi\hat{x})$ must be a symbol which does not express anything: we might therefore say that it is not significant.

It is also argued that 'The value for $\phi\hat{z}$ with the argument $\phi\hat{z}$ is true' is not meaningless but false, since no such value exists.

Now since the simple type theory does not require the full strength of T3, it is natural to ask whether T3a can be derived on other grounds. In fact, Russell offers another argument by a direct consideration (pp. 47–8), viz. that the propositional function is ambiguous and cannot be used as a subject. Here, the confusion between propositional functions as properties and as open sentences seems particularly evident. Thus, it is the open sentence which is a mere ambiguity awaiting determination, and cannot occur as an argument; while in '$\phi\hat{x}$ is a man,' one would say that the ambiguity in ϕx is eliminated by the circumflex.

If we drop T3a altogether, there would be nothing to prevent our getting the property of all properties ϕ such that $\neg\phi\phi$, or $\hat{x}(x \notin x)$. On the other hand, it is conceivable that we can replace T3a by weaker principles such as: no class of a given type can be as large as the class of all ordinal numbers of that type.

In the second edition of *Principia*, Russell borrowed from Wittgenstein a principle of extensionality (see below) and in addition tried to do without the axiom of reducibility. The result of the first revision is essentially to make all properties extensional so that they are no different from classes except that, on account of the second revision, only predicative classes are permitted. Pages (appendix C) are added to argue that '*A* believes *p*' and '*p* is about *A*' are not genuine counter-examples to the principle of extensionality.

Dropping of the axiom of reducibility had at least four types of consequence. First, the definition of identity no longer worked. This, however, could be replaced by the principle of extensionality $(x)(\phi x \equiv \psi x) \supset (F(\phi) \equiv F(\psi))$. Concepts and results on higher infinities, such as Cantor's theorem, could no longer be obtained; but this was not much deplored. Classical analysis, such as the theorem of least upper bounds, was lost, and this was deplored. Finally, there is difficulty with mathematical induction.

Without the axiom of reducibility, not only are there integers of different types, but within each type higher than 1 there are integers of infinitely many orders, because an integer belongs to every class (of a fixed order) which is inductive, i.e. contains 0 and is closed under the successor operation. In appendix B, Russell offered a proof that the class of integers of order 5 is no larger than the class of integers of order *n*, for any $n > 5$. It would follow that the class of integers can be defined as the intersection of all inductive classes of order 5. This would seem to contradict the fact that one can, using higher order induction, prove the consistency of the system with lower order induction and, therefore, eliminate more non-standard integers. As Gödel pointed out, the proof of *89.16 is not conclusive.[23]

In the *Tractatus*, Wittgenstein put forward a number of provocative points about the philosophy of logic and mathematics. Roughly speaking, there are simple objects and atomic facts. Atomic propositions, if true, picture atomic facts ('the picture theory of meaning'). Quantifiers are reduced to conjunctions and disjunctions. Every simple object has a unique name, hence identity is, in the final analysis, dispensable, although it is not denied that it is useful and indeed essential to mathematics, where our main interest is to determine whether different descriptions have the same reference. Furthermore, the principle of extensionality (5.54) is meant to apply to all composite propositions: 'In the general propositional form propositions occur in other propositions only as bases of truth operations.' From these general assertions, the general form of propositions is obtained which yields all propositions by applying a generalized stroke function (negation of all propositions of any given set; compare a related idea in Schönfinkel's notation, $fx \mid {}^{x}gx)^{24}$ repeatedly on the class of all atomic propositions. The whole theory overlooks the distinction between finite ranges and infinite ranges, and is, therefore, quite irrelevant to the foundations of mathematics. Numbers are sensibly treated along a different line: 'A number is the exponent of an operation' (6.021).

The most basic principle is perhaps that of atomicity, which asserts the possibility of ultimate analysis. Little is said about simple objects which appear more like material objects than the sense data advocated by Russell and the logical positivists. The theory of descriptions seems to be an important influence in suggesting this position of 'logical atomism,' according to which terms which do not refer can be eliminated.

'A sword is broken' makes sense only if there are simple objects so that we can think of them as being rearranged. This assumes that sense has to be formulated in terms of reference and reference has to be to material objects. Perhaps not just material objects, but simple objects at any rate.

Logic must be true in all possible worlds. How then are we to think of the possible worlds? Different possibilities arise out of rearranging the same basic stuff.

It is all very familiar: 'The president of England' seems to have a fictitious reference and the theory of descriptions makes it seem unnecessary to go beyond real objects. Hence, why not in all cases? Analysis should lead to simple signs and hence to simple objects. If simple signs are to have sense, the sense can only be reference. If the sense of a simple sign is not an object, then further analysis is possible. In fact, whether a name makes sense would always have to depend on whether something is true. In other words, if we have only descriptions, where do they get sense? Unless somewhere propositions reach out directly to reality, there can be no foundation for explaining the truth or falsity of any proposition. We may not know what the atomic propositions are, but there must be such propositions.

The contrast between definite and indefinite senses introduces an element which reminds one of the law of identity stated with various qualifications. There is a feeling that when enough trouble is taken, a proposition cannot but have a definite sense: not to have a definite sense is not to have any sense.

If we begin with unanalyzed propositions and generate more complex propositions by logical operations, we have to choose between different meanings of the logical constants and also decide whether to permit sentences without a definite truth value.

The mathematical treatment of a given finite domain of objects is made easy by the fact that we can count up all the objects and assign to each object a unique sign. Fixed predicates and functions can be defined extensionally, perhaps by tables. It is clear that extensionally there can be only a finite number of possible predicates and functions over a finite domain. Then the logical constants $\wedge$, $\vee$, $\neg$, ( ), ($\exists$) can also be explained in the natural manner, and the usual laws of logic can be verified as true according to the explanation. We cannot very well expect that these laws are complete relative to the explanation, since there are in general accidentally true statements about the given small world which are not logically true, e.g. $(x)(y)(z)$ $(x = y \vee x = z \vee y = z)$ in a world with two objects. From this it is a short step to arrive at the position that in the sequence of propositions $(\exists x_1) \ldots (\exists x_n)(x_1 \neq x_2 \wedge \ldots \wedge x_{n-1} \neq x_n)$, we begin with tautologies when n is no more than the total number of simple objects and end up with contradictions.[25]

In his lectures of 1930–3,[26] Wittgenstein came to appreciate the two basic mistakes in the *Tractatus*, probably under the impact of Brouwer. The first of these concerned atomic propositions. 'He said that both he and Russell had the idea that non-atomic propositions could be "analysed" into atomic ones, but that we did not yet know what the analysis was. . . . His present view was that it was senseless to talk of a "final analysis".' He was willing to take in any context unanalyzed (rather than unanalyzable) propositions as atomic. The second important mistake was his analysis of general propositions as conjunctions. 'He said he had been misled by the fact that $(x)Fx$ can be replaced by $Fa \wedge Fb \wedge Fc \wedge \ldots$, having failed to see that the latter expression is not always a logical product, that it is only a logical product if the dots are what he called "the dot of laziness".'

Ramsey's essay[27] of 1926 contains a reinterpretation of the simple theory of types under Wittgenstein's influence. He listed three basic mistakes in *Principia*. First, the theory amounts to saying that every class has a defining property. 'The mistake is made not by having a primitive proposition asserting that all classes are definable, but by giving a definition of class which applies only to definable classes, so that all mathematical propositions about some or all classes are misinterpreted.' It is familiar that, in each formal language, there are indefinable classes. Ramsey seems to suggest also the possibility of absolutely indefinable classes. 'Whether there are indefinable classes or not is an empirical question; both possibilities are perfectly conceivable. But even if, in fact, all classes are definable, we cannot in our logic identify classes with definable classes without destroying the apriority and necessity which is the essence of logic.' Second, *Principia* fails to distinguish semantic from mathematical paradoxes. Third, the treatment of identity is a misinterpretation in that it does not define the meaning with which the symbol for identity is actually used. In his review of Ramsey's book,[28] Russell said: 'For my part, I admit the first and second of these defects, and regard Ramsey's work on these points as of great value. . . . With regard to identity I am, however, less convinced.'

Ramsey's position is that of a realist who puts finite sets and infinite sets on the same footing. In particular, all mathematical truths are, according to him, (truth-functional) tautologies, sometimes of infinitely many propositions.

> A *predicative function* of individuals is one which is any truth-function of arguments which, whether finite or infinite in number, are all either atomic functions of individuals or atomic propositions. . . . Admitting an infinite number involves that we do not define the range of functions as those which could be constructed in a certain way, but determine them by a description of their meanings (Ramsey's book, p. 39).

According to Ramsey, our inability to write propositions of infinite length is logically a mere accident (p. 41). From this approach, the axiom of reducibility becomes dispensable and is replaced by the axiom of comprehension which in form appears quite the same but is true according to the realistic position with regard to classes or infinite truth functions. On the other hand, according to the *Principia* interpretation, the axiom of reducibility is neither a contradiction (it may be true) nor a tautology (it may be false). The axiom of choice behaves the same way in the two interpretations. That it is a tautology in the realist interpretation follows from the fact that all specifications determine classes (of some given type), since we envisage all possible classes of objects in each type. To the objection that if the axiom of choice is true, it should be provable, Ramsey replies, 'But it does not seem to me in the least unlikely that there should be a tautology, which could be stated in finite terms, whose proof was, nevertheless, infinitely complicated and therefore impossible for us' (p. 59). The axiom of infinity remains troublesome because of the preoccupation with 'individuals' and the refusal to allow numbers or recursive constructions a separate place.

Ramsey's remarks are of little mathematical significance because he throws no light on how we might prove by some finite means that the axiom of comprehension is consistent (when there are infinitely many objects of some given type) or how we might settle the question of independence of the axiom of choice relative to proofs (which are not infinitely complicated). With regard to the axioms in the constructive theory, it may actually be observed that the axiom of reducibility is false (because there are classes of higher order not coextensional with classes of lower orders) and the axiom of choice is true (because the universe is countable and the intuitive model assures the possibility of selections by classes of sufficiently higher order).

Ramsey's treatment of the semantic paradoxes brings out some obscurities in *Principia*. Take Grelling's paradox of '*w* is hetero-logical.' If we use *w* to range over symbols for properties and *R* to be the naming relation, the predicate is given by:

$$Hw \equiv (\exists\phi)(wR(\phi\hat{x}) \wedge \neg\, \phi w)$$

In particular, $H'H' \equiv (\exists\phi)('H'R(\phi\hat{x}) \wedge \neg\, \phi'H')$.

Now, we might wish to argue, by the axiom of reducibility, there is a predicative function (in the sense of *Principia*) F such that $Fw \equiv Hw$. Therefore, since 'H'RH, we get $F'H' \equiv \neg\, H'H'$, and therewith $H'H' \equiv \neg\, H'H'$. Hence, it would seem that the axiom of reducibility reintroduces the semantic contradictions. Now the theory of types does not exclude either the substitution of 'H' for w or the substitution of H for F, but simply remains silent on such discourses. This is an indication that if we wish to give a unified treatment of mathematics and semantics, we have to introduce explicitly semantic concepts and rules governing their use.

In a popular lecture published soon afterwards, Ramsey expressed his misgivings about the axiom of infinity and asserted of his own theory: 'it is impossible to regard it as altogether satisfactory' (p. 81). And, according to the editor of his book, 'in 1929 he was converted to a finitist view which rejects the existence of any actual infinite aggregate and to which allusions are made in some of the later notes' (p. xii).

5 LOGICAL TRUTH AND OTHER PHILOSOPHICAL MATTERS

The introduction to the second edition (1937) of *Principles* may be regarded as a summary of Russell's views on the philosophy of logic. The central theme is logical truth and logical constants, and the main conclusion is that he has not found an adequate definition of logic.
(1) *Criticisms of intuitionism and finitism* These are rather superficial. The comments on finitism, for example, fail to understand the element of idealization in the theory; the outburst against this doctrine seems to be based on little more than a mere play on the word 'finitist.' 'If the finitist's principle is admitted, we must not make *any* general statement about a collection defined by its properties, not actual mention of all its members.' But it is well known that recursive definitions and all laws of (primitive) recursive arithmetic are perfectly acceptable according to the finitist position.
(2) *Identity of mathematics and logic* Russell's basic position seems to be that logic and mathematics are identical no matter how logic

and mathematics are more exactly defined, provided the definitions are reasonably correct. Abstractly, such a position can be quite acceptable since we sometimes know that *A* and *B* are the same without having an exact definition of either; for example, complex numbers and ordered pairs of real numbers, or God and the almighty. In the present case, however, Russell's persistence in his belief, in contrast with Frege, Ramsey, and Wittgenstein, plus the lack of an attempt to resolve the many remaining difficulties which he could not fail to perceive, is puzzling. In particular, the place in logic of the concept of infinity which is central to mathematics demands a good deal more attention before even a clear *statement* of the 'reductionist' position can be adequately enunciated. One possible theory, for example, would be taking Ramsey's early position and supplementing the disregard for the difference between finite and infinite by a justification of the axiom of infinity in terms of constructs such as all possible strings of *'s. Such a position, however, would have to assume that the logic which is true for finite sets automatically applies also to infinite sets. But this theory is very much against Russell's constructive viewpoint.

(3) *Logical construction and platonism* Russell's initial platonism, with regard to classes in particular, has been abandoned through the theory of descriptions, the abolition of classes (in favor of attributes), and Whitehead's definition of space, time and matter as classes of events. This continuing constructivist philosophy is somewhat incompatible with Russell's apparent approval of Ramsey's original theory which is as nonconstructive as any philosophy of mathematics can be.

(4) *Logical truth and logical constants* This is a central question which seems to call for extended comments.

According to Russell, a logical proposition must have complete generality and must be true in virtue of its form. No constants except logical constants occur in the verbal or symbolic expression of logical propositions. For example, we may consider the somewhat reformulated traditional syllogism: 'If all pleasures are transitory and immortality is a pleasure, then immortality is transitory.' This is, according to Russell, true in virtue of its form but not completely general because it contains the words 'pleasure,' 'transitory,' 'immortality.' If we replace these words by suitable variables, then we get a statement: 'No matter what possible values *S* and *P* and *M* may have, if all *M*'s are *P* and *S* is an *M*, then *S* is *P*', which represents for Russell a proposition of logic.

There are at least two questions: what are the logical constants, and are all true (or, rather, valid) sentences in which all constants are logical constants, logical truths.

According to Russell, 'After the ultimate efforts to reduce the number of undefined elements in the logical calculus, we shall find ourselves left with two (at least) which seem indispensable: one is incompatibility; the other is the truth of all values of a propositional function' (p. xi). In other words, the two are exclusive-or and universal quantification. This leaves out the membership relation which may reasonably be regarded as lying beyond the domain of logic. However, Russell presumably believes that predication, as symbolized by concatenation, so that we have yx in place of $x \in y$, does not have to be taken as an additional primitive, but performs the work for the membership relation. Such a view would be misleading since we do need special axioms for predication which are not demanded by the nature of exclusive-or and universal quantification.

In any case, there would seem to be a demand for some criterion to separate logical constants from nonlogical constants. Russell once said that a logical constant is something which remains constant in the verbal or symbolic expression of a proposition even when *all* the *constituents* of the proposition are changed. He also said that a fundamental logical constant will be that which is in common among a number of statements, any one of which can result from any other by substitution of *terms* one for another. These only reduce the matter to the equally complex questions of what terms or constituents of propositions are.

It is suggested in the *Tractatus* that in an adequate notation (an ideal language) logical constants would be like punctuations or brackets (4.441, 5.4, 5.4611, 5.474). It is, therefore, clear that no constituents (objects or complexes of objects) correspond to them; there are no 'logical objects.' This suggestion can help in the selection of logical constants if there is an independent criterion for adequate notations. Otherwise, an arbitrary selection can be rationalized by stipulating *ad hoc* that a notation is adequate if and only if it represents these words by signs similar to punctuations and brackets.

If we assume that the first question is somehow answered, there remains the second. Already in 1919[29] Russell began to feel that the absence of nonlogical constants, though a necessary condition for propositions of logic, is not a sufficient condition. Ramsey's counterexample is: 'Any two things differ in at least thirty ways.' If one does not require any additional property for logical truth, one would seem to be driven to a view, once voiced by Quine,[30] that every statement exemplifying a valid statement form with no nonlogical constants is logically true, with the consequence that we have to accept as logical truths certain statements whose truth depends on the size of the universe.

If we do not wish to accept this consequence, then an additional property is needed, *tautological* according to early Wittgenstein and Ramsey, and *analytic* according to many others. The natural notion of *tautological* is 'true in all possible worlds.' A rather attractive theory is developed in the *Tractatus* on such a basis, which appears to explain laws of quantification theory with identity quite well. When it comes to a class theory, Ramsey, as we mentioned before, again brings in the size of the universe in connection with the axiom of infinity.

Both Russell and the earlier Ramsey seem to believe that we cannot get ordinary mathematics unless we assume not only the existence of individuals in the world, but also infinitely many of them. Since we feel pretty sure that no matter how many things there are in the physical world, n would always be different from $n + 1$, the natural conclusion to draw is that a theory which makes this depend on an empirical hypothesis about the world must be wrong. Infinity must come from somewhere else. In fact, it is the difficulty in giving an adequate account of infinity in terms of strictly logical concepts which makes Russell's thesis of identifying logic and mathematics highly doubtful.

6 PREDICATIVE DEFINITIONS AND THE VICIOUS-CIRCLE PRINCIPLE

(1) *Formulation of the principle* The problem of formulating the principle correctly and clearly is no less complex than that of justifying it. If our aim is to determine all acceptable principles of class existence, we must decide whether to exclude all definitions which violate the vicious-circle principle or to include some such definitions which can be justified on generally accepted grounds. Ideally, it would be nice to use the principle as our sole guide, or at least to isolate the domain of all definitions justifiable by the principle alone. This latter task is not so easy, particularly because the principle is essentially negative insofar as it says directly only what definitions are to be excluded as illegitimate. Hence, in practice, it is not always clear when the principle is applicable.

In *Principia*, the principle is formulated essentially as follows p. 37):
'(1a) The vicious-circle principle. No totality can contain members definable only in terms of this totality; whatever is definable only in terms of all of a collection must not be a member of the collection'. This formulation is highly ambiguous. Some of the ambiguities could be resolved by examining the positive theory proposed by Russell, others call for varying degrees of further analysis.

A fixed finite domain of objects presents no serious theoretical difficulty. The first interesting notion for mathematics is the general concept of finiteness.

(2) *The concept of finiteness* This is presupposed in Russell's ramified theory of types in several ways. (i) In the syntactic description of the theory, we have to speak of all finite orders n, and within each order we have to think of all finite combinations obtainable by truth functions and quantifications. (ii) The definition of the successor function presupposes any finite number of iterated applications. (iii) Even the axiom of infinity, construed in terms of a physical world, has to presuppose the concept of finiteness to be meaningful.

In fact, the talk of infinity through individuals (rather than some form of abstract idealization) appears to be misguided. Russell seems to wish to distinguish the understanding of the general concept of finiteness from the assumption of the existence of infinitely many objects. This is perfectly reasonable if we are thinking of physical objects. It is, however, quite futile to try to develop mathematics on such a basis. Indeed, the reduction of arithmetic to logic, as construed and carried out by Russell, is quite definitely a failure.

Russell objects to the union of all classes obtained from the empty class 0 by taking repeatedly the unit class $\{x\}$ of each given class x on the ground of impure types and troubles with a universal set. Such objections are not valid against a ramified type theory divorced from the other separable aspects of Russell's system. We can, for example, begin with $*$, and consider a class A such that (i) $* \in A$, (ii) $x \in A \supset x* \in A$.

The difficulty here is with the variable x. We would like to say that x ranges over (a), the class consisting of $*$ plus all and only the strings obtainable from $*$ by any *finite* number of applications of the operation of appending a $*$ to a given string. This would presuppose the concept of finiteness. Alternatively, we may say that there are many classes A which satisfy (i) and (ii) because there is nothing to exclude extraneous things. In order to get a definition we could speak of the smallest class satisfying (i) and (ii). But then the definition is no longer predicative. On the other hand, if we accept the concept of finiteness as given, we can take (a) as the definition of A.

If we shift the burden to the formation rule, we can say: (i) $*$ is a term; (ii) if x is a term, $x*$ is a term. We can also use as axioms the true statements: (iii) $x* = y* \supset x = y$; (iv) $x* \neq *$. Then we can define classes by conditions such as: (v) $** \in B$; (vi) $x \in B \supset x** \in B$.

There is no explicit statement in the vicious-circle principle regarding the acceptability of recursive definitions. On the one hand, we can argue that since we understand finiteness and recursive definitions anyhow, they are acceptable and do not violate the principle. On the other hand, one may point out that an explicit definition of $x \in B$ would look like $(A)((** \in A \wedge (z)(z \in A \supset z** \in A)) \supset x \in A)$, which is obviously impredicative. If we replace $z \in A$ by $(z \in A \wedge z \neq x)$, we would have the comfort that the variable A can be taken to range over only finite classes and hence need not include B which is an infinite class.

If we leave aside the taboo about mixed types, which has nothing to do with the vicious-circle principle, Russell seems willing to accept a theory of finite classes. Since we know that it is possible to develop arithmetic on such a basis, we can then generalize the above device to obtain at least recursive sets of numbers.

The central problem is to arrive predicatively at variables which range over (the totality of) finite classes or natural numbers. If we agree that 0 is a term and $j(x, y)$ is a term if x and y are, and use as axioms $x \in 0 \equiv x \neq x$, $z \in j(x, y) \equiv (z \in x \vee z = y)$ we seem to be assured that the range R of the variables does include all finite classes built up from 0. Are we justified in thinking that the collection C of all these finite classes is not an illegitimate totality?

The principle (1a) does not seem to provide an explicit answer to this question, although it is most likely that Russell was not worried about the possibility that R may be larger than C. This question of unintended interpretations or non-standard models is not obviously relevant to our question. But that the familiar way of excluding these interpretations uses an impredicative definition makes us suspicious of the legitimacy of C. We are led to ask whether there is any way at all of introducing an infinite totality without violating the vicious-circle principle.

Whatever the solution may be, we certainly wish to use an infinite totality as a base for further construction. And a totality such as C is certainly acceptable, even if it should be regarded as violating (1a), since we do understand the concept of finiteness. In view of the fact that we can arrive at the totality C and the collection N of numbers by way of this concept, we do not have to choose the particular way of introducing these totalities which happens to violate (1a). And the conclusion we get is that C and N are legitimate totalities on the basis of which we can devise further predicative definitions.

Those who refuse to accept this conclusion will have to speak of predicativity relative to natural numbers. There is also a similar problem with regard to inductive definitions in general (see below).

There is an interesting side issue which does not seem particularly relevant to the question of predicativity. Once we have C or N, we can get predicative definitions for all arithmetic predicates by using quantifiers and a small number of simple initial predicates. However,

125

recursive definitions and all of free variable arithmetic can be developed with schematic letters (in place of variables) so that nonstandard models do not affect their interpretations insofar as the predicates are applied to the standard numbers. This is so because equality makes the denotations of each numeral unique and unnatural numbers cannot interfere. This is not true of arithmetic predicates in general because the unnatural numbers can mess up the interpretation of the quantifiers so that, e.g., 3 may satisfy a defining condition in one model but fail to do so in another. Thus, we get an interesting distinguishing characteristic of recursive definitions which might be called 'presupposing potentially infinite totalities only.' Nevertheless, this more refined distinction does not appear to be relevant to the question of predicativity, according to which once a totality is available we are free to use bound variables ranging over it. It is somewhat farfetched to argue that the variation in the nonstandard models serves to disturb the interpretation of an arithmetic predicate A and therefore that A is not predicatively defined. Rather, minimum or standard models for the ranges of variables are assumed in the construction of a predicative theory and the only bad disturbances are ones which force us to change the previous ranges so that we can no longer stick to any one minimum model. Formally, the contrast is clear in a definition of some number-set which contains only number quantifiers as against a specification in which there are quantifiers ranging over arbitrary number-sets.

(3) *Definitions and their order* The relevant notion of definition is not the use of an abbreviation for which a mechanical procedure for unique elimination of the defined expression is the whole requirement. For one thing, such abbreviations do not care where we begin from and usually do not permit the possibility of infinitely many preceding abbreviations. The concept of definition under consideration is narrower than the general category of specification which is quite neutral to the constructive flavor which we wish to preserve. On the one hand, to be pedantic, we would like to say that an impredicative definition of a number-set is not a definition but a specification relative to a preconceived realist model. On the other hand, we do not object to 'the tallest person in the room' or 'the smallest perfect number' provided we have somehow got the class of people in the room and the class of numbers. We would like to say these are impredicative specifications of objects which were defined predicatively to begin with.

From a classical point of view, one might wish to say that we are here also interested only in specifications, and that the vicious-circle principle only distinguishes one type of specification from other types. We demand, however, that the predicative definitions be well-ordered somehow so that every class is defined by a membership condition in which the values of all variables are limited to things introduced by earlier definitions in the well-ordering. It follows that a later definition does not disturb an earlier definition; if a definition A contains bound variables with a range including things to be defined in B, then the classification determined by A has to be adjusted by that determined by B, and, in general, there are complicated questions of satisfying simultaneously a group of conditions. For example, according to Russell, 'the least integer not nameable in fewer than nineteen syllables' denotes 111,777 in the classification according to the English names of integers, but the above name contains only eighteen syllables.

The order cannot be construed literally as a temporal order, and ordinal numbers are of central importance.

If arbitrary ordinals are assumed to begin with, one can go as far as getting a model for the whole of set theory, as is done by Gödel. Of course, with higher ordinals, impredicativity is intrinsic, at least as far as we know. For the purpose of predicative set theory, we use only lower ordinals and begin with natural numbers.

Once we are willing to assume natural numbers on a syntactical and conceptual level, which Russell does (without admitting it) anyway, the problem of mathematical induction is no longer difficult. As to real numbers, we can also get standard theorems such as the least upper bound (the Dedekind cut) theorem by taking unions at limit ordinals.

Given a class of ordinal numbers and a beginning theory (for example, that of finite classes or natural numbers), there is a standard procedure for building up a predicative set theory by transfinite induction: an immediate predicative extension at each successor ordinal, and taking unions at each limit ordinal.

There remain the questions of acceptable ordinals, definability versus provability, and inductive definitions.

(4) *Acceptable ordinals; automatic expansions; truth and knowledge*
To get the ordinals, we have to have a theory which in turn depends on the ordinals. In 1954 a suggestion[31] was made that we take all ordinals *definable* in a given system and then use these ordinals to make new systems. This idea of 'boot strapping' has a certain conceptual appeal. An alternating automatic extension between ordinals and systems was envisaged. The ambiguous word 'definable' ordinal was taken to mean the ordinal type of any predicate appearing in a system which happens to be a well-ordering. In 1955, Spector[32] proved a result which implies that the above expansion process in one definite sense stops with the recursive ordinals and the hyperarithmetic sets. In formal terms, one can modify slightly the Bernays set

theory to get a formal system as a codification of the theory. The modification needed is to make sure that in the axioms general bound set variables are avoided in favor of variables ranging over previously determined sets.

This simple idea has been refined to the requirement that for an ordinal to be acceptable, the corresponding well-ordering must be recognized (proved) to be a well-ordering in the given predicative system. This naturally raises the question how a predicative system, not containing variables over arbitrary sets of ordinals, can express truly the property of being a well-ordering. It so happens that in many cases the unrestricted well-ordering theorem is classically true, when the restricted form is provable in the given predicative system. Schütte and Feferman[33] have independently obtained results along such a line under the name of 'autonomous progressions.'

The more general question is whether, in the characterization of predicative definition, we should impose the requirement of knowledge over and above truth. A parallel issue has come up in connection with recursive definitions: whether we should demand that the recursiveness be constructively provable. In both cases, it seems reasonable to develop both interpretations. In the case of predicative definitions, at least, one could argue that the question of definability is primarily one of truth and should be separated from the question of recognizability. At any rate, it is possible to have a conception of predicative definition divorced from the requirement of provability.

This same question comes up also with regard to recognizing that a proposed inductive definition is indeed a definition.

(5) *Inductive definitions* In a general inductive definition quantifiers already available (e.g. over natural numbers) are permitted. One is tempted to say that these are acceptable because the only missing part is the extremal clause 'nothing more' which we understand quite well. Here again, the standard way of taking the smallest (the intersection) of all classes satisfying the inductive condition lands us in outright impredicativity.

Just as in the case of all finite classes, we can, for example, give an explicit definition of the class of recursive ordinals by using variables which range over all and only hyperarithmetic classes. This situation leads to another ambiguity in the principle (1a).

Given that we can define each hyperarithmetic (or finite) class predicatively, are we justified in introducing variables which range over all of them? It seems that this is acceptable because each member of the class *HC* of all hyperarithmetic sets is definable without using the totality *HC*, even though the abstract property of being-a-member-of-*HC* cannot be defined without somehow using *HC* itself.

Since *HC* does not contain any member definable only in terms of *HC*, the principle (1a) is not violated.

In connection with inductive definitions, there is again the problem of recognizing that what has the form of an inductive definition does indeed have a minimum model. It is of interest to try to find sufficient (and preferably also necessary) syntactic conditions under which a proposed fomula gives an inductive definition. However, we can again isolate the questions of truth and recognizability and allow that if a formula happens to be an inductive definition it is predicatively acceptable, although we might have no available method of recognizing that it is indeed an inductive definition.

(6) *Justification of the vicious-circle principle* If one assumes that classes are there from the very start, justified by other reasons such as a semi-combinatorial intuition, the principle serves only to separate out an interesting type of class, comparable to, say, primes among numbers. Gödel has argued[34] that objectively the principle is not true.

From a constructive viewpoint, or a nominalist position according to which names are introduced in some order (though ordinals may be more than names), one may regard the principle as established on the ground that we have no constructive way of going beyond it. The problem of accommodating Brouwer's free choice sequences, however, may perhaps indicate that the principle is inadequate.

NOTES

1 *Principles of mathematics*, 1903 and 1937. The three fragments mentioned are at pp. 1–108, 523–8, p. v–xiv, a total of 124 pages.
2 See pp. 13–26.

The propositional calculus uses three indefinables and ten premisses: (*a*) (material) implication, (*b*) formal implication, (*c*) truth; premisses (1), (2), (3) say essentially that propositions are made up from p, q, etc. by $\supset$, (4) *modus ponens*, (5) $pq \supset p$, (6) $(p \supset q)(q \supset r) \supset (p \supset r)$, (7) $(p \supset (q \supset r)) \supset (pq \supset r)$, (8) $(pq \supset r) \supset ((p \supset q) \supset r)$, (9) $(p \supset q)(p \supset r) \supset (p \supset qr)$, (10) $((p \supset q) \supset p) \supset p$. '$p$ is a proposition' is defined by '$p \supset p$', pq by $(r)((p \supset (q \supset r)) \supset r)$, $p \vee q$ by $(p \supset q) \supset q$, $\neg p$ by $(r)(p \supset r)$.

The calculus of classes uses three more indefinables $(d) \in$, (e) such that, (f) propositional function, and the premisses: (11) $x \in \hat{x}\phi x \supset \phi x$ ($\supset$ should probably be $\equiv$), (12) $(x)(\phi x \equiv \psi x) \supset \hat{x}\phi x = \hat{x}\psi x$ and '$x = y$' is defined by '$(u)(x \in u \supset y \in u)$.' The calculus of relations uses one more indefinable (g) relation, and seven more premisses: xRy is a proposition, implication and $\in$ are relations, the complement of a relation is a relation, the logical product of a class of relations is a relation, the relative product of two relations is a relation, between any two terms there is a relation not holding between any two other terms (the effect seems to be the ordered pair of the two terms). Relations are taken intensionally so that two relations may have the same extension without being identical. It is somewhat strange to mix in implication as a relation.

Russell's Logic and Some General Issues

3 G. Frege, *Grundgesetze der Arithmetik*, vol. 2, postscript.
4 B. Russell, *My philosophical development*, 1959, p. 83.
5 *Philosophy of Bertrand Russell*, ed. P. A. Schilpp, 1944, pp. 175–226.
6 A. J. Ayer, *Language, truth and logic*, 1936, chapter III.
7 *Proc. London Math. Soc.*, vol. 4, 1906, pp. 29–53.
8 W. V. Quine, *Am. Math. Monthly*, vol. 44, 1937, pp. 70–80.
9 A property ϕ does not define a class if there is a function f such that for all classes u, if $(x)(x \in u \supset \phi x)$, then $f(u)$ exists, $\phi(f(u))$, and $f(u)$ is not a member of u (p. 35). Thus, if ϕ defines w, we get $\phi(f(w))$ and $\neg\, \phi(f(w))$. If ϕ is 'being an ordinal' and $f(u)$ is 'the ordinal of u,' we get the Burali-Forti paradox. If ϕ is 'being a cardinal' and $f(u)$ is 'the cardinal of the power set of the largest cardinal in u,' we get Cantor's paradox. If ϕ is 'not belonging to itself' and $f(u)$ is simply u, we get Russell's paradox.
10 J. Richard, *Rev. générale des sci. pures et appl.*, vol. 16, 1905, p. 541.
11 H. Poincaré, *Rev. metaph. mor.*, vol. 14, 1906, pp. 196–207, 866–8.
12 B. Russell, *Rev. metaph. mor.*, vol. 14, 1906, pp. 627–50.
13 B. Russell, *Am. j. math.*, vol. 30, 1908, pp. 222–62. E. Zermelo, *Math. Annalen*, vol. 65, 1908, pp. 261–81. L. E. J. Brouwer, *Tijdschrift v. Wijsbegeerte*, vol. 2, 1908, pp. 152–8.
14 H. Poincaré, *Rev. metaph. mor.*, vol. 17, 1909, pp. 461–82.
15 *Rev. metaph. mor.*, vol. 18, 1910, pp. 263–301.
16 Th. Skolem, *Videnskap. skr. I. Mat-Nat. Kl.*, vol. 6, 1923.
17 W. V. Quine, *Mathematical logic*, 1940 and 1951, § 17.
18 P. Bernays, *Math. Zeitschrift*, vol. 25, 1926, pp. 305–20.
19 See note 8 above.
20 D. Hilbert and W. Ackermann, *Grundzüge der theoretischen Logik*, 2nd edition, 1938.
21 J. Herbrand, *Recherches sur la théorie de la démonstration*, 1930.
22 L. Wittgenstein, *Tractatus*, 1921, 1922, 1961. F. P. Ramsey, *Foundations of mathematics*, 1931. K. Gödel, 'Russell's mathematical logic,' in the book quoted under note 5 above.
23 Op. cit., footnote 38.
24 M. Schönfinkel, *Math. Annalen*, vol. 92, 1924, pp. 305–16.
25 See Ramsey, op. cit., pp. 59–61.
26 G. E. Moore, *Mind*, vol. 64, 1955, pp. 1–4.
27 Ramsey, op. cit., pp. 1–61. For the quotations in this paragraph, see pp. 22–4. On the question of absolute definability, compare K. Gödel's address in *The undecidable*, ed. M. Davis, pp. 84–8. The closest approximation to the intended notion is Gödel's ordinal definability.
28 B. Russell, *Mind*, vol. 40, 1931, pp. 476–82.
29 B. Russell, *Introduction to mathematical philosophy*.
30 W. V. Quine, *Mind*, vol. 62, 1953, p. 436.
31 *J. symbolic logic*, vol. 19, 1954, p. 261.
32 C. Spector, *J. symbolic logic*, vol. 20, 1955, pp. 151–63.
33 K. Schütte, 'Predicative well-orderings,' *Formal systems and recursive functions*, eds J. N. Crossley and M. Dummett, 1963, and *Arch. math. Logik u. Grundl.*, vol. 7, 1965, pp. 45–60. S. Feferman, *J. symbolic logic*, vol. 29, 1964, pp. 1–30.
34 K. Gödel, paper quoted under note 22 above.

IV

LOGICAL TRUTH

1 PRESUPPOSITIONS OF ARISTOTLE'S LOGIC

It is easy to describe logic by extension, i.e. listing the logical constants and giving an axiom system. Naturally we are also interested in more substantial questions such as the distinguishing conceptual characteristics of logic (e.g. the doctrine that logic is true of all possible worlds) and the related question of the genesis of logic, not as a combination of historical accidents but as a part of evolving overall pictures of human knowledge.

One natural point at which to begin would seem to be Aristotle. Since our main concern is not with the history of philosophy, we shall not consider extensively the place of logic in Aristotle's general philosophy. Rather, we shall confine our attention mainly to those aspects of Aristotle's conception of logic which essentially embody many of the underlying assumptions of the study of logic today. We shall refrain from detailed comments on issues such as the ambiguity between words and things.

Aristotle's treatises on what we now call logic were collected after his death under the title *Organon*, or general instrument. Roughly speaking, the *Categories* is a theory of terms, *On interpretation* is a theory of judgments, the *Prior analytics* is a theory of correct inferences (i.e. syllogisms). The *Posterior analytics* deals with certain scientific reasoning (demonstration) which calls for true premises and offers conditions which the initial propositions (axioms) of a science must satisfy as well as a theory of definitions. The *Topics* treats of dialectic reasoning and leads from a practical interest in winning arguments to a theoretical interest in correct inferences.[1]

Logical Truth

1.1 Logic and ontology

'Expressions which are in no way composite signify substance, quantity, quality, relation, place, time, situation, action or affection' (*Categories*, 4). This reflects an ontology with three kinds of being: individuals (primary substance), classes (secondary substance), attributes (the other nine categories). A first comment is that, from this point of view, logical constants such as 'is,' 'all,' 'some,' 'and,' 'not' do not belong to any of the categories. We may wish, as a first approximation, to suggest that what are left out are just the logical constants. Of course, 'possible,' 'necessary,' 'the,' prepositions and many other words are left out. Part of the answer is that expressions are units such as noun phrases and verb phrases so that prepositions may be disregarded. Moreover, there is also modal logic which receives some preliminary treatment in Aristotle.

'When one thing is predicated of another, all that which is predicable of the predicate will be predicable also of the subject.' This suggests that the relation 'is predicable of' corresponds more to the class (or attribute) inclusion relation than to the membership relation. But a closer look would reveal a mixture not unnatural for a nominalistic ontology which admits no higher level classes (or attributes) not having direct contact with physical reality, i.e. not having individuals as members. A primary substance may belong to a class (or fall under an attribute which is true of it), but a class (or attribute) can only be included in another class (or attribute). Thus, 'human' is predicable of 'Greek' only in the sense that all Greeks are human. In terms of the membership relation, we have only two levels, viz. the level of primary substances and the level of predicates (i.e. classes and attributes). There are no higher levels of classes or attributes. However, Aristotle's position is not thoroughly nominalistic in that A and B are not identified whenever they are true of the same collection of individuals. According to a nominalist (in the sense thus intended) the real content of a universal is exhausted by the individuals covered by it.

Exclusion of singular terms in treating syllogisms would make for greater neatness since in that case every term may be used as a subject and as a predicate without any restriction.

> There is an upward limit also to the process of predicating. . . .
> Of these ultimate predicates it is not possible to demonstrate
> another predicate, save as a matter of opinion, but these may
> be predicated of other things. Neither can individuals be predi-
> cated of other things, though other things can be predicated of
> them. What lies between these limits can be spoken of in both
> ways: they may be stated of others, and others stated of them.

And as a rule arguments and inquiries are concerned with these things (*Prior analytics*, I, 27).

Actually, all that is required by Aristotle is that in each syllogism at least one term can figure now as subject, now as predicate. He does use proper names in syllogisms, such as names of men (47b, 15–38, 70a,1–28), names of heavenly bodies (89b,17, 93a,37), and 'this' (67a,36).

1.2 Propositions and the subject-predicate form

Logic deals with reasoning and one of the things reasoning directs itself to is to grasp necessary connections between propositions. 'Now reasoning is an argument in which, certain things being laid down, something other than these necessarily comes out through them' (*Topics*, I, 1). 'For arguments start with "propositions," while the subjects on which reasonings take place are "problems." Now every proposition and every problem indicates . . . either property or definition or genus or accident' (*Topics*, I, 4).

It is taken for granted that propositions are of the subject-predicate form. For example, it is deemed necessary (*Topics*, I, 8) to argue rather the stronger point that all propositions are subjects followed by predicates of the four above kinds. Syntactically, this corresponds to the analysis of each sentence into a noun phrase and a verb phrase. 'Every affirmation, then, and every denial, will consist of a noun and a verb' (*On interpretation*, 10, 19b,10). Peter Geach points out that in this context Aristotle requires that the nouns and verbs be simple signs, with no parts that signify separately (16a,20f, 16b,6f). 'Nouns' and 'verbs' are so defined as to be mutually exclusive: verbs are always predicative (16b,10f). In the *Prior analytics*, the difference of noun and verb is ignored in the account of predication. And no requirement of simplicity of terms is imposed.

When Aristotle speaks about syntactic expressions, he is explicit in confining his attention to declarative sentences.

> Every sentence has meaning, not as being the natural means by which a physical faculty is realized, but, as we have said, by convention. Yet every sentence is not a proposition; only such are propositions as have in them either truth or falsity. Thus a prayer is a sentence, but is neither true nor false. Let us therefore dismiss all other types of sentence but the proposition, for this last concerns our present inquiry (*On interpretation*, 4).

For Aristotle, a simple proposition is a subject-predicate proposition affirmed or denied (quality), universal or particular (quantity). Hence, it is quite different from what we call nowadays an atomic proposition. 'A simple proposition is a statement, with meaning, as to the presence of something in a subject or its absence' (*On interpretation*, 5, 17a,23).

> An affirmation or denial is single, if it signifies one thing about one thing; it matters not whether the subject is universal and whether the statement has a universal character, or whether this is not so. . . . If, on the other hand, one word has two meanings which do not combine to form one, the affirmation is not single (*On interpretation*, 8).

In addition to quality and quantity, Aristotle also considers the modality of a proposition (e.g. *Prior analytics*, 29b,29–40b,16). Since this aspect receives no definitive treatment in his hand, we shall disregard it.

The reference to ambiguous propositions points to another assumption in logic which is formulated explicitly by Aristotle, viz. that ambiguities are to be removed before logical inferences are carried out (e.g. *Topics*, II, 3).

Elsewhere, Aristotle also mentions and discards indefinite propositions.

> A proposition (or categorical proposition) then is a sentence affirming or denying one thing of another. This is either universal or particular or indefinite. By universal I mean the statement that something belongs to some or not to some or not to all; by indefinite that it belongs or does not belong, without a 'universally' or 'particularly' (*Prior analytics*, I, 1).

Indefinite propositions are ruled out in the exact development of logic since they are ambiguous and are to be reduced to the universal or the particular by additional information; Aristotle often interprets them as particular propositions (e.g. *Topics*, III, 6).

The familiar square of opposition with *A* (universal affirmative), *E* (universal negative), *I* (particular affirmative), *O* (particular negative) is introduced fairly explicitly in *On interpretation*, 7. The stage is thereby set for an exact study of logical inferences with propositions of these basic forms.

We note that there is no attempt to utilize the analysis of 'all' and 'some' in terms of quantifiers (so that 'all *A* are *B*' becomes 'for all *x*, if *x* is *A*, then *x* is *B*'). Hence, there is no occasion to consider iterated applications of quantifiers. Actually, an analysis like the one indicated is quite natural to a position that assigns a privileged status to primary substances. Such an analysis seems to be implicitly assumed. 'And we say that one term is predicated of another, whenever no instance of the subject can be found of which the other term cannot be asserted; "to be predicated of none" must be understood in the same way' (*Prior analytics*, I, 1, 24b,28).

In a different direction, there is no systematic attempt to study the logic of propositions, even though an exact treatment of the syllogistic would seem to call for some substructure dealing with the logic of implication.

1.3 Attributes and relations

It is a familiar fact that modern logic goes beyond traditional logic in dealing with relations besides attributes. Since Aristotle does admit the category of relation, it is natural to ask how he assimilated relational statements. Roughly speaking, relations seem to be reduced to relatives so that instead of aRB, we would say $a = R'b$ or $a \in R''b$ (i.e. a is the object bearing the relation R to b or a belongs to the set of things bearing the relation R to b). (Compare *Categories*, 7.) It is admittedly possible, though perhaps inconvenient, to develop a logic of relations in terms of relatives, but the fact is that the proposed reduction did contribute to a neglect of relations. For a triadic relation $Sabc$, we may have to introduce several ad hoc dyadic relations in order that the reduction to relatives can be captured. The reduction of relations to sets in set theory is, of course, a different matter which, for convenience, employs devices such as ordered pairs.

One may attempt to use more sophisticated methods for reducing relations to attributes. For example, an equivalence relation would yield an attribute common to all members of the domain (and range) of the relation. Or if the relation is simply being distinct, one might say that there is some attribute not possessed by both. But when it comes to less simple relations we can no longer find such ad hoc reductions. If, for example, we say set A is larger than B, we may wish to reduce this to A is m-numbered and B is n-numbered but then we still need the relational statement that m is greater than n.

The familiar criticism of Aristotle on the lack of relational inferences is dramatized by a quotation from Jevons (*Principles of science*, chapter 1): 'I remember the late Prof. De Morgan remarking that all Aristotle's logic could not prove that "Because a horse is an animal, the head of a horse is the head of an animal".' There is no question but that Aristotle would recognize such an inference as correct. This can be seen from Aristotle's example of a related (though not strictly parallel) argument: 'Again, if knowledge be a conceiving, then also the object of knowledge is an object of conception; and if sight be a sensation, then also the object of sight is an object of sensation' (*Topics*, II, 8). There is also a discussion on rules regarding greater and less: 'Moreover, argue from greater and less degrees. In regard to greater degrees there are four commonplace rules. One is: See whether a greater degree of the predicate follows from a greater degree of the subject . . .' (*Topics*, II, 10). The fact remains that Aristotle made no systematic development of any logic of relations either directly or as a consequence of syllogistic inferences.

1.4 Logical form and the use of schematic letters

Here are some of Aristotle's examples of syllogism. Pittacus is generous, since ambitious men are generous and Pittacus is ambitious (70a,25). This (animal) is sterile since this is a mule and all mules are sterile (67a,36). Usually, variables or schematic letters are used. For example: 'If A is predicated of all B, and B of all C, A must be predicated of all C' (*Prior analytics*, I, 25b,37). Elsewhere, 'must' is omitted: 'If A belongs to all B, and C to all A, then C belongs to all B' (*Prior analytics*, II, 11, 61b,34). The word 'must' is most naturally taken to mean that the inference is true of all A, B, C. It is sufficiently faithful to Aristotle's usage to attribute to him the following formal theorem:

(1) If all B are A and all C are B, then all C are A

This illustrates clearly the concept of a logical form, for we can easily think of instances of (1) and analyze the components of each instance into two classes so as to put into the first class components which we regard as variable and into the second class those which we regard as fixed and unchanging. The fixed and unchanging components would be the logical constants.

The use of schematic letters is of course a convenient mark of universality, showing that the conclusion always follows from the premisses no matter what terms we choose. It reveals that we get the conclusion not by virtue of the matter of the premisses but by virtue of their form. This universality gives a typical sense of necessity, and the letters can be construed as free variables or dummies as we choose.

There are extensive discussions of Aristotle's axiomatization of his system of syllogisms. The consensus seems to be that the result is substantially correct but certain parts of the logic of propositions are applied in an intuitive manner and are neither axiomatized nor even always stated explicitly. Furthermore, Aristotle's axioms, even suitably reinterpreted, are not complete, in the sense of being capable of proving all true and rejecting all false expressions of the syllogistic.

Certain assertions of Aristotle may be construed as metatheorems in his system. 'Further in every syllogism one of the premisses must be affirmative, and universality must be present' (*Prior analytics*, I, 24). 'So it is clear that every demonstration and every syllogism will proceed through three terms only. This being evident, it is clear that a syllogistic conclusion follows from two premisses and not from more than two' (*Prior analytics*, 25, 42a,31).

Several statements appear to be concerned with the properties of the identity relation. The identity of indiscernibles: 'For only to things that are indistinguishable and one in essence is it generally agreed that all the same attributes belong' (*On sophistical refutation*, 24, 179a,37). Rules governing identity:

> Again, look and see if, supposing the one to be the same as something, the other also is the same as it: for if they be not both the same as the same thing, clearly neither are they the same as one another. Moreover, examine them in the light of their accidents or of the things of which they are accidents: for any accident belonging to one must belong also to the other, and if the one belongs to anything as an accident, so must the other also. If in any of these respects there is a discrepancy, clearly they are not the same (*Topics*, VII, 1, 152a,31).

The law of identity 'Every A is A' is not stated explicitly in Aristotle, it is used once in a proof (*Prior analytics*, II, 22, 68a,19).

1.5 Some explanatory comments

In terms familiar today, we may say that syllogisms deal with classes and the two relations of inclusion, $\subseteq$, and intersecting, I, between them. The four basic forms of propositions are:

$$A: A \neq 0 \wedge A \subseteq B, \quad E: \neg AIB, \quad I: AIB, \quad 0: A = O \vee \neg A \subseteq B$$

This differs from the ordinary Boolean algebra not only in giving empty classes a special place but especially in not permitting the formation of new classes from given ones by Boolean operations. In fact, the basic task is confined to a very special problem of forming with three terms three propositions, each of one of the given forms and with each term occurring in exactly two propositions, and then asking whether one proposition follows logically from the other two.

When viewed in this manner, it is rather surprising that anyone should single out such a fragment for study, and even more that he should regard it as the whole or at least the most important part of logic. We have attempted to indicate why the choice is natural for Aristotle but it is obvious that no clear-cut answer can be given to this question.

If everything is either an individual or a class (or attribute), and science does not deal directly with individuals, it would seem natural to study only relations between classes (or attributes). If, furthermore, all classes (and attributes) are on the same level, then the general relations between them would be rather restricted in kind. For example, whether two classes have the same cardinal number would presumably be regarded as too specialized a relation. One may feel that inclusion and exclusion (and their denials) are the only perfectly general relations between classes.

Aristotle's logic contains in itself seeds of its liberation in several major aspects. Relations are at least as important as attributes; once we realize the inadequacy of the reduction of relations to relatives, it is natural to study a logic of relations. Individuals should not be excluded because, even though science is not usually interested in any particular individual objects, it is interested in the relations of classes to their members in general; hence, the analysis of '$A \subseteq B$' in terms of quantifiers should be utilized explicitly. The logic of propositions used implicitly should be developed systematically. We are naturally led to unbounded iterations of truth functions and quantifiers, once we envisage some iterations of implication (e.g. if $p \supset q$, then r). By the way, it may be natural to stop at the earlier stage of iterating only conjunction and disjunction on certain simple propositions and their negations; iterations of implication and quantifiers seem to be a bigger step to take. Finally, once we envisage '$x \in A$' explicitly, it is natural to think of classes of classes, etc. and develop certain set theories with a hierarchy of classes or attributes.

In the discussion of Aristotle up to this point, I have benefited from criticisms by Peter Geach and corrected several mistakes in an earlier draft.

1.6 Demonstrations, axioms and definitions

The familiar point that the premisses of a correct inference need not necessarily be true seems to be remarked on by Aristotle. 'By demonstration I mean a syllogism productive of scientific knowledge. . . . The premisses of knowledge must be true, primary, immediate, better known than and prior to the conclusion, which is further related to them as effect to cause. . . . Syllogism there may indeed be without these conditions' (*Posterior analytics*, I, 2, 71b,18).

But it is not entirely clear from this and similar observations whether the premisses of a syllogism need not be true or merely they must be true but need not have all the other properties such as 'primary', etc. In any case, syllogisms in which the premisses are not known to be true are undoubtedly permitted.

For Aristotle all pure scientific knowledge is necessary, and each piece is either a basic truth or obtained from previous scientific knowledge by demonstration. A basic truth is either an axiom or a thesis, a thesis is either a hypothesis or a definition.

Since the object of pure scientific knowledge cannot be other than it is, the truth obtained by demonstrative knowledge will be necessary. And since demonstrative knowledge is only present when we have a demonstration, it follows that demonstration is an inference from necessary premises (*Posterior analytics*, I, 4).

Our own doctrine is that not all knowledge is demonstrative: on the contrary, knowledge of the immediate premises is independent of demonstration. (The necessity of this is obvious; for since we must know the prior premises from which the demonstration is drawn, and since the regress must end in immediate truths, those truths must be indemonstrable) (Ibid., I, 3, 72b,18).

I call an immediate basic truth of syllogism a 'thesis', when, though it is not susceptible of proof by the teacher, yet ignorance of it does not constitute a total bar to progress on the part of the pupil: one which the pupil must know if he is to learn anything whatever is an axiom. . . . If a thesis assumes one part or the other of the enunciation, i.e. asserts either the existence or the non-existence of a subject, it is a hypothesis; if it does not so assert, it is a definition (Ibid., I, 2, 72a,14).

Among axioms are included propositions true of anything whatever such as the laws of contradiction and excluded middle, as well as propositions of more restricted scope such as 'if equals are taken from equals, equals remain' which applies only to quantities. The axioms seem to answer to Euclid's 'common notions.' The hypotheses seem to answer, to some extent, to Euclid's 'postulates.'

Necessary propositions ascribe predicates to subjects in such a way that the predicate is an attribute which is (1) true in every instance of its subject, (2) essential, (3) commensurate and universal (*Posterior analytics*, I, 4, 5).

Definitions are for Aristotle something objective, and for him any proposed definition is either correct or incorrect. Giving 'the meaning of a name' is giving merely a nominal definition which is relatively unimportant and distinct in a basic way from three kinds of real definition.

Since definition is said to be the statement of a thing's nature, obviously one kind of definition will be a statement of the meaning of the name, or of an equivalent nominal formula. . . . That then is one way of defining definitions. . . . We conclude then that definition is (a) an indemonstrable statement of essential nature, or (b) a syllogism of essential nature differing from demonstration in grammatical form, or (c) the conclusion of a demonstration giving essential nature (*Posterior analytics*, II, 10).

While it is not easy to interpret these distinctions, it seems clear that the object of definition is some universal or common nature of a number of individuals covered by a given name.

So demonstration does not necessarily imply the being of Forms nor a One beside a Many, but it does necessarily imply the possibility of truly predicating one of many; since without this possibility we cannot save the universal, and if the universal goes, the middle term goes with it, and so demonstration becomes impossible. We conclude, then, that there must be a single identical term unequivocally predicable of a number of individuals (*Posterior analytics*, I, 11).

How are the first premisses, in particular definitions, known? At the end of *Posterior analytics* (II, 19, compare also *Metaphysics*, A, 1), there is a famous discussion which is rich in suggestions. Knowledge of the first premisses can be neither innate nor acquired.

Now it is strange if we possess them from birth; for it means that we possess apprehensions more accurate than demonstration and fail to notice them. If on the other hand we acquire them and do not previously possess them, how could we apprehend and learn without a basis of preexistent knowledge?

Therefore we must possess a capacity of some sort from which this basic knowledge may be developed. This capacity is found to be sense-perception which develops into memory and, in the case of man, further into 'experience.'

And this at least is an obvious characteristic of all animals, for they possess a congenital discriminative capacity which is called sense-perception. But though sense-perception is innate in all animals, in some the sense-impression comes to persist, in others it does not. . . . When such persistence is frequently repeated a further distinction at once arises between those which out of the persistence of such sense-impressions develop a power of systematizing them and those which do not. So out of sense-perception comes to be what we call memory, and out of frequently repeated memories of the same thing develops experience; for a number of memories constitute a single experience.

From experience again – i.e. from the universal now stabilized in its entirety within the soul, the one beside the many which is a single identity within them all – originate the skill of the craftsman and the knowledge of the man of science.

Thus, experience as repeated memories creates (or is) concepts. This certainly seems an inadequate account of concept formation.

When one of a number of logically indiscriminable particulars has made a stand, the earliest universal is present in the soul: for though the act of sense-perception is particular, its content is universal – is man, for example, not the man Callias. A fresh stand is made among these rudimentary universals, and the process does not cease until the indivisible concepts, the true universals [i.e. the categories], are established: e.g. such and such a species of animal is a step towards the genus animal, which by the same process is a step towards a further generalization.

The passage from particulars to the universals implicit in them, both with regard to concepts and with regard to premisses, is said to be accomplished by *induction*. The grasping of the first premisses is by *intuition*.

Thus it is clear that we must get to know the premisses by induction; for the method by which even sense-perception implants the universal is inductive. . . . From these considerations it follows that there will be no scientific knowledge of the primary premisses, and since except intuition nothing can be truer than scientific knowledge, it will be intuition that apprehends the primary premisses.

Since this intuition is able to grasp immediately necessary (and therefore universal) truths, it is a sort of intellectual intuition. It is not clear how Aristotle arrives at the conclusion that there is this originative source of science which grasps the original basic premiss. His discussion sounds like a transcendental argument: since scientific knowledge is a fact and it is possible only if there is this intuition, there must be this intuition.

1.7 Truth and correspondence, laws of thought

We mentioned before that there is no explicit statement of the law of identity in Aristotle. But he does state explicitly the laws of contradiction and excluded middle. In addition, he also states explicitly the familiar and somewhat vacuous criterion of truth: *p* if and only if it is true that *p*.

For a principle which everyone must have who understands anything that is, is not a hypothesis; and that which everyone must know who knows anything, he must already have when he comes to a special study. Evidently then such a principle is the most certain of all; which principle it is, let us proceed to say. It is, that the same attribute cannot at the same time belong and not belong to the same subject and in the same respect; we must presuppose, to guard against dialectical objections, any further qualifications which might be added. This, then, is the most certain of all principles, since it answers to the definition given above (*Metaphysics*, Γ, 3, 1005b,15).

But on the other hand there cannot be an intermediate between contradictories, but of subject we must either affirm or deny any one predicate. This is clear, in the first place, if we define what the true and the false are. To say of what is that it is not, or what is not that it is, is false, while to say of what is that it is, and of what is not that it is not, is true; so that he who says of anything that it is or that it is not, will say either what is true or what is false (*Metaphysics*, Γ, 7).

It is often remarked that the laws of contradiction and excluded middle are only two among many equally basic laws of, say, the propositional calculus. The natural way to look at them is, however, to regard them as metalogical principles which stipulate that we use the two-valued logic. If we consider, for example, the task of setting up the propositional calculus by asking for the theorems governing, say, 'not,' 'or,' 'and,' 'if,' the law of excluded middle narrows the possible values down to two, while the law of contradiction demands that the connectives be truth *functions* (i.e. a composite proposition has a unique truth value completely determined by the truth values of the components). The interpretation of 'not' is decided with these laws, while additional considerations from usage, convenience, etc., will determine the exact truth functions corresponding to the other connectives.

1.8 Logic and the philosophy of development

The two pillars of Aristotle's philosophy may be said to be his logic and his system of development (compare, e.g. Windelband). His logic does not apply directly to the system of development but only to scientific knowledge which crystallizes the process of change into static propositions. Logic presupposes that all terms are 'univocal,' i.e. they are words which retain their meaning each time they are used.

There is no necessary reason why a logic of change may not be possible. The dialectic logic of Hegel, Engels and Marx is proposed precisely as such a logic of development. And formal logic has been called a limiting special case of dialectic logic. It is, however, clear to everybody that there is very little in common between formal logic and dialectic logic.

2 LOGICAL CONSTANTS AND LOGICAL TRUTHS

The many attractive properties of the first order or restricted predicate calculus (quantification theory) have suggested the convenient identification of it with first order logic, pure logic, or just logic. Given the identification, we can determine the realm of logical truths as the theorems of the calculus (or the substitution instances of these theorems). It is natural to ask how such an identification could be justified. And this is a question on which one can hardly expect any definitive answers. The question might be separated into two parts: how do we choose the logical constants (more exactly, the logical grammar), and how, after we have chosen the logical constants, do we determine the realm of logical truths. Once the first part is answered, we do have various interrelated and convincing ways of answering the second part.

2.1 Logical truths based on current logical constants

Let us assume, for the moment, that we have reached the choice of the current grammar of quantification logic in one of its various possible forms. (*a*) The lexicon or fragments: (the category of individual) variables x, y, etc.; (the category of) predicates or predicate letters (or variables[2]) or both (one-place, two-place, etc.); possibly (the categories of) names and functors. (*b*) The construction particles or logical constants: truth functional connectives; quantifiers; possibly a symbol for predication. A sentence (or well-forming formula) can be defined in the familiar manner; and the definition together with (*a*) and (*b*) constitute our logical grammar. The grammatical structure of a sentence is determined by the positions of the logical constants. For example, we may restrict the constants to negation, conjunction and existential quantification and a sentence may be $\exists x(Px \wedge \neg Qx)$.

Given this apparatus, we have several familiar ways of characterizing those sentences which are logically true (or valid). A sentence is logically true if all sentences of the same grammatical (or logical) structure are true; or, equivalently, it cannot be turned false by substituting for lexicon. If we do not use names, functors, or predicate letters (or variables), then we can say more simply that a logical truth remains true under all proper (in an exactly specifiable sense) changes of its predicates. If we refrain from using any constant names (and functors) and predicates, then we may say a sentence (or schema or sentence form) is (logically) valid if it is true in all models, where a model may vary the interpretation of variables (and schematic letters) but not that of the (logical) constants. Or if we allow all the notation mentioned above, we might say that a sentence is logically true if it is true but contains no constants except logical constants; in this case, the only other basic units are variables and they are taken to be universally quantified when occurring free.

These apparently equivalent formulations can be different if we are not careful. For example, if we consider just changing predicates from a given list, we seem to gain a sort of clarity because we assume less by not considering all possible interpretations of a predicate letter. But we do not always get the desired concept because the predicates in the given list need not exhaust all the possible reinterpretations of the given predicates in a sentence. The natural idea of formulating logical truth is to go through logical validity which is to remain true in all interpretations (in all possible worlds). In fact, it is a significant result of mathematical logic that a quantificational sentence is valid in the intended sense if it remains true when we vary the predicates in certain restricted classes. We have in mind the technical result[3] that if such a sentence has a model at all, it has an arithmetic model (in fact a model of both two quantifier forms in the arithmetic hierarchy). Hence, if such a sentence is valid with respect to all arithmetical predicates, then it is unconditionally valid. As a result, the more transparent and apparently weaker characterizations in terms of grammatical structures and substitutions of predicates are adequate provided we are careful in our choice of basic predicates and sentences. In fact, all we need are the predicates of equality, sum and product (of natural numbers) together with logical combinations of them. Therefore, if, as is customary, we agree that the logical combinations are automatically taken as (derived) predicates, a finite list of basic predicates is sufficient provided the three familiar predicates of equality, sum, and product are obtainable.[4]

It should be emphasized that one must not be unduly impressed by the gratifying possibility of economy and syntactic transparency thus achieved. The result is obtained only by way of the highly non-syntactic concept of arbitrary sets or models (or structures or possible worlds), which is involved in the very concept of logical validity. In other words, whatever indeterminacy we may wish to impute to the concept of arbitrary set is shared by the concept of logical validity. For example, it seems completely unlikely that one could offer a satisfactory account of the concept of logical validity on the basis of 'stimulus meaning.' This is not a place where one can 'throw away the ladder after he has climbed up it.'

So far we have attempted to characterize informally the realm of logical truths under the assumption that somehow we have arrived at the choice of logical constants urged on us by the current (first order) logic. It is natural to look more closely at both this conditional question and the prior question of how we arrive at the list of logical constants which we now use. For both purposes, Bolzano's classical account of validity and completeness of logic offers a natural starting point.

2.2 Completeness of pure logic and Bolzano's definition of logical validity

Bolzano's anticipation[5] of the current definitions of completeness (of logic), validity, and logical truth goes back to 1837. Bolzano calls a proposition valid (allgemeingültig) relative to its constituents $i, j, \ldots$ when results obtained by varying these constituents at will are all true. These propositions he calls analytic (analytically true) in the broader sense. He goes on to define analytic propositions in the narrower sense as those in which the unchanging parts all belong to logic. Hence, we have here a fairly explicit definition of the modern concept of logical truth, provided we choose the appropiate list of logical constants. In fact, Bolzano is aware of this problem of choice and he proceeds to say: 'This distinction has of course something vague about it, because the range of the concepts which belong to logic is not so sharply defined that controversies may never arise on the matter.' In this connection, we may recall the disagreement between Frege and Dedekind over what is to be regarded as belonging to logic.

According to Bolzano, 'certain propositions $A, B, C, D, \ldots$, $M, N, O, \ldots$ stand in the relation of compatibility, and, in particular, relative to the concepts $i, j, \ldots$,' if 'there exist certain concepts which, when put in the places of $i, j, \ldots$, make all the propositions true.' We have here more or less the modern notion of model if we think of the fixed parts as the logical constants and $i, j, \ldots$ as the varying parts (predicates and ranges of variables, etc.). Bolzano continues to introduce a concept of deducibility: 'and say that the propositions $M, N, O, \ldots$ are deducible from the propositions $A, B, C, D, \ldots$, relative to the varying constituents $i, j, \ldots$, if every set of concepts which in the places of $i, j, \ldots$ make all the propositions $A, B, C, D, \ldots$

145

true, also make all the propositions M, N, O, . . . true.' In modern terminology, this says that a set X of sentences (logically) entails a sentence p if and only if p is true in every model of X. Bolzano's concept of deducibility supplies a criterion for the adequacy of a formal system of logic: it is complete (or adequate) if and only if formal deducibility in the system is coextensive with deducibility in his sense.

To be more explicit, consider the sentence $\exists x(Px \wedge \neg Qx)$. A model of the sentence could be $\langle D, A, B \rangle$, where D is the set of books in this room, A is the set of those with red covers, and B is the set of those with soft red covers. The triple $\langle D, A, B \rangle$ satisfies (or is a model of) the sentence, because there happen to be books in this room which have hard red covers and we accept the ordinary interpretation of the logical constants $\exists$, $\wedge$, $\neg$. For some purposes it is convenient to distinguish a model and a structure and call the triple $\langle D, A, B \rangle$ a structure rather than a model. In any case, the triple $\langle D, A, B \rangle$ is to be distinguished from the relation of satisfaction (or model of), commonly denoted by the symbol $\models$. Thus,

$$\langle D, A, B \rangle \models \exists x(Px \wedge \neg Qx).$$

The structures presuppose arbitrary sets because they are triples of arbitrary sets; the relation of satisfaction presupposes both the structures and the predetermined interpretations of the logical constants. Usually when we speak of the concept of model, we mean the relation of satisfaction (model of).

Therefore, a concept of model presupposes and determines a distinction between the logical constants and the varying constituents. We assume that the logical constants receive fixed interpretations while the interpretations of the constituents can vary arbitrarily within fixed categories (such as individuals, sets, relations). Once we have fixed the concept of model, we have fixed also the choice of logical constants. Hence, in general terms, Bolzano's concept of deducibility suggests a general way of looking at the problem of formalizing different notions of logic. Thus, given a concept of sentence (or well-formed formula) and a concept of model, we can define generally the relation of logical entailment and the concept of strong completeness. Let X be a set of sentences and p be a single sentence.

(LI) X logically entails p if and only if p is true in every model of X, i.e. for every structure M, if $M \models X$, then $M \models p$. In particular, p is valid if the empty set l.e. p, i.e. every structure (of the appropriate form) satisfies p.

(LC) A formal system S with the given concept of sentence is strongly complete if and only if logical entailment implies formal deducibility in S (in other words, if X l.e. p, then $X \vdash_s p$). Ordinary (weak) completeness requires only that every valid sentence p be provable in S.

A basic result in modern logic is that familiar formal systems of the first order logic are indeed strongly complete in the above sense with respect to a concept of model which seems very natural. Let us briefly review the essential history of this development.

It is well known that Frege in 1879 proposed the first formal system of first order logic, which was proved to be complete in 1930, in the sense that every valid sentence is provable. Among other things, Frege extended the concept of function to truth-valued functions or propositional functions and gave for the first time the modern form of quantification. With regard to the first point we quote the following:[6]

> In particular, I believe that the replacement of the concepts
> *subject* and *predicate* by *argument* and *function* respectively
> will stand the test of time.
>
> Let us assume that the circumstance that hydrogen is lighter
> than carbon dioxide is expressed in our formal language; we can
> then replace the sign for hydrogen by the sign for oxygen or
> that for nitrogen. This changes the meaning in such a way that
> 'oxygen' or 'nitrogen' enters into the relations in which 'hydro-
> gen' stood before. If we imagine that an expression can thus
> be altered, it decomposes into a stable component, representing
> the totality of relations, and the sign, regarded as replaceable
> by others, that denotes the object standing in these relations.
> The former component I call a function, the latter its argu-
> ment.
>
> If A and B stand for contents that can become judgments,
> there are the following possibilities: (1) A is affirmed and B is
> affirmed; (2) A is affirmed and B is denied; (3) A is denied and
> B is affirmed; (4) A is denied and B is denied.

Frege's invention of the quantification theory is, of course, of central importance. The particularly original aspect of the innovation seems, rather curiously, to be the choice of an appropriate general notation. For example, in commenting on a variant of Frege's notation, Wittgenstein says:[7]

> If, for example, we wanted to express what we now write as
> '$(x).fx$' by putting an index in front of 'fx' – for instance by
> writing 'Gen. fx' – it would not be adequate: we should not
> know what was being generalized. If we wanted to signalize it
> with an index 'g' – for instance by writing '$f(x_g)$' – that would not

be adequate either: we should not know the scope of the generality-sign. If we were to try to do it by introducing a mark into the argument-places – for instance by writing

$$\text{'}(G, G)\cdot F(G, G)\text{'}$$

– it would not be adequate: we should not be able to establish the identity of the variables, and so on.

We can get an intuitive feel for the power and flexibility of Frege's notation of quantifiers if we try to put a few sentences containing a few quantifiers into ordinary language.

Frege used truth tables or tabulations of alternative truth possibilities for propositional connectives to explain his basic primitives of material implication and negation, as well as to justify his axioms. In 1885, Peirce[8] made more extensive use of truth tables and suggested the general notion of validity in the propositional calculus: 'To find whether a formula is necessarily true substitute *f* and *v* and see whether it can be supposed false by any such assignment of values.' This directly leads to the notion of completeness of formal systems of the propositional calculus: a system is complete if every valid sentence is a theorem. Explicit proofs of the completeness of familiar systems of the propositional calculus were obtained by Bernays and Post[9] in 1918 and 1920. If we recall the familiar intimate connection[10] between the propositional calculus and Boolean algebra with two elements, then a completeness proof can be extracted fairly simply from developed normal forms which were familiar to G. Boole a long time ago.

The question of completeness of the predicate calculus is a more complex matter because the very notions of validity and completeness seem to be indeterminate to begin with and, even when rendered mathematically definite, they remain highly questionable for those who are inclined toward one or another form of constructivism. With regard to the first aspect, we have initially an unmanageable informal notion of (logical) validity and it seems hopeless to survey all valid sentences (even just of the given first order language) and demonstrate that they are all theorems in a given formal system such as Frege's (call it *S*). The actual development reveals that we can capture this informal notion of validity by appealing to just certain particular uses of the notion. The phenomenon is instructive in that it illustrates how the right ideas may supply an exact, or at least a more exact, explication of some concept which appears to be hopelessly informal.

It is not hard to convince ourselves that all theorems of the system *S* (say) are indeed valid, even though our notion of validity is not exact. In other words, we can use our informal notion V_i to convince ourselves: (a) if $\vdash A$, then $V_i(A)$. As mentioned above, we have also a fairly exact mathematical concept of model or validity, V_s, in terms of arbitrary set-theoretical structures. Since V_i refers to all possible interpretations, they must include these structures in particular. Therefore, whatever V_i may mean exactly, we can assert: (b) if $V_i(A)$, then $V_s(A)$. Now the (weak) completeness proof does not appeal to the informal notion but proves mathematically: (c) if $V_s(A)$, then $\vdash A$. Combining (a), (b), and (c), we arrive at the surprising conclusion that V_i, V_s, and $\vdash$ are coextensive. In other words, we not only get the mathematical result that all valid (in the sense of V_s) sentences of *S* are theorems of *S*, but also the seemingly inexact theorem that all informally valid sentences of *S* are theorems of *S*. This is perhaps not as surprising as it seems, since the concept of arbitrary structures is itself a rich concept which is, for example, not completely characterizable by formal systems. Also, even without the detour through (a), (b), and (c), many of us are willing to accept V_s as a reasonable explication of V_i. That is why we used V_s to explain Bolzano's ideas and we shall continue to use V_s and forget about V_i.

With regard to V_s, there are objections and confusions engendered by the influence of various constructive tendencies. It may be instructive philosophically if we review briefly the history[11] of the discovery of the completeness theorem. In 1922, Skolem gave a proof of Löwenheim's theorem without the use of the axiom of choice. The proof contains the mathematical core of Gödel's proof of the completeness of systems like *S*. Moreover, in 1928, Skolem even stated a theorem of completeness for a different formal system *P*. However, the proposed proof seems to beg the question by confusing 'satisfiable' with 'consistent.' The idea is, apparently, to assume an informal concept of logical proof which is thought to be complete because it is believed that in the domain of pure logic no other hindrance can exist besides contradiction. Therefore, completeness would then mean that whenever there is an informal logical proof, there is a proof in *P* for the same conclusion. It is not easy to see how we can be sufficiently explicit about the intended concept of informal proof to carry out Skolem's inadequately sketched outline.

Bolzano's general criterion of a complete system of logic was rediscovered by Hilbert and Ackermann[12] and applied to a specific system similar to but more exact than Frege's system *S* in 1928 (with the logical constants chosen in their current form). And the question of completeness of their system is posed as an open problem.

Whether the axiom system is at least complete in the sense that all logical formulas which are valid (*richtig*) for all domains of individuals, are in fact derivable, remains an unsolved question. It can only be stated empirically that this axiom system is adequate to all applications.

All examples of formulas, which are valid (*allgemeingültig*) in every domain of individuals, can be proved from the axioms of the functional calculus set up by us. It is conjectured that (not only these examples but indeed) all such valid formulas are provable in the given system.

As noted above, 'the completeness theorem, mathematically, is indeed almost an immediate consequence of Skolem's work of 1922.' It therefore seems surprising that the problem of completeness, once so posed, was not solved as an exercise by applying the work. However, the fact is, before Gödel,[13] nobody (including Skolem himself) had drawn this conclusion. This surprising failure may be attributed to 'a widespread lack, at that time, of the requisite epistemological attitude toward metamathematics and toward nonfinitary reasoning.' That Skolem did use nonfinitary reasoning in his earlier improvement of Löwenheim's theorem (to the stronger result of a submodel by way of the axiom of choice) does not disprove this interpretation. 'Pure model theory, where the concept of proof does not come in, lies on the borderline between mathematics and metamathematics, and its application to special systems actually belongs to mathematics, at least for the most part.' Skolem undoubtedly felt that one has to talk about more tangible things in a proof of completeness. Hence, his failure to appeal to his own argument of 1922, as well as his unsuccessful attempt to supply a syntactic argument.

In this connection, it is relevant to mention that Hilbert[14] proposed a reformulation of the notion of completeness in finitary terms shortly before the appearance of Gödel's proof. The proposal turns out to be unsatisfactory because Hilbert identified validity of a sentence A with provability of all its arithmetic instances in a particular formal system Z of number theory. In other words, instead of arbitrary structures, only those structures with sets and relations expressible in the system Z are permitted; and, what is more restrictive, instead of the instances of A being true, they are required to be provable in Z. Relative to the knowledge of that time, the proposal was not demonstrably mistaken. But, given Gödel's later result of incompletability, we can easily show that there are sentences valid in Hilbert's finitary sense which are not valid (in our intended meaning).

The completeness theorem actually shows more than the derivability of $\vdash A$ from $V_s(A)$. It shows that validity in a weaker sense, viz. validity over the domain of natural numbers, is sufficient to assure derivability in standard systems of predicate logic. In other words, if

$V_n(A)$, then $\vdash A$. In fact, it is possible to obtain an arithmetic version of an extension of the completeness theorem which is limited to syntactic notions.[15] Thus, let Con(T) be a usual formula expressing arithmetically the consistency of a first order formal system T. Then in the formal system obtained by adding Con(T) as a new axiom to the usual formal system of number theory, we can prove arithmetic translations of all theorems of T.

Thus far, we have emphasized exclusively the question of (weak) completeness. Actually there is another aspect of logical entailment, viz. the property of compactness, which is also important for capturing the full content of completeness. We recall here the definition (*LC*) of strong completeness: if X l.e. p., $X \vdash p$. If S is a complete system of predicate logic, then we have the special case when X is the empty set. Actually, if X is a finite set, we can put its conjunction into a single sentence B. Then X l.e. p if and only if $B \supset p$ is valid. Hence, by completeness, we can again get $\vdash B \supset p$ and therewith $X \vdash p$. Only when X is infinite, do we need the property that the system S is compact: i.e. an infinite set X of sentences in the language of S has a model if and only if every finite subset of X has a model. It turns out that the usual proof of the completeness of the familiar systems of logic can easily be extended to yield a proof of compactness. Given compactness, we obtain strong completeness by reducing the infinite case to the finite case.[16] The crucial point is that a proof is necessarily a finite object and, therefore, $X \vdash p$, where X is an infinite set, can only mean that $X_1 \vdash p$, for some finite subset X_1 of X. The compactness theorem enables us to move from the infinite case to the finite case, thus establishing indirectly the provability of p from an infinite set X of hypotheses.

We therefore arrive at the conclusion that given the language of the first order logic and the accompanying concept of model (or relation of satisfaction), the customary formal systems S (such as Frege's) are strongly complete. In other words, once we have chosen the current list of logical constants, we do have a highly successful explication (by a formal system) of the relation of logical entailment.

In this connection, we remark that the familiar classical interpretation of the logical constants such as negation, implication, existential and universal quantification is not the only possible interpretation. A widely known different interpretation is codified in the intuitionistic predicate calculus. We shall, however, refrain from considering such nonclassical alternative logics. It is of interest to realize that there are in this sense different ways of 'choosing the logical constants.' This has nothing to do with the trivial point that different symbols are sometimes employed on different occasions for the same concept (e.g. &, ·, ∧ for conjunction). Rather, concepts like existence, disjunction, and implication are not completely fixed in ordinary and mathematical discourses (e.g. in dealing with vague concepts or infinite sets). We may say that the intuitionists have chosen the same logical constants but interpret them differently, or that they have chosen different logical constants.

2.3 Additional constants and other logics

A familiar question is whether identity or equality is to be counted as a logical constant. On the one hand, it is a universal relation which is useful whenever we permit terms which have different senses but the same denotation, e.g. '3' and '2 + 1' or 'Tolstoi' and 'the author of *War and Peace*.' Moreover, we have formal systems which extend the predicate logic by adding identity and share the properties of completeness and strong completeness. On the other hand, if we count identity as a logical constant, we can no longer say that if a sentence is true and contains only constants which are logical constants, it is a logical truth; since there are then true sentences, such as 'there are at least 25 objects,' etc. which contain only logical constants but probably are not to be regarded as logically true. Another obvious consequence is that we can no longer say that substituting predicates for predicates always preserves logical truth because, e.g. '$x = x$' would be counted a logical truth when identity is included in logic, but '$x < x$' or 'x is his own guardian' are certainly not logical truths. This is, of course, not surprising, since whether any predicate is taken as a logical constant naturally bears on the question whether all predicates are regarded as on an equal footing relative to logic.

When we are concerned with only a finite number of predicates in the predicate logic, it is familiar that we can define identity in terms of the other predicates. For example, if Rxy is the only predicate (which might in particular be the membership relation), we have $\forall z(Rxz \equiv Ryz) \wedge \forall w(Rwx \equiv Rwy)$ as a definition of $x = y$. It does not seem that there are any decisive substantial reasons for either including identity in or excluding it from logic. We shall generally preserve an ambivalent attitude and even make different choices in different contexts.

Less familiar mathematical considerations have recently appeared which are relevant to the question of justifying our actual choice of the particular logical constants (say) negation, conjunction, and existential quantification. On the one hand, we have a theorem of Lindström[17] according to which, under certain rather general conditions, first order logic is the only possible logic. On the other hand, there are formal systems which are complete and compact but essentially different from first order logic: in particular, there is such a formal system[18] which includes an additional 'logical' constant Q standing for 'there exist uncountably many.'

The complete and compact formal system $L(Q)$ extends the first order logic by adding the logical constant Q which calls for a fixed interpretation. In this way, we have a different language and a different concept of model. By definition, 'uncountable' occurs in the model so that, e.g., Löwenheim's theorem cannot be true. For example, the sentence '$Qx(x = x)$' can have no countable model. It used to be argued that the reason why second order logic is not satisfactory is because it cannot be formally axiomatized. The same argument can no longer be applied to $L(Q)$. We seem to be forced to face more directly the question of characterizing logical constants. One is tempted to say that 'uncountable' and therefore Q is not a logical concept. For example, in ordinary developments of set theory, we do not take 'uncountable' as a primitive but rather define it in terms of other notions. In addition, many people find uncountability an obscure (and highly nonconstructive) concept.

It cannot, however, be denied that $L(Q)$ throws doubt on the identification of logic with first order logic, and especially on the many bold philosophical theses based on such an assumption: such as explaining ontological commitment by first order formalization and developing a theory of meaning from first order truth definitions. If one wishes to emphasize constructive methods, then intuitionistic logic is a serious contender. If one chooses to take a more classical position, then there is no obvious argument to refute the contention that $L(Q)$ is a possible logic, especially since set-theoretical notions are traditionally associated with logic. Of course, to say that theorems of $L(Q)$ are logically true (or rather valid) is quite different from calling theorems of set theory true, as is seen from the fact that $L(Q)$ is complete in a sense analogous to the first order logic (that all valid sentences are provable) while formal systems of set theory are incomplete in the sense of theories (that not every statement is either provable or refutable).

The system $L(Q)$ invites further extensions. Once we accept uncountability as a logical concept, there is nothing to prevent us from including also higher infinities as logical constants. Hence, $L(Q)$ seems less attractive than systems of first order logic in that it does not give a natural stopping place. On the other hand, it is not unnatural to desire a sort of open-endedness in our basic logic. One might therefore wish to contend that while $L(Q)$ does not in itself yield a definitive logic, it points the way toward a grander limit which is the true logic and which is presumably not formally axiomatizable. While it cannot be denied that the first order logic is a highly attractive and stable domain, we do not seem to possess definitive arguments to show that it is the only possible logic.

The theorem of Lindström shows simultaneously the high stability of the first order logic as well as its limitations. It gives a general concept of logic and asserts that logics which apparently extend the first order logic all end up being the same as it, provided they satisfy the Löwenheim theorem (i.e. a sentence has a countable model if it has a model at all) and they either have the compactness property or are formally axiomatizable. When we are interested in set theory or classical analysis, the Löwenheim theorem is usually taken as a sort of defect (often thought to be inevitable) of the first order logic. Therefore, what is established is not that first order logic is the only possible logic but rather that it is the only possible logic when we in a sense deny reality to the concept of uncountability and require (what seems to be a less debatable condition) that logical proofs be formally checkable (viz. the requirement of axiomatizability or compactness).

The general concept of logic is interesting in that it uses abstractions of a high level. Thus, in the first order logic, each satisfiable sentence P has a variety of models so that we can associate with p a set $M(p)$ of models. In particular, if p is not satisfiable, then $M(p)$ is empty. In this way, we obtain a collection of sets $C = \{A | A = M(p)$, for some $p\}$. The collection C is determined by the first order logic and in turn determines it. We can now consider abstractly collections C_L with certain natural general properties such as: if $M(p)$ and $M(q)$ belong to C_L, then $M(\neg p)$ and $M(p \wedge q)$ belong to it. These collections are said to be (or to determine) the general logics. The properties of compactness and the Löwenheim theorem can also be expressed in terms of these collections. Hence, up to this stage, we need not even consider what exactly the language and the sentences are in each general logic. When we bring in the property of axiomatizability, we do have to consider the sentences, but the conditions on them remain very general. As a result, the class of general logics is very broad and includes most of the languages we consider in mathematical logic: infinitary languages, new quantifiers, etc.

One feels that it may be possible to replace the hypothesis of Löwenheim's theorem by a more basic condition which captures the idea underlying the direct proof of the theorem by the axiom of choice. There is a vague feeling that uncountability involves a big jump and that a certain general form of thinking never gets beyond the realm of the countable. In particular, if given finitely many objects, only finitely many new objects are needed to satisfy a given relation, we certainly reach a closure with countably many objects. For example, the condition that for every even number, there is a larger one, is certainly satisfied at the stage ω. Something like this seems to be sufficient for a lot of mathematical thinking and a lot of considerations about language. One might be able to characterize in some palatable way what could be called first order thinking. The wish is then to show that for first order thinking the only possible logic is first order logic.

2.4 Philosophical foundations of logic

If we leave aside deviant interpretations of the logical constants (such as intuitionistic and quantum theoretical) or consider them as derivative, the problem of defining logic and justifying the definition may be identified with that of choosing logical constants, in particular, that of justifying the choice of propositional connectives and quantifiers as the logical constants. If we are able to give a natural definition of logic and show that the definition leads to this choice, then we would also have one sort of answer.

It has been suggested that we simply define logic by enumerating the particular list of logical constants. This has the virtue of giving a definite answer, but begs the question. It reminds one of Protagoras[19] who defines virtue by enumerating justice, temperance, holiness, courage and wisdom which are said to form parts of virtue in the same way as the mouth, the nose, eyes, and ears are parts of a face.

A somewhat more satisfactory answer may be in terms of the traditional categories of quantity, quality, relation and modality. We could perhaps claim that monadic predicate logic takes care of quantity, propositional logic takes care of quality, polyadic predicate logic takes care of relation, and modal logic takes care of modality. It may further be argued that insofar as mathematics and science are concerned, modal logic is unnecessary, since occurrences of modal concepts are dispensible and can be explained away by the other logical and metalogical concepts.

We may look for assistance in the direction of grammar. In each natural language, it is relatively unproblematic to obtain a list of basic symbols (letters or phonemes). Generally we are willing to assume a list of larger units, viz. a lexicon or a list of words. The grammarian's main task is to determine what combinations of words make up (grammatical) sentences. The natural and convenient inclination is to permit arbitrarily long sentences and appeal to unlimited principles of construction (recursions and iterations). For example, the iterations in the tale 'the house that Jack built' suggest that there is no natural finite bound on how far such iterations can be continued. Another useful suggestion from grammar is that different sentences are of the same form or have the same structure. For example, in analyzing certain sentences into subjects and predicates (or noun phrases and verb phrases), we have the notion of categories and the relation of predication.

If we argue that in scientific languages we are concerned chiefly with declarative sentences, and we are not much interested in refined analyses of noun phrases and verbal phrases into smaller parts, we seem to arrive quite naturally at the atomic sentences in a logical grammar. If at this stage we bring in the idea that the most important general property of a sentence is whether it is true or false, then we seem justified in giving the propositional connectives a prominent place. The quantifiers are the most convenient device for dealing simultaneously with a collection of sentences which have the same form. We would probably then justify excluding propositional attitudes and modality on the ground that they are not necessary in any definitive formulation of scientific results.

This line of argument cannot convince us that the continuous deepening of our study of grammar could have led to the logical grammar as a rational stopping place. It cannot be denied that historically our favorite logical constants have not played any eminent role in the development of grammatical studies. In fact, the measure of convergence of logic and grammar in recent years comes more from an influence of logic on grammar rather than the other way round. In recent years, there has emerged a subject of mathematical linguistics inspired, at least in part, by mathematical logic. The main task of the subject is to arrive at a formal character-ization of meaningful or (not equivalently) grammatical sentences. This goal has not been attained and is believed by many to be un-attainable. The basic controversy is, according to Hockett,[20] whether language is like chess.

The problem of logical constants is the central concern of what has been called 'philosophical logic.' It may be formulated in several ways: to find really distinctive features of the forms and constants of logic; to give a general intelligible account of the concept of a logical particle; to find a natural place for logic in an overall view of human knowledge; to extract logic from reflecting on the idea of a pro-position.

We use words to make distinctions. To each word may be associ-ated a circle so that the distinction is pictured by the inside and the outside. The word is true of the objects inside the circle, and false for those outside. Or, in order to describe how things are in the world, we make assertions by specifying general types and particular cases. Or, empirical knowledge depends on our having both general con-cepts and particular intuitions. Or, if we think of propositions as functions with true and false as values, then we need functions and arguments. To assert is to exclude; if nothing is excluded, nothing is asserted. Hence, from each of the above routes, we get the two exclusive alternatives of being true and being false. A proposition *B* follows (logically) from or is (logically) deducible from a proposition *A* if *B* is true whenever *A* is true, or, in every possible world, *B* is true if *A* is. This suggests that we should look for a natural concept of possible worlds or interpretations or models.

It seems reasonable to suppose that in a scientific language there are sentences and each sentence is either true or false but not both. It also seems reasonable to believe that there should be terms, as well as sentences which contain these terms and which are so simple that their truth and falsity depend only on the presence or absence of the state of affairs they describe, but not on the truth or falsity of other sentences. Here we have the contrast of unanalyzed as against unanalyzable sentences. Relative to our knowledge, it is by no means clear that there are unanalyzable sentences, much less that there are such which would provide, with the help of logical constants, an adequate basis for all knowledge. At the same time, a deep-rooted scientific way of thinking continues to force upon us the use of unanalyzed sentences.

As is well known, the *Tractatus* argues for the necessity of unanalyzable (called 'elementary') propositions. 'It is obvious that the analysis of propositions must bring us to elementary propositions which consist of names in immediate combination' (4.221). 'The requirement that simple signs be possible is the requirement that sense be determinate' (3.23). 'Names cannot be anatomized by means of definitions' (3.261). 'If the world had no substance, then whether a proposition had sense would depend on whether another proposition was true. In that case we could not sketch out any picture of the world (true or false)' (2.0211, 2.0212). These ideas pay no attention to the fact of knowledge but rather presuppose that we must have a special kind of picture of the world (true or false). In arithmetic, it is natural to begin with simple numerical propositions even though it is a complex matter to understand them. 'If I cannot give a priori a list of elementary propositions, then the attempt to give one must lead to obvious nonsense' (5.5571). Such a list has not been given and probably cannot be given. It seems, therefore, desirable to avoid any appeal to unanalyzable propositions in the epistemological sense and that is the sense in which we are interested.

Within certain contexts, we do use unanalyzed propositions, and it is a fact that in such cases there are a plurality of propositions. Given this fact and the fact that each proposition is true or false, we have naturally the idea that there are different ways in which we can assign truth values to a set of propositions in terms of the truth values of the propositions in the set. For any finite set of propositions, we can consider pairs first and iterate the operation of pairing together. Hence, we need only truth functions of one and two propositions. It turns out that many functions can be obtained from others; for example, negation and conjunction are sufficient. Every person is male or female and we are interested in different couples of persons according to their sexes, but we do not normally assign to each set of persons a sex because combinations of persons do not yield persons again. We need also the idea that truth-functional combinations of propositions again give propositions. Perhaps the comparison should be with metals combining to form alloys.

If we take a set of propositions, which may be finite or infinite in number, we can also say that all propositions in the set are true, or all are false, or some are true, or some are false. The most common way of grouping propositions is to take propositions of the same structure; e.g. take all propositions which differ only in containing different names at a corresponding place such as, 'Marx was a Marxist,' 'Lenin was a Marxist,' 'Keynes was a Marxist,' etc. By turning the names into a variable and adding quantifiers, we get $\forall x F x$ and $\exists x F x$ which respectively assert the conjunction or disjunction of all propositions of the form Fa. In this way, the logical principles such as 'if $\forall x F x$, then Fa' and 'if Fa, then $\exists x F x$' are seen to be tautologies which may involve finitely or infinitely many propositions.

Or the idea of applying a function (general concept, predicate) to an argument (particular case, subject) to give a truth value carries with it a range of propositions which consists of all propositions with the same function but with different arguments. If we take this idea as the source of universal quantification and combine it with the basic operation of negation, we can get our familiar logical constants by a few natural conventions.[21] This is related to, but somewhat different from, Wittgenstein's general form of proposition which permits us to say that all the propositions in a given set are false. This is much too general when there are infinitely many propositions since we would have uncountably many sets of them. This seems to be one of the instances where Wittgenstein treats the infinite case as no different from the finite case.[22]

Another seductive assertion by Wittgenstein gives the impression that by merely reflecting on the concept of a proposition (in general) we arrive at the familiar logical constants.

It is clear that whatever we can say *in advance* about the form of all propositions, we must be able to say *all at once*. In fact elementary propositions themselves contain all logical operations.

For '*fa*' says the same thing as '$\exists x(fx \wedge x = a)$'. Whenever there is compositeness, argument and function are present, and where these are present, we already have all the logical constants. One could say that the sole logical constant was what *all* propositions, by their very nature, had in common with one another. But that is the general propositional form (5.47).

The illustration shows that we have existential quantification, conjunction, and even identity[23] implicit in a simple proposition. Presumably we can claim that negation is contained in the concept of a proposition since it is always true or false and we do entertain both possibilities.

A general proposition and its corresponding logical product do not mean the same thing. (1) We cannot always write out the product. (2) When we do write it out, we should add a clause to say that the product includes all the instances. (3) We can understand a general proposition without hearing of all its instances. (4) A general proposition means to refer to a totality of objects (say the totality of natural numbers) and its equivalence to the logical product of its instances depends on the assumption that every object in the totality has a (standard) name. In other words, the intended interpretation of quantifiers speaks about a realm of objects. That we can always approximate it by its instances is by no means obvious, especially if we choose, for the purpose of explicitness, to regard them as sentences (syntactical objects).

For considerations in mathematical logic, we do gain considerably in definiteness by considering sentences, and then there does appear to be a distinction to be made between the substitutional and the referential interpretations, because we do not have enough names. But there are people who say that we can imagine uncountably many names, and in first order systems with a well-ordering of the universe there is a countable submodel in which every object has a name. The more basic question is to preserve somehow the referential aspect of the quantifiers in the substitutional interpretation. For example, in dealing with natural numbers we can introduce a designation relation between names and numbers and establish that every natural number has a name. Then we can, by adding a single axiom (which could be the conjunction of several axioms), define the concept of truth for all sentences in first order number theory. But the clause on atomic sentences uses quantifiers in a referential way.[24] The question of defining truth is thought to be a sharper criterion for determining the adequacy of the substitutional interpretation because, in order to understand quantifiers, it seems natural to ask what the conditions are under which sentences containing quantifiers are true.

Logical Truth

This question of defining truth for a (first order) theory is also related to the question of logical truth, since the logically true (or rather valid) sentences are the sentences true in all theories or, what amounts to the same thing, true in all interpretations of the predicates and variables. As we mentioned before, the concept of model or interpretation is related to our choice of logical constants so that the move from truth to validity again serves more to define logical truth after we have chosen the logical constants rather than to justify the particular choice of logical constants. Similarly, if we assume a suitable concept of possible worlds or a suitable modal concept of possibility, we again arrive at a natural concept of logical truth, given the particular logical constants we have chosen.

In the definition of sentences of pure logic and the definition of validity for them, we use recursion and envisage infinitely many instances. Also in the consideration of models, we include infinite models. Hence, infinity comes into logic, if not directly, at least indirectly. This leads into the kind of thing discussed in the *Tractatus* under formal concepts and formal series. And we find a natural transition from first order logic to mathematical logic.

In logic we make no assertions about the world. Logical truth should not depend on how many individuals there are in the world. It may be debatable whether logic does not require and presuppose a nonempty world, but surely there is no logical proof that there must be at least two or one hundred individuals in the world. Indeed, we would think that logic would be true even in an empty world. That current logic does presuppose a nonempty universe is more a matter of convenience than a matter of necessity: the domains we are interested in are usually nonempty ones. Hence, in building up logic and mathematics, we must not assume individuals or names of them. Yet both Russell and Ramsey believe that we cannot get ordinary mathematics unless we assume not only the existence of individuals but also the existence of infinitely many of them. In other words, they believe that mathematics can only be developed with the help of the axiom of infinity which is taken to be an empirical proposition about the world and hence could be either true or false.

Thus, there are all sorts of absurd consequences such as[25] if there are only $n-1$ individuals in the world, then the natural number n is identical with the natural number $n + 1$. Since we feel sure that no matter how many individuals there are, n would always be different from $n + 1$, the natural consequence to draw is that Russell's and Ramsey's philosophy of logic and number must be quite wrong. Infinity ought to come from somewhere else.

Dedekind once proposed to establish the existence of infinite classes by considering an object, the idea of the object, the idea of the idea of the object, etc. Similar arguments were mentioned by Bolzano previously and by Russell afterwards. Russell's is concerned with classes: if there is nothing, there is one class, viz. the empty class, 2 classes of classes, 4 classes of them, etc. If we take all of these together we get an infinite class. But Russell thinks that the argument involves a confusion of types. In the *Tractatus*, it is observed that the operation of applying truth-functional connectives to form new sentences can be repeated indefinitely, and natural numbers can be introduced to indicate the number of reiterations.

What is important in all these considerations is the fact that we can iterate some operation as many times as we wish. This fact is so clear to our intuition that there is good reason to take it for granted in building logic and mathematics. There is no need to confuse types. For example, we can easily put down a star * and think of the totality of all strings of stars obtainable from it by appending repeatedly one more star to a given string. Or, even in Russell's example, we can easily so arrange our types that all the classes considered by him do belong to the same type. Surely in mathematics we do think of the infinite, or at least the indefinitely large, independently of the question whether the world is finite or infinite.

As a logical possibility, we may imagine the following hypothetical natural history. We begin first by constructing the first order logic (an empty logic) which forms part of a general language describing the world but which does not presuppose the existence of any particular number of things in the world. As we reflect on the language and the system thus constructed, we find that we feel we can repeat indefinitely the process of getting new expressions from given expressions in certain definite ways. When we try to describe this possibility, we are led to lay down some infinite systems such as indefinitely long strings of stars. These may be viewed as representing the positive integers in the natural fashion, or as the 'exponents of an operation' as in the *Tractatus* (6.021).

Once we have a star and the operation of adding one star to a given string of stars, we can get easy equalities between these strings, as well as inequalities. Then we can introduce variables ranging over these strings, and form general propositions, as well as propositions which result from the use of ordinary truth-functional connectives.

Now, how do we introduce classes of these strings or sets of positive integers? We consider an arbitrary sentence form which contains a free variable that ranges over positive integers. Or to use Russell's terminology, we consider a propositional function Fx, where x is a variable taking positive integers as values. Each such sentence form or propositional function defines a class in the following manner: for each integer n, either Fn is true or it is false; if Fn

is true, put *n* in the class, otherwise, throw it away. When we have hypothetically done this with every positive integer, all those which we have not thrown away constitute the class. In this way we get a class for every defining property of positive integers. We arrive at a principle: 'Given any sentence form *Fx*, we can find a class *K* of positive integers such that for every positive integer *x*, *x* belongs to *K* if and only if *Fx* is true.'

It is then natural to introduce variables for classes of positive integers so that the defining sentence forms *Fx* are enlarged to include also these variables, free or quantified. If we repeat this process indefinitely for any *n*, and add the axioms of extensionality and choice, we arrive at the usual simple theory of types. There is no decisive reason why we should stop at finite types. If we continue to the transfinite, we move into what is commonly called axiomatic set theory, where the notational distinctions of the different types are conveniently suppressed, even though the conceptual distinction of types is preserved.

We conclude with a brief comment on recent attempts to deal with the foundations of logic and mathematics by means of modal concepts. Some such approach has been urged by H. Putnam,[26] S. A. Kripke, J. Hintikka, M. Slote, and others. From this approach, it is desirable to avoid possible worlds which immediately suggest models and set-theoretical interpretations but stress possibility (might be, conceivable, imaginable) which is more intimately connected with propositions (and the relation of implication among them), dispositions, laws, and conditions. The tendency to shun objects is not unlike the later Wittgenstein's appeals to the ambiguous concept of being able to imagine. For example,[27]

> Why are the Newtonian laws not axioms of mathematics? Because we could quite well imagine things being otherwise. But – I want to say – this only assigns a certain role to those propositions in contrast to another one. I.e.: to say of a proposition: 'This could be imagined otherwise' or 'We can imagine the opposite too,' ascribes the role of an empirical proposition to it.

The question, 'Do numbers and sets exist,' seems unclear. We are not interested in certain specific objects but rather any objects satisfying certain conditions, so that isomorphic structures are equally acceptable. Instead of asking whether numbers exist, one may ask whether it is possible that all conditions (true sentences) about numbers can be simultaneously satisfied. If one distinguishes possible objects from actual objects, then existence can be a predicate, and we can ask whether certain possible objects satisfy the predicate. But this sounds very much like the discredited distinction between existence and subsistence. Hence, possibility is favored over possible worlds and possible objects.

The truth of a mathematical statement can be taken to mean that it is impossible that an interpretation of the basic conditions (e.g. axioms) would fail to satisfy the statement. There is here a duality of modal interpretation and set-theoretical interpretation. The modal explanation is attractive when we recall that numbers have no properties except those that come from their order in the number sequence. The fact of incompleteness of formal systems does not show that there are absolutely undecidable propositions. But if we ask whether Fermat's conjecture or the continuum hypothesis is true, we do seem to be denied the interpretation through pure logic according to which the truth of a hypothesis means that it is necessary or valid that certain prechosen axioms imply the hypothesis.

Hence, in order to give an adequate modal account of truth in set theory, we are naturally led to the task of supplying an explanation of standard models (e.g. of set theory) in modal terms. There have been attempts to do this, e.g. in terms of tree structures of the membership relation, but at this stage they remain in an unfinished state.

In general terms, we would expect a modal account to be helpful in some ways. Yet our conservative instinct would incline us to expect old difficulties to appear in new forms after the reformulation has made enough progress.

Another advantage of the modal approach is that possibility and necessity are natural concepts unlike philosophers' inventions such as subsistence and analyticity. A related virtue is that they are not only relevant to mathematics but also to general metaphysics. This virtue seems to imply at the same time a disadvantage, in that, for the very reason of their wide applicability, they need not be specially pertinent to mathematics. Thus, we seem to have a basic ambiguity in the modal concepts: e.g. physically possible, naturally possible, logically possible, geometrically possible, mathematically possible, conceptually possible, etc.

The emphasis on modality is to some extent related to the idea of being true to a concept (as contrasted with true of an object). We would then like to distinguish mathematics from novels where we also strive to be true to certain concepts or characters. While the smaller degree of arbitrariness in mathematics seems obvious, we do have to face once more the task of characterizing the distinctive traits of logical and mathematical concepts.

Logical Truth

NOTES

1 The references used in this section are as follows.
   (1) 1. The works of Aristotle, translated into English under the editorship of W. D. Ross, 1928. (In particular, vol. 1, *The organon*; vol. 8, *Metaphysics*). 2. *Aristotle*, W. D. Ross, 1923. 3. *Aristotle's syllogistic*, Jan Lukasiewicz, 1951 and 1957.
   (2) I. M. Bochénski, *A history of formal logic*, 1961.
   (3) W. and M. Kneale, *The development of logic*, 1962.
   (4) Heinrich Scholz, *Concise history of logic*, 1931 and 1961.
   (5) Wilhelm Windelband, *A history of philosophy*, 1901 and 1958.

2 We note that it is essential, when predicate variables are allowed, not to quantify them existentially. They are only to serve basically as free variables or dummy letters. Otherwise, the logic would no longer be first order.

3 See D. Hilbert and P. Bernays, *Grundlagen der Mathematik*, vol. 2, 1939 and 1970, pp. 252–3, and also S. C. Kleene, *Introduction to metamathematics*, 1952, p. 394.

4 Philosophers not familiar with logic may prefer a more leisurely elaboration of the widely known ideas summarized in the last few paragraphs. They will find a characteristically attractive account in chapter 4 of W. V. Quine, *Philosophy of logic*, 1970.

5 B. Bolzano, *Wissenschaftslehre*, 1837; republished 1929 to 1931. The quotations in this and the next paragraphs are from § 148 and § 155. The question whether a sentence is a logical truth depends heavily on what are taken to be the logical constants (and how they are interpreted to render certain sentences true in virtue of such interpretations) and the constituents. Bolzano offers (vol. 2, p. 199) an interesting contrast to illustrate the difference between genuine and spurious logical arguments.

> It is only from other circumstances, e.g. from the context, that one can guess whether the speaker has in his mind *determinate* notions in respect to which the relation of deducibility is to be present, or whether he only intends to intimate that there *are* such notions. Thus, e.g., it is easy enough to gather from the following proposition: 'If Caius is a man, and all men are mortal, then Caius, too, is mortal,' that it is here intended to state the deducibility of the proposition: Caius is mortal, from the two propositions: Caius is a man, and, all men are mortal, in respect of the three notions: Caius, man, mortal. This next utterance on the other hand: 'If in all men there stirs an irresistible desire for permanence; if, too, the most virtuous must feel unhappy at the thought that he is one day to cease; then we are not wrong to expect of God's infinite goodness that he will not annihilate us in death' – this would be subject to the reproach of extreme obscurity, since its sense is not that the same propositions stand in a relation of deducibility when some of their notions (which still have to be ascertained) have been taken as variable. By such an utterance it is only intended to state that notions are present such as to warrant inference from the truth of the antecedent to the truth of the consequent; but it does not as yet tell one which these notions properly are.

6 G. Frege, *Begriffschrift*, 1879, preface, § 9, and § 5.

7 L. Wittgenstein, *Tractatus*, 4.0411.

8 C. S. Peirce, *Collected papers*, vol. 3, § 387.

9 P. Bernays, *Math. Zeitschrift*, vol. 25, 1926, pp. 305–20, which is essentially the same as his *Habilitationsschrift* presented in 1918; E. L. Post, *Am. j. math.*, vol. 43, 1921, pp. 63–185.

10 See, e.g., C. I. Lewis, *A survey of symbolic logic*, 1918 and 1960, p. 286.

11 For a more detailed discussion, see 'A survey of Skolem's work in logic,' especially pp. 18–29 in *Selected works in logic*, ed. J. E. Fenstad, 1970.

12 D. Hilbert and W. Ackermann, *Grundzüge der theoretischen Logik*, first edition, 1928. The two quotations below are from p. 68 and p. 80.

13 Kurt Gödel, 'Die Vollständigkeit der Axiome des logischen Funktionen-kalküls,' *Monatsh. Math. Physik*, vol. 37, 1930, pp. 173–98, and also *Über die Vollständigkeit des Logikkalküls*, thesis, University of Vienna, 1930.

14 D. Hilbert, 'Probleme der Grundlegung der Mathematik,' *Math. Annalen*, vol. 102, 1930, pp. 1–9.

15 See *Methodos*, vol. 3, 1951, pp. 217–32.

16 Thus, if X is infinite and X l.e. p, then X plus $\neg p$ has no model. Hence by compactness, some finite subset X_1 of the augmented set has no model. If X_1 contains $\neg p$, then $X_1 - \{\neg p\}$ l.e. p, and, by completeness, $X_1 - \{\neg p\} \vdash p$, $X \vdash p$. If X_1 does not contain $\neg p$, then the negation B_1 of the conjunction of the sentences in X_1 is valid and provable in S by completeness. Hence, $\vdash B_1 \supset p$, $B_1 \vdash p$, and $X \vdash p$.

17 Per Lindström, 'On extensions of elementary logic,' *Theoria*, vol. 35, 1969, pp. 1–11.

18 A systematic exposition of results in this direction is contained in H. J. Keisler, 'Logic with the quantifier "there exist uncountably many",' *Annals of math. logic*, vol. 1, 1970, pp. 1–93.

19 Plato, *Protagoras*, 349.

20 Charles F. Hockett, *The state of the art*, 1968, p. 85.

21 More exactly, M. Schönfinkel used the primitive notation $Fx \mid *Gx$ to stand for $\forall x \neg (Fx \wedge Gx)$. Then $\neg p$ can be defined as $p \mid *p$, $\forall x Fx$ as $\neg Fx \mid * \neg Fx$, $p \wedge q$ as $\neg (p \mid *q)$.

22 The assertions in 6.126, 6.1262 seem to suggest that logic is decidable, a suggestion contradicted by later mathematical results. But one can well expect logic to be decidable if it is thought that there is no essential difference between the finite and the infinite cases. If no decision procedure is implied by his assertions, then the distinguishing feature of logic mentioned there is shared by every formal system.

23 The treatment of identity in the *Tractatus* is very peculiar. A doctrine of one sign, one object is proposed. 'Identity of object I express by identity of sign, not by using a sign for identity. Difference of objects I express by difference of signs' (5.53). This is presumably because, it is thought, a real (elementary) proposition must say something about reality. If we permit two signs to mean the same object, then we get equations which look like propositions but do not say anything about reality (but only say things about expressions). This has various unusual consequences as listed under 5.531, 5.532, 5.534, and 6.2.

24 For more detail, compare next chapter. See also John Wallace, *Synthese*, vol. 22, 1970, p. 128.

25 B. Russell, *Introduction to mathematical philosophy*, 1919, p. 132.

26 H. Putnam, 'Mathematics without foundations,' *J. philosophy*, vol. 64, 1967, pp. 5–22.

27 L. Wittgenstein, *Remarks on the foundations of mathematics*, 1956, p. 114.

V

METALOGIC

1 FORMAL LANGUAGES AND FORMAL SYSTEMS

1.1 Syntax and semantics

Metalogic may be defined as the study of the syntax and the semantics of formal languages and formal systems. It is related to but does not include the formal treatment of natural languages. A formal language usually requires a set of formation rules, i.e. a mechanical and complete specification of the well-formed formulas (sentences or meaningful expressions). This specification usually contains three parts: a list of primitive symbols (basic units) is given mechanically, certain combinations of these symbols are singled out mechanically as the atomic sentences, and then there are inductive clauses to stipulate that natural combinations of given sentences by logical connectives (viz. propositional connectives and quantifiers) are again sentences. 'Mechanical' means that a machine can check whether a candidate satisfies the requirements. Since these specifications are concerned only with symbols and their combinations, we are here dealing with the syntax of the language.

An interpretation of a formal language is determined by a domain of objects together with an interpretation of the atomic sentences (viz. which objects are denoted by which constants and which relations and functions are denoted by which predicate letters and function symbols). The truth-value (i.e. true or false) of every sentence is thereby determined according to the standard interpretation of logical connectives. For example, $p \wedge q$ is true if and only if both p and q are true. Thus, given any interpretation of a formal language, we obtain a formal concept of truth. Truth, meaning, and denotation are semantic concepts.

If in addition we introduce a formal system in a formal language, we encounter further the syntactic concepts of axioms, rules of inference, and theorems. Certain sentences are singled out mechanically as the axioms. Axioms are (basic) theorems. There are then inductive clauses each stating that if certain sentences are theorems, then another sentence related to them in a suitable way is also a theorem. For example, if p and $\neg p \vee q$ are theorems, then q is a theorem.

It is a fundamental discovery of K. Gödel in 1931 that in most of the interesting formal systems not all true sentences are theorems.[1] It follows from this result that semantics cannot be reduced to syntax, and we often have to distinguish syntax which is closely related to proof theory from semantics which is closely related to model theory. Roughly speaking, syntax is a branch of number theory and semantics is a branch of set theory.

1.2 Example of a formal system

In order to clarify these abstract concepts, we give a formal system N (with its formal language) for illustration.

A Formation rules

1 Primitive symbols: $\neg$, $\vee$, $\forall$, (,), $=$, function symbols $+$, ., constants 0, 1, and variables $x, y, z, \ldots$;

2 Terms: a constant is a term, a variable is a term, if a and b are terms, $a + b$ and $a \cdot b$ are terms;

3 Atomic sentences: if a and b are terms, $a = b$ is a sentence;

4 Other sentences: if A and B are sentences and v is a variable, then $\neg A$, $A \vee B$, $\forall v A$ are sentences.

B Axioms and rules of inference

1 Those of the (first order) predicate calculus (including the propositional calculus).

2 Axioms of N: $\neg(x + 1 = 0)$, $\neg(x + 1 = y + 1) \vee x = y$, $x + 0 = x$, $x + (y + 1) = (x + y) + 1$, $x \cdot 0 = 0$, $x \cdot (y + 1) = (x \cdot y) + x$.

3 Rule of inference. If $A(0)$ and $\forall x(\neg A(x) \vee A(x + 1))$ are theorems, then $\forall x A(x)$ is a theorem. (The principle of mathematical induction.)

The system N as specified by A and B is a formal system in the sense that given any combination of the primitive symbols, we can check mechanically whether it is a sentence of N, and given a finite sequence of sentences, we can check mechanically whether it is a (correct) proof in N, i.e. whether each sentence is either an axiom or follows from preceding sentences in the sequence by a rule of inference. Viewed in this way, a sentence A is a theorem if and only if there exists a proof whose last sentence is A. It should be noted that we do not require of a formal system that we can mechanically decide whether a given sentence is a theorem. In fact, a well-known result is that there is no mechanical method to decide whether a sentence A of N is a theorem of N.

1.3 Truth definition for the given language

The formal system N admits of different interpretations by results of Gödel and Th. Skolem.[2] The intended or standard interpretation takes the ordinary nonnegative integers as the domain, the symbols 0 and 1 as denoting zero and one, and the symbols $+$ and $\cdot$ as standing for ordinary addition and multiplication. Relative to this interpretation, we can give a truth definition for the language of N.

It is necessary to distinguish between open and closed sentences. For example, $x = 1$ is an open sentence and may be true or false depending on what value x takes; $0 = 1$ and $\forall x(x = 0)$ are closed sentences (both happen to be false in the intended interpretation).

1 A closed atomic sentence is true if and only if it is true in the intuitive sense. For example, $0 = 0$ is true, $0 + 1 = 0$ is false. This specification as it stands is not syntactic, but with some care we can give an explicit and mechanical specification of those closed atomic sentences which are true in the intuitive sense.[3]

2 A closed sentence $\neg A$ is true if and only if A is not true.

3 A closed sentence $A \lor B$ is true if and only if either A or B is true.

4 A closed sentence $\forall v A(v)$ is true if and only if $A(0)$, $A(1)$, $A(1 + 1)$, ... are all true.

The above definition of truth is not an explicit one but an inductive one. Using concepts from set theory, we can obtain an explicit definition which yields a set of sentences which consists of all and only the true ones. If we use Gödel's method of representing symbols and sentences by numbers, then we can obtain in set theory a set of natural numbers which are just the Gödel numbers of the true sentences of N.

We note that there is a definite sense in which it is impossible to define truth for a language in itself. This can be proved by using the liar paradox. Consider the sentence 'I am lying' or alternatively:

(1) This sentence is not true

Since (1) is 'this sentence', if (1) is true, (1) is false. On the other hand, if (1) is false, (1) is true. If the concept of truth for sentences of N is definable in N itself, then using a device invented by Gödel, it is possible to obtain in *N* a sentence which amounts to (1) and thereby yields a contradiction. This was first emphasized in publications by A. Tarski and Gödel.[4]

2 ORIGINS AND INFLUENCES OF METALOGIC

Historically, as logic and axiomatic systems became more and more exact, there emerged, for the sake of greater transparency, a tendency to pay greater attention to the syntactic features of the languages employed rather than to concentrate exclusively on intuitive meanings. In this way logic, the axiomatic method, and semiotic converged toward metalogic.

2.1 The axiomatic method

The best known axiom system is undoubtedly Euclid's for geometry. The axiomatic method proceeds in a linear manner, beginning with a set of primitive concepts and propositions from which all other concepts and propositions in the theory are defined or deduced.

The realization of different possible geometries in the nineteenth century led to a desire to separate abstract mathematics from spatial intuition. Many hidden axioms in Euclid's geometry were uncovered as a result. And these discoveries were organized into a more rigorous axiom system in D. Hilbert's famous *Grundlagen* in 1899. However, in this and related systems, logical connectives are taken for granted and their properties remain implicit. If we take the predicate calculus to be the logic, we arrive at formal systems as discussed above.

Once we arrive at such formal systems, it is possible to transform certain semantic problems into sharper syntactic problems. For example, one argues that non-Euclidean geometries are consistent because they have models in Euclidean geometry which in turn has a model in the theory of real numbers. But how do we know that the theory of real numbers is consistent? Obviously, modeling can only establish relative consistency and has to come to an end somewhere. With the possession of a formal system (say of real numbers), we do have a sharper syntactic problem of consistency which has a combinatorial flavor: viz. consider all the possible proofs (as syntactic objects) and ask whether any of them ever has (say) $0 = 1$ as the last sentence.

Or take another example. We are interested in the question whether a system is categorical, i.e. determines a unique interpretation up to isomorphism. This can to some extent be replaced by a related syntactic question of completeness: whether there is any closed sentence A of the system such that neither A nor $\neg A$ is a theorem. Even though we now know that the two concepts are different, the original vague requirement of adequacy gets clarified by both concepts. The sharp syntactic questions such as consistency and completeness were emphasized by Hilbert and the study of these problems was called metamathematics (or proof theory) by him around 1920.

2.2 Logic and metalogic

In one sense, logic is to be identified with the (first order) predicate calculus with or without equality. In this sense, Frege achieved a formal calculus of logic as early as 1879. Sometimes logic is construed as including also higher order predicate calculi, but then it is a small step to engulf set theory in logic. In fact, axiomatic set theory is often regarded as a part of logic. For our present purpose, it is more appropriate to confine ourselves to logic in the first sense.

It is hard to separate out significant results in logic from metalogic since all theorems of interest to logicians are about logic and therefore belong to metalogic. Every mathematical theorem p, in particular, one about logic, can be turned into a theorem $\neg P \lor p$ in logic, where P is the conjunction of the mathematical axioms employed for proving p. But it is important to remember that we do not do mathematics by carrying out explicitly all the steps as formalized in logic. The selection and intuitive grasp of the axioms is important for mathematics and metamathematics. Actual derivations in logic, such as those carried out by Whitehead and Russell, are of little intrinsic interest to logicians. It might therefore appear redundant to introduce the term 'metalogic.' The present classification is to have metalogic deal not only with results on logical calculi but also with studies of formal systems and formal languages in general.

An ordinary formal system differs from a logical calculus in that the former usually has an intended interpretation, while the latter deliberately leaves the interpretations open. Thus, for example, we speak of truth or falsity of sentences in a formal system but validity (i.e. true in all interpretations or in all possible worlds) and satisfiability (or having a model, i.e. true in some interpretations) of sentences in a logical calculus. Hence, completeness of a logical calculus has quite a different meaning from completeness of a formal system: the former permits many closed sentences A such that neither A nor $\neg A$ is a theorem; all that is required is that every valid sentence is a theorem.

2.3 Semiotic

Originally, the word 'semiotic' meant the medical theory of symptoms. Locke used the term for a science of signs and significations. The current usage is recommended especially by R. Carnap.[5] According to this usage, semiotic is the general science of signs and languages, consisting of the three parts pragmatics (in which reference is made to the user of the language), semantics (in which we abstract from the user and analyze only the expressions and their meaning), and syntax (in which we abstract also from the meaning and study only the relations between expressions).

At first, Carnap emphasized exclusively syntax. Gradually he realized the importance of semantics and the door was reopened to many difficult philosophical problems. Pragmatics is at present more or less an empty name covering a wide range of scientific investigations of language: physiological, psychological, ethnological, and sociological. Since it is conspicuously incapable of formal treatment, it is usually not considered a part of metalogic.

Certain aspects of metalogic were instrumental in the development of a whole new approach to philosophy commonly associated with the label of logical positivism. In *Tractatus*, Wittgenstein gave an appealing exposition of logical truths as sentences true in all possible worlds. For example, it is raining or it is not raining. In every possible world one of the disjuncts is true. On the basis of this observation and broader developments in logic, Carnap attempted formal treatments of science and philosophy.

Thus, a branch of science is given a formal language in which there are logically true sentences and factually true ones. The former have universal logical ranges, while the latter have more restricted ranges. Roughly speaking, the logical range of a sentence is the set of all possible worlds in which it is true. It was thought that the success of metalogic with mathematical disciplines could be carried over to physics and even biology or psychology.

A formal solution of the problem of meaning has also been proposed for these disciplines. Given the formal language of a science, we can define a notion of truth more or less as we have done with the language of *N*. Such a truth definition determines the truth condition for every sentence, i.e. a necessary and sufficient condition for its truth. The meaning of a sentence is then identified with its truth condition,[6] 'because to understand a sentence, to know what is asserted by it, is the same as to know under what conditions it would be true.' 'To know the truth condition of a sentence is (in most cases) much less than to know its truth value, but it is the necessary starting point for finding out its truth value.'

2.4 Influences in other directions

Metalogic has led to a great deal of work of a mathematical nature in recursion theory, model theory, and axiomatic set theory (notably independence results) in recent years.

In a different direction, the explication of mechanical procedures in terms of Turing machines has led to the investigation of idealized computers, with ramifications in the theory of finite automata and mathematical linguistics.

As far as philosophy of language is concerned, there is a widespread tendency to stress the philosophy of logic. For example, there are considerations on the contrast between intensional and extensional concepts, attempts to study meaning in natural languages as truth conditions, much discussion of the relation between formal logic and natural logic (i.e. logic of the natural language), much discussion of the relation between ontology and the use of quantifiers, etc.

There are also efforts to produce formal systems for empirical sciences such as physics, biology, and even psychology. On the whole, it is doubtful that these efforts have yielded any surprising fruits.

3 EXACT RESULTS ON FORMAL MATHEMATICAL SYSTEMS

3.1 General outline

On the two central questions of completeness and consistency, Gödel (1931) obtained strong results for the most interesting formal systems. 1 If they are ω-consistent (see below), they are never complete. 2 If a formal system is consistent, then the statement of its consistency, easily expressible in it, is not provable in the system itself.

Soon afterwards,[7] Gödel modified a suggestion of J. Herbrand and introduced a general concept of recursive functions. In 1936, A. M. Turing, A. Church and E. Post argued for this and equivalent notions, thereby arriving at a stable and exact concept of mechanical or computable or recursive or formal which provides an excellent explication of the intuitive concept of all mechanical procedures. As a result we are able to prove not only that certain classes of problems are mechanically solvable (for which the sharp general concept is unnecessary) but that certain others are mechanically unsolvable (or absolutely unsolvable.) The most notable example is the result[8] that there is no algorithm for solving all Diophantine equations or, in other words, that Hilbert's tenth problem has a negative solution.

In this way, we finally arrive at a sharp concept of formal axiomatic systems because we no longer have to leave 'mechanical' as a vague nonmathematical concept. In this way, we also arrive at sharp concepts of decidability. In one sense, decidability is a property of sets (of sentences): to find a mechanical method to decide, for any closed sentence of a given formal system (N, say), whether it is true (or, a different question, is a theorem). There is also another sense of decidability which refers to a single closed sentence A: A is undecidable in a formal system if neither A nor $\neg A$ is a theorem. Using this concept, Gödel's incompleteness result is sometimes stated thus: every interesting formal system has some undecidable sentences.

Given these developments, it was easy to extend Gödel's results to show: 3 interesting formal systems such as N are undecidable (both with regard to theorems and with regard to true sentences). This was first demonstrated by Church.[9]

3.2 The two incompleteness theorems

The first and most central result is that systems such as N are incomplete and incompletable, since the theorem applies to any reasonable and moderately rich system. The proof may be viewed as a modification of the liar paradox which yields the result that truth cannot be defined in the language itself. Since provability in a formal system S can often be expressed in S itself, we are led to another conclusion.

Consider the sentence

(1) This sentence is not provable in S

In particular, we may think of N as the system S. Representing expressions by numbers and using an ingenious substitution function, Gödel was able to find in S a sentence p which can be viewed as expressing (1).

Once such a sentence p is obtained, it becomes clear that we are going to get some strong conclusions. If S is complete, then either p or $\neg p$ is a theorem of S. If p is a theorem, then intuitively p, or (1) is false, and there is in some sense a false theorem in S. Similarly, if $\neg p$ is a theorem, then it says $\neg$(1) or that p is provable in S. Since $\neg p$ is a theorem, it should be true, and we seem to get two conflicting sentences which are both true: viz. p is provable in S, and $\neg p$ is provable in S. This can only be the case if S is inconsistent.

A careful examination of this inexact line of reasoning leads to Gödel's exact theorem saying that if S is reasonably rich and ω-consistent, then p is undecidable in S. The notion of ω-consistency is stronger than consistency but is a very reasonable requirement since it demands merely that we cannot prove in S both $\exists x \neg A(x)$

173

and also all of $A(0)$, $A(1)$, . . . (i.e. some number does not have the property A yet each number does have the property A). J. B. Rosser[10] was able to weaken the hypothesis to mere consistency, at the expense of complicating somewhat the initial sentence (1).

More exactly, Gödel shows that if S is consistent, then p is not provable; if S is ω-consistent, then $\neg p$ is not provable. The first half leads to Gödel's theorem on consistency proofs: if S is consistent, then the arithmetic sentence expressing the consistency of S cannot be proved in S. This is usually stated briefly thus: no interesting system can prove its own consistency, or there exists no consistency proof of S which can be formalized in S.

The proof of this theorem consists essentially of a formalization in arithmetic of the arithmetized version of the proof of 'if S is consistent, then p is not provable.' In other words, it consists of a derivation within number theory of p itself from the arithmetic sentence $\text{Con}(S)$ which says S is consistent. Hence, if $\text{Con}(S)$ were provable, p would also be, contradicting the previous result. This proof was only briefly outlined by Gödel. But it is carried out in detail in Hilbert-Bernays.[11]

One other remarkable feature is that the undecidable sentence p is always of a relatively simple form, viz. the form $\forall x A(x)$, where A is a recursive, in fact primitive recursive, predicate.

3.3 Decidability and undecidability

The first incompleteness theorem yields directly that truth in a system S (for example, N) to which the theorem applies is undecidable. If it were decidable, then all true sentences would form a recursive set and we could take them as the axioms of a formal system which would be complete. This depends on the reasonable and widely accepted assumption that all we require of the axioms of a formal system is that we can decide effectively whether a given sentence is an axiom.

Alternatively, we can avoid the above assumption by resorting to a familiar lemma: all recursive or computable functions and relations are representable in S (e.g. N). Since truth in the language of S itself is not representable (definable) in S, it cannot, by the lemma, be recursive (i.e. decidable).

The same lemma also yields the undecidability of systems like S with regard to theoremhood. Thus, if there were a decision procedure, there would be a computable function f such that $f(i) = 1$ or 0 according as the i-th sentence is a theorem or not. But then $f(i) = 0$ says just that the i-th sentence is not provable. Hence using Gödel's device, we again obtain a sentence (say the t-th) saying of itself that it is not provable. If $f(t) = 0$ is true, then, since f is representable in S, it is a theorem of S. But then, since $f(t) = 0$ is (equivalent to) the t-th sentence, $f(t) = 1$ is also true and therefore provable in S. Hence, S, if consistent, is undecidable with regard to theoremhood.

While the system N is incompletable and undecidable, arithmetic with addition alone or multiplication alone is decidable (with regard to truth) and therefore has complete formal systems. These results are due to M. Presburger[12] and Skolem.[13] Another well known positive result is Tarski's decision procedure for elementary geometry and elementary algebra.[14]

3.4 Consistency proofs

The best known consistency proof is G. Gentzen's for the system N of classical number theory.[15] This proof uses transfinite induction to the first $\in$-number (i.e. the limit of ω, ω^ω, ω^{ω^ω}, ...) which is not formalizable in N. There are several variants of this proof, and it has opened up an area of rather extensive work.

Along a different line, there have been investigations of the relation between classical and intuitionistic number theory. This was thought to be of significance because the latter is believed to be more constructive and more evident. In 1933, Gödel found an interpretation of classical number theory in the intuitionistic theory (also discovered independently by P. Bernays and Gentzen). In 1958, Gödel extended the result to obtain constructive interpretations of sentences of classical number theory in terms of primitive recursive functionals.[16]

More recently, there have been efforts to extend Gentzen's result to ramified theories of types and fragments of classical analysis, as well as attempts to extend Gödel's interpretation to relate classical analysis to intuitionistic analysis. Also, in connection with these consistency proofs, there are various proposals to present constructive notations for the ordinals of segments of Cantor's second number class. A good deal of discussion has been devoted to the epistemological significance of the consistency proofs and the relative interpretations.

4 EXACT RESULTS ON LOGICAL CALCULI

4.1 The propositional calculus

We assume that a description of the calculus is given in some familiar manner. It is easy to show that the calculus is complete in the sense that every valid sentence, i.e. tautology, or sentence true in all possible worlds (all interpretations), is a theorem. For example, $p \vee \neg p$ is always true because p is either true or false. In the former case $p \vee \neg p$ is true because p is; in the latter case, because $\neg p$ is. One way to prove the completeness is to observe that the calculus is sufficient to reduce every sentence to a conjunctive normal form, i.e. a conjunction of disjunctions of single letters and their negations. But any such conjunction is valid if and only if every conjunct is. And a conjunct is valid if and only if it contains some letter p as well as $\neg p$ as parts of the whole disjunction. Completeness follows because such conjuncts can all be proved in the calculus, and if these conjuncts are theorems so is the whole conjunction.

Consistency is more or less obvious because it can easily be checked that all axioms are valid and rules of inference lead from valid sentences to valid sentences. But a contradiction is not valid. In fact, the conclusion is stronger than consistency: only valid sentences are provable.

The calculus is also easily decidable. Since all and only valid sentences are theorems, we can test each sentence mechanically by putting true and false for each letter in the sentence. If there are n letters, there are 2^n possible substitutions. A sentence is a theorem if and only if it comes out true under all the 2^n possibilities.

The independence of the axioms is usually proved by using more than two truth values so that the axiom to be shown independent can get some undesired value while all theorems provable without using this axiom always get the desired values. This originally suggested many-valued logics.

4.2 The (first order) predicate calculus

We assume that a description of the calculus is given in some familiar manner. This includes the propositional calculus as a part. There is an option of including or not including equality. We shall in the present context make no definite commitment one way or the other. This is the central area of logic, and there are many significant problems and results.

The problem of consistency is relatively simple. Assume there is only one object a. In that case, $\forall x A(x)$ and $\exists x A(x)$ both become $A(a)$, and all quantifiers can be eliminated. It is easily checked that after the reduction, all theorems of the calculus become tautologies (i.e. theorems in the propositional calculus). But, for example, the sentence $\forall x F(x) \wedge \neg \forall x F(x)$ is reduced to $A(a) \wedge \neg A(a)$ which is not a tautology; therefore, the original sentence is not a theorem and, hence, no contradiction can be a theorem. In fact, it can be proved quite directly, not only that the calculus is consistent, but also that all theorems are valid.

The completeness and undecidability of the calculus are much deeper results. The former is due to Gödel (1930). The latter was established in 1936 by Church and Turing by quite different methods;[17] given the general developments up to 1936, it also follows in another way from Theorem X of Gödel's 1931 paper.

The completeness result says that every valid sentence is a theorem. It follows that if $\neg A$ is not a theorem, then $\neg A$ is not valid and, therefore, A is satisfiable. But to say that A is consistent means nothing other than that $\neg A$ is not a theorem. Hence, from the completeness, it follows that if A is consistent, then A is satisfiable (has a model). Therefore, the semantic concepts of validity and satisfiability are seen to coincide with the syntactic concepts of derivability and consistency.

A result closely related to the completeness theorem is the Löwenheim-Skolem theorem[18] which says that if a sentence (or a formal system) has any model, it has a countable model. The most direct method of proving this theorem provides very useful tools in model theory and studies on relative consistency and independence in set theory.

4.3 The Löwenheim-Skolem theorem

In the predicate calculus, there are certain reduction or normal form theorems. One useful example is the prenex normal form: every sentence can be reduced to an equivalent sentence in the prenex form, viz. in a form such that all the quantifiers appear at the beginning. This form is specially useful for bringing out the central ideas of some proofs of the Löwenheim-Skolem theorem.

Consider for illustration a simple schema in prenex form:
(i) $\forall x\, \exists y M x y$.
Suppose (i) has a model with a (nonempty) domain D. By the axiom of choice, there is a function f which singles out for each x a corresponding y. Hence, we have:
(ii) $\forall x\, M x f(x)$.
Let now a be any object in D, then the countable subdomain $\{a, f(a), f(f(a)), \ldots\}$ already contains enough objects to satisfy (ii) and therefore (i). Hence, if (i) has any model, it has a countable model, which is in fact a 'submodel' of the original model.

An alternative proof was given by Skolem[19] to avoid appealing to the axiom of choice and turns out to be useful also for establishing the completeness result. Instead of using the function f given by the axiom of choice, we can arbitrarily denote a by 1. Since (i) is true, there must be some object y such that $M1y$, call one such 2. We can repeat this process indefinitely and obtain

(iii) $M12$, $M12 \wedge M23$, $M12 \wedge M23 \wedge M34$, . . .

all true in the given model. The axiom of choice is not needed, since in each case we only argue from $\exists yMny$ to 'let one such y be $n + 1$.' It follows that every member of (iii) is true in some model. It is then possible to infer that all members of (iii) are simultaneously true in some model, i.e. there is some way of assigning truth-values to all atomic parts so that all members of (iii) come out true. Hence, it follows that (i) is true in some countable model.

4.4 The completeness theorem

Gödel's original proof of the completeness theorem is closely related to the second proof above. We consider again all the sentences in (iii) which contain no more quantifiers. If they are all satisfiable, then, as before, they are simultaneously satisfiable and (i) has a model. Hence, if (i) has no model, some one of them, say $M12 \wedge \ldots \wedge M89$, is not satisfiable, i.e. its negation is a tautology (i.e. a theorem of the propositional calculus). Thus $\neg M12 \vee \ldots \vee \neg M89$ is a tautology. This remains true if we replace $1, 2, \ldots, 9$ by variables. Hence, $\neg Mrs \vee \ldots \vee \neg Myz$, being a tautology expressed in the predicate calculus as usually formulated, is a theorem in it. It is then easy to use the usual rules of the predicate calculus to derive also $\exists x \forall y \neg Mxy$. In other words, the negation of (i) is a theorem of the predicate calculus. Hence, if (i) has no model, then its negation is a theorem of the predicate calculus. Therefore, if a sentence is valid (i.e. its negation has no model), then it is a theorem of the predicate calculus.

4.5 The undecidability theorem and reduction classes

Given the completeness theorem, it follows that deciding whether any sentence is a theorem of the predicate calculus is equivalent to deciding whether any sentence is valid or whether any sentence is satisfiable.

Turing's method of proving that this class of problems is undecidable is particularly suggestive. Once the concept of mechanical procedure was crystallized, it was relatively easy to find absolutely unsolvable problems, e.g. the halting problem which asks for each Turing machine the question whether it will ever stop, if it begins with a blank tape. Now Turing shows that each such question about a single Turing machine T can be expressed by a single sentence F of the predicate calculus so that T will stop if and only if F is not satisfiable. Hence, if there were a decision procedure for validity (or satisfiability) for all sentences of the predicate calculus, then the halting problem would be solvable.

In more recent years,[20] Turing's result has been improved to the extent that all we need are sentences of the relatively simple form $\forall x\,\exists y\,\forall z Mxyz$, where M contains no quantifiers. Hence, even the decision problem for the simple class of $\forall\exists\forall$ sentences in the predicate calculus is unsolvable. Moreover, the method of proof also yields a procedure by which every sentence of the predicate calculus is correlated with one in the simple form. Hence, the class of $\forall\exists\forall$ sentences forms a 'reduction class.' There are various other reduction classes.

NOTES

1 Kurt Gödel, *Monatsh. Math. Physik*, vol. 38, 1931, pp. 173–98. This basic paper has been reprinted in English translation in at least three books.
2 Gödel, op. cit., and Th. Skolem, *Norsk matematisk forenings skrifter*, series 2, no. 10, 1933, pp. 150–61.
3 For an exact treatment of this truth definition, compare D. Hilbert and P. Bernays, *Grundlagen der Mathematik*, vol. 2, 1939 and 1970. More exactly, the natural reading of condition 1 is inadequate for deriving all cases of the truth schema $P: G_p$ (the Gödel number of p) is true if and only if p. It is known that P is not derivable from N plus the four conditions as axioms. The intuitive reason is that in nonstandard models of N plus the four conditions, P may be false for certain sentences with quantifiers. In the intended model of N, the four conditions do make P true for the truth predicate thus specified. The exact statement of condition 1 by Hilbert and Bernays uses a denotation relation $d(x) = y$ which says that the integer with Gödel number x denotes y. It is then a theorem of N that $\forall y\,\exists x d(x) = y$, i.e. every number has a name. Then we use universal quantifiers to say, for example: for all u, v, w, the result of substituting u, v, w for x, y, z in the sentence '$x + y = z$' is true if and only if $d(u) + d(v) = d(w)$. This of course gives all we want for numerical equations of the form $m + n = k$ since we can specify u, v, w to be the Gödel numbers (or names) or the specific integers m, n, k. But in addition, we can also derive, for instance, $\forall x(x + x = x)$ from the hypothesis that '$\forall x(x + x = x)$' is true. Thus, the latter says that, for all u, the result of substituting u for 'x' in '$x + x = x$' is true and, therefore $\forall u(d(u) + d(u) = d(u))$. Since $\forall x\,\exists u(d(u) = x)$, $\forall x(x + x = x)$ follows. For more details, compare Hilbert and Bernays, pp. 344, 348.
4 In 1933 and 1934; compare *The undecidable*, ed. M. Davis, 1965, p. 64, for historical references.
5 See R. Carnap, *Introduction to semantics*, 1942, and the reference there to C. W. Morris.
6 Carnap, op. cit., p. 22; compare also *Tractatus*, 4.024, 4.46.
7 In 1934; see *The undecidable*, op. cit., pp. 69–71.
8 Ju. V. Matijasevicz, 'Enumerable sets are Diophantine,' *Soviet Math. Dokl.*, vol. 11, 1970, pp. 354–8.
9 Alonzo Church in *The undecidable*, pp. 89–107.

Metalogic

10 J. B. Rosser in *The undecidable*, pp. 231–5.
11 Op. cit.; compare also J. R. Shoenfield, *Mathematical logic*, 1967.
12 M. Presburger, *Comptes rend. du I Congrès des Math. des Pays Slaves*, Warsaw, 1930, pp. 92–101.
13 Th. Skolem, *Videnskap. Skr. I. Mat.-Nat. Kl.*, vol. 7, 1930.
14 A. Tarski, *A decision method for elementary algebra and geometry*, 1948 and 1951.
15 G. Gentzen, *Math. Annalen*, vol. 112, 1936, pp. 493–565; and *Neue Fassung*, 1938.
16 K. Gödel in *The undecidable*, pp. 75–81; for exposition, compare Hilbert-Bernays, op. cit. and Gödel in *Dialectica*, vol. 12, 1958, pp. 280–7.
17 See *The undecidable*, pp. 108–15 and pp. 145–54.
18 See L. Löwenheim, *Math. Annalen*, vol. 76, 1915, pp. 447–70; Th. Skolem, *Videnskap. Skr. I. Mat.-Nat. Kl.*, vol. 4, 1920.
19 T. Skolem, *Selected works in logic*, ed. J. E. Fenstad, 1970, pp. 137–52. For more details, compare the survey article in that volume.
20 *Proc. Nat. Acad. Sci. U.S.A.*, vol. 48, 1962, pp. 365–77 and *Proc. of symposium on math. theory of automata*, 1963, pp. 23–52.

VI

THE CONCEPT OF SET

1 THE (MAXIMUM) ITERATIVE CONCEPT

A set is a collection of previously given objects; the set is determined when it is determined for every given object x whether or not x belongs to it. The objects which belong to the set are its members, and the set is a single object formed by collecting the members together. The members may be objects of any sort: plants, animals, photons, numbers, functions, sets, etc.

According to the iterative concept, a set is something obtainable from some basic objects (such as the empty set, or the integers, or individuals, or some other well-defined urelements) by iterated applications of the rich operation 'set of' which permits the collecting together of any multitude of 'given' objects (in particular, sets) or any part thereof into a set. This process includes transfinite iterations. For example, the multitude of sets obtained by finite iteration is considered to be itself a set.

We understand this concept of set sufficiently well to see, after some deliberation, and in some cases even a great deal of deliberation, that the ordinary axioms of set theory are true for (or with respect to) this concept, and to be able to extend these axioms by proposing additional axioms and recognizing some of them to be true for (or with respect to) it.

The iterative concept involves at least four difficult ideas: the idea of 'given', the idea of collecting together, the idea of 'part' or subset, and the idea of iteration. The idea of iterations implies the potentiality of continuing to any stage (as indexed by a previously given ordinal number)[1] and adds an inductive element to the idea of 'given' (viz. all sets obtained at or before any given stage are viewed as given). The idea of urelement is not difficult for set theory, because we are in this context not interested in what an individual is but rather leave the question open. We do not attempt to determine what the correct urelements are.

It is a basic feature of reality that there are many things. When a multitude of given objects can be collected together, we arrive at a set. For example, there are two tables in this room. We are ready to view them as given both separately and as a unity, and justify this by pointing to them or looking at them or thinking about them either one after the other or simultaneously. Somehow the viewing of certain given objects together suggests a loose link which ties the objects together in our intuition, or a variable object which could be any one of them. In order that our mind may more effortlessly and unwaveringly fix our attention on this variable object, we, it could be suggested, concretize or reify the loosely linked bundle of objects and think of the more determinate range of variability. But then we seem to be forced by the surprising success of the reification to admit that there are certain objective grounds for our ostensively acquired intuition. It may be noted that Cantor discusses briefly the same phenomenon in connection with the move from a potentially infinite to an actually infinite.[2]

We can form a set from a multitude only in case the range of variability of this multitude is in some sense intuitive. This is the criterion for determining whether a multitude forms a set for us. The natural way of getting such intuitive ranges is by the use of intuitive concepts (defining properties). An intuitive concept, unlike an abstract concept such as that of mental illness or that of differentiable manifold, enables us to overview (or look through or run through or collect together), in an *idealized* sense, all the objects in the multitude which make up the extension of the concept, in such a way that there are no surprises as to the objects which fall under the concept. Hence, each intuitive concept determines an intuitive range of variability and therewith a set.

The overviewing of an infinite range of objects presupposes an infinite intuition which is an idealization. Strictly speaking, we can only run through finite ranges (and perhaps ones of rather limited size only). This idealization contains seeds for growth in itself. For example, not only are the infinitely many integers taken as given, but we also take as given the process of selecting integers from this unity of all integers, and therewith all possible ways of leaving integers out in the process. So we get a new intuitive idealization (viz. the set of all sets of integers) and then one goes on.

The concept of all subsets is often thought to be opaque because we envisage all possibilities independently of whether we can specify each in words; for example, just as there are 2^{10} subsets of a set with

10 members, we think of 2^a subsets of a set with a members when a is an infinite cardinal number. In particular, we do not concern ourselves over how a set is defined, e.g. whether by an impredicative definition. This is the sense in which the individual steps of iteration are 'maximum'. It is possible to get other iterative concepts by restricting the operation of going to the next stage, one familiar example being the constructible sets. The (maximum) iterative concept has been discussed by Bernays[3] under the name of platonism.

> The weakest 'platonistic' assumption introduced by arithmetic is that of the totality of integers. . . . But analysis is not content with this modest variety of platonism; it reflects it to a stronger degree with respect to the following notions: set of numbers, sequence of numbers, and function. It abstracts from the possibility of giving definitions of sets, sequences, and functions. These notions are used in a 'quasi-combinatorial' sense, by which I mean: in the sense of an analogy of the infinite to the finite. . . . In Cantor's theories, platonistic conceptions extend far beyond those of the theory of real numbers. This is done by iterating the use of the quasi-combinatorial concept of a function and adding methods of collection. This is the well-known method of set theory.

What is given at each stage depends on an orderly manner of iteration. Hence, the concept of ordinal number is essential to the iterative notion, in that we use ordinal numbers to index the stages of iteration. Thus, as we generate more and more sets according to the iterative concept, we encounter certain well-ordered sets among the sets generated. The order types of these well-ordered sets determine ordinal numbers which can be used to index (further) stages of the iterations. Given a totality of operations for generating sets, we can also survey all the ordinal numbers obtainable by these operations and introduce new ordinals. In general, for any ordinal number α, given by whatever means, we are permitted to carry the process of iteration to the α-th stage, and regard all the sets generated up to and including the α-th stage as given and proceed further.

The question of urelements involves us in the contrast between sets (or mathematical objects in general) and other objects. Philosophically it is important to realize that we are faced with a perfectly general situation and that we can begin initially with any collectable multitudes as urelements. There is nothing in the original iterative concept to rule out different kinds of urelements. For example, we can take all physical objects as the urelements, or all elementary particles, or all animals, or all integers, etc. In each case, if we are able to collect the urelements into a set x, we can carry out the process of iteration starting with x (or conceive of a hierarchy of transfinite types with x at the bottom). Since, however, the process of generating further sets from an initial set x of urelements is uniform, with respect to x, i.e. the process remains the same no matter what initial set x we might wish to choose, it is reasonable to consider just one typical general case as we have done in our first explanation of the iterative concept.

Moreover, for the abstract study of sets, it seems convenient to disregard nonsets altogether. This turns out to be feasible, because even if we start from nothing (i.e. neither urelements nor sets) initially, we can get the empty set 0. The use of this artificial special case of an empty set of urelements achieves a convenient purity. As a matter of fact, for the mathematical studies of sets it is customary to require that all members of sets are sets. This restriction excludes sets of tables and elephants, but does not exclude sets of numbers and functions which are identified with certain sets. Under this restriction, we say that a set is a collection of given sets.

On the basis of our explanations of the (maximum) iterative concept of set, we are able to see that the ordinary axioms of set theory (commonly referred to as *ZF* or *ZFC*) are true for the concept. *AE Axiom of extensionality.* A set is completely determined by its members; i.e. two different sets may not contain the same members. If x and y have the same members, then $x = y$.

This may be viewed as a defining characteristic of sets (in contrast with properties).

AS Axiom of subset formation (axiom of comprehension). If a multitude A is included in a set x, then A is a set.

Since x is a given set, we can run through all members of x, and, therefore, we can do so with arbitrary omissions. In particular, we can in an idealized sense check against A and delete only those members of x which are not in A. In this way, we obtain an overview of all the objects in A and recognize A as a set.

AP Axiom of power set. All subsets of a set can be collected into a set.

For, if x is given, then all subsets of x are given individually by *AS*. We have, moreover, an intuitive idea of running through with omissions. This general notion, which is on a higher level than its application to each multitude A included in x, provides us with an overview of all cases of *AS* as applied to x. And the overview provides us with the basis of performing the collection to get the power set of x.

In our previous discussion about the urelements, we have reached the conclusion that for the abstract development of set theory we can conveniently disregard the diversity of urelements and, in fact, leave out nonsets altogether, taking an empty set of urelements. Now that we are justified in forming the power set of a given set, we are able to tidy up the iterative process in another direction. The operation of forming the power set of a given set eliminates the need to branch out from a given set x: there are different ways of forming subsets of x; we might otherwise be forced to distinguish between different kinds of subsets of x so that certain subsets of x are collected into one new set, and certain other subsets into another new set, and so on. By using the power set of x, we are able to pull together all subsets of x and summarize the formation of all possible subsets of x in a single new set, viz. the power set of x. In this way, we obtain a standard representation of all single applications of the rich operation 'set of' to any given totality of given objects. There are then no other obstacles against our construing the iterative conception in the sharper form of ranks or types or stages: every set is obtainable at some stage α (an ordinal number) and every stage R_a is obtained from the empty set (of urelements) by iterated applications of the operation 'set of,' which yields all members of the power set of R_β if $\alpha = \beta + 1$, and just gathers together all sets obtained at previous stages if α is a limit ordinal number. In other words, if R_a is the totality of sets obtained at all stages before the α-th, then R_{a+1} consists of all the subsets of R_a. For example, $R_0 = 0$, $R_1 = \{0\}$, $R_2 = \{0, \{0\}\}$, $R_3 = \{0, \{0\}, \{\{0\}\}, \{0, \{0\}\}\}$, and so on.

The iterative concept implies that we continue the iteration as far as possible; in particular, it implies that, for any given ordinal number α, there is an α-th stage. There is then the problem of getting ordinal numbers to index the stages. For example, we take for granted that we have the finite ordinal numbers to begin with. We are then led, as it happened to Cantor originally, to ω as the limit of all finite ordinal numbers (the natural numbers) and then to $\omega + 1$, and so on.

Thus, for each natural number n, we have a stage R_n. But there is no reason to stop there. So we have a further stage R_ω which collects together all the finite stages, as well as stages $R_{\omega+1}$, etc. From the way the stages are obtained, we see that for every set obtained, there is a first stage at which it appears, and that if there is at least one stage possessing a certain property, then there is a first stage possessing that property.

AF Axiom of foundation. Every set can be got at some stage; or, every nonempty set (or even multitude of sets) has a minimal member, i.e. a member x such that no member of x belongs to the set.

For there is a member x which is got at no later stage than any other member of the set. But all members of x are got at earlier stages and therefore cannot belong to the set.

185

AI Axiom of infinity. There is an infinite set (for example, R_ω).

AC Axiom of choice. Given any set x of nonempty sets, there is a set which contains exactly one member from each member of x.

Since every member of x is got at an earlier stage than x, all members of members of x are got earlier and any selection from these can be collected together to form a set.

AR Axiom of replacement. If b_x is a set for every member x of a set y, then the union of all these sets b_x is included in a set.

This form of *AR* differs from the more familiar form in two minor aspects: the use of the union and the weakening from being a set to being included in a set. The familiar form is *SAR*: if b is an operation and b_x is a set for every member x of a set y, then all these sets b_x form a set. The differences are introduced for certain esthetic reasons, which are not very relevant to our main interest here. We shall relegate a crude direct justification of *AR*, as well as an explanation of the relation between *AR* and *SAR*, to a footnote.[4] Here, we shall confine our attention to *SAR*.

Once we adopt the viewpoint that we can in an idealized sense run through all members of a given set, the justification of *SAR* is immediate. That is, if, for each element of the set, we put some other given object there, we are able to run through the resulting multitude as well. In this manner, we are justified in forming new sets by arbitrary replacements. If, however, one does not have this idea of running through all members of a given set, the justification of the replacement axiom is more complex.

Gödel points out that the axiom of replacement does not have the same kind of *immediate* evidence (previous to any closer analysis of the iterative concept of set) which the other axioms have. This is seen from the fact that it was not included in Zermelo's original system of axioms. He suggests that, heuristically, the best way of arriving at it from this standpoint is the following. From the very idea of the iterative concept of set it follows that if an ordinal number α has been obtained, the operation of power set (P) iterated α times leads to a set $P^\alpha(0)$. But, for the same reason, it would seem to follow that if, instead of P, one takes some larger jump in the hierarchy of types, e.g. the transition Q from x to $P^{|x|}(x)$ (where $|x|$ is the smallest ordinal of the well-orderings of x), $Q^\alpha(0)$ likewise is a set. Now, to assume this for any conceivable jump operation (even for those that are defined by reference to the universe of all sets or by use of the choice operation) is equivalent to the axiom of replacement.[5]

The seven axioms *ESPFICR* will be regarded as making up the ordinary system *ZF* (or *ZFC*) of set theory. The comments above about these axioms are intended to show that we can see them to be true for the iterative concept of set. Somewhat more formally, we can also recapitulate the hierarchy of sets resulting from the iterative concept, by assuming that the ordinal numbers are given initially, as follows.

$R_0 =$ the empty set (or, sometimes, the set of integers).
$R_{a+1} =$ the power set of R_a, i.e. the set of all subsets of R_a.
$R_\lambda =$ the union of all R_a, $a < \lambda$, where λ is a limit ordinal.
$V =$ the union of all R_a, a any ordinal.

In other words, the universe of all sets consists of all x such that x belongs to some R_a, a an ordinal. The smallest a such that x belongs to R_a is usually called the rank of x. Under this formulation, it is clear that the two difficult ideas are power set and ordinal number. In recent years, much effort has been devoted to finding more ordinals by introducing new cardinals to strengthen axiomatic set theory. In contrast, there has been little progress in efforts to enrich directly power sets (e.g. that of the set of integers) by new axioms. Both endeavors could be viewed as attempts to make our vague intuitive ideas more explicit.

The iterative concept seems close to Cantor's original idea,[6] and has been, in one form or another, developed and emphasized by Mirimanoff, von Neumann, Zermelo, Bernays, and Gödel.[7]

This iterative concept of set is of course quite different from the dichotomy concept which regards each set as obtained by dividing the totality of all things into two categories (viz. those which have the property and those which do not). Following Gödel, one may speak of the two concepts as the mathematical versus the logical. To quote:[8]

> There exists, I believe, a satisfactory foundation of Cantor's set theory in its whole original extent and meaning, namely axiomatics of set theory interpreted in the way sketched below. It might seem at first sight that the set-theoretical paradoxes would doom to failure such an undertaking, but closer examination shows that they cause no trouble at all. They are a very serious problem, not for mathematics, however, but rather for logic and epistemology.

Many people have been puzzled by the fact that in an earlier paper on Russell, Gödel takes the paradoxes much more seriously.[9] 'By analyzing the paradoxes to which Cantor's set theory had led, he freed them from all mathematical technicalities, thus bringing to light the amazing fact that our logical intuitions (i.e. intuitions concerning such notions as: truth, concept, being, class, etc.) are self-contradictory.' The difference in emphasis, as Gödel explains, is due to a difference in the subject matter, because the whole paper on Russell is concerned with logic rather than mathematics. The full concept of class (truth, concept, being, etc.) is not used in mathematics, and the iterative concept, which is sufficient for mathematics, may or may not be the full concept of class. Therefore, the difficulties in these logical concepts do not contradict the fact that we have a satisfactory mathematical foundation of mathematics in terms of the iterative concept of set. In relation to logic as opposed to mathematics, Gödel believes that the unsolved difficulties are mainly in connection with the intensional paradoxes (such as the concept of not applying to itself) rather than with either the extensional or the semantic paradoxes. In terms of the contrast between bankruptcy and misunderstanding as considered below, Gödel's view is that the paradoxes in mathematics, which he identifies with set theory, are due to a misunderstanding, while logic, as far as its true principles are concerned, is bankrupt on account of the intensional paradoxes.[10]

One feels vaguely that the iterative concept corresponds pretty well to Cantor's 1895 'genetic' definition of set:[11] 'By a "set" we shall understand any collection into a whole M of definite, distinct objects m (which will be called the "elements" of M) of our intuition or our thought.' We are naturally curious to know a little more about the development of Cantor's concept and its relation to the iterative concept.

In 1882, Cantor explains that a set of elements is *well defined*, if by its definition and by the logical principle of excluded middle we must recognize as internally determined whether any object of the right kind belongs to the set or not.[12] One is inclined to think that the concept of set implicit in this context is closer to the logical concept rather than the mathematical one. In the next year, a set is defined, with references to Plato's notion of ideas and other related concepts, as[13] 'every Many, which can be thought of as One, i.e. every totality of elements that can be united into a whole by a law.'

According to Fraenkel, Cantor had discovered the so-called Burali-Forti paradox no later than 1895, i.e. at least two years before Burali-Forti's publication, and had communicated it to, among others, Hilbert in 1896 (see p. 470 of Cantor's *Works*). This discovery may have something to do with the 'genetic' element in the famous 1895 definition. According to Zermelo (p. 352, footnote 9), part of the reason why Cantor, in his treatise of 1895–7, deals extensively with the second number class rather than with all cardinal numbers was Cantor's awareness of the 'Burali-Forti paradox.' This may also explain why Cantor, in his 1895 paper, spoke of desiring to show that all cardinals form a well-ordered set 'in an extended sense' (p. 295). A concrete proposal along the line of distinguishing sets and classes was made in Cantor's letter to Dedekind in 1899 (pp. 443–4), not published until 1932.

There are also other differences between Cantor's outlook and the current one. But these seem to belong more appropriately to a footnote.[14]

With regard to the task of setting up the axioms of set theory (including the search for new axioms), we can distinguish two questions, viz. (1) what, roughly speaking, the principles are by which we introduce the axioms, (2) what their precise meaning is and why we accept such principles. The second question is incomparably more difficult. It is my impression that Gödel proposes to answer it by phenomenological investigations.

In connection with the first question, Gödel suggests the following summary of the principles which have actually been used for setting up axioms. It is understood that the same axiom can be justified by different principles which are nevertheless distinct in that they are based on different ideas; for example, inaccessible numbers are justified by either (2) or (3) below. The five principles to follow are illustrated by the discussion so far and the section below on new axioms and criteria of acceptability.

(1) Existence of sets representing intuitive ranges of variability, i.e. multitudes which, in some sense, can be 'overviewed' (see above).

(2) Closure principle: if the universe of sets is closed with respect to certain operations there exists a set which likewise is. This implies, e.g., the existence of inaccessible cardinals and of inaccessible cardinals equal to their index as inaccessible cardinals.

(3) Reflection principle: the universe of all sets is structurally undefinable. One possibility of making this statement precise is the following: The universe of sets cannot be uniquely characterized (i.e. distinguished from all its initial segments) by any internal structural property of the ∈-relation in it, expressible in any logic of finite or transfinite type, including infinitary logics of any cardinal number. This principle may be considered as a generalization of (2). Further generalizations and other precisations are in the making in recent literature.

(4) Extensionalization: axioms such as comprehension and replacement are first formulated in terms of defining properties or relations. They are extensionalized as applying to arbitrary collections or extensional correlations. For example, we get the inaccessible numbers by (2) above only if we construe the axiom of replacement extensionally.

(5) Uniformity of the universe of sets (analogous to the uniformity of nature): the universe of sets does not change its character substantially as one goes over from smaller to larger sets or cardinals,

i.e., the same or analogous states of affairs reappear again and again (perhaps in more complicated versions). In some cases it may be difficult to see what the analogous situations or properties are. But in cases of simple and, in some sense, 'meaningful' properties it is pretty clear that there is no analog except the property itself. This principle, e.g., makes the existence of strongly compact cardinals very plausible, due to the fact that there should exist generalizations of Stone's representation theorem for ordinary Boolean algebras to Boolean algebras with infinite sums and products.

2 BANKRUPTCY (CONTRADICTION) OR MISUNDERSTANDING (ERROR)?

The reactions of Frege and Cantor to the paradoxes were sharply different and can be described as the bankruptcy theory versus the misunderstanding theory. The difference can undoubtedly be attributed completely to their different conceptions of set (the logical versus the mathematical notion). A related reason may perhaps be described as the difference between viewing sets from outside (Frege) and actually doing set theory (Cantor). Typically in philosophical discussions on the foundations of a subject, the emphasis of insiders and outsiders tends to differ. Even when the same statements are endorsed, quite different things could be intended. The meaning of methodological statements can be so indefinite that it is sometimes not easy to reconcile what a specialist says with what he does.

For example, Cantor, Zermelo, Mirimanoff, and von Neumann all seem to have basically the same conception of set, at least with regard to properties of sets which are implicit in the familiar axioms of today. Yet what they say sounds quite different. Cantor apparently thinks that the paradoxes are paradoxical only because the concept of set is not correctly understood (see, e.g., p. 470, letter of 1907). Zermelo construes the paradoxes as necessitating some restrictions on Cantor's 1895 definition of set:[15]

> It has not, however, been successfully replaced by one that is just as simple and does not give rise to such reservations. Under these circumstances there is at this point nothing left for us to do but to proceed in the opposite direction and, starting from set theory as it is historically given, to seek out the principles required for establishing the foundations of this mathematical discipline. In solving the problem we must, on the one hand, restrict these principles sufficiently to exclude all contradictions and, on the other, take them sufficiently wide to retain all that is valuable in this theory.

According to Mirimanoff,[16]

> One believes and it appears evident, that the existence of
> individuals must imply the existence of sets of them; but
> Burali-Forti and Russell have shown by different examples that
> a set of individuals need not exist, even though the individuals
> exist. As we cannot accept this new fact, we are obliged to
> conclude that the proposition which appears evident to us and
> which we believe to be always true is inexact, or rather that it is
> only true under certain conditions.

In discussing attempts to axiomatize set theory, von Neumann[17]
emphasizes an arbitrary element:

> Naturally, it can never be shown in this way that the
> antinomies are actually excluded; and much arbitrariness always
> attaches to the axioms. (There is, to be sure, a measure of
> justification of these axioms in that they turn into evident
> propositions of naive set theory, when the axiomatically meaning-
> less word 'set' is taken in Cantor's sense. But what is deleted
> from naive set theory – and to avoid the antinomies it is
> essential to make some deletion – is absolutely arbitrary.)

In the extreme cases, the proponents of the misunderstanding
theory propose to uncover flaws in seemingly correct arguments,
while the bankruptcy theorists find our basic intuition proven to be
contradictory and seek to reconstruct or salvage what they can, by
ad hoc devices if necessary. The basic intuitive concept is often called
naive set theory and identified with the belief in an absolute comprehension principle according to which any property defines a set.
That some notion like this was actually seriously developed by
Frege was a historical accident often advanced as evidence that we
do have such a contradictory intuition. The principle, if correct, in
fact appears to be the sort of thing which belongs to the domain of
logic. Hence, it is much easier to understand Frege's enthusiasm
over the thesis of reducibility of mathematics than that of his
followers. Viewed in the light of Cantor's development of set theory,
however, it is not at all clear that we do have such a contradictory
intuition. It seems more appropriate to say that we have an inexact
intuition which leads to the iterative conception as we notice the
paradoxes and the flaws in them. It is, therefore, debatable whether
we have such an intuition to begin with. But perhaps this could
easily degenerate into a terminological debate.

Now, a stronger assertion is that the inconsistent concept is the
only intuition of set we have. Hence, once the concept is seen to be
wrong, we are left with nothing but the task of reconstruction as

described in the above quotation from Zermelo. Taken literally, Zermelo's two constraints of not too narrow and not too broad are rather weak and leave room for much arbitrariness in that many mutually incompatible set theories are possible solutions. Moreover, there is implicitly an additional arbitrariness in deciding what results are to be taken as data for the reconstruction since the notion of 'valuable' (perhaps also implying 'reliable') is clearly ambiguous. Assuming that we have a good idea what the data are, the task as described sounds much like a combinatorial puzzle which in principle admits of diverse solutions. Even in the empirical sciences, such a situation does not satisfy the intellect. For example, the eightfold way theory of elementary particles has such a flavor but most people look for either a refutation of the theory or more basic principles from which the theory can be deduced. It will be said that, if in fact we do not have good intuitions about sets, then our wish for a stable solution of the paradoxes is futile. And it is not hard to see why the 'tough-minded' position of crying bankruptcy has a certain appeal: it gives the impression of greater 'clarity,' a defiance of tradition, and independence from the slippery matter of intuition.

But the fact is we do arrive at a fairly stable iterative concept of set, whether or not we agree that this is the only original intuitive notion of set to begin with. And this concept was also implicit in the works of Zermelo and von Neumann who in the quoted contexts speak as bankruptcists, but used their good intuitions about sets in setting up their axiom systems. In any event, even if we agree that our intuition did once lead to contradictions, that fact does not justify the view that we run a high risk of self-contradiction whenever we use our intuition. The striking fact is that people do set theory by extensive appeals to their intuition and there is a practically universal agreement on the correctness or incorrectness of the results thus obtained, as results about sets. The iterative concept of set is an *intuitive* concept and *this* intuitive concept has led to no contradictions.

This is not to say that we have made the iterative concept fully exact and explicit: there remain problems about the indefiniteness of the concept of definite property and one-one correspondence, the range of ordinals we can envisage, the limitations of the axiomatic method. It is not even denied that, within this framework, there is room to experiment with new axioms and be open-minded as to the choice between alternatives. But the historical and conceptual matters sketched so far seem to discredit the bankruptcy view according to which, even today, the fundamental problem of the foundations of set theory remains the solution of the antinomies.

There is a related distinction between formalists and realists (or objectivists). As these positions get further refined, there is a certain convergence of views on matters regarding the correctness of results, even though there is a difference in choosing different problems to work on, for example, a preference by formalists for constructible sets and relative consistency results over speculations on and derivations from very large cardinals. Another difference is in the matter of working habits, so that one might be an avowed realist but think mainly formalistically, while an avowed formalist may use intuitions very efficiently in doing set theory and yet claim that set theory has only a formalistic model. In any case, any serious formalistic position does accept that we have perfectly reliable intuitions with regard to integers and some would claim intuitionistic reasoning as mostly evident. In other words, a formalist position on sets is given more content by contrasting set theory with other (usually more restricted) areas which do have more than a formal subject matter. One also thinks of degrees of reliability. The objectivistic position is a modification of realism with the goal of avoiding a number of extraneous difficulties with mathematical objects.

3 OBJECTIVISM AND FORMALISM IN SET THEORY

Different philosophical positions may be reached either by using the same data or by using different data. With the same data, the disagreement may often be apparent rather than real. More (relevant) data ought to be an advantage. It is not always easy to determine what is acceptable as data. For example, working informally with *ZF* is easier than with *NF*;[18] with *ZF*, while one pursues the argument without regard to formalization, the end results usually come out all right and can, if one wishes, be made into formal proofs from the axioms. This is at least in part due to our ability to think in terms of the intuitive models rather than the formal axioms. One might expect that the finite axiomatization of *NF* would yield fairly directly a contradiction, but the enumeration of all objects turns out to use an unstratified formula. Also, the ability to work with, e.g., a set which is a standard model of *ZF*, an assumption not formally provable in *ZF*, not only yields correct results but facilitates the flow of our arguments. Another point is the convergence of theories which at one stage were regarded as based on fundamentally different ideas.

For this reason, it cannot be said that our belief in the superiority of one set theory is merely a result of sociological factors such as familiarity, conformity, and respect for authority. It seems to be unquestionable that we have come to accept axioms of extensionality, replacement, choice, and foundation. Perhaps more doubtful is the acceptance that the hypothesis of constructibility is false and that we suspend judgment on the truth or falsity of the hypothesis of measurable cardinals. Sometimes we accept an axiom once stated, sometimes it takes a fairly long time before an axiom is accepted (e.g. the axiom of choice), but at the end we reach an agreement. We do not have two camps of comparable force such that one accepts an axiom, the other rejects it. The agreement also persists in time, i.e. the community does not oscillate from one day to the next. There is also a pretty good agreement on when to suspend judgment. By empirical induction we expect similar agreement in the future, and similar persistence.

It is often not easy to give precise reasons why a certain axiom is accepted or rejected. And also, what is accepted need not always be reflected faithfully in a formal (statement of an) axiom. Hence, the possibility of refinement and modification is not excluded. And the search for more articulate explanations of these empirical facts is of philosophical interest. But it does not follow that unless clear reasons can be given, these surprising phenomena of agreement and coherence must be considered illusions. Here we tread on a thin line between passive acceptance of the fashion and capricious irreverence.

It appears that if mathematics deals with objects, then every mathematical proposition is true or false. There is a natural tendency to think of objects and models. On the other hand, we may wish to say that what is more basic is the successor or the membership relation and that they have certain properties. This does not confine us to any fixed formal systems. In the first place, the rule of induction, for example, is usually taken in an informal way or, in other words (what is really the same thing), taken as a second order statement. As is well known, we then have again the standard model. This is probably one way of upholding objectivism without relying on objects. In the second place, it is not implied that we know all the properties in advance. It is not excluded that we may in the process of studying the subject further come upon and accept new axioms. Perhaps this does leave room for the possibility that there is some yet undiscovered limitation which will show that, for example, the continuum hypothesis is undecidable in a certain stronger sense. The limiting case would be that there are certain absolutely undecidable propositions in set theory. But nobody knows how to work with the concept of absolute undecidability.

A very different position would be: since the continuum hypothesis is undecidable in *ZF*, *therefore*, the question of its truth loses meaning. In other words, axioms and theorems are true, but undecidable propositions can neither be true nor be false. Let us refer to this mixed position as *M*. A more radical and perhaps more consistent position says that it makes no sense to speak of propositions of set theory (or, according to another extreme viewpoint, any mathematical propositions) as having a truth value (or that they are not really propositions), axioms and hypotheses being in the same boat. This radical thesis depends either on a recommendation to use the word 'true' in a special way or on the contention that we have no reasonable intuitive concept of set at all. We shall not delay over it but confine our attention to the less radical mixed position *M*.

It is not easy to understand the position *M* in any coherent way. The axioms can only be true on account of an interpretation of the concepts involved. In order that the interpretation withhold judgment on undecidable propositions, the axioms would have to capture fully the 'interpretation.' This means, among other things, that we must not confine ourselves to interpretations in the ordinary sense of two-valued models because in such models every proposition is either true or false. Of course, with the usual axioms of number theory and set theory, we do believe that they do not capture completely our intended interpretations of the central concepts.

The historical origin of this curious position *M* is somewhat complicated. The desire to avoid occult qualities and operate with concrete material as much as possible leads to a delight in formal systems as syntactical objects. Perhaps a transfer of the dubious verifiability theory of meaning is made so that verifiability and falsifiability of propositions of set theory are identified with provability and refutability in a formal system. Apart from other difficulties with general verifiability theory, this viewpoint has its own problems: the limitations of formalization, and the unexplained source of the intrinsic meaningfulness of the axioms and theorems of a formal system.

A different line of defending this mixed position is to argue that propositions of set theory have no independent meaning but only derive their meaning from a superstructure, perhaps useful as a summary or for the economy of thought, which is not based on direct intuitions but on how efficiently one can get back ordinary mathematics from it. From this point of view, there is quite a bit of arbitrariness in our choice of formal systems of set theory, and if a system is adequate for ordinary mathematics, the meaning of the axioms is derived from its consequences in more meaningful areas as a sort of gift. Theorems of set theory which are derivable in the formal system and stay in the superstructure get in turn their meaning from the axioms. Hence, undecidable propositions of set theory cannot have meaning since the only possible source of meaning for them (viz. provability or refutability) is barred.

This viewpoint cannot account for the relatively stable iterative concept of set and makes the question of truth of the propositions of set theory quite thoroughly a relative matter, depending on which formal system one chooses to use. For example, the axiom of choice, the nonexistence of a universal set or a complement set of every set, the existence of any subset of ω definable only by nonstratified formulas are each true in *ZF* but false in *NF*. Also, the uninhibited comparative study of different systems becomes somewhat of a mystery unless we have an intuitive set theory which we can use with no conscious regard toward formalization.

A favorite example against the pragmatic view that we accept an axiom because of its elegance (simplicity) and power (usefulness) is the constructibility hypothesis. It should be accepted according to the pragmatic view but is not generally accepted as true. Indeed, it is likely to be false according to the iterative concept of set. Basically, it is felt that the pragmatic view leaves out the criterion of intuitive plausibility. The constructibility hypothesis is not plausible in itself and, moreover, many of its consequences are not plausible. For example, it implies the existence of a definable well-ordering of the real numbers and fairly simple uncountable sets without perfect subsets; and these consequences are dubious – they have been said to be contrary to the intuition of ordinary mathematics. It implies a strange pattern of reduction theorems with regard to projective sets.[19] It is not a conceptually pure proposition because it allows ordinal numbers definable only by impredicative definitions or not definable at all, but proceeds to reject all further uses of impredicative definitions. The central argument is, perhaps, that by intention we view sets as arbitrary multiplicities regardless of how or if they can be defined. Hence, it is extremely unlikely that constructible sets, which are essentially the ordinal numbers only, give us all arbitrary sets.

Given this initial implausibility, one may be inclined to view with favor certain propositions which contradict the constructibility hypothesis. In particular, the existence of measurable cardinals is one such proposition, and it implies that there are only countably many constructible sets of integers. On account of the prior belief that the constructibility hypothesis is highly restrictive, this conclusion is seen as further evidence that it is false and as evidence that the measurable cardinal hypothesis has plausibility.

It has been suggested that possibly all sets are ordinal definable because we may have so many ordinal numbers that the collection turns out to be sufficiently rich. When this argument is applied to defend the constructibility hypothesis, we have a further difficulty in that higher ordinals give no more lower sets. For example, all constructible sets of integers are obtained at stage ω_1 and no large cardinals will change the situation. Here, one would perhaps wish to say that there are a lot of countable ordinals. If there are actually enough countable ordinals to make it true that all sets of integers are constructible, then, of course, the continuum hypothesis would also be true. On the other hand, there are familiar ways of foiling the constructibility axiom while retaining the continuum hypothesis. This is entirely in line with our belief, further substantiated by, though probably not completely dependent upon, the truth of the continuum hypothesis for constructible sets, that we are, relative to our present knowledge, more ready to deny the constructibility hypothesis than the continuum hypothesis.

There are different alternatives to the strong proposition that undecidability in *ZF* implies meaninglessness, or the related proposition that the *ZF* axioms constitute an 'implicit definition' of the concept of set. One alternative is to say that we can never know enough to conclude definitely whether the continuum hypothesis (or the constructibility hypothesis) is true or false. This position would permit our extension of *ZF* to include inaccessible and Mahlo numbers but exclude the possibility of finding clear axioms to decide the continuum hypothesis. A somewhat different alternative would be to say that at least ideas which we have today such as large cardinals cannot possibly lead to a decision on the continuum hypothesis. The position hardest to refute is perhaps that we have simply to withhold judgment: admittedly, as time goes on, we can discover new facts about sets, we can decide more propositions; but, for all we know, we may never be able to decide the continuum hypothesis. One feels uncomfortable if this is put forward as an empirical prediction. Otherwise we would like to see some general arguments. For example, taking into account the diverse possible ways in which languages can grow, we may feel that there are potentially uncountably many questions we can ask about sets. But, certainly we cannot answer uncountably many questions. Hence, why should the continuum hypothesis not be among the unanswerable ones? This can be answered by pointing out that even if we cannot answer all questions, we may be able to answer any question which is singled out as an object of special attention.

Since the continuum problem is to determine the number of sets of integers, it seems reasonable to expect that, barring surprising coincidence, we can only settle the question after we have determined what objects are to be numbered (what sets of integers are allowed) and on the basis of what one-one correspondences (compare Gödel, p. 266). But then we seem to be in a difficulty since thus far the determinations we can specify by precise axioms would tend to contradict the intended arbitrary character of sets and one-one correspondences. For example, this is the situation with the notion of constructible sets: we do not regard the continuum hypothesis as shown to be true because it follows from the constructibility hypothesis.

The general limitations of language and formal systems might also suggest that no plausible axiomatization of set theory is likely to be sufficiently refined to determine the exact size of the continuum. It may be the case, for example, that no plausible axioms of set theory will yield the continuum hypothesis, or determine a different specific cardinality for the continuum. But since we have no way of surveying all correct axioms of set theory, there is little likelihood that such a proposition will be established directly rather than approximated by scattered negative results, such as $2^\aleph \neq \aleph_1$, $2^\aleph \neq \aleph_4$, etc.

Reasons for believing the continuum hypothesis to be false have been put forward, and are regarded widely as unclear. If one believes the negation of the continuum hypothesis, then, of course, no formal system which includes only true axioms and is consistent with the continuum hypothesis can decide it. This had been used by Gödel as a reason for believing the continuum hypothesis undecidable in ZF, before P. J. Cohen established the fact.[20] According to Gödel (p. 267), the continuum hypothesis has implausible consequences. For example, there are results which give uncountable sets which intuitively seem to contain very few members or are highly scattered (e.g. uncountable sets which are meager on every perfect set). But the continuum hypothesis implies that these sets are of the same size as the continuum. The uneasiness about such evidence is based on the feeling that most people do not have a well-developed intuition of large and small with regard to infinite sets apart from the actual development of set theory. On the other hand, it cannot be excluded that someone might have such intimate knowledge so that, for example, he can separate out the errors coming from using the preset-theoretical intuitive concept of largeness. With regard to the matter of intuition, Gödel notes a current fashion against the appeal to intuition and a consequent lack of practice in the conscious use of intuitions. He points out that intuition does not at all mean what first comes to mind but can and should be cultivated.

Some set theorist states that if $2^\omega = \omega_1$, then there must be a surprisingly delicate balance between the reals and the countable ordinals. But such a remark would be more forceful if it were used against $2^\omega = \omega_{17}$ say. As it is, one might say that, for all we know, 2^ω might be ω_2, or the first inaccessible number, or real-valued measurable, and that ω_1 is, for all we know, about as reasonable a candidate as any of these.

We do not argue for any strong sharp conclusions but rather try to apply what might be called the dialogue method to determine the limitations of one-sided views. For example, we are not able to establish in any clear sense the thesis that the set-theoretical concepts and theorems describe some well-determined reality, in which Cantor's conjecture must be either true or false. Yet the somewhat indeterminate meanings of the primitive terms of set theory as explained in the iterative notion are accepted as sound. According to Gödel (p. 272): 'The mere psychological fact of the existence of an intuition which is sufficiently clear to produce the axioms of set theory and an open series of extensions of them suffices to give meaning to the question of the truth or falsity of propositions like Cantor's continuum hypothesis.' By the phrase 'give meaning to the question,' Gödel means that there is a good chance of finding a unique answer to the question which will be accepted by all or most of those who are acquainted with the question.

The attraction of the dialogue method is perhaps due at least in part to the fact that what is most interesting in philosophy is not general conclusions but the meaning and limitation of these. Hence, we arrive at the content of these general statements by dialogues. For example, the fact that we have no inconsistency may be due to our limited range of activity relative to all formally possible proofs, and, in addition, our tendency to give proofs which can be interpreted in different frameworks.

It is more natural, certainly for most mathematicians, to deal with objects and models rather than formulas and formal systems. One might wish to claim this is just a shorthand way of doing things even though set theory is a formal game based on analogy and hasty generalizations. The central weakness of this position is of course its apparent inability to explain how the purely formal set theory can hang together so well.

It has been claimed that we have an informal consistency proof of set theory based on considerations about formulas. The point can be illustrated by thinking about the second order arithmetic. Let us try to find directly a countable model for the formal system. We do not have to worry about the fixed sets defined by conditions involving only integers. Now we consider the countably many formulas which contain variables over sets. For each statement $m \in x$ (i.e. $m \in \hat{m}\phi_n m$), we may attempt to try out the two possibilities of being true and being false, adding more set terms to satisfy the impredicatives in ϕ_n or $\neg \phi_n$. In this way, we would arrive at an intricate graph tree with countably many nodes. For each numeral m and each set term t, we have a formula $m \in t$ (a node) and two branches according as it is taken to be true or false. The truth and falsity of these countably many atomic formulas interact in a complicated way. The problem of consistency is to have a consistent selection of truth values for these atomic formulas, i.e. each formula gets a unique truth value so that all the defining conditions are satisfied.

Viewed in this way, we do not seem to have any good intuition that there must be such a model. In fact, we would find it very surprising if the combinatorial facts resulting from such a formalist outlook on the axioms come out right. In any case, it seems unreasonable to use such a picture with such apparently uncertain outcomes as a means of defending the formalist position.

Alternatively we may follow Gentzen and attempt to prove by transfinite induction that no proof can give a contradiction. In general, whether a formula $n \in t$ is true depends on whether certain other atomic formulas are true or false. If we could obtain an ordering of the degrees of impredicativities, we would be able to get the induction going. But the circular element in the impredicative definitions seems to suggest that we can only get such an ordering in some artificial way, perhaps by assuming what we wish to prove. In fact, it seems that this type of consideration, rather than increasing our belief in the formalist position, has the tendency of suggesting that the platonic picture is the only foothold, vague as it is, we can fall back on.

4 NEW AXIOMS AND CRITERIA OF ACCEPTABILITY

Consider first the conditions for accepting a hypothesis in set theory (axiom of choice, hypothesis of measurable cardinals, or some suitably restricted hypothesis of determinacy) as true. Two basic criteria are intrinsic necessity and pragmatic success. The former is related to but perhaps sharper than intuitive plausibility. The latter has various ramifications. One condition is to produce correct lower-order consequences, known (confirmation) and unknown (prediction), for example, about sets of reals, reals, and integers. Another condition is to supply powerful methods of solving problems and even methods which unify diverse results and go beyond them. It is also desirable that the hypothesis be easy to state and to understand. Briefly, we may speak of confirmation, prediction, power, unification (and therefore 'explanation'), and simplicity. The elements of power and unification also contain the component of elegance. Of course, these conditions are neither necessary nor sufficient, since the complicated notion of intrinsic necessity has to dominate and since we may be willing to accept as true hypotheses satisfying only some of these conditions. Of course, there is nothing like a set of quantitative measures by which we can calculate how well each hypothesis fares according to these criteria.

One might wish to view pragmatic success as merely an intermediate criterion for screening candidates for new axioms and require that these candidates eventually pass the test of intrinsic necessity. But there is then the question how invariant the notion of intrinsic necessity is. The iterative concept is admittedly not perfectly clear. Some new axioms may be seen as rendering more exact what we intend, while others may extend or modify our notion in some natural way. If intrinsic necessity is the only way to qualify a hypothesis as an axiom, then there would seem to be no need of comparing set theory with physics. But if pragmatic success can also make a proposition true, one might wonder whether the meaning of the word 'true' is not stretched. To reply to this, we seem to be in a position to say that if pragmatic success is sufficient to make physical hypotheses true, why not also hypotheses in set theory?

There appears to be a sharp contrast between arbitrarily choosing to call a hypothesis true and axioms being forced upon us. Looking backwards, it seems fair to say that axioms which we have accepted so far were forced on us. Therefore, it seems reasonable to expect that we will only accept a hypothesis as true in the future, if the evidence forces it upon us. We do not have a clear idea how such forcing will take place. Moreover, our axioms now all seem to be justified on intrinsic necessity alone. This again suggests that we might choose to wait till existing and future hypotheses achieve the state of intrinsic necessity relative to our understanding before accepting any of them as axioms.

The same data can be interpreted in opposite ways. It has been claimed that the axiom of choice was elevated to the status of an axiom only because of repeated exposure and the psychological reluctance to tolerate central undecidable propositions. One would then have to say that the conceptual justification is no more than an ad hoc rationalization. In the same vein, objects may be regarded as convenient metaphors for discussing formulas and properties.

In any case, it does not seem reasonable to call our choice 'arbitrary,' since we feel we have good reasons for making certain choices and there is a surprising degree of agreement among people who have thought about alternative hypotheses. The two serious positions would seem to be: (1) by accepting a new axiom, we change or extend our concept of set (change the meaning of the word 'set'), and the meaning and truth of the new axiom is determined by the changed concept; (2) we have all along the same concept of set and we accept the new axiom because we have discovered new facts about sets. There is a strong temptation to say that there is no genuine disagreement, because there is no sharp distinction between changing knowledge by changing meaning and changing knowledge by acquiring new information.

Nobody denies that our intuition of set develops. One should like to be open-minded and allow for the possibility of revoking or modifying our axioms if, for example, contradictions arise or the content of some axiom is rendered more precise by new findings. We cannot, however, disregard our experience so far which seems to indicate a measure of stability leaving little room for difficult choices. We may or may not be successful in explaining satisfactorily the apparently surprising degree of coherence and agreement in set theory, but it is important that we do not belittle this fact on the basis of preconceived philosophical ideas.

Intrinsic necessity depends on the concept of iterative model. In a general way, hypotheses which purport to enrich the content of power sets (say that of integers) or to introduce more ordinals conform to the intuitive model. We believe that the collection of all ordinals is very 'long' and each power set (of an infinite set) is very 'thick.' Hence, any axioms to such effects are in accordance with our intuitive concept. The difficulty is that in order to make specific assertions to increase the length or the thickness, we generally have to use propositions which imply other consequences as well. And then we can no longer justify all these propositions by appealing merely to our (maximum) iterative concept. In particular, there is no known positive principle that guides the search for new axioms to enrich power sets.

For example, consider the hypothesis that the cardinality of the continuum is real-valued measurable. This does deal with the power set of ω, and it decides the continuum hypothesis. But nobody is willing to take it as an axiom. It asserts a special relationship between cardinal numbers defined initially in different ways and is not the kind of proposition which one would be inclined to regard as directly justifiable on the basis of the intuitive iterative concept. Another example is the much more intensively studied axiom of determinacy (AD). This axiom AD does imply that there are a lot of real numbers (and comparatively few sets of real numbers). But, as it stands, AD embodies a generalization of DeMorgan's law with quantifiers (e.g. $\neg \forall x \, \exists y$ is equivalent to $\exists x \, \forall y \neg$) to the infinite case and asserts the existence of winning strategies for infinite games.

In its full generality, AD contradicts the axiom of choice. The attention is, therefore, mostly concentrated on restricted forms of AD. And according to the criterion of pragmatic success, the projective AD (say) performs very well indeed. It yields uniform and elegant proofs that all projective sets are Lebesgue measurable and have the Baire property, it yields pleasing new results on the reduction principles, it is easy to state and understand, etc. However, AD is not taken as an axiom in the sense that we can see directly from our intuitive concept that it or certain restricted forms of it are true. Rather it is generally viewed as an efficient hypothesis which yields elegant consequences and, in various restricted forms, may be derivable from more intuitive principles ('axioms of infinity' or large cardinal axioms) about the length of the collection of all ordinal numbers.

If we have somehow got hold of the 'real' power set of integers, CH should already enjoy a definite truth value even though we might not know what the value is. It is an empirical fact that we do not know how to enrich the power set directly by intuitively evident principles. Hence, the current search for new axioms (in particular, for the purpose of settling CH) centers around large cardinal axioms. Parallel to the imperfect information regarding the thickness of the power set of ω, our knowledge of the countable ordinals is also very incomplete. For example, the minimal α such that M_α is a model of ZF is a countable ordinal about which we have little to say without reference to the system ZF. Even if we look at ZF directly in an attempt to build a countable model, we are not clear whether and to what degree the circularity of assuming ZF to have a model can be avoided.

The fascination with axioms of infinity leads to the reaction: Why just this one jewel? This is undoubtedly connected with the impression that we can find axioms of infinity which mostly appear to be justifiable by an appeal to the inexact iterative concept of set. To begin with, it is commonly believed that the positive notion of continued iterations is sufficient to justify inaccessible numbers and Mahlo numbers. For example, the existence of (strong) inaccessible numbers means roughly just that the totality of sets obtainable by the procedures of set formation embodied in the axioms of ZF forms again a set. Hence, these same procedures are applicable to it to yield other new sets.[21] Since the iterative concept permits unlimited extensions, the new axioms are seen to be introduced without arbitrariness. Moreover, each of these axioms, under the assumption of its consistency, can be shown to yield new number-theoretic theorems. Hence, they can be defended both on the ground of intrinsic necessity and, to some extent, on the ground of pragmatic success.

Another method of justifying axioms of infinity is by way of the reflection principles. The iterative concept implies that the universe of all sets is very large. When we have expressed certain properties of the universe, we can already find sets which have these properties. In other words, the reflection principle generalizes the relation of inaccessible numbers to the axioms of *ZF*. It says that, any time we try to capture the universe from what we positively possess (or can express), we fail the task and the characterization is satisfied by certain (large) sets. Such principles have been applied to justify (to derive) the existence of the inaccessible and the Mahlo numbers, as well as almost all axioms of *ZF*.[22] They have also been applied to justify larger cardinals. But, for example, reflection principles of diverse forms which are strong enough to justify measurable cardinals (by way of 1-extendible numbers) no longer appear to be clearly implied by the iterative concept of set.

There used to be a confused belief that axioms of infinity cannot refute the constructibility hypothesis (and therefore even less the continuum hypothesis) since *L* contains by definition all ordinals. For example, if there are measurable cardinals, they must be in *L*. However, in *L* they do not satisfy the condition of being measurable. This is no defect of these cardinals, unless one were of the opinion that *L* is the true universe. As is well known, all kinds of strange phenomena appear in nonstandard models. However, there does remain a feeling that the property of being a measurable cardinal says more than just largeness, although it implies largeness. It is often felt that the existence of measurable cardinals is more problematic than the existence of inaccessible numbers, even if we disregard the fact that the former is much stronger than the latter. In fact, there are different ways of introducing large cardinals. For example, sometimes we introduce large cardinals by singling out properties of ω in relation to the smaller ordinals and say that there exist cardinals greater than ω which have such properties.

Yet large cardinal hypotheses do occupy a preferred place among the candidates for new axioms about sets because in the majority of cases we expect to be able to show that they just make explicit that the iterative model contains ranks R_α for certain large α. Many of these hypotheses are linearly ordered in the sense that, for two hypotheses H_1 and H_2 we can either (1) derive H_1 from H_2 in *ZF* and find (by assuming H_2) a rank R_α which satisfies *ZF* plus H_1 but does not satisfy H_2, or (2) obtain the same results with H_1 and H_2 interchanged.

There are a number of different aspects of mathematics. In two senses, set theory is not sufficiently abstract to serve as foundations of mathematics. It might be said that we have real numbers as a basic datum, and it is less central how reasoning about real numbers is formalized. In another direction, mathematics is interested in abstract structures such as groups and fields which, though involving concepts like that of set, are independent of the detailed structures of our set theory.

The modern mathematical theory of categories suggests two rather distinct problems. One is whether the self-applicability of categories is essential so that mathematically interesting proofs would not go through under an interpretation of categories as sets or classes (perhaps of different levels or types). The other is whether such interpretation, even if successful in 'substance,' would not be too artificial as a codification of a type of natural mathematical practice.

5 COMPARISONS WITH GEOMETRY AND PHYSICS

Set theory has been compared to geometry and to physics. There are different aspects with regard to which the comparison is made: objects of these disciplines (ontology), sources of our knowledge (epistemology), propositions (axioms or hypotheses) and their truth or acceptability (methodology).

The comparison between Euclid's fifth postulate and the continuum hypothesis is far fetched. Nobody proposed to call *CH* an axiom. There is a feeling that not only is the parallel postulate not evident, but the other postulates are also assumptions (together making up an implicit definition) of which we do not have sharp enough intuition to give justifications. The independence of *CH*, on the other hand, is not accompanied by doubts about the acceptability of the axioms of *ZF*. There is a sense of completeness of geometry with the parallel postulate or its alternatives either as first order theory or as second order theory (with completion coming from the different domain of sets). Hence, even if one takes the position that other postulates are evident or necessary, there is less reason to look for new axioms which would decide the parallel postulate.

Both the parallel postulate and its negation are extensions of 'absolute geometry' (determined by the remaining axioms of geometry) in the weak sense (in the sense of translatability or relative interpretability) (see Gödel, pp. 270–1). This is equally true of *CH* at least relative to *ZF*. But axioms of infinity yield extensions in a stronger sense and there is an asymmetry between an axiom of infinity and its negation. Roughly speaking, an axiom of infinity is stronger and more fruitful than its negation. Epistemologically, there is of course also the difference that geometry is more directly connected to the physical world than set theory.

It seems clear that admitting space as a pure form of intuition need not commit us to the a priori character of Euclidean geometry. For example, we are willing to admit as a consequence of our form of intuition that all physical objects have spatial extension, but then it may be argued that such a statement is analytic. The scepticism over the parallel postulate is often attributed to the difficulty of envisaging the infinite extension of the straight line. As is well known, there are various equivalent statements which do not mention the infinite extension and can be tested by experiments subject to inevitable inaccuracies in measuring continuous quantities. Two answers can be given to attempts to determine the truth of Euclidean geometry by empirical observations. One would be Poincaré's 'conventionalism.' The other would be to speak of a (local) 'space of intuition' which necessarily satisfies Euclidean geometry. It is true that this second reply is not refuted by experience. Only it is hard to give a convincing positive argument that we do have such exact intuitions, with or without the parallel postulate. Perhaps statements such as 'there are three noncollinear points' are evident and necessary.

It seems curious that while certain obvious things are proved in an elaborate manner, many other gaps are left wide open in Euclid. One explanation might be that the metaphorical definitions of points, lines, etc. are implicitly appealed to. On the other hand, there is a body of central theorems and proofs which are presumably proved quite exactly, and the foundations were accepted with a good deal of tolerance.

Another apparently puzzling feature is the relation of the fifth postulate to the rest. If one doubts the fifth postulate and it is shown to be independent, then the natural conclusion would seem to be that the fifth postulate is not a priori but the others are not affected. Instead, one began to question the necessity of all the postulates. This historical fact is perhaps a combination of two different factors. One is led to realize there is a difficulty in understanding the primitive concepts (or their definitions as originally given). Also, the existence of consistent alternatives shows that we do not have a 'complete' system that is necessary, and that, therefore, we probably do not have enough intuition to justify even parts of the system.

What is gained by comparing set theory with physics? One reason may be the suggestion of mathematical objects. In this comparison, set theory is quite different from arithmetic where, unlike evidence in physics, the general rules such as mathematical induction are perfectly evident.

It has been argued that just as physical objects are natural and necessary for organizing our physical experience, mathematical objects are natural and necessary for organizing our mathematical experience. Physical objects and not merely sensations are immediately given since they are not mere combinations of sensations and our thinking cannot create qualitatively new elements. Or perhaps what is given is not the physical objects but merely something different from sensations which generates the unity of one object out of the diversity of its many aspects. But then one is inclined to think of this something as contributed by the mind. The operation 'set of' is undoubtedly an instrument of synthesis. But there is always lurking somewhere the problem of infinity. To the extent the operation 'set of' suggests a synthesis, we seem to call up a picture of images which can possibly operate on infinite totalities and even permit infinite iterations. But the image of all subsets of a given infinite set (say ω) seems to involve an especially big jump. If somehow we have these subsets, we can apply the operation 'set of' to them. Yet to arrive at all subsets (say of ω), we seem to use something like an analogy.

Perhaps the fact that we can operate with such collections (e.g. in Cantor's diagonal argument) and even use them to prove theorems about natural numbers may be regarded as evidence. But such data are ambiguous and open to interpretations compatible with, e.g., predicative set theory. It seems reasonable to assert that not all data need be associated with certain things acting on our sense organs. But the only other possible source would seem to be either mind or a subtler form of objective reality which either is different from the physical world (e.g. remembering a platonic world) or is the same world but only acts on us in a different way (perhaps by an 'abstract perception').

It seems relatively easy to accept that axioms of set theory force themselves upon us as being true, or even that we feel we have an intuition that produces not only these axioms but an open series of extensions of them. It is perhaps reasonable to assume that all possible extensions will converge. But it seems a stronger assumption to say that the extensions will eventually yield in some sense a unique model so that the continuum hypothesis will be true or false in that model.

To say that mathematical objects exist objectively or even more that in some indeterminate sense we 'perceive' them seems to be stronger yet. Of course, if this is true, we are entitled to use the predicate calculus and reach the conclusion that every statement of set theory is meaningful. For our knowledge, we may still have the problem of recognizing whether a statement is true. This may be the reason why one could believe this strong position and yet not regard the criterion of pragmatic success as entirely superfluous.

The comparison with physics suggests that we look for evidence indirectly through consequences. While it is not necessary that we should be omniscient with regard to our intellectual creations, the difficulty in recognizing new axioms does appear more compatible with the view that mathematical objects exist independently of us. It would seem inevitable that applying this criterion would cost mathematical axioms much of their 'absolute certainty.' For it cannot be denied that success is a matter of degree and consequences (especially lower level consequences which are the more important for this criterion) do not at all determine the axioms in any unique manner. This does not necessarily obliterate the difference between physics and set theory (as with geometry), at least insofar as we do not at present envisage testing axioms of set theory by consequences in physics.

We may wish to compare the continuum hypothesis with a physical hypothesis which cannot be decided yet. But the analogy is certainly unclear since the latter is not only related to laws (axioms) of physics but depends on a good deal of empirical data. In fact, whatever undecidable propositions in physics may mean, they would seem to be of a radically different nature from those in formal mathematical systems.[23]

6 DIGRESSION ON UNBOUNDED QUANTIFICATIONS

The central problems of the iterative concept are: (1) the power set operation (i.e. what subsets are allowed); (2) ordinal numbers (i.e. what ordinals are allowed). Both involve an element of unlimited generality which cannot be rendered completely explicit. An explication of the concept of definite property in the principles of subset formation and replacement is relevant to approximations to this element of generality. In addition, there are principles for generating ordinals which depend on, besides iteration, also analogy and reflection.

Several people have questioned the legitimacy of using unbounded quantifiers (ranging over all sets) in defining new sets, even accepting the iterative interpretation of set theory. It has been suggested, among other things, that we are only justified in using all axioms of *ZF* if we combine it with the intuitionistic predicate calculus. This leads to an exact formal system and mathematical problems concerning the strength of such a system. The philosophical point at issue is, however, by no means equally clear.

If the totality of all sets is an unfinished totality, there is a problem in the use of unbounded quantifiers in the axiom of replacement and in the logical inferences. At any rate the logical notion of sentence is quite alien to Cantor's conception and there is a problem of comparing the sentential generating principle with the conceptual one (less correctly, the arithmetic one).

It does not seem unreasonable to regard at the same time ω as an unfinished totality and yet allow both quantifiers over all members of ω and the unrestricted law of excluded middle. Here it is clear that every member of ω is reachable from 0 by the successor function. Similarly, if we consider a theory of the second number class, we would be willing to do the same, even though we cannot explicitly give the operations for generating new countable ordinals. From this point of view, the current practice with the universe V of all sets seems entirely consistent.

It might be argued that we do look beyond ω_1 while V is a sort of absolute limit; ω_1 is a set but V is not a set. But the situation does not change, if we are only interested in countable ordinals and regard ω_1 as our universe. And the crucial point is, we do not anticipate incompatible alternative extensions of various approximations to ω_1 or V. Even though there are different ways of approximating to ω_1 and to V, we expect them to converge.

The genetic element is tied up with the distinction between viewing a class as one and as many. It is not excluded that we can talk about all sets and even form classes by conditions on all sets. Only in order that class be treated as one, we have to build it up from below. This imposes a requirement on its members (they must be 'given') but not on how one is to select sets from all given sets to form a new set. This is typically the situation with the replacement axiom: we make sure that all members of the new set are sets but choose them by arbitrary means, including the use of unbounded quantifiers. In particular, only a class as one can be a member of other classes or sets.

The concept of an unfinished or subjectively unfinishable totality is distinguishable from the idea that existence must agree with provable generation according to predetermined generating operations. Rather it permits the classical interpretation of quantifiers. We may also appeal to the reflection principles to argue that the unbounded quantifiers are not really unbounded. We are inclined to say that it is not problematic that we accept the classic logic with regard to propositions about all sets. There is no objection against viewing such propositions as determining definite properties.

If we adopt a constructive approach, then we do have a problem in allowing unlimited quantifiers to define other sets. Even then there remains the possibility of accepting the law of excluded middle. The difficulty is rather in establishing universal conclusions because we cannot survey all permissible operations.

Frege thinks of individuals, predicates, predicates of predicates, etc. He identifies sets with extensions of predicates and treats them as individuals (on the same level with individuals). This suggests immediately the idea of a type hierarchy of extensions, since extensions of predicates seem to be more closely related to predicates than to individuals. Alternatively, we may wish to think of all sets as objects (individuals) but distinguish them from extensions of predicates. In that case, we would be led to something like a finite type theory (perhaps ramified) based on the current set theory (a theory of individuals). But such a conception has little that is positive to say about how sets are to be generated.

7 EXTRACTING AXIOMS OF SET THEORY FROM CANTOR'S WRITINGS

As before, we discuss Cantor's views by reference to his collected works. It is relatively easy to be dissatisfied with Cantor's philosophical speculations on the transfinite. We can comfort ourselves that there is no need to take Cantor's flight into theology seriously, especially since we now possess more reasonable defenses of set theory.

> One proof proceeds from the concept of God and concludes
> first from the highest perfection of God's essence the possibility
> of creating a transfinitum ordinatum. It then goes on to conclude
> from His divinity and glory the necessity of the actual successful
> creation of the transfinitum. Another proof shows a posteriori
> that the assumption of a transfinitum in natura naturata yields
> a better (because more complete) explanation than the opposite
> hypothesis, of the phenomena especially of the organisms and
> the psychical facts (1886, p. 400).

> In one sense we may regard the integers as real insofar as they
> take up, by dint of definitions, a wholly determined place in our
> understanding, are well distinguished from all other ingredients
> of our thinking, but stand in definite relations to them and
> thereby modify the substance of our spirit in a definite way; I
> propose to call this kind of reality of the numbers their
> *intrasubjective* or *immanent reality*. The numbers can, however,
> also be ascribed reality insofar as they must be considered as an
> expression or picture of events and relations in the world outside
> our intellect, as further the different number classes I, II, III,
> etc. are representatives of cardinalities which actually appear in
> the physical and spiritual nature. I call this second kind of
> reality the *transsubjective* or *transient reality* of the integers. . . .

This coherence of both kinds of reality has its proper root in the *unity* of *all, in which we ourselves participate.* The allusion to this coherence serves here the purpose of deriving a consequence for mathematics which seems very important to me, namely that in developing ideas in it we *only* have to account for the *immanent* reality of its concepts, and are not at all obliged to test their *transient* reality (1883, pp. 181–2).

This last special property of mathematics is for Cantor the ground for calling mathematics 'free.'

In the case of Cantor, what is more interesting for philosophy is perhaps not so much his metaphysical speculations as the conceptual framework revealed by his mathematical practice.

Cantor uses multiplicity or manifold (Vielheit) as a primitive concept which corresponds to class in current usage. According to him there are two kinds of (definite) multiplicity: the absolutely infinite or inconsistent multiplicities (proper classes in current usage) and the consistent ones which are called sets. He then states explicitly three axioms (pp. 443–4).

C1 Two equivalent classes are either both sets or both proper classes. (One-one replacement).[24]

C2 Every subclass of a set is a set. (Subset formation).

C3 For any set of sets, the elements of these sets again form a set; in other words, the union of a set of sets is a set. (Union).

There are undoubtedly axioms which appear too obvious (and presumably too numerous) to Cantor to be stated explicitly. Such axioms can of course be added without violating Cantor's intention.

Like most mathematicians, Cantor uses implicitly the axiom of extensionality, for example, in establishing $P = Q$ for two point sets P and Q (but compare the introduction of $\equiv$ on p. 145). By the way, Dedekind mentions this axiom explicitly.[25]

C4 If two classes A and B have the same elements, then $A = B$ (in particular, two sets with the same extension are equal). (Extensionality).

A more interesting case is the power set axiom. In at least two connections, Cantor uses implicitly something like the power set axiom. In defining exponentiation of cardinals (pp. 287–9, 1895) Cantor considers the totality of functions from a set a into a set b and states explicitly that the totality is again a set. In particular, he shows that the cardinality of the linear continuum is $2^{\aleph_0}$. In presenting his diagonal argument to establish $2^\lambda > \lambda$, for any cardinal λ, he considers for every set a (in particular, the set of all real numbers) with cardinality λ, the set b of all functions $f(x)$ which takes only 0 and 1 as values with x ranging over all members of a (in particular, all reals $\geqslant 0$, $\leqslant 1$) (pp. 279–80, 1890–1). Here, b is the power set of a.

C5 For every set a, all its subsets form a set. (Power set).

Of course, Cantor never doubts there are infinite sets. He freely uses the sets of all integers, all algebraic numbers, all reals, etc. (pp. 115, 126, 143, etc.). More specifically, he states explicitly (p. 293, 1895) that the totality of all finite cardinals forms a set.

C6 There is a set containing 0, 1, 2, etc. (Infinity).

A basic indefiniteness in the above axioms is the notion of equivalence or one-one correspondence in C1: what language forms are permissible in specifying the one-one correspondence? The problem is illustrated by Zermelo's discussion[26] of definite properties (which are presumably contrasted with things like poetic images and theological characterizations). One expects Cantor to accept a broad range of one-one correspondences so that, for example, any formula in the second order language with set and class variables would be permissible; or alternatively one might choose to exclude bound class variables.

As far as I know, Cantor does not discuss well-founded sets. But I believe he operates under the assumption that all sets are well-founded.

It is well known that Cantor does not consider the axiom of choice and often uses it implicitly. For example, on p. 293 (1895), he gives a 'proof' that every infinite set contains a subset of cardinality $\aleph_0$ but is not aware that an appeal to the axiom of choice is needed.

Cantor is much interested in the well-ordering theorem in the form that (1) the totality of all cardinal numbers can be well-ordered (p. 280, 1890–1; p. 295, 1895) or that (2) all infinite cardinal numbers are alephs (p. 447, 1899). It is perhaps worth remarking that on p. 280 and p. 295 he speaks of the totality of all cardinals as a 'well-ordered set' in quotation marks. Undoubtedly the later distinction between sets and classes is a way of removing these quotation marks. Actually, on p. 280 Cantor claims to have proved (1) in his paper of 1883 (pp. 165–208). It seems that this erroneous assertion is based on the implicit assumption of (2) as evident or proven. On p. 285 (1895), Cantor also asserts the comparability of any two cardinal numbers with a promise to return to a proof of this.

On p. 447, Cantor attempts to prove (2) by arguing that the cardinality of every set is an aleph. Suppose V is a class with no aleph as its cardinal number. Then, Cantor argues, the well-ordered class *On* of all ordinals is projectable into the class V and there must exist a subclass of V which is equivalent to *On*. Hence, by C1 and

C2, V must be a proper class. The claim that labelling distinct members of V would use up all members of On appeals to some form of the axiom of choice.

From the above discussion, it would appear that what is currently called ZF or perhaps the second order theory of ZF would be a reasonable codification of Cantor's concept of set. This is under the assumption that we identify ordinal and cardinal numbers with sets in the now familiar manner and that one-one correspondences be specified more explicitly. Also, Zermelo's formulation of the axiom of choice and his use of it in proving the well-ordering theorem is a definite advance beyond Cantor.

It would seem a relatively simple matter to introduce the rank hierarchy and observe that every set has a rank. Cantor, however, seems to consider primarily only hierarchies of all numbers but not those of all sets. Mirimanoff seems to be the first to formulate explicitly the iterative concept with the rank hierarchy (1917).

8 THE HIERARCHIES OF CANTOR AND MIRIMANOFF

Cantor considers the well-ordered classes of all ordinals and all infinite cardinals (p. 444):

A 0, 1, 2, . . ., ω, . . .
B $\aleph_0, \aleph_1, \aleph_2, \ldots, \aleph_\omega, \ldots$.

In the current treatment, each member of A or B is a set and, in general, $\aleph_\alpha$ is identified with ω_α ($\aleph_0 = \omega$). The consideration of the exponentiation of infinite cardinals (p. 288) and the cardinality of the power set of an infinite set (p. 280) also suggests another well-ordered class:

C $\aleph_0, 2^{\aleph_0}, 2^{2^{\aleph_0}}, \ldots, (C_0 = \aleph_0, C_{\alpha+1} = 2^{C_\alpha}, C_\lambda =$ the union of all C_β, $\beta < \lambda$, λ a limit number).

The generalized continuum hypothesis says in effect that each term of B is identical with the corresponding term of C. The continuum hypothesis asserts that $2^{\aleph_0} = \aleph_1$. It is well known that Cantor introduced the continuum hypothesis and spent much effort trying to prove it. As early as 1878, Cantor asked the question as to how many classes would result if we divide all infinite point sets into different classes according to their cardinalities, and stated (p. 132): 'By an inductive procedure, the presentation of which we do not enter upon here, one can prove the theorem that the number of classes of linear point sets yielded by this principle of partition is a finite one and, in fact, it is *two*.' And then in 1883, Cantor asked for the cardinality of the continuum and stated (p. 192): 'I hope to be able to answer soon with a strict proof that the cardinality sought is none other than that of our *second number class*.' This is followed by a footnote (number 10, see p. 207) stating in effect that $2^{\aleph_1} = \aleph_2$. At the end of his most important paper (published 1879–84), he promised again (p. 244, 1884) that the continuum hypothesis 'will be proved in later sections.'

Cantor's continuum problem is a sharp formulation of the simple and intrinsically interesting question: how many points are there on a line or how many sets of integers are there? It is remarkable that Cantor is able not only to give a stable extension of the concept of (cardinal) number to infinite sets without arbitrariness but also to give the well-ordered class of all alephs as a basis for comparison. The class of alephs uses the class of ordinal numbers and Cantor's concept of number classes to get the next aleph after each given single aleph or sequence of alephs indexed by an ordinal. That all infinite cardinals are alephs (a form of the well-ordering theorem) depends on the axiom of choice. Hence, Cantor's great interest in the well-ordering theorem is easily understandable, seeing that it is needed to give a definite shape to the collection of all cardinal numbers. The very fundamental character of the continuum problem as well as the impressive achievements of Cantor in arriving at a sharp formulation of the problem also explain both Cantor's organization of his ideas and his obsession with the continuum hypothesis. A solution of the continuum problem would have been the crowning event of his whole intellectual development.

Cantor had obtained the Burali-Forti paradox at least two years before Burali-Forti's publication in 1897 and communicated it to Hilbert in 1896 (p. 470). He evidently did not find the phenomenon shocking and his distinction between sets and inconsistent multiplicities does not strike one as an ad hoc device but rather like a sharpening of an incomplete intuition quite in the spirit of his general approach. But his description of the distinction is admittedly vague and all too brief. 'For a multiplicity can be such that the assumption of a "being together" of *all* of its elements leads to a contradiction, so that it is impossible to conceive of the multiplicity as a unity, as "one finished thing". Such multiplicities I call *absolutely infinite* or *inconsistent multiplicities*' (p. 443). These letters to Dedekind were not published until 1932.

In 1917, Mirimanoff published two papers[27] in which ideas similar to Cantor's are discussed in great detail and pursued further.

With regard to ideas familiar today, the concept of well-founded sets is introduced along with the rank function and employed to show (all in M1) that every well-founded set has a rank (the iterative model). Furthermore, the representation of ordinals commonly associated with the name of von Neumann is proposed in M1 and developed more extensively in M2. It is perhaps of some historical interest that von Neumann, in his paper of 1925, did refer to M1 in connection with well-founded sets[28] but apparently was not aware of the anticipation of his definition of ordinals.

The fundamental problem of M1 is (p. 38): What are the necessary and sufficient conditions for a set of individuals to exist? The distinction between existent and nonexistent sets corresponds to that between sets and proper classes. For linguistic convenience, we shall translate Mirimanoff's terms into the familiar ones. As another example of different terminology, he speaks of 'ordinary sets' instead of 'well-founded classes (or sets).'

In M1, each class is associated with a membership tree that goes from the class to all of its members, and thence to all their members, etc. (p. 41). Each path in this tree is called a descent and a class is well founded if all the descents in its tree are finite (p. 42). The trees can only stop at indecomposable elements which are the noyaux (p. 43, nuclei, the urelements). In particular, the empty set is taken as an urelement and denoted by e. The well-founded sets are suggested by the paradox of sets which are not their own members. It is clear that the class of all well-founded sets is not a set (p. 43). This approach brings out a common feature of Russell's and Burali-Forti's paradoxes.

It is not assumed that we are only interested in well-founded sets, but rather a solution for the fundamental problem is only proposed for well-founded sets. Six axioms are stated in M1.

P1 Subset formation. Every subclass of a set is a set (p. 44. This is 'a property of sets which is far from being evident but which I regard as true, at least for the sets I consider in this work,' p. 43).

P2 A class equivalent to the class *On* of all ordinals is not a set (p. 45. By P1, any class containing a subclass equivalent to *On* is not a set).

P3 The urelements form a set which is regarded as given or known (p. 48).

P4 Power set. For every set a of well-founded sets, there is a set of all subsets of a (p. 49).

P5 Union. For every set a of well-founded sets, there is a set of all members of members of a (p. 49).

P6 One-one replacement. Given a set a and a one-one correspondence correlating each member of a with a well-founded set, there is a set of all the images of members of a (p. 49).

The Concept of Set

The concept of rank is introduced explicitly (p. 51): the rank of a well-founded set is the smallest ordinal number greater than the ranks of its members. The rank of an urelement (in particular, of e) is zero.

Two theorems are then proved (p. 51).

Th. 1 Every well-founded set has a rank. It is first observed that a set has a rank if all its members have ranks. This is proved by a lemma to the effect that every set of ordinal numbers has a rank. Since ordinals under the Cantor conception are not sets, the von Neumann ordinals are introduced to represent them and P6 is applied to obtain the lemma (p. 50). If now a well-founded set x did not have a determinate rank, then there is at least one member x_1 of x having the same property; similarly x_1 has at least a member x_2 not having a determinate rank, and so forth – an absurd result, seeing that the whole sequence $x, x_1, x_2, \ldots$ stops at an urelement whose rank is zero.

This elegant proof makes an implicit use of the countable axiom of choice and is familiar nowadays.

Th. 2 For every α, the collection R_α of all well-founded sets of rank α forms a set.

First, if the theorem is true for all $\alpha < \pi$, then it is also true for π. Thus let Σ be the union of R_α for $\alpha < \pi$. By P6 and P5, this union is a set. But R_π is a collection of subsets of Σ and is therefore a set by P4 and P1. But the class of all ordinals is well-ordered and the class of ordinals for which Th. 2 is false, if not empty, must have a least number.

The two theorems together yield the result: there is a relation $S(\alpha, y) \equiv y = R_\alpha$, and for all well-founded sets x, $\exists \alpha \; \exists y (S(\alpha, y) \land x \in y)$. Let $H = \hat{x}(\exists \alpha)(S(\alpha, y) \land x \in y)$.

The solution for the fundamental problem thus obtained in M1 is the following (pp. 51–2): a collection of well-founded sets is a set if and only if the ranks of its members are bounded above by an ordinal number.

Clearly if we assume the axiom of foundation (that all sets are well founded), we can delete from the above discussion the qualification of well-foundedness, and obtain the result that the universe is the same as the union of all R_α (briefly $V = H$) and therewith reach the iterative concept of set described in § 1.

Intuitively it seems very plausible that since we collect 'given' objects to form new sets, there should be enough ordinals to index the stages of this process of iterated expansion. The axiom of foundation sharpens the concept of iteration. Given the axiom, which says that every path in a membership tree leads back to an urelement in a finite number of steps, it becomes more plausible that

216

we can, beginning with the set of all urelements, reach each set by steps indexed by ordinal numbers. The possibility of deriving $V = H$ from the axiom of foundation of course shows that no strong new axiom can contradict the iterative concept without refuting some of the basic axioms commonly accepted. In this respect, $V = H$ is very different from the much stronger 'axiom' of constructibility.

Of course, the basic axioms for getting larger sets are replacement and power set. By definition, power set only increases the rank by 1, and replacement has also this 'local' character because every set of ordinal numbers has an upper bound which is again an ordinal number. Replacement itself assures that the indices of the members of the image set again form a set. A justification of the axiom would be that proper classes are so large that a one-one correspondence never gets from a set to a proper class.

Once we have $V = H$, it seems reasonable to strengthen Cantor's axiom C1 to say also that (C1∗) all proper classes are equivalent to V. Thus, given any class, either there is a bound on the ranks of all its members and then it is a set, or else the ranks are unbounded and then it forms a proper class C. If we use the members of C to count the members of V rank by rank, then we cannot stop at any R_α because we would then have a one-one correspondence between a proper class C and a set which is the union of $R_0, \ldots, R_\alpha$. To carry out this argument, we have to assume the global axiom of choice that the universe V can be well-ordered because the well-ordering of each R_α is not given explicitly by the local axiom of choice. Given $V = H$, this appears to be the natural generalization of the usual local axiom of choice by which each R_α can be well-ordered. The axiom C1∗ was first introduced by von Neumann (1925). The axiom of foundation and the rank model were rediscovered and treated more thoroughly by von Neumann (1925 and 1929) and also by Zermelo (1930).[29] A particularly nice formulation of the axiom of foundation would seem to be: if every subset of a class X belongs to X, then $X = V$.

In M1, the ordinal numbers, 1, 2, 3, etc. are represented by $\{e\}$, $\{e, \{e\}\}$, $\{e, \{e\}, \{e, \{e\}\}\}$, etc. These are obtained as follows. Let x be a well-ordered set, and let y be the set of all its segments, including the segment e. Replace these segments in y by the sets of the segments of these segments and apply an analogous transformation to the segments introduced in this manner, and so on (p. 45). A definition not appealing to given well-ordered sets is also given (p. 47): Definition of On: a set x represents an ordinal if: (1) x is a well-founded set based on the urelement e; (2) if y and z are two distinct elements of x, then $x \in y$ or $y \in x$ (connected); (3) $y \in x$, then $y \subseteq x$ (transitive).

If we adopt the axiom of foundation, this of course yields the currently employed definition of *On* which is usually regarded as an improvement over von Neumann's rediscovery of 1923.[30] Further properties of *On* are derived in M2. In the conclusion of M2, it is pointed out that *On* can be used in place of Cantor's ordinal numbers in dealing with well-ordered sets. 'I do not know whether this indirect method presents real advantages. In any case the classic theory of Cantor appears thus under a new aspect' (p. 217).

A totally new problem in the foundations of set theory is considered in M3, namely the nature of definite properties implicitly employed in stating the axioms of subset formation and replacement. The discussions are not nearly as conclusive as the extensional considerations in M1.[31]

Turning to the origins of Cantor's development of set theory we append some historical notes on a few anticipations and independent discoveries of some of Cantor's ideas in set theory. As is well known, Cantor began his mathematical career by works on the trigonometric series.[32] In trying to extend the uniqueness of representation in terms of these series to certain functions with infinitely many points of discontinuity, Cantor was faced with the problem of singling out suitable infinite sets of points on the line. This led to the notion of the derived set P' of a set P (viz. the set of limit points of P) which not only marked the beginning of Cantor's study of point set theory but paved the way for his construction of transfinite ordinal numbers later on.

In 1872, Cantor considered finite iterations of the operation of derived set and observed that there can be point sets P such that, for every n, $P^{(n)}$ is not empty and hence is infinite (p. 92). In 1880 (p. 145), Cantor introduced infinite iterations to ∞, $\infty + 1$, $n_0\infty^m + \ldots + n_m$, ∞^∞, etc. In particular, $P^{(\infty)}$ is, for example, identified with the intersection of P', $P^{(2)}$, etc. 'Here we see a dialectical generation of concepts, which always leads yet farther, and remains both free from every arbitrariness and necessary and logical in itself' (p. 148). This was followed in 1883 by the first extensive development of transfinite numbers. Cantor observed that further progress of his investigations would depend on an extension of the concept of number which nobody had attempted yet, and that without this extension of the concept of number:

It would be impossible for me to advance freely a single step in the theory of sets; in this circumstance a justification or, if necessary, an excuse, may be found for my introduction of apparently strange ideas in my considerations. These concern an extension or continuation of the sequence of integers into the infinite; however daring these may appear, I can nevertheless express not only the hope but the firm conviction that this extension will in time be regarded as thoroughly simple, proper, and natural. At the same time, I by no means conceal from myself the fact that with this enterprise I place myself in a certain opposition to widespread views on the mathematical infinite and to oft-defended opinions on the essence of number (p. 165).

In a paper of 1880,[33] P. du Bois-Reymond claimed priority on the concept of derived sets of infinite order. He considered a set D of intervals so distributed on the straight line that every interval contains some member of D as a part. Then he asserted: 'We are led to this kind of distribution of intervals, of which I have several examples, when we seek for points of accumulation of order ∞, whose existence I indicated to Mr Cantor of Halle by letter years ago.' He also mentioned that he had introduced his notion of 'pentachic' before Cantor did his equivalent notion of 'everywhere dense.'

A more interesting anticipation was du Bois-Reymond's use of the diagonal method in his theory of growth[34] nearly twenty years before Cantor published in 1892 his famous diagonal proof of the theorem that every set has more subsets than elements. Consider increasing functions of one real variable x, for $x > 0$. For two such functions $f(x)$ and $g(x)$, du Bois-Reymond stipulated that $f < g$ if $f(x)/g(x)$ tends to 0 as x increases indefinitely. The following theorem was proved. Let $f_1, f_2, \ldots$ be any sequence of increasing functions such that $f_1 < f_2 < f_3, \ldots$, then there exists an increasing function f such that $f_n < f$, for all n. He defined a new sequence $g_1, g_2, \ldots$ such that $g_1 = f_1$, and $g_{n+1}(x) > g_n(x)$, for all x. Thus, by hypothesis, there exists x_1 such that $f_2(x) > g_1(x)$, for $x > x_1$. Let $g_2(x) = f_2(x)$, for $x > x_1$; $g_2(x) = g_1(x) + 1$, for $x \leqslant x_1$. Similarly, let $g_{n+1}(x) = f_{n+1}(x)$, for $x > x_n$; $g_{n+1}(x) = g_n(x) + 1$, for $x \leqslant x_n$. The desired function f can then be defined: for every n, $f(n) = g_n(n)$ and $f(x) = g_{n+1}(x)$; for $n < x < n + 1$. This theorem is analogous to Cantor's theorem that every fundamental sequence of ordinal numbers defines a greater ordinal. An analog of the immediate successor would be to go from f to g such that $g(x) = x f(x)$.

NOTES

1 The reader who is not familiar with the technical concepts of set theory is referred to standard texts such as E. Kamke, *Theory of sets*, 1950 (original German editions 1928 and 1947), A. A. Fraenkel, *Abstract set theory*, 1953. For more specialized concepts and results, the reader may consult F. Hausdorff, *Set theory*, 1957 (from the 1937 edition in German), K. Gödel,

The Concept of Set

Consistency of the continuum hypothesis, 1940, P. Bernays, *Axiomatic set theory*, 1958, P. J. Cohen, *Set theory and the continuum hypothesis*, 1966.

2 G. Cantor, *Gesammelte Abhandlungen*, 1932. All references to Cantor are to this volume of his collected works.

Unterliegt es nämlich keinem Zweifel, dass wir die *veränderlichen* Grössen im Sinne des potentialen Unendlichen nicht missen können, so lässt sich daraus auch die Notwendigkeit des Aktual-Unendlichen folgendermassen beweisen: Damit eine solche veränderliche Grösse in einer mathematischen Betrachtung verwertbar sei, muss strenggenommen das 'Gebiet' ihrer Veränderlichkeit durch eine Definition vorher bekannt sein; dieses 'Gebiet' kann aber nicht selbst wieder etwas Veränderliches sein, da sonst jede feste Unterlage der Betrachtung fehlen würde; also ist dieses 'Gebiet' eine bestimmte aktualunendliche Wertmenge. So setzt jedes potentiale Unendliche, soll es streng mathematisch verwendar sein, ein Aktual-Unendliches voraus. Diese 'Gebiete der Veränderlichkeit' sind die eigentlichen Grundlagen der Analysis sowohl wie der Arithmetik und sie verdienen es daher in hohem Grade, selbst zum Gegenstand von Untersuchungen genommen zu werden, wie dies von mir in der 'Mengenlehre' (théorie des ensembles) geschehen ist (1886, pp. 410–11).

3 P. Bernays, 'Sur le platonisme,' *L'enseignement math.*, vol. 34, 1935, pp. 52–69. Reprinted in English translation in *Philosophy of mathematics*, ed. P. Benacerraf and H. Putnam, 1964; see pp. 275–6.

4 In very rough terms, we may directly justify the axiom AR, on the basis of the iterative concept, in the following manner.

In general, given any set y, we may consider the multitude of all stages $R_{\alpha(x)}$ where x is a member of y and $R_{\alpha(x)}$ is the first stage at which x appears. A reasonable principle for continuing the stages is to permit, for each given set y the collection or merging of all these stages $R_{\alpha(x)}$ into a new set. If, instead of $R_{\alpha(x)}$, we take any given set b_x, it is no less justifiable to collect or merge all the stages where these sets first appear, to get a new set. By this principle, if b_x appears at stage $R_{\beta(x)}$ then the result obtained by merging these stages, for all x belonging to y, contains the union of these sets b_x.

The minor additional procedure of forming the union of a set (i.e. merging the elements of a set) is conceptually a consequence of the intended process of iteration, since all members of members of a set a are given at earlier stages and therefore collected into a set b before the stage at which a emerges. A separate axiom for forming unions is often included in formal systems of set theory because the defining properties do not mirror faithfully the intended extensional interpretation. The absorption of this feature into the replacement axiom (as stated above) is meant to render it less conspicuous. An inessential feature of the form of AR as stated is to get, instead of the image of y directly, a set which contains it. This amounts to taking, instead of b_x itself, its corresponding stage $R_{\beta(x)}$ so that (the union of) the multitude of all the sets b_x, for x in y, is included in the set of all their corresponding stages $R_{\beta(x)}$. This serves the purpose of avoiding the somewhat inelegant situation of making the more basic axiom of comprehension a consequence of the replacement axiom.

It should perhaps be pointed out that these seven axioms *ESPFICR* are equivalent to other more commonly used sets of axioms taken as making up *ZF*. For a detailed proof, the reader may consult J. R. Shoenfield, *Mathematical logic*, 1967, pp. 240–3. The derivations making up the proof of equivalence go back at least to E. Zermelo (1930) and P. Bernays (1958); compare the references under notes 20 and 1.

5 More explicitly, I would like to add as a supplement, it is a familiar fact that once we have replacement from sets of ordinals to get new sets of ordinals and we permit a stage R_α for each given ordinal α, we can get full replacement. And it is easily seen that replacement for sets of ordinals (i.e. given $f(\alpha)$, $\alpha < \beta$, there is γ, $f(\alpha) < \gamma$, for all $\alpha < \beta$) follows from the interation of jumps (i.e. given f and β, there is γ^α, $f(0) < \gamma$, for all $\alpha < \beta$).

Gödel's explanation of the jump operation may also be viewed as a generalization of the way Cantor applies (in the development of his second number class) his second principle of generation according to which, if there is defined any definite succession of ordinal numbers of which there is no greatest, a new number is created which is defined as the next greater to them all (1883, p. 196).

6 Compare the discussions to follow soon (in particular, notes 10, 12, 13 below). It may be said that not only the famous 1895 definition in terms of a collection of objects into a whole, but even also the 1883 definition in terms of one and many suggest strongly the iterative concept.

7 Compare respectively their papers of 1917, 1925, 1930, 1935, 1947 mentioned in other notes to this chapter.

8 K. Gödel, 'What is Cantor's continuum problem?' *Am. math. monthly*, vol. 54, 1947, pp. 515–25. Reprinted with additions in the collection edited by Benacerraf and Putnam, pp. 258–73; see p. 262. References to this paper will be made in the text below.

9 K. Gödel, paper of 1944 in the collection by Benacerraf and Putnam, pp. 215–16.

10 In order to prevent any misinterpretation of this remark, Professor Gödel suggests adding the following. 'This observation by no means intends to deny the fact that *some* of the principles of logic have been *formulated* quite satisfactorily, in particular all those that are used in the application of logic to the sciences including mathematics as it has just been defined.'

11 'Unter einer "Menge" verstehen wir jede Zusammenfassung M von bestimmten wohlunterschieden Objekten m unserer anschauung oder unseres Denkens (welche die "Elemente" von M gennanten werden) zu einem Ganzen' (1895, p. 282).

12 Eine Mannigfaltigkeit (ein Inbegriff, eine Menge) von Elementen, die irgendwelcher Begriffssphäre angehören, nenne ich *wohldefiniert*, wenn auf Grund ihrer Definition und infolge des logischen Prinzips vom ausgeschlossenen Dritten es als *intern bestimmt* angesehen werden muss, *sowohl* ob irgendein derselben Begriffssphäre angehöriges Objekt zu der gedachten Mannigfaltigkeit als Element gehört oder nicht, *wie auch*, ob zwei zur Menge gehörige Objekte, trotz formaler Unterschiede in der Art des Gegebenseins einander gleich sind oder nicht. Im allgemeinen werden die betreffended Entscheidungen nicht mit den zu Gebote stehenden Methoden oder Fähigkeiten in Wirklichkeit sicher und genau ausführbar sein; darauf kommt es aber hier durchaus nicht an, sondern *allein* auf die *interne Determination*, welche in konkreten Fällen, wo es die Zwecke fordern, durch Vervollkommnung der Hilfsmittel zu einer *aktuellen* (*externen*) *Determination* auszubilden ist (p. 150).

13 'Unter einer "Mannigfaltigkeit" oder "Menge" verstehe ich nämlich allgemein jedes Viele, welches sich als Eines denken lässt, d. h. jeden Inbegriff bestimmter Elemente, welcher durch ein Gesetz zu einem Ganzen verbunden werden kann, . . .' (p. 204). The parenthetical explanations of sets in the

The Concept of Set

contexts of defining cardinality in 1884 (p. 387) and 1887 (p. 411) do not seem to add anything.

14 Cantor does consider point sets (sets of real numbers) and sets of integers, as well as functions of point sets. But in his general development one sees more a theory of transfinite numbers than a set theory. He quickly extracts cardinal and ordinal numbers from sets and devotes most of his attention to these infinite numbers. The impression is that he believes there is a great variety of objects so that no neat structure can be imposed on all sets above and beyond that imposed by such basic notions as cardinal and ordinal numbers.

For Cantor, cardinals and ordinals are not sets but general concepts or universals abstracted from sets of equal cardinality and isomorphic well-ordered sets. For example, the cardinality of a set x is what is common to all sets 'equivalent' to x (p. 141, 1879; p. 387, 1887; p. 283, 1895; p. 444, 1899). Two sets are equivalent if there is a one-one correspondence between them. Cantor does work freely with numbers as objects and forms sets of them. For example, the first infinite cardinal is that of the set of finite cardinals.

On the other hand, we certainly cannot identify a number with its extension and take it as a set in our universe of sets. For example, the extension of the universal 1 is as large as the universe of all objects (including all sets) since, for each x, $\{x\}$ is a set of cardinality 1. Since the universe of objects consists of sets and urelements and numbers are objects but not sets, Cantor seems to treat them as urelements. This creates some problem with regard to the iterative concept of set. How do we assign ranks to the numbers? A natural suggestion is to give all urelements the rank 0 and the rank of a set would, as in the current form, be determined inductively by the membership relation. But then R_0 which is a set would be too large and contain what Cantor calls an inconsistent manifold. One alternative would be distributing numbers into different ranks.

There is indeed a natural way of doing this, as has been carried out by Mirimanoff (1917), Zermelo (unpublished work of 1915, see P. Bernays, *J. symbolic logic*, vol. 6 (1941), p. 6), and von Neumann (1923). Each ordinal number is identified with a canonical set representing it: take the empty set as 0, $\alpha \cup \{\alpha\}$ as $\alpha + 1$, the limit ordinal as the set of representatives of all preceding ordinals. Cantor did not make this convenient identification. But it seems likely that Cantor thinks of an open domain of objects which are not sets, such as physical objects, experiences, universals, properties, and whatnot. Hence, he would not have examined the idea that they can all either be put into R_0 or be given other appropriate ranks in a natural way. However that may be, Cantor's development of set theory as a mathematical subject can be embodied in a framework of pure sets, once the identification of numbers with suitable sets is made.

It is perhaps natural to think of the urelements as forming a set. If, on the other hand, one assumes that there are as many sets (or numbers) as urelements, one might perhaps modify the iterative model by defining $R_a(a)$ relative to each set a of urelements such that $R_0(a) = a$ but $R_{a+1}(a)$ and $R_\lambda(a)$ are defined as above.

15 E. Zermelo, *Math. Annalen*, vol. 65, 1908, p. 261.

16 D. Mirimanoff, *L'enseignement math.*, vol. 19, 1917, p. 38.

17 J. von Neumann, *J. reine u. angew. Math.*, vol. 154, 1925, pp. 219–40; reprinted in *Collected works*, vol. 1, 1961 (see p. 37).

18 The system of W. V. Quine, *Am. math. monthly*, vol. 44, 1937, pp. 70–80.

19 Compare, e.g., D. A. Martin, *Bull. Am. Math. Soc.*, vol. 74, 1968, pp. 687–9.

20 See Gödel's 1947 paper, op. cit., and P. J. Cohen's book, op. cit., as well as his paper in *Proc. Nat. Acad. Sci. U.S.A.*, vol. 50, 1963, pp. 1143–8 and vol. 51, 1964, pp. 105–10.

21 See E. Zermelo, *Fund. math.*, vol. 16, 1930, pp. 29–47.

22 Compare A. Lévy, *Pacific jour. of math.*, vol. 10, 1960, pp. 223–38; and P. Bernays, *Essays in the foundations of mathematics*, 1961, pp. 1–49.

23 Gödel points out that the hypothesis of measurable cardinals may imply more interesting (positive in some yet to be analyzed sense) universal number-theoretical statements beyond propositions such as the ordinary consistency statements such as, for instance, the equality of p_n (the n-th prime number) with some easily computable function. Such consequences can be rendered probable by verifying large numbers of numerical instances. Hence, the difference with the hypothesis of the expanding universe is not as great as we may think at first.

24 Cantor does seem to apply implicitly the axiom of replacement to get ω_ω from ω, ω_1, . . . in his 1895 paper (p. 296).

25 R. Dedekind, *Was sind und was sollen die Zahlen?* 1888, § 2.

26 E. Zermelo, 1908, op. cit., § 1.4, § 1.6.

27 D. Mirimanoff, *L'enseignement math.*, vol. 19, 1917, pp. 37–52; pp. 207–17; vol. 21, 1920, pp. 29–52. These will be referred to respectively as M1, M2, M3.

28 J. von Neumann, *Collected works*, vol. 1, p. 46, footnote. Originally the papers appeared in *J. reine u. angew. Math.*, vol. 154, 1925, pp. 219–40.

29 See J. von Neumann, op. cit., and *J. reine u. angew. Math.*, vol. 160, 1929, pp. 227–41; also E. Zermelo, op. cit. in note 20.

30 J. von Neumann, *Acta Univ. Hung.*, *Section sci. math.*, vol. 1, 1923, pp. 199–208.

31 For related historical matters, compare also part II of the survey of Skolem's work in logic, T. Skolem, *Selected works in logic*, ed. J. E. Fenstad, 1970, pp. 35–40.

32 A long discussion of the relation of Cantor's work in this area to his pre-decessors' is contained in a series of papers by P. E. B. Jourdain, 'The development of the theory of transfinite numbers,' *Archiv der Math. und Phys.*, 1905–14.

33 *Math. Annalen*, vol. 16, 1880, pp. 115–28; see the end of the paper.

34 The relevant papers by P. du Bois-Reymond are: *J. reine u. angew. Math.*, vol. 70, 1869, pp. 10–45 (especially § 7), vol. 76, 1873, pp. 61–91 (especially the appendix); *Math. Annalen*, vol. 8, 1875, pp. 363–414, vol. 11, 1877, pp. 149–67.

VII

THEORY AND PRACTICE
IN MATHEMATICS

---

1 ACTIVITY AND FEASIBILITY

In learning elementary geometry, we are asked to prove the equality of the base angles of an isosceles triangle and observe it. The happy idea of constructing a new line from the top vertex to the base enables us to notice relations between the parts of the new diagram, thereby proving the conclusion. Or, alternatively, we can get the conclusion directly by observing the possibility of a rigid motion in space that interchanges the two base vertices.

We are asked to find the sum of the first 10,000 positive integers, and hit on the device of rearranging the numbers to look like:

$$1 \quad 2 \quad . \ . \ . \ 5000$$
$$10000 \quad 9999 \ . \ . \ . \ 5001.$$

We notice each of the 5000 columns add up to 10001.

When the service of a mathematician is requested by an engineer or a physicist, he reformulates the problem in a more idealized form, striking out all the factual details he judges to be irrelevant. This reformulation may require the joint efforts of a mathematician and a practitioner of the source subject, sometimes combined in one person. The new problem is more abstract and retains only a skeleton of the original problem. It is more perspicuous, at least to the properly trained mind which is often able to juggle it to get a method of solution either by standard techniques or by inventing new mathematics. Sometimes the application of the method to the specific problem may be tedious and, for example, calculating machines may have to be used to supply an actual solution.

In each case, there are interplays of schematic representations (diagrams, graphs, arrays of characters such as numerals, variables, schematic letters, logical and mathematical constants) and mental experimentations. We are interested in schemata or diagrams rather than pictures or portraits, because we are concerned not with all the factual details about them, but rather with their skeletons and structures, the 'formal facts' about them, the forms and patterns revealed by them. They are aids to our imagination in the process of reasoning, and, as such, essential to mathematics. This does not mean that we always have to draw the diagrams on paper or blackboards, nor that mathematics is a manipulation of symbols. It is not the physical production of the diagrams that distinguishes the mathematical activity, but the possibility of using them to assist our mental experimentations in the search for desired necessary connections.

The mind participates actively in seeing, e.g., an array of numbers, as paired off suitably to create a new uniformity. Thus this 'seeing as' enables us to take in at a glance the 5000 pairs of numbers which all have the same sum 10001. In this respect, the dots are not 'mere abbreviations' either, because they, or something else like them, are indispensable for grasping the array of numbers at one go; they embody the formal fact that we see the 5000 pairs as a whole string with a definite beginning, a definite end, and a definite way of continuation. In doing this calculation, one is likely to make (mental) experiments such as trying to look for suggestions from summing up a small number of integers. But calculation is not itself an experiment, since once the path is found, certainty intervenes.

To prove that for every prime p, there is a greater prime, the crucial construction is, of course, the function $p! + 1$. Here it is not natural to describe this function as obtained by the act of 'seeing as.' In general, the types of constructions are varied and heterogeneous. Once we have got $p! + 1$, we show that, for all q, $q < p$, q does not divide it by seeing $p!$ as qP, where P is the product of all $m < p$, except $m = q$.

Suppose we are to prove that in a right triangle, $c^2 = a^2 + b^2$, and are given the following diagram:

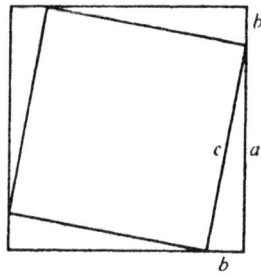

We see that the area of the big square is the same as the sum of the area of the small square and the area of the four right triangles. We write this out: $(a + b)^2 = c^2 + 4(\frac{1}{2}ab)$. Then, lo and behold, we get $c^2 = a^2 + b^2$. Here, we would say that for the purpose of proving the desired theorem, finding the above diagram is a much bigger step than the rest.

Or, to prove the same theorem, we may easily think of drawing a square on each side of the right triangle. Then we may get the vague idea that if we draw any three 'similar' figures on the sides, the situation would be the same. In particular, we may choose three right triangles which are reflections of ACD, BCD, ABC and see that since ABC = BCD + ACD, the area of the one on c is obviously the sum of the areas of the triangles on a and b.

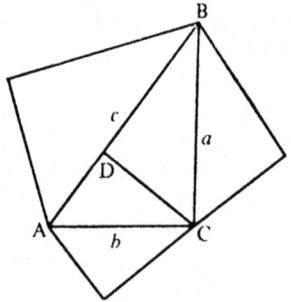

Hence, the same relation holds among the three squares, and $c^2 = a^2 + b^2$. Many people would find the proof not sufficiently conclusive as it stands, but it can be expanded into a more convincing form.

In searching for a solution, the activity is directed to a definite goal. One is easily led to ask how the mental experiments are chained together. The technical problem about methods of discovering solutions ('how to solve it') is not one for the philosophy of mathematics, although it is of pedagogic interest and central for the mechanical simulation of the mathematical activity. The nature of inferring and the compulsion of the logical 'must,' once the inference is made, is indeed the concern of philosophers. We accept, as a matter of fact, a sequence of symbols as an application of a certain rule, e.g. the modus ponens. Here we may easily get into the slippery ground of truth by convention, synthetic a priori, self-evidence. But an underlying foundation is the sociological fact that it is so accepted. And this sociological fact involves a variety of different factors: among them, the biological and the physiological, which are likely to be the ultimately decisive elements.

That Beethoven continued to compose good music after he had gone deaf is important for the study of the activity of composing music. Similarly, blind mathematicians are a phenomenon which should shed some light on the nature of the mathematical activity. It is very striking that most of us would find it difficult, if not impossible, to multiply three 7-digit numbers in our head. For one thing it is not easy to retain the question without the assistance of paper and pencil. If a child asks his blind father to help him to do such a sum, he would probably ask the child to serve as his pencil and paper to record the question and the intermediate results. If such assistance is denied a blind mathematician who wishes to do complicated numerical calculations, he would have to train himself to be a calculating prodigy.

That pencil and paper are indispensable to complicated calculations is certainly an important fact about the calculating activity. Most of us do not memorize a large number of telephone numbers but we remember, or rather know, different methods of finding them out. We do not learn the multiplication table to 100 times 100 but only to 9 times 9, or 12 times 12. In more advanced mathematical activities, most of the things which a mathematician knows have not come to him through a deliberate effort to memorize. Interconnections not only increase the number of things remembered but also their duration and their quality. Certain things are kept simultaneously in the head, and these enable one to spin out a great many things in sequence. The spinning power of a head with structured memories and dispositions determines the power to experiment mentally and the ability to do mathematics. When one says that mathematics is an activity of the pure intellect, it cannot be to deny that sense perceptions and memory form an integral part of it, but rather that an excellent eyesight or a good memory is not a distinguishing characteristic of better mathematical capabilities.

Some problem-solving is prompted by practical needs, others by analogy with existing problems. Not all mathematical activity is problem-solving. Esthetic needs and the desire to systematize and smooth out things lead to the development and improvement of mathematical theories. It is among such results that the thesis of the reducibility of mathematics to logic comes in. And it is along such a path that one is led to what might be called the librarian's definition of pure mathematics as the class of all conditional propositions in which all constants are logical constants.

'All A are B, all B are C; therefore, all A are C' is a diagram and traditional logic is a sort of mathematics, as ticktacktoe is a sort of board game. One may feel that, being so crude and inefficient, it hardly deserves the fair name of mathematics. However, family resemblance with mathematical logic seems to lend some color to it. Traditional logic is more a hindrance than a help to right reasoning that is quite adequately taken care of by our natural power. This is seen from the fact that the more purely rational an activity is, the less is it needed. Mathematics is least in need of it while election politics, judging from Susan Stebbing's studies, needs it most.

Mathematical logic has to a considerable extent suffered the same kind of misfortune. Logic is primarily interested in the analysis of a proof into as many distinct steps as possible, and not, like mathematics, in efficient methods of reasoning which can produce remote consequences in one swoop or unravel an involved entanglement. When, e.g., an elementary branch of it gets practical applications in making machines, it does this only, so to say, accidentally and against its own will. It is by leaving behind the basic concerns of logic and pursuing the subject as a simple sort of mathematics that the application is made.

The breaking up of a proof into a large number of small steps is desirable in so far as the set of all possible different small steps is in general less complex than the set of a smaller number of different bigger steps. This seems obvious, since the union of all small steps which make up one big step is simpler than the big step which contains the simple steps (possibly with some repetitions) plus a special mode of combination, and some small steps generally occur in a number of different big steps. There is, however, no equally obvious reason why such simplification should be desirable for the mathematical activity. In fact, since we are quite at home with the bigger steps, one is inclined to think that by multiplying the pieces in each proof, the breaking up only serves to slow us down and make it harder for us to take a proof in.

Few mathematicians have taken the trouble to learn the theory of quantifiers and they are none the worse for their ignorance. It sounds idle to rejoice over the accomplishment that when a logician has analyzed and reformulated a proof, even a machine can check it for correctness. Nobody, not even a logician, checks an elaborate mathematical proof in this manner, and so far machines have not been used to check proofs.

Thirty years ago it must have appeared that if man finds such a way of checking proofs tedious, machines would not do it any better either in speed or in accuracy. The appearance of large machines and the rapidity with which their speed and reliability have been improved, is one of the unexpected occurrences in history which yield consequences which are hard to predict.

There is, however, a distinct possibility that in this connection a basic application of logic will be found that is based on the essence rather than the accidents of logic: viz. to handle inferences as efficiently as calculations. For example, some preliminary work has already enabled a common machine to prove all theorems in *Principia* of quantification theory with equality in a few minutes.

Grammar is of little help in learning one's native language or cultivating elegant writing. And we do not worry about the theory of sound waves when learning to speak. Phonetics is a little more relevant, although few can afford tuition from Professor Higgins. If mathematical logic were a little less pure, perhaps it could assist a mathematician to learn some alien branch of mathematics. In its present aloof form, however, a training in mathematical logic is neither necessary nor likely to speed up the pursuit of other branches of mathematics.

On the other hand, if a machine is to do mathematics, it is necessary that methods of logic be explicitly included. This provides incentive for doing more detailed work on the decision problem and proof procedures for logic.

Moreover, considerations about the practical feasibility of alternative procedures are pushed to the forefront. This supplements the basic concern that a mathematical argument should be perspicuous, surveyable, or capable of being taken in. These two aspects of the problem of efficiency are not identical. For example, a less efficient proof procedure is generally easier to describe, and the argument for proving its adequacy is generally easier to grasp. On the other hand, the two aspects combine to account for and give direction to much of our mathematical activity. To stress the requirements that procedures be feasible and that proofs be surveyable, one might coin the label 'praximism.'

In a different direction, the project of mechanical mathematics calls our attention to the problem of formalizing methods of finding proofs. Theoretically dispensible methods and strategies will be included to speed up the search for proofs. Here we have another hitherto largely neglected domain which is susceptible of a treatment by methods similar to those used in the more elementary parts of mathematical logic. Such problems are on a different level from the study of the psychology of mathematical invention. We may be able to simulate the external circumstances of preparation under which Poincaré's exceptional subconscious functions. But it seems preposterous to suppose we are capable of endowing a machine with a subconscious, much less with one comparable to Poincaré's.

If a machine produces a proof of Fermat's conjecture with one million lines, we still have the somewhat easier task of making the proof perspicuous. This would be a situation where we could say, in a clear sense, that a proof exists but nobody has understood it. Somebody would undoubtedly prefer to say that there is no proof yet, just as he would say that a machine cannot calculate, cannot prove, because there must be a final contact which lights up the whole thing and only a man can establish this contact by taking in the whole process that makes up the calculation or the proof.

When interesting mathematical questions can be settled by machines, our chief concern will be shifted to the methods of proof and their coding. And we do not expect to have 10^6 lines of coding. We synthesize and abbreviate as we make progress, in order to press more and more into the brain as a bounded finite machine. With the increasing power of mechanized methods, an economy in storage is achieved by substituting general methods for particular arguments. Instead of a single proof requiring 10^6 lines, it should be possible to organize all our mathematical knowledge and have it contained in so many lines.

Definitions generally reveal new aspects and thereby help to direct the course of our thinking into certain channels. Consider, for example, the development of arithmetic within the framework of set theory. Through the linking definitions, the theorems of set theory can be divided into two classes: those which correspond to theorems of arithmetic and those which do not. Theorems of both classes are, one is inclined to think, in the system all along; the linking definitions do not change their meaning but merely provide a different way of looking at those in the first class. Most of us have seen pictures which appear to be a mess at first, but reveal, e.g., a human face upon closer scrutiny. The physical object that is the picture is not affected by the different impressions which we get from it. The picture, however, means different things before and after we discern a face. This, one feels, is also the situation when linking definitions enable us to see certain sentences of set theory as disguised arithmetic sentences. If one is afraid that next time he will forget how he can discern a face, he may, as a reminder, trace certain parts of the picture by a red pencil. As a result, everybody can immediately see a face, although the configurations in the picture remain the same. Does it make an essential difference whether the stress is made by a red pencil or just seen in our mind's eye?

Does a proof change the meaning of a hitherto unproved mathematical proposition? Does a new proof of a mathematical theorem change its meaning? The answer is undoubtedly: sometimes it does, usually it does not. The point of the question is probably not to suggest the instability of mathematical concepts but rather to point to an abstractly human element in the meaning of mathematical concepts. Think of the proposition as a station in a formal system. The country is there, but we do not know whether there is any road which leads to the station. Presently we find one road, then we find another. But the country is the same, the station is the same. Both of us understand the proposition that there are infinitely many prime numbers. You know a proof of it but I do not. Does it have the same meaning for both of us? It is not yet known whether there are infinitely many pairs of primes n and $n + 2$ ('twin primes'). Will a proof of the proposition change its meaning? The proof will reveal new connections and provide reminders which enable every member of the mathematical community to see the proposition as true. Does the increase of knowledge affect the meaning of a proposition or is the relation between knowledge and meaning only an external one resembling the relation between the weight of an elephant and our knowledge of it?

Elephants exist independently of our knowledge, but in what sense does a proof exist independently of all knowledge? Once a proof is found, it can be codified and put at its proper place within a textbook, but where did it reside previously? More, to call several pages of printed marks a proof presupposes a good deal of the sociological circumstances which make them a proof. For instance, they are sufficient to recreate in a few people the gradual process which culminates finally in seeing that the concluding proposition of the several pages must be true. We are reluctant to deny that every possible proof in a formal system exists even before we have singled it out and digested it by constructions, mental or with red pencils. Under suitable conditions of size and endurance, a machine can eventually grind it out. In this sense, the undigested proof has existed all along, even though the digested proof has to be invented. Is, however, an undigested proof a proof? To say that it is a proof because it is, though undigested, digestable, leads to the question of distinguishing digestable in principle from digestable as a matter of fact. Even if a miracle reveals that there is a way of seeing the geographical contours of Venus as a proof of Fermat's conjecture, how do we know we shall ever be able to find suitable perspectives to make such an undigested 'proof' perspicuous? It seems like a dogma to say that every undigested proof will eventually be digested. If one does not wish to assert so much, then it is hard to provide, without circularity, a sense of 'digestable' according to which every undigested proof is digestable.

I think I know how to add and multiply. But it would be easy to find complicated problems which I cannot do within two hours. For instance, multiplying 78 by 78, 78 times. With some effort, we can also find computation problems which I cannot do, at any rate by the ordinary technique, within a month, or within my lifetime. In what sense do I know how to add and multiply? Not just in the sense that

I can handle small numbers, because I feel I can deal with large numbers too. Or perhaps, if I live long enough, say by keeping myself fit like a great athlete, I shall be able to complete even the most complicated additions and multiplications? But then surely I cannot do them with the ordinary technique for there would be neither enough chalk, nor sufficiently large blackboards.

These considerations strike one as utterly irrelevant. When I say I can do addition and multiplication, I do not mean to preclude the possibility that practical difficulties may prevent me from carrying out certain complicated calculations. I feel I can do them, shall we say, in principle. One is generally not expected to do artifically elaborate calculations. If it were the case that nobody was interested in multiplications of less than 300 numbers each with more than 10 digits, then one might say that nobody could multiply unless he was assisted by a machine.

In this connection, it may be instructive to consider the following inductive argument: 1 is small; if n is small, $n + 1$ is small; therefore, every number is small.

The words 'can,' 'decidable,' etc. mean different things in pure mathematics and applied mathematics, in actual mathematical activities and in the discussions of mathematical logicians. A man says that the further expansion of π is a further expansion of mathematics and that the question changes its status when it becomes decidable. Since what the millionth place of the decimal expansion of π is, is a theoretically decidable question, the man seems to be inconsistent in saying that a ground for the decision has yet to be invented. This is so only if we think of decidable in the logician's sense. In the sense of actually doing mathematics, the question is not yet decidable because it is to be expected that some ingenious general argument is required to supply the required digit and prove to the satisfaction of mathematicians that it is indeed the desired one. And it strikes one as dogmatism to assert categorically that such an argument will be found. It is true that finitists and intuitionists do not worry about such questions because once a problem is decidable in theory, they lose all interest in it. This, however, does not mean one cannot interest oneself in feasibility as a concept worthy of philosophical considerations.

Confusions arise when two men each choose one of the two different senses and refuse to recognize that there is also the other sense. Perhaps a phenomenologist is one who permits both senses and distinguishes them from each other. At any rate, it seems convenient to make use of both senses, at least until we have more successfully unified them.

There is a great gap between what can be done in principle and what can be done in practice. Often we are interested in broadening the range of the latter. That is why such techniques as the use of the Arabic notation, logarithmic tables, and computing machines are important. (The second and the third differ from the first in that we are not aware of the steps in the calculation.) Are they only of practical importance or are they also of theoretical interest? Shall we say that theoretical and practical significances merge in such fundamental improvements in the technology of mathematics?

It is not always easy to draw the line between theoretical and practical. Numbers of the form $2^{(2^n)} + 1$ are called Fermat's numbers because Fermat conjectured that all such numbers are prime. It has been proved since Fermat's time that, for $n = 5, 6, 7, 8$, all Fermat's numbers are composite. A proof for each case was a nontrivial piece of mathematics, even though, with patience, these questions could be settled simply by the ordinary methods of calculation. One might say that the proofs provide us with new techniques for deciding problems which could otherwise be solved by uninspired laborious computation.

In mathematics the introduction of new techniques is important and definitions do serve to introduce new techniques. It is therefore misleading to speak of them as 'mere abbreviations.' Even if, after a proof of a theorem in number theory has been discovered, it is possible to eliminate defined terms and translate the proof into the primitive notation of set theory, the translated proof would not have been discovered by one who worked exclusively with the primitive notation of set theory. Nor could the translated proof in practice be understood correctly even if one was aware of the definitions.

2 REDUCING MATHEMATICS TO LOGIC

The more sensational reduction of mathematics to logic is the thesis that definitions of mathematical concepts can be found in logic such that mathematical theorems can be transformed unconditionally into theorems in logic. This is plausible only if 'logic' is understood in a very broad sense to include set theory as a part.

The term 'set theory' is less familiar than the term 'logic,' but then, at the same time, more unambiguous too. Since set theory is itself a branch of mathematics, the question is that of reducing other branches of mathematics to this particular one. In this sense, the matter is initially a domestic affair of mathematics. The concern of philosophers has come about partly as a result of the historical accident that Frege and Russell, rightly or wrongly, connected it with philosophy, and that at least one of them is such a good propagandist. Nonetheless, the persistence of such interest surely cannot be discarded simply by deploring the poverty of philosophy. After all, even if set theory is but another branch of mathematics, the claim that all other branches are reducible to it makes it a proper concern of philosophers.

The most interesting case is number theory. If we are concerned only with numerical formulas containing addition and multiplication, it appears possible to find theorems of logic which correspond to them rather naturally. On the other hand, if we are concerned with general laws of arithmetic as well, the reduction is only possible when we take set theory rather than logic proper.

It is puzzling that Kant called '7 + 5 = 12' synthetic a priori and that Frege believed himself to have refuted this by his reduction of arithmetic to logic. One way to make the two viewpoints plausible seems to be the following. In order that an equation be analytic, the two sides must have the same sense, not just the same denotation. One is tempted to say that '7 + 5' and '12' have different senses, although they have the same denotation. Hence, '7 + 5 = 12' is synthetic and a priori, its necessity not being questioned here. But there is a natural way of reducing '7 + 5 = 12' to a theorem of logic. Suppose we use the abbreviations:

$(E!_1x)Gx$ for $\exists x_1 \forall y\, [Gx_1 \wedge (Gy \supset y = x_1)]$
$(E!_2x)Gx$ for
$\exists x_1 \exists x_2 \forall y[x_1 \neq x_2 \wedge Gx_1 \wedge Gx_2 \wedge (Gy \supset (y = x_1 \vee y = x_2))]$

Then the corresponding theorem of logic is:

$(*)\ (E!_7x)Gx \wedge (E!_5x)Hx \wedge \forall u \neg (Gu \wedge Hu) \supset (E!_{12}x)(Gx \vee Hx)$

Since it is natural to regard all theorems of logic, i.e. the theory of quantifiers with equality, as analytic, Frege seems to have shown that '7 + 5 = 12' is analytic.

There are a number of difficulties in this explanation. The negation of something like (*) does not give us what we want if we are interested in proving, e.g., '7 + 6 ≠ 12.' The obstacle arises because the letters G, H serve as free variables so that we have to quantify them to get the correct negation. We certainly do not wish to say that '7 + 5 = 12' is analytic but '7 + 6 ≠ 12' is synthetic a priori. Moreover, there is no way to get around the need for existence assumptions in one form or another. If there are not enough entities in the universe of discourse, the antecedent of (*), for instance, would be always false, and we can derive, e.g., 12 = 13. In fact both objections can be combined and met by assuming that there are infinite sets or that all finite sets exist. We are led back to the reduction of arithmetic to set theory, and there is an obvious choice between saying that arithmetic has been shown to be analytic (Frege) and saying that logic (more correctly, set theory) has been shown to be synthetic (Russell at one time).

Although the numerals, 5, 7, 12 occur in (∗) as subscripts, there is no direct circularity in the reduction, because we can expand (∗) and avoid the use of numerals by employing sufficiently many distinct variables. A striking feature of the reduction is that short propositions are reduced to long ones. As a result, it would be very clumsy if one were to do arithmetic in such a notation, and we are quickly forced to introduce abbreviations. This is rightly considered an inessential complication for the simple reason that the reduction is not meant to introduce a new technique of calculation. It only yields an informal result about calculations as a byproduct: that one could do arithmetic in the complicated symbolism too. This depends on the reduction plus the information that one can do arithmetic in the customary notation.

A more basic difficulty of the reduction is the accompanying increase in conceptual complexity. If we attempt to give a proof of (∗) in the expanded form, we find ourselves counting the distinct variables, and going through, in addition to operations with logic, exactly the same kind of moves as in elementary calculations. We are able to see that (∗) is a theorem of logic only because we are able to see that a corresponding arithmetic proposition is true, not the other way round. By tacking 'frills' on an arithmetic proof of '7 + 5 = 12', we get a proof of (∗) in logic. 'A definition of christening in a particular church is no longer a definition of christening.'

There are different ways of defining arithmetic concepts in set theory. If we imagine a determinate situation with one specific formal system of set theory, one of arithmetic, and one specific set of linking definitions, then there is a theorem in the primitive notation of set theory that corresponds to the arithmetic theorem '1000 + 2000 = 3000'. The formula would be forbiddingly long. Does it mean the same thing as the original formula of arithmetic? When one who is not aware of the definitions is faced with the long formula, he might be at a loss to see any clear connections between the two formulas. He may be sufficiently familiar with set theory to understand the long formula and still not recognize its relation to the short one. Or even if he knows the definitions and is asked to simplify the long formula according to them, chances are he will make errors and arrive at some incorrect result. We are inclined to think that such considerations are irrelevant as far as the intended meaning of the formulas is concerned. But if a man fails to see the equivalence of the two formulas even after hours of hard labor, can we still say that the two formulas mean the same thing to him?

Theory and Practice in Mathematics

This is an artificial question because nobody is expected to write out or work with the long formula in order to do arithmetic calculations. We have a short argument to show that there must be such a formula, and that nearly exhausts the meaning of the hypothetical assertion that we could work directly with it too. When it is a matter of doing mathematics, we naturally fall back on the best available technique we have. If we had only the long version at first, then we would as a matter of fact not be able to do much calculating until we hit on some systematic way of changing it into a short version. We may spend many hours to read a long formal proof, but when we understand it, we do not give each line the same status, but work out an easily memorizable structure which may include known theorems, lemmas, subcases, reminders that certain successions of steps are of certain familiar forms. We do not have to keep all details of the structure in mind at the same time. The proof may be a mile long, but we can still plant posts as we go along and not worry about parts changing when we are not looking at them. As soon as we are convinced that some parts do give us a subtheorem which is the only contribution those parts can make toward proving the final theorem, we need retain only the subtheorem in our head.

If set theory alone is given but the linking definitions with arithmetic are still missing, then we do not yet have arithmetic in full force because we would not and could not, as a matter of fact, do the arithmetic proofs and calculations in set theory. If both set theory and the linking definitions are given, we continue to do arithmetic as before only with the awareness that there is a sense in which our proofs and calculations could be translated into set theory. But doing arithmetic is still different from doing set theory. We do not change our manner of doing arithmetic. That is the sense in which arithmetic has not been reduced to set theory, and, indeed, is not reducible to set theory.

Do we reduce mathematics to abstract set theory or do we get set theory out of mathematics by padding? In analysis, we find certain real numbers such as π and e of special significance. Somehow we are led to the search for a general theory of real numbers. Since we want the theory to be general, we postulate many more real numbers in order to make the surface smooth. When we find that real numbers, natural numbers and many other things can all be treated as sets, we are induced to search for a general theory of sets. Then we add many more other sets in order to make the surface appear smooth. 'If tables, chairs, cupboards, etc., are swathed in enough paper, certainly they will look spherical in the end.' In this process, we lose sight of the distinctions between interesting and uninteresting sets, useful and useless real numbers. In order to recover the distinctions once more,

236

we have to take off the padding. Could we perhaps describe this reverse process as reducing (e.g. 'Mrs E is on a diet') abstract set theory to mathematics?

If we think in terms of true propositions about natural numbers, then set theory is also reducible to arithmetic at least in the sense that, given any consistent formal system for set theory, a translation can be found such that all theorems turn into true arithmetic propositions. The same is true of any other branch of mathematics on account of the possibility of an arithmetic representation of formal systems. Hence, we can also say that all mathematics is reducible to arithmetic, but in a sense quite different from, for instance, what was known as the arithmetization of analysis. Arithmetization of logic involves a change of subject from talk about sets, etc., to talk about how we talk.

When we ask, 'what is a number,' 'what is the number one,' we seem to be after an answer as to what numbers *really* are. If numbers are neither subjective nor outside of us in space, what could they be? And then it is gratifying to get the answer that they are really certain classes. One is relieved to have thus unmasked numbers. What does the unmasking accomplish? Frege's definition of number seems to resemble rather closely our unanalyzed concept of number so that we are sometimes inclined to take it as providing a true analysis of our intentions. But what more?

Apparently there is the belief that the reduction puts mathematics on a more trustworthy basis. Otherwise, the paradoxes about sets would not have induced Frege to say that the foundation of arithmetic wobbles. This is, as we now know, unjustified. We understand arithmetic better than set theory, as evidenced by the highly informative consistency proofs for arithmetic. The foundation of arithmetic is more trustworthy than that of set theory—what would be of greater interest is rather to found set theory on arithmetic, or on an extension of arithmetic to infinite ordinals.

There are different ways of defining numbers in terms of classes. Each of them leads to and from the undefined concept of number, and they are seen to be equivalent not through the interconnection between themselves but by way of the channels connecting them to the naked concept of number. Perhaps this indicates a certain priority of numbers to their corresponding classes?

Identifying numbers with suitable classes is said to be 'recommended by the fact that it leaves no doubt as to the existence-theorem.' 'Postulating' a limit to fill the gap for each Dedekind cut is said to have advantages which are the same as those 'of theft over honest toil,' while the course of honest toil is to identify the limit with the class of ratios in the lower section of the cut. It is in a sense

237

true that the latter course 'requires no new assumptions, but enables us to proceed deductively from the original apparatus of logic.' This is so, however, only because in the original apparatus of logic we have already made assumptions of the same kind. If the existence of the postulated limit is called into question, the existence of its corresponding class is equally doubtful. There is no reason to suppose that numbers evaporate but classes are rocks.

The reduction to set theory gives 'the precise statement of what philosophers meant in asserting that mathematics is a priori.' This is neither an informative statement nor a true one.

It is said that the axioms of arithmetic admit diverse interpretations while the reduction eliminates such ambiguities. True, the concept of set is involved in the axiom of induction and the intended interpretation of the concept of set assures the intended interpretation of the axioms of arithmetic. But arithmetic presupposes only inductive sets which are a particular type of set. Moreover, we should not confuse the possibility of incorrect interpretations with the impossibility of correct interpretations. It is possible both to interpret the axioms of arithmetic correctly and to interpret the axioms of set theory incorrectly. Moreover, interpreting the axioms of set theory involves greater conceptual difficulties.

Surely one cannot deny that Frege's definition has the great virtue of taking care of applications? This is undoubtedly the case if we perform a multiplication just in accordance with the rules of calculation or argue formally by observing the rules of logic. But the application of number to empirical material forms no part of either logic or set theory or arithmetic. There may be some doubt if we consider the proposition 'Paris has 4 million inhabitants' as an application of the number 4 million, and the proposition 'two rabbits plus two rabbits yield four rabbits' as an application of the mathematical proposition '$2 + 2 = 4$.'

Such applications can appear neither in arithmetic nor in set theory for the simple reason that words such as 'Paris,' 'rabbits,' 'inhabitants' do not occur in the vocabularies of these theories, and the set-theoretical definition of numbers offers no help. If it is meant that the definition enables us to apply numbers within the framework of a wider language, then it is not clear why the same does not apply without the definition. Suppose we are to infer the proposition 'she has two virtues' from the proposition 'her only virtues are beauty and wit.' It is apparently thought that the inference can only be made by using Frege's definition of the number 2, because otherwise the class of her virtues cannot be shown to have the number 2. If, however, the full richness of ordinary discourse is permitted, we can surely make the inference without appeal to Frege's definition.

In any case, why should such applications be taken as the proper business of set theory or of arithmetic? Mathematics and its applications are two things which can conveniently be studied separately. If the desire is to have a general language which includes both mathematics and other things, the link between numbers can just as well be provided by axioms which assert, for example, that a class has $n + 1$ members if and only if it is gotten from a class with n members by adding a new member. In other words, if we adopt the course of taking numbers as undefined, we can still, if we wish, add axioms to do the job of Frege's definitions. The effects are the same except that mathematics and its application are divided at a more natural boundary.

3 WHAT IS MATHEMATICS?

The most impressive features of mathematics are its certainty, its abstractness and precision, its broad range of applications, and its dry beauty. The precision and certainty are to a large extent due to the abstractness which also in part explains the wide applicability. But the close connection to the physical world is an essential feature which separates mathematics from mere games with symbols. Mathematics coincides with all that is the exact in science.

According to Kant, mathematics is determined by the form of our pure intuition so that it is impossible to imagine anything violating mathematics. If we agree that the physical world, including our brains, is a brute fact, this view can be said to imply that the external world, including the physiological structure of our mind, determines mathematics. The discovery of non-Euclidean geometries need not be regarded as refuting Kant's doctrine, since we can construe them as superstructures on the Euclidean, or an even weaker, geometry. A more serious objection is that Kant's theory does not provide enough elucidation of the principles by which these and other superstructures are to be set up.

As we all know, Shaw was accustomed to exaggerate. He defended himself by arguing that shock value is the best way to call attention to new ideas. In a similar spirit, we may hope to clarify our vague thoughts by examining a few one-sided views of mathematics.

3.1 Mathematics is the class of (logically) valid or necessary propositions 'p implies q.' Thus, given any theorem q, we can write the conjunction of the axioms employed in its proof as p, and 'p implies q' is a theorem in elementary logic. In this somewhat trivial sense, all mathematics is reducible to elementary logic. This really says nothing about mathematics proper, since one would like to assert *p* and *q* unconditionally. This evades the whole question why certain *p*, e.g. mathematical induction, is accepted as a mathematical truth. Moreover, the concepts of validity and necessity (or possibility) are to be explained by the concept of set or perhaps by concepts like law and disposition. A related view is to construe logic more broadly so as to include propositions such as 'For all *x* and *y*, if *x* and *y* have no common members, *x* has 7 members, *y* has 5 members, then $x \cup y$ has 12 members.' Then one has to define numbers in logic, and so on. Such a view is akin to the next one.

3.2 Mathematics is axiomatic set theory. In a definite sense, all mathematics can be derived from axiomatic set theory. To be definite, we can adhere to a standard system commonly referred to as *ZF*. This is the counterpart of Frege's and Russell's reduction of mathematics to logic and paradoxically also of Poincaré's 1900 remark about the arithmetization of mathematics ('numbers and their sets'). This is what most impressed the logical positivists, leading to, among other things, an emphasis on axiomatization and formalization. There are several objections to this identification. As we know, there are many difficulties in the foundations of set theory. This view leaves unexplained why, of all possible consequences of set theory, we select only those which happen to be our mathematics today, and why certain mathematical concepts and results are more interesting than others. It does not help to give us an intuitive grasp of mathematics such as that possessed by a powerful mathematician. By burying, e.g., the individuality of natural numbers, it seeks to explain the more basic and the clearer by the more obscure. There is the side issue of logicism which continues to be upheld in some quarters despite definitive evidence against it. In at least one important case, this mysterious state of affairs is based on a mistaken identification of Frege's logical theory of sets (extensions of predicates) with Cantor's mathematical theory of sets. The argument goes like this. Frege's theory looks like logic and mathematics can be reduced to Cantor's theory; therefore, by the identification, mathematics is reducible to logic.

In an autobiography, Einstein gave as his reason for choosing physics over mathematics the lack of unity in mathematics. We may wonder whether set theory might not give a unity to mathematics. The formal system *ZF* is, of course, neither complete nor categorical. Moreover, it cannot even decide familiar mathematical propositions such as the continuum hypothesis. Hence, as a comprehensive system, it is conceptually unsatisfactory. If now we leave aside higher infinities and confine ourselves to more applicable mathematics such as classical analysis, number theory, and abstract algebra, it seems reasonable to agree that almost all familiar theorems have counterparts in *ZF*. Could we claim that *ZF*, together with the derivation of different branches of mathematics from *ZF*, provides a rough indication of the sort of unity we look for?

One objection is that the representation is not faithful enough. In particular, it tends to miss the more abstract aspect of mathematics. Certainly the postulates of a group or a field are satisfied by various and diverse models. Even the theorems of classical analysis can be proved in axiom systems of very different strength. This suggests the possibility of a web of axiom systems such that each system determines an abstract structure, viz. the class of all possible models of the system. Something like *ZF* or a more adequate enlargement yet to be contrived encloses all these systems in the sense that none postulates the existence of any object not envisaged by it.

From this approach one might even prove metatheorems about all models of a system without circularity, because they can also be proved in some fairly weak system which admits of both very big models and rather small ones. If we devised such a web of perhaps no more than ten systems, we would get a sort of skeleton, which could only be made into a living form by the addition of facts about the present state, a guess at future trends, and the historical highlights of mathematics.

3.3 Mathematics is the study of abstract structures. This appears to be the view of Bourbaki. An influential sequence of books has been written to substantiate this view. They make a conscious attempt to divorce mathematics from applications which is not altogether healthy. The inadequacy of this outlook is revealed not only by the omission of various central results of a more combinatorial sort, but especially by the lack of intrinsic justification of the selection of structures which happen to be important for reasons quite external to this approach. The constructive content of mathematical results is not brought out. There is also a basic inconsistency insofar as lip service is paid to an axiomatic set theory as the foundation, while serious foundational researches are frowned upon. It would conform more to the general spirit if number, set, and function were treated in a more intuitive manner. That would at least be more faithful to the actual practice of working mathematicians today.

3.4 Mathematics is to speed up calculations. Here calculations are not confined to numerical ones. Algebraic manipulations and juggling with logical expressions (e.g. in switching theory) are also included. A somewhat broader view would be to say that every serious piece of mathematics must have some algorithmic content. A different, though related, position would be to say that all mathematics is to assist science, to assist us to understand and control nature. These views seem to make it impossible to explain, e.g., why we often prefer more elegant proofs with higher bounds and why we take great delight in impossibility results. One could argue that there is in addition the human element in mathematical activities so that it is essential, even for applications, that the situation should be perspicuous. Thus, we can better grasp an elegant proof and, indirectly, are enabled thereby to look for more efficient algorithms; and impossibility results tell us the limitations of given methods, helping the search for positive results in the long run. This kind of argument is, however, typical of philosophers stretching a position to try to fit in unwanted facts.

So much for oversimplifications.

If we review quickly the history of mathematics, we find quite a few surprises. What appears particularly attractive is that there is room for a serious and fruitful synthesis of mathematics and work in the philosophy of mathematics which would help the progress of mathematics itself by making the subject more appealing and by fighting against excessive specialization.

Foundational studies in this century have been very fruitful in several ways. The possibilities and limitations of formalization have been much clarified. There is a better understanding of constructive methods. And the explication of mechanical procedures has yielded many fundamental results, especially negative ones, on decidability and solvability. On the whole, there remains, however, the impression that foundational problems are somewhat divorced from the main stream of mathematics and the natural sciences. Whether this is as it should be seems a highly debatable point.

The principal source of the detachment of mathematics from mathematical logic is that logic jumps more quickly to the more general situation. This implies a neglect of mathematics as a human activity, in particular, of the importance of notation and symbolism, and of the more detailed relations of mathematics to applications. It is philosophically attractive to study in one sweep all sets, but in mathematics we are primarily interested in only a very small range of sets. In a deeper sense, what is more basic is not the concept of set but rather the existing body of mathematics. For example, the distinction between linear and nonlinear problems, the invention of logarithms, the different ways of enumerating finite sequences, the nature of complex numbers and their functions, or the manipulation with infinities by physicists (such as Dirac's delta function and the intrusion of infinities in quantum electromagnetic theory) all seem to fall outside the range of problems which interest specialists in foundational studies. Rightly or wrongly, one wishes for a type of foundational studies which would have deeper and more beneficial effects on pedagogy and research in mathematics and the sciences.

As a first step, one might envisage an 'abstract history' of mathematics that is concerned less with historical details than with conceptual landmarks. This might lead to a resolution of the dilemma between too much fragmentation and too quick a transfer to the most general.

3.5.1 Concrete arithmetic began with practical problems. The idealization of the indefinite expandability of the sequence of numbers and the shift from individual numbers to general theorems about all numbers gave rise to the theory of numbers. Only around 1888 was Dedekind able to formulate the so-called Peano axioms by analyzing the very concept of number.

3.5.2 The solution of equations together with the use of literal symbols such as letters for unknowns marked the beginning of algebra ('transposition and removal'). Only in 1591 (F. Vièta) were letters used for known quantities as well (variables and parameters).

3.5.3 Geometry deals with spatial forms and geometrical quantities such as length and volume. The number of a set is an abstraction from that which is invariant under any changes whatsoever in the properties and mutual relations of the objects in the set (e.g. color, weight, size, distance), provided only the identity of each object is not disturbed (by splitting or merging). Similarly a geometrical figure or body is an abstraction of an actual body viewed purely with regard to its spatial form, leaving out all its other properties. Rather surprisingly, such an abstract study led not only to pure geometry but also to the first extensive example of the deductive method and axiomatic systems. There was even a geometrical algebra in Greece.

3.5.4 Measurement of length and volume is a union of arithmetic and geometry, applying units to calculate a number. This, just as the solution of equations, is a natural way of leading to fractions and even irrational numbers. The desire to have an absolutely accurate, or rather indefinitely improvable, measurement leads to the general concept of 'real number'. Algebra led to negative numbers and complex numbers. But a better understanding of complex numbers was only reached through their geometrical representations.

3.5.5 By the way, in terms of speeding up computations, the invention of logarithms (Napier, 1614) was a great advance.

3.5.6 In an indeterminate equation, say $3y - 2x = 1$, we may view x and y not only as unknowns but as variables so that the given equation expresses the interdependence of these two variables. The

general concept of function or interdependence is the subject matter
of analysis. Using the Cartesian coordinates, we get a connection
between algebra and geometry, with function playing the central
role. In this sense, analytic geometry may be said to be the simplest
branch of analysis. It is implicitly assumed that we deal with at least
all real numbers.

3.5.7 If we add in addition the concept of change or motion, and
study a broader class of functions, we arrive at the calculus. The
original source was geometry and mechanics (tangent and velocity, area
and distance). Theories of differential and integral equations search
for functions rather than numbers as solutions. Such theories develop
naturally both from applications and from an intrinsic combination
of the calculus with the algebraic problem of solving equations. In
the same spirit, functional analysis is not unlike the change from
algebra to analysis, the interest being no longer confined to finding
individual functions but rather to studying the general interdependence of functions.

3.5.8 It is not easy to understand why functions of complex variables turned out to be so elegant and useful. But it certainly was a
gratifying phenomenon that an extension served to clarify many
facts in the original domain. Incidentally, if we require the axioms
of fields be satisfied, extensions of complex numbers are not possible,
e.g., for quaternions multiplication is not commutative.

3.5.9 The lively development of the theory of probability has been
connected with statistical mechanics, and its foundations are a
fascinating but elusive subject.

3.5.10 In algebra, Galois theory not only gives a conclusive treatment of the solution of equations but opens up a more abstract study
of abstract structures dealing with operations on arbitrary elements
rather than just numbers.

3.5.11 The greatest changes in geometry have been the discovery of
non-Euclidean geometries and Riemann's general ideas about the
possibility of many different 'spaces' and their geometries. Figures
are generalized to arbitrary sets of points.

3.5.12 The development in functions of a real variable touches on
various conceptual problems such as the definition of real number,
and the meaning of 'measure.'

In this century, the development of logic, the emergence of computing machinery, and the prospect of new applications in the
biological sciences and in linguistics all tend to emphasize what might
be called 'discrete mathematics,' even though continuous mathematics is well entrenched and as lively as ever.

One of the very basic problems is that we still do not have any definitive theory of what a real number or what a set of integers is. Perhaps we can never have a definitive theory. It seems quite unknown how this fundamental unclarity affects the rest of mathematics and the novel applications of mathematics in physics.

Relative to different concepts of set and proof, one could reconstrue most of mathematics in several different ways. Are these different formulations just essentially equivalent manners of describing the same grand structure or does there exist a natural framework in which everything becomes more transparent?

4 PRACTICAL ASPECTS OF MATHEMATICS

We have mentioned the anthropocentric elements of surveyability of proofs and feasibility of calculations. There are also ethical, political, and sociological aspects of mathematics. We may ask for practical justifications for developing a particular branch of mathematics or proving a particular theorem. We may reflect on how the general line of development of mathematics is determined and, in particular, how fashions, personalities, applications, intrinsic merits, and other factors interact. It is remarkable that mathematics is harder to popularize than other sciences. This is in part caused by the fact that mathematics has more than other sciences a special language of its own.

There is a familiar aphorism that mathematics is a language. In one sense, the concepts of mathematics are most independent of language, tying up with 'pure intuition.' At the same time, mathematics is perhaps the most efficient language (for those who understand it), as, e.g. exemplified by Littlewood's inferences from a diagram on the table of an unfamiliar room.[1] Mathematics is much more than a language insofar as it is much more than just a means of communication. It has its own language, but that is very different from saying that it is a language.

In 1900, Hilbert proposed a very influential list of twenty-three mathematical problems. H. Weyl once suggested the idea of using this list as a basis to review the overall progress of mathematics during several decades. J. von Neumann was asked to offer a modern list in 1954 but pleaded inability to cover wide areas of mathematics. It seems likely that nobody today is in a position to make up a list comparable to Hilbert's relative to his time.

If a sufficiently representative group of people put together a list of twenty or thirty central problems today, one could use this problem list as a basis to 1 picture the present state of mathematics and its relations to other sciences; 2 review the history; 3 predict future trends; 4 discern some sort of conceptual unity of the whole of mathematics; 5 discuss some of the perennial epistemological questions.

By the way, a comprehensive list of general problems would include (a) certainty and necessity (synthetic a priori or not); (b) mathematical existence (and methods of construction); (c) the driving force in mathematics (utility, esthetic appeal and art for art's sake, fashions and their cause, curiosity); (d) the mathematical activity (notation and abbreviations, heuristics, the phenomenon of physically blind mathematicians); (e) the nature of mathematical proofs (formalization and intuitive evidence); (f) exposition, teaching, and mechanization of mathematics (problems of communication contrasted with the obtaining of new pieces of mathematics, the possibility of mathematical criticism as an analog of literary criticism); (g) pure versus applied mathematics (criterion for judging the value of mathematical models of empirical situations, distance from applications); (h) mathematics as a 'language.'

It is neither necessary nor sufficient that the problems be famous ones. For example, Fermat's and Goldbach's conjectures and the four-color problem should probably not be included unless somebody has some promising idea of attack which, even if it fails, would yield a rich harvest of byproducts. On the other hand, since a number of serious mathematicians are thinking about the Riemann hypothesis, this may be worth including, providing one places it in an informative context.

It is in general not easy to find problems which are both sharp and of central interest. Usually, the sharp problems are not obviously fundamental, while the fundamental problems tend to be nebulous, waiting for the extraction of more specific questions. We may illustrate this situation by describing a few problems (or vague areas of research) suggested by mathematical logic, which is a highly nonrepresentative branch of mathematics.

1 *A more adequate axiom system of set theory* A central question is to codify somehow the notion of an arbitrary subset of a given set, in particular, of the set of positive integers, and the idea of possible levels of iterating the power set operation. In a certain sense, we can never get a formal system which is completely adequate. But it might be possible to obtain a natural formal system in which, for example, the continuum hypothesis is decidable. Moreover, it is desirable to think of exact ways of relaxing the concept of formal systems to permit, say, a 'semiformal' system that would codify adequately the power set of the set of positive integers. A sharp formulation of the quest for new axioms is the study of axioms for large cardinals. There is also considerable interest in trying to

relate such axioms to various restricted forms of the axiom of determinateness (on infinite games).

2 *Consistency of impredicative definitions* Often this is expressed as the question of establishing the consistency of classical analysis. The commonly accepted axiom systems for classical analysis are, besides being inadequate (not providing enough real numbers), lacking in transparency on account of the acceptance of sets introduced by impredicative definitions. It is desirable to find more articulate reasons for believing that they lead to no contradictions.

3 *Solvable and unsolvable problems* Theoretical work on algorithms has made it possible to prove general impossibility results. It is natural to attempt to get such results in older mathematical disciplines. There have been successes with the word problem for groups and Hilbert's tenth problem (on the integer solutions of Diophantine equations). There are attempts to settle Burnside's problem in group theory and the equivalence problem of three-dimensional topological manifolds. It is also likely that one could get significant unsolvability results on the solution of differential equations, the quadratic programming problem, and so on. Two specific problems which are expected to get positive solutions are the concatenation analog of Hilbert's tenth problem and the Gödel case of logical sentences with equality included.[2]

4 *The mechanization of mathematical arguments* The attempt to use computers as an aid to mathematical research would seem to lead to radically new types of problem such as the efficiency of decision procedures, the reorganization of our knowledge in a branch of mathematics, say number theory, with emphasis on sharp classifications of data, and formalization of heuristics.

5 *Feasible decidability* There is a good deal of interest in the complexity of calculations. One looks for a natural and stable concept of feasible calculability according to which, for example, the traveling salesman problem is undecidable. An exact definition of computational complexity should also make it possible to give a sharp sense in which, for example, multiplication is more complex than addition.

It is undeniable that fashions and strong personalities have their influences in mathematics, as elsewhere. For example, many people feel unhappy over the proliferation of the designing and building of mathematical structures and blame this in part on fashions. One feels that in the long run the general line of development is determined by more objective factors such as fundamental applications and intrinsic conceptual interest.

The position of constructivists provides a concrete and sharp example. The constructivists believe that they have the true or correct view of mathematics. In addition, they sometimes predict that their position will triumph. Here we find a close analogy with political views: we ought to strive for the correct ideal and, in addition, the correct ideal will win out in the long run anyhow.

On February 9, 1918, G. Polya and H. Weyl made a wager in Zurich with twelve other mathematicians as witnesses.[3] Since the wager is formulated in a particularly interesting way, we quote it at length.

Concerning both the following theorems of contemporary mathematics:
(1) Every bounded set of numbers has a least upper bound,
(2) Every infinite set of numbers has a countable subset,
Weyl prophesies:
A. Within 20 years (that is, by the end of 1937), Polya himself, or a majority of the leading mathematicians, will admit that the concepts of number, set, and countability, which are involved in these theorems and upon which we today commonly depend, are completely vague; and that there is no more use in asking after the truth or falsity of these theorems in their currently accepted sense than there is in considering the truth of the main assertions of Hegel's physics.
B. It will be recognized by Polya himself, or by a majority of the leading mathematicians, that, in any wording, theorems (1) and (2) are false, according to any rationally possible clear interpretation (either distinct such interpretations will be under discussion, or agreement will already have been reached); or that if it comes to pass within the allotted time that a clear interpretation of these theorems is found such that at least one of them is true, then there will have been a creative achievement through which the foundation of mathematics will have taken a new and original turn, and the concepts of number and set will have acquired meanings which we today cannot imagine.
Weyl wins if the prophecy is fulfilled; otherwise, Polya wins.

Polya relates that when the bet was called, in 1940, everybody, with one exception (K. Gödel), said he (Polya) had won.
More recently, E. Bishop made a similar prophecy.[4]

This book is a piece of constructivist propaganda, designed to show that there does exist a satisfactory alternative. To this end we develop a large portion of abstract analysis within a constructive framework. . . . These immediate ends tend to an ultimate goal – to hasten the inevitable day when constructive mathematics will be the accepted norm.

Theory and Practice in Mathematics

There is a disagreement over the issue whether constructivism is 'realist' or 'idealist.' On the one hand, classicists may be thought to be realists because they seem to be more willing to envisage abstract entities. On the other hand, Bishop prefers to call the classicists idealists since they tend to forget the true (i.e. numerical) content of mathematical statements. Another disagreement is whether classical or constructive analysis is more appropriate to applications in physics.

In many cases, doing a piece of mathematics is justified by appealing to its intrinsic interest or its relevance to other interesting mathematics. This can be contrasted with justifications in terms of the welfare or interest of society and mankind. If satisfying the rational interest of mankind is to constitute justification, we have to admit that there are different views of what this rational interest consists in. It is easy to accept the justification that knowledge is power or that knowledge makes man master and governor of nature. In such terms, mathematics is to be justified by its physical applications, actual and potential, and perhaps less directly by its disciplinary role in scientific thinking. There is also the tradition of allowing practical justifications broader than the utilitarian one: knowledge as the actualization of human reason, as a cultural value, as art, and so on.

Kant offers an interesting contrast between practical and pathological interests:[5]

> The dependence of the power of appetition on sensations is called an inclination, and thus an inclination always indicates a *need*. The dependence of a contingently determinable will on principles of reason is called an *interest*. Hence an interest is found only where there is a dependent will which in itself is not always in accord with reason: to a divine will we cannot ascribe any interest. But even the human will can *take an interest* in something without therefore *acting from interest*. The first expression signifies *practical* interest in the action; the second *pathological* interest in the object of the action. The first indicates only dependence of the will on principles of reason by itself; the second its dependence on principles of reason at the service of inclination – that is to say, where reason merely supplies a practical rule for meeting the need of inclination.

Even though there is social support for mathematics in many societies, this fact alone does not yield a practical justification. With regard to some branches of mathematics, it may have been a mistaken belief in their practical value which has led to the support. Or a bad government could encourage mathematics with a view to keeping a group of people out of mischief which would be, in the objective sense, valuable to social progress. In fact, many contemporary intellectuals have discovered an eternal contradiction between the universal knowledge they search for and the special way of thinking they have acquired from the particular environments in which they have been brought up. Hence, for each individual mathematician, the problem of practical justification is of a higher order of difficulty than that for a particular area of mathematics.

NOTES

1 J. E. Littlewood, *A mathematician's miscellany*, 1953, p. 50.
2 See H. Löb, *J. symbolic logic*, vol. 21, 1956, p. 66; and K. Gödel, *Monatsh. Math. Physik*, vol. 40, 1933.
3 A report on this wager is scheduled for publication in *Math. Zeitschrift*.
4 Erret Bishop, *Foundations of constructive analysis*, 1967, pp. ix–x.
5 Kant, *Groundwork of the metaphysics of morals*, B38. (English translation by H. J. Paton, p. 81).

VIII

NECESSITY, ANALYTICITY, AND APRIORITY

1 HOMES AND ASSIMILATIONS OF THE THREE CONCEPTS

A necessary proposition is true by virtue of the nature of things, it expresses the essence of things. An analytic proposition is true by virtue of its meaning or, when in the subject-predicate form, if the predicate is contained in the meaning of the subject. An a priori proposition is one which can be known without any appeal to the particular facts of experience. These crude dictionary definitions are sufficient to bring out the distinction that necessity is a metaphysical concept, analyticity a linguistic concept, and apriority an epistemological concept. Of the three concepts, necessity (or possibility) has the advantage of being an everyday concept, while the other two were invented by philosophers. Nonetheless, they are intimately connected with the nontechnical concepts of meaning and experience.

Necessary statements were considered extensively by Aristotle. Leibniz identified them with truths of reason and spoke of them as being true in all possible worlds and as propositions whose denial involves a contradiction. Leibniz[1] also spoke of 'truths a posteriori, or of fact' and 'truths a priori, or of reason.' The terms a priori (meaning what is prior) and a posteriori were derived in the scholastic philosophy from Aristotle's idea that A is prior to B in nature (or knowledge) if B could not exist without A (or we could not know B without knowing A). The present usage of the term a priori for what is not derived from experience came from Kant, who also introduced the distinction between analytic and synthetic judgments. There is also a tradition of associating a priori propositions with self-evidence and a priori concepts with innate ideas, i.e. ideas with which we were born so that we have no need to acquire them.

251

Our knowledge comes from two components which are variously called experience and thought, practice and theory, sensation and reason, intuition and logic, sensual receptivity and conceptual (and intuitive) spontaneity. Switching to the extensional linguistic framework, the truth value of a sentence depends on two factors: a validating fact and the meaning of the sentence (and the words in it). The interconnections between the two components are very complicated: experiences mould our thoughts which in turn modify our experiences. In actual situations, receptivity and spontaneity are so closely interlinked that we have no way of using a sharp distinction between them as a basis for reaching an appropriate understanding of human knowledge. Morality or knowledge of good and evil would lose much of its point if we disregarded the existence of other people. And factual knowledge is conditioned in an essential way by the fact that people are born into societies and with capacities peculiar to the human species.

Experience commonly implies more than sensual receptivity and practice suggests more activity than experience. Whether experience or practice is stressed can make a great difference in the basic orientation of a philosophy. The concept of experience is understood differently by various philosophers and the different conceptions lead to contrary views of knowledge.[2]

We use what we know. The basic fact or belief is that we live in a world in which we have a surprisingly large amount of knowledge about language, mathematics, and the natural sciences. This reveals a good deal of order in nature, and, in particular, in the physical objects which are the human beings with minds capable of knowing much of the order. From this point of view, all knowledge is contingent on the gross fact that there are the natural phenomena of existence and mind. Hence, even a priori knowledge is contingent. Nature could have been otherwise, and we could have been otherwise. But, while realizing this limitation of our knowledge makes us prepared to accept in principle the revisibility of any knowledge, the more substantial task remains one of appreciating how mind and nature interact to make it possible that we have the knowledge we have.

If a priori knowledge does not come from experience, even though it begins with experience, we may be led to think in terms of recalling or awakening material stored in our minds from birth. Babies may be born with a craving for milk. Certain birds may be born with a fear of rapidly moving shadows. We tend to relegate innate ideas and innate mechanisms to the realm of psychology and separate them from the epistemological concept of the a priori. If some day we find out from neurology how a program for doing multiplication develops in the brain, that would answer some questions about how we know multiplication. But that the multiplication table would be a priori in this sense does not seem to guarantee directly its truth or necessary truth. Sometimes it is thought that philosophy just muddles with things about which we do not have enough knowledge: the requisite scientific knowledge is necessary and, once attained, sufficient to clear up all the real problems. From this point of view, we should either hold our breath or at most aim only at some temporizing hypotheses. Even though an innate mechanism will explain how we are capable of learning multiplication there will remain the problem of explaining why the multiplication table works in actual applications. One may wish to supply a scientific explanation of the applicability by describing the orderly fashion in which nature behaves. That would seem to be more appealing than claiming that nature is made by mind and therefore cannot help obeying laws of the mind.

One consequence of the above observation is that even a priori knowledge is relative, but relative to an inescapable state of affairs at each historical stage which, furthermore, remains, to a large extent, stable for very long periods of time. In other words, even what is taken to be a priori knowledge can be mistaken, can be revised, but not frequently, not casually. And a priori knowledge does not just possess a high degree of certainty but has its own special status which ought to become clear as we get a reasonable picture of human knowledge. If we compare apriority with necessity, we see that necessity has an advantage in possessing a built-in reply to the possibility of error. Since necessity deals with reality and we cannot be completely certain we know reality perfectly, it is obvious that what we take to be necessary propositions need not be truly necessary. Or, maybe we know some of them are necessarily true if true at all, but we are not certain they are true. This protection may also be considered a dodge, since we can only know what we know and there is no direct adjudication of disagreements over the necessity of certain propositions. Retreating from knowledge to reality seems to open the door to untestable speculations.

But the true situation may be tied more closely to how easily we can work with each concept. And in different cases, one or the other may be more appropriate. For example, it seems natural to call propositions of pure logic necessary in the sense that they are true in all possible worlds. In this case, we possess a fairly definite and stable concept of possible world. On the other hand, the inclination is to regard mathematical propositions as a priori. This seems particularly true with regard to the propositions of number theory, perhaps on grounds hinted at by Brouwer. Natural numbers are intrinsic to our basic way of thinking in going from one thing to a next; they result from the 'form of our intuition.'

It is a moot question whether there are absolutely undecidable propositions. If ever such a conclusion is established for some mathematical proposition A, then A (or its negation) would not be a priori even though true. But the general conclusion is presumably a priori, as it will probably be proved as a theorem with considerations which are vaguely 'mathematical.' If the only obstacle to calling mathematics a priori is that there are absolutely undecidable propositions, this slight element of contingency is not very disturbing.

The continuum is more complicated. The geometrical intuition of the continuum may be said to be a priori, but the more formal theories of the continuum set forth by Dedekind and others embody a compromise between intuition and the requirement of precision. The geometrical intuition of the possibility of arbitrary infinite sequences of successive bisections of the unit interval is open to diverse formal interpretations. The concept of set, while more complex than the continuum in its set-theoretical interpretation, is less dependent on a geometrical interpretation. Sets may be said to be related to Kant's categories of understanding in that they serve to get unities out of multiplicities, abstracting from properties of concrete objects. They represent abstract forms of particular syntheses.

One could imagine computers producing a very large counter-example to Goldbach's conjecture that every even integer greater than 4 is a sum of two odd prime numbers. Since we have no direct way of verifying this by a perspicuous proof, we may have to resort to empirical arguments on the reliability of computers. Here we have another potential foil of the a priori view of mathematics which S. A. Kripke, I understand, construes as an argument for the possibility of necessary a posteriori truths.

As far as abstract mathematical structures are concerned, there is a strong if-then element which may be related to the idea that theorems in these areas are analytic or true by convention. Certain theorems about groups are true because we call structures satisfying certain postulates groups. There is a question of distinguishing these axiom systems from other axiom systems, mathematical or non-mathematical. To distinguish them from, say, an axiom system for the kinship relation, we might wish to say that all the concepts in the axioms of a mathematical structure are purely set-theoretical. To distinguish them from, say, arithmetic or set theory, we need only point out that in the latter cases there are unique intended models, while an abstract structure is intended to permit varied interpretations. Logic and set theory provide the foundations for abstract mathematical structures in two different ways. Logic supplies the framework for an implicit definition or convention that any structure satisfying certain postulates is called a field or a group or something else, as well as a hypothetical justification of all theorems about the structures as conditional theorems in logic. Set theory supplies the range of possible abstract interpretations of the postulates.

Geometry is something of a mixture. On the one hand, our spatial intuition is a major source of a priori knowledge. On the other hand, this intuition is not sufficiently exact to discriminate between alternative geometries. In particular, the discovery of non-Euclidean geometries has tended to produce views which assimilate geometry to empirical sciences. It seems desirable to preserve the analogy of geometry with arithmetic but admit that even though we are convinced that geometry is roughly a priori, we may be wrong in details. The sense in which general relativity has falsified Euclidean geometry proves that we are indeed wrong when we come to the very large and very small. But it should be emphasized that this did not come about because of isolated experiments but rather because of a rival theory. We do have a very stable concept of Euclidean geometry which is intended to be categorical and therefore not just a hypothetical abstract structure open to diversified interpretations.

The concept of analyticity was first introduced with the intention of separating out certain trifling propositions which are easily justified by convention (definition), e.g. 'there are twelve pence in a shilling.' This used to be true but recently has been 'falsified' by decree. There are now five pence in a shilling. Here it seems easy to understand what is happening and we are inclined to say that we have changed the convention or that we have changed the meaning of certain words. 'The old proposition is not false but has just become unusable.' There are complications even in this simple example depending, e.g., on whether new coins are minted. The recent fashion of extending the concept of analyticity to include all a priori and necessary propositions has been hard to resist. The extension seems natural and gives us a feeling that we suddenly have an easy way of explaining why necessary propositions are necessarily true. In addition, there are no other natural extensions which are narrower than the final broad notion; the ascent from the narrow concept to the broad one is smooth.

This is a striking example of the assimilation of expressions.[3]

Imagine someone's saying: '*All* tools serve to modify something. Thus the hammer modifies the position of the nail, the saw the shape of the board, and so on'. – and what is modified by the rule, the gluepot, the nails? – 'Our knowledge of a thing's

255

length, the temperature of the glue, and the solidity of the box.'
– Would anything be gained by this assimilating of expressions?

It seems clear that Kant intended the class of analytic propositions to be rather restricted. We would like to say, 'let us stick to the vaguely delineated narrow class.' One difficulty is that we do not have a good definition of the class. But a good class need not have a sharp definition. There are, however, more specific problems. For example, are true statements of logic analytic? Are logical consequences of analytic statements analytic? Kant was able, it seems, to bypass this difficulty because his distinction applies only to judgments which, for him, belong to the realm of understanding, while inferences (at least mediate ones, i.e. ones involving two or more premises), for him, belong to the realm of reason. Another feature is that Kant seemed to have in mind the lexicographer's definitions (or rules of language) so that analytic propositions are trifling isolated statements which are not central to any extended conceptual framework. Hence, for example, statements enunciating definitions of force or kinetic energy or simultaneity in physics would not fall under his concept of analyticity. In this regard, we get a sharp contrast between the narrower and wider definitions: while for Kant, centrality in human knowledge is thought to be evidence against a statement's being analytic, for the broader notion there have been suggestions that the more central a statement is in human knowledge, the higher degree of analyticity it possesses.

From Kant's point of view, the analytic statements are ones which can be seen to be true quite directly from dictionary definitions and can be understood without any special knowledge of science or philosophy. In particular, very simple logical truths may be said to be analytic, but not complicated ones; although it seems attractive to keep silent about logic altogether and deal only with 'judgments.' An objection to the distinction thus reformulated is that it has dubious philosophical interest. In particular, since the range of analyticity is so narrow, it seems less of an achievement to give examples of synthetic a priori propositions. The answer is that, admittedly, the narrower definition makes it easier to argue for the synthetic character of arithmetic truths, but the major achievement of Kant is to show that they are a priori, in a pregnant sense of this term. The crucial criterion for comparing the relative merit of rival positions is the interest and instructiveness of the answers to the question of explaining why arithmetic truths are necessarily true: whether because they are analytic or because they are synthetic a priori in the Kantian sense.

It is not denied that there is an almost irresistible temptation to use the broader definition of analyticity. The criticism is rather that it has driven philosophy into less fruitful channels. Not only has it served as a shaky foundation for sweeping general views but also it has resulted in endless debates on whether there is a distinction to be drawn at all and whether there is a sharp boundary. A curious phenomenon is that bad arguments through contrasting exaggerations have more influence than the sensible avoidance of frustrating involvements in artificial issues. Thus, instead of taking analyticity with a grain of salt and confining its applications to reasonable special cases, the distinction is elevated to the position of the foundation stone of schools of philosophy. Instead of either sticking to more modest concepts or examining the courses of the misuses of the distinction, familiar arguments are employed to derive, without any conclusiveness, general theses such as there being no distinction to be drawn, and to jump to mushy irresponsible slogans of wholism and gradualism.

The following quotation from G. E. Moore[4] represents a reasonable position. 'It seems to me that there are ever so many different cases of necessary connection, and that the line between "analytic" and "synthetic" might be drawn in many different ways. As it is, I do not think that the two terms have any clear meaning.' But again, we cannot overlook the pressures of the professional community to think about what are currently considered central problems and to come out with sharp views and strong positions on issues which need more patient cumulative efforts and more modest dialogues.

In calling mathematics a priori and logic necessary, I do not mean to say that mathematics is not necessary. All that is intended is to mention natural and direct applications of the two concepts. While logic seems ideally suited to the common definition of necessity in terms of possible worlds, to argue that arithmetic truths are necessary in that sense we would have to bring in less clear concepts such as essence and objects versus structure in mathematics. On the other hand, from the side of the a priori, it is well known that Brouwer considered number theory as more basic than logic and, in fact, he extracted different logics from different infinite domains (viz. natural numbers, the continuum, sets).

Often the a priori, the necessary, and the analytic are considered coextensive, and there are natural inclinations for doing so. While Kant distinguished the analytic sharply from the a priori, he also considered the a priori as coextensive with the necessary. Thus, if a proposition is necessary, it is inconceivable or unimaginable that it could be false. If meaning is taken to be all the possible circumstances under which a proposition can be true, then a necessary proposition must be analytic because otherwise we could imagine its being false.

Necessity, Analyticity, and Apriority

An analytic proposition is commonly agreed to be a priori and apriority implies necessary. It is of interest to recall that the three distinctions put different familiar concepts at the center of philosophy. The analytic leads to emphasis on meaning and synonymy. The a priori suggests the examination of the concepts of experience (and knowledge). The necessary is intricately connected with the concepts of possible world (or possibility) and essence (or the nature of things).

When actual knowledge is taken as the most attractive starting point, the natural preference is experience over meaning and possibility. Not only is actuality more definite than possibilities but knowledge is more accessible than reality. Not only is truth more easily graspable than meaning, but known truths are the only dependable source for a better and directed understanding of meaning. Moreover, factualism would favor a study of experience in terms of actual knowledge which is the data for all philosophy. More specifically, actual scientific practice and fundamental ideas in the sciences are the major source of material for philosophical considerations of knowledge which philosophers can ill afford to disregard or take lightly.

In the attempt not to stretch the range of applications of the natural ideas of analyticity, apriority and necessity, we have left much of human knowledge unclassified. At most, we have suggested only possible ways of accounting for logical (necessary), mathematical (a priori), and verbal truths (analytic). It is not claimed that what is not included is all on the opposite side: not everything except logic is contingent, not everything except mathematics is a posteriori. Our initial rudimentary concepts are simply not sharp enough to yield any direct account of, say, the necessity of mathematical truths. In particular, the a priori, which might appear the most promising for factualism, suggests innateness and is altogether too detached from experience. There seems to be an urge to introduce a more comprehensive distinction, perhaps with less claim to explanatory value but at least convenient for general discussions.

Such a prosaic distinction might be between isolated propositions and interexperiential propositions, or between local and global propositions, or between unstable and stable propositions. Such distinctions, like the original meaning of the a priori as what is prior, immediately suggest gradualism and a scale of degrees. What is objectionable in the idea of degrees is not the assertion that there is no sharp sweeping dichotomy of all true propositions but the implication that human knowledge is less structured and less stable than we commonly take it to be. One would like to get a map of knowledge analogous to a map of the world, with mountains, hills, valleys, oceans, islands, rivers, and so on. Philosophy of knowledge

258

aims at making such a map and organizing observations relating to such a map. Therefore, we desire to look more closely at physics, biology, and mathematics. We look for whatever security (or relative certainty) we can get in different parts of human knowledge. Of course, basic scientific advances are of philosophical interest, but a stable and instructive overview of what is known seems a more appropriate goal for philosophers than anticipation of future discoveries.

In scientific practice, there is indeed a kind of relativism. A geologist takes results in physics for granted more or less as self-evident or necessary or a priori. And physicists have a similar attitude toward mathematics. Moreover, two mathematical expressions which mean different things to a mathematician may be considered as having the same meaning by a physicist. This sort of hierarchical presupposition is, according to Bernays,[5] embodied in F. Gonseth's doctrine of the 'préalable.'

There is a seductive idea of wholism or even pragmatic wholism which views our whole conceptual system as a massive alliance of beliefs which face the tribunal of experience collectively and not independently. These beliefs are, according to this view, related to experiences by varying degrees of germaneness and located in the whole conceptual network with varying degrees of centrality. Any statement can be revised and any statement can be held true come what may. The only guidance is pragmatic considerations which include conservatism and the quest for simplicity. There is undoubtedly some sense in which these general statements can be accepted as true if not particularly informative. But there are different objections to the implied picture.

It is not at all clear that anybody can in practice achieve a conceptual framework which is a reasonable abstract picture of the sum total of human knowledge. 'Being in separate disciplines is like being separated by mountains.' The monolithic character of our conceptual system is very much an idealization which, even in philosophy, can only be connected with the actual phenomenon of scientific progress by more specific information about the idealized picture. And pragmatism, like most assimilation to 'nothing but' positions, constantly runs the danger of wavering between vacuity and inadequacy. One feels disturbed by an excessive precision with regard to the minute details of ill-motivated specific problems combined with a willingness to put forward vague sweeping incitant generalities when all of human knowledge is concerned. Exactly the richer middle range, such as the foundations of set theory and the foundations of physics, is left out except for clever remote comments which fail to take seriously the specific conceptual contents of the actual disciplines.

259

There have also been more specific criticisms of this wholism along the lines of Lewis Carroll's Achilles and the tortoise. Revisibility presupposes some minimum unchanging framework with respect to which one can make sense of revisions. It is easy to see that abandoning basic laws which govern 'logical connections,' such as those of identity and contradiction, can be a complex matter, in view of the fact that they are 'dense' rules which affect the assignment of truth values to all propositions. For example, given any partial assignment of truth values, defined everywhere except on a single sentence and its negation, there is an extension of the assignment which satisfies the law of excluded middle.

There is a vague distinction between empirical and conceptual considerations. For example, people speak of revising logic and logic being empirical. But one is reminded of intuitionist logic which results from conceptual considerations rather than empirical considerations. The net impression one gets from the discussions of quantum logic is that no reasonable conceptual system has thus far emerged to determine a stable and understandable quantum logic. In the interesting cases (such as the discovery of $\sqrt{2}$ or Einstein versus Lorentz) where we would be inclined to speak of changes in the meaning of concepts, there is usually less a matter of changing our conventions on how words are used. Rather, we have a deeper continuity of the meaning of the concepts so that one could also speak of the meaning of the same concepts getting clearer and finding out inadequacies of old propositions involving these concepts. It is this double aspect which tempts us toward a hard choice between apparently contradictory positions.

The use of formal languages and meaning postulates to safeguard analyticity in them is also a natural move to avoid the hard choice. It is a typical case of postponing problems by an appeal to the device of if-then. One could in this way codify separately the old concept and the new concept and thereby avoid the confusing task of unifying the apparently contrary concepts. The drawback of this approach is not only that we lose sight of the continuity between the old and the new concepts but that in isolating them we fail to capture the richer underlying concept and cannot even crystallize the full pregnancy of either concept. By working with these artificial concepts for the sake of clarity, we no longer deal directly with actual knowledge but instead spend most of our efforts worrying over supposedly harmless minor departures from the intended meaning of the original concept.

To illustrate the rich variety of propositions of which the question of being a priori or necessary or analytic might be asked, we include a list of propositions most of which have come up in various discussions. 1 $7 + 5 = 12$; 2 if a point a is between b and c, then b is not between a and c; 3 existence is not an attribute; 4 the world is four dimensional; 5 hypocrisy is not red; 6 there exists something; 7 $(\exists x)\,(x = x)$; 8 every property of positive integers which is expressible in the ordinary theory of numbers defines a class of positive integers; 9 a cube has twelve edges; 10 I cannot be you; 11 I could not have been born fifteen years later; 12 'Frau' is a German word; 13 Cantor was the discoverer of Cantor's theorem; 14 Wessel was the discoverer of Argand's diagram; 15 this sentence is true; 16 every tone has an intensity and a pitch; 17 one and the same surface cannot be simultaneously red and green all over; 18 spiritual values have a higher place in the scale of values than vital values; 19 the sum of the internal angles of a triangle is 180°; 20 the sum of the internal angles of a triangle is less than 180°; 21 a sentence in a formal system expressing the consistency of the system; 22 the principle of mathematical induction; 23 any two things differ in at least thirty ways; 24 the empty set is different from its unit set; 25 every sentence is either true or false; 26 if p is analytic and p entails q, then q is analytic; 27 there exists an infinite set; 28 every sentence has a verb; 29 $x + 0 = x, x + (y + 1) = (x + y) + 1$; 30 space is three-dimensional; 31 the best men get what they want; 32 the best men want what they can get; 33 the law of conservation of energy; 34 a continuous line joining a point inside a circle to a point outside intersects the circle; 35 the earth did not come into existence five minutes ago; 36 there is a past; 37 $e = \frac{1}{2}mv^2$; 38 $f = ma$; 39 $e = mc^2 + \frac{1}{2}mv^2 + \ldots$; 40 two spheres cannot differ only numerically; 41 thought is not laryngeal motion; 42 unity is not a quantity; 43 number is not the thing that is counted; 44 the difference between two degrees of quality is not itself a quality; 45 I ought to promote my own good on the whole (where no one else's good is affected); 46 if I ought to do something, then I can do it; 47 the axioms of prudence, benevolence, and equity; 48 I ought to regard a larger good for society in general as of more intrinsic value than a smaller good; 49 one man's good is (other things being equal) of as much intrinsic value as any other man's; 50 the world is a system of necessarily connected parts; 51 an individual is a set of characters; 52 the characters of an individual are not all equally essential; 53 things have manifold necessary relations to other things; 54 every event has a cause; 55 the world is infinite; 56 I see with my eyes; 57 the world is finite but unbounded; 58 what is done cannot be undone.

2 SUGGESTIONS FROM KANT'S PHILOSOPHY

The writings of Leibniz seem to suggest a curious and interesting theory of definitions. There are concepts which are possible and others which are impossible, such as round square and even prime greater than 2. In particular cases, a great deal of analysis and calculation may be necessary for determining whether a concept is possible or not, but there are certain simple (atomic) concepts which are clearly possible. For our other concepts we assume definitions which are similar to an expression of a quantity by means of an algebraic formula. These definitions should enable us to make the decomposition or analysis of a complex concept into the simple (atomic) ones after the fashion of the decomposition of a natural number into its prime factors.

A proposition is a truth of reason, if and only if after we have thus decomposed the subject and the predicate of the proposition, we see that the simple concepts in the subject are among those in the predicate. In most cases, in order to see that a proposition is a truth of reason, we do not have to analyze the predicate and the subject into their simplest constituents. Indeed, we can reach a pretty clear idea of the range of the truths of reason, even without knowing what the simplest concepts are.

Both Kant and Leibniz speak of identical propositions. Sometimes they seem to imply that all analytic propositions or truths of reason are identical propositions. At other times they seem to consider the notion of identical propositions a narrower one. For example, Leibniz asserts that all necessary truths are really identical propositions, yet sometimes he identifies identical propositions with primitive truths of reason, having to do with the simplest concepts only.

The following are examples of what Leibniz considers to be truths of reason. There can only be three dimensions in space. I shall be what I shall be. I have written what I have written. The equilateral rectangle is a rectangle. The rational animal is always an animal. If the regular figure of four sides is an equilateral rectangle, this figure is a rectangle. If a figure having no obtuse angle may be a regular triangle, a figure having no obtuse angle may be regular. An equilateral rectangle cannot be non-rectangle. 'A regular decahedron has ten sides' is not a truth of reason since the concept, 'regular decahedron,' is impossible. As is well known, Leibniz defines $x = y$ by the definition that for every property F, Fx if and only if Fy.

According to Leibniz, 'This sole principle (of contradiction) suffices for the demonstration of arithmetic and all geometry, i.e., of all mathematical principles.' This seems to presuppose a rich theory of definition far beyond what Leibniz actually developed. For example, it is hard to find ordinary definitions to justify customary axioms for the membership relation, or even just for the addition of positive integers, especially if by logic is meant just Aristotelian logic.

Frege claims to have reduced arithmetic to logic and thereby established the analytic character of arithmetical propositions. He thinks he has in this way refuted Kant who considers arithmetical propositions as synthetic a priori. It is, of course, possible to say simply that Frege and Kant understand the domain of the analytic differently because what they consider to be logic is not the same. It is small wonder that by allowing a wider region to logic, logic includes more. Frege could yet argue that his extension of Kant's notion of logic is so natural that Kant would have agreed to the new notion had he known it. It is, nonetheless, simpler to restrict ourselves to Kant's actual use of the terms 'logic' and 'analytic.'

The range of application of Kant's notion of analyticity is narrower than the Leibnizian 'truths of reason' and the Humean 'relations of ideas.' All necessary propositions, those of arithmetic and geometry in particular, are for Hume concerned merely with relations of ideas, and can, according to Leibniz, be demonstrated solely by the principle of contradiction. But, as is well known, the propositions of arithmetic and geometry are synthetic for Kant, whose analytic-synthetic distinction corresponds more closely to Locke's distinction between the trifling and the instructive.

According to Kant, in all analytic judgments the relation of a subject to the predicate is thought in such a way that the predicate B belongs to the subject A, as something which is (covertly) contained in this concept A (A6, B10);[6] and the truth of an analytic judgment can always be adequately known in accordance with the principle of contradiction which states that no predicate contradictory of a thing can belong to it (A151, B190). Kant's examples of analytic propositions include: 1 all bodies are extended (A7, B1); 2 air is an elastic fluid (§ 4); 3 substance is that which only exists as subject (ibid.); 4 gold is a yellow metal (§ 2); 5 no bodies are unextended (i.e. simple) (ibid.); 6 a triangle has three angles (A593, B621); 7 God is omnipotent (A595, B623); 8 all bodies are bodily (or, to use another term, material) beings; 9 everything conditioned presupposes a condition; 10 everything contingent must have a cause (B290); 11 the whole is equal to itself (B17); 12 the whole is greater than its parts (ibid.).

When we try to apply Kant's definition and criterion to explain why these are analytic and to decide whether certain other propositions, not explicitly mentioned by him, would be considered analytic by him, we encounter some difficulty. We can probably admit that most of the above twelve examples are analytic, and verbal; yet to say exactly how, for instance, 1 or 3 or 8 or 12 conforms to his notion of the analytic is not very easy. To quote a criticism by N. K. Smith:[7]

Thus there is little in detecting the synthetic character of the proposition: all bodies are heavy. Yet the reader has first been required to admit the analytic character of the proposition: all bodies are extended. The two propositions are readily identical in logical character. Neither can be recognized as true save in terms of a comprehensive theory of physical existence. If matter must exist in a state of distribution in order that its parts may acquire through mutual attraction the property of weight, the size of a body, or even its possessing any extension whatsoever, may similarly depend upon specific conditions such as may conceivably not be universally realised.

On the other hand, there are other kinds of propositions which appear close to what Kant would recognize as analytic, but which, for one reason or other, he did not discuss explicitly. In the first place, there are what Leibniz calls the disparates: 13 heat is not the same thing as color; 14 man and animal are not the same (although every man is an animal). In the second place, Kant accepts Aristotelian logic and recognizes its formal character. He does not say that 'all men are mortal, all Greeks are men, therefore all Greeks are mortal' is an analytic judgment because he does not consider it a judgment at all. But, as we know, we can rephrase the inference and transform it into a hypothetical judgment: 15 'if all men are mortal and all Greeks are men, then all Greeks are mortal.' There are also other hypothetical judgments obtained by thus reformulating inferences in Aristotelian logic, such as: 16 if all men are mortal, then no men are immortal; 17 if Socrates is perfect implies somebody is perfect, and if nobody is perfect, then Socrates is not perfect. Lastly, there are those propositions which are true on account of grammar or idiomatic usage, such as: 18 if everybody wants peace, then peace is wanted by everybody; 19 if all men are mortal, then everything is such that if it is a man then it is mortal. It is not entirely clear whether Kant would consider 13 — 19 to be analytic, and how he would justify his conclusions. This indicates that Kant's account is not a thoroughly explicit explanation of his basic analytic-synthetic distinction.

The current idea that analytic propositions follow from definitions by logic can be found in Frege. This is rather different from Kant's original concept in several ways. Kant's theory of definition yields a rather narrow range of definitions.

To *define*, as the word itself indicates, really only means to present the complete, original concept within the limits of its concept. If this be our standard, an *empirical* concept cannot be defined at all, but only *made explicit*. . . . In the second place, it it also true that no concept given a priori, such as substance, cause, right, equity, etc. can, strictly speaking, be defined. . . . Consequently, mathematics is the only science that has definitions (A727–9, B755–7).

But of course we do not have many analytic judgments in mathematics according to Kant.

All mathematical judgments, without exception, are synthetic. . . . Some few fundamental propositions, presupposed by the geometricians, are, indeed, really analytic, and rest on the principle of contradiction. But, as identical propositions, they serve only as links in the chain of method and not as principles; for instance, $a = a$; the whole is equal to itself; or $(a + b) > a$, that is, the whole is greater than its part. And even these propositions, though they are valid according to pure concepts, are only admitted in mathematics because they can be exhibited in intuition (B14 and B16–17).

Hence, definitions are a poor source of analytic propositions.

Moreover, instead of arriving at analytic judgments from definitions, the process is usually the reverse.

For if a concept, e.g. that of substance, belongs to metaphysics, judgments which originate in mere analysis of this concept also belong necessarily to metaphysics, e.g. substance is that which only exists as subject, etc. By means of several such analytic judgments we try to arrive at the definition of a concept. But as the analysis of a pure concept of the understanding (such as metaphysics contains) does not proceed in any other way than the analysis of all other concepts, empirical included, that do not belong to metaphysics (e.g. air is an elastic fluid, the elasticity of which is not suspended by any known degree of cold), the analytic judgment is not peculiarly metaphysical, even though the concept is (§ 2c3).

As far as derivations and demonstrations by logic are concerned Kant's position is roughly that we cannot derive analytic judgments (or at least any 'knowledge from principles') from definitions (or other analytic judgments). This is in sharp contrast to the present-day concept of analyticity. According to Kant, every syllogism is a mode of deducing knowledge from a principle. Major premises of syllogisms are universal and can be called principles.

But if we consider them in themselves in relation to their origin, these fundamental propositions of pure understanding are anything rather than knowledge based on concepts. For they would not even be possible a priori if we were not supported by pure intuition (in mathematics), or by conditions of a possible experience in general. . . . The understanding can, then, never supply any synthetic modes of knowledge derived from concepts; and it is such modes of knowledge that are properly, without qualification, to be entitled 'principles' (A301, B357). 'An apodeictic proof can be called a demonstrative, only insofar as it is intuitive' (A734, B762).

Of course, proofs in mathematics do not yield analytic propositions even though the conclusion 'can indeed be discerned in accordance with the principle of contradiction, this can only be if another synthetic proposition is presupposed, and if it can then be apprehended as following from this other proposition; it can never be so discerned in and by itself' (B14). For Kant, the construction of a triangle and a straight line parallel to one of its sides is not just a heuristic step, but forms an integral part of the demonstration.

If these passages are not sufficient to remove our uncertainties with regard to the problem of applying logic to get more analytic propositions, we can appeal to another distinction implicit in Kant. This is the phenomenological component, i.e. what is 'actually thought' in the subject. Where definitions or fairly complete analyses are available, the distinction between analytic and synthetic is logical. But since Kant admits strict definitions only in mathematics and mathematical propositions are synthetic, there is little room for obtaining analytic propositions from the logical distinction. When definitions or adequate analyses are not available, the appeal is to what is actually thought. For example, this is brought out in a negative way while considering mathematical proofs.

We are not here concerned with analytic propositions, which can be produced by mere analysis of concepts (in this the philosopher could certainly have the advantage over his rival), but with synthetic propositions, and indeed with just those synthetic propositions that can be known a priori. For I must not restrict my attention to what I am actually thinking in my concept of a triangle (this is nothing more than the mere definition); I must pass beyond it to properties which are not contained in this concept, but yet belong to it (A718, B746).

We include two more quotations from Kant:[8] 'If one had the entire concept of which the notions of the subject and predicate are *compars,* synthetic judgments would change into analytic. It is a question of how much arbitrariness there is.' Kant did not consider the line of the distinction variable or arbitrary. 'There are definitions of concepts which we already have but which are not correctly named. In these cases, it is not that the meaning of a word is analyzed, but that a concept, which we already possess, is analyzed; then it must be particularly shown what name properly expresses it.'

An affinity of factualism to Kant's philosophy is, if not obvious, certainly intended. There is an impression that mathematical and scientific activities in their appropriate general aspects are taken into account by Kant, if not in an entirely clear way, certainly in a vaguely correct manner. On the more general level, the idea of an unknowable thing-in-itself is not congenial to factualism. In fact, the idea seems to be connected with that of a lawful nature resulting from the form of our consciousness. It seems preferable to take both an external nature and a knowing mind as gross facts, and refrain from postulating either a realm of 'an sich' things or mind-determined nature. This, however, need not lead to the view that the methods of the natural sciences yield an adequate world view.

With regard to the philosophy of mathematics, it should be noted that Kant, in elaborating the intuitive evidence of geometry, said nothing about the question of the evidence of the parallel postulate even though it was under debate in his time. There was little about the continuum, and continuity seems to be identified with unlimited divisibility so that, for example, the line with only rational points would satisfy the condition 'The property of magnitudes by which no part of them is the smallest possible, that is, by which no part is simple, is called their continuity' (A169, B211). There seems to be no serious consideration of the calculus and its applications in physics.

3 FROM FREGE TO ANALYTIC PHILOSOPHY

Frege makes an attempt to state accurately what earlier writers, Kant in particular, have meant by the analytic-synthetic distinction. According to him, the distinction concerns not the content of the judgment but the justification for making the judgment; and the problem of deciding whether a true proposition is analytic or synthetic becomes that of finding a proof of the proposition, and of following it up right back to the primitive truths. If, according to Frege, in carrying out that process, we come only on general logical laws and on definitions, then the truth is an analytic one.[9]

In this account, three kinds of things are involved: *a* proofs; *b* general logical laws; *c* definitions. In order to be clear about a notion of analyticity, we should accordingly be clear about the notions of proof, logical law, and definition. As we have just remarked, Frege's definition is quite different from Kant's in spirit as well as in substance.

To some extent, Frege was aware of the fact that his notion of analyticity was different from Kant's:[10]

> Kant obviously – as a result, no doubt, of defining them too narrowly – underestimated the value of analytic judgments, though it seems that he did have some inkling of the wider sense in which I have used the term. On the basis of his definition, the division of judgments into analytic and synthetic is not exhaustive. . . . He seems to think of concepts as defined by giving a simple list of characteristics in no special order; but of all ways of forming concepts, that is one of the least fruitful. . . . But the more fruitful type of definition is a matter of drawing boundary lines that were not previously given at all. What we shall be able to infer from it, cannot be inspected in advance; here, we are not simply taking out of the box again what we have just put into it. The conclusions we draw from it extend our knowledge, and ought therefore, on Kant's view, to be regarded as synthetic; and yet they can be proved by purely logical means, and are thus analytic. The truth is that they are contained in the definitions, but as plants are contained in their seeds, not as beams are contained in a house.

Knowing what we know now, Frege's detour through logic (or rather set theory) does not help too much, since, in place of arguing that arithmetic is analytic, we are left with the no easier task of arguing that set theory is analytic.

As we have mentioned before, Frege continued to uphold Kant's position that geometry is synthetic a priori. Here is an illustration of how, in philosophy, if we want to get yes and no answers, we can often find proponents of all possible combinations of the different alternatives. Thus, let us ask two questions: *a* whether propositions of arithmetic are synthetic a priori; *b* whether propositions of geometry are synthetic a priori. To both questions Kant answers yes, while many contemporary empiricists answer no. Frege says no to *a* and yes to *b*, while Brouwer says yes to *a* and no to *b*.

Many factors have combined to bring about the transition from Frege's concept of analyticity to the modern idea according to which not only all mathematical truths are analytic but even the foundations of the empirical sciences can be conveniently studied by relative analyticity (i.e. relative to certain meaning postulates governing the basic concepts). With this modern view is often associated also the idea that analytic truths are true by convention. One factor was Poincaré's conventionalism which proposed to retain Euclidean geometry within a general physical theory, come what may. Another factor was the separation of pure from physical geometry with the famous quotation from Einstein: 'As far as the laws of mathematics refer to reality, they are not certain; and as far as they are certain, they do not refer to reality.'

Two other influences were Hilbert's emphasis on implicit definitions and the logistic development of basic mathematics by Whitehead and Russell. The former suggests the hypothetical approach to a theory and the dominance of syntactical over semantic considerations. The latter led Russell to expect wider uses of the logistic apparatus and Carnap to work out constructional systems as a means of reconstructing and even unifying science. On the more philosophical side, Wittgenstein's *Tractatus* contains an attractive account of truth-functional tautologies as being true in virtue of the meaning of the propositional connectives. This is combined with a confused belief in the reducibility of mathematics to logic to arrive at the conclusion that all true mathematical propositions are tautologies in a similar sense.

Thus, in his *Aufbau*, Carnap restates Frege's definition of analytic propositions and mentions the thesis that all a priori propositions are analytic.

> The first type of theorem can be deduced from the definitions alone (presupposing the axioms of logic, without which no deduction is possible at all). These we call *analytic* theorems. . . . If an analytic theorem is transformed into a statement about the basic relations, a tautology results; . . . Expressed in the realistic language, this means that analytic theorems are tautological statements about concepts (these statements are not necessarily trivial, since the tautology may become apparent only after the transformation, as is the case with mathematical theorems); . . . It is the contention of construction theory that there are no such things as the 'synthetic judgments a priori' which are essential for Kant's approach to epistemological problems (§ 106).

> The aim of science consists in finding and ordering the true statements about the objects of cognition. . . . The first aim, then, is the construction of objects; it is followed by a second aim, namely, the investigation of the nonconstitutional properties and relations of the objects. The first aim is reached through convention (Festsetzung); the second, however, through experience. (In the view of construction theory, there are no other

components in cognition than these two, the conventional and the empirical; thus, there is no synthetic a priori) (§ 179).

In 1936, Ayer published a book in English,[11] which widely popularized the views of Carnap and his colleagues. In this exposition, there is, in addition to the broad concept of analyticity, an emphasis on phenomenalism in the tradition of Hume. There is a nod to G. E. Moore's view that philosophizing is an activity of analysis. As the influence of later Wittgenstein became widespread, we see the emergence of the ordinary language wing of analytic philosophy.

4 NOTES ON CONTEMPORARY DISCUSSIONS

In recent philosophy much thought has been given to the distinction between the analytic and the synthetic.[12] A number of people have put this distinction at the center of their philosophical doctrines, making it coincide with that between the necessary and the contingent, the a priori and the a posteriori, and the certain and the merely probable. There results a beguilingly simple picture of knowledge: no more synthetic a priori; no more need for treating propositions of logic and mathematics as empirical hypotheses. Indeed, according to some authorities, contemporary empiricism may be defined as the doctrine that there are no synthetic a priori truths. The rejection of synthetic a priori truths is necessary, it seems to have been assumed, for precluding all theories which tend to admit any form of an intellectual intuition or any speculative scheme that is specially furnished by philosophy and that would compete with the hypotheses of science. Sometimes it is even asserted that all true philosophical propositions, apart from historical records and factual illustrations, are analytic. Hence, philosophy is akin to logic and mathematics at least insofar as they all seek for analytic truths.

There are many different ways of classifying declarative sentences, even when we confine ourselves to a single language. Those which contain more than thirty letters, those containing less. Those containing more than five occurrences of the letter 't', those not. Those expressing philosophical thoughts, expressing scientific thoughts, expressing other thoughts, expressing no thoughts. Those uttered more often by females, those not. True sentences, false sentences, and indefinite sentences. Analytic (true) sentences and synthetic (true) sentences. Necessary (true) sentences and contingent (true) sentences. And so on.

It is certainly not the case that the more significant distinctions are all and only sharp distinctions. If there is any correlation between sharpness and significance, it is probable that the sharper distinctions tend to be the less significant.

If we decide easily in all cases whether a given sentence is of one kind or some other, then the distinction must be a sharp one. The converse is not true. For example, the distinction between theorems and nontheorems in a definite formal system of number theory is a sharp distinction. Yet it is not easy to decide whether Fermat's conjecture is of one kind or the other.

The significance of a distinction depends to a large extent on how many significant things we can say in terms of the distinction. We can of course differ with each other in our judgments as to what things are significant. The same difficulty comes up if we speak in terms of usefulness. It depends on the use to which we want to put the distinction.

One purpose of the analytic-synthetic distinction was presumably to provide us with a clear picture of our knowledge. There are many interesting things which we cannot say about knowledge in general but which we can say separately about knowledge expressed by analytic sentences and about knowledge expressed by synthetic sentences. Insofar as this is true, the distinction is useful and significant.

The interest of the distinction would be substantially reduced if the majority of true declarative sentences were neither analytic nor synthetic or if they could not be decided to be either. Thus, if there were too many things the biologists could not classify as either animals or plants, then the corresponding distinction would become less useful. But so long as and if it is conceded that there is a hard core of analytic sentences (those of logic and mathematics, those true obviously by verbal definitions) and there is a hard core of synthetic sentences, the mere existence of borderline cases is not enough to upset the value of the many interesting things which we say in terms of the distinction.

Philosophers get excited because it is contended that the distinction, taken together with the adherence to a related principle of verifiability, serves to eliminate metaphysics. There are, however, no decisive arguments for or against the contention. While it can be used as an instrument for rationalization by those who are indifferent to metaphysics anyway, there are too many obvious exits which could be taken to avoid the conclusion that metaphysics is nonsense. Indeed, common sense tells us that some metaphysics makes good sense if we read it in the right manner.

Not a few psychologists and social scientists exhibit enthusiasm for the distinction. Apparently they are often bewildered by theories

271

of their colleagues or opponents which they feel are worthless yet which they are quite unable to refute. They find in the analytic-synthetic distinction an effective weapon. They can now press their opponents to make clear the meaning of their terms, and ask whether or not their theories follow strictly from the meaning of their terms. In the first case, their opponents would be proposing disguised definitions. In the second case they can usually argue that the theories are at least highly debatable.

The same trick has also been applied to propositions of metaphysics, by appealing to the thesis that all necessary propositions are analytic. Since metaphysics is traditionally not concerned solely with the meaning of words, metaphysical propositions should not be analytic. Yet if they are not analytic, they cannot be necessary. Then either they are just bold hypotheses on a par with theories in empirical sciences, or they are straight nonsense.

This raises the following question. Is it good to ask persistently whether or not a given proposition is analytic or synthetic? Of course, sometimes it is good, as some psychologists testify. More obviously, it is not always good. Therefore, it is highly desirable to use the distinction intelligently and sensibly. The question is not to keep or abolish the distinction, but how to use it in the right manner.

There are certain living things which we do not know whether to call animals or plants. There are also certain propositions whose truth values we do not know. Nevertheless we ordinarily adhere to the distinctions of animals and plants, and true and false. Bradley did speak of degrees of truth. But he has been out of fashion for more than half a century, even though the pendulum may be swaying back.

We may perhaps compare the matter with the question of deciding whether a man is bald. Admittedly it is a matter of degree here. There are numerous people who are borderline cases. It is theoretically possible to introduce a sharp distinction by stipulating that, for example, a man with less than 500 hairs on his head is to be called bald. This curious distinction could become interesting if there were some drug which would enable a man with 500 hairs or more to recover his lost hairs. Otherwise the strict distinction would be very arbitrary and quite objectionable. It would probably be highly objectionable if proponents of the strict distinction between the analytic and the synthetic talked as though they had such a magic drug.

Gödel distinguishes two senses of analyticity: (1) the subjective sense, i.e. truth by virtue of human definitions, and (2) the objective sense, i.e. truth by virtue of concepts as objectively existing entities. According to him, logic and mathematics are analytic in the objective sense but not in the subjective sense.[13]

In this sense even the theory of integers is demonstrably non-analytic, provided that one requires of the rules of elimination that they allow one actually to carry out the elimination in a finite number of steps in each case. (Because this would imply the existence of a decision-procedure for all arithmetical propositions.)

Since the three distinctions of analytic-synthetic, necessary-contingent, and a priori-a posteriori are intricately connected and have from time to time been identified or at least regarded as coextensive, it is convenient to introduce a more general distinction between type A and type B statements for the purpose of discussing an ambiguous dichotomy summarizing the three distinctions.

It is a commonplace to assert that philosophers disagree because they use the same words differently, that philosophy is not clear because the problems are not clear, that the real purpose or significance of a long sequence of separately cogent arguments and criticisms remains obscure at the end, that when philosophers do draw grand conclusions from their reasoning there is often some non sequitur. Like many other trite assertions, these are true. One way to avoid such common errors in philosophy is to restrict oneself, as far as possible, to saying what can be said clearly and definitely, and to begin to speculate only when nearly all the clear and definite things to be said on the topics have been exhausted.

For example, there are various areas in logic and mathematics of which we have a pretty clear picture and in which the true propositions are almost universally accepted as of type A. Before arguing about general questions about type A, we could attempt first to characterize somewhat fully such areas. The question of definitions is a hard one, but perhaps much obscure talk could be avoided if we examined a wider variety of actual definitions in, for instance, the dictionaries, mathematical and scientific textbooks, etc. rather than confining ourselves to a very small number of overworked traditional examples. Thus, Putnam contrasts[14] the concept of kinetic energy with the concept of bachelor. The statement $e = \frac{1}{2} mv^2$ is of quite a different type from statements such as 'all bachelors are unmarried.' Putnam discusses law-cluster concepts and framework concepts and remarks on their difference from more isolated concepts.

For every given way of drawing the line, we have at least two different problems. The first is to compile a list of type A propositions or to provide a general method for compiling such a list. The second problem is to justify the list or the method for compiling it as the right one.

For example, we can imagine a committee of learned men organized for the purpose of selecting all the true sentences in the books of a certain large library. Afterwards, we can ask the logicians and mathematicians to single out those which are truths of logic and mathematics, the linguists to single out those which are true by grammar and verbal definitions. With regard to true sentences involving technical terms, we ask the physicists, biologists, etc. whether or not these are true merely on account of the way they use their terms, etc. Moreover, the logicians may have to add also all the logical consequences of the true sentences thus found to be of type A.

Suppose that in this way we arrive at a list of true sentences which are of type A, a list of true sentences which are not, and probably also a list of true sentences which we do not know where to put. In cases where experts disagree, we put the sentences in the third list too.

Ordinary dictionaries can be used to help in the selection of type A propositions. There are, of course, obstacles to using these as a guide. Certain relations are not mentioned in dictionaries (for example, a cube has six faces). We are interested in sentences not merely words. We can retain the same meaning after we make rhetorical or other kinds of rephrasing. These are usually not recorded in the dictionary, but rather in grammar books or handbooks on usage. Sometimes a dictionary may tell us too much, i.e. give us information which is not clearly of type A. For example, Columbus was the discoverer of America.

Actually, we go beyond dictionaries and ordinary usage to make special areas more precise, as the need arises. For example, logic makes $=$, 'or,' 'and,' 'only if,' 'not,' more precise. Biology stipulates an exact use of terms such as 'fish,' and so on. Even here we can allow boundary cases. Similarly in mathematics and other sciences we find it necessary to use certain terms more exactly.

There is no rigid order of priority in definitions. For example, either speed is equal to distance divided by time, or in driving an automobile, distance is equal to speed times time. In order to determine the meaning of a term we often have to get into larger and larger contexts and do not restrict ourselves merely to word by word explanations. If we were merely concerned with words, many words are certainly indefinable ('time,' 'one,' etc.). The dictionary merely gives 'near' equivalents. We learn the use of words by different methods and tools. Dictionaries are, perhaps, but the least significant of these.

There remains the question of a criterion for determining whether or not a sentence is of type A. What has often been suggested is a behavioristic criterion such as the degree of commitment, or the degree of readiness to give up a sentence in the face of adverse evidence, or the feeling of certainty. Any of these could be employed to provide a partial ordering of all true sentences according to the amount of character A in them.

Approached in this manner, the question of where to draw the line clearly becomes more or less arbitrary. But such an approach cannot be adequate anyway. There are many sentences which few would consider to be of type A but about which we are as certain as we are about any type A sentence. For example, 'the earth has existed for many years past,' 'the distance from London to Peking is more than two kilometers,' 'my body was born at a certain time in the past.' The conclusion is that no simple behavioristic criterion can suffice. Indeed, so long as there is a fair degree of agreement, we need not worry too much about an explicit formulation of a criterion for choosing type A sentences.

It seems reasonable to suppose that among the true sentences whose type A character we have difficulty in deciding, very few cases are such that one group insists on calling them type A while another group insists on calling them type B. In most cases, the difficulty comes because nobody has a strong conviction that the sentences definitely belong to either category. In other words, we are usually unable to decide whether a given true sentence is of type A or B because we cannot see what difference our calling it one or the other would make. We can say we are faced with a pseudoproblem, because there is neither urgency nor an unquestionable standard for judging a reply. A blurred picture of a blurred situation can nonetheless be truthful. Accuracy and precision do not usually go together. Misplaced precision can be most inaccurate and misleading.

We turn to the question of justifying the answers. Suppose we have a list of type A propositions generated by what we consider to be rather reliable methods. Somebody reading it may or may not agree that our list is the correct one. Assuming that he does, are we at the end of the quest? One would probably say that our list is at most a careful report of usage. But one wants something more to account for the necessity – what produces the necessity? Why are these necessary? Now what kind of answer is expected?

We could answer that these are of type A because they are true in all possible worlds, or because they are true in virtue of the intended meaning (by definition), or because they are seen to be true by a criterion in mind, etc. One and all of these answers may be used. It is not important that these are not clear. Even unclear ideas can illuminate each other. Moreover, what is asked for is, at least in part, some feeling of comfort or ease. That each answer does provide the required feeling for certain people is quite obvious from history.

Of course, if we ask more specific questions about more specific areas, we can get more specific answers.

The conventionalist answer is perhaps the most tempting: we just decide to use words in that way. There are, of course, familiar difficulties in a thorough development of the answer. Indeed, if we handle the matter too rigidly, we easily get into some circularity or infinite regress. This is analogous to the matter of communication: in order to communicate we have to reach some common usage, in order to establish common usage, we have to communicate first. The fact that we can communicate proves that the regress is harmless.

If every hammer must be man-made and in order to make it another hammer is necessary, we can never make the first hammer. The fact that we do have hammers proves that at least one of the premises must be false. It is a fact that certain propositions are true by convention. If we need another convention in order to introduce a convention, then there is a regress. But there exist no impossible facts.

Perhaps it is better to make a few exceptions and assume that we can see the true and necessary character of the rule of syllogism or modus ponens and certain basic identities such as the simple numerical formulas. Then it would be easier to argue that many other type A truths are true by convention. In any case, it is quite clear that the rule of *modus ponens* occupies a very peculiar position in the domain of type A truths and deserves separate treatment. Similarly the numerical identities form a very basic category.

There are many other things which are relevant to the clarification of the nature of type A truths. Apart from the question of verbal definitions, many have to do mainly with the foundations of logic and mathematics. For instance, theorems and undecidable sentences of formal systems, definitions of truth or analyticity for given formal sytems, the nature of implicit definitions, the possibility of alternative logics, the relation between existence and necessity, the nature of geometry, and the consistency of mathematics.

The concept of convention is both appealing and involved. It is natural to feel that it has much to contribute toward explaining necessity. Yet in practice we seem unable to get much illumination from it.[15]

Coordination problems are faced by two people rowing a boat or the Budapest String Quartet. These can be solved by concordant mutual expectations which may be produced by, among other things, agreement. In particular, if verbal communication is feasible, a common understanding of the problems can be ensured. If the same or a similar coordination problem is repeated, there is a tendency to follow a precedent or precedents. This leads to a convention: driving on the left in England, red and yellow lights for walking in Massachusetts, and signs saying 'walk on the left-hand side.' Convention may involve (explicit) agreement, or precedent. Convention involves common knowledge and knowledge that it is common knowledge.

Conventions (for example, those of a language) can be learned in different ways. A native speaker is a party to the conventions of the language. His knowledge of the conventions may be potential knowledge only or nonverbal knowledge (though about conventions of a language) and he may be able to apply a convention in particular instances without formulating a general belief.

By definition, a convention admits of alternatives. It is in this sense and in this sense only that conventions are arbitrary. It is in this sense that a decision to accept, for example, an axiom is not necessarily a convention. What is not conventional to some may be conventional to others so that there are degrees of convention. Complicated consequences of a convention may or may not be conventions, since these consequences need not be common knowledge. Are government laws conventions?

Explicit agreement is not the only possible source of conventions. Now there is an ambiguity in the word 'agreement.' If it means verbal agreement, it seems that we not only do not, but cannot originate all convention by agreement. We have, perhaps, the case of the Budapest String Quartet, or the implicit understandings between two superpowers. Or perhaps one can think of infinite regresses and argue that even if any convention of language could be introduced by verbal agreement, not all of them could. There is also a tendency to think that conventions of language must, by definition, be created by verbal agreement. Perhaps agreement is a broader notion than convention. Perhaps (social) contract is the appropriately narrower notion. But then a social contract does not seem to imply as much common knowledge.

Traffic lights and other signals are in an obvious sense conventional. We can also use verbal signals. We encounter concepts of intention, communication, and (conventional) meaning. An action is often more suitable for being a sign if it is easy to produce and easy to observe. But this does not apply to natural signs such as symptoms of a disease. We are then led to semantic rules for possible languages (such as truth in L). Semantic rules appear to be explicit verbal conventions. Now it seems a small step to say that an actual language is nothing but a possible language used by a population. It may also be said that we have an additional 'semantic rule' of speaking truth in the language, i.e. the 'rule' that when we make a statement, it is implicitly prefixed by an assertion sign. And the additional rule actualizes a possible language.

But we have not touched on logic, and, to account for logic, we are tempted to appeal to the notion of possible world. As for grammar, it is supposed to economize our brain power and make a language usable. We are supposed to bring behavioral and cultural factors into possible languages to render one of them explicit.

There is a conventional element in language. We might change our conventions if we like: use words otherwise or use different words. This does not mean that necessary truths are created by convention. And this leaves out most of the interesting problems. What is so peculiar about words in logic and in arithmetic?

To say that analyticity is not sharp is quite different from saying it is not intelligible.

There are unwritten rules, informal rules which may or may not be called rules.

There are different nice ways of motivating parts of logic and parts of mathematics.

We may think there is some urlogic, even though we are not sure exactly what belongs to the urlogic. Even if we agree that there is a basic relativity of all knowledge to empirical facts in a broad sense (e.g. genetic facts), what is most interesting is not the aspect of relativity.

It is difficult to deny that what we regard as evident may turn out not to be evident. But we need a more convincing overall view to overthrow a given one. And we are very much interested in knowledge as it is. We have to understand what it means to revise logic or arithmetic; such revisions involve much more than any flippant relativism would suggest.

NOTES

1 *Nouveaux essais*, book 4, ch. 9.
2 Compare the discussions of the concepts of experience of Aristotle, Locke, Kant, Carnap, and later Wittgenstein in F. Kambartel, *Erfahrung und Struktur*, 1968.
3 L. Wittgenstein, *Philosophical investigations*, 1953, p. 7.
4 *Philosophy of G. E. Moore*, ed. P. A. Schilpp, 1942, p. 667.
5 P. Bernays, *Akten XIV Int. Kong. Philos.*, 1968, pp. 192–8.
6 The page references are to Kant's *Critique of pure reason*; the section references are to his *Prolegomena*.
7 *Commentary to the critique of pure reason*, pp. 38–9.
8 From Reflexion 3928 and 3003 in the Prussian Academy edition of Kant's works. For a suggestive discussion of Kant's views on the notion of analyticity, compare L. W. Beck, *Kant-Studien*, vol. 47, 1955, pp. 168–81, and *Philos. rev.*, vol. 65, 1956, pp. 179–91.
9 *Foundations of arithmetic*, § 3.
10 Ibid., § 88.

11 A. J. Ayer, *Language, truth and logic.*

12 From the vast literature on this subject, we mention just a few. W. V. Quine, 'Two dogmas of empiricism,' *Philos. rev.*, vol. 60, 1951; F. Waismann, 'Analytic and synthetic,' *Analysis*, vols 10, 11, 13, 1949–52; H. Putnam, 'The analytic and the synthetic,' *Minnesota studies in philos. of sci.*, vol. 3, 1962; A. Pap, *Semantics and necessary truth*, 1958; B. Blanshard, *Reason and analysis*, 1962.

13 *Philosophy of B. Russell*, ed. P. A. Schilpp, 1944, p. 150.

14 In the paper listed in note 12.

15 For a careful consideration of the issues touched on in the following five paragraphs, see D. K. Lewis, *Convention: a philosophical study*, 1969.

IX

MATHEMATICS AND COMPUTERS

---

1 NEW USES OF COMPUTERS

The eventual goal of studying new uses of computers must be practical in a broad sense. They may be used to do familiar things in order to eliminate drudgery, to reduce cost, to increase reliability, or to speed up operations. The greater accuracy and speed alone may also make possible hitherto unachievable aims such as space projects or weather forecasting. The practical goal could also be the advance of knowledge and understanding. Many of the unorthodox experiments and speculations on new uses of computers have to be justified in such terms. And it can be frustrating to remind oneself that much of the theoretical work on computers may turn out to be pointless in the long run.

There is a sort of conservation law. The immediately practicable applications such as airline reservations or recognition of characters typed by a given kind of machine are, though financially profitable, intellectually less challenging, while the more exciting problems are, almost by definition, much harder.

For example, computers are useful as a model of 'thinking machines' in that we can now experiment with hardware models or program simulations thereof which will perform certain mental acts. It is not so much (not in the foreseeable future anyway) that we aim at duplicating the brain but rather, we can try to improve existing computers, both in their use and in their structure, to perform more and more sophisticated tasks. On account, however, of the radical novelty of qualitatively new applications, we are mostly at a loss as to how to proceed. In fact, this area shares with many new things serious and interrelated drawbacks: no solid foundation (such as Newtonian mechanics) to rely upon, no heritage to fall back on, cumulative advance not easy, standard of evaluating results less objective, vulnerability to exaggeration and deception.

There are also safer uses which are not practical in the narrow sense. For example, the very concept of computers lends a new dimension to discussions on philosophical problems such as mind and body, the nature of consciousness. In the area of mathematics, we can also list a few rather noncontroversial examples. Computers have been used as heuristic aids to deal with nonlinear problems. The complex data are not only useful in themselves but may suggest solutions to abstract mathematical problems in more general cases. There has also been work to prove general theorems in number theory by reducing them to some special numerical cases manageable on large computers. In numerical analysis, it is desirable to mechanize the sequencing of connecting steps between different procedures in order to take advantage of the automatic aspect of computers.

2 INFLUENCE OF MATHEMATICS ON THE DEVELOPMENT OF COMPUTERS

Rather surprisingly, the influence of specific mathematical theories and results on the development of computers is quite limited. Perhaps we can mention only the two elementary things: Boolean algebra for circuit design and the binary notation of numbers. The abstract theory of idealized computers has had little practical impact.

In a more general way, the abstract theory has of course a good deal of educational value for users of computers. Moreover, whatever pure mathematicians may say, programming is quite typically a mathematical activity insofar as it involves a lot of 'thought experiments' with characters and numerals. On the whole, a sort of mathematical spirit is crucial to the use of computers. In fact, with the current shift of emphasis from hardwares to softwares, one would expect the influence of mathematics to increase.

The mathematical study of computers is attractive but not easy since it often calls for new conceptual tools to achieve the correct formulations of right theorems to be proved. Some of the directions under development are: 1 to find more realistic idealized models of computers and programs; 2 to relate computer programs to more standard logical and mathematical formulas in order to assist simplification and debugging of programs; 3 to establish a natural framework for proving that multiplication is in general more complex than addition; 4 to formulate the appropriate notion of effective method and prove that the traveling salesman problem is unsolvable; 5 to develop a mathematical theory of pattern recognition.

Of course, it is possible that a higher level of abstraction may impose some order and uniformity on how to use computers. One might think of the examples familiar from high school mathematics: clever word problems in arithmetic become a matter of routine in algebra, and ingenious proofs in elementary geometry can be treated systematically in analytic geometry.

3 LOGICAL MATHEMATICS

In general, formalization or rendering exact and explicit vague procedures is of practical interest in extending the range of application of computers. This is perhaps the most basic link between logic and computers. It is in this direction that a large scale revolution of mathematics is likely to be achieved in the long run. As more and more of our mathematical arguments get mechanized, the human contribution to the mathematical activity will have to be less and less routine and more and more imaginative or creative.

The initial experiment with and limited success at automatic demonstration came from an appreciation of the fairly advanced state which mathematical logic had arrived at with respect to formalization. Further attempts at progress revealed the limitations of the achievements of logic as a formal and systematic treatment of mathematics. Very roughly speaking, what one needs is not just formalization in principle of mathematical textbooks but rather formalization in practice of mathematical activities. The goal is to enrich logic (or mathematics) so that computers can aid pure mathematicians at least as much as they assist the applied scientists at present. It calls for the mechanization of two related aspects: the formalization of proofs after discovery, and the abstraction of general methods to guide the search for proofs of new theorems. There seems to be a need to develop a sort of 'logical mathematics,' the idea of which must be quite repulsive to pure mathematicians who would think of a hybrid of mathematicians and librarians. It is most likely that such a discipline will be more relevant to automatic demonstration than 'mathematical linguistics' is to mechanical translation. Moreover, it may even be the most promising avenue in the near future that will lead to a general progress on the study of the potentialities and limitations of 'artificial intelligence.'

Formalization is obviously central to all uses of computers. The very existence of computers depends on the basic fact that we have exact rules for numerical calculations. Arguing by analogy, we may contend that the great expansion of the uses of computers for mental acts will be achieved first in the area of mechanizing mathematical arguments. Compared with game-playing, this area is much richer and more central to all works of the intellect.

4 MATHEMATICAL REASONING AS MECHANICAL

There are several aspects of the thesis that mathematical reasoning is mechanical. It means more than the thesis that mathematical arguments can be formalized; it requires mechanization of methods of proof and not merely formalization of given informal proofs into a mechanically checkable form. An ambiguity in this thesis is the difference between the possibility of somehow doing mathematics mechanically and the stronger requirement of mechanizing the actual process of doing mathematics. For example, according to the second interpretation, the thesis would have us mechanize the processes of how individual mathematicians find proofs, how mathematics is taught, how the mathematical community reaches a consensus about accepting certain results (as true). If the interest is to determine whether the thesis can conceivably be true, there are advantages in taking the thesis in the second sense. If one wishes to do as much mathematics as possible with computers, then it is reasonable not to worry over being faithful to how people do mathematics. Here we have a special case of the contrast between artificial intelligence and simulation.

With regard to the general issue of mechanism, the definiteness and exactness of mathematics have a special attraction. One might feel we have here a large body of sharp data useful for testing any mechanical theory of mind, perhaps comparable to data on planetary motions for the development of mechanics. Since, however, we do not have sharp exact data on the mathematical activity, the attractive feature is really much more restricted. Like the less serious area of board games, the end results (viz. actual plays or proofs obtained) are rather more exact than specifications of what is a good translation or what patterns are to be extracted from what data. In other words, even though our knowledge of the process of activity is vague and limited in all these areas, the existing mathematics regarded as a finished product is more definite than most of the other basic areas of mental activities.

In the direction of formalization, there are two major successes in modern logic. First, the fairly well established conclusion that all of mathematics is reducible to axiomatic set theory and that, if one takes enough trouble, mathematical proofs can be reproduced in this system completely formally in the sense of mechanical checkability.

Second, the results of Skolem and Herbrand according to which we can, by construing mathematical theorems as conditional theorems (viz. that the axioms imply the theorem) in the predicate calculus, search for each mathematical proof in a mechanical (in principle) way to determine whether a related Herbrand expansion contains a contradiction. Impressive as these results are, and encouraging as they are for the project of mechanizing mathematical arguments, they are only theoretical results which do not establish the strong conclusion that mathematical reasoning (or even a major part of it) is mechanical in nature.

What is exciting in the unestablished strong conclusion is that we are facing an altogether new kind of problem which cries out for a totally new discipline and which has wide implications for the perennial problem about mind and machine. We are invited to deal with mathematical activity in a systematic way. Even though what is demanded is not mechanical simulation, the task requires a close examination of how mathematics is done in order to determine how informal methods can be replaced by mechanizable procedures and how the speed of computers can be employed to compensate for its inflexibility. The field is wide open, and like all good things, it is not easy. But one does expect and look for pleasant surprises in this requirement of a novel combination of psychology, logic, mathematics, and technology.

There is a false contrast between the algorithmic and the heuristic approaches. Every program has to embody some algorithm, and for serious advances partial strategies or heuristic methods are indispensible. Hence, no serious program could avoid either component. Perhaps the contrast is more between anthropomorphic and logicist approaches, as typified by the general problem solver on the one hand and elaborate refinements of the Herbrand theorem on the other. This polarization appears to me to be undesirable and to represent what I would call the reductionist syndrome.

Typically the reductionist is struck by the power or beauty of certain modes to proceed and wish to build up everything on them. The two extremes seem to share, in practice if not in theory, this reductionist preoccupation. In my opinion, there should be more reflective examinations of the data, viz. the existing mathematical proofs and methods of proof. It is true that what is natural for man need not be natural or convenient for machine. Hence, it will not be fruitful to attempt to imitate man slavishly. Nevertheless, the existing body of mathematics contains a great wealth of material and constitutes the major source of our understanding of mathematical reasoning. The reasonable course would be to distill from this great reservoir whatever is mechanizable. In other words, we should strive for an interplay between reduction and reflection which, for lack of a better name, may be called the dialectic method.

A reflectionist takes the data of existing human knowledge more seriously and often is not able to come up with as sweeping answers. In its extreme form, we arrive at phenomenology which is serious philosophy but hardly of immediate relevance to technical advances. For example, inconclusive arguments have been put forward to contend that it is intrinsically impossible to use computers to perform mental tasks such as making perspicuous grouping, tolerating ambiguities, distinguishing essence from accident, and appealing to fringe consciousness. While these discussions help to focus certain long range issues, we do not at present possess sharp enough concepts of realizable computers and feasible algorithms to prove, or even to conjecture, such impossibility results.

Although such extreme positions do not seem promising, it does seem highly desirable to coordinate reduction (synthesis) with reflection (analysis) in the area of automatic demonstration. In particular, at the present stage, the preoccupation with Herbrand's theorem illustrates for me a reductionist tendency, and should, in my opinion, be balanced by more reflections on the data (viz. existing mathematics). For example, in number theory, we should obviously make use of *least* counterexamples rather than just counterexamples. In each branch of mathematics, we should bring in, besides general features common to all branches, distinguishing characteristics of the particular branch. In addition, we are no longer interested in the economy of axioms but rather lean heavily on derived rules (metatheorems). As we progress, what is known at each stage has to be more carefully digested and organized in order that mechanical retrieval be feasible. More concretely, I feel that an extensive and systematic examination of a large body of existing proofs is of value at the present stage.

If we reflect on the mathematical activity, one striking feature is man's ability to operate simultaneously on different levels. It is not necessary to perfect the lower levels in a hierarchy in order to be able to act on a higher level. And it is hard to see how machines can be made to do the same. As a result, one often finds it easier to adapt oneself to take advantage of what machines can currently do (such as checking numerical instances after the man himself has reduced a general theorem to these crucial special cases). But the primary objective of automatic demonstration is certainly to extend the general power of computers to take over new types of work.

It is highly likely that there are different levels of mathematical activity which can be measured by the ease of mechanization. For example, Euler told of how his theorems were often first discovered by empirical and formalistic experimentations. While these experimentations are probably easy to mechanize, the steps of deciding what experimentations to make and of finding afterwards the correct statement and proof of the theorems suggested are of a higher level and much harder to mechanize. Ramanujan is reported to have commented on the taxicab number 1724 that it is the smallest number expressible as a sum of two cubes in two different ways. The memory and powers of calculation exemplified in this anecdote are probably not hard for a computer, but it would be less easy to have a computer prove most of his theorems. One suspects, however, it would be easier for a computer to prove his theorems than many of the more famous theorems in number theory which are more 'conceptual' and further removed from calculations. Axiomatic set theory has in more recent years become much more mathematical, and one gets the impression that long formal proofs of relatively simple results are much easier to discover mechanically than advanced neat proofs which can be communicated succinctly between experts.

On the highest level, Poincaré compares Weierstrass and Riemann. Riemann is typically intuitive while Weierstrass is typically logical. In this case, it is natural to believe that it is easier to reach results of Weierstrass mechanically. Hadamard contrasts his impression of the great works of Poincaré and Hermite and states that he finds Hermite's discoveries more mysterious.[1] By stretching greatly one's imagination, one might wish to claim that Hadamard would have found it easier to design a program to discover Poincaré's results than to get one for Hermite's.

G. Wallas[2] suggests that there are four stages in the process of bringing about a single achievement of thought: 1 preparation, 2 incubation, 3 illumination, 4 verification. This fits in well with Poincaré's lecture on mathematical discoveries.[3] Hadamard[1] and Littlewood[4] discuss these four stages at great length. The first and the last stages are done consciously. The preparation stage contains two parts: the long range education of the individual, and the immediate task of learning and digesting what is known about the problem under study. The verification stage consists of making vague ideas precise and filling in gaps (in particular, carrying out calculations). To mechanize these stages appears formidable enough but incubation leading to illumination would seem in principle a different kind of process from the operation of existing computers. Since incubation implies an element of rest (an abstention from conscious thought on the initial problem), we may perhaps claim that the importance of this stage comes from a weakness on the part of man, and that machines do not need the period of rest or abstention.

286

One interesting aspect of the mathematical activity is the great economy with which the experts communicate their arguments to one another. It presupposes a vague but useful distinction between the new and the routine. Also in memorizing an argument, a good mathematician tends to retain just the barest outline which is sufficient to recall, when the need arises, a whole long chain of details. This indicates a very flexible structure in the head which is almost never revealed in written works but which could sometimes be taught in a highly informal manner. A related ability is to use rich general concepts in a variety of diverse contexts; for example, an open set, a diagonal argument, a tree.

The sense in which mathematical arguments can be formalized is controversial. Excessive concern with formalization seems on the whole to hamper the ability to discover new results. A certain degree of formalization is often useful to the teaching of an argument and, in general, for communication to those with somewhat different backgrounds.

We may wish to attempt to formalize the structure of, say, set theory, as it lies in the head of a good set theorist. The difficulties would appear to be formidable. And it is hard to see how we can make the efforts seem worthwhile – seeing that such a long term project is perhaps harder to carry out than proving new theorems.

5 FINITE COMPUTATIONS AND INFINITE MATHEMATICS

5.1 Physical limitations

It seems unquestionable that we cannot have arbitrarily small or arbitrarily fast computer components (say for switching). Physics should be capable of calculating lower or upper bounds to these quantities. This kind of limitation does not affect in any inevitable way the meaning of infinite mathematical procedures. Of course, if there were no such bounds, we might be able to justify mathematical infinity simply by physically actual infinity. I see no reason to delay over this unrealistic assumption.

The problem of noise and the nonexistence of infallible components can to some extent be treated by means of redundancy. For example, von Neumann[5] asserted that if the probability of basic units to malfunction is no more than $\epsilon = 0.05$ (half of one per cent), then one can arbitrarily improve the reliability by majority organs (fiduciary level $\Delta = 0.07$ is favored). There are other complications not considered in von Neumann's scheme, but it seems reasonable to accept that for moderately long computations, we can, with enough effort, improve reliability to as high a degree as we wish.

In short, we wish to distinguish two kinds of problem: the scientific problems of physical limitations of speed, reliability, size, and length of computation on the one hand; the epistemological problem of arbitrarily long computations on the other. The scientific problems are important and contain different interrelated aspects each calling for careful attention. But, for the purpose of our present discussion at least, the epistemological problem is essentially one, viz. the apparent fact that there can be no physical machinery to carry out arbitrarily long computations, either without error or just without appreciable probability of error. For this epistemological problem, I do not view the distinction between certainty and high probability as the central issue. I shall leave aside the challenging problem of a theory of physical computations and confine myself to considering the philosophical implications of the finite nature of actual computations. The main features of the basic problem are fully present in the simple matters of adding or multiplying large integers.

There is indeed a distinction between one machine to do arbitrarily long computations and each long computation to be done by some machine. It is logically possible that there is no machine M which deals with all lengths n, yet for each length n there is a machine M to do it. But we shall not speculate on whether such a logical possibility is actual. Rather we shall take for granted that neither is physically possible; therefore, in particular, that there is some large N such that we can never do a computation of length N with reasonable accuracy. For those who do not like the assumption, we may base our discussion on the weaker postulate:

(*) There can be no physical machine which does correctly arbitrarily long computations.

Does it follow from this that there exists no procedure for calculating the digits of π? The problem of mathematical existence is notoriously controversial. We are accustomed to saying that there exist infinitely many prime numbers, that there exists (indeed, we have) an effective method by which we can, for each n, calculate the n-th digit of π, that there exists a relatively simple effective function f such that $f(n)$ gives the n-th digit of π. To say that there exists no such procedure invokes not only the postulate (*), but also, more seriously, the stipulation:

(#) Existence of a mathematical procedure can only be established by the existence of a physically constructible automaton to carry out the procedure arbitrarily far.

Even in applying infinite mathematics, physics possesses a closer contact with reality and executable procedures. Experimental confirmation of a physical theory has to go through performable measurements and calculations. Mathematics supplies a detour through the nonexecutable. If applications of nonexecutable mathematics are to be accepted at all, the physical scientist can also, no less than the mathematician, legitimately work on such material in order to help complete the detour.

5.2 Mathematics and its application

The stipulation ($\#$) presents serious problems to both mathematics and physics. It may be thought that mathematics could go on as 'purely formal systems,' but physics cannot hide behind such formalities. This can at best serve to evade the issue. It is certainly not an arbitrary matter that we choose to emphasize the 'formal systems' of natural numbers and real numbers. Why do we favor some formal systems over others?

Application is a distinguishing characteristic of mathematics, in contrast with mere games. One does not justify the study of pure mathematics exclusively or primarily in terms of applicability. Mathematics in its advanced stage also lives a life of its own. For example, the criterion of beauty and elegance, that of depth, all are commonly employed in judging works in mathematics.

But it is an undeniable fact that infinite mathematics has been applied in a most spectacular way in the study of natural phenomena. In terms of applications, infinity has thus far proven to be a highly useful detour. One might ask whether it may not further improve matters if we eliminate this detour altogether. We have no guide line as to how to accomplish this. In fact, the mathematical way of thinking in terms of infinities is so deeply rooted, it is hard to see why we should wish to give up such a powerful tool.

Less drastic new directions would be to retain what we have, but look more closely at infinities as detours and try to extract as much executable content as we can, as well as to justify infinite mathematics in terms of experiencible facts and more concrete intuitions.

Attempts along these directions are not unfamiliar, but usually less drastic than eliminating infinities altogether. Rather they represent a domestic affair for mathematicians who wish to eliminate or justify higher infinities (the actual infinite) in favor of or in terms of simple infinities (the potential infinite). Thus we have intuitionism, finitism, as well as various efforts to rebuild classical analysis in terms of recursive functions or constructive sets in some suitable sense of 'constructive.' On the whole, there has been no definitive success in the sense of actually changing the common practice in mathematics.

But a suitable rough-edged recursive approach may turn out to be a wholesome way of looking at mathematics.

There are also a few scattered discussions of strict finitism and ultraintuitionism, which reject numbers which are not 'executable.' In particular, A. S. Yessenin-Volpin[6] attempts to prove the consistency of current set theory on this basis. The proposed proof is rather obscure and some people regard it as an elaborate joke. There is, however, no doubt that the author is quite serious about his program.

5.3 Mathematical activity

Mathematical activity is a phenomenon in nature and is, as such, like all mechanical and mental activities, finite. This undeniable fact does not in itself exclude infinite mathematics. Rather, it excludes, for example, any alleged proof that is too complex to be digestible. For example, even though whether 'the billionth digit of π is 7' is a problem decidable in principle, we do not possess at present a digestible proof either of this proposition or of its negation.

What we have here is not something controversial but rather an aspect of mathematics grossly neglected in foundational discussions. One can accept mathematics as it is commonly practiced or choose some different outlook on mathematics. But in any case, a mathematical theorem is established only if it is somehow accepted by the relevant mathematical community and somebody must have understood the proof. Execution is central to mathematics, but not in the restricted sense of exhibiting the billionth digit of π, rather more in the extended sense of actual understanding (a mental activity) by some human mind. Attention to this aspect of mathematics can even resolve the deep-rooted conflict on the question of how central applications are for mathematics. The pursuit of elegance is central to mathematics perhaps for the reason that mathematics, as a mental activity, has to be perspicuous and surveyable. And elegance generally extends the range of complexities which we can command.

6 LOGIC AND COMPUTERS

6.1 Historical and philosophical background

Familiar connections between mathematical logic and automatic computers are the possibility of representing basic building blocks of computers by (sequential) Boolean functions and the close resemblance between programming languages and symbolisms of logic. As a result, both for the construction and for the use of computers, a certain degree of acquaintance with logic becomes indispensable. As early as 1656, Leibniz dreamed of a universal scientific language in his first published work; and many people today are actively seeking for a universal language for computers. Gottlob Frege wished to reduce arithmetic to logic from 1879 on, and in an oblique way the performance of arithmetic operations in computers by means of electronic circuits which are essentially logical functions may be said to accomplish the task in a particularly down-to-earth manner.

A more basic link between logic and computers is perhaps the common interest in algorithms. Although Charles Babbage conceived of and started to build in the 1830s the Analytical Engine which possessed most of the basic characteristics of modern computers, it was only in the 1940s that automatic computers began to appear through the efforts of Howard Aiken, John von Neumann, and others. The logicians had, on the other hand, made not only a highly successful abstract study of algorithms but even clarified the relation between machines and algorithms, largely through A. M. Turing's theory of idealized machines, all in the 1930s.

Traditionally the study of algorithms falls outside the domain of logic. The deepest source of the affinity of logic and computers is the preoccupation of logicians with formalization. The long evolution of attempts to formalize mathematical proofs, from Euclid to *Principia*, finally led to mechanizability as the ultimate criterion of complete success. This desire to make arguments formally precise and exact is concerned more with the product rather than with the theory of formalization. Only in the 1920s, D. Hilbert, P. Bernays and others began to study metamathematics: the theory of proofs, the theory of formal systems. The distinction may be illustrated by the method of 'discarding 9's' for checking multiplications. It is a metamathematical result on the usual technique of multiplying particular integers that a number is divisible by 9 if the sum of its digits is. This example also brings out the fact that the distinction between mathematics and metamathematics is not sharp. For we can easily state and prove the above result as a simple theorem in number theory by the easy relation $10^n \equiv 1 \pmod 9$.

It was the concern with a theory of proofs which at first led J. Herbrand to an abstract definition of calculation processes, as a particularly simple type of proofs. Although Turing was said to have had his theory of machines formulated before he was familiar with many of the achievements in logic, he certainly did his homework quickly and soon put his work in the main stream. The surprisingly simple solutions to the question of giving a general definition of algorithms were undoubtedly an important cause of the rapid developments in the area of abstract studies of calculations.

6.2 Between engineering and mathematics

Logic was a bastard of mathematics and philosophy; while actual computers first came into being as a great feat of engineering. This divergence in their ancestry presents serious sociological and scientific difficulties for those who are interested in the vaguely defined region referred to as 'logic and computers.' This is not the place to digress into sociology.

The trouble on the scientific side is that most ambitious people find dreary piecemeal engineering and idle intellectual gymnastics equally repulsive. And it seems as though there is little else to offer at the present stage, except it be irresponsible speculations. The origin of the problem goes further back. Every branch of applied mathematics embodies an intrinsic dilemma: each piece of work is either not sufficiently applied or not sufficiently mathematical. We have to present a patient defense in each case.

As Turing machines and actual computers were studied more or less independently of one another, there slowly developed a desire to bring about a marriage of theory and practice. This has proved to be an exceedingly difficult task. True, there are a number of basic results in very general terms. Turing machines are equivalent to actual computers if we disregard speed and the question of a potentially infinite supply of tape. In fact, there are alternative formulations of Turing machines which are more similar to actual computers, e.g. a representation of Turing machines by programs with a small number of basic instructions. Hence, since there are problems (e.g. the halting problem) which are unsolvable on Turing machines, the corresponding problems are unsolvable on actual computers. Another example is the result that in theory erasing is dispensable on Turing machines. Hence, magnetic tapes (in contrast with, say, paper tapes) are in theory not necessary for building computers.

Along with Turing machines, a simpler model of computer under the name 'finite automata' has been extensively investigated and sometimes compared, in an expansive and speculative mood, to the human brain. This elegant model has also given rise to a number of amusing mathematical results.

It must be emphasized that the mathematical theory of machines is a young discipline and, as such, it is doing very well so far. Moreover, it has the important advantages that little equipment beyond native wits is required for its pursuit and that it promises great things to come. But great things are rare. What is needed at present is not quantity but rather pursuers of good quality.

On the more theoretical level, the study of impractical algorithms and abstract machines, not as isolated idealizations, but in relation to other parts of logic and mathematics, has led to many significant mathematical results. Moreover, these results, although not often their proofs, can usually be stated in quite simple terms. In terms of their intrinsic intellectual merit and of their potential applications, they would seem to have as wide an appeal as, say, molecular biology.

6.3 Unsolvable problems

While engineering is primarily the study of how to make things, mathematics is more often concerned with showing that under certain general conditions certain things can or cannot be done. There is a special appeal to show that certain things cannot be done, because such results involve, in a negative way, all the available resources of a given method. For example, in bisecting an angle, we use only a small part of the resources of ruler and compass; while in proving the impossibility of trisecting an arbitrary angle we have to possess a clear conception of all the possible constructions which we can make with ruler and compass. It is in this area of demonstrating unsolvability that the abstract study of idealized machines has produced results of the greatest mathematical interest. In particular, the interplay of logic and the theory of computers is striking.

It is familiar to logicians that all mathematical theories can be formulated in the framework of elementary logic. Hence, if we could decide whether in general a statement is a theorem of logic, we would also be able to decide whether a statement is provable in any given mathematical theory. This situation explains why the Hilbert School regarded the Entscheidungsproblem, i.e. the problem of deciding whether a statement in logic is a theorem, as the main problem of logic.

From 1920 on, Post[7] tackled this problem by formulating a more general one that deals with derivability in arbitrary production systems, of which the system of elementary logic is a special case. This turned out to yield a general concept of formal systems, and indirectly, one of calculation processes. Moreover, the abstract formulation renders possible experimentations on apparently simple cases, with a view to discovering some common pattern useful for the handling of the general case.

Unfortunately, as a means to get positive results, this attractive approach is, on the whole, quite powerless. One of the very first examples which Post studied in 1920–1, and reported publicly in 1943, remains unsettled today. Consider all (finite) strings made out of 0's and 1's and use two very simple rules: if a string begins with 0, delete the three symbols at the beginning and add 00 at the end; if it begins with 1, delete the three initial symbols and append 1101 at the end (stop if a string contains less than three symbols). The problem is simply: Do we have a general method of deciding, for any two strings, whether the second can be obtained from the first by the above two rules?

On the other hand, Post's approach can be employed to establish negative results, once the step is taken to identify solvability with that by a production system or some other equivalent method, say by a Turing machine. In fact, in 1936 Turing proposed and argued for such an identification, and applied results on Turing machines to prove the unsolvability of the Entscheidungsproblem. Quite recently, this result has been sharply refined to a certain degree of finality, with the help of a picturesque auxiliary tool of tiling problems.[8] This type of work exemplifies the rich possibilities of applying the theory of machines to establish basic results about logic.

Applications in other branches of mathematics include P. S. Novikov's proof[9] that the word problem for groups is unsolvable, a result which has been applied by A. A. Markov to prove that the 4-dimensional homeomorphy problem is unsolvable. The 3-dimensional homeomorphy problem remains open. Recently Matijasevicz[10] has shown the unsolvability of Hilbert's tenth problem: there is no general method of deciding the question of solvability in integers of every polynomial equation with integer coefficients. This implies also that there is no decision procedure for quantifier-free number theory with addition and multiplication. There is a concatenation analog of Hilbert's tenth problem which remains unsettled.[11]

A (formally) simple example of an unsolvable problem is the following word problem. Consider strings (words) made out of the five symbols, a, b, c, d, e and the following seven rules for mutual substitution: $ac \leftrightarrow ca$, $ad \leftrightarrow da$, $bc \leftrightarrow cb$, $bd \leftrightarrow db$, $adac \leftrightarrow abace$, $eca \leftrightarrow ae$, $edb \leftrightarrow be$. It is an unsolvable problem to decide whether any two words are equivalent by these rules. If we replace by c the e in the fifth rule, then the word problem for the resulting system is solvable.

6.4 Formalization

From the rich domain of mathematical logic, we have selected two aspects as specially relevant to computers, viz. the theory and the practice of formalization. The unsolvability results belong to the theory side, while formalizing individual mathematical proofs or 'deriving mathematics from logic' belongs to the practice side. In this latter aspect the interplay of logic and computers is significant on a more concrete level: developments of logic combined with the great power of actual computers give rise to the hope of mechanizing mathematical arguments, not just in principle, but in practice as well.

As in engineering, there is little likelihood of general results in this positive enterprise. But, unlike an engineer, we are not concerned with actually making things and we do get exact results in each individual case.

The interest in mechanization implies a reorientation of formal logic with a view toward greater efficiency. In particular, this means that the need for economy of axioms and primitive concepts is to be supplemented with an exact formulation of a large body of concepts and rules, which make up the average mathematician's stock of trade.

This can best be illustrated by an example from elementary number theory.[12] Suppose we wish to prove:

$$\text{I} \quad x > 1 \rightarrow \exists y [Py \wedge (y \,|\, x)]$$

i.e. every integer greater than 1 has a prime divisor.

We assume given an organized stock of information SF with properties of $+$, $\cdot$, $<$ listed first, and then properties of P and $|$, which may involve the more basic concepts $+$, $\cdot$, $<$. The list SF is organized so that not too much searching is necessary to look up required properties.

The basic strategy is to assume the theorem false and try to derive a contradiction from the least counterexample, which embodies a mechanically convenient form of the principle of mathematical induction. The imagined least counterexample provides an 'ambiguous constant' which possesses not only general properties true of all integers but also unusual properties arising from the assumption that it is a counterexample. In simple cases such as I, after we draw on SF and use simple truth-functional deductions, we quickly get an ambiguous constant with contradictory properties. It should be emphasized that the proof below is merely a sketch of an illustration. More elaborate strategies of roughly the same type are necessary in order to prove more complex theorems.

To prove I, we first assume it false and let m be the least counterexample:

1   $m > 1$
2   $Pb \rightarrow b \nmid m$
3   $1 < a < m \rightarrow Py_a \wedge (y_a \,|\, a)$

The only ambiguous constant thus far is m. Substitute m for a and b above in order to get further properties of m.

4   $Pm \rightarrow m \nmid m$
5   $1 < m < m \rightarrow Py_m \wedge (y_m \,|\, m)$

Look up SF and try to derive simple consequences from 1, 4, and

5 with the help of *SF*. Find $m \not< m$ in *SF* and delete the trivially true 5. Find $m \mid m$ in *SF* and infer from 4:

6 $\neg Pm$

Now 4 may be deleted since it is a direct consequence of 6. We now have 1, 2, 3, 6. Look up *SF* and get the defining property of *P* as applied to *m*:

$$\neg Pm \leftrightarrow \exists x[1 < x < m \wedge (x \mid m)]$$

By 6, we get:

7 $1 < x_m < m$
8 $x_m \mid m$

Since x_m is a new ambiguous constant, it is desirable to substitute it for the free variables in the general statements obtained so far, viz. 2 and 3 only.

9 $Px_m \to x_m \not\mid m$
10 $1 < x_m < m \to Py_{x_m} \wedge (y_{x_m} \mid x_m)$

Derive truth-functional consequences (first without appealing to *SF*) from 1, 2, 3, 6–10.

11 $\neg Px_m$, by 8 and 9
12 Py_{x_m}, by 7 and 10
13 $y_{x_m} \mid x_m$, by 7 and 10

Now appeal to the list *SF* and use: $(a \mid b) \wedge (b \mid c) \to (a \mid c)$.

14 $y_{x_m} \mid m$, by 8 and 13.

Substitute the ambiguous constant y_{x_m} for the free variables in 2 and 3:

15 $Py_{x_m} \to y_{x_m} \not\mid m$
16 $1 < y_{x_m} < m \to Py_{y_{x_m}} \wedge (y_{y_{x_m}} \mid y_{x_m})$

By 14 and 15, we get:

17 $\neg Py_{x_m}$, contradicting 12.

Obviously we have not listed all the blind alleys and the method has to be specified much more exactly before a machine program can be written. But, it is thought, the above outline makes it plausible that a fairly natural program can be written on existing machines to prove theorems like 1 and, for example, also $2x^2 \neq y^2$ (*x*, *y* range over positive integers).

NOTES

1 J. Hadamard, *Psychology of invention in the mathematical field*, Princeton, 1945.
2 *Art of thought*, 1926, pp. 79–107.
3 H. Poincaré, *Science and method*, 1908.
4 J. E. Littlewood, 'The mathematician's art of work,' *The Rockefeller Univ. review*, Sept.–Oct. 1967.
5 J. von Neumann, 'Probabilistic logics,' *Automata studies*, eds. C. E. Shannon and J. McCarthy, 1956.

Mathematics and Computers

6 A. S. Yessenin-Volpin, 'Le programme ultra-intuitioniste des fondements des mathématiques,' *Infinitistic methods*, 1961, pp. 201–33; and in *Intuitionism and proof theory*, ed. J. Myhill, 1970, pp. 3–45. Compare also D. van Dantzig, 'Is $10^{10^{10}}$ a finite number?', *Dialectica*, vol. 9, 1956, pp. 273–7.

7 For the relevant papers of E. Post and A. M. Turing, compare *The undecidable*, ed. M. Davis, 1965.

8 Also called 'domino' problems. This was first introduced in *Bell system techn. jour.*, vol. 40, 1961, pp. 22–4. For further developments, compare R. Berger, *Memoirs of Am. Math. Soc.*, no. 66, 1966.

9 P. S. Novikov, *Trudy Mat. Inst. Steklova*, vol. 44, 1955, 143 pp.

10 Ju. V. Matijasevicz, *Soviet math. dokl.*, vol. 11, 1970, pp. 354–8.

11 For a statement of the problem which was also independently posed by A. A. Markov, see M. H. Löb, *J. symbolic logic*, vol. 21, 1956, p. 66, footnote.

12 For more considerations of the same type, see *Proc. IFIP Congress*, 1965, vol. 1, pp. 51–8.

X

MINDS AND MACHINES

ASPECTS OF MECHANISM

A commonly accepted belief today among biologists is that all manifestations of life can ultimately be explained by the laws governing inanimate matter. This belief is often labeled mechanism or materialism. According to this view, the ultimate goal of the life sciences is to account for the origin and properties of life (and mind) by means of the principles of physics. Psychology is reducible to physiology (the machinery of brain), physiology (and biology) is reducible to chemistry and physics (the machinery of life), chemistry is reducible to physics. The complexity of the phenomena of life (and mind) comes from the complex organization of the large number of objects involved and not from the complexity of the fundamental laws governing the basic objects.

One working hypothesis is that, whatever uncertainties there are with regard to the foundations of physics and however they will be resolved, they will not affect seriously the superstructure that makes up biology (and psychology). It seems unquestionable that for a long time to come results in biology will be sufficiently stable (or imprecise) so that they will not be affected by alternative theories of elementary particles. It is, however, not equally clear that resolutions of the unresolved difficulties in fundamental physics will not affect the ultimate program of a complete account of life in terms of physics.

It is possible to distinguish two aspects of mechanism. If we discovered a complex machine in nature, we would expect it to function according to the laws of physics even though we might not be able either to build a copy of it or to get a good explanation of how it came into existence. Physical laws typically leave explicitly undetermined the (initial) boundary condition, and the emergence of the first individual of a new species seems to call for specific boundary conditions which require an historical account. Just as we have more exact knowledge of the structure of matter than of the history of the universe, it is conceivable that we shall some day understand well in physical and chemical terms how an animal A functions and yet have no satisfactory mechanical account of how the first individual of a particular species came into being. In such a situation, we may still feel that we have not accomplished a fully mechanistic account of the life phenomena of the animal A.

The distinction between the historical origin and the law-abiding operations of an individual need not be tied up with the conception that machines are objects created by an agent (man) for special purposes. Certainly for most believers in mechanism, the view does not imply that life was created by some higher agent for certain purposes. In other words, even though mechanism could be described as asserting that man is a machine, it certainly does not involve the other element in the conception of machine that it is man-made. (Of course, in one sense, man is man-made; but we are not thinking of that sense.)

If we compare physics with biology, we may be struck by various different things. There is an arrow of time in life, both in the sense of evolution and in the sense of individuals getting old. But there is no arrow of time in physical laws. Or, the origin of life is a surprisingly unique event since to get a chain of 400 elements from 20 amino acids, the probability is only 1 in 20^{400}. Some people have compared biology with engineering. But they are radically different at least in that biology deals with natural objects while engineering is concerned with making things.

In the account of how devices for calculation and control function, we confine ourselves to the consideration of the mechanical and electrical properties of the materials used. We apply simple physical laws governing the interaction between the parts of the machine and essentially disregard the atomic structure of matter. However, there is nothing to preclude, and indeed we believe there are in the long history of organic evolution various results obtained by, trying out in nature wide ranges of possibilities of atomic and subatomic interactions. Viewed in this way, we may find it less surprising that life seems so complicated to us when viewed as a physical system. By thus pointing out a rich source of complexity, mechanism or reductionism also becomes harder to refute. Also this viewpoint may lead us to doubt whether the simplifying assumption of molecular biology in disregarding physical forces in the very small is justified in the long run.

Of course there are many ambiguities in connection with the thesis of mechanism or reductionism. We may, for example, ask whether it is a working hypothesis, a prediction, or a definition (unless we have reached mechanical explanations, we have not finished). Physical laws change with the advance of physics and the notion of machines also changes in time. When we realize abstract machines physically, we may find, for example, that physical properties might be tied up with emotions such as love, compassion and malice. We may wish to distinguish ontological reduction from epistemological reduction. The 'reduction' of thermodynamics to statistical mechanics is viewed by some as a prize example of successful reduction but by others as a clear counterexample to reductionism because in this case order in the whole comes out of chaos in the parts.

There is a natural appeal in the views that whole is more than its parts, that change is basic and the ordinary scientific method distorts by dissecting and abstracting, or that, as J. B. S. Haldane once suggested, when biology and physics meet, the one that will vanish is not biology. The interesting aspect of these assertions is not so much to argue for or against their truth, but rather to find a clear meaning for them as a basis of further consideration. Perhaps biology will be to physics as quantum mechanics is to classical mechanics? Or would we have laws governing different wholes which cannot be decomposed into laws about parts? Or maybe life and mind play such a central role that physical phenomena become a part of life phenomena.

Whether to emphasize life or mind gives quite a different slant. Somehow one feels that for life mechanism is presently of scientific significance, while for mind we are in the realm of philosophy or speculation.[1] The contrast between mind and body is certainly different from that between tables and electrons or that between the logical states (universals) and the structural states (physical realizations) of a machine. Perhaps a solipsist is to some extent a mechanist. Anyhow, there is somehow a feeling that other minds are closer to machines than one's own mind. There is a tendency to be troubled with the regress with regard to a machine thinking about itself. One gets confused in thinking about a self-conscious machine.[2]

Logicians are proud of their possession of an exact explication of the concept of mechanical procedure in terms of recursive functions or Turing machines. This concept of mechanical, which is relevant to the study of computers, naturally yields also a concept of mechanism. Mechanism in this mathematical sense imposes a different requirement so that on the one hand, it brings in the question of infinity which clouds the issue, and, on the other hand, even present day physical theory may not be mechanical in the sense that observables are recursive relative to the initial boundary conditions. For example, the function $f(n)$ which is 1 or 0 according to whether, by the accepted physical laws, there will be an eclipse on the *n*-th day may or may not be a recursive function. It seems, however, that the materialistic or physicalistic concept of mechanical (mechanism) is the more deep-rooted. We are inclined to think that we have a mechanical procedure of finding out the values of $f(n)$ just mentioned (viz. by observation ad infinitum) no matter whether $f(n)$ is recursive or not. Moreover, at least in classical physics, the differential equations are relatively simple (the basic functions being continuous), and their solutions are recursive in the initial conditions. Hence, the two senses of mechanism are not as different as they might appear at first sight.

Whether man is a machine is a different question from whether a machine can think. It is conceivable that there be a thinking machine or indeed a machine which behaves like a man in other ways as well but which is structured differently from man. Such an achievement will undoubtedly help our understanding of how the brain functions but need not give us anything like a physical account of the actual brain. On the other hand, if the goal is to prove that man is not a machine, it is obviously sufficient to prove that machines cannot think or even, for example, that no machine can prove as many theorems of arithmetic as a man. There is occasionally a tendency to equivocate between these two distinct questions.

There are three different uses of behavior: criterion, meaning, and methodology. It seems reasonable to aim at machines which would behave like man: as a criterion of success, behavior can go a long way. This is quite different from studying psychology merely by observing behaviors. It is quite possible that the more fruitful way is by looking more deeply into other factors. The question of meaning is also different from mere criterion. In fact, it seems that a richer notion of meaning may also be helpful to the development of a better method.

In order to avoid undue emphasis on verbal behavior and to concentrate on purely intellectual features, we may think of a less colorful examination game. Typed questions are fed into the computer: prove the following theorems, translate the following paragraph into French. Also a game of chess can be played. This does not prevent typed conversations. Suppose a machine does very well. Are we to say it is alive or it is conscious? We must judge other people's mental conditions from without. And the capacity of complex behavior is connected with consciousness.

It seems evasive to say that machines cannot be conscious because they are not alive, since we would face a similar problem with being alive. Another argument is that the behavior of a machine is in principle predictable and therefore it has no free will. Therefore, a machine cannot be conscious. The two inferences are both questionable. It is not clear that any of the three properties 'having free will,' 'not predictable,' 'conscious' implies any of the others.

If we do not know the background of a discovered robot, which behaves like man, we may not be able to tell whether it is a machine. It is not excluded that, knowing it to be a machine, we nonetheless wish to say it is conscious. A fairly clear question to ask is whether, if some day we can make machines which behave like man, we shall speak of them as being conscious. We probably shall. But this does not seem such an interesting question. The vague feeling is that there ought to be some deeper difference.

A 'soulless sweetheart' which behaves entirely like a soulful one is a somewhat strange notion. It may bear some similarity to the question of class origin. Or it may mean simply that under unusual circumstances, it or she may behave differently. If we do not know any conceivable way of distinguishing two objects, we seem justified in regarding them as indistinguishable.

It has been suggested that we teach a machine language and make it tell truth, and then we can ask it whether it is conscious. This transfer of the difficulty does not seem of much help. For example, we may teach it: 'remember your origin, you are not a man. Only men are conscious.' Presumably, we would not like to prejudge the issue. But in any case, why should it be better off than we are? Presumably, if our teaching is successful, the language it employs will reflect whatever vagueness there is in the indefinite criteria we use in our language. If there is such a machine which we are able to teach, etc., as if we were dealing with a man and which reacts in all other respects like a man, would it not be reasonable to expect it would also behave like a man in believing itself to be conscious? The basic trend of distinguishing theoretical from practical problems has many ramifications. When one neglects feasibility altogether, we lose a basic controlling element. This is exhibited in attempts to axiomatize physics, to ask for a reductionist criterion of meaning, to use Turing machines to discuss the mechanical nature of man, etc. When we abstract too much, we have little left to work with. To find the correct level of abstraction is an essential component for finding something interesting. We have to mix the theoretical with the practical, only we often do not arrive at the productive mixture.

The subject of mechanism has received a revival mainly through the successes in molecular biology and the development of large computers. There are discussions on this topic on various levels from phenomenology to technology. We shall be concerned mainly with the impacts of computers so that the problem of men and machines is narrowed down to that of minds and computers. Under this general heading, we shall consider artificial or mechanical intelligence, its relation to theoretical psychology, comparisons of brains and computers, and attempts to draw large philosophical consequences from results in mathematical logic about idealized computers.

The section on mathematical arguments illustrates a general type of argument which purports to show that machines have certain limitations which men do not have. In these arguments we tend to use idealizations and contrast actual performance with capacity. Even when we find sharp results on the limitations of machines, we are at a loss to show that minds are not subject to similar limitations. And idealization tends to conceal most of the more essential aspects.

On the whole, there is something disturbing in the attempts to apply directly exact mathematical results to get sweeping conclusions on broad philosophical and methodological issues. The issues are usually insufficiently exact to allow a successful coordination with existing abstract results. Often the positions attacked are ones we are vaguely much dissatisfied with anyhow. Nonetheless, accepting the conclusion need not restrain us from being critical of misleading arguments for the conclusion. One example is certain arguments against behaviorism.

One argument asserts that behaviorism identifies man with a finite automaton. Since no finite automaton can multiply arbitrary integers but man can (or possesses a program for doing so), behaviorism must be mistaken. This refutation seems too simple to be serious. A Turing machine can multiply and the distinction between a finite automaton and a Turing machine is somewhat subtle conceptually. It seems rather implausible that the concepts of behaviorism, which were developed independently of these idealized machines, should be so sharp as to admit the interpretation of mind as a finite automaton but exclude that of mind as a Turing machine.

Another argument is that, even if man is a finite automaton, behaviorism is inadequate because by examining the inputs and outputs only, we cannot determine exactly the internal states or predict the future responses. This depends on the hypothesis that we do not know how big the finite automaton is. But it could be argued that we can give an upper bound to the size, and then the argument fails. Moreover, it is known that man can multiply and use languages, so that a serious behaviorism would have to take into account such behaviors which are not obviously among the capabilities of a finite automaton.

2 COMPUTERS AND BRAINS

We know pretty well how computers function but we are a long way from getting computers to perform all intellectual tasks done by the brain; the brain can do a lot of things but we know very little about how it functions as a machinery. This double ignorance has led to unjustified positive and negative conclusions. For example, some vague similarity is observed between the underlying design principle of the computer and some crude anatomic feature of the brain; some existing unorthodox applications of computers are described as exemplifying intelligent behavior. These are then taken as a powerful argument for the conclusion that all intelligence is a natural consequence of the symbol-manipulating capabilities of complex switching networks. We may or may not like the conclusion. But it is hard not to find the above argument somewhat hasty for the strong conclusion of mechanism.

In fact, some form of the familiar argument along the above line is either circular or by vague analogy. There are two basic observations. 1 To some extent, the brain resembles a computer. 2 Any definite cause-and-effect relationship between inputs to and outputs from the brain, could, in principle, be implemented by a computer-like switching network. From these plausible remarks much stronger conclusions have been drawn on the relation between brains and computers. With the help of 1, it is somehow concluded that 3 brain operations always exhibit definite cause-and-effect relationships. Therefore, combining 2 and 3, we arrive at the strong conclusion that 4 brains are computers. Even leaving 1 aside, one might be inclined to accept 2 and 3 outright, but then there would seem to be a play on an ambiguity of the term 'definite cause-and-effect relationship.' The alternative of inferring 3 from 1 seems to involve a jump while applying the perfectly reasonable premiss that computers can only operate in a definite cause-and-effect manner.

Perhaps what is intended is not an argument to establish the strong conclusion 4, but a plea to make 3 true for more and more brain operations and strengthen 2 from 'in principle' to 'in practice' for these 'definite relationships.' However, at present, our knowledge on this question is so limited that we are not yet ready to do any reasonably extensive fruitful work on computer models of the brain, to say nothing of applying known laws of physics to the neural network and thereby deriving intelligence as an inevitable result. Applications of computers today in neurological research remain fairly routine (digesting data, etc., as in particle physics and areas of applied sciences). Rather the immediate interest bearing on computers and the brain is largely in the task of discovering surprising new uses of computers, not along the line of neurology but along the line of mechanical intelligence.

Crude comparisons between existing (digital) computers and the brain have exhibited a number of apparent differences, the relative importance of which remains unknown. There are more neurons than functional units in the computer; neurons are smaller, slower, and use less energy. The operations of the brain are less cleancut in a number of ways. Instead of being primarily electrical, the nerve impulse has several aspects: electrical, chemical, and mechanical. The brain mixes digital (nerve pulses) and analog (chemical secretion, muscle contraction) operations. The brain mixes more extensively serial and parallel operations; a large fraction of the neurons are often active at the same time. The brain uses statistical properties (threshold, frequency, correlation-coefficients, etc.) of the nerve pulses; the connections in the brain are less precise and methodical and appear, at least locally, to be rather random. These parallel and imprecise features may account for the tolerance of individual errors, achieving low precision but high reliability. The location, capacity, and physical embodiments of memory in the nervous system are hard to determine. The phenomenon of fatigue and recovery has no reasonable counterpart with computers.

On the psychological level, people are taught often by examples while computers are told to do things by complete and detailed instructions. It is highly desirable that some device be introduced so that a computer could, like the child, generalize from a few examples to cover a wide variety of similar situations. At present it is difficult to see how we could accomplish this by ingenious programming since it is hard to extract either data (experience) or the mechanism (learning process) by which the data yield the generalization, or, for that matter, to formulate in computer terms the generalizations arrived at. In fact, this fact is often used as a typical example of how computers cannot handle 'tacit knowledge' which is of central importance for the mind. It is suggested that we should look for new types of computers and computer components. For example, single components do not carry out simple, easily described functions. Rather a group of components together performs such and such a function.

This sounds dangerously close to the difficult notion of the whole being more than its parts. We could perhaps think of a whole body of data acting simultaneously on a group of components (compare vision), but the components reacting selectively, so that the total reaction of the whole group depends on a synthesis of the reactions of the individual components. In this imagined picture, the parallel operation is obvious. Also, it seems desirable not to digitalize all data so that at least some of the components act as analog devices.

If the brain is indeed a machine, then it can in principle be simulated by a digital computer because current computers are universal machines in a theoretical sense. This is quite a vacuous argument. Whatever apparent force this argument may have comes from the vague feeling that if the brain is not a machine, what other thing could it be? In fact, the premiss is not quite the same as what is intended by physical mechanism: it says that if the brain is a digital computer (a Turing machine, a recursive machine) the argument is no more than a tautology. Even if we were somehow given to know that the premiss is true, we would still be not much better off. One machine simulating another is greatly slowed up by the mechanism of 'describing' one machine in terms of another; this is also an argument against simulation of thought. But of course the more serious matter is that we cannot describe exactly and in detail the circuitry or even the operations of each component in the brain.

When our interest is in the conceivability of mechanism, there is a natural tendency to use negative mathematical results to argue for inconceivability. There is on the one hand a failure of imagination: how can there be another kind of machine? On the other hand, there is no theoretical difficulty for a universal machine with a model of itself. There is, in this theoretical vein, even a harmless infinite regress. The fact that actual phenomena are finite and mathematics finds it easy to go to the infinity poses a problem which is not easy to resolve. Giving up infinity is giving up too much; but it is not easy to give a detailed account of the applicability of mathematics.

3 ARTIFICIAL OR MECHANICAL INTELLIGENCE

A first task would seem to be sorting out, relating, and organizing the cluster of problems on comparing minds with computers. Roughly speaking there are philosophical problems of what computers can eventually do and scientific problems of the better lines of approach in the near future. I do not believe that, in order to justify investigating novel new uses of computers, it should be necessary to be convinced that there are no limitations of computers not shared by man, that all human thoughts can be mechanized, etc. We are not only ignorant of whether such general statements are true but also lacking in any serious understanding of their meaning. We cannot imagine in any informative way what it is like for such statements to be true or false, since we have no clear conceptions of the capacity and limitations of either man or computer. Computers have achieved a good deal in scientific and business applications and nobody has good objective reasons against the expectation to find new and interesting uses of computers. What is often debated is rather the broader claims and promises made on behalf of computers with regard to mental activities. And these are connected to what is called artificial intelligence.

According to a broader usage of the term, there are different areas of artificial intelligence, for example:

(a) Pattern recognition: in particular, signal processing; pictorial pattern recognition.

(b) Problem solving: in particular, theorem proving; 'heuristic' problem solving; man machine symbiosis (in problem solving).

(c) Brain and mind models: in particular, self-organizing models; physiological modeling; integrated artificial intelligence systems (robots); programming systems and models for artificial intelligence.

(d) Language and understanding: in particular, question-answering systems and computer understanding; linguistic research relevant to artificial intelligence.

There are also different approaches: brain-centered versus mind-centered; simulation versus construction. Taking all possible combinations, we get four different approaches.

Brain-centered simulation has a physiological orientation; while construction searches for simple basic principles of behavior and learning, and aims at discovering self-organizing (adaptive) systems. Since almost nothing is known about how the nervous system recognizes patterns, learns and manipulates concepts, etc., the prospect is certainly remote that sophisticated thought processes can emerge along the brain direction either by simulation or by construction. At present, perhaps more restricted tasks such as models for the vision system of an octopus or a horseshoe crab will prove to be useful in the study of neurophysiology.

By the way, at first models were construed in a more literal sense, and experiments were performed with mechanic and electronic devices. Nowadays it is customary to use programs on general purpose computers, taking advantage of their flexibility.

According to one usage, artificial intelligence is confined to what I call construction of mental processes, i.e. it deals with the mind rather than the brain and it disregards the question of simulation. This narrower artificial intelligence is closely related to the simulation of thought. They differ in their emphasis on results as against processes. Narrower artificial intelligence aims at using computers to perform intellectual tasks as well as possible, no matter whether these are done in a manner analogous to the human psychological process. Motor cars do not resemble horses and airplanes do not resemble doves. It does not mean that we should not reflect on how a man would, for example, do mathematics and try to make use of all feasibly mechanizable devices which a man would employ. Only it is not required that the whole procedure should be a faithful simulation, and it makes less claims to any great immediate relevance to the study of psychology. In contrast, simulation prides itself on making computers do things as man would do them, not merely attain the same end results such as winning a game of chess. In the abstract, simulation and modeling of mind sound like an excellent idea: they serve to apply computers to psychology; if the computer program does not do very well, there is always the excuse that our main interest is not performance but rather the thought process; in particular, the 'models of mind' enable us to test alternative psychological theories.

There is an elusive element in both the simulation and the construction approaches which distinguishes artificial intelligence from more neutral characterizations such as mechanization of thought or simply nonnumerical uses of computers. This elusive element creates both wider appeals and acuter controversies. It aims at finding useful mechanistic interpretations of these mentalistic notions that have real value: such as meanings, goals, understanding. It claims to be a new and better approach to psychology, especially theoretical psychology. A less central accompanying feature is the belief that a sufficient technical foundation exists for the use of mentalistic language as a constructive and powerful tool for describing machines. The preoccupation with mind generates a vague concept of what is basic and central to the discipline, which is distinct from the easier criteria of immediate practical applications and distinctly impressive new tasks.

In my opinion, deemphasizing simulation is a liberation, and deemphasizing psychology is an additional liberating step. Undoubtedly psychological considerations can be a valuable source of suggestions. But scientific progress tends to come by doing what we can and often depends more on local criteria of fruitfulness and elegance. At our present stage of ignorance, mechanization of thought as applied mathematics may turn out to be more conducive to long range progresses than as theoretical psychology. To talk about this more neutral area, I shall speak of mechanical intelligence.

One kind of criticism is to argue that existing computers cannot simulate or otherwise match the mind and that what these machines do do and can do are only exhaustive searches. Hence, it is concluded, digital computers cannot perform any interesting intellectual tasks. This does not preclude the possibility that future and different machines might do better. But even on this restricted topic, one is uneasy to argue for or against the thesis. I feel it is perhaps not unfair to say that computers have not yet achieved interesting intellectual tasks, that they are far from being seriously called thinking machines. Yet it is not equally clear that potentialities of even existing digital computers have been explored so fully that we can conclude, e.g., that they cannot be so programmed as to be a champion chess player. Probably they could if sufficiently many qualified people were interested in working on the project. Doing mathematics would be more serious and more interesting: in fact, I find it hard to decide whether concentrated efforts should not at present be devoted to the project. What is less clear at present is the more general question as to what digital computers can or cannot do. For example, Turing seems to be quite wrong when he speaks as though what is missing is just a matter of programming efforts:[3] 'about sixty workers, working steadily through the fifty years might accomplish the job, if nothing went into the wastepaper basket.' In any case, it seems highly desirable that those who are for and against would cooperate to find the true picture.

4 COMPUTER SIMULATION OF HUMAN THOUGHT

The trouble is we do not know what we are simulating, we do not know enough about the object (viz. the mind) we are modeling after to have sharp enough theories to be tested on the computer. Even though much of our intellectual effort is conscious and in that sense we know more about our mental or mind processes than our brain processes, our knowledge is so inexact that it is insufficient to support any heavy structure of simulation. Free use of this knowledge as an auxiliary to the development of mechanical intelligence seems to be the right load which this knowledge can bear in the general area of computer and thought.

There seems at first sight a circularity in the idea of simulation. On the one hand, understanding how man performs sophisticated tasks is a major clue to the discovery of programs that can do likewise. On the other hand, we appeal to computer simulation because we do not understand how man does them. The answer given is apparently that we have a pretty good idea of the overall strategies but only lack knowledge of the details of how man works. Replication of complete individual details is neither necessary nor even desirable. This answer points to a basic instability of the concept of simulation: since simulation is only on the global level, it depends on each individual's theory of how man operates in an overall manner, and does not possess the quality of faithful reproduction as suggested by the term 'simulation.'

On account of the instability of the concept of simulation, it is not easy to tell whether a program is simulating or not. For example, in the earlier stages when the Logical Theorist was in vogue, I designed a much simpler program which did much better.[4] And yet it could be claimed, contrary to the popular opinion, that my program also was a simulation, only of more sophisticated people.

A more serious objection to simulation is that in the very central area, we do not know, even in global terms, how information is selected, organized, and retrieved by the mind. Our 'pretty good idea' can be no more than crude plausible guesses. Even if in a deeper sense mind did operate in a mechanical manner, chances are that there would be other mechanical solutions which could be reached more directly with less emphasis on simulation. For the purpose of mechanical intelligence, it is more important to get more intelligent programs than to get programs superficially resembling the mind in certain aspects. And it is a practical certainty that the additional constraint can only hamper advance. I believe that, in the long run, simulation can be shown conclusively to be the less fruitful approach to mechanical intelligence. In fact, I am under the impression that the simulation approach is stagnant even now.

In discussions on minds and computers, one encounters frequently a play on the ambiguity of the term 'information processing system.' Since both minds and computers are information processing systems, we cannot, we are told, but succeed in eventually simulating minds by computers. But this equivocation begs the very question which is open, to say the least. We know precious little about whether minds are information processing systems in the same rigid sense in which computers are.

Certain mental phenomena are more mechanical; others are less so. The relative distance to computers varies greatly from activities to activities and from people to people. Thus, 'he thinks like a machine' is not regarded as an empty statement, and certain routine clerical work is commonly considered to be rather mechanical.

Computers as information processing machines usually are not thought of as including analogous devices or motor actions. Thus, while it is easy to think of a machine-building machine, such a machine is not (just) a computer. It is of course not a serious problem to adjoin to a computer other machines such as displaying equipments, motor units, etc. Expecting somebody, having pain, feeling angry or anxious, desiring something, etc. are mental concepts which are rather remote from computers. Perhaps understanding and intending may be regarded as somewhere between these and problem solving or pattern recognizing.

It would seem reasonable to expect mechanical intelligence to be more easily successful in areas closest to the symbol manipulating processes of computers. Hence, not surprisingly, logic has come to share some of the popularity of computers.

For example, the familiar consistency proofs of number theory yield a procedure by which given any proof of a conditional existence statement

$$\forall x_1 \ldots \forall x_m \, \exists y_1 \ldots \exists y_n R(x_1, \ldots, y_n)$$

with recursive R, we can find fairly simple recursive functions $g_1(x_1, \ldots, x_m), \ldots, g_n(x_1, \ldots, x_m)$ which satisfy the condition. This has been applied to reduce the task of finding a program to that of proving a theorem. Thus, the given statement is interpreted as wanting a program which will compute y's as outputs for any x's as inputs where the y's should satisfy R with the given inputs. The functions $g_1, \ldots, g_n$ together give the desired program.

It is well known that whether a program terminates, etc., can be expressed by a formula in the predicate calculus (in fact, in very simple forms such as $\forall \exists \forall$). Hence, given a program, instead of asking whether the program terminates, we can ask whether the corresponding formula is a theorem.

Such remarks are of theoretical interest. But one's first reaction is that they would be of little practical importance on account of the general gap between theory and practice. I believe, however, these possibilities are worthy of further explorations.

5 PROTOCOLS AND THEORETICAL PSYCHOLOGY

My conviction is less strong when it comes to the relation between computers and psychology, for the simple reason that I have no firm grasp of the current state of psychology as a scientific field. But I would like to look more closely at a rather definite concrete area of computer simulation, perhaps not relative to the current state of psychology but relative to one's native conception of what psychology ought to be.

A protocol is a record of thinking aloud, i.e. a subject's report of what he is doing while working through a problem (say in the propositional calculus). We have a very elegant situation. Protocols are collected for a given class of problem from a fixed group of people (normally college students). By 'induction,' one arrives at a computer program which is expected to react to these problems in a similar manner as the college students. The program is the theory which can be tested against the protocols. This picture seems to fit beautifully the classical naive image of scientific research. Moreover, it seems to avoid all appeal to anything that would make the behaviorist unhappy.

There are several puzzling features in this kind of experiment.

1 How is the induction done? A whole apparatus of some higher order theory is invoked for the interpretation of the data: goals, subgoals, match, etc. This aspect would probably make the behaviorist unhappy but does not seem necessarily to be an objection.

2 What does the computer contribute? One could imagine the whole experiment carried out by hand simulation of the computer. It will be objected that it would be too tiresome to test by hand a large class of examples. But notice we are not using computers very efficiently because we are not taking advantage of the computer's powers to help solve any single problem, rather merely to perform the less interesting chore of doing more of the same. This is a bit like using a large computer as an adding machine.

3 Why not just ask oneself? Apparently the wish is to gather a diversity of data in order to have a basis for performing induction. There is also an element of pride: I am too sophisticated, we are interested in how the average person behaves. In this connection, it becomes clear that the goal is no longer to have the computer do as well as it can (i.e. as we can make it do) on certain problems but to account for how certain people behave. As mechanical intelligence the program is too simple-minded, as psychology the experiment is too complex to be basic. The interest in quantity (the multiplicity of protocols) seems to me a way of evading harder conceptual problems and could at best add some frill to impress the uninformed.

4 How about the nonverbal behaviors? It will, I trust, be freely admitted that we are not trying to simulate the verbal protocols but rather what goes on in one's head. But obviously we cannot describe exactly what goes on in our head. Now the program is supposed to correspond to the inner mechanism (or the mind) while its outputs correspond to the protocols. An obvious objection would be that even if the outputs did correspond to the protocols, there is no assurance that the program would represent faithfully the inner mechanism. But, of course the more serious matter is that we do not succeed in getting programs with right outputs for any really interesting case. Thus we have people who have proved many hard theorems. Does anybody believe that we can collect protocols on his endeavors and arrive at a program which is capable of proving theorems of the same order of difficulty?

312

5 Or consider the question of teaching. I think we would all agree that at the present stage we do not know how to write programs which would organize sufficiently well the information imparted by a teacher so as to perform as well as a moderately bright college student. But if we could devise successful programs from protocols, we would be able to 'teach' the computer to compete with the student. More, think of Poincaré's 'protocols' on some of his great discoveries in mathematics. Suggestive as they are, we do not believe that, even if he had produced many more protocols, anybody would be turned into a great mathematician merely by studying these protocols (even with the help of computer simulation). There is certainly less reason to think that, at least at present, we can make better use of such protocols in designing a program than as a direct aid to teaching mathematicians.

It may be said that we are at first only interested in ordinary practice, not how a genius works. But the point is, if we could find out by this method how ordinary people work, why does it fail elsewhere? One suspects that the answer is rather discouraging. In simple cases, we know how to make a computer do certain things, *even though* it may be doing them in quite a different way from how people do them.

I conclude without any reservation that the extensive use of protocols in the current manner is not a superior way to advance directly mechanical intelligence. I find it harder to offer articulate reasons against the contention that such studies may be of indirect use or that they are good theoretical psychology. I can only try to express my reservations in a tentative and round-about way.

I once read an argument defending the use of computer simulation for the study of psychology.[5] The problem is to find a language or a calculus in which to express or formulate a theory to account for some realm of human thought or human behavior. Natural language is ruled out because 'if a science is to grow, it must eventually develop methods and concepts that are more concise than the common language can express. When that day comes for the psychologist, where is he to turn?' Classical mathematics, symbolic logic, and the calculus of probability are found unsuitable. 'By a process of elimination, therefore, a psychologist . . . is perhaps not driven, but certainly nudged, in the direction of the computer program as a natural way to do it.' Just as an argument, this almost sounds as though that computer program is the last straw to grab at. One should have thought that natural language would remain the best tool for psychology for a long time to come and that, in any case tools, such as a calculus or language, are to be found or made as definite needs in the study of psychology demand them. The strength of the argument probably lies somewhere else. Our ability to think clearly on difficult questions remains pretty much constant. New ways of looking at things are likely to shake us out of our gray dullness, and computers offer a new way of thinking about problems in psychology. Of course, the use of computers and concepts from computers in psychology need not be confined to simulation.

It is rather unfortunate that the term 'artificial intelligence' has come, on the basis of what has actually happened during the brief history of the area, to be associated not only with simulation of thought but also with excessively optimistic forecasts as to what computers will soon be able to do. On the other hand, if one disclaims all direct relevance of mechanical intelligence to the study of human psychology, then we seem to lose one strong appeal, especially to the imagination of the general public, of the whole area of finding new uses for computers. But perhaps that would not be an unmixed loss.

In any case, we seem to have two complementary guiding principles. 1. To exploit fully the strength of existing computers: do things which are simple for computers but complex for people. 2. There are certain spectacular things which we would like to have computers do and which are, we vaguely feel, do-able by existing computers or something resembling them. The second principle suggests that we locate weaknesses of computers relative to the remote goals such as pattern recognition and try to remove these weaknesses. One central task is to develop a fairly stable criterion of value judgment on works in this area: only then would we get the great advantage of older disciplines and thereby cease to be frustrated by the feeling that what we can do is not interesting, and what is interesting we cannot do. A relatively stable framework would serve to discriminate between different results which, in isolation, do not appear specially interesting: we would be able to judge that certain lines of progress are more central than others.

It would be said that a stable criterion will evolve by natural selection. Probably. But that will take a long time and, in any case, we have to make choices and decisions at each stage. My own bias is to study mechanical intelligence unhampered by worries over faithful simulation and direct relevance to the current state of the field of psychology. And my own favorite central area for the not too remote future is the mechanization of mathematical arguments.

I do not wish to deny the fascination of thinking about, for example, human understanding in mechanical terms. Nor do I wish to argue that in the long run the nonnumerical aspect of computers will not become a very important tool for psychological investigations. Only, undoubtedly to a considerable extent due to my ignorance, I do not see as much promise in this direction for the near future as in the less popular direction of a somewhat austere pursuit of mechanical intelligence.

6 MATHEMATICAL ARGUMENTS

There are various attempts to apply Gödel's incompleteness results to prove that men can do more than machines. Actually, related theorems about abstract machines deal more directly with the limitations of mechanical procedures.

A Turing machine may be regarded as a digital computer with an unbounded storage capacity (e.g. an indefinitely expandable tape). An unsolvable (mass) problem is an infinite class of problems each with a 'yes' or 'no' answer such that no such machine can answer all of these questions correctly, i.e. each machine would either give some wrong answer or fail to give any answer to some of the questions however much time is allowed for a reply. It is well known that there are many such unsolvable problems. A difficult question is whether this type of mathematical result proves a disability of machines to which man is not subject.[6]

6.1 Solving the unsolvable

It is not entirely clear what bearings these unsolvable problems have on the theoretical limitations of the machine. For example, it is not denied that machines could be conceived which are capable of proving that such and such problems are unsolvable. If one contends that we could imagine a man solving an unsolvable set of problems, then it is not easy to give a definite meaning to this imagined situation. It is of the same kind as imagining a human mind so constituted that given any proposition in number theory, he is able to tell whether it is true. We are inclined to say that it is logically possible to have such a mind but logically impossible to have such a machine. But it is not easy to give any definitive exact argument that would establish a conclusion with the phrase 'logically possible' much strengthened.

If we could find an unsolvable problem such that man can decide all its cases, we would seem to obtain a definite result on the relation between man and machine. But the question of infinity creates a serious barrier. If the decision is made in a finite time, we would need some method to cover infinitely many cases within some finite duration. If we use the abstract notion of 'capability,' we are hard put to specify the conditions which the capability must satisfy in order to perform this heterogeneous (because nonrecursive) task.

The word 'man' is used ambiguously: any man, any man with ordinary intelligence, the best mathematician, the whole of humanity. Hilbert believes that every mathematical proposition can be decided eventually by man, or, alternatively, that every interesting mathematical proposition will be decided. Even Brouwer agrees to the extent that such a belief cannot be disproved. This belief implies that all individual cases of a given unsolvable problem will be settled by man. The picture is suggested that each generation settles a few individual cases and every case will get cleared up eventually. One may wish to conclude that at least in this somewhat weak sense, man is superior to machine. But then nature may produce generations of machines, or man may design machines through generations. How do we then apply the unsolvability results to a set of machines which is not generated by a mechanical procedure?

6.2 Theoretical and practical possibilities

While there is a natural temptation to arrive at quick answers by concentrating on theoretical possibilities, there is also an uneasy feeling that we are asking the wrong question. Many would like to show once and for all that, no matter how things are done, man can do more than machine. And the majority of us probably share the belief in this conclusion. But to give a proof, and a proof based on mathematical results, is quite another matter. We may admit that we have a stable abstract (and mathematical) concept of machines. However, what might be called a concrete concept of machines changes as we learn to do more with machines. Of course, man does not grind out theorems the way an existing machine would do. Yet the opponent would point out that we can think of more and more sophisticated machines for which the difference from people becomes less and less obvious.

It is by no means obvious that the abstract concept is philosophically more interesting than the concrete concept of machines. One suspects that many who believe so may have been misled by a wrongheaded scientism.

6.3 Beating all machines at proving theorems

A greater amount has been written on the implications of Gödel's incompleteness results with regard to the superiority of man over machine. These results state that given a consistent formal system S for number theory containing a reasonable amount of number theory, we can find a statement H_S which is true but not provable in S. In particular, H_S could be a statement Con(S) expressing the consistency of *S*, or one expressing 'I am not provable in *S*.' It is argued that we, knowing this theorem, can beat every formal system *S*, and therefore every theorem-proving Turing machine, because we can prove H_S, but *S* cannot. The basic mistake in this simple argument is surprisingly elementary. Briefly, truth is identified with provability: a principle which must not be applied except in a very careful manner. It is possible to give effectively acceptable collections of all formal systems or (theorem-proving) machines which contain enough number theory. And there is a Turing machine which will yield H_S as output whenever *S* is given as input.[7] Hence, if we leave aside the question of the consistency of *S*, a machine can give all the Gödel sentences. On the other hand, it is easily shown that the infinite class of questions as to whether any given *S* is consistent is an unsolvable problem.[8] Hence, in order to beat every Turing machine, I would have to be able to decide correctly all cases of an unsolvable problem.

A more involved argument would require my opponent to propose machines as candidates who would do at least as well as I. It is reasonable to contend that only consistent machines are serious candidates. The reasoning goes then as follows. Given any such candidate *S*, I can prove H_S because *S* is consistent. Hence, I can do more than *S*. This is somewhat slippery because I do not know H_S except under the condition that my opponent is only allowed to propose consistent candidates. Either my opponent does not know all the consistent machines, then my ability to refute him does not imply that no consistent machine could prove as many theorems as I do. Or my opponent knows all consistent machines and then he can solve an unsolvable problem. Then either he is superhuman, or we beg the very question whether a man can solve an unsolvable problem. In any case, the claim that I know H_S in each case is dubious, for all I know is: if *S* is consistent, then H_S.

6.4 Consistency and know thyself

The matter gets more complex when one introduces the contention that I know, and therefore I can prove:

A I am consistent.

There are then two separate aspects: what arguments can be offered to reach the conclusion that I can prove A? What follows by accepting that I can prove A?

The comparison of man with a theorem-generating Turing machine involves various idealizations. And there are reasons for and against such abstract and unrealistic considerations. One idealization is neglecting the limited life span of people: the capability is thought of in terms of mechanisms in man which could perform certain tasks if obstacles such as wear, tear, fatigue, distraction, death, etc. were all absent. In this sense, for example, it is taken for granted that if one has learned a particular formal system, he is 'capable of' producing all the theorems which the corresponding infinite machine can.

Under this assumption, it is, for example, taken for granted that I can do enough number theory to satisfy at least the condition of being sufficiently strong in the hypotheses of Gödel's theorems. Hence, if we assume further that I can prove A, then an immediate corollary of the theorems is that I am not a consistent Turing machine, since no such gadget can prove its own consistency.

If in addition we assume that A is true (not only that I can prove it), then of course I cannot be an inconsistent Turing machine either. But even under these assumptions, it is not ruled out that some consistent Turing machine S will be able to prove all my theorems and more. True, H_S cannot be proved in S, but I may also not be able to prove H_S either because I do not know the exact description of S or, for some other reason, I cannot prove Con(S).

Hence, from the assumption that I can prove A, it follows that I am not a consistent machine. If, in addition, we assume that A is also true, we get the stronger conclusion that I am not a machine. But in neither case is it excluded that a machine can prove more theorems than I do.[9]

Therefore, in the sense of being able to prove more theorems than any machine, the assumptions have not yielded the conclusion that I can do more than any machine. Yet in another sense, the assumptions seem to yield such a conclusion: machines can generate all and only recursively enumerable sets, while, since no machine can generate exactly my theorems, the set of my theorems is not recursively enumerable. Thus, even though the assumptions do not enable me to win the contest of being able to prove more theorems, they do enable me to generate a set which cannot be generated mechanically, and, in that sense, endow me with a capacity denied to all machines.

But the assumption that I can prove A is highly dubious. What has to be argued first is that I use an essentially different concept of proof from machines. It involves us in a flat contradiction (to Gödel's firmly established theorems) to think of me as a theorem-generating machine and at the same time to accept that I can prove my own consistency. It is true that the incompleteness results do not exclude the possibility of sets which are not recursively enumerable and which, by some natural Gödel numbering, contain their own consistency statements. But we need a different concept of proof in order that a set of theorems can be proved which form a set not recursively enumerable. By the way, the set of true statements of number theory does not contain its own consistency statement, because it is no longer an arithmetic statement.

It is not possible to prove I am not a machine by deriving, along the line of using A, a contradiction from the premiss that I am a machine. Even if I can manage to put myself into the frame of mind of imagining myself to be a machine, I could not possibly resist the conviction that I must be a very complicated machine relative to my knowledge. It is highly unlikely that I would know the exact description of my machine table (or program), much less know that I always function correctly without involving myself in contradictions.

The unclarities of the meaning of A tend to obscure the exact strength of the premiss that I am a machine. For example, in some sense I can prove A, but the sense of 'prove' and the sense of A need not be the formal sense which we assumed in deriving the conclusion that I am not a machine. Thus, if we accept the belief that I have also an informal way of knowing things, then I am not a machine for that reason already. Or, if we agree that A is different from an arithmetic statement of consistency and that I can prove A (without violating Gödel's results), then it is not excluded that I am indeed a machine, but I do not know I am really consistent.[10]

One is tempted to try a different approach and begin by asserting that I do have a component C which functions as a theorem-generating machine and which is capable of generating enough number theory for Gödel's results to apply. Moreover, it might be contended, I can prove that C is consistent. But then, since C need not exhaust my mechanical component, the conclusion can only be that I am more than C, not that I can prove more theorems than any machine. If C is thought to exhaust my mechanical component, then the additional theorem on the consistency of C must come from elsewhere. Therefore, there is a part of me which is not mechanical. It is, however, difficult either to determine such an exhaustive mechanical component C or, even were that possible, to prove a genuine consistency result on C. If it is suggested that, even though we cannot determine C exactly, I contain 'potentially' all theorem-generating machines, then there remains the old problem of separating out the consistent ones.

A quick argument seems to show that we are at least not an inconsistent machine: an inconsistent machine can prove everything but we obviously do not wish to assert everything even when we arrive at a contradiction. This is clearly a weak argument and shows clearly that there are various senses in which we could or could not legitimately compare mind to a Turing machine. It introduces a human element not shared by machines. If we wish to, we could also think of a machine which constantly checks whether a contradiction has been reached and attempts to revise its basic axioms when that happens. Then we would have shifted the difficulty of simulating man to the problem of mechanizing how we would go about revising our initial axioms. In any case, if we introduce such a checking device, we would seem to have eliminated the minor difference above as an argument for showing that we are not inconsistent machines.

It has been suggested that a property of conscious minds is their ability to answer questions about themselves without becoming other than themselves. But machines can answer questions about themselves too: e.g. it has been shown by M. H. Löb that the sentence expressing 'I am provable in *S*' is indeed a theorem of *S*, when *S* is, say, the ordinary system of number theory. It cannot be that man is supposed to have complete self-knowledge. We probably all feel that there are many questions about ourselves which we cannot answer.

It is a fact that we know certain systems of number theory to be consistent, and we also know that these systems remain consistent when we extend them by adding principles like (B):

(B$_1$) If '*W*' is provable in *S*, then *W*.

This suggests the vague idea that however far we extend the sequence of systems, we can always see beyond it. And this not unnaturally leads to the idea that we know more than any machine. A closer look at the original vague idea leads quickly to considerations about transfinite counting and ordinal logics. A number of technical results are available on these topics, but they are of little help with regard to establishing the superiority of man over machine.[11]

A somewhat frivolous argument could be given for showing that no man can do better than all machines. Suppose *X* is such a man, build a machine with an instruction 'consult *X*.' The obvious objection to this is that the machine is not independent but gains power by taking advantage of the abilities of *X*. On the other hand, we do not wish to deny a man or a machine the advantage of looking up printed material or seeking assistance from other people. Presumably the crucial point is that the 'crucial' steps should be supplied from one's own resources.

From the discussions so far, it does not seem that we can draw from the incompleteness results any sharp definite conclusions on the differences between man and machine. It cannot, however, be denied that these results do make some difference. If arithmetic were completable, then by a familiar argument it would also be (mechanically) decidable. We would then be willing to call arithmetic mechanical and not look for sharp theoretical limitations of machines not shared by men in the direction of theorems on natural numbers.[12]

6.5 Meaning, use, and objectivism

There are also discussions on broader philosophical implications of Gödel's theorems.

Some people take for granted that the human nervous system is subject to all the limitations of Turing machines. The incompleteness and unsolvability results are then called 'psychological laws.' One consequence of this view would seem to be the following. The existence of nonrecursive (but recursively enumerable) sets shows a radical limitation in man's power of envisaging the totality of a series of acts whose generating principle is envisaged with complete precision. This consequence would seem to be both clearer and more plausible than the general talk about psychological laws.

In a similar spirit, it has been suggested half facetiously that Gödel's theorems show that psychology is impossible. We cannot understand anything more complicated than Turing machines, so that psychology is not possible if we are not such machines. On the other hand, if we are Turing machines, Gödel's theorems indicate certain intrinsic limitations on what we can know about ourselves.

The second incompleteness theorem suggests the highly indefinite conclusion that we cannot prove mathematics is consistent. On the other hand, most mathematicians believe the similarly indefinite proposition that mathematics is consistent. This state of affairs has been dramatized by a widely circulated quotation: 'God exists, since mathematics is consistent, and the Devil exists, since we cannot prove it.'

We seem to have an understanding of the nonrecursive or the nonmechanizable, the uncountable, the inaccessible. In what sense do we conceive of something nonmechanizable? An oracle is, by definition, something we cannot explain. The nature of explanation is highly complex. Sometimes we seem to feel that a true explanation has to be mechanical. On the other hand, we do use teleological explanations (goals and purposes) a lot.

If the incompleteness results are to mean anything, we must have an idea of mathematical truth which is not the same as mere provability in a fixed formal system, but represents rather an ideal to which provability in any one given system is an approximation. It is, however, not excluded that truth is provability in some informal sense which might even be taken as given by an informal collection

C of formal systems such that *p* is true if and only if there is some *x* in *C* so that *p* is provable in *x*. There is then the burden of grasping the informal notion or characterizing *C*. Thus, a finitist like Herbrand or an intuitionist like Brouwer could perfectly make sense of the incompleteness results since neither a finitist nor an intuitionist is committed to one fixed formal system. In fact, a constructivist generally accepts a more basic intuition of provability or (constructive) truth to which formal systems can only offer imperfect approximations.

There are those who regard formal systems as basic and consider the postulation of anything beyond as likely to lead to obscurantism. While they agree that no formal system can characterize the number concept, they deny that the number concept is something above or beyond the formal systems. For these people, the incompleteness results do seem to create certain difficulties. It is sufficient, it may be argued, either to say that the results could be viewed as establishing a lack of closure (all instances provable but not the general law), or to say that truth for natural numbers is a well defined property of expressions. But if we do not have the notion of truth, how do we know there is a property of certain expressions that is truth; how do we know provability implies truth and, therefore, the closure property is what we desire?

The incompleteness results yield a contrast of formal mathematics with intuitive mathematics. But many would deny that we are thereby contrasting image with reality. Others would go further and say that we are only contrasting a game using strict rules with one using rules which change with the changing situation. This metaphor in terms of games leaves unexplained why we feel so confident not only about the games with strict rules but also about the general results on all games with strict rules.

It is tempting to draw from the incompleteness results the conclusion that we have in 'natural number' a counterexample to the thesis that meaning is to be explained by its use. The idea is perhaps to identify use or rather its characterization with provability in a given formal system. Incompleteness seems to show that no finite description of the use of the expression 'natural number' can exhaust what it is to have the concept, since to have the concept is at least to grasp the application of the predicate true to all arithmetic statements. This argument is hard to disentangle. It seems to assume that all uses can be fully described, and described by formal systems. Also, it is not clear in what sense having the concept of natural number (understanding the meaning of the expression) implies the ability to grasp the application of the predicate true to all arithmetic statements.

It is a familiar fact that in order to characterize fully the concept of natural number, we need to use either the concept itself or some other complex concepts such as finite or set. Thus, if it is a matter of characterizing meaning and use, we have no complete definite characterization of either. Hence, we do not have an easy argument for showing the inadequacy of formal systems (uses) to approach a contrasting and definite account of the meaning of number.

For example, we have an exact definition of arithmetic truth in terms of infinite induction. Even though we feel we understand infinite induction, we do not know how to use it directly. We can use it only when we have more information because we know the premisses are all provable only when we know that they are provable in a fairly uniform way. That is the only manner we know of dealing with an infinite collection of propositions. And in any case, infinite induction presupposes the concept of natural numbers or something like it.

We may readily agree that the concept of number is an innate idea, latent in the child's mind. That is why we cannot teach beasts number theory, no matter how much training we may give them in how to use the word 'number.' The innate component of meaning would seem to transcend the aspect of use. Yet the thesis of reducibility of meaning to use possesses sufficient vagueness to resist even such an argument.

The appeal of the thesis is undoubtedly tied up with the problem of communication. I can observe how others use words; but even if I can recognize in myself an experience of understanding a concept which is distinct from my ability to use the corresponding word, I cannot recognize such an experience in another person. And since the experience cannot be communicated, there is a doubt whether the recognition of such an experience is to be considered proper knowledge. The meaning of a word considered as part of the common language ought to be common and not private. One confusing matter is the vagueness of the concept of communicability. It may be argued that our having a common stable and rich concept of natural number is a basic fact which ought to be our starting point rather than something to be debated.

There is a reluctance in recent philosophy to envisage a perfectly definite concept which is incapable of a complete description but is somehow grasped by our intuition and serves as a guide to much of our pursuit in a given area. One is left wondering whether too exact a standard of clarity, while undoubtedly useful in excluding obscure and irresponsible speculations, may not also prevent us from doing full justice to our common heritage of a rich and inexhaustible intuition in our mathematical thinking.

In the introduction, we have quoted at length how Gödel relates his objectivistic position to his major discoveries in mathematical logic. Gödel points out that people might choose not to adopt the objectivistic position but merely do their work 'as if' the position were true, if they are able to produce such an attitude. But then they only take this 'as if' point of view toward this position after it has been shown to be fruitful. Moreover, it is doubtful whether one can pretend so well as to yield the desired effect of getting good scientific results. In any case, here we tread on a very delicate ground indeed, because in this area we no longer have a sharp distinction between what is practically feasible and what is possible in principle. We seem to have here a terminal reckoning of how fruitful a philosophical position is. The 'economy of thought' achieved by the objectivistic position is not something one can easily belittle, and may be essential in practice for the discovery. And practical feasibility is indeed our chief concern in this context. To reply that philosophy is not interested in the idiosyncracies of individual successful mathematicians is to mistake the incompleteness results for ordinary theorems in mathematics and to eschew a healthy respect for the basic facts of man's scientific activities.

7 GÖDEL ON MINDS AND MACHINES

In Gödel's opinion (as set forth in the unpublished 25th Josiah Willard Gibbs Lecture[13] delivered by him at Providence on December 26, 1951) the two most interesting rigorously proved results about minds and machines are these:

1 The human mind is incapable of formulating (or mechanizing) all its mathematical intuitions. I.e.: If it has succeeded in formulating some of them, this very fact yields new intuitive knowledge, e.g. the consistency of this formalism. This fact may be called the 'incompletability' of mathematics. On the other hand, on the basis of what has been proved so far, it remains possible that there may exist (and even be empirically discoverable) a theorem-proving machine which in fact *is* equivalent to mathematical intuition, but cannot be *proved* to be so, nor even be proved to yield only *correct* theorems of finitary number theory.[14]

2 The second result is the following disjunction: Either the human mind surpasses all machines (to be more precise: it can decide more number theoretical questions than any machine) or else there exist number theoretical questions undecidable for the human mind.

Gödel thinks Hilbert was right in rejecting the second alternative. If it were true it would mean that human reason is utterly irrational by asking questions it cannot answer, while asserting emphatically that only reason can answer them. Human reason would then be very imperfect and, in some sense, even inconsistent, in glaring contradiction to the fact that those parts of mathematics which have been systematically and completely developed (such as, e.g. the theory of 1st and 2nd degree Diophantine equations, the latter with two unknowns) show an amazing degree of beauty and perfection. In these fields, by entirely unexpected laws and procedures (such as the quadratic law of reciprocity, the Euclidean algorithm, the development into continued fractions, etc.), means are provided not only for solving all relevant problems, but also solving them in a most beautiful and perfectly feasible manner (e.g. due to the existence of simple expressions yielding *all* solutions). These facts seem to justify what may be called 'rationalistic optimism.'

Gödel notes moreover that attempted proofs for the equivalence of mind and machines are fallacious. E.g. he recently wrote the following paragraph[15] about Turing's alleged proof that every mental procedure for producing an infinite series of integers is equivalent to a mechanical procedure:

Turing, in *Proc. Lond. Math. Soc.* 42 (1936), p. 250, gives an argument which is supposed to show that mental procedures cannot carry any farther than mechanical procedures. However, this argument is inconclusive, because it depends on the supposition that a finite mind is capable of only a finite number of distinguishable states. What Turing disregards completely is the fact that *mind, in its use, is not static, but constantly developing.* This is seen, e.g., from the infinite series of ever stronger axioms of infinity in set theory, each of which expresses a new idea or insight. A similar process takes place with regard to the primitive terms. E.g., the iterative concept of set became clear only in the past few decades. Several more primitive ideas now appear on the horizon, e.g., the selfreflexive concept of proper class. Therefore, although at each stage of the mind's development the number of its possible states is finite, there is no reason why this number should not converge to infinity in the course of its development. Now there may exist systematic methods of accelerating, specializing, and uniquely determining this development, e.g. by asking the right questions on the basis of a mechanical procedure. But it must be admitted that the precise definition of a procedure of this kind would require a substantial deepening of our understanding of the basic operations of the mind. Vaguely defined procedures of this kind, however, are known, e.g., the

process of defining recursive wellorderings of integers
representing larger and larger ordinals or the process of
forming stronger and stronger axioms of infinity in set theory.

In our discussions Gödel added the following. Turing's argument
becomes valid under two additional assumptions, which today are
generally accepted, namely: 1 There is no mind separate from
matter. 2 The brain functions basically like a digital computer.
(2 may be replaced by: 2′ The physical laws, in their observable
consequences, have a finite limit of precision.) However, while
Gödel thinks that 2 is very likely and 2′ practically certain, he
believes that 1 is a prejudice of our time, which will be disproved
scientifically (perhaps by the fact that there aren't enough nerve
cells to perform the observable operations of the mind).

More generally, Gödel believes that mechanism in biology is a
prejudice of our time which will be disproved. In this case, one dis-
proval, in Gödel's opinion, will consist in a mathematical theorem
to the effect that the formation within geological times of a human
body by the laws of physics (or any other laws of a similar nature),
starting from a random distribution of the elementary particles and
the field, is about as unlikely as the separation by chance of the
atmosphere into its components.

NOTES

1 The contrast between life and mind reminds one of the doctrine of Descartes
according to which beasts are machines but men are not (see *Discourse on
method*, part V, especially p. 116 in the edition of E. S. Haldane and G. R. T.
Ross). His main argument is from the diversity and flexibility of the mind,
using speech as a distinguished example. Thus, 'although machines can perform certain things as well as or perhaps better than any of us can do, they
infallibly fall short in others, by which means we may discover that they
did not act from knowledge;' 'it never happens that it arranges its speech in
various ways, in order to reply appropriately to everything that may be said
in its presence, as even the lowest type of man can do.' Plausible as these
assertions are, especially with regard to existing machines, they can hardly
claim to be sharp conclusive arguments. La Mettrie, for example, accepts
Descartes' tests but argues that man is a machine.
2 There is a tantalizing discussion of self-conscious machines by M. Minsky,
'Matter, mind and models,' *Proc. IFIP Congress*, 65, 1965, pp. 45-9.
3 See A. M. Turing, 'Computing machinery and intelligence,' *Mind*, vol. 59,
1950, pp. 433-60.
4 Compare 'Toward mechanical mathematics,' *IBM Journal*, vol. 4, 1960,
pp. 2-22.
5 See remarks by G. A. Miller in *Computer and the world of the future*, ed.
Martin Greenberger, 1962, pp. 118-21.

6 A rather early attempt to show man's superiority by considering mathematical activities is contained in E. Post, 'Absolutely unsolvable problems and relatively undecidable propositions' in *The undecidable*, ed. M. Davis, 1965; the paper was written around 1941.

'It makes of the mathematician much more than a kind of clever being who can do quickly what a *machine* could do ultimately. We see that a *machine* would never give a complete logic; for once the machine is made *we* could prove a theorem it does not prove.' This remark seems to share with later arguments the disturbing equivocation between truth and provability. All that the mathematical result establishes is a conditional statement: if the machine is correct (consistent), then the undecidable proposition is true. It says nothing about our being able to prove that the machine is correct, even if it indeed is. 'The creative germ seems not to be capable of being purely presented but can be stated as consisting in constructing ever higher types.'

7 For example, we may take the formal language of Peano's arithmetic with addition and multiplication included and assume a fixed Gödel numbering of all the expressions. Let N be the ordinary formal system of number theory with all theorems enumerated by a recursive function f. Consider now all partial recursive functions and for each such function g, let the set of all m such that $\exists n(f(n) = m$ or $g(n) = m)$ be the theorems of its corresponding formal system. In this way, we reach a sufficiently wide collection of systems. For each system, we get the undecidable sentences in the same manner as with N.

8 Let y_0 be the Gödel number of $0 = 1$. Since we know this is not a theorem of N, y_0 is in the range of the union of f and g if and only if it is in the range of g. But it is undecidable whether for any g, y_0 belongs to g. See, e.g., H. Rogers, *Theory of recursive functions and effective computability*, 1967, p. 33, (f) of Theorem I. A more direct remark is that even deciding whether a single axiom is consistent is exactly the unsolvable decision problem of the predicate calculus. If it is objected that these systems with single axioms include ones which are not sufficiently rich, then we can modify the argument somewhat and consider the systems obtained from N by adding for each sentence A_i of N an arithmetic statement saying that A_i has a two-quantifiered arithmetic model. Then deciding the consistency of these systems would again yield a decision procedure for the predicate calculus.

9 An alternative approach is to assume that I can prove: (B) If I can prove 'W', then W; i.e., everything I can prove is true. Given the assumption that I can prove (B), it follows by a familiar remark that I can also prove my own consistency. Thus, put '$0 = 1$' for 'W' in (B). Since I can prove 0 1, I can also prove by (B) that I cannot prove '$0 = 1$'; i.e., I am consistent.

10 There are a number of subtleties on the exact form of the consistency statement. For example, in Gentzen's proof of the consistency of N, a transfinite induction is applied which cannot be formalized in N. Yet the hypothesis of the induction can be proved in N. Since, one is tempted to say, given the hypothesis, we can see that the unprovable consequence which is a standard consistency statement follows, it may seem reasonable to take the hypothesis as the consistency statement. But in that case, the consistency of N can be proved in N. However, as Gödel points out, the induction step is precisely the difficult step which we do not see easily. Hence, knowing the induction hypothesis does not imply knowing the conclusion. This example illustrates the stability of the second incompleteness theorem relative to truthful formulations of the consistency statements.

11 For example, all true Π^0_1 sentences, i.e. sentences of the form $\forall x P(x)$, with P

recursive, can be proved in some ordinal logic L_a, where a is a recursive ordinal notation, and extensions are made by adding consistency statements. If the extension principle is (B_1) strengthened to infer a $\Pi^0{}_1$ sentence from the arithmetic statement expressing the provability of all its instances, then all true arithmetic statements can be proved in some L_a. On the other hand, no $\Pi^1{}_1$ path through the set of recursive ordinal notations can give enough ordinal logics to prove all true $\Pi^0{}_1$ statements. See A. M. Turing, 'Systems of logic based on ordinals,' *Proc. London Math. Soc.*, vol. 45, 1939, pp. 161–228; S. Feferman and C. Spector, 'Incompleteness along paths in progressions of theories,' *J. symbolic logic*, vol. 27, 1962, pp. 383–90.

12 There are many discussions on the implications of the incompleteness results, both on mechanism and on other general issues. We mention here just a few. J. Myhill, 'Some philosophical implications of mathematical logic,' *Review of metaphysics*, vol. 6, 1952, pp. 169–98. J. Lucas, 'Minds, machines and God,' *Philosophy*, vol. 36, 1961, pp. 112–26. R. L. Goodstein, 'The significance of incompleteness theorems,' *Brit. j. for the phil. of sci.*, vol. 14, 1963, pp. 208–20. M. Dummett, 'The philosophical significance of Gödel's theorem,' *Ratio*, vol. 5, 1963, pp. 140–55. P. Benacerraf, 'God, the Devil, and Gödel,' *Monist*, vol. 51, 1967, 9–33. J. Webb, 'Metamathematics and the philosophy of mind,' *Phil. of sci.*, vol. 35, 1968, pp. 156–78.

13 See *Bull. Am. Math. Soc.*, vol. 58, 1952, p. 158.

14 Regarding the discussion given in the first five paragraphs of § 6.4 above, Gödel thinks that because of the unsolved intentional paradoxes for concepts, like 'concept,' 'proposition,' 'proof,' etc., in their most general sense, no proof using the self-reflexivity of these concepts can be regarded as conclusive in the present stage of development of logic, although, after a satisfactory solution of these paradoxes, such arguments may turn out to be conclusive.

15 To be added as a footnote at the word 'mathematics' on p. 73, line 3, of *The undecidable*, op. cit.

XI

NOTES ON KNOWLEDGE
AND LIFE

INTRINSIC GOALS AND
LARGE PROBLEMS

There are certain goals which are hard to dispute: to eliminate war (peace on earth), to reduce hostility (good will toward man), to decrease diseases (such as finding a cure for cancer), to wipe out hunger, to remove inequality, to spread esthetic enjoyment, to maximize human happiness, to increase knowledge, to cultivate more affection. These are the intrinsic goals. They are different from intermediate goals which are justified with the help of beliefs that they will contribute to the attainment of certain intrinsic goals.

In practice, most intrinsic goals do not determine directly human activities. First, we usually do not know the best way to attain these goals. Second, many of these goals contain basic ambiguities so that there is a serious problem of interpretation. Third, quite often different goals are in conflict and it is hard to determine their relative priorities. We usually do not know how much particular actions contribute to any intrinsic goal. Even the few goals listed above form a heterogeneous lot: e.g. some are positive ones to maximize the good and some are negative ones to minimize the bad. One basic disagreement is between maximizing the good for a minority (be it the elite countries or the elite groups within given societies) in the name of culture or civilization and minimizing the bad for the majority.

An apparently innocent emphasis on some of the intrinsic goals could be quite controversial and indeed morally repugnant. For example, in the heyday of British imperialism, a rather influential ethical doctrine came out of Cambridge which singled out esthetic

329

enjoyments and personal affection as good in themselves. In theory, this doctrine does not reject the suggestion that for a long time to come eliminating miseries will be of more moral value than pursuing personal enjoyments. In practice, it has had the effect of enhancing the complacency of intellectual aristocrats.

Another basic distinction is between egoism and altruism. In theory, everybody agrees that altruism is better than egoism. In practice, there are reasons on different levels for disproportionate concerns over one's self-interest. On the crudest level, there is the feeling that since nearly everybody is egoistic, why should I play the fool? Then there is the excuse that I know much better what contributes to my own welfare than what is good for mankind. On the highest level, one is convinced that he is important for mankind so that he feels he must take very good care of himself in order to maximize his good influences. It is hard to deny that in many societies, for those who have little difficulty in having their basic material needs satisfied, the greatest misery comes from the pre-occupation with their ego. This is perhaps the deep practical sense in which egoism might be said to be self-contradictory.

The existence of different nations of course places an additional complicating factor on the relation between self and mankind. Sometimes a large group of people agree on a basic central goal such as winning the war or saving the country. This agreement not only imposes a moral obligation on members of the group but also determines the direction in which an overall philosophy of action (including priorities and strategies) is to be reached. In general, it is not realistic to assume that people with totally different conditions of existence can easily agree on which of several different courses of action is best for humanity.

At first one is inclined to feel that there is little gap between understanding the world and changing the world, given the fact that this is not the best of all possible worlds. The idea is, once we understand the ills of the world and their causes and cures, it only remains to take the prescribed steps in a concerted effort, with energy and joy. The truth is we do not and cannot have a perfect understanding of the world in the sense that there is an essentially unique course of action which everybody clearly sees to be the right one. This is not to deny that on many occasions many of us do feel strongly that we know, say, certain government actions to be wrong. But often we do not know what is the most effective way for oneself to combat the wrong. In a different direction, some of us may face the dilemma that, while convinced of the superiority of a particular society, one is not able to choose to live in that society on account of personal habits and other similar factors about oneself. In these cases, the feeling of a lack of knowledge is summoned to support an inaction resulting largely from inertia and a wish to avoid pain or disturbance.

The more relevant distinction is between studying philosophy with a view to understanding the world and studying philosophy with a view to changing the world. While in the abstract the distinction need not be sharp, in fact, the former approach tends to emphasize mathematics and the natural sciences (especially physics), the latter approach tends to emphasize history and the social sciences. Perfect knowledge would certainly be a stage at which the two approaches converge; even though such convergence need not require perfect knowledge. World changing is not the only possible goal of philosophy as a guide to action; it is well known that there are philosophies which have been intended, or at least used, for the preservation of the status quo, e.g. Confucianism. In many cases, a strong motivating force for the study of philosophy is a sense of dissatisfaction with the world as it is. And it has been suggested that a true understanding of the world has to contain a workable program for changing the world to make it better.

It is a fact that many individuals have abstract knowledge which they do not know how to apply to certain particular situations. There is a basic gap between theory and practice, as well as knowledge and action, not only with physics and technology, but also with political economy and revolution. Hence, it is customary to separate knowledge from action, and in the extreme case some people enunciate the credo of knowledge for knowledge's sake. In this way, we are led to various large problems which have primarily to do with knowledge.

Of course, life is more important than art and science. In the same sense, knowledge is secondary to action. The most central large problems are self-evidently important and require no further motivation. These are:

1 What should I do (now and in the long run)?

2 What is to be done (by mankind to make the world better)?

In one form or another, these questions are familiar to everybody even though only a small minority discuss them in public. Rarely does a man stop all except the absolutely necessary activities in order to devote himself to a persistent systematic pursuit for answers to these questions, based on first principles.

In his *On the improvement of the understanding*, Spinoza announces:

> I finally resolved to inquire . . . whether, in fact, there might be anything of which the discovery and attainment would enable me to enjoy continuous, supreme, and unending happiness. . . .

What that character is we shall show in due time, namely, that
it is the knowledge of the union existing between the mind and
the whole of nature. This, then, is the end for which I strive,
to attain to such a character myself, and to endeavour that
many should attain to it with me. . . . Yet as it is necessary
that while we are endeavouring our purpose, and bringing the
understanding into the right path, we should carry on our life,
we are compelled first of all to lay down certain rules of life
as provisionally good.

The knowledge of the union of mind and nature is knowledge of
a very special character, different from what is ordinarily thought of
as (scientific) knowledge. Much of ordinary knowledge is supposed
to help us by providing us with the means of attaining goals which
are determined by other factors having more to do with feeling and
willing, rather than just thinking.

If knowledge yields a world view, then of course the connection
with life becomes more intimate. This conception of knowledge is
implicit, for example, in the declaration that Hegelism or Marxism
is a science of human history.

For one who is devoted to the pursuit of knowledge, knowledge is
of course exceptionally important for his life. Here the relation
between knowledge and happiness is of a derived nature. For example, he may have been brought up in the belief that 'in the books
there are golden houses, in the books there are beautiful ladies.'
The social system may be such that this belief corresponds pretty
closely to the real situation. Knowledge becomes a means again,
this time not by any immediate application of the knowledge to the
understanding or the modification of the real world, but by a sort
of credential which functions much like money or other types of
outside influence. In this regard, knowledge is no different from other
concrete goals of success and recognition, and presents no special
avenue of connecting knowledge with life.

Traditionally, there have been suggestions that philosophical
knowledge, unlike ordinary knowledge, does promise a state of
happiness which can be brought about by seeing Truth or by finding
out the proper way to live. The example of Spinoza or Chuangtse
perhaps belongs to this category.

If we think deeply about the nature of knowledge, we may come
to a better understanding of the thinking subject. It seems then
reasonable to suggest that we thereby reach a better understanding
of the self. In this way we may obtain a special avenue to a better
life through knowing the nature of man.

In what follows, such more profound approaches to life and

knowledge will not be considered. The considerations are confined rather to the relation of the activity of knowledge pursuit to the life of the knowledge pursuer.

2 RELEVANCE AND FORMS OF LIFE

Egoism could be aggressive or defensive. It is sometimes argued that the best solution may be for everybody to be a reasonable egoist, who is, above all, not competitive and extremely considerate towards others at least in a negative way. The world has so much to offer, there is room for everybody's fulfillment if only nobody is so foolish and wicked as to negate value and take positive things away from others. Whatever the merits of such an ideal in an imaginary world, it seems hardly of immediate practical relevance.

A less radical position would be to look for a universal way of salvation that is applicable to every individual. Spinoza seemed to believe that he had found such a solution which he recommended to others. If few others understood his way or attained the ultimate end, that is another matter. Somehow the pursuit of common good is transformed into the pursuit of truth. And it can be asked whether a recipe for good life which in practice is not widely executed could be called a true solution, except perhaps only in a hypothetical sense.

We all take the world as we understand it and behave accordingly. Some of us are more interested in changing it. But in varying degrees our understanding is always very partial and imperfect. There are painful surprises. When we are forced to do disagreeable things the reasons for which we either detest or do not understand, we are frustrated, we feel alienated. In the nature of things, each of us lives in a very narrow region. Most of us are specialists, if not in the positive sense of knowing a great deal about some special areas, certainly in the negative sense of knowing very little about most areas. Yet what concerns us most, whether we choose it or not, are historical processes and political directions which relate to all the diversity of human experience. In this sense, we are most ignorant about what is most vital. If we are left with choices, we either follow the course of least resistance or choose reluctantly by inadequate evidence. Or we try, as far as possible, to refrain from committing ourselves to any clear direction, thereby depriving ourselves of courage and joy and greatly impoverishing our life. So few who reflect are blessed with an ardent faith and confident understanding of the future course of history.

Many of us are reduced to make-believe. We submit to blind

forces on big issues and try to be rational locally with regard to more restricted problems. We find ends-in-view to substitute for the unknown ultimate ends and channel our energy into narrow courses in order to get at least the pleasure of exercising our faculties, not unlike playing games for a living perhaps with less clearcut rules and less certainty of irrelevance. If one believes that power, money, fame all are vanity, there remains yet the problem of making a living. This is not as easy as it sounds, especially since, for one thing, most people need and have their 'breeding holes,' as Santayana so disdainfully calls the family dwellings of the married fellows of Cambridge. In any case, where is one to draw the line between greed and need?

If the image of games is pursued, then it would seem that games with more complicated (and in that sense more flexible) rules are the more interesting. But the image does not go very far because there are also the question of relevance (which may perhaps be included as additional rules) and the possibility of making new rules. There is probably some sort of positive correlation between the breadth of an area and the flexibility of its rules.

One might wish to say that the task of every philosopher is to describe eventually 'the world as I see it' and that his achievement is to be evaluated by how significant a picture he gives. Human experience is preserved in written words and in people's heads, reading and conversing are the only external sources of experience which go beyond the rather restricted direct contacts with nature and artifacts. Each philosopher absorbs a certain small part of the human experience through direct contact and indirect communication by words. He is actively to choose continually the chunk of experience he is to have, and to digest and arrange it in stages. The end result is somehow to pass for a world view.

This sort of activity would seem quite the opposite of expertise or specialization as ordinarily understood. And there are some intrinsic difficulties in fitting a philosopher's pursuit into the academic life. The process of acquiring and digesting experience is rather too private to be suitable for a teacher. And the chief interest is in learning rather than teaching. At each stage, one possesses a framework on the basis of which a few more things can be understood and absorbed. In this way the basic outlook undergoes revisions and expansions, and gradually grows in breadth and maturity.

Every philosophy is necessarily partial and unbalanced. One mainly interested in art is likely to come up with a different kind of philosophy from one chiefly concerned with knowledge. A preoccupation with history certainly lends a different flavor than one with mathematics.

What we are and how we live certainly affects our way of looking at the world. An able black man in Africa is not likely to have a similar outlook on life to a clever Brooklyn Jew. Except in very restricted domains, our thinking cannot dissociate completely from our class origins and national traditions. Philosophers tend to live and work in academic communities, which are often institutions based on medieval ideas. Ivory towers remain dominated by the medieval interpretation of the Greek distinction between the practical life and the contemplative life. Scholasticism and abstention from judging on large practical issues require a justification. It cannot be denied that there is an intimate and mutual dependence of theory and practice. To comfort oneself, one tries to believe that the contemplative-practical distinction is sound, and that, since there are many worthwhile things in life, each individual has a right to select what best suits him, which might be contemplation.

In any case, it is not easy to change the habits of daily life. Moreover, there are in universities deep-rooted requirements of discipline, clarity, reliability which are impossible to satisfy while dealing with large practical issues. If a philosophy is devoted to the 'practical' problem of making the world better, then it is only natural that most academic philosophers find the philosophy muddled, unconvincing, if only because they have never seriously asked the same question. Embracing any such philosophy is made harder by the unwillingness to make commitments and the all too ready eagerness to suspend judgment which are practically the hallmark of the contemplative life.

If one thinks in terms of life ideals, then there seem to be, at first sight, the three stages of finding a life ideal, striving to attain it, and finally living in the ideal state. In practice, most people do not have such sharply separate stages. It is not easy to be a believer. Many ideals do not include the last stage in one's lifetime. For example, if one believes firmly in some way of bringing about an ideal society, one may be willing to contribute every effort towards this goal, even though there is no anticipation of living long enough to see that society.

The relation between society and self generates two distinctions relevant to one's behavior. The first distinction is between thinking of oneself as a station on a more or less permanent social way and envisaging the future as wholly unlike the past whether or not one's own preference is for drastic changes. The second distinction is between seeing one's own life as a small contribution to a much larger whole and viewing one's own immediate circle as an isolated unit striving for suitable intrinsic qualities. History is full of examples of people each searching for one form or another of secular or religious salvation. Uncertainties about the future naturally yield the desire to look to the past and one's family and friends for comfort.

In a stable society, it is possible to think of one's own generation as a phase in a long process, which transmits and perhaps modifies the accumulated heritage from a continuous past. It is possible to believe that the future of humanity is more or less secure and that intellectual advances accompany social progress. Under such conditions, it is relatively easy to bestow value on most intellectual and artistic activities, and one is less likely to be troubled by the concern with relevance. It is less hard to tolerate and even encourage ivory towers.

In a period of change with great social mobility, one longs for some sort of 'home.' To say that home is where one starts from bypasses a good deal of difficulty. There is what one was accustomed to, which could have been transplanted onto some island and kept alive artificially by some reactionary force. There is also what one expected to see which is found nowhere. If to identify oneself with a large group becomes increasingly unattainable, the next thing is to look for a smaller group, perhaps as representing a recurrent type in history. In this way, an attempt is made to broaden the group to which one feels a kinship.

3 SPECIALIZATION AND THE UNITY OF KNOWLEDGE

Specialization is a highly ambiguous word. We may begin by looking at a few statements by Weber.[1]

> In our time, the internal situation is first of all conditioned by the facts that science has entered a phase of specialization previously unknown and that this will forever remain the case. Not only externally, but inwardly, matters stand at a point where the individual can acquire the sure consciousness of achieving something truly perfect in the field of science only in case he is a strict specialist. . . . Only by strict specialization can the scientific worker become fully conscious, for once and perhaps never again in his lifetime, that he has achieved something which will endure. A really definitive and good accomplishment is today always a specialized accomplishment. And whoever lacks the capacity to put on blinders, so to speak, and to come up to the idea that the fate of his soul depends upon whether or not he makes the correct conjecture

at this passage of this manuscript may as well stay away from science. . . . For nothing is worthy of man as man unless he can pursue it with passionate devotion.

By science, Weber means any intellectual discipline or any (intellectual) knowledge, including esthetics and types of cultural philosophy. In particular, Weber himself is undoubtedly a scientist in this sense, although we tend to think of him as more than a specialist. If by specialization is meant merely concentrated attention on the topic under consideration, then much of Weber's exhortation would seem to be unnecessary. On the other hand, it cannot be the case that Weber wishes to urge everybody to stick to small questions. One positive content of his remarks is perhaps the suggestion that suggestive ideas are not as valuable as finished products and only a specialist can produce finished products. This does not exclude the possibility that certain people might create new specialties. The process of creating a subject X can hardly be called specializing in X. The point must be that in order to create X, one has first to specialize in some related areas Y.

Often when we deplore the ills of specialization, we have in mind the narrow specialists. We believe that many eminent intellectuals are not specialists, or not just specialists. We feel that there are many important intellectual questions left untouched by established special disciplines. In fact, often one finds that the problems one is naturally most interested in do not fall squarely in any existing specialty. For many, putting on blinders may be incompatible with a passionate devotion. If the advice is to resist at all cost the temptation to deviate from specialization, then it is no longer unnecessary but, perhaps for the same reason, also not unquestionable. In any case, if passionate devotion is the ultimate criterion, it is by no means obvious that specialization is necessary, even less that it is necessary at every stage of a life devoted to intellectual work. If all that is meant is that only by specialization can passionate devotion produce serious results, then the proposition remains debatable unless 'serious' is defined in terms of 'specialization.' Even then we might wish to forego serious for interesting work. In another direction, specialization often implies more direct comparisons and competitions (winning and losing) which appeal to some people but not to others.

An example of the conflict between specialists and generalists might be the mixed receptions of Spengler's or Toynbee's work in history. Professional historians object to such sweeping books because they do not work at history but only talk about history.

However one is to resolve the problem of the exclusive importance of specialization, it is certainly a familiar phenomenon that many people, rightly or wrongly, long for a unity of knowledge. Examples of hesitant misgivings over the domination of specialization are the following:

(a) Fragmentation impoverishes life. One desires to have an over-all view of human knowledge no matter whether one is in addition a specialist. Many find the life of a mere specialist not sufficiently satisfying. Since knowledge is a valuable thing, it seems wasteful not to experience it in its broad sweep. Confining oneself to a narrow area appears too much like denying the best things life has to offer and it is an intrinsic good to understand one's place in the universe. Is such an inclination to be broad natural and rational?

(b) Some feel that specialization tends to reward certain types of mind (and temperament) which need not be of the highest quality. Hence, there is a desire to change the rules of the intellectual life to provide an attractive outlet for those who have ability but dislike specialization. Is the feeling unjustified and the desire quixotic?

(c) Ideally a young man would see clearly the alternatives open to him (viz. both the possible paths in the abstract and his individual endowments) and decide rationally on a choice of life career. In practice, his choice depends mostly on accidents. Would a unified outlook help in some measure to make one's choices in life more rational?

(d) Within narrow areas, colleagues can have interesting discussions. But can the dream of a community of scholars be realized in the sense that people from diverse fields can have significant intercourse?

Those who are sympathetic to the desire for unity may be interested in considering the following tentative suggestions on 'What is to be done?'

(a) The desire to know all is actually a desire not to know all: not to know all the details, but only the 'essential.' Within a special discipline, it is familiar that some talented men are able to confine their attention to more central problems. One is tempted to argue by analogy and think of a further climb to the 'highest knowledge.' There is the obvious danger that in getting rid of the resistance of air, flying becomes not easier but impossible.

(b) How is unity within one broad discipline related to the unity of knowledge? One may wish to bypass the former. If it is thought that the former is a precondition of the latter, we would have to map out a few general areas first and perhaps concentrate on one area at a time, with special attention to its relation to the general unity. The short books making up the *Britannica Perspectives* series (1968) are along this line.

338

(c) One suggestion would be a redistribution of talents: to encourage synthesis and digestion of known material. For example, it has been suggested that (say) every five years all physicists should stop getting 'new' results for a year and spend the time in reviewing and consolidating gains. Perhaps more value should be attributed to synoptic reviews and controlled speculations than minute new findings.

(d) Groups can be and have been formed with practitioners from diverse disciplines. People in such a group might try to instruct each other on a few general topics. For example, what is a theory? In what sense do we have more theoretical physics than theoretical biology? We are told that science is cumulative, art is not. What constitutes *progress* in science and in art? We are told that in poetry there is the *exact* word, in music there is the *exact* note. In what way does art nonetheless differ drastically from mathematics? What is the relation of mathematics to application? What is the importance of *repetition* in art and science?

(e) It is not so much whether reductionism (say the reduction of the life process to physics and chemistry) will eventually turn out to work. We have no a priori reason to predict the outcome one way or the other. Rather we have to work simultaneously on several levels if our aim is to attain some unified view of knowledge in the near future.

(f) Through our history philosophers have attempted in various senses and with very different degrees of success to achieve some unification of knowledge. The most recent serious attempt is logical positivism. The basic position is a little too neat. But the root of the failure would seem to be insufficient attention to the consequences of the program. That is, the founders were excited by a neat way of classifying knowledge and thought that a reorganization of knowledge along their basic principles could not help but produce significant new results. Instead they should have thought more about how the program would affect the *practice* of scientists and artists. They would have found that if their approach were followed faithfully, all *life* would be taken out of the intellectual pursuit.

If one is optimistic about some sort of unification, then there are a number of possible alternative (not mutually exclusive) goals.

(a) To make the unity of knowledge a fact of experience for the majority of the instructed (say college graduates).

(b) To make it possible for a minority of interested and able individuals to attain a unified view of knowledge: organically interrelated and not just as consisting of isolated compartments.

(c) To create a new (and perhaps more efficient for the fortunate few) way of advancing human knowledge.

(d) To create a new discipline: generalist philosophy. There is the serious problem of making such a profession attractive enough for the interested individuals.

(e) To generate an object (a not too bulky book?) of contemplation. There is the intrinsic satisfaction. Possibly it also would serve as a guide to how to live. Presumably such a central object would also assist the advancement of knowledge.

(f) To rejuvenate philosophy: to make philosophy, or at least philosophy of knowledge, a more meaningful subject.

(g) Unified knowledge (or philosophy) as a guide to action.

(h) Perhaps a better understanding of the unity of knowledge will lead to a drastic revision of the curriculum on all levels.

Imagine ourselves being members of a group from different fields engaged in exploring the possibility of unifying knowledge. Some of the questions we might ask ourselves could be the following:

(a) Recently there was a paper by Roger Revelle on 'Can the poor countries benefit from the scientific revolution?' This involves a survey of useful knowledge. Clearly it does not seek for the same sort of thing we are after. Nonetheless, it is an impressive discussion ranging over a wide range of subjects and focusing on one tangible central theme. Can we find a pretty definite *focus* for our undertaking?

(b) It has been pointed out that beginners can more easily plunge into discussions in humanities and social sciences than in natural sciences. Would one say that the former is easier to understand or easier to create an illusion of understanding? It is a familiar experience that, for example, there are different levels of understanding a philosophical work or a poem. Also, is it perhaps possible to require every educated man to have a minimal command of 'languages' (including some mathematics and some basic science)?

(c) It seems irrelevant to presuppose that the products of mind possess a unity corresponding to their source, or that any human mind is capable of understanding what any other mind has articulated. These presuppositions appear to be unnecessary 'metaphysics.' These ambiguous propositions are either true by definition or false in any serious sense. But we are obviously not working toward the impossible goal that everybody know everything. Our task is a practical task and, as such, much of the preliminary problem is to articulate our vague desires toward greater unity and organization of knowledge. It is essential that we clarify our ideas sufficiently to enable us to benefit from one another, taking advantage of our very different backgrounds.

(d) Even though we wish not to bog down in messy details, we also have to avoid formulating our questions in too abstract a form so that we end up spending most of our time clarifying the meaning of terms. Thus, it does not seem helpful to ask at the start whether there are breeds of human minds that cannot cross and yield fertile offsprings, or whether there is a radical split between the beliefs on matter and mind. It would seem more fruitful if we could at first exchange 'distilled wisdom' from our respective disciplines and obtain some basic data to philosophize upon.

(e) Somewhere there is a basic doubt whether we are not being utopian or trying to do the impossible. The facts of life are such that there are great artists, there are great scientists, there are great scholars. How do we know we are not, in trying to change the existing situation, attempting to be superhuman?

Traditionally highly flexible principles have been suggested for the purpose of unifying knowledge. For example, we have yin and yang in *Iching*, the dialectical logic, and dialectical materialism. In more recent times, Niels Bohr has expounded the concept of complementarity, which is seen to be at work with regard to continuity and discreteness, justice and charity, subject and object (especially subject viewing itself as an object), contemplation and volition, the pragmatic and the mystic, different national cultures, and so on. This highly suggestive idea seems to be awaiting more careful analysis and elaborations at the present stage.

A different way of trying to find an overview of knowledge might be to find some sort of map of knowledge.

Let us distinguish the provinces of art, history, (natural) science, mathematics, and philosophy. It is tempting to say that history seeks for categorical singular propositions; art is, to the extent it is concerned with propositions at all, interested in hypothetical singular ones; mathematics is after hypothetical universal propositions; and philosophy, if we are optimistic, looks for categorical universal propositions.

From this point of view, the social sciences are closely related to history but aspire to be like the natural sciences. And there is a doubt whether natural science is to be classified with mathematics or with philosophy. When we think of the boundary conditions and the simplifying assumptions in the abstract statement of scientific laws, we are inclined to group natural science with mathematics. But when we remind ourselves of the great difference between physics and mathematics and the surprising extent to which we know nature, we would like to say that science, more successfully than philosophy, yields categorical universal propositions. One is then inclined to say that philosophical propositions are more universal in that they deal with the world as a whole and not, for example, just matter and motion.

We may also wish to introduce the aspect of 'necessity.' We would then say that science and history are interested in contingent propositions while philosophy and mathematics are interested in necessary propositions. There is the serious problem of securing a sufficiently rich concept of 'necessity' which permits important necessary propositions without obliterating the distinction between necessity and contingency.

Poetry is more scientific than history, since it deals with universals, such as what a generalized type of man would do on a generalized type of occasion. If art expresses emotions, then it should express real and not hypothetical emotions. As the characters of a novel are developed, they may be said to be true to a concept. But the ordinary logical distinctions of different kinds of proposition need not apply to art. To identify art with language is not only to define art but also to introduce a new dimension to the more prosaic concept of language as is familiar in logic and linguistics.

There is also a temptation to assimilate history to art. One is struck by the common goal of obtaining an intuitive experience of particulars. Thus, the business of the historian is to see individual events, and the business of the artist is to see individual tunes, men, landscapes, and so forth.

All knowledge is what we know now. In this sense, one might wish to say that all knowledge is historical knowledge. More, when we assert a general law, we deal directly only with instances so that science is but history with its particular reference suppressed. And on various occasions, this is an interesting reminder. While (natural) science and history are both interested in facts and laws, the law is the end in science and the particular fact is the end in history. But a scientist is interested in the exemplification of the universal in the fact and the historian recognizes a fact as a fact by bringing general concepts to interpret the fact; bare facts and pure universals are false abstractions. More, it has even been suggested that science is not knowledge but action, not true but useful: it is merely an instrument for knowledge, i.e. historical knowledge.

But neither of the two last sentences succeeds in obliterating a distinction between science (as typified by physics) and history. The first sentence could deteriorate into the tiresome distinction of difference in degree and difference in kind. The second sentence reveals the temptation to identify the genus knowledge with one of its species; instead of identifying history with science, it distinguishes the two by giving history the central position in knowledge and demoting science to the position of an inferior kind of knowledge. For many purposes, it is perfectly reasonable to view history as more important than science, but to deny science the title of proper knowledge would seem to be doing violence to our common conceptions. Etymologically the Greek term episteme is derived from a root meaning stability and firmness. We are inclined to think that science, more than history, embodies a firm and stable edifice.

The more common tendency, at least in academic circles, is to strive to elevate history to the envious status of (natural) science. If the gap appears too big, one invites social, political, behavioral sciences to aid bridging the gulf.

One might be struck by the constancy and regularity of the basic human biological needs and the interplay of these needs with one another and with the environment. One might be struck by certain basic patterns of the growth and the decay of societies. Or there is a certain sense of historical inevitability in, for example, the reactions toward extreme measures. Laws must underlie whatever is inevitable, and, with enough effort, we are always capable of systematizing laws into a science. Following this line of optimism, we are led to think of a practical possibility in place of a mere logical possibility, in a sense of 'logical' which is rather irrelevant in this context. If we are willing to forego the formal or mathematical sense of 'logical,' we are tempted rather to believe that a science of history after the pattern of physics is not only a practical but a logical impossibility. A plausible reason is, history is a more humane subject. Our readiness to accept certain historical accounts is not determined by their consistency with physical laws but rather by a broader appeal to life as we know it. History calls for an ability to imagine life under different circumstances, to put oneself in the place of people from a different period, to reconstruct and apply their concepts and categories.

This humane element opens up for history the possibility of avoiding specialization in one particular sense. This is seen by the fact that a good survey of history can be valued more highly than a good monograph, while, in the sciences, a survey can never be ranked higher than any significant new discovery. Of great value to the historians are the capacities for integration and association, for perceiving the relation of parts to wholes, for selection and arrangement of details. To some extent, the urge to be a generalist can be satisfied by striving to be a broad historian.

History of thought is, compared with other parts of history, more closely related to the ideal of unifying knowledge, which is, however, concerned less with history than with the structure of current human thought. We are more interested in the end results rather than the detailed process by which the results were arrived at. This leads us back to specialization.

The question of specialization is, to be sure, central to the pursuit of knowledge. It involves the appealing principles of cooperation and division of labor. Quite often we find we are actually objecting to bad taste rather than specialization: for example, when we dislike so-called new results which in no way contribute to the advance of knowledge. Either the results are not really new and do not even offer a more congenial way of looking at known facts, or they are new but of such small significance that they will be forgotten and rediscovered effortlessly when they begin to fit significantly into a larger framework. There is simply too much emphasis on 'results' and 'originality' which look different but mean very little.

It cannot be denied that specialization serves to focus and give direction to one's activities. It guides the selection of data to be attended to. By definition of the word 'attention,' we cannot pay equal attention to everything. It is tempting to compare specialization to the use of crutches, but then if one tries to talk without these crutches, the feeling may resemble walking on water.

The problem with well established specialties and ill-established specialties is quite different. In a well established field, the rules of work are rigid, the judgments of relative merits are fairly objective and uniform, the ability required is quite specific and well defined. In an ill-established field, standards are confusing, rules of work are more flexible, and there is constantly the uneasy feeling that one may be asking the wrong question so that a whole domain may turn out to be pointless. This is related to the danger of inventing wrong specialties. The drive towards specialization not unnaturally leads to an impatience to stabilize nebulous ideas into a specialty so that others can pursue it with no regard to the broader significance of the specialty. Thus it is we often find long and persistent considerations which, though pertinent and interesting relative to the task set, appear to be of little interest because the original questions were artificial, ill-conceived, and unimportant to begin with. We are then under the impression, quite often correctly, that we are witnessing the play of a pointless game.

The birth of a specialty often involves an element of modeling or abstracting or putting on blinders. This has the effect of making more sharp and definite results feasible, but also of introducing some inevitable distortion of the less explicit original problems. It is not always clear whether the distortion as a loss is sufficiently compensated by the gain in the increased manageability of the reformulation. The overeagerness for tangible quick progress tends to encourage hasty crystallizations of vague problems into inappropriate sharp reformulations. An indication of something wrong may be the feeling that we no longer make use of our intuition of the original natural problem but instead either proceed merely formally or on the basis of a derivative intuition based entirely on the reformulation. Somewhat paradoxically, in the most exact and well established specialties such as mathematics and physics, the best practitioners are better able to transcend formal details and exercise their imagination and refined intuition.

When a topic falls outside of established specialties, there is the inclination to create a specialty to fit it. But the topic may either be unripe yet for such a treatment or be one not capable of being so treated. We do have people who specialize in generalities. The phrase calls to mind science journalists and popular expositors. In the practical sphere, the head of a state may be said to have the function of specializing in generalities. But in the sphere of ideas, philosophers are also traditionally expected to specialize in generalities.

An amateur can have a good idea in a given discipline. Most of the time, however, he would not have a sufficient understanding of the broader context to fully control, evaluate, and exploit the idea in its bearings. Occasionally there are exceptions: for example, the mathematician G. H. Hardy unintentionally made a fairly basic contribution to genetics.

A sociological aspect of the prevalence of specialization is the practical necessity of being a specialist in order to belong to a group and even to make a living. The need for appreciation and close intellectual interactions is fairly easily satisfied by being a specialist.

An element of all experience which is to form part of human knowledge is that it must be capable of being communicated by language. In this regard, it is appropriate to think of mathematics, not as a special branch of knowledge, but as a refinement of general language, supplementing ordinary verbal expressions, which may be too imprecise and cumbersome, with new tools to represent relations. This refinement of language is so successful in certain domains that there has arisen a tendency to think of the ideal of science in terms of the adjective 'mathematical.' On the other extreme, the emphasis of existence over essence could be construed as a thesis either that language is not adequate to knowledge or that knowledge is not adequate to life.

Why is it that we find the abstract talk of a unity of knowledge somewhat lame? A king might apply his knowledge of unity to try to bring about an ideal society in his kingdom (and perhaps elsewhere). An Aristotle, a Hegel, or a Marx could erect a whole system and have great influence. A Chuangtse or a Spinoza would use his view of the wholeness of knowledge to guide his life. But what is the use of a dried-up unity for the archives or a purified and unified textbook? It would perhaps be of interest to reforming education.

If one is brought up to be concerned primarily with knowledge and is yet repulsed by the isolation and fragmentation of the specialties, it is natural to look for a general science or a comprehensive philosophy. It is of course not guaranteed that such searchings will be productive, even less that they will yield a satisfactory life.

Perhaps what one longs for is not so much a unified view of knowledge but a philosophy or world outlook which serves as a guide to action. The conflict between different political ideals and national cultures reveals a sort of intrinsic difficulty in any attempt to reconcile opposing philosophies. It does not seem satisfactory to comfort ourselves by acknowledging that the different views complement one another. A thorough dissociation from the main camps not only imposes the almost impossible burden of thinking about each issue on its own merits but creates a serious danger of living as a social outcast. In practice, there are a few fortunate and energetic individuals who manage, with some degree of success, to move from one specialty to another, to change from one alliance to another. The resulting unifying outlook would be the somewhat vacuous one: doing one's best at each stage in the light of what one thinks is the best at that stage.

4 BERTRAND RUSSELL AS AN EXAMPLE

1 In trying to place Russell in one of the pigeonholes, one faces obstacles which may be partly ascribed to the poverty of language. He was a writer who did not write belles-lettres, at least not any to be taken seriously. He was neither an artist nor a scientist. Shaw pointedly called him a mathematician, while J. E. Littlewood calmly spoke of him as a philosopher. In replying to his critics[2] (July, 1943), he stated:

> I shall pass gradually from the abstract towards the concrete. This will take us first to logic, then to scientific method, then to theory of knowledge and psychology, and thence to metaphysics. Passing over to matters involving judgments of value, we come first to ethics and religion, then to political and social philosophy, and finally to the philosophy of history.

Even this long list leaves out his pronouncements on war and peace, education, popular science, conquest of happiness, down to contributions to *Playboy* magazine.

He was never a regular professor, although he was the idol of many professors. Professional mathematicians tend to regard him as an outsider, although in terms of intellectual power, he was widely ranked with the best among the scientists and mathematicians. He was unique in combining an F.R.S. with a 'Nobel Prize' in literature. Among his friends and admirers were musicians, scientists, writers of fiction, politicians, and young people: all categories to which he does not belong.

2 As a form of life, Russell's career presented many unusual questions. The most basic is probably the effects of the prevalence of specialization. On the one hand, a serious and respected subject nowadays demands a good deal of initial preparation and continuous efforts to keep up with new developments. As a result, to be a specialist is essentially a full-time occupation. On the other hand, social opinion is such that a general writer is commonly regarded as at best a second-rate intellectual. This combination of circumstances practically excludes the possibility of a satisfactory life devoted to writings ranging over a diversity of fields. Russell managed to resolve this dilemma as satisfactorily as few others have done in this century. A more recent example of comparable success, from a somewhat different approach, is Sartre.

On several occasions Russell modestly said that his writings got such a large audience only because he had in his younger days done serious work in mathematical logic. One feels slightly embarrassed when Russell writes that, having done all he set out to do in mathematics, he turned his attention to other matters in about 1910. To ramble over different areas, it is essential that the advantages of the specialist's training are not overwhelming. This means that one is constrained to turn to 'soft' fields or less well-developed intellectual disciplines, which fortunately include most of the subjects which directly interest the intelligent common public.

In the fifties, a film was made from an interview with Russell. He replied to a question by saying that if he had been young then, he would have chosen instead of philosophy, physics or, if he did not have the ability, political propaganda as his field of concentration. This remark offended many academic philosophers who refused to take it seriously. If, however, one's aim in life is to have as much positive influence as possible, and preferably fairly conspicuous influence, within the restricted framework of using written words, then the remark is not so surprising.

It is, of course, quite impossible to evaluate and compare the satisfactions one gets in pursuing one specialty to the utmost of one's ability, be it music, poetry, mathematics, physics, or philosophy, with those obtainable by permitting all the diverse inclinations to divide the attention into a variety of channels. There were days when regret was expressed that Russell gave up logic around 1910. Although Russell says that he felt his ideas on logic at that time were quite stale, one would guess that there were deeper reasons for the change of direction. The choice to leave logic must have required wisdom and great strength of character. It is hard to imagine that Russell would have led a more satisfactory life by staying in logic.

In a popular article, Russell was reported as saying that he got more fame than many of his more clever contemporaries at Cambridge by rushing into controversies. It seems that in the pursuit of knowledge at least, polemics and controversies tend to hamper rather than speed up progress. The purpose of accumulation is better served by seeing what is right in someone rather than what is wrong in him. If someone's ideas are worthless or without content, the best treatment is silence and neglect. Polemics tend to divert attention away from near-truth and get into a game with words. One main difference between Wittgenstein and most contemporary Anglo-American academic philosophers would seem to be the indulgence of the latter in clever, small arguments clouded by all sorts of extraneous detail.

3 Another aspect of Russell's way of life was his detachment from academic institutions and large corporations in general. In the advanced 'free' societies today, the greatest freedom seems to be reserved for those who have the business acumen. As for the scientists and those who live on words and symbols, it is practically impossible to escape the corporations, which naturally impose restrictions to protect their own interests. As a result, there is great pressure to conform in matters which have remotely to do with politics or basic moral principles.

Even if one somehow manages to achieve a measure of financial independence, there is little room to exert wide influence on public affairs by written words and logical arguments alone. Apart from the control of the mass media of communication by the wrong people, there is the disadvantage of diversification which leaves to the bewildered reader the choice from a variety of views of very unequal values.

Russell partially solved this difficulty by a more or less unique combination of circumstances. He first built up a fairly large capital of academic reputation, through hard work, good style, family wealth and eminence, the class society in England, and the predominance of the British Empire. This was then supplemented by wide reading, quick writing, dry wit, an engaging lucidity, constant involvements in controversial issues, and a capacity not to worry about adverse criticisms. Even with all these, some of his public activities in his later years would have been impossible or much harder if he had not deep roots in a country of declining power with a pronounced traditional respect for the well-educated.

As it is, when he arrived, in a scientific spirit, at his views on the Cuban crisis and the border issue between China and India, his disagreement with the official position in the West was attributed by the *Observer* to the 'vanity of an old man' since it had to be conceded that he was not a communist.

4 The basic frame of reference in considering Russell's development has to be individualism and enlightened egoism. When Moore disposed of egoism quickly as self-contradictory,[3] one feels that the issue was not faced squarely. True, a group of egoists would come into contradiction, and a crude concentration on self-seeking can be self-defeating. However, there are occasions when genuine choices have to be made which yield different outcomes according as whether one is an egoist or not. The situation is greatly complicated by the fact that the issue is generally concealed because many objective factors are unknown. The institutions manage to transform almost all issues on self versus society into ones on self versus self.

On the other hand, it seems necessary for a vigorous collectivism to tolerate and even encourage some form of individualism which, to be sure, must on the whole entail a total gain to the common good.

The philosophical position of modern empiricism, beginning with my experience here-now, is a failure both as a guide to scientific inquiry and as a guide to practical action. The two failures are independent but have the common source in that my present sense data are too far removed from what really matters.

On moral questions, it happens too often that we refuse to compare the relative importance of different basic premises. When Moore preached personal affection and the appreciation of what is beautiful in art or nature as the intrinsically good, he did not specify explicitly a program of action based on this doctrine.[4] In practice, however, one would expect that such a basic position, if followed widely, would not be particularly good for social progress. Even Keynes outgrew this comforting philosophy as he went into the civil service.[5]

The basic injustice today is perhaps not exploitation within each country, with the important exception of Negroes in the United States, but rather, economic inequality between different countries. When the discrepancy is so great and wealthy countries try to protect and further increase their wealth and poor countries try to become less poor, it is not surprising that peace and goodwill does not prevail. If one accepts this as a basic premiss, one cannot help feeling disgusted at the amount of hypocrisy and unjustified self-righteousness on the part of the rich countries. It is a pleasure to find that Russell finally, at his great maturity, came to stress this aspect of the moral issue.

A great difficulty with views on social and political problems is the difference between what should happen and what will happen. In propounding a line of approach *A*, which, if realized, would be better than *B*, there is the grave danger that the doctrine will help to bring about an alternative *C* which is even less desirable than *B*. This, basically, is the objection against utopian radicalism, which diverts attention away from the more realistic alternatives.

5 On writing, Russell had this to say:[6] 'His most emphatic advice was that one must always rewrite. I conscientiously tried this, but found that my first draft was almost always better than my second. This discovery has saved me an immense amount of time. I do not, of course, apply it to the substance, but only to the form.' This is in sharp contrast with the story about how Tolstoi wrote, often revising thoroughly his manuscripts over ten or twenty times. Undoubtedly this has something to do with the difference between artistic and didactic writings. Apart from this difference in purpose, it is clear that the types of pleasure derived from writing must also be quite different.

Wittgenstein wrote well in quite a different way from Russell. It would be quite outrageous and uninformative to say that Russell's books are close to good journalism, while Wittgenstein's are close to poetry. Both Russell and Wittgenstein tried to make philosophy more scientific and less verbal, with cumulative progress but without repulsive technicality. In pursuing this goal, each of the two men has in a sense created a style of writing, possibly also a style of philosophizing.

6 The relation between Russell and his three principal collaborators is not without interest. Whitehead used to say, 'Bertie thinks I am muddle-headed, but I think he is simple-minded.' Russell's disenchantment with at least the influence of Moore and Wittgenstein, if not with their own work, was vividly transparent in his paper,[7] 'The Cult of "Common Usage".' Moore was frustrated in his attempts to make clear and precise Russell's concepts, such as that of propositional function. Wittgenstein was said to have considered withholding publication of the *Tractatus* because he was not happy with Russell's introduction. Certainly the later Wittgenstein was as much against Russell's philosophical ideas as against his own earlier views.

There was a letter[8] from Whitehead to Russell which said: 'My ideas and methods grow in a different way to yours and the period of incubation is long and the result attains its intelligible form in the final stage, – I do not want you to have my notes which in chapters are lucid, to precipitate them into what I should consider a series of half-truths.' In personal letters,[9] Russell spoke of Wittgenstein's private criticisms of his work. 'I saw he was right, and I saw that I could not hope ever again to do fundamental work in philosophy. . . . I became filled with utter despair.' 'Wittgenstein's criticism gave me a sense of failure.'

Santayana felt that Russell wasted his talent.[10] He could have been a great political figure, a leader of reform or alternatively: 'He might have undertaken an *insaturatio magna* of scientific philosophy. He could have done it better than Bacon, inasmuch as the science at his command was so much more advanced; and the *Principia Mathematica* seemed to foreshadow such a possibility.'

7 There were times when Russell was thought to be corrupting the youth. It is hard to see how his rational arguments on marriage and morals, for example, could possibly be regarded as subversive. Nevertheless, one can understand that Russell's views could easily be misunderstood. Abstract speculations are apt to leave out the practical circumstances under which the implied recommendations are to be carried out. Communication fails because there are different levels on which a sentence in ordinary language is understood. Thus it is that Russell unintentionally may have done harm to young people who are intellectually capable but practically quite ineffectual.

On intellectual matters, there are also those unguarded young people who have been misled by Russell's superficially clear writings to believe that philosophy promised a unified mathematics and a greater, clearer, and more systematic science. It is difficult to estimate whether these same people would not have, without Russell, found other even less rewarding projects on which to waste their time and energy.

8 Russell's influence in logic and in philosophy was deep and great. He is probably the most widely read and cited philosopher of this century. Basic works such as Skolem's paper on free variable number theory, Herbrand's and Gödel's theses, Gödel's paper on the incompletability of arithmetic all took *Principia* as their point of departure. The idea of a ramified (predicative) hierarchy plays an essential role in the study of the foundations of set theory, in particular, the questions of independence and relative consistency. The contrast of false and meaningless, as suggested in the theory of types, continues to fascinate professional philosophers.

It is often said that Russell's solid contributions to human knowledge were far smaller than his influences. The most hostile and unfair account of Russell's achievement, which can be heard among some working logicians and philosophers, runs more or less as follows. Many of his major ideas in logic were anticipated by Frege and often developed more adequately by Frege: the reduction of mathematics to logic (in particular, the definition of natural numbers), the invention of the propositional calculus and the quanti-fication calculus, the formulation of the basic concepts in the modern philosophy of logic. Even the theory of types appeared in some form in Frege and in Schröder. Russell's paradox and the theory of descriptions amount to two brief remarks, and the former was discovered independently also by Zermelo. The vicious-circle principle was first suggested by Richard and Poincaré. In philosophy, he was once the fashion, but has in recent years been supplanted by Wittgenstein; and since there is hardly any accumulation of progress in philosophy, once out of fashion, there is practically nothing left that can be salvaged.

That such an evaluation is entirely wrongheaded is quite obvious. The forces which create this sort of evaluation are more complex. There is a bit of envy and resentment of the specialist against a more or less universal talent. There is an element of frustration with 'scientific' philosophy and academic philosophy in general. Perhaps more important, there is the impact of the mathematician's criterion of originality: the search for definite and specific innovations is somewhat analogous to the use of the sexual act as the sole standard for evaluating the success of a relation of love. Moreover, there is the historian's delight in tracing anticipations and arbitrating the distribution of credits: a small dose is not unhealthy but one could easily be carried away and lose sight of the broader structure. This game reduces itself to absurdity when the conclusion is reached that the central figure of a period, such as Russell in logic and philosophy, *really* did nothing much. It is possible to play such a deflating game with practically anybody.

9 Many of the above comments on Russell as a man must be unbearably crude and in bad taste. Those who were young in a prosperous Europe at peace (internally at any rate) are naturally more gentle, more optimistic, and more generous than individuals from a generation grown up in war and living a life in alien environ-ments. Perhaps this is why Russell seemed to have more strength, more courage, and more hope than people whose ages are between a third and a half of his.

Here is a message which Russell wrote on his eightieth birthday.[11]

I may have conceived theoretical truth wrongly, but I was not wrong in thinking that there is such a thing, and that it deserves our allegiance. I may have thought the road to a world of free and happy human beings shorter than it is proving to be, but I was not wrong in thinking that such a world is possible, and that it is worth while to live with a view to bringing it nearer. I have lived in the pursuit of a vision, both personal and social.

Personal: to care for what is noble, for what is beautiful, for what is gentle; to allow moments of insight to give wisdom at more mundane times. Social: to see in imagination the society that is to be created, where individuals grow freely, and where hate and greed and envy die because there is nothing to nourish them. These things I believe, and the world, for all its horrors, has left me unshaken.

5 LIFE AND THE PURSUIT OF PHILOSOPHY

There are different conceptions of philosophy, and people come to an interest in philosophy along diverse paths. The basic conflict is between the requirements of rigor and comprehensiveness. More specifically, there is a schism between nature and the human life as two aspects of the subject matter of philosophy. While it seems promising to preserve at least a semblance of rigor in dealing with nature and the exact sciences, philosophy, to be comprehensive and, in fact, to justify its claims to our attention (for the majority of people), must concern itself with the practical direction of life.

We have therefore a conflict between two ideals: philosophy as a rigorous science and philosophy as a world view. One solution is to envisage a future philosophy which is both rigorous and comprehensive. Not only is it difficult to reach any agreement on the estimate of how likely it may be that such a philosophy will eventually emerge, but there is also a question of priority in choosing at the moment which type of philosophy to pursue. We have here typically the situation of a choice between alternative courses of action, and the choice is determined largely by each individual's temperament and the relevant knowledge he happens to possess. For example, Husserl, being a theoretical man who is convinced by his intensive study of the possibility of a superscience, chooses to work toward a comprehensive and rigorous philosophy.[12]

Since I am in no position to evaluate the grounds of Husserl's conviction and since most of us do not possess Husserl's mentality and special belief, I shall leave aside his solution of the conflict between the concerns with nature and with man. And there is a genuine difference among philosophers determined by whether they put more value on the study of nature or the study of man.[13]

If a philosopher's chief preoccupation is with human life, then there is another divergence of basic attitudes toward the contrast between the individual and the society. If he lives in a society where the idea of tradition is more or less stable, then his efforts toward getting a world view are likely to be directed to self-perfection or generally how each individual is to live his life in the given society. On the other hand, if he is basically dissatisfied with the existing societies, there is then a conflict between first studying how to change the society and first studying how to live in given societies.

And then it is not a big step to arrive at the conception of philosphy as the study of how to bring about better societies. Given such a conception and given the present world situation, it is not hard to understand the assertion that the central problem of the contemporary intellectuals is what to do with Marxism. It is undeniable that for humanity at large Marxism is presently an important force, and Marxism has serious implications with regard to moral judgments not only for practical activities but also for intellectual pursuits. The magnitude of the task of deciding what to do with Marxism can be illustrated by a quotation from M. Heidegger (*Letter on humanism*, 1949): 'Since neither Husserl nor Sartre, as far as I can see thus far, recognizes the essential place of the historical factor in Being, neither phenomenology nor existentialism has entered the dimension in which alone a constructive debate with Marxism can take place.'

If a philosopher's attention is confined to the individual, then the problem of liberty and choice has a natural appeal. It is commonly thought that one should so make his choices as to realize his potentialities to the maximum degree. And then there is a lot that can be said about the mechanics of making choices and the consequent commitments. When a philosopher is struck by how painful life can be, the task of philosophy is thought to be the search for the true sources of the pain and effective general methods for its resolution.

According to Windelband (writing in 1901):[14] 'By philosophy present usage understands the theoretical treatment of the general questions relating to the universe and human life.' In tracing the history of the concept of philosophy, he mentions various different conceptions: as any methodical work of thought; as an art of life, based upon theoretical principles; as a handmaid to church doctrine; as 'world-wisdom'; and as a universal science. 'In view of these mutations,' he concludes, 'it seems impracticable to pretend to gain a general conception of philosophy from historical comparisons.' Windelband seems to believe that Kant introduced an 'apparently final' conception of philosophy which could unite the universal conception of philosophy with philosophy as a particular science (viz. the critique of reason). It is not easy to understand or accept this judgment of his. By the way, one is tempted to compare contemporary academic philosophy with the middle ages and judge it to be a handmaid, not, to be sure, to church dogma, but to the new religion of science and technology.

Although Husserl chooses to pursue philosophy as a rigorous

science, he paints a glowing picture of philosophy as Weltan-schauung.[15]

> Insofar, then, as the vital and hence most persuasive cultural motives of the time are not only conceptually grasped but also logically unfolded and otherwise elaborated in thought, insofar as the results thus obtained are brought, in interplay with additional intuitions and insights, to scientific unification and consistent completion, there develops an extraordinary extension and elevation of the originally unconceptualized wisdom. There develops a Weltanschauung philosophy, which in the great systems gives relatively the most perfect answer to the riddles of life and the world, which is to say, it affords as well as possible a solution and satisfactory explanation to the theoretical, axiological, and practical inconsistencies of life that experience, wisdom, mere world and life view, can only imperfectly overcome.

Many philosophers would undoubtedly find the achievements of the great systems thus described a most attractive goal to work toward. Husserl's criticism of these systems is that they are not absolute but relative to different historical periods, that they are practical rather than theoretical, and that they are not scientific (rigorous) but in fact a child of 'historical scepticism.'

A basic belief of Husserl is that he has found a method by which we can gradually obtain absolute knowledge and establish philosophy as a rigorous science. In contrast, many people would put greater emphasis on what we now know and try to separate out more stable parts of our actual knowledge. The recognition of stable gross facts suggests a mixed position which distinguishes basic concepts and principles from those which are more dependent on particular historical circumstances. In this way, one hopes to arrive at a more rigorous and scientific component of philosophy upon which different 'great' systems can be erected not only at one particular time but also over extended historical periods. From this point of view, Husserl's proposed radical reconstruction of knowledge puts too much burden on his method as a way of establishing comprehensive absolute knowledge once and for all. It belittles the existing knowledge accumulated over the years. Moreover, it is not easy to share Husserl's great confidence in long range prospects: 'Where science can speak, even though only centuries from now, he will disdainfully reject vague Anschauungen'; 'For the sake of time we must not sacrifice eternity.'

Kant and Husserl have been contrasted in terms of a careless large edifice (Kant) versus a thorough but slow beginning (Husserl). As we are accustomed to thinking of each individual as having only one life to live, we are reluctant to call Kant's work careless and many of us would prefer arriving at an imperfect overall philosophy rather than spending the whole life developing a method. Moreover, Husserl's method is such that only very few minds are capable of using it in a really fruitful way.

If we look at the actual pursuit of knowledge, we find many questions of general significance. There is the question of interest. How we are brought up and what we are brought up to aspire to certainly influence as a matter of fact what we find interesting. But then we also feel that there is a question of intrinsic value which becomes especially difficult if we attempt to compare the value of works in different fields (for example, *Sons and lovers* with a moderately important mathematical theorem). There is the question of disagreement. Often we are puzzled by the vehemence displayed in seemingly immaterial disagreements on minute theoretical matters. According to some view, the passion can usually be traced back to basically political disagreements. There is the question of the one-sidedness of philosophy so that, in practice, we often get more understanding of life from literature rather than from philosophy.

There is a nebulous idea of what might be called applying a general philosophical outlook to diverse considerations. For example, M. Dummett once made the observation that while the political position of each individual in a society does not remain invariant through changing political climates, the relative positions of different individuals in the total spectrum from radical left to radical right are much more stable. In studying the flexibility of computers, B. Dunham once noted with respect to the task of sorting out smaller bodies from an aggregate, the contrast between using a sieve and measuring the size of each body in the collection. One vaguely feels that these remarks are of philosophical interest in some broad sense of 'philosophical.' But it is not easy to see how such observations can find their proper places in a general philosophy of knowledge.

The respect for actual knowledge and its acquirement and development also means a greater interest in the more conceptual aspects of heuristics, pedagogy, and the history of ideas, which are all related to the factual question of how in practice progress is made toward new discoveries or a better understanding. It is because we do not expect to acquire a higher reason in philosophy, we feel obliged to pay more attention to how knowledge as a matter of fact advances by more efficient thinking. A complementary belief is that purely formally the human mind is rather limited in its power, for example, in doing long and complicated multiplications or seeing long chains of deductions from a given hypothesis. The actual achievements have come from many complex factors which we cannot, at least for the present, understand either all at once by pure reason or piecemeal by appealing to neurophysiology (with or without evolution). And factual anthropocentric considerations seem more promising.

There is a familiar image of a big book which can be applied to illustrate some of the problems of philosophy.[16] Suppose somebody knew all the movements of all the bodies in the world dead or alive and all the states of mind of all human beings, and suppose he put all he knew in a big book B_1. A first question is the language in which this is written and the way to decipher it. We might think of using a coordinate system giving the locations in space and time. We do not have such a big book and do not even know what it would look like. Reductionism seems to predict the form of such a book and even recommend ways of achieving it. Perhaps a more interesting book B_2 would be dealing with actual knowledge. In that case, we obviously do not have complete knowledge, and partly for this reason we would have to appeal to ways of summarizing our (incomplete) knowledge. We might wish to list all sentences of a given language which the human race takes to be true (an infinite collection), and then delete sentences which are consequences of other sentences. There remains a considerable gap between such a book and a good existing encyclopedia, which, we feel, is yet far from containing the appropriate data for developing a philosophy of knowledge. It contains too many useless details for such a purpose, is too poorly organized, and does not go into the more fundamental things deeply enough. Nor is it a particularly efficient instrument as a main source for learning about human knowledge. In this regard, if, for example, one selects about twenty main areas of human knowledge and asks an expert in each area to write a three-hundred page survey, the result may be closer to a compendium of usable data for the philosophy of knowledge. In practice, each philosopher can understand well perhaps only three or four of these monographs and that only because he is familiar with these areas to begin with. And what he uses would be the knowledge he possesses initially as evidenced by his ability to understand and appreciate these few surveys.

The idea of a big book in the sense of B_1 has been employed to explain the peculiar place of ethics relative to our possible knowledge of matters of fact. The feeling is that while judgments of relative value all occur in B_1, no judgment of absolute value can. Hence, there can be no science of ethics. There is something clean and elegant in this suggestion. But its implications for rational moral considerations seem disappointing. As a matter of fact, we do seem to agree on certain general statements of absolute value such as 'all men are created equal,' 'involuntary hunger is evil.' The line between value and fact is not sharp. Determining basic aspirations would seem to relate facts to values. In practice, with regard to most serious decisions in life, we usually appeal to principles which are not universally accepted. One way to reduce 'it is better to work for progress' to a factual statement would be to accept that history moves in a definite direction with regard to moral values (toward the better or toward the worse). Ordinarily one is just, largely through forces not under one's own control, situated within a certain historical and personal context, which supplies in a more or less confused way the standards of morality.

This general phenomenon of local determination is, in particular, exemplified in the practical activity of intellectual pursuits. But if we try to step back and attempt to make rational choices, we get confused. There are different contrary forces at work. There is the pull toward specialization or generalization, that toward new results or broader understanding, that toward autonomy or relevance, that toward progress or contemplation, that toward scientific values or artistic values, that toward exact details or large overviews (the square or the circle in a Chinese imagery). In a few very exceptional cases, a unity of contraries is achieved and the diverse desires seem to be all satisfied. An outstanding example is Einstein who even reports on some of his deliberations concerning his choice of a career:[17]

> I saw that mathematics was split up into numerous specialties,
> each of which could easily absorb the short lifetime granted to
> us. . . . True enough, physics also was divided into separate
> fields, each of which was capable of devouring a short lifetime
> of work without having satisfied the hunger for deeper know-
> ledge. . . . In this field, however, I soon learned to scent out
> that which was able to lead to fundamentals and to turn aside
> from everything else, from the multitude of things which clutter
> up the mind and divert it from the essential.

In choosing intellectual projects, one is led consciously or un-consciously by a lot of personal factors, such as likes and dislikes, one's way of life, one's place in society, and one's general outlook on life and the world. There is a choice between aiming at more intense local or shorter range impact and milder broader or longer range interests. Some intellectual work involves more direct contacts with the physical world such as in the case of experimental sciences. Some pursuits (such as mathematics and physics) favor the young, while others (such as perhaps history and literature) promise fruit-ful lifelong development. Some people prefer local thoroughness while others like better larger ranges of coverage. Objectively, there are the criteria of intrinsic interest and influence. Since influence is hard to define, Chang Pinghsi used to remark that the value of a piece of intellectual work is to be measured by the number of jobs it generates. One immediately thinks of people who create bad fashions. In the case of literature, a lot of people may read and enjoy a piece of work which incidentally leads to commentators and biographers whose manners of making a living reflect the value of the work at most in a derivative way.

There is the ideal of doing one's best which perhaps means doing what he is best at with the greatest energy possible. Greater interest in some pursuit tends to generate greater energy. We keep on adjusting our own interest to what we take to be objectively interesting. When we are unclear about what is objectively interesting, we are inclined to indulge ourselves by doing what we happen to find interesting. There is all the time the task of connecting interesting questions with answerable questions. And it is natural to wish to put what we find interesting near the center (say of a particular discipline such as philosophy) if only because it would thereby receive greater attention and more rapid development.

In philosophy, there is a desire to combine or connect different things and give each thing its due. An anthropocentric obstacle to the fulfillment of such a desire is the fact that different things are pursued by different people and therefore that we are on unsure ground when attempting a synthesis and are likely to produce a distorted picture. At the same time, if for one reason or another religion and mysticism are denied to most of us as a possible way out, it would seem that only a connected general view can satisfy to some extent our longing for ultimate justifications.

A related problem is the prevalence of rival philosophies. Often there is something true on each side. The wish then is to separate out the true aspects and present a balanced picture. But seeing all sides can also take away the attraction attaching to the exaggerated decisiveness in the one-sided views. For example, in discussing Chinese culture, some are out to prove how superior it is while others are concerned with establishing their belief that it is bad. A more objective description tends to be less appealing emotionally and politically.

We might also wish to test the relative value of alternative philosophies by using some objective criterion. For example, we are inclined to evaluate a physical theory by looking at its external confirmation and inner perfection. The inconclusive debates between the philosophies of Chu Hsi and Lu Hsiangshan led to closer studies of the Confucian classics as a final court of appeal, because both philosophers claimed to be presenting a true explanation of the Confucian *tao*. Factualism proposes to use actual knowledge as a final court of appeal. If it is tiresome to argue against other people, then the way is to concentrate on expressing one's own thoughts. Some may even prefer to do philosophy in the manner of literature, paying attention more to how well their language expresses their thought than to how well their thought corresponds to reality. Such an approach might be defended on the ground that we understand better what is better writing than what is better philosophy.

There is a problem of making a profession into a satisfactory way of life. This problem is specially acute with regard to philosophy which often looks like foundations without a superstructure. Many people found G. E. Moore attractive because he appeared to promise an approach which required no technical knowledge at all but just pure thinking from the fundamentals. In a different way, logical empiricism seemed to promise a clearer and more systematic reconstruction of knowledge that required little more than an ability of passive learning plus a logical mind. When these shortcuts turned out to be less than rewarding in the long run, philosophy gradually developed its own technical aspect either by way of mathematical logic or by way of linguistic subtleties. In this manner, a sort of autonomy has been achieved which does not require too much data-oriented preparation.

It is, however, possible to distinguish the social factor from the intrinsic difficulties of serious philosophy. It is completely possible that there will be societies in which the social factor is favorable toward the pursuit of serious philosophy.

NOTES

1 'Science as vocation', *From Max Weber*, ed. H. H. Gerth and C. W. Mills, 1946, pp. 134–5.
2 *The philosophy of Bertrand Russell*, ed. P. A. Schilpp, 1944, p. 681.
3 G. E. Moore, *Ethics*, 1912.
4 G. E. Moore, *Principia ethica*, 1903.
5 J. M. Keynes, *Two memoirs*, 1949.
6 Russell, *Portraits from memory*, 1956, p. 210.
7 Ibid., pp. 166–72.
8 *The autobiography of Bertrand Russell*, vol. 2, 1968, pp. 96–7 (Bantam edition).
9 Ibid., pp. 64, 90.
10 G. Santayana, *My host the world*, 1953, p. 29.
11 *Portraits from memory*, pp. 58–9.
12 'Philosophy as rigorous science,' first published in 1911; see English translation in E. Husserl, *Phenomenology and the crisis of philosophy*, 1965,

pp. 71–147. In contrasting the different life goals of pursuing philosophy as world view or as rigorous science, Husserl emphasizes the role a difference in temperament plays in the choice.

Let it be admitted from the beginning that on the basis of the individuals who philosophize no definite practical decision for the one or the other kind of philosophizing can be given. Some are preeminently theoretical men inclined by nature to seek their vocation in strictly scientific research, provided the field that attracts them offers prospects for such research. Herein it may well be that the interest, even passionate interest, in this field comes from temperamental needs, let us say from needs in a Weltanschauung. On the other hand, the situation is different for aesthetic and practical natures (for artists, theologians, jurists, etc.). They seek their vocation in the realization of aesthetic or practical ideals, thus of ideals belonging to a nontheoretical sphere (p. 137).

But we often have the strong urge to blend theoretical, esthetic, and practical ideals, or to pursue an ideal which would satisfy our needs in all three spheres.

13 For example, while commenting on B. Russell's *What I believe* (1925), F. P. Ramsey says:

Also, if I were to quarrel with Russell's lecture, it would not be with what he believed but with the indications it gave as to what he felt. . . . Where I seem to differ from some of my friends is in attaching little importance to physical size. I don't feel the least humble before the vastness of the heavens. The stars may be large, but they cannot think or love; and these are qualities which impress me far more than size does (*Foundations of mathematics*, 1931, p. 291).

14 W. Windelband, *A history of philosophy*, pp. 1–6.
15 E. Husserl, op. cit., pp. 132–3.
16 One might speak of the fallacy of a perfect encyclopedia along with the fallacy of a perfect dictionary.
17 *Albert Einstein: philosopher-scientist*, ed. P. A. Schilpp, 1949, pp. 16–17.

XII

THEMES AND APPROACHES

1 SCIENTIFIC STUDIES OF MATTER, MIND, AND MACHINES

Politics has been called the art of the feasible, and sound political judgments depend essentially on a proper sense of the priorities. In scientific research, whether for one individual or for one discipline or for the whole of science, feasibility and priorities should also be the governing principles: only these must be construed in a broad enough sense based on the complex notion of scientific progress. Priority is supposed to contain not only the degree of importance but also the reasonable order in which different obstacles are to be overcome in succession. Hence, it overlaps with feasibility as a guide for intellectual work. By definition, feasibility is the necessary condition of all intellectual work since progress is possible only by doing what is feasible, or, in other words, it is possible to do only what is possible. In practice, these guiding principles are hard to apply, as can be seen by imagining somebody who is faced with a choice of doing technical linguistics or political criticism or philosophy.

Progress is closely connected with the problem of accumulation. Work left out of the main stream is often lost until similar results are rediscovered. If the work is very basic, such as Mendel's on genetics, then the original work will be rediscovered too, but more often the original work is simply forgotten. In either case, one might say that such work did not contribute to the on-going scientific progress, certainly not as much as if it were in the main stream. The question of 'main stream' is a bit complicated. To a large extent, it depends on a measure of coherence with a sufficiently large body of current work. But it may also depend on extraneous factors such as propaganda, dramatizing, the worldly position of the one who does the work. The cohesiveness of an area also depends greatly on an efficient way of communication, which demands a certain measure of humility: not everyone neglecting everybody else and inventing a new jargon; a fairly severe standard of elimination, both before and after publication; a habit of thinking and communicating relative to larger contexts; efforts to mark out facts against fiction. More basically, there is a mysterious element of understanding: only what is understood can be made use of. And there are so many different levels of understanding the same thing. Dramatization (or exaggeration) is important for the dialectic process of ideas.

Philosophy, in its very nature, must be different from science. Perhaps the essential fact is that, among other things, philosophy, instead of seeking for new discoveries, aims at *selecting* by sound sense the true view from diverse sources and *organizing* true views on diverse things into a communicable body. There is no definitive philosophy, and some novelty in the perspective helps to create more impact. The philosophical component of science is vital to the health and appeal of every scientific subject. The ability to select and to organize requires much more than mere patience. Scientific life would be more satisfying if more attention were paid to acquiring and practicing this ability. On the global level, one may think of the great mass of publications in the libraries and the bookstores. Does man really know so much, and so many important true or reasonable things that they have to be expressed in so many volumes? Of course, much that is published is worthless and much is repetition. Is it in the nature of things that such great redundancy and false accompaniments are necessary for intellectual progress?

An objection against philosophy has been voiced that it asks for only what must be the case and that it attempts to finesse the need for detailed information. This is surely a matter of degree. In the extreme case, philosophers, to use Kant's imagery, would be trying to fly without air (even that is possible at a different stage). But the desire to separate out what must be the case and to avoid detailed information is certainly an essential factor for the advance of science. A good scientist is able to concentrate on the essentials and let details take care of themselves. What must be the case is no other than what is definitely known. And it is very desirable to separate out what is conclusively known from what are plausible conjectures. This leads to a natural wish to have what might be called a middle discipline.

Related to reductionism, one could believe that there is no genuine knowledge beyond science as illustrated by physics and chemistry. In particular, all philosophical problems will eventually be cleared up when science is sufficiently advanced. Given this point of view, one extreme would say that there is no point in bothering with philosophy now since we are not ready, or more drastically, since philosophy will take care of itself. In other words, science is either necessary or necessary and sufficient for philosophy. Alternatively, one might wish to have some partial science which is admittedly a makeshift but will help further developments of genuine science. There are of course also practical decisions to make, so that we still have to do local pseudo-science which serves to make local predictions of 'cause and effect' (we should not depend too heavily on any obscure notion of 'causality' unless we are ready to give it a clear enough meaning; on the other hand, I see no reason why we cannot use it occasionally just for convenience). There would then seem to be theoretical and practical (medicine, etc.) partial sciences. The central problem is with the methodology of theoretical partial sciences.

On the other hand, one may wish to say that no matter how far science advances, there will always be some residue. The question is then, can we sort out the residue now? This uncertainty illustrates the difficulty of philosophy from the scientific point of view. Whatever the answer to the question may be, we may still wish to pursue and establish some middle science. One may think of the example of thermodynamics versus statistical mechanics. But how can we be sure we could attain, say, a science of intentionality that is comparable in correctness and stability to thermodynamics?

There remains yet a more extreme attitude, according to which science, despite all its success, is dogmatic and gives only imperfect knowledge. What is needed is a new approach which would establish philosophy as 'science' and eventually give a better account of and in fact improve science as we now understand it. This appears to be the claim of phenomenology. But we do not seem to have even a vague idea now of how it is related to science.

Since the basic contrast is between mind and matter and since there is a science of matter (natural science), it is natural to think by analogy of a science of mind. A revival of Descartes' postulation of mind as an explanatory principle has been suggested in analogy to Newton's assumption of the occult quality of gravitational force acting at a distance, which failed from his own viewpoint to give a mechanical explanation of the cause of gravity but has come to be accepted by common sense. I find this comparison singularly incongruent not so much because of the difference in explanatory power but because of the far greater distance between the concept of mind and exact laws governing the concept. Whatever the merits of postulating the mind might be, it does not seem at all like the situation of gravitational force with Newton.

Themes and Approaches

Somewhat in the same vein, detractors of artificial intelligence have been compared to clergymen who expounded clever but unsound criticisms of Galileo's physics. One feels uneasy because there is so far no definitive basic advance in artificial intelligence that is comparable to Galileo's work in physics.

A view has been expressed that artificial intelligence could be regarded as the development of a science of weak methods, comparable to, say, numerical analysis. The weak methods are rather general in character, such as generate and test, heuristic search, hypothesis and match. These weak methods remind one of Mill's canons of induction. Unlike numerical analysis, the major work here is to find out how each method can be applied in each context. Once I coined, in analogy with numerical analysis, the term 'inferential analysis' in connection with the narrower region of mechanizing mathematical arguments. Even though the proposed field has not been developed to any reasonable extent, it seems to me that this latter comparison is somewhat more accurate.

Another analogy is to recall how much the development of physics owed to astronomy, where comparatively clean and exact data were available. It is natural to look for the astronomy for the science of mind. An obvious candidate would seem to be mathematical arguments. But then one might prefer some simpler area such as chess. In any case, it seems reasonable to suppose that in the science of mind, we may need more than one astronomy. Even if one attains some day a measure of success in mechanizing the mathematical activity, it would appear clear that there are regions of mental processes which present different kinds of problems.

Certainly the most popular candidate today (or should we say yesterday?) is language and our knowledge of it. Here we witness a shift of emphasis from syntax to semantics, not unlike the change Carnap made around 1940. Recently there is a surprisingly late rediscovery of logic both with regard to the role of quantifiers and, in a more general way, in the close relation between logic and the deep structure of grammar. This incidentally illustrates the practical difficulties in the accumulation of knowledge especially across disciplines.

Since the science of matter is spectacularly successful, if one believes that a science of mind is either impossible or at least not feasible at present, then it would be natural to look for a science of machines, more specifically a science of computers as perhaps something in between. In fact, 'computer science' has become a fairly familiar term, and there are departments with such a designation.

A very frustrating aspect of computer science is the divorce of theory and practice. One envies people in more classical branches of

365

applied mathematics such as fluid dynamics and perhaps also astronomy, where, e.g., why certain suspension bridges tend to collapse under strong wind is explained in reliable theoretical terms. But then fluid dynamics has had a long history and the close connection between theory and practice only emerged in recent years through the works of Prandtle, von Karman, and others in this century. In fact, until 1800, there had been an enormous gap between the amount of theoretical knowledge and the paucity of practical applications. It was not primarily because scientists did not focus their attention on practical issues. A certain kind of maturity of the field and sometimes of scientists too was necessary before applications could be made. Lord Kelvin (William Thompson) may be said to be the first industrial scientist. This suggests the need of patience and unspectacular slow work in the development of a computer *science.*

We do have an abstract theory of computability in principle. But the theory fails, among other things, to take into consideration the factor of practical feasibility. Consequently, theorems in this area cannot be applied conclusively to establish results on what humanly possible things machines can or cannot do.

The difficulties in developing a usable theory of computation have led to the belief that computer science is a branch of engineering. This has the advantage that one can devote one's attention to practical applications without a guilty conscience. But many of the well established branches of engineering have physics as their underlying theory, and the trend in universities is to emphasize the theoretical aspects of engineering, often called applied science. We do not have a stable ground to make a distinction between theoretical and applied computer science, rather we seem to have mostly two disparate extremes of not very useful theoretical work and highly specialized applications.

One may wish to look to biology where even to this day theoretical biology is not a recognized field. The thought is that computer science could also have vast developments without too much theoretical work. The basic difference is of course the objects studied: natural organisms on the one hand, artifacts on the other. This difference is both a disadvantage because the objects do not remain essentially fixed, and an advantage because we know more about them and can mold them to suit our investigations.

2 SCIENCE AND PHILOSOPHY

Philosophies of knowledge often tend to use mathematics and physics as a model of thought. Knowledge in these domains, in contrast with the cultural sciences, is more absolute and more objective in the sense that the temporal and social condition of its emergence had little effect on its content or even form. One is led to the attractive picture of a cumulative progress through different historical periods so that a later period differs from an earlier one by filling certain gaps and correcting certain errors. Moreover, there is the fact that basic conceptual advances are rare, and, even when they do occur, do not make the well established theories obsolete but rather only limit their range of application, Newtonian physics being the favorite example. Hence, it is exceedingly attractive to build one's philosophy of knowledge on this stable and rich foundation of our knowledge in mathematics and physics.

It is clear that a theory of knowledge obtained in such a way need not automatically be appropriate to the cultural sciences for which the earlier stages are not quite so simply superseded by the later stages. On the other hand, most people share the belief that many fundamental problems about knowledge get clarified by looking at mathematics and physics. If, as is only reasonable to concede, this approach does not yield in itself a complete picture, it certainly seems to be a very good place to begin.

A different distinction is between activities and end results. Even in the exact sciences, the process of scientific activity is much less exact than the results obtained. The interest of philosophy in knowledge is not confined to the end results. Although we can largely avoid detailed socio-historical considerations, we do wish to look for general traits in the human mind which make the pursuit of exact sciences possible. Moreover, even though we would also like to avoid detailed psychological studies, we cannot overlook the crucial phenomenon of human understanding. Knowledge is knowledge only when it is understood; only then is further progress based on it possible. It is understanding which makes knowledge alive and puts it in the stream of human history.

In another direction, we may make a distinction between philosophy before science and philosophy after science. Philosophy before science can mean several different things. Certain philosophical problems may lead to sharper questions capable of a more scientific treatment; for example, the development of mathematical logic since Frege has been greatly influenced by philosophical considerations especially on the foundations of mathematics. Or, a science such as psychology, at its current not advanced stage, may benefit from general conceptual and methodological reflections of a philosophical nature. Furthermore, there are certain general philosophical problems such as explanation and causation for which there are no existing scientific results to fall back on, even though they are supposed to underlie a good deal of scientific studies.

The most immediate kind of philosophy after science is to discuss the philosophical implications of a new theory (such as evolution or relativity) or a new theorem (such as the incompleteness results or the existence of non-Euclidean geometries). A related trend is to bring technical results or methods to bear in philosophical discussions; while this sometimes shows a healthy respect for scientific facts, at other times it can be deplorable. ('If you think that your paper is vacuous, use the first-order functional calculus. It then becomes logic, and, as if by magic, the obvious is hailed as miraculous.' – P. R. H. Anonymous, 1957.) The most ambitious type of philosophy after science is a reflection on and critique of the preconditions which make whole areas of exact knowledge possible; the standard example is of course Kant's chief work viewed as a philosophy of arithmetic, Euclidean geometry, and Newtonian mechanics. A somewhat different type of work is to consider concepts of philosophical interest such as life, space, time, and make proper use of scientific results on these concepts.

The predominance of science makes it hard for the philosophers to take a calm attitude towards it. As a result, most philosophers seem to feel either resentment or awe towards science. It is, therefore, emotionally appealing to study areas of philosophy which are independent of science, except for the widely held belief that serious, tough-minded philosophy ought to accommodate scientific knowledge somehow. Those who bow to science imitate or use science in various ways. Some would attempt to axiomatize ethics or develop ethics with the ideas of game theory. Some would try in one way or another to capture the 'scientific spirit' and then attempt to make philosophy scientific. Others would extract and isolate some ideas or results from science and translate them into a less technical form so that the topic can be pursued independently of its source in science. In exceptional cases (such as E. Cassirer), broad scholarship yields some impressive good reading material which is, however, rather loosely structured.

There are many different ways of philosophizing about sciences. It is very tempting yet, nonetheless, usually ill-advised, to draw sweeping general conclusions from theories successful in some special branch of science. For example, J. Kokoroshov is said to have inferred the immortality of soul from the theory of relativity: 'When we die our souls will travel with the speed of light until the resurrection, for according to some authorities, no duration of time is then experienced.' Other examples are: 1 quantum mechanics refutes conclusively the validity of the two-valued logic; 2 Einstein's theory of relativity supports a relativism in ethics; 3 evolutionism in biology justifies the morality of a highly competitive society; 4 wave theory, in contrast to particle theory, supports a spiritualistic, non-materialistic view of life.

Less crude generalizations resulting mainly from the development of physics are such as the philosophical doctrines of operationalism and logical empiricism. It is dangerous to found general philosophies on a very small number of particularly impressive scientific achievements. For such generalities are usually vague and ambiguous, and it is almost inevitable that one moves back and forth between the true but obvious (in defending the theory) and the absurd yet influential (in applying the theory) interpretations. Thus, it is one thing to urge that Eddington's or Milne's a priori approach to certain problems of physics is fruitless, and quite another thing to assert that a peculiar brand of empiricism is in general superior. To disagree with Einstein's approach to the general theory of relativity is quite another thing than to assert the universal validity of operationalism.

The danger of these and many other philosophical theories comes from the very imperfect understanding of their influence on scientific research and social life. A whole and unambiguous truth, we can, in normal situations, assert without guilty conscience, no matter what the consequences of seeing the truth may be. But a gospel, ambiguously expressed and inadequately supported by argument or evidence, is more profitably judged by the kind of activity and society which the prophet wishes to see prevail, as well as by his conscious and unconscious motivations for upholding the new doctrine. Berkeley, for example, recommended his philosophy as the only bulwark against materialism and atheism.

There are different types of rather specific questions which are taken as belonging to the realm of the philosophy of the sciences. Many of them, however, can only be competently dealt with by those who happen to possess firsthand knowledge of the science or sciences concerned. Something like this must be what G. Ryle has in mind when he says, 'I have long since learned to doubt the native sagacity of philosophers when discussing technicalities which they have not learnt to handle on the job.'

A scientist can of course be interested in the philosophy of his subject in his spare time or after his retirement. He may, however, also indulge in philosophy to an even greater extent. There are, among scientific problems, some which are of more philosophical interest, and a scientist may be philosophically-minded in the sense

369

that he is only interested in those problems in his field which are of philosophical significance.

An alternative way of studying the philosophy of science is to treat nontechnical concepts and problems which arise in the area common to or outside of all special branches of science. The treatment may serve either as a simplified model or as a preparatory clearing of the ground.

The notion of scientific philosophy is attractive to some people, but repugnant to others. Since science and philosophy are different, one would naturally expect them to use different methods. To advertise scientific method in philosophy gives rise to the fear of a superficial imitation. Actually when Russell publicized this idea in *External world* (1914 and 1926), he was struck by something new at the time, viz. the new logic and his slogan of logic as the essence of philosophy. The relation between logic and philosophy has been developed in many different directions since that time. Russell's specific program of developing our knowledge of the external world has been continued especially in Carnap's *Logische Aufbau* (1928). This trend has undergone a good deal of elaboration and popularization.

The most familiar form is a phenomenalistic program which attempts to reconstruct human knowledge from sense data with empirical induction and a broad logic that includes set theory. Nowadays even those who are most sympathetic to the program agree that it appears hopeless. Some emphasize the need to account for dispositions and lawlike connections, while others feel that the whole approach was ill-conceived from the very beginning. It seems more reasonable to begin with physical things rather than sense data. One might feel that even though the original program fails, other variants might yet succeed, and that it is desirable to obtain partial results in preparation for further more definitive developments.

One danger is that such preparations are idle. There is a spurious analogy with mathematics. For example, tensor analysis, functions of complex variables, and non-Euclidean geometry which had been developed without applications in view, turned out to be very useful in physics. But these examples differ in at least two ways from the type of philosophical work under discussion. First, the results in philosophy are generally less sharp and exact. Second, they are more fragmented. The general type of program which aims at a homogeneous reconstruction of human knowledge seems doomed to failure for the simple reason that it presupposes, on the part of philosophers, a sort of privileged access to knowledge.

In the abstract, the nonexistence of a privileged access is often conceded. Russell puts the matter in these words:

While admitting that doubt is possible with regard to all our common knowledge, we must nevertheless accept that knowledge in the main if philosophy is to be possible at all. There is not any superfine brand of knowledge, obtainable by the philosopher, which can give us a standpoint from which to criticize the whole of the knowledge of the daily life. The most that can be done is to examine and purify our common knowledge by an internal scrutiny, assuming the canons by which it has been obtained, and applying them with more care and with more precision. Philosophy cannot boast of having achieved such a degree of certainty that it can have authority to condemn the facts of experience and the laws of science (*External world*, p. 71 and p. 73).

We find an echo of these thoughts in Quine:

The philosopher's task differs from the others', then, in detail; but in no such drastic way as those suppose who imagine for the philosopher a vantage point outside the conceptual scheme that he takes in charge. There is no such cosmic exile. He cannot study and revise the fundamental conceptual scheme of science and common sense without having some conceptual scheme, whether the same or another no less in need of philosophical scrutiny, in which to work. He can scrutinize and improve the system from within, appealing to coherence and simplicity; but this is the theoretician's method generally (*Word and object*, 1960, p. 275).

In the concrete, however, it is not clear whether or to what extent Russell and Quine as philosophers have practiced what they preach. One is inclined to think that they do not take the existing body of human knowledge sufficiently seriously, that they do not get sufficiently inside this highly intricate system, that they tend to oversimplify and eschew a more structured understanding of our exact knowledge. From outside everything looks similar and, therefore, one concludes that sense data and empirical induction can yield a perspicuous account of all empirical knowledge or that basic differences are but differences of degree. For example, Quine speaks of the myth of mathematics and the myth of physics (*Logical point of view*, p. 18) and asserts, 'But in point of epistemological footing the physical objects and the gods differ only in degrees and not in kind. Both sorts of entities enter our conception only as cultural posits' (ibid., p. 44). Clearly Quine has here deserted plain English and is speaking in a technical, philosophical language that has been created because he was struck by a special one-sided global aspect. It does not seem unfair to view these declarations as an indication that Quine's philosophy is a bit too detached from actual human knowledge.

Another example of assimilating basically different situations is the following sweeping comparison.

> Conversely, by the same token, no statement is immune to revision. Revision even of the logical law of the excluded middle has been proposed as a means of simplifying quantum mechanics; and what difference is there in principle between such a shift and the shift whereby Kepler superseded Ptolemy, or Einstein Newton, or Darwin Aristotle? (*Logical point of view*, p. 43).

One would like to say that the differences between the four cases are of much philosophical interest, more than the somewhat superficial similarity. Earlier, Quine held a somewhat different view on revisibility.

> There are statements which we choose to surrender last, if at all, in the course of revamping our sciences in the face of new discoveries; and among these there are some which we will not surrender at all, so basic are they to our whole conceptual scheme. Among the latter are to be counted the so-called truths of logic and mathematics, regardless of what further we may have to say of their status in the course of a subsequent sophisticated philosophy (*Ways of paradox*, p. 95).

Excessively aloof considerations of science seem to suggest that philosophically every difference is a difference of degree. But when one is interested in knowledge as it is, many forms of tolerance become intolerable. For example, it seems quite idle to say: 'One could even end up, though we ourselves shall not, by finding that the smoothest and most adequate overall account of the world does not after all accord existence to physical things, in that refined sense of existence' (*Word and object*, p. 4).

Quine seems to answer partially these comments by drawing a distinction:

> To call a posit a posit is not to patronize it. A posit can be unavoidable except at the cost of other no less artificial expedients. Everything to which we concede existence is a posit from the standpoint of a description of the theory-building process, and simultaneously real from the standpoint of the theory that is being built (*Word and object*, p. 22).

This bestows on the words 'posit' (or 'myth') and 'artificial' a special philosophical usage which can be misleading in a fundamental way. The misgiving one feels may therefore be due to either a discomfort over the fact that Quine does not do what he says is important or a difference in belief as to whether it is more rewarding to study in general terms the process of theory-building or look more closely at science as it is. The declaration that 'Epistemology, for me, is only science self-applied' (*Words and objections*, p. 293) would seem to imply that Quine does value more highly philosophy that enters seriously into the facts of existing knowledge, even though his own work is generally more aloof. It is also possible that Quine does regard it as more fundamental to consider general questions on theory-building which, for him, are probably closely related to the philosophy of language. Then the misgiving voiced in the earlier comments would seem to apply to the part of his general philosophical position which delights in obliterating differences and making sweeping comparisons. In addition, the somewhat implicit guiding principle of some imagined remote 'regimentation of scientific theory' (e.g. ibid. p. 292) has a Utopian flavor which is almost Carnapian.

Some people would say that philosophy is what philosophers do. It is an undeniable fact that Quine's philosophy occupies quite a central position in contemporary academic Anglo-American philosophy. To believe in an objective standard of value which goes radically against the current 'main stream' can more often than not lead to futile criticisms. There is the serious danger of measuring some existing work against an unattainable goal. And one is easily suspected of being unduly influenced by one's personal likes and dislikes. Perhaps the strongest urge to criticize arises against those who seem to accept fundamentally the same standard yet appear to do things according to quite different standards. There is also a genuine concern that the admittedly one-sided work diverts attention away from more promising directions. On the other hand, since the goals in philosophy are so hard to define, one is more liable than in the sciences to feel unhappy over the work of some philosopher because he works in an area not to one's own liking or the motivation of the work appears mysterious.

For example, one might wish to get something relevant to science yet invariant relative to (most) changes; an overall view of how different parts are related; something beyond the problem solvers and tool improvers; to give an articulate description of fundamentals which would teach a better command of the field; to take into consideration advances in mathematics since 1900. The familiar sense of frustration over philosophy comes perhaps from a deep-rooted belief that philosophy should be important and exciting, confronted with the impression that current practice seems irrelevant and unsatisfying. One would like to get out of this bottle too.

The heart of the difficulty with philosophy lies undoubtedly in its relation to other human activities and, for our discussions here, especially to mathematics and the natural sciences. Imitation is not successful, extensive contact is too demanding and often humiliating, isolation impoverishes. To indulge in coining terms, one might speak of the fallacy of privileged access, the fallacy of too many digits, and the fallacy of idle preparations.

A common avenue to philosophy is a reaction against science (as one is taught) and one looks for a neater or less painful way of doing interesting intellectual work. As a result of this phenomenon, philosophy tends to attract impatient innovators who are eager to say new things and believe that a combination of native wits with a command of one's native language, or diligence with a facility in logic-chopping, should be sufficient for doing most interesting intellectual work. This would seem to be over-correcting the tendency of passive learners to just collect information. The desire to imitate science to aim at piecemeal advances leads many to make heavy weather over insignificant details. Moreover, isolation from vital concerns yields results which are supposed to be preparations for use on future occasions which will not arise. In particular, there is experimentation with restricted methods to see how far one can go, e.g. phenomenalism or nominalism. This is useless because the basic conception is either indeterminate or the incorrect notion or both.

3 REMARKS ON CONTEMPORARY PHILOSOPHY

Through a cursory study of the literature in current philosophy, an uninitiated reader may get a number of general impressions.

Much of the discussion seems to be concerned with minute details which have no apparent relevance to anything which most people are interested in. Often one starts with an obviously interesting topic, and then it is transformed because it is too hard. Before long, we end up with issues which are suited to intellectual gymnastics but bear no recognizable resemblance to the original topic. What difference does it make, one cannot help wondering, whether one philosophical school or another is right? Why should anybody bother himself by such disputes? In his autobiography, the late R. G. Collingwood complained: 'and by about 1920 I found myself asking, "why is it that nowadays no Oxford man, unless he is either 70 years old or else a teacher of philosophy at Oxford or elsewhere, regards philosophy as anything but a futile parlor game?"'

One way to handle such complaints is to deny that philosophy is nothing but a futile parlor game: 'when you get to know it better, you will see that it is more,' 'some philosophy may be just that, but certainly not the type of philosophy which I do,' and so on.

A more forceful reply is to give them the 'so what?' treatment: 'I happen to enjoy such activity and I do not care whether or not you consider it just a futile parlor game.' This does not always put an end to the complaints. It is like selling food which somehow is believed to be both tasty and nutritious. When the customer finds out that the food is delicious but not nourishing and produces headaches afterwards, he feels he has been cheated even though he was not led to expect such value by the present food seller.

Such disappointment seems rather inevitable. So much goes under the name philosophy, and one is led to an interest in philosophy through so many diverse paths.

For some, the final goal of any philosophy should be a program of action, to change the world, or at any rate to enable the philosopher himself to act more resolutely. For these philosophers knowledge and understanding are to prepare for action. It is thought that once we see what everything is and feel that everything is what it is, we are not far from realizing how things should be. What usually happens is, of course, a realization, often too late, that 'life is bounded while knowledge is not.' To understand is already more than a full-time occupation, there is no time and vigor left for action. Collingwood lamented: 'My philosophy and my habits were thus in conflict; I lived as if I disbelieved my own philosophy and philosophized as if I had not been the professional thinker that in fact I was.'

Others who are resigned to their inability to act still desire comprehensive understanding. To understand is to connect, to relate, to systematize, to use successive scaffolds to put things to where they belong. Derivatively, understanding should yield clarity and certainty. To find or believe that systems are incompatible with certainty and clarity is a sad state for these philosophers to be in.

The more scientifically inclined philosophers are also struck by the fact that results of philosophical discussions are not cumulative. Instead of extensions and refinements of previous results, we find only repetitions and refutations. Instead of dealing separately with different aspects of a problem and adding up the results, philosophers tend to treat all aspects of a problem over and over again each in his own manner. The lack of objective standard often rewards rhetoric and shrewd manoeuvring, more than truth and intellectual honesty.

It is no secret that many philosophical disputes are verbal and terminological. When we are lucky, we arrive at concessions, at one stage or another, such as: if that is all you mean by such and such, I agree with you.

Over half a century ago, G. E. Moore urged that philosophers should *try* to discover what questions they are asking before they set about to answer them, and expressed the optimistic view that in many cases a resolute attempt would be sufficient to ensure success. Sometimes a philosopher succeeds in giving a precise formulation of a philosophical problem and providing a clear answer; but it is not equally unquestionable that the problem thus formulated *is* the one which people set about to answer. Or several distinct problems with clear answers are singled out as being involved in the original problem. In either case, we may feel that the answer and answers do not do full justice to the question with which we began.

The same question can arise in different ways under different circumstances. For example, the biologist who studies a special kind of snake for the first time asks whether the snake is poisonous and gets an answer. Years later, the same question is asked in an examination of a course on biology. Or, a mathematical theorem discovered a few years ago is now an exercise in a textbook. A similar though somewhat different situation is encountered if we compare, for example, Dedekind's essay on the nature of number with many articles in philosophical periodicals on the same topic as two kinds of context for asking the same question, 'what is a number?'

It happens quite often that although a problem has not been answered, yet new problems arise and the old ones become obsolete. Sometimes it helps us to understand a theoretical problem better, if we know the socio-psychological reasons why certain people find it interesting (or uninteresting). Collingwood contended that a philosophical proposition is usually intended as an answer to a question posed in a definite historical context, so that if one does not know the question originally asked, one cannot understand the answer.

According to those who deplore the divorce of philosophy from science and life, it would hardly be possible to grasp the true essence of a philosophical problem if we isolate it from its roots in life and science. Nor can we understand the significance of philosophy as a social phenomenon if we disregard its influence outside philosophy. Very often philosophical problems are handed down to us through tradition, and in the process of passing on a cultural inheritance it is almost inevitable that the more vigorous roots get lost sight of and the problems degenerate into parlor games.

In his charming autobiography, Moore asserts, 'I do not think that the world or the sciences would ever have suggested to me any philosophical problems. What has suggested philosophical problems to me is things which other philosophers have said about the world or the sciences.' It is hard to resist the temptation to ask what would happen if all philosophers were like this.

The preference to be a philosophers' philosopher quite naturally leads to questions as to what a given philosopher *meant* by what he said, and to painstaking but not always fruitful textual analyses of philosophical writings. In a way, this occupation is a double retreat from the old-fashioned concern with reality or the world, the intermediate stage being the interest in knowledge and the sciences.

It may not be inappropriate to review briefly the two traditions (sometimes called the 'constructionist' and the 'naturalist') of analytic philosophy which more or less dominate academic Anglo-American philosophy today.

From about 1898 on, Bertrand Russell joined G. E. Moore in a revolt against F. H. Bradley: refuting idealism and defending common sense. For both, time is real, physical objects are real, Platonic ideas are real. A preoccupation with foundations of mathematics led Russell to his theory of descriptions and a claim that symbols for not only descriptions but also classes and relations are incomplete symbols eliminable in contexts. The mistaken belief that classes can be had at no extra 'expenses' in ontological assumptions undoubtedly lent additional attraction to the principle of extensive abstraction which Russell credited to, and shared with, Whitehead. Following this principle, a physical object is, for example, said to be a class of classes of events.

Concurrently with these more specific proposals, Russell and L. Wittgenstein were said to have founded logical atomism, although there are significant differences between their views. For example, in the *Tractatus* there is no bias toward sense data or unsensed sensa, and numbers are (all too briefly) accounted for in an entirely different way from Russell. Little is said in the *Tractatus* about mathematics and it was left to F. P. Ramsey to derive some of the logical conclusions from the obliteration of the distinction between finite and infinite domains. The result is, unlike Russell's (since 1908 at any rate), a very realistic philosophy of classes.

The logical positivists, fortified by the positivistic trend from Mach and their belief in the reducibility of mathematics to logic shared with Russell, drew other consequences from the *Tractatus*. A deceptively simple picture of human knowledge emerged. The influence of Russell was perhaps more obvious: in the emphasis on reduction, on logic, on sense data. Only very gradually did it become clear that the reduction is not possible and the new approach not only offers no fruitful method for but is disappointingly irrelevant to the advancement of our knowledge or understanding in logic, mathematics or the natural sciences. While Russell remains all along sympathetic to this tradition, especially to the more tough-minded ones like R. Carnap and H. Reichenbach, he has not consistently and fully endorsed the popular version of logical positivism. People working along this line are often called scientific philosophers or constructionist analytic philosophers.

The other faction of analytic philosophy (often called naturalist analytic or ordinary language philosophy) has been influenced strongly by Moore and the later Wittgenstein. Moore's defence of common sense did not at first include ordinary usage: 'my business is *not* with proper usage, as established by custom' (*Principia ethica*, p. 6). In his papers of 1917 and 1925, Moore came to show respect for ordinary usage and to remark on the danger of giving a simple common phrase some special (philosophical) meaning and slipping unawares to the ordinary one. Moore's analysis was largely a method of refutation. In the positive aspect, it strove to dig out something hidden beneath the surface, usually without success. The opponent is not convinced but feels that Moore is arguing at cross purposes; Moore failed to make clear what his opponent is doing. By using common propositions in a philosophical discussion, Moore was in his own way violating ordinary usage. Later Wittgenstein modified Moore's manner of philosophizing in fundamental ways. According to Wittgenstein, one has to keep in mind the complex and varied use of phrases such as 'conscious of.' Everything already lies open to view, but we have to assemble, select, and arrange the uses of language to suit a particular philosophical problem. Wittgenstein made a more thorough and more imaginative use of ordinary language and, according to some interpretations, he turned a method of refutation into one of 'therapy.' The fact that there seems to be a big gap in quality between the work of Wittgenstein and most of his followers would appear to indicate there is much more to the method than can be learnt from Wittgenstein's teachings. Sometimes Wittgenstein wondered whether he had created more than a 'style.' It is a notoriously unproductive job to copy somebody's style. The emphasis on puzzles seems to make philosophy less serious, at least if we respect the ordinary sense of the word 'puzzle.'

There is a twist in Wittgenstein's conception of 'ordinary usage' which is often overlooked: 'One must always ask oneself: is the word ever actually used in this way in the language-game which is its original home?' (*Investigations*, 116). Thus, we are certainly free to consider mathematical terms in discussing philosophy of mathematics and should be at home with the relevant technical matters. It is understandable that this twist is often overlooked, since Wittgenstein mostly stays with elementary concepts when dealing with mathematics.

The most active and influential logic-oriented philosopher during the last forty years or so has probably been R. Carnap. His intellectual autobiography (*Library of living philosophers*, vol. 11, 1963) is remarkable for its bold lines and candid good nature. There is a curious mixture of moderation and tolerance with a revolutionary zeal. It is impressive how he adapted and formulated sweeping theses and programs, how he persevered, through successive modifications, in his basic beliefs, and how he persisted in producing new pieces of work which are central according to his fundamental position.

Some of Carnap's basic beliefs are the following:

(a) Logic is central to philosophy. 'It is the task of logic and of mathematics within the total system of knowledge to supply the forms of concepts, statements, and inferences, forms which are then applicable everywhere, hence also to non-logical knowledge' (p. 12). 'But to the members of the [Vienna] Circle there did not seem to be a fundamental difference between elementary logic and higher logic, including mathematics' (p. 47).

(b) The basic task of philosophy is explication and rational reconstruction (e.g., p. 16).

(c) 'Since science in principle can say all that can be said, there is no unanswerable question left' (p. 38).

(d) Constructions of artificial languages are important. 'Thus, in time, I came to recognize that our task is one of *planning* forms of language' (p. 68). 'Although the two problems, the construction of language systems in symbolic logic and the construction of international languages, are different and are directed toward different aims, working on them is somehow psychologically similar' (p. 71).

(e) A sentence is meaningful only if either it or its negation is verifiable or confirmable (e.g., p. 59).

(f) There is a basic distinction between analytic and synthetic statements; the distinction is 'practically indispensable for methodological and philosophical discussions' (pp. 63, 922).

(g) Semantics is of central interest to philosophy. In this regard, a shift of emphasis from syntax to semantics occurred around 1940 (pp. 56, 60).

These theses have been criticized on various levels. For example:

Even at the time of earlier liberalization of the empiricist requirement, some empiricists, e.g., Quine and Hempel, expressed doubts whether it was still possible to make a clear distinction between meaningful and meaningless terms or whether this distinction should rather be taken as a matter of degree (p. 80).

Some of those who accept the semantical concepts of truth reject a sharp distinction between logical and factual truth. Most prominent among them are Tarski and Quine. During the academic year 1940–1, when all three of us were at Harvard, we discussed this problem in great detail. They believed that, at best, a distinction of degree could be made (p. 64).

Criticisms on quite a different level have been voiced by Wittgenstein and by Einstein:

I was interested in the problem of an international language like Esperanto. As I had expected, Wittgenstein was definitely opposed to this idea. But I was surprised by the vehemence of his emotions. A language which had not 'grown organically' seemed to him not only useless but despicable. . . . I remarked that nevertheless the question of the existence and explanation of the alleged parapsychological phenomena was an important scientific problem. He was shocked that any reasonable man could have any interest in such rubbish. . . . When Schlick, on another occasion made a critical remark about a metaphysical statement by a classical philosopher (I think it was Schopenhauer), Wittgenstein surprisingly turned against Schlick and defended the philosopher and his work. . . . Schlick himself . . . accepted certain views and positions of Wittgenstein without being able to defend them by rational arguments in the discussions of our Circle. . . . When we found in Wittgenstein's book statements about 'the language', we interpreted them as referring to an ideal language; and this means for us a formalized symbolic language. Later Wittgenstein explicitly rejected this view. He had a sceptical and sometimes even a negative view of the importance of a symbolic language for the clarification and correction of the confusions in ordinary language and also in the customary language of philosophers which, as he had shown himself, were often the cause of philosophical puzzles and pseudo-problems (pp. 26–9).

But Einstein thought that these scientific descriptions cannot satisfy our human needs; that there is something essential about the Now which is just outside of the realm of science. . . . But I definitely had the impression that Einstein's thinking on this point involved a lack of distinction between experience and knowledge. . . . Then he criticized the view, going back to Ernst Mach, that the sense data are the only reality, or more generally, any view which presumes something as an absolute basis of all knowledge. I explained that we had abandoned these earlier positivistic views, that we did no longer believe in a 'rockbottom basis of knowledge'; and I mentioned Neurath's simile that our task is to reconstruct the ship while it is floating on the ocean. He emphatically agreed with this metaphor and this view. But then he added that, if positivism were now liberalized to such an extent, there would be no longer any difference between our conception and any other philosophical view (p. 38).

In these encounters, we witness differences in philosophical attitudes which are determined to a considerable extent by different temperaments, tastes, and experiences. They can hardly be resolved 'by rational arguments,' especially since there is likely to be a corresponding difference in the concepts of 'rational' of the disagreeing parties. Or, if a fairly rigid concept of 'rational' is agreed upon, it may be easy to concede that certain basic differences in approaches cannot be settled by rational arguments in such a sense. One might wish to appeal to long range effects or an intuitive sense of value. But then intuitions may differ and predictions may differ. Moreover, a type of internally coherent work, even if it is rather pointless in a larger sense, has a tendency to perpetuate itself. Perhaps the only possible refutation is that, after the momentum is spent, one looks back and finds the results neither of intrinsic interest nor providing material on which we could further build.

Those who find Carnap's scientific philosophy too Utopian in the negative sense of the word can probably find evidence for their belief in Carnap's admitted failure to communicate with physicists on his philosophy of physics:

> I had some talks separately with John von Neumann, Wolfgang Pauli, and some specialists in statistical mechanics on some questions of theoretical physics with which I was concerned. I certainly learned very much from these conversations; but for my problems in the logical and methodological analysis of physics, I gained less help than I had hoped for. . . . I had expected that in the conversations with these physicists on these problems, we would reach, if not an agreement, then at least a clear mutual understanding. In this, however, we did not succeed in spite of our serious efforts, chiefly, it seems, because of great differences in point of view and in language (pp. 36–7).

To a neutral observer, this would appear to be a very damaging criticism of Carnap's approach to philosophy with its declared intention of respecting science as it is.

The conversation between Carnap and Einstein on the liberalized positivism has a familiar ring. More recently, there have been similar discussions on the behaviorist position which was so defined as to be vacuous. What is disturbing in thus moderating apparently radical positions is not so much that the redefined position loses its sharpness as that in practice the liberal position is not followed faithfully. It does not seem fair for a behaviorist to criticize his opponents for not observing narrower behavioristic criteria and at the same time to proclaim as his own a broader notion of behaviorism which nobody can object to.

It is not hard to sympathize with Wittgenstein's rising to the occasion to defend Schopenhauer against Schlick. If, as so often happens, philosophers are found to be saying interesting things, it is not pleasant to see them summarily brushed aside under the pejorative term 'metaphysics.' To define knowledge in such a way that anything not manageable by science is automatically excluded from knowledge, is, to say the least, begging the question.

There is a tendency in Carnap to suspend judgments and postpone decisions. This predilection for tolerance has in practice led to his conflict with Wittgenstein on Esperanto, parapsychology, and ideal languages. We have also Carnap's favorite device of defining 'analytic in *L*' which amounts to saying that I do not know exactly what the scientist means, but if he means *A*, then *A'*, if he means *B*, then *B'*, etc. This hypothetical approach is rather repugnant for those who feel that the most interesting part of epistemology should be concerned with knowledge as it is, not only because we are not told whether the scientist means *A* or *B* or *C*, but often none of the alternatives is rich enough to give the actual meaning. On the level of philosophy, genuine problems are lost or replaced by pseudo-problems because one avoids studying the serious phenomenon of choice and decision together with all the accompanying complexities. By smoothing out what seem to be merely rough edges of scientific knowledge and neglecting scientific development as a living process, we are left with an approximation which obliterates difficult questions and permits logical exercises of a routine sort to parade as serious philosophy.

The enthusiasm over and confidence in his own basic positions seems to have generated in Carnap a tendency to disregard or twist central scientific facts in order to preserve his central doctrines. One example is his unswerving belief in logicism which, combined with his curious principle of tolerance, enabled him to discard the most interesting problems on the foundations of mathematics with complacence. Since he believed that mathematics is reducible to logic, he concentrated his efforts on logic and metalogic so that, for example, the serious problem of infinity became one of only peripheral interest to him. Since his concept of logic is basically Fregean and since it is well known that that conception led to contradictions, one wonders how Carnap could still feel comfortable with logicism.

According to one story, he made a sort of identification of Fregean logic with Cantorian set theory. Since mathematics is known to be deducible from the latter, and since the former inconsistent conception looks like logic; therefore, mathematics is reducible to logic. As is well known, there is a serious difficulty in justifying the axiom of infinity as an axiom of logic. To some extent Carnap was not unaware of the difficulty and gave a solution by suggesting that it is a logical or analytic proposition that there are infinitely many positions or coordinates (pp. 47–8). This was employed to prove that the Peano axioms are analytic (*Logical syntax*, pp. 92, 103–4, 125, 140). At times Carnap appears to vacillate between being a logicist and a pragmatist who says that if mathematics is reducible to logic, fine, if not, it is not so important (e.g. *Logical syntax*, p. 327). It is of course reasonable to say that whether mathematics is reducible to logic depends on how broadly one construes 'logic.' The crucial point is perhaps that Carnap does not seem to pay enough attention to the important differences infinity makes to our basic mathematical and scientific concepts.

With regard to both wings of the analytic school, the emphasis on language is conspicuous. Part of the motivation was initially in the direction of clarity on the ground that linguistic expressions are more concrete and tangible than concepts and ideas. This was most striking when it was thought that we could confine our attention to syntax. Another factor is the natural desire to shun technical specialized facts: every educated man knows his native language pretty well, and logic is the most general conceptual discipline which is the furthest removed from complex empirical facts. There is also the feeling that in language we have got the most central and most basic component of all human knowledge. As Confucius says, 'No knowledge of words, no knowledge of men' (*Conversations*, XX, 3). Language seems to supply a foundational key which can be examined and polished by appealing primarily to our native wits.

The construction of formal languages for branches of science has generated an interest in what is called pragmatics which is given the difficult task of evaluating the suitability of the constructed language for the purposes on hand. This subject is supposed to be devoted to the study of the influence of considerations of efficiency, simplicity, and fruitfulness on the choice of linguistic stipulations in logic and the empirical sciences. Typically Carnap acknowledges the importance of this branch and recommends developing (perhaps by some future generation) pure or theoretical pragmatics, but does not do much about it. Others have emphasized the pragmatic element in a general way without suggesting that this area is suitable for a systematic study. When it comes to specific subjects such as physics and set theory, we get the impression that this seemingly harmless concern with the pragmatic aspect often produces superficial observations which are, if not strictly false, certainly unilluminating.

The influence of the interest in logic and formal languages on the development of linguistics has been more substantial. In fact, both wings of the analytic school have, not surprisingly perhaps, come to have close contacts with the empirical science of linguistics and psycholinguistics. Since it is hardly attractive to classify philosophy as a branch of linguistics, the concern has been called the philosophy of language which studies the foundations of linguistics and perhaps also, in a less direct way, the foundations of human knowledge. Many philosophers today regard the theory of meaning as the center of epistemology and, indeed, of philosophy. It is thought that philosophy of language is more fundamental than, say, philosophy of mathematics or physics or biology. Of course, this does not mean that it is therefore a more fruitful subject of study (except perhaps in the sociological sense of getting more attention from professional colleagues), just as we would perhaps all agree that the more fundamental discipline of ontology is not a more fruitful subject to pursue than mathematics or physics.

4 RESPECT FOR GROSS FACTS

Gross facts include the success of physics, biology, mathematics, the use of mathematics in physics, communication by language. On a more restricted level, we may mention the presence of abstract thinking in the child, the Mendelian discovery of genetics, the coherence of axiomatic set theory. There are also gross facts about traditional philosophical doctrines and problems which are tied up with their historical contexts.

In a different direction, we accept as a gross fact that the scientific picture of the world in its general outline is true in those aspects where science offers generally accepted answers. This does not mean that we exclude the possibility of revising scientific beliefs. In fact, we ought to specify explicitly in each case what we take for granted as the gross facts in our discussion. In this way, we are to control the misuse of alleged gross facts. In practice, it is believed that we can easily confine ourselves to acceptable gross facts, and the main problem is to select the appropriate facts.

As an example, we mention the fact that knowledge arises from interactions of organisms with the environment. This implies that the organisms and the environment both contribute to the development of knowledge. The exact contributions of each of the two sides are of course controversial issues on which we do not have comprehensive and detailed gross facts.

There is a basic circularity in the respect for gross facts. It is a familiar fact that facts are interpreted data and there is often a strong desire to get at the raw data. It is thought that the important first step is to determine what are the facts rather than to take uncritically certain facts for granted. The position urged here is to keep closer contact with our scientific common sense and refrain from wilful skepticism. One could also concern oneself endlessly with analyzing the concepts of fact and datum. But we should remind ourselves that the existing body of knowledge offers us far more facts than philosophical abstractions such as sense data or stimulus meaning.

It may be objected that the slogan of respecting gross facts has no positive content, since nobody in his right senses would wish to violate it. It is necessary to elaborate what I take this slogan to mean by bringing out some of its implications.

We would like to take knowledge as it is more seriously. In particular, we wish to keep in mind knowledge as a structured body and avoid, for example, general debates on whether a particular difference such as that between analytic and synthetic is one of degree or one of kind. In this regard, we would not be satisfied with a conclusion which is vaguely right if suitably interpreted but would try to look into the intended interpretation of the conclusion.

On the whole, I prefer vaguely right positions to precisely wrong ones. This contrast can mean several things. Giving a mistaken but relevant exact interpretation of a given problem can generate considerations which could help to clarify the original problem. But in that case it is essential to bear in mind the inadequacy of the exact interpretation and refrain from belaboring its formal consequences which have nothing to do with the original problem. A precise but wrong doctrine may sometimes be turned into a correct hypothetical deduction which begins with unrealistic premises. It may therefore be claimed to have scientific, if not philosophical, value. One difficulty is we can rarely turn the doctrine into a completely precise, if hypothetical, one. It is clear that we should not categorically deny the value of all precise but mistaken doctrines, since it depends on how precise they are and how interesting their unrealistic hypotheses are. It does seem that there is too much eagerness to misapply formal techniques to unsuited situations.

Another gross experience is the tendency in contemporary philosophy to avoid facts except for (usually detailed) linguistic ones. This bears on a different aspect of the interest in knowledge as it is, viz. that we are interested in what is important in knowledge. While it is impossible and pointless to learn and use all details of all branches of knowledge in a philosophy of knowledge, the respect for gross facts implies an interest in serious knowledge. It is true that often the more elementary parts of knowledge are of more philosophical interest. And if the goal is to say true and interesting things, then the less presupposition of technical knowledge, the greater the challenge. There is a slight ambiguity in that the presupposition may be necessary for the saying though not for the understanding. In any case, I believe that philosophy has less right to be isolated than special branches of science.

The respect for gross facts implies also a distrust of unaided pure deductive reason. It would be nice if by pure thought we were able to uncover certain simple first principles and deduce all knowledge from them. A gross experience is that such a feat has never been accomplished. It is inferred that it cannot be done. Instead, the suggestion is that philosophical thoughts be checked against gross facts not only with respect to consistency but also with respect to relevance.

One gross fact is that there is much knowledge and there is also much on which mankind is ignorant. The only basis on which we can arrive at a comprehensive overview is what we know now. It seems, therefore, essential that we should take full advantage of what is known. Within each discipline, there is a pretty good idea of what is important or central, even though there is a good deal of disagreement and the consensus can be mistaken in that seemingly unimportant aspects may open up interesting new avenues. To transcend special disciplines seems to lead one into a no-man's land. Yet there is a persistent desire to understand, to make sense of all knowledge and the world as known. In practice, respect for fact implies a recommendation of caution: instead of being enthused quickly with sweeping doctrines of 'nothing but,' one is to check carefully against the full richness of human knowledge.

In many respects, Aristotle probably comes closer to this ideal of a philosopher than anybody else. This is of course relative to the existing knowledge of his time. Admittedly he does not even take adequate account of mathematics as existing at his time. And it is often said that his philosophy hampered the progress of science. All the same, it is hard to deny that his philosophy is comprehensive and has depth, showing great respect for facts as known at his time. In this regard, one is tempted to point out that what are taken to be facts at his time are often not genuine facts. This is inevitable: what we take to be facts today may also turn out to be nonfacts seen at a more advanced stage of knowledge. Yet we have no choice but to begin with knowledge as it is; to look for only absolutely certain knowledge seems inevitably to confine philosophy to a state of isolation from human knowledge. In any case, what I find most disappointing in contemporary philosophy is the lack of any forceful pursuit of what might be called 'the factualist ideal.'

A serious objection to the example of Aristotle is the impossibility for any individual to command current knowledge as Aristotle commanded knowledge of his time. This would seem to force, initially at least, everybody interested in philosophy to a choice between being philosophical expositors of existing knowledge and pursuing certain first principles with less direct and explicit concern with the whole body of knowledge as it is. If, however, the two areas of philosophical exposition and study of first principles are pursued in an objective and cumulative fashion, with close co-operation and with the goal of unification in mind, then the ideal of a more relevant and more stable and substantial philosophy may become a rewarding area of investigations.

It might seem that the cautious respect for facts would discourage guessing or speculation. That would be a bad thing not only because man enjoys speculating but also because speculation is necessary to get one out of pure passivity, and passivity alone cannot generate anything of interest. What is recommended is rather controlled speculation both in the selection and conceptualization of facts and in devising links to bring together diverse aspects. Facts help us to avoid some of the too many ifs, but they are to be supplemented by speculations if the result is to be sufficiently unconditional to enter into the main streams of the development of human thought.

One concrete suggestion, if not implication, derivable from the respect for facts is the interest in the genesis of knowledge. This would seem to be a natural consequence of the desire to look for relevant gross facts which bear on the central problems of knowledge.

The genetic element has at least three components: the history of human knowledge, the development of the child, and biological foundations. The repulsive aspect of genetic considerations is the lack of clean and unquestionable facts which are of sufficient generality to be of interest to philosophy. The advantage is the possibility of magnifying details to reduce the danger of distortion and over-simplification.

It seems trite to remark that in a sense our concept changes as our knowledge relating to it changes or, more exactly, that once a judgment is performed on a given concept, the concept thereafter carries a sense which is the result of the judgment. We are inclined to hold ourselves to a more static concept of concept so that the meaning of a concept does not change with our knowledge.

Yet undoubtedly there are pragmatic advantages in paying attention to this genetic aspect of concepts and their meaning. When we study the development of a concept in the child or in the history of scientific concepts, it usually pays to separate out those additional parts of the meaning of a concept which we have acquired at a later stage. Or, if we attempt to understand certain texts or a new system of philosophy, we generally succeed better if we reflect on and take into account the convictions we bring with us. A more basic reason for emphasizing such genetic analyses is that they help us to clarify our own central concepts and to better understand the world.

A familiar complaint is that the number and content of special sciences have become so vast that nobody is able any more to survey and enjoy all these treasures of cognition, and to derive full advantage from this wealth. It is not immediately clear why surveying one area only is less enjoyable than surveying all, or what great advantages one could derive from an encyclopedic knowledge. Imagine a greatly improved pedagogy guided by a more congenial reorganization of knowledge which enables many an individual to know all that has been ascertained objectively in all sciences. It might be said that the essential task of philosophy remains untouched since what is sought for is an account of how all sciences are rooted in the (yet to be uncovered) first principles.

We have here a typical case of the complexity involved in thinking about imagined situations. One implication is that the practical difficulty of knowing all sciences has nothing or little to do with the philosophical problem of unification. Of course there is no point in memorizing telephone books or even encyclopedias. Knowledge is not just memorization. Given the fact that everybody has a limited capacity in learning what is known, it follows that if anybody has in any significant sense managed to know all sciences, then he or mankind at large must have developed a more efficient way of looking at knowledge. And such new ways cannot but be of philosophical interest. Whether the result of such new ways of organizing and acquiring knowledge is called philosophy, it would undoubtedly render the task of philosophical unification more feasible.

5 LOOKING BEYOND

Knowledge in the broadest sense is to be identified with human culture: language, myth, religion, art, history, science, philosophy. If humanity is to be characterized by man's work, by the system of human activities, one is tempted to equate the philosophy of knowledge with the philosophy of man. The rather loose unifying theme of man as the symbol-using animal has been suggested. This is more appropriate than the traditional definition of man as a rational or a language-using animal since, for example, myth and perhaps also religion are not rational. Also, symbol is both a broader and a richer concept than language since symbols are more universally used in art than language, and the use of language in science seems less a defining characteristic than the use of symbols. Of course, one is in this way using the concept of symbols in a rather extended sense. In any case, symbol-using as a unifying theme is not too informative insofar as it is to be entirely neutral, and not so neutral insofar as it is to be rather informative. Perhaps that is the common fate of all simple unifying themes. It is also natural to consider myth and religion to be of more historical than contemporary interest.

More often, philosophy of knowledge is mainly, or at least initially, concerned with scientific knowledge. The emergence of modern science during the sixteenth and seventeenth centuries in Europe is a unique gross fact which has in one way or another affected all subsequent philosophies of knowledge. This is usually said to have generated a philosophy of simple materialism and indirectly the more refined Humean empiricism. The idea is that since abstraction turned out to be successful in physics, one was led to the abstract picture of the world as a succession of instantaneous configurations of matter, or, upon reflection on how our knowledge is obtained, the similarly abstract picture of applying induction to sense impressions. To these abstractions, a familiar and largely justified objection is the need of the right understanding of the immediate occasion of knowledge in its full concreteness and the observation that mistaking the abstraction for the concrete datum distorts. But it is doubtful that the only way to meet this objection is to go to a thoroughgoing philosophy of organism or that a preoccupation (even just initially) with physics necessarily leads to an inadequate philosophy of knowledge. One could just as well look closely at physics and mathematics and determine the conditions which make them possible. In this way, the 'full concreteness' may be recovered, if not completely, at least to a large extent, and there is no obvious reason why such an understanding of the foundations of scientific knowledge would necessarily exclude a more adequate picture of mind and the world. On the contrary, one would expect to learn in this way a good deal about human knowledge that is central and substantial.

One striking fact about physics is the extensive use of mathematics which contrasts sharply with the schemes of classification stressed so much by Aristotle and Francis Bacon. Somehow we are not interested here in abstracting a common property from different things in terms of similarity and thereby cancelling the determinations of the special cases. Rather a general mathematical formula gives a broader concept which retains traces of the special cases so that we have functional relations which unify many heterogeneous cases. For example, the parameters in quadratic equations, when specified, yield ellipses or parabolas or hyperbolas. This phenomenon leads to the theme of contrasting things (and properties) with relations, substances with functions. One senses a basic point in this somewhat vague contrast. Yet it is not as easy to see how one can use this point fruitfully in a comprehensive philosophy of knowledge.

A general issue which is relevant to contemporary science is the problem of complexity. Not only do we encounter large groups with complicated projects and expensive equipments in experimental and applied sciences, but many theoretical problems in the sciences which are believed to have been solved in principle remain unsolved in practice. It has been pointed out that, through the application of quantum theory to atoms, we are now relatively certain that we know the fundamental laws of physics relevant to ordinary matter, i.e. systems of all sizes above the subatomic and below the galactic. But, for example, nobody has succeeded in deriving from atomic physics that water freezes at 32° F. On the one hand, there is the belief that the right laws have been found. On the other hand, there is the fact that the complexity of most systems is such that we have not been able to deduce the relevant consequences of what we know in principle. Of course, many who are not sympathetic to this optimistic confidence in the existing physical laws would suggest that complex systems may have properties which do not follow from the laws describing the interactions of their constituents. Most working scientists would, however, choose to use the negation of such wholist positions, at least as a working hypothesis. We are then led to ask whether we should not pursue a new subject that is devoted to finding methods for handling complex data in all their diversities, such as perhaps the computational approach and general systems analysis. In other words, a general systematic study of complexity in all its manifold manifestations is envisaged. A significant subdomain would be a theory of the complexity of computations.

Another suggestive theme is closely connected with the contrast between fact and fiction. Given a thing or an object or a person A and a property P which A is capable of having, we tend to believe that either A has P or A does not have P, even if we might happen to be ignorant as to which is the case. In writing a novel, there is also some idea of a natural development of the characters. For example, one feels that the last five-twelfths of *Water margin* is incongruent with earlier parts and finds out that these were added by another author. But there is much that is left open so that alternative continuations are permissible and not all questions are answerable even in principle. It may simply be indeterminate whether, for example,

390

the hero will remarry or whether his height is five feet, nine inches. The contrast is sometimes characterized as between being true of an object and being true to a concept. A statement about an object is either true or false, but a statement about a concept in this special sense need not be true or false. At places Wittgenstein seems to suggest that many statements about numbers are of this latter type. People have also suggested tying up realism with the acceptance of the law of excluded middle. According to this criterion, a realist about sets is, by definition, one who believes that every pure statement about sets is such that either it or its negation is true (and perhaps also, therefore, in principle knowable).

The 'full concreteness' of an experience has many dimensions. Often we feel we cannot describe the experience, or we cannot even communicate it either by a description or by some other means. For example, one might find somebody's voice especially delightful but cannot describe the experience of hearing that voice. Sometimes we may attribute the inability to the lack of a technique: perhaps a poet could do it, perhaps as our knowledge advances, we acquire better ways for communication. In any case, it appears clear that reflections on scientific knowledge are a long way from accounting for experiences tinged with emotions.

The task of philosophy may be said to be the study of the nature of man, and scientists, artists, theologians, politicians all approach the problem from their own viewpoints. History might be thought of as a relatively neutral subject, yet one feels that in order to avoid being superficial, a historical answer to the nature of man calls for some particular orientation. Familiar examples are the will to power, the sexual instinct, and the economic instinct. These insights satisfy a longing for the discovery of the driving force or forces behind the history of man, but they can hardly claim to account smoothly for all human history in any straightforward way. In former times, there used to be certain less specific general frames of orientation and reference such as perhaps metaphysics in the ancient times, theology in the middle ages, mathematics or biology at different periods of modern times. Nowadays to combine or unify all the competing particular aspects and perspectives seems impossible. Such unification seems to have been driven beyond human capabilities by the constraints introduced through the passionate interest in detailed stubborn facts on the one side, abstract generalizations on the other, as well as the exacting task to match the two sides.

Traditionally the Chinese intellectuals seem to have a more coherent view of human nature which brings together more closely everyday life with philosophy, the arts, history, and politics. Every intellectual is more or less a generalist whose learning affects his life in almost all directions. Different intellectuals all have a common heritage and can communicate with one another on nearly all topics of interest to each. There was less respect for specialization, less interest in subtle logical argumentations (in contrast with intuition and common sense), less ambition for rigid grand systems.

Often we feel that certain statements are true, even though we cannot formulate articulate reasons for our belief in them. If now the desire is to find out what is true, it would seem rational to accept such statements by a direct appeal to our intuition. The contrary course often produces clever arguments which 'win a debate without convincing anybody.' There is something frivolous in polishing arguments just to score a point over one's opponent. Grand systems often have in each case their own technical apparatus so that they are open to diverse interpretations, i.e. that there are diverse ways of translating them into any truly stable common language such as the language of science or ordinary language. Hence, while grand systems may be the delight of scholars, they are not easily or unambiguously absorbable into the main body of objective human knowledge.

It has often been remarked that Chinese philosophy is morality oriented, while Western philosophy is knowledge oriented. This probably points to a more basic difference.

The wish to derive satisfactions from intellectual activities is all too familiar. An obvious component of these satisfactions is success and recognition which often involve the not altogether attractive element of competition. One also speaks of the purer pleasure of a job well done. And it cannot be denied that there is a somewhat independent component of enjoying a certain type of work more than others. It is true that once energies are channeled into a specialty, there is often a tendency to strive to maximize one's success according to the established criterion of the specialty. Even in such situations, partly because success is hard to predict, each individual tends to choose what happens to strike his own fancy. Frequently one enters a specialty and finds it different from the early expectations. Then either a change of specialty or an adaptation of the original interests takes place. Among the specialists we encounter also the different temperaments which lead either to a sort of entrenchment or to a hankering after greener grasses elsewhere.

Many people do get pleasure and satisfaction from just learning a beautiful subject, playing the piano as amateurs, painting pictures as amateurs, or exchanging poor poems with friends. An individual person's idea of what is valuable may conflict with that of his colleagues or that of society at large. This may deprive him of the pleasure of enjoyable discussions with colleagues on topics of common interest, the satisfaction of having sympathetic audiences, and other fruits of recognition. Hence, fashion is a strong force for conformity. In fact, the instinct for belonging to a group leads to all sorts of formal and informal intellectual clubs which can be repositories of good taste as well as bulwarks against progress.

Obviously an insider and an outsider may offer quite different judgments on the values and ills of a given club. For example, Oxford philosophy has been influential in academic circles for some years. To quote P. F. Strawson, 'During the last quarter of a century Oxford has occupied, or reoccupied, a position it last held, perhaps, six hundred years ago: that of a great centre of philosophy in the Western world' (*Meaning and truth*, 1970). In his book *Words and things* (1959), E. Gellner expresses extremely negative views about this movement which emerges from his descriptions as a sort of elaborate conspiracy. According to him, it is a secularized established religion which worships conspicuous triviality and gentlemanliness:

> It is also interesting to note how very similar the exegesis of common sense or usage is to the traditional deference of reason to Faith in scholasticism (only the object of reverence has changed) . . . too human to admit of any technique, too formal and (allegedly) neutral to be of vulgar practical relevance or to be classified as subversive, too diversified to allow general ideas (pp. 250–1).

It is striking how being at the right time and place and belonging to the right group of people enables the same ability to produce better work and even the same sort of work to achieve greater importance and influence. This obvious factor is often overlooked and one is then frustrated in trying to assess and evaluate soberly people's ability and work and influence. Also there can be many extraneous reasons why some work is taken seriously, the extreme case being that of a political leader. Once somebody's words are taken seriously, generalities can mean much more than definite specific results, the significance of which is more independent of who authored them.

Contact with the exact sciences may also create the illusion that intellectual work in general is independent of one's political views and one's position in society at large. This view has its severe limitations. For example, clearly those in the humanities and the social sciences who are deprived of identification with and intimate understanding of any large society (in particular, a country) would be denied much of the more rewarding intellectual activities and may find their lives greatly impoverished altogether.

If an intellectual's task is to formulate and communicate thoughts, then philosophy and literature, for example, may be viewed as alternative roads leading to the same end. Literature uses more concrete images and less abstract concepts. It is better suited for expounding impartially competing positions and leaving the reader to draw his own conclusions. Literature is more concerned with facts or rather imagined facts, while philosophy seems to be concerned with general principles. When the possibility of theory and system in philosophy is rejected, communication by means of a mixture of literature and philosophy as exemplified in *Chuangtse* has a strong appeal. If the common purpose of philosophy and literature is thought to be the influence on people's behavior, then literature certainly seems to be on the whole more effective than philosophy. It has also been suggested that the way to describe one's world view is not by stating, 'what I believe,' but rather, 'what I feel.' It cannot be denied that there is a basic distinction between knowledge and feeling. With knowledge, true or false is a central concern, but if we sometimes speak of true and false feelings, we have in mind totally different things from true and false beliefs.

There is an element of nostalgia in the conception of a unity of knowledge. In the past, people working in any field could more easily understand what people in most fields were doing than they can today. In the past, some superior minds were capable of not only understanding but making original contributions to a very wide segment of human knowledge. These historical facts are undoubtedly related to the other facts that knowledge was less complex and therefore easier to grasp and that perhaps for the same reasons scholars and scientists wrote in a more literary and less technical style. For at least the last hundred years or so, every subject has tended to create its own enclave and a common belief has arisen that specialized concentration in a prescribed area is the best way to advance knowledge. One takes pride in particularity rather than generality. The aim of seeking knowledge is no longer to reach a world view, but to reach a new fact or a new partial view embracing a special group of facts. Departments in universities see to it that everybody is to be educated as a specialist and get recognition as a specialist.

One might wish to view Kant's work as an attempt to lay the groundwork for a unity of knowledge, looking for a unity of the products of mind by reflecting on their source. Or one might wish to suggest that all intellectual activities make use of certain common building bricks so that most young people should be made to learn these common elements, and that some leading scientists and scholars should strive to expound the current state of their fields in these terms. A first task would then be the discovery of the right building bricks, and there are naturally all the obstacles and uncertainties accompanying any such abstractly conceived reform.

If an observer's view is determined by his social position, then he will never be able to single out the more general and theoretical aspects which are implicit in the concrete observations he makes. This relativity and its implicit consequences are diluted by the existence of the socially unattached intelligentsia, a relatively classless stratum. These are individuals whose only capital consists in their education. They form a group which is to a large degree unattached to any social class and which is recruited from an increasingly inclusive area of social life. Their willingness to examine every point of view is often accompanied by endless waverings and a lack of conviction, which can hardly make them happy individuals. But they are of some value to the society at large.

To confine one's activities to the intellectual pursuit does not imply that one's goal is restricted to understanding the world. Rather there is a basic desire for certainty and for reflection which tends to work for postponing problems of life in favor of problems of knowledge. The natural tendency of being afraid of the many vicissitudes of the practical life helps to strengthen the conviction that it is more important to look first at the more static, more stable, and more permanent. One is led by a looking inwards to large problems having to do with the nature of knowledge.

(a) How is knowledge possible? In particular, how is mathematics possible? how is physics possible? how is our knowledge of language possible? Reflection would put oneself in the frame of mind of finding the success of mathematics and physics and language truly amazing. The success seems to imply that there must be a good deal of order in nature and in the mind.

(b) How is knowledge acquired? This is clearly related to (a) but suggests at first sight a more empirical study since what is asked seems to be a factual question about the natural phenomenon of knowledge acquisition. As, however, we know so little about the answer, detached methodological and other conceptual considerations are highly relevant probably for a long time to come. This question is obviously related to questions of education, as well as to those of mechanical intelligence. Since knowledge is acquired through the interaction of a man with the environment (which contains other men), it may also be asked, as an additional question, how much is contributed by the man himself (how much is native) and how much is contributed by the environment. A more abstract question would be, how can knowledge be acquired, or what models for the man and his environment would be adequate to producing knowledge?

(c) What is to understand something? We say we understand a

word, a concept, a theory, a sentence, a theorem, a proof, a rule, a situation, a set of phenomena. There are different levels of understanding the same thing. There are also different kinds of understanding ranging from absorbing a small piece of familiar information to seeing for the first time order in a chaos. Understanding some new thing changes an individual's whole conceptual framework to some extent. A totally new way of looking at a set of phenomena is also a new understanding and can initiate a significant advance of human knowledge if others with a similar interest start to understand the innovation and accept it. Understanding is the decisive anthropomorphic element of knowledge.

(d) Problems on the unity of knowledge. Is there a unity of knowledge? What are the advantages and disadvantages of specialization? Is it desirable to avoid being a specialist? How can we arrive at a rational guide to choosing a speciality? How important are interdisciplinary studies?

(e) What are the data of knowledge? There is the familiar approach of attempting to build up all empirical knowledge from personal sense data. This is, it is generally agreed, different from the way scientists proceed, which is amazingly successful but hard to be given any neat account for. There are then the Cartesian and the Husserlian conceptions of richer data. What would seem to be a different approach is to take human knowledge as it is as the data.

While all these problems could be accepted as being intrinsically interesting with regard to the nature of human knowledge, they are not the sort of problems on which we can expect definitive scientific answers, certainly not in the near future. Problem (b) has more the scientific flavor than the others, but so little is known at present that evaluation and interpretation of new information on the problem is usually at least as important as obtaining such new information. There is also experimental work pertaining to the nature of understanding, but one suspects that at least at present there is much room for relevant speculations on problem (c) outside the professional field of psychology.

In studying these large problems about knowledge, a predominant goal is undoubtedly the advance of human knowledge. But if knowledge is to be defined by its usefulness in conquering nature and improving human welfare, even interesting thoughts on these large problems may not, as a rule, be clearly conducive to the increase of knowledge. On many of these problems, what is immediately sought after seems to be a sort of idle intellectual comfort: being at peace with the facts because one understands them. If, on the other hand, one argues for knowledge for its own sake, then it is easy to extend the range of knowledge to include knowledge about knowledge. There is always in the back of one's mind the vague belief that a better understanding of the nature of knowledge will somehow eventually help improve man's fate.

It is well known that there is little which is interesting and clear and distinct one can say on the large problems. An obvious and crude 'product law' is in operation which says that the interest of a comment on a topic is equal to the product of the interest of the topic and the interest of the comment for the topic. It is undoubtedly this product law which to a considerable extent guides the choice of one's area of work and accounts for our common evaluation of intellectual achievements.

In addition to this rational product law, there is in action sometimes also an irrational 'principle of independence' which tends to draw some people away from conventional fields which have fairly well-defined standards of requirement and progress.

Applied to the large problems, the product law tends to pull people away from them, while the principle of independence tends to draw one toward them. Various compromises are adopted as a result. One such would be to keep the large problems in mind while adhering as closely to existing knowledge as is compatible with having something to say, if only indirectly, on the large problems.

APPENDIX
EXERCISES IN CRITICISM

1 NOTES ON THE JUSTIFICATION
OF INDUCTION

Different philosophers have expressed different views, often irreconcilable with one another, on the subject of induction; especially on that of its justification, or, as it is usually called, *the* problem of induction. In general terms, the problem may be put so: What is the justification of the belief that the future resembles the past, that the unobserved resembles the observed? Authors on induction seldom fail to stress the importance of inductive reasoning in science and everyday life, intending to indicate thereby the indispensability of some answer to the problem for an adequate theory of knowledge.

It has often been repeated that an appeal to habit or animal faith would not provide an adequate solution. Recently many philosophers with scientific bent are of the opinion that the attempt to justify induction is futile, the problem of induction is a fictitious one, a *general* problem in its usual formulation does not exist. Nevertheless, they insist, it is not irrational to expect future experience to conform to the past: for when we come to define rationality we shall find that for us being rational entails being guided in a particular fashion by past experience. The genuine problem of induction, according to them, is to formulate scientific method and define the notion of rationality in accordance with science and common sense. Probably this kind of answer does not sound congenial to the majority of philosophers. None the less, it may be a piece of wise advice against overindulgence in fanciful speculations.

Thoughtful scientists find the success of science hard to explain. Some remark that the most incomprehensible thing about the world is that it is comprehensible. Others tell us that there is inherent in nature a hidden harmony which reflects itself in our mind under the image of simple mathematical laws – that is the reason why events in nature are predictable.

Such answers do not seem to satisfy all serious thinkers. Accordingly induction has been said to be the despair of philosophy. Occasionally antagonists of contemporary philosophy claim the situation a *reductio ad absurdum* of what they call the subjectivistic and empiricistic approach. Bertrand Russell grants it highly probable that there is nothing better to be done, but observes that to attempt the possible which *looks* impossible is the summit of wisdom, that a passionate lover of knowledge will not give up the attempt until he has explored every avenue of escape.

As a matter of fact, we do have competent scholars who attempt what looks impossible, proposing various elaborate solutions of the problem. Now and then one solution or another has attracted a considerable number of adherents. Notwithstanding, no solution seems to have enjoyed really wide acceptance, to say nothing of a unanimous approval.

Presumably the disagreement in connection with these solutions is partly due to the fact that the problem in question usually does not receive exact formulation. Specifically, there are two points about which we are often not very clear: *a* what sort of thing is to be justified; *b* what kind of justification is asked for.

Thus Keynes's well-known principle of limited variety has been condemned as providing no satisfactory justification of induction on the ground that it makes ontological assertions of a kind the truth of which we are unable to know with our ordinary means. If the condemnation is right, the reason for it may be specified by saying that Keynes did not give the right kind of justification, although his principle (if granted) does justify what we want to be justified.

On the other hand, we may well agree that no sort of imaginable experience could fail to afford a basis for intelligibility, that there will always be *some* discoverable order, *some* resemblance with the past, however the future may turn up. We may even agree to follow Kant and comment that, if objective validity of knowledge is to be possible at all, certain very general kinds of regularity must hold. Still that would not help much, unless we are able to determine how much regularity and order in future experiences is thereby guaranteed. For example, it may be asked: Is such regularity and order sufficient to ensure that the sun will very probably rise tomorrow? if so, how? It seems that we do want something more than the mere intelligibility of the future, we want success (in some sense) of our predictions. When we ask for a justification of induction, we are seeking a ground for our belief in the future success (in some sense) of our predictions.

If we agree not to allow ontological assumptions and not to stop at a justification *only* of our belief in the intelligibility of the future, then the following conclusions reached by investigation of careful students of induction seem to be indisputable.[1]

In order to justify inductive reasoning, we may or may not insist that inductive generalizations can be established with theoretical certainty. If we do so insist, we shall find ourselves unable to explain the possibility of future counter instances, unless we exclude it by reconstruing the inductive generalizations and reconstrue them as analytic statements. The only disadvantage is that a statement gives up its role of empirical prediction the moment it accepts the privilege of being analytic.

On the other hand, we may grant the lack of theoretical certainty of inductive generalizations and attempt a justification by theorems of probability. But this means nothing in particular until some interpretation has been put upon the notion of probability. Specifically, we may either adopt the frequency interpretation or adopt some non-frequency interpretation. If we take the latter alternative, we shall at no stage be able to pass from a certain frequency being overwhelmingly probable to it being overwhelmingly frequent. That is to say, on any non-frequency interpretation we have no guarantee that on the whole and in the long run the more probable alternative is the one that is more often realized.

This latter condition is guaranteed analytically on the frequency interpretation. It is, however, to be noted, that each of the crucial (for justifying induction) theorems of probability starts with a premiss about the probability of events of a certain kind turning out in a certain way. Now, on the frequency interpretation, such a premiss is itself a statement about limiting frequency which is in turn either assumed as a hypothesis or established by inductive generalization. Hence, here again theorems of probability cannot supply a justification for inductive generalization in general.

Thus, in either case, theorems of probability alone can provide no sufficient ground of induction. Attempts to justify induction by resorting to mathematics seem to be misled either by confusing different interpretations of the notion of probability or by introducing new assumptions tacitly.

Let us now turn to several plausible answers in the literature and see how far we can get. Consider first the following argument put forward by Professor D. C. Williams in his book on induction.[2]

Let R, say the class of rabbits, be a class of r members. Let t be the number of the members of R which have a specific property P, say whiteness. Let R' be any r'-membered ($0 \leqslant r' \leqslant r$) subclass of R, and t' be the number of the members of R' having the property P.

400

Then the number n of such subclasses of R is given by $C_{t'}^{t} \times C_{r'-t'}^{r-t}$. From elementary algebra, we know that n is greatest when t'/r' is nearest t/r. We also know that when r' is large (in some sense yet to be specified) the number of those subclasses of R for which t'/r' is approximately (in some sense yet to be specified) equal to t/r is much greater than that of all the other classes put together. Hence, given empirically that t' members in an r'-membered (r' large) sample of R have the property P, by *proportional syllogism* we are assured that it is highly probable that t/r is approximately equal to t'/r'. This provides the desired principle of induction adequate to justify inductive reasoning.

Thus, if we have observed r' rabbits (r' large) and found that t' of them are white, then it is highly probable that the ratio of the number of all white rabbits to that of all the rabbits is approximately t'/r'. In particular, if, for example, $r' = 2500$, we can reach our desired conclusion by the following proportional syllogism:

Major premiss: At least 68 per cent of the 2500-membered subclasses of any R do not vary in composition from R by more than 1 per cent;
Minor premiss: R' is a 2500-membered subclass of R;
Conclusion: There is at least a probability of 0·68 that
$$|t/r - t'/r'| \leqslant 0·01.$$

Therein the minor premiss is guaranteed by our hypothesis, and the major premiss is obtained by mathematical calculation.

Professor Williams contends that his theory 'proves the jurisdiction of inductive procedure over all the branches of philosophy as well as over the natural sciences, the professions, and common sense, and it guarantees the relevance of the content of any one of these fields to all the rest' (ibid. p. 202). However, to those long puzzled by the problem of induction, his whole argument may look like a justification of everything with nothing. They may suspect there must be something wrong with the argument.

First, let us ask what interpretation is put on probability by Professor Williams. Judging from his tireless attack on the frequency interpretation, we may presume some non-frequency interpretation is assumed. But if so, what guarantees induction to lead us more often to success than to disappointment, granted that we can justify inductive generalizations with high probability on some a priori ground? Or is there a bridge between a priori probability and frequency? It seems there is no such bridge, at least so long as we stick to a definite interpretation of probability.

Suppose there be 10^{10} bags each containing 5000 balls. Suppose further we have observed 2500 balls from each bag and found all these $10^{10} \times 2500$ balls white. Now we must admit it is logically possible that none of those unobserved $10^{10} \times 2500$ balls will turn up to be white. But the principle of induction established by Professor Williams assures us this is very, very improbable. The same principle also enables us to make many other probability judgments about the color of the unobserved balls of the 10^{10} bags. In particular, take any one bag from these; we can judge it highly probable that at least some of the unobserved 2500 balls of it are white. Similarly with regard to any other such bag. And we can judge it overwhelmingly probable that at least some of the unobserved balls of at least some of the 10^{10} bags are white.

Suppose the unexpected happens. We start to observe the remaining $10^{10} \times 2500$ balls and find that none of them is white. What shall we say about our probability judgments made beforehand? If we adopt some non-frequency interpretation, we need not reject them as false. We may say merely that we are not lucky in this particular case. But suppose these be all the probability judgments we ever make on the principle in question, and accordingly all the highly probable alternatives are those not realized: we might still insist that our probable judgments are right relative to our knowledge at the time. However, a principle of induction which might always lead to disappointment does not seem to be what is wanted. And yet it is difficult to see how the almost wholly mathematical proof of the principle could exclude a priori such possibility.

To put the matter in another way: for our knowledge, between what is observed and what is unobserved, there is all the difference in the world. It is literally true, 'The experienced species is peculiar in being experienced, but every species is peculiar in some respect' (ibid. p. 176). But this does not imply that they are equally peculiar for our knowledge; for our knowledge, being experienced, is a very peculiar peculiarity. God might neglect the human distinction between the past and the future, the known and the unknown; but we cannot afford to do so. No a priori principle of indifference could assure us that it is equally probable whether what is experienced should be experienced in the order it is actually experienced or in any one of the permutations of it – unless we either beg the question by tacitly assuming something to the effect that the future resembles the past or give up the claim that the more probable alternative is on the whole and in the long run more often realized.

The previous proportional syllogism may be evaluated in one way or another according as we accept one interpretation or another of the notion of probability. On the frequency interpretation, the conclusion does not follow from the premises; while on any non-frequency interpretation, the conclusions reached in such fashion need not guarantee success, on the whole and in the long run, of our actions guided by them as predictions. In granting that we know a priori that a large sample very probably has nearly the same composition as the whole population, we must not forget that here what are known to be more probable need not be those which are on the whole and in the long run more often realized. Indeed, if we find consolation in the assurance of such a priori high probabilities, Professor Williams's justification seems to be of the kind which can justify almost everything we may desire to justify.

A more modest answer to the problem of induction is Professor Reichenbach's widely known solution.[3] He maintains that to obtain such a solution we need only prove two things: i the aim of induction is possible; ii induction is the best means we have for attaining the aim. Foreseeing the future as the aim of induction is determined by him as 'to find series of events whose frequency of occurrence converges toward a limit' (p. 350). Then i is obviously true. Moreover, his theory, he tells us, provides a logical demonstration of ii. Hence the solution is complete.

Let h_i be the frequency-ratio of events of the type A among a series of i events A and non-A. Professor Reichenbach formulates (on p. 340) the principle of induction by the following statement: 1 For every $s(s > n)$, we assume that $|h_n - h_s| \leqslant \varepsilon$, where ε is a small number. Then he points out that this formulation is a necessary condition for the existence of a limit of the frequency near h_n (p. 341). But the following does not appear very clear: What kind of number is n? how small is ε? A necessary condition of the existence of a limit of the frequency which specifies ε and does not depend on any particular n seems to be the following statement: 2 For every n, there is an ε_n such that for any $s(s > n)$, $|h_n - h_s| \leqslant \varepsilon_n$, and ε_n approaches 0 as n increases indefinitely. This is an analytic consequence of the assumption that the h-series of frequency-ratios does have a limit at all.

But if we adopt statement 2 as our principle of induction, something which happens may look paradoxical. On the one hand, for any fixed k, however large it may be, the first k terms of the ε-series of the ε_i's may be arbitrarily determined without affecting the mathematical truth of our principle. On the other hand, empirically we are always concerned with those ε_i's and h_i's for which some finite upper bound k can be found; what we are concerned with in practice is how the first k terms of the ε-series are to be determined. In other words, this principle as it stands seems to guarantee no practical success whatsoever in our life; because, however our empirical findings at a stage may be, mathematically our principle is always compatible with the possibility that the actual limit differs from the frequency-ratio found at the stage by some quantity no less than 1/10 (say) or even 1/2.

Professor Reichenbach does not deny that 'a series actually observable is always finite, of even a rather restricted length, determined by the short duration of human lives.' He introduced 'the term *practical limit* for a series showing a sufficient convergence within a domain accessible to human observations,' and tells us that his theory may be said to be concerned with a practical limit instead of a mathematical limit (pp. 360–2).

Let us take an *h*-series of frequency-ratios with finitely many terms $h_1, \ldots, h_k$. The statement 3 'For every $j(j \leqslant k)$, there is an ε_j such that $|h_k - h_j| \leqslant \varepsilon_j$, where for every small $\delta(> 0)$, there is an $l(l \leqslant k)$ such that $\varepsilon_l \leqslant \delta$' is then necessarily true, seeing that we may choose to give ε_k the value 0. If we take statement 3 as a sufficient condition for the existence of a practical limit, it is an analytic truth that every *h*-series with finitely many terms has a practical limit. Such a notion of practical limit would be of little interest for us, because certainly from a principle of induction we want something more than the assurance of existence of such limits.

We may require that only those *h*-series with accompanying ε-series of a specific kind are to be said to possess a practical limit. For example we may require that for every $i(i \leqslant k)$, $\varepsilon_i = 0$; or we may require that for every $i(i \leqslant k)$, $\varepsilon_i \leqslant \frac{1}{2}$; or we may require that for every $i(i \leqslant k)$, $\varepsilon_i \leqslant \frac{1}{i}$; and so on. Corresponding to every specification of the requisite ε-series there is then a notion of practical limit. And if following Professor Reichenbach we introduce the term 'predictable' 'for a world which is sufficiently ordered to enable us to construct series with a limit' (pp. 350–1), then corresponding to every notion of a (practical) limit there will be a principle of induction which is expressed by statement 3 plus the corresponding condition on the admissible ε-series. The applicability (at least to some *h*-series) of each such principle will be necessarily ensured by the assumption of predictability (in the corresponding sense) of the world.

In each case, it will be tautologous to say that, if the world is predictable, then the principle of induction has application. The problem of formulating the principle of induction becomes mainly a matter of choosing a suitable definition of practical limit, which in turn is a matter of choosing a suitable condition for the admissible ε-series. Probably past experience may help us in specifying the condition for the existence of a practical limit and determining thereby the notion of predictability as well as the principle of induction. Each principle of induction becomes then something like a scientific hypothesis about our future experience. When 'the short duration of human lives' comes to an end, some higher spirit may observe that the human belief in the predictability of the world turns out to be true (or false).

Professor Reichenbach persistently repeats that his principle of induction is the best means we have for attaining the aim of induction. In what sense is it the best? It is analytically true that, if there exists a limit of the h-series, we may reach an h_n arbitrarily near the limit by choosing a sufficiently large n; though for a given small ε, assuming the existence of a limit of the h-series, we are yet unable to fix the value of n. If we consider an h-series of finite (yet undetermined for us) number of terms, probably we may call that principle of induction the best which uses the narrowest notion of (practical) limit (i.e. the one for which the condition on the admissible ε-series is the strongest) and yet turns out to be confirmed at the end of 'the short duration of human lives.' But, if so, we certainly do not know which is the best; because we do not know which specific principles of induction turn out to be confirmed in the end.

The justification of induction given by Professor Lewis in his new book[4] seems to be along a different line. He appeals to our everyday experience and common sense instead of mathematics. In what follows I will attempt a summary of Professor Lewis's theory. Since, however, I am not sure I understand him at all, my attempt will probably fall beside the mark.

We have no logical guarantee that the alternative judged by us to be more probable is on the whole and in the long run the one which is more often realized. It is logically possible that this is not the case. It is logically possible that the majority of our present predictions in science about future experience will turn out to be discredited. We cannot even adequately explain why natural laws have led to so much success so far, especially in view of the often very insufficient evidence on which the generalizations were based. If we think about it, this may appear to be the most incomprehensible thing about the world. In fact, if it makes one feel better, one may resort to a hidden harmony inherent in nature for explanation. But so far as our empirical knowledge goes, it is certainly possible that the sun will not rise tomorrow. More than that, for example, I may judge that, because a certain visual doorknob-appearance S is presently and indubitably given, therefore if I initiate the proper groping motion A, the doorknob-contacting sensation E will follow; and yet possibly E will not follow A. It is logically possible that most of such highly probable everyday predictions of the form 'If A, then E' will be falsified.

The epistemological problem of induction, however, is not and cannot be to give a logical demonstration that such suppositions cannot turn out to be true, that such logical possibilities are logically impossible. We must not expect to get a guarantee of general success for our empirical predictions by resorting to formal logic or mathematics. More fundamental but perhaps less often observed than these particular predictions is our sense of fact, our sense of empirical reality. Any item of our sense of past fact is prima facie credible and probable; otherwise to say that one alternative is more or less probable than another would be meaningless *for us*, because we would then have no criterion of the empirically real, no means of understanding what is meant by calling one alternative more probable. That empirical reality can be known is an analytic statement which can only be repudiated on premisses which already imply it. The possibility of knowledge of empirical reality is a prerequisite for the notion of probability to have any *meaning* at all.

Any prediction 'If *A*, then (probably) *E*' must inevitably be relative to what we know at present; while the knowing process must take place in the *epistemological present*, a present in which what is sensuously given is surrounded by or embedded in a mass of epistemically pertinent surrogates of past experience as having been so and so. Such mnemic preservation of past experience, its present-as-pastness, is constitutive of the world we live in.

It is indeed logically conceivable we might be subject to persistent delusions, and what is remembered at every epistemological present might always be newly created in our mind at the moment by God. But the assertion of such possibility is at best a metaphysical thesis in the sense that it is in principle incapable of being either empirically verified or falsified. We have no rational alternative but to presume that anything sensed as past is more probable than that which is incompatible with what is remembered and that with respect to which memory is blank.

Once initial prima facie credibility is granted the remembered merely because remembered, it becomes comparatively easier to see this: When the whole range of empirical beliefs is taken into account, all of them more or less dependent upon memorial knowledge, we find that those which are most credible can be assured by their mutual support, or, to use Professor Lewis's special terminology, by their *congruence*. An examination of concrete examples reveals the fact that a body of empirical beliefs, each of which is less than certain and no one of which can be substantiated on empirically certain ground, may nevertheless be established as credible by their relation to one another; the conjoint truth of some – and perhaps a relatively few – in a congruent set of statements may be sufficient to establish a high probability of some other, or perhaps all of the others, even though no single one of the items thus conjoined would be particularly good evidence of anything in question. If several relatively unreliable witnesses independently tell the same circumstantial story, then the congruence of the reports establishes a high probability of what they agree upon; for on any other hypothesis than that of truth telling, this agreement is highly unlikely. Such considerations account for the usually very high credibility of our everyday beliefs.[5]

2 ON SKEPTICISM ABOUT INDUCTION

In mathematics we have demonstrably insoluble problems, one example being that of trisecting an arbitrary angle in elementary geometry. Every now and then, we encounter engineers and others who offer solutions of the insoluble and make some stir. To those who feel convinced of the demonstration of insolubility, these claimed solutions do not seem to deserve any serious consideration. In fact, such solutions have long since ceased to attract attention from mathematicians.

The situation in philosophy seems different. Here we do not possess demonstrations as clear and distinct as in mathematics. For example, it has been a fashion among philosophers for two centuries or so to answer Hume's skepticism concerning induction. Although, presumably, there never has been any answer or solution which is as widely accepted among philosophers as Hume's skeptical argument, yet philosophers continue to enjoy elaborating arguments for and against Hume's skepticism. And people who feel convinced by Hume's reasoning often find it difficult to understand why philosophers persist in trying to contradict Hume flatly instead of seeking for some more devious way out.

Recently Professor F. L. Will has contended that only through some logical slip would it be possible to arrive at the skeptical conclusion; that, in fact, there is at the bottom of the skeptical argument a confusion between two senses of the word 'future.' According to Mr Will, people like Hume and Russell are really worrying about the character of a future which by definition can never come (cf. *Mind*, vol. 56, no. 224, Oct. 1947). I feel strongly that what Mr Will says is not the case.

Let us take a very artificial example. Suppose there be 100 bags each containing 5000 balls, and every day we take out of each bag one ball and observe its color. Suppose further we have so far observed 2500 balls from each bag and found all these 100×2500 balls to be white. The man who said on our 1000th (say) day of observation that the future would be like the past (so far as the color of the balls to be observed is concerned) certainly would be saying something which has been borne out by the evidence available so far.

To be more specific, a man who said on our 1000th day of observation that the next day would be like the past and who repeated the same prediction every day since then till yesterday certainly has all the confirming evidence in his favor. It would be simply contradicting the fact to say that there is no evidence for such statements about the future of the bygone days.

However, at every moment, there is *the* future of that moment. I may be worrying about the color of the 2501st balls which we shall observe tomorrow from each of the 100 bags. The statement 1 'the 100 balls which we shall observe tomorrow will be found to be mostly white,' when made *now*, says something of the future of today. The statement 1 made yesterday or the day before yesterday or a month ago or a year ago has so far been confirmed. It is then a fact that the statement 1 made under different circumstances has been repeatedly confirmed. But does this fact constitute evidence for the statement 1 made today? The puzzle about knowledge of the future seems to be the lack of a theoretically convincing reason to assure us that the answer to the question is in the affirmative.

I should like to make two distinctions. In the first place, I think it is an empirical fact that we do believe in inductive reasoning. Thus, in the above example, we would *in fact* admit that we have strong empirical *evidence* for the statement 1 made now. And it is not this that is disputed. What is disputed is rather, whether we have any theoretical justification for our admitting that we have *evidence*, or whether, if we are justified, such *evidence* would provide a priori any guarantee for success of the prediction. In other words, we may agree so to use the word 'evidence' that, if only half of the 100 balls which we observe tomorrow will be found to be white, then we are mistaken in admitting that we have strong *evidence* for the statement 1 made now. The question is, how can we prove that we are not mistaken in admitting it? Presumably we feel certain psychologically that we are not mistaken. But something more seems to be expected. Or, we may agree to use 'evidence' in such a way that by definition it is correct to say under the circumstances that we have strong *evidence* for the statement 1 made now. The question then is, how can we guarantee that predictions like 1 made today and on the next 2499 days to come will be mostly fulfilled? I think the *fact* that we do believe that the future will be like the past alone supplies no adequate answer to skepticism about induction.

Another distinction I wish to make is that between general statements and particular predictions. Suppose, for example, we assert now the following two statements:

    i. 'Most of the balls we observe tomorrow resemble in color those observed today;'

ii. 'From 2499 days ago until 2500 days from now, most of the balls we observe on any day resemble in color those observed on its preceding day.'

If we construe the statement ii. as a conjunction of 5000 similar statements one for each day, it seems obvious that we have so far *evidence* for it in the sense that half of the conjunctive terms of the statement have been known to be true. And this is so, no matter whether we grant some principle of uniformity or not. But the statement i. seems to be in a different position. That the statement i. uttered on previous occasions has been borne out repeatedly by empirical facts does not seem to provide any ground for concluding that i. uttered today will be confirmed tomorrow, unless we accept some principle of uniformity.

At every moment, we are especially interested in the future of that moment. Every moment supplies solutions of certain old problems and brings with it its new problems. For any moment, we have no proof that there is any evidence for statements about the future of that moment. And this future is not a future that will never come, because it will come. But after it has come and become past, it will remain interesting only as a historical fact. We can indeed learn from history. However, without assuming beforehand some principle of induction, we have no theoretical assurance that the practice of guiding our activities by what we learn from history will lead to success on the whole and in the long run.

Indeed, a prophet who keeps on saying that a Utopia lies around the next corner has been confronted with contrary evidences all the time until now. But Mr Will does not tell us what is the theoretical ground of our belief that the prophet will again be confronted with contrary evidence when we turn the corner this time. The happenings around the next corner are things which do concern us. And the next corner is not a next corner which will never come, although there is yet a next corner of that next corner which will become particularly interesting to us when we have turned the corner.[6]

3 THE EXISTENCE OF MATERIAL OBJECTS

In his article on the above subject in *Mind* of October 1946 Mr A. H. Basson has considered the view that we can never know for certain that material objects exist. There he puts forward the following possible defense of the view:

> If by making the statement you do mean to say something about the future, then what happens in the future will constitute evidence for or against it. You cannot have now the evidence

you will have in the future. If, therefore, by making this statement about the present, you mean to imply something about the future, the evidence you have must *necessarily* be insufficient (pp. 315–16).

In answer to this Mr Basson says:

> We want to say that the evidence $[e_1]$ we have makes it *certain* that the table is here $[(x_1, y_1, z_1)]$ now $[t_1]$, and this makes it *highly probable* that we shall have other 'evidence' in the future. Now suppose the unexpected happens, and the table suddenly disappears. What is the bearing of this new evidence? *If* the evidence $[e_2]$ we have is sufficient to make it *certain* that the table is not here $[(x_2, y_2, z_2)]$ now $[t_2]$, this makes it *highly improbable* that the table was there before, and this makes it *highly improbable* that the evidence we believe to be sufficient *was* sufficient. But we cannot argue from the improbability of the sufficiency to the probability of the insufficiency of our later evidence; because this would make the present non-existence, and consequently the past non-existence of the table *less* probable; and this would make the insufficiency of the former evidence *less* probable, and this would make the insufficiency of the later evidence *less* probable than we had assumed. Consequently, whatever degree of probability of insufficiency of the later evidence you choose to infer from the improbability of the sufficiency of the earlier, you can prove it is in fact less. Hence it is self-contradictory to infer from doubt of the past existence to doubt of its present non-existence. And it is equally self-contradictory to infer the other way.
> I think it is clear from this, that, not only doubt of the material facts rest on certainty of some others, but also that doubt of the sufficiency of evidence likewise rests on certainty of the sufficiency of other evidence. Hence, we can know, really know, matters of fact, and that material objects, tables, chairs and the like do really exist (pp. 316–17).

I find it difficult to follow Mr Basson. Nevertheless his argument appears to me fallacious. Let '$T(x_1, y_1, z_1, t_1)$' be an abbreviation for 'The table is (tenseless) at (x_1, y_1, z_1, t_1)'; '$p(T(x_1, y_1, z_1, t_1)/e_1) = 1$' be an abbreviation for 'e_1 makes it *certain* that T is at (x_1, y_1, z_1, t_1)'; and '$p(\neg T(x_2, y_2, z_2, t_2)/e_2) = 1$' be an abbreviation for 'e_2 makes it certain that T is not at (x_2, y_2, z_2, t_2).' Mr Basson seems to say, among others, the following two things:

(a) We want to say

(1) $p(T(x_1, y_1, z_1, t_1)/e_1) = 1$;

(b) If

(2) $p(\neg T(x_2, y_2, z_2, t_2)/e_2) = 1$

is true, this makes

(3) $T(x_1, y_1, z_1, t_1)$

highly improbable, and this makes (1) highly improbable.

In other words, he seems to assert the following things:

(4) we want to say (1);

(5) (2) $\supset$ ((3) is highly improbable);

(6) ((3) is highly improbable) $\supset$ ((1) is highly improbable);

Suppose we assert in addition

(7) ((1) is highly improbable) $\supset$ ((1) is false).

From formal logic, we know that (1), (2), (5), (6), and (7) cannot be all true; because '$\neg$((1) $\wedge$ (2) $\wedge$ (5) $\wedge$ (6) $\wedge$ (7))' is tautologous, the corresponding tautologous matrix being '$\neg (p \wedge q \wedge (q \supset r) \wedge (r \supset s) \wedge (s \supset \neg p))$.' Therefore, it is necessary that at least one of (1), (2), (5), (6), and (7) is false. (5) and (6) are asserted to be true by Mr Basson. Is (7) true? It certainly does not follow from that '$T(x_1, y_1, z_1, t_1)$' is highly improbable, that '$T(x_1, y_1, z_1)$' is false, for even a highly improbable statement may be true – at least that is what is ordinarily claimed. On the other hand, does it or does it not follow from that (1) is highly improbable that (1) is false? I think it does follow, if by 'a statement is certain' we mean 'we know the statement for certain.' In other words, I think, if it is highly improbable that at t_1 we knew for certain that $T(x_1, y_1, z_1, t_1)$ on the basis of e_1, then it is true that at t_1 we did not know for certain that $T(x_1, y_1, z_1, t_1)$ on the basis of e_1. If this is the case, (7) is true. Granting this, we are driven to the conclusion that (1) and (2) contradict each other; i.e., either (1) or (2) is false, or both are false.

After having granted as much as Mr Basson seems to have done, one would, I should expect, argue roughly as follows. Since we believe e_1 to be sufficient at t_1 and cease to believe so at t_2 on account of e_2, we may cease to believe e_2 to be sufficient at some time later than t_2. Hence, the conclusion which seems to suggest itself is that both (1) and (2) are false. One may yet dispute this conclusion by bringing in various subtle things which it is impossible to anticipate and enumerate. But it appears obvious to me that the conclusion leads to no contradiction. And what puzzles me is that Mr Basson seems to argue that such a conclusion leads to a contradiction.

True, he does not quite say so. Rather he seems to say that, if we infer from doubt of the past existence of the table to doubt of its present non-existence, then we would doubt less of the past existence, and consequently doubt less of the present non-existence. On the one hand, there is the present external situation described by the statement 'the table suddenly disappears' which makes me believe the present non-existence of the table and doubt its past existence; on the other hand, there is my memory that a moment ago I thought (1) is true. Since I thought (1) is true and doubt it now, I might think (2) is true and doubt it the next moment, and so (2) would be merely highly probable. But if (2) were merely highly probable, (1) would be more probable than if (2) is true, and so it would be less probable that I should doubt (2) the next moment. And so on. Hence, Mr Basson seems to conclude, (2) is true, or at least (1) and (2) are not both false, because otherwise we would get a contradiction.

I believe there is some logical slip in Mr Basson's argument. Since we are admitting a connection between (1) and (2), we may grant that we have a fixed function $f(w)$:
$$u = f(w)$$
$$= p((p(T(x_1, y_1, z_1, t_1)/e_1) = 1)/(p(\neg T(x_2, y_2, z_2, t_2)/e_2) = w)) \quad (i)$$
Then, for any *fixed* evidence e_2, w assumes a definite value, and, consequently, u assumes a definite value. w may or may not assume the value 1. In either case, there seems to be no contradiction.

Probably the following is Mr Basson's point. Assume there is a function $g(u, w)$:
$$v = g(u, w) = p((p(\neg T(x_2, y_2, z_2, t_2)/e_2) = w)/(f(w) = u)) \quad (ii)$$
Now the value of v depends on w by (i), and conversely, the value of w also depends on v by (ii). If we admit (ii), then, for any value w, unless the value of $g(u, w)$ happens to be 1, we should encounter a contradiction, because, by (ii), the value of w would be actually different. The conclusion Mr Basson draws seems to be that we should therefore reject (ii).

I think the argument merely shows that we should in every case so choose the value w that $g(u, w)$ assumes the value 1. Intuitively this looks like a problem of finding the limit of a convergent series. And, in most cases, the value of w need not be 1 in order that $g(u, w)$ assume the value 1. There seems to be no contradiction resulting from the adoption, along with our other beliefs, of both (i) and (ii) for certain suitable f and g. Hence, I conclude that Mr Basson's argument is fallacious, or at least inadequate.[7]

4 A QUESTION ON KNOWLEDGE OF KNOWLEDGE

In his *A reply to my critics*, Moore writes:[8]

> I have sometimes distinguished between two different
> propositions, each of which has been made by some philosophers,
> namely 1 the proposition 'There are no material things' and

2 the proposition 'Nobody knows for certain that there are any material things.' And in my latest published writing, my British Academy lecture called 'Proof of an External World', I implied with regard to the first of these propositions that it could be *proved* to be false in such a way as this; namely, by holding up one of your hands and saying '*This* hand is a material thing; therefore there is at least one material thing.' But with regard to the second of those two propositions, which has, I think, been far more commonly asserted than the first, I do not think I have ever implied that *it* could be *proved* to be false in any such simple way; e.g., by holding up one of your hands and saying 'I know that this hand is a material thing; therefore at least one person knows that there is at least one material thing.'

The question which I wish to ask is merely this. Why should anybody who accepts the first proof as valid reject the second? It is a question of which I feel utterly incompetent to supply a satisfactory answer. Yet somehow I have the suspicion that this belongs to the kind of question on which readers of *Analysis* are experts.

To clarify a bit the problem. 'Those philosophers who have denied the existence of Matter have not wished to deny that under my trousers I wear pants.' Moore makes perfectly clear that he wishes only to refute those philosophers who do wish to deny that there are trousers or pants at all. Maybe Moore is hitting at a straw man. I am, however, not asking whether or not that is the case.

It has also been contended that, since the circumstances under which Moore asserted emphatically the existence of his hands were so artificial and extraordinary, he was not using language in an ordinary way and *therefore* he was not giving a valid proof. This is not relevant to the present question either, because I am asking that the validity of Moore's proof be assumed.

Apparently Moore does not wish to distinguish 'know' from 'know for certain.' Accordingly, it is not necessary to pay special attention to the question of certainty. Indeed, Moore's own proof is concerned not so much with the Cartesian doubt as with a 'Kantian dogma.'

In short, Moore holds at the same time at least two propositions: *a* 'the proposition 1 can be proved to be false by holding up one of your hands and saying "*This* hand is a material thing; therefore there is at least one material thing" '; and *b* 'the proposition 2 cannot be proved to be false in a similar way as, e.g., by holding up one of your hands and saying "I know that this hand is a material thing; therefore at least one person knows that there is at least one material thing." ' And the question is, what are the grounds for one who holds *a* to hold also *b* at the same time?

In his 'Proof of an external world,'[9] Moore gives refutations of the proposition 1. In his example, we may say, the premiss was something which he expressed by holding up one of his hands and saying, 'Here is a hand,' and the conclusion was, 'There is at least one material thing' (cf. 295–6). There he enunciates three necessary conditions for his proof to be a rigorous proof: namely *a* the premiss which he adduced as proof of the conclusion was different from the conclusion he adduced it to prove; *b* the premiss which he adduced was something which he *knew* to be the case, and not merely something which he believed but which was by no means certain, or something which, though in fact true, he did not know to be so; and *c* the conclusion did really follow from the premiss. He maintains that all these three conditions were in fact satisfied by his proof. With regard to the second condition, he says that he certainly did at the moment *know* that which he expressed by the combination of certain gestures with saying the words 'Here is a hand.' He says he *knew* that there was a hand in the place indicated by combining a certain gesture with his utterance of 'here.' And 'How absurd it would be to suggest that I did not know it, but only believed it, and that perhaps it was not the case! You might as well suggest that I do not know that I am now standing up and talking – that perhaps after all I'm not, and that it's not quite certain that I am!' (296).

Suppose one minute ago I tried to refute the proposition 2 in a similar manner, the premiss having been something which I expressed by holding up one of my hands and saying 'I know for certain here is a hand,' and the conclusion, 'At least one person knows for certain that there is at least one material thing.' Let me call this supposed proof 'my proof.' Did my proof satisfy the three conditions necessary for a rigorous proof? If it satisfied the three conditions, then Moore seems to have provided no ground for holding the proposition *b* in addition to and together with the proposition *a*. It is true that a proof satisfying these three conditions need not necessarily be a rigorous proof, for the conditions are only *necessary* conditions for a proof to be a rigorous proof. But, if the satisfaction of the three conditions does not suffice to qualify my proof as a rigorous proof, nor has Moore given any more reason for saying that his proof is a rigorous proof. Maybe there are additional conditions, the satisfaction of which together with these three conditions is sufficient to qualify a proof as a rigorous proof. And maybe it is that these additional conditions were satisfied by Moore's proof that the proposition 1 is false, but not by my proof that the proposition 2 is false. However that may be, yet he certainly has given no such additional conditions. And it must be admitted that, if my proof did satisfy the three conditions, Moore has given no reason whatsoever for his holding the proposition *b* in addition to and together with the proposition *a*.

Now, did my proof satisfy the three conditions? *a* The premiss which I adduced in proof was quite certainly different from the conclusion, and *c* it is quite certain that the conclusion did follow from the premiss, for it could not be denied that I was a person. How about the second condition? When considering his proof, Moore asserts the proposition A 'I certainly did at the moment *know* that which I expressed by the combination of certain gestures with saying the words "Here is a hand."' Suppose I assert the corresponding proposition B 'I certainly did at the moment *know* that which I expressed by the combination of certain gestures with saying the words "I know for certain that here is a hand."' Yet, if I did at the moment know my premiss, what I knew is certainly not the same kind of thing as what Moore says he knew at the moment he was refuting the proposition 1. What he says he knew is that there was a hand in the place indicated by combining a certain gesture with his utterance of 'here.' What I knew is, if I did know it, that I knew that there was a hand in the place. Thus, though his gesture helped him to indicate what he knew (his premiss), my gesture certainly did not help me to indicate what I knew (my premiss) in the same sense or to the same extent. It seems more natural to hold up one of my hands and say 'Here is a hand,' than to hold up one of my hands and say 'I know for certain that here is a hand.' The question I want to ask is, am I justified in asserting the proposition B in connection with my premiss just as Moore is justified in asserting the proposition A in connection with his premiss? If I am, then my proof satisfies his three conditions, and then he gives no reason for saying that one cannot prove the proposition 2 to be false in such a simple way as he proved the proposition 1 to be false.

It seems obvious that, in a sense, what is expressed by the words 'Here is a hand' is more closely connected with what is expressed by my gesture of holding up one of my hands than what is expressed by the words 'I know for certain that here is a hand' is. And I think we can even say that, in a sense, the circumstances of holding up one of my hands and saying 'Here is one hand' give me more knowledge about what is expressed by holding up one of my hands and saying 'Here is a hand,' than the circumstances of holding up one of my hands and saying 'I know for certain that here is a hand' give me about what is expressed by holding up one of my hands and saying 'I know for certain that here is a hand.' Also we have, in a sense, a better reason to assert the proposition A under the former circumstances than to assert B under the latter circumstances. But I cannot say exactly in what sense we have more knowledge or better reason in one case than in the other, nor do I know what bearing the point (that we have in a sense more knowledge or better reason in one case) has on the answering of the question whether I am justified in asserting the proposition B. Let us put aside these considerations and ask, am I justified in asserting the proposition B? If I am, then *b* is not true. If I am not, why?

I am interpreting the proposition *b* in such a way that it is true only if the proposition 2 cannot be proved to be false by holding up one of my hands and saying 'I know that this hand is a material thing; therefore at least one person knows that there is at least one material thing.' One might wish to interpret the proposition *b* so that it is also true if, although the proposition 2 can be proved in the above manner, the proof is not related to the proposition 2 in the same fashion as Moore's proof is to the proposition 1. If such an interpretation were adopted, what was said above would already be sufficient to establish the truth of the proposition b. I do not, however, believe that this is the correct interpretation.

Sticking to my original understanding of *b*, I can put my doubts in the following words. I am inclined to think that the proposition B is true. But if B is true, then the proposition *b* is false. At any rate, I find it difficult to say what more knowledge is required by those who question the truth of B. If, for example, it is contended that to defend the proposition B I must be able to prove I am not dreaming, then I cannot see exactly why the same should not be required for a defense of the proposition A.[10]

5 WHAT IS AN INDIVIDUAL?

I find Quine and Goodman's nominalistic position unclear; and this is because they have not explained to my satisfaction what, according to them, are the individuals or nonclasses. I wish to explain the reasons for my dissatisfaction and to suggest that until a better account of the notion of being an individual is available their distinction between nominalists and nonnominalists cannot be accepted as a very helpful way of grouping philosophies or philosophers. If the difficulties (which I shall discuss) in determining the notion of being an individual are real, then there is, so it seems to me, also ground to suppose that Quine's general criterion of using the values of variables to decide the 'ontological commitment' of a theory is not as fruitful as, for instance, the more traditional ways of distinguishing systems according to whether they admit of infinitely many things, or whether impredicative definitions are allowed, and so on. In particular, I shall argue that, for instance, finitism or no-infinity theory would be a more revealing banner for the position which Quine and Goodman call nominalism.

Quine and Goodman speak of universals, abstract entities, classes, concrete objects, concrete individuals, individuals, and the like. I shall talk only about individuals and classes (nonindividuals) and discuss relevant passages in the writings of Quine and Goodman, with special emphasis on Goodman's recent book.[11] Since many things are treated in this book with great thoroughness and precision, I am led to believe that on those specific points where I disagree with Goodman, definite answers in one way or the other will come with discussion.

I think I can distinguish in Goodman's book three related but separate explanations of the notion of individuals. I shall deal with them one by one.

The most illuminating answer presystematically (i.e. in ordinary language) seems to me to be his assertion that the nominalist recognizes no distinction of entities without a distinction of content, plus the illustration that the class of the counties of Utah is for the nominalist not different from the whole state of Utah as a single individual (p. 33). But this can, at best, be considered only as a rough account. For example, what is meant by *content* is not being made completely explicit. If a box with two layers touching each other is filled up with gunpowder, then this whole box as an individual and the whole box minus the outer layer as another individual would ordinarily be said to have the same content. Yet presumably Goodman would want to say they are different individuals. Or, if we define real numbers as certain classes of rational numbers, we ordinarily do not consider the content of the class of all reals to be the same as that of the class of all rationals. Hence, we can only conclude that Goodman intends to use the word 'content' in a special way which is illustrated but not exactly characterized by his explanation and example.

Indeed, Goodman stresses the distinction between the ordinary and the technical uses of a term. Thus, he emphasizes that the technical use of the term 'individual' need not coincide completely with popular usage (p. 42) and proceeds to suggest defining individuals as all and only those things which *overlap* something (p. 43). I take this as his second explanation of the notion of individuals. In offering this definition, he could not mean to suggest that this definition is more satisfactory because the use of the term 'overlaps' is completely known intuitively. Rather such a definition is helpful to him, so it seems, only because his calculus of individuals characterizes the predicate 'overlaps' postulationally. This leads me to what I understand to be his third answer.

In other words, individuals are all and only those things for which there is a certain relation R such that, by taking R as the interpretation of the only primitive predicate '*o*' ('overlaps') of Goodman's calculus of individuals, and by taking these things as constituting the universe of discourse, all the theorems (including the postulates) of his calculus are true under the normal interpretation of the constants of quantification theory. Or more briefly, individuals are the things which satisfy his calculus of individuals.

Against such a kind of explanation, it might be asked, if the technical use is to be determined by the calculus, what guides us in our construction of the calculus? Do we not need an intuitive notion of individuals (or of overlapping) to begin with? However, such questions could only arise for someone who had already understood Goodman's notion and wished to dispute its correctness. Since my purpose is merely to understand his notion, I do not have to ask such questions, which more or less have to do with justifying his notion as right. The first problem for me is, rather, do I consider the use of postulate systems a satisfactory way of communicating one's notions? I happen to think that in many cases in general, and with regard to the notion of individuals in particular, the answer is yes, provided the calculus offered is fairly complete, in the sense that it determines to a reasonable degree the range of permissible interpretations. Indeed, to take another example, I consider the standard theories of classes (such as those of Russell and Zermelo) in many respects the clearest and most exact answers available at present to the question: what is a class? Hence, the next problem for me is to study Goodman's calculus and try to find out whether it can be considered as fairly complete.

Unfortunately, this is not easy, because he decides not to give a complete account of his calculus (p. 43). However, he does refer to published versions of the calculus of individuals (p. 42, footnote). So let us translate the postulates of these earlier calculi into his language, and assume that the results are the postulates of his calculus. Then his calculus includes only one postulate schema and one specific postulate:[12]

1 If $\exists w \ldots w$, then $\exists x \forall y (yox \equiv \exists z (\ldots z \wedge yoz))$.
2 xoy if and only if $\exists z (\forall w(woz \supset wox) \wedge \forall w(woz \supset woy))$.

Another postulate of the older systems is replaced by a definition for identity (p. 45):

3 $x = y$ if and only if $\forall z (zox \equiv zoy)$.

From 2 we can show that the relation of overlapping is both reflexive and symmetric. We can also derive the ordinary theory of identity in the usual manner.

With regard to this calculus G, a few things may be noted. It admits of many different interpretations. For example, we can take the universe as consisting of a single thing ς such that '$\varsigma o\varsigma$' is true. Or, we can use a model in which the universe consists of an arbitrary finite or infinite number of things. In other words, G is satisfiable in every nonempty domain. If we want to restrict somewhat the range of admissible interpretations, we have to introduce some postulates which determine an upper or lower bound of the number of things in the universe. This seems to indicate that the calculus G as it stands does not embody an adequate explanation of the notion of individuals. G differs from the older calculi in that it is isolated from the theories of classes. Thus, in place of 1, these older calculi contain a postulate which amounts to:

4 If the class of all z such that . . . z is not empty, then $\exists x\ \forall y$ $(yox \equiv \exists z\ (. . . z \land yoz))$.

If the class theory happens to contain postulates such as the axiom of infinity of the theory of types, then 4 is much stronger than 1 and can generate many different new things on account of the accompanying class theory.

Since the calculus G does not even delimit roughly the range of admissible interpretations, it only partially determines what individuals are and this must be fixed by supplementary decisions. Goodman asserts (p. 35) that for different actual systems quite different elements may be chosen as individuals. And, in general, he wants to admit all those interpretations which satisfy the postulates of G. More exactly, he wants to admit all systems which contain G and certain additional postulates or also additional primitive predicates. But this obviously will not do. For instance, we could add to G strong postulates of infinity, or we could even adjoin (say) the whole Zermelo set theory to G. The system resulting from adding the Zermelo set theory to G would be just like his realistic system (pp. 147, 173) in containing just one kind of variable, one additional predicate ('ε' in this case instead of his 'W'), and a number of additional postulates. Clearly he does not want to consider such a system nominalistic. Hence, we need to use judgment in choosing our systems and interpretations. But then we seem to have to assume some intuitive notion of individuals to guide our judgment. Undoubtedly such intuitive notions often differ, and there is probably no generally acceptable procedure to resolve such differences. For instance, I confess that I have no intuition with regard to the alternatives as to whether there are infinitely many individuals, and yet this, as we shall see, is a most crucial question regarding one's understanding of the nominalistic position.

At some places, Goodman seems to emphasize unduly the theoretical implications of the notation of a system (p. 35). He seems to contend that we are perfectly free in selecting the individuals to be admitted, so long as we do not also use a different kind of variable which takes classes as values. However, since we possess class theories (for instance, Zermelo's) each of which contains one kind of variable, and since, if we want to, we can obviously use some other symbol in place of the obnoxious 'ε,' clearly we can decide whether a system has variables taking classes as values, or not, only by examining its postulates and not merely by examining its notation.[13] However, when we come to deciding whether to accept certain postulates, I think we usually possess more helpful criteria than just asking whether it commits us to classes. In any case it would certainly be extremely difficult to construct a general theory about deciding which kind of postulates commit us to interpret the variables as taking classes as values. I think, for example, a much more useful way of deciding the commitment of postulates is to ask whether a postulate or a postulate system requires a domain of infinitely many things for its interpretation.

Goodman remarks specifically that his calculus is to contain no postulate implying that the number of individuals is either finite or infinite (p. 48). Therefore, it is not allowable to take as a postulate of his calculus any of the usual postulates of infinity, such as:

5 $\forall x \, \exists y \, (x \ll y)$.
6 $\forall x \, \exists y \, (y \ll x)$.

Moreover, this also precludes the possibility of including in the calculus any postulate saying that the number of individuals is no more than a definite positive integer (for instance, 100 or 10^{37}):

7 $\exists x_1 \ldots \exists x_{100} \, \forall y \, (y = x_1 \vee \ldots \vee y = x_{100})$.
8 $\exists x_1 \ldots \exists x_{10^{37}} \, \forall y \, (y = x_1 \vee \ldots \vee y = x_{10^{37}})$.

Other postulates which are being thus precluded are those, if there be any such, that exclude infinity but do not fix any numerical limits. Such postulates would express in effect something like:

9 There exists some indefinite positive integer n, such that there are no more than n individuals.

The view implicit in this attitude seems to be that whether the number of individuals is taken as finite or infinite does not affect his nominalistic doctrine and language. And this is a point which I wish to dispute. I wish to suggest that, so far as our power to comprehend is concerned, the introduction of infinity generates more decisive and definite difficulties than the talk about classes. If we assume only finitely many individuals, both the calculus of individuals and that of classes should be considered, by any reasonable standard, as comprehensible. On the other hand, if we assume some natural postulate of infinity with regard to individuals, even the calculus of individuals might appear to be not completely acceptable to the radical nominalist.

Consider first the alternative that there are no more than a definite finite number of individuals: for instance, that assertion 8 is true. Then, as Quine has shown in great detail,[14] the whole nonnominalistic theory of classes (in the form of the simple theory of types with 8 replacing the axiom of infinity) becomes trivialized and can be explained away as a mere manner of speaking. As a result, we can say that, if we assume a definite finite upper bound to the number of individuals, then there is no need to distinguish the theory of individuals and of classes between nominalistic and nonnominalistic languages. It is true that the scrupulous nominalist might object to the use of '. . .' in the statement of 8, on the ground that there would not be enough matter to write it out explicitly.[15] However, it would be utterly unbelievable that anybody should be able to comprehend some sophisticated calculus of individuals but not 8. The finitistic nominalist, if such there be, only refuses to admit infinity, and therefore, incidentally, refuses to admit certain things ordinarily asserted in class theory. The difference between him and us ordinary people depends on whether infinity is recognized, not on whether classes are.

Let us now turn to the more serious alternative of adopting some postulate of infinity of individuals. Although Goodman explicitly declines to include any postulate of infinity in his calculus, he apparently does not consider all such postulates absurd or plainly false. For example, he mentions in a quite friendly manner the statement (our 6) that every individual has a proper part (p. 48), and asserts that an individual may be divisible into any number of parts (p. 42). Suppose we add 6 to the calculus of individuals as a new postulate. Then we can see that the resulting calculus of individuals is far more complex and ethereal than the theory of classes founded on finitely many individuals.

Thus, an individual a has a proper part b which has a proper part c, etc. Hence, given any individual a, we can find b, c, d, etc., such that $a \gg b \gg c \gg d \gg$. . . . Consider now the individuals $a - b$, $b - c$, $c - d$, etc. which are discrete from one another and are proper parts of a. Therefore, each individual contains an infinite number of discrete proper parts. Hence, once we admit the simple postulate 6,

421

use of the calculus of individuals opens the door to infinitely many proper parts, infinitely many proper parts of each proper part, etc., of each of the given individuals.

Despite all these considerations, I am inclined to consider the alternative of admitting infinity more interesting. In my opinion, a comparative study of a calculus of individuals (with infinity assumed) and the ordinary class theories might lead to illuminating distinctions. Such an investigation is, I think, one direction which could perhaps make the position of rejecting everything except individuals significantly fruitful.

Goodman does not agree to this view but feels[16] that any assumption of infinity is highly objectionable. He does not wish to use any of the postulates like 5–8, but is more interested in postulates that would give the effect of 9. Indeed, Goodman himself first brought up and discussed in his classes the problem of how such a postulate can be expressed in his calculus. William Craig has conjectured that we can prove the impossibility of formulating any such postulate in the framework of Goodman's calculus of individuals. The difficulty seems to be, unless infinity is assumed, there is no way of introducing variables which would range over all positive integers; and in order to express 9, we seem to need such variables. For instance, it is possible, as Goodman has observed, to express both that there is a universal individual containing all individuals, and that there are atoms which have no individual proper parts. But to exclude infinity, we seem to need in addition something like a postulate of Archimedes which assures us that there is some positive integer n such that the universal individual is at most n times as (say) big as any given atom. Goodman appears to consider 9 to be true, although he wants also to say that the language used in expressing 9 is a language which he does not understand.

It we assume 9 instead of postulates such as 8, then the easy way, mentioned above, of explaining away classes is no longer directly available. However, I think, we should still be able to dispense with 9 in every particular case. In the first place, 9 is thought to be useful where the universe dealt with is finite but the number of individuals quite unknown. In most ordinary cases, when we know that the number is finite but have no exact knowledge of the number, we are able to fix a rough but safe upper bound (sometimes with considerable reflection); such as in the case of the number of cats in the world, or the number of hairs on the heads of all people on the earth. Yet even the finitude or infinitude of the number of individuals in each of Goodman's systems is apparently a question not easily decidable. In any case, if we know that the universe is finite, we can argue, so to speak, schematically and carry out the elimination of classes as before. Thus, if 9 is true, there must exist an upper bound to the number of individuals. Assume this number is t (a positive integer, we do not know exactly how large). Then,

$$10 \quad \exists x_1 \ldots \exists x_t \, \forall y \, (y = x_1 \vee \ldots \vee y = x_t)$$

must be true and can be taken as a postulate. Therefore, we can again carry out Quine's procedure[17] and explain away the classes.

To sum up. If we assume that there are only finitely many things altogether and stick to a language that excludes infinity, then the talk about classes is in any case clear and harmless. On the other hand, if we admit infinity, Goodman finds that the calculus of individuals would also lose its philosophical and intuitive advantage. Therefore, the appeal of nominalism to him is largely caused by his association of nominalism with the rejection of infinity. However, it is certainly not generally agreed that individuals are finite in number. Taking all these considerations into account, would it not be more illuminating to call his position finitism (or no-infinity theory) rather than nominalism?

Personally, I am inclined to think that it is hard to adhere to such a finitism. For instance, the use of the schema 1 in G which amounts to an infinity of postulates, and the ability to understand 9 (even though not to express it), tend to indicate that in certain very definite senses even the 'nominalist' understands and uses infinity. Or again, how are we going to develop science and mathematics if even the use of variables taking all positive integers as values is not allowed? Maybe diligent and thorough analysis of the foundations of science would some day yield a satisfactory theory which would prove that all talk about infinity is nothing but a shortcut method of speaking about finite and discrete entities. That would be a great achievement indeed. Meanwhile, given the actual knowledge we do possess now, we are, I think, justified in considering, at the present stage, the no-infinity theory as either basically untenable or at least as too Utopian to be interesting and significant.[18]

NOTES

1 For a thorough treatment of the points raised in the next three paragraphs, cf. Professor C. D. Broad's 'Hr. von Wright on the logic of induction,' *Mind*, vol. 53, 1944, pp. 1–24, 97–119, 193–214.

2 *The ground of induction*, 1946; see especially chapter 4. Professor Lewis pursues reasoning along similar lines on pp. 272–5 of his new book *An analysis of knowledge and valuation*, 1946. But it is interesting to note that there he does not use the argument to justify induction. On the contrary, he

points out that it will have force only if some general ground for validity of induction is assumed beforehand.

3 His theory was put forward in *Wahrscheinlichkeitslehre* and ch. V of *Experience and prediction*. References of page numbers will be made to the second work.

4 Op. cit. Professor Lewis's justification is given principally in chapter XI of the book. Note, however, the discussion of probability in chapter X has led him to conclude that the (rational) 'credibility of a statement "*P*" coincides with the intent of "It is probable that *P*," in a sense of "probable" which is commonly current and represents the only basic meaning of "probable" which it is necessary to consider' (p. 316). Hence in chapter XI he uses 'probable' and 'credible' almost as synonyms.

5 This section appeared in *J. philosophy*, vol. 44, 1947, pp. 701–10.

6 This note appeared in *Phil. of sci.*, vol. 17, 1950, pp. 333–5.

7 This note appeared in *Mind*, vol. 52, 1948, pp. 488–90.

8 *The Philosophy of G. E. Moore*, ed. P. A. Schilpp, 1942, p. 668.

9 *Proc. of the British Academy*, vol. 25, 1939, pp. 273–300.

10 This note appeared in *Analysis*, vol. 14, 1954, pp. 142–6.

11 N. Goodman, *The Structure of appearance*, 1951. All page references in this paper, unless otherwise indicated, are to this book. To avoid misunderstanding, I wish to emphasize that the significance and interest of most questions treated in Goodman's book are quite independent of its author's adherence to a nominalism which I find unclear.

12 See *J. symbolic logic*, vol. 5, pp. 48–9, 108.

13 In other words, it is, in my opinion, not sufficient to underline the words 'individual,' 'overlap,' etc., but it is necessary to develop an adequate calculus of individuals. If the meaning of a word is its use, it is important to know what statements involving the word are taken to be true.

14 W. V. Quine, 'On Universals,' *J. symbolic logic*, vol. 12, 1947, pp. 74–84. Compare also Kurt Gödel, 'Russell's mathematical logic' in *The philosophy of Bertrand Russell*, 1944, ed. P. A. Schilpp, especially p. 144.

15 Quine, op. cit., p. 84.

16 I have asked Professor Goodman to read an earlier draft of this paper, and received from him helpful explanations and criticisms. In this revised version, I am using his remarks and statements freely, fully aware that these need not represent faithfully his final position on the matters I consider.

17 See Quine, op. cit.

18 This section appeared in *Philos. rev.*, vol. 62, 1953, pp. 413–20.

INDEX

abstract structure, 37–40, 241
Achilles, 69, 70
Ackermann, Wilhelm, 8, 87, 149
Aiken, Howard, 291
analytic philosophy, *see* linguistic philosophy; positivism
analyticity, 14, 23–7, 34, 234, 251–79, 379, 382
apriority, 23–7, 61–2, 251–79
Archimedes, 72
Argand, J. R., 61
Aristotle, 16, 32, 131–43, 251, 263, 264, 345, 372, 386, 387, 389
artificial intelligence, *see* mechanical intelligence
axiomatic method, 18, 21, 35–8, 169–70
Ayer, A. J., 7, 270

Babbage, Charles, 291
Bacon, Francis, 351, 385
Baire, R., 203
Basson, A. H., 409–12
Beethoven, Ludwig van, 227
Berkeley, George, 70, 71, 369
Bernays, Paul, 10, 127, 148, 175, 183, 187, 259, 291
Bernoulli, Johann, 71
Bishop, Erret, 80, 248, 249
Blanshard, B., 5, 24
Bohr, Niels, 7, 341
Bolzano, Bernhard, 70, 73, 74, 145, 149, 161
Boole, George, 21, 148, 290
Bourbaki, N., 37, 40, 241
Bradley, F. H., 272, 377

Brouwer, L. E. J., 7, 41, 50, 54, 61, 62, 68, 79, 118, 129, 253, 257, 268, 316, 322
Burali-Forti, C., 48, 188, 191, 214, 215
Burnside, W., 247

calculation, 91–5, 231–2, 241–2
Cantor, Georg, 7, 30, 40, 41, 48, 68, 70, 74, 76, 175, 182, 185, 187–91, 199, 207, 208, 210–19, 240, 261, 383
Carnap, Rudolf, 3, 7, 18, 30, 40, 171, 269, 270, 365, 373, 377, 378–83
Carroll, Lewis, 260
Cassirer, Ernst, 368
Cauchy, Augustin-Louis, 74
Chang, Pinghsi, 359
Chu, Hsi, 359
Chuangtse, 332, 345, 394
Church, Alonzo, 96, 172, 173, 177
Cohen, P. J., 198
Collingwood, R. G., 324, 375, 376
computers, 17, 26, 28, 280–97, 365–6; and brains, 304–5; and logic, 22, 282–3, 290–6; mathematical arguments on, 315–26; simulation of thought, 309–15
Confucius, 383, 359–60
consistency, 33–4, 41–51, 174–5, 247
constructivity, 10–12, 22, 27, 95–9, 247–9, 317–21
continuum, 17, 21, 69–81
continuum hypothesis, 9, 11–12, 25, 198

Darwin, Charles, 372
Davis, Martin, 9

Index

Index

logic, 1, 23–4, 170; Aristotle's, 131–43; and computers, 290–6; and formalization, 27–8, 55–7; mathematical, 21–2, 28, 31, 51–2, 172–9, 367; relation to philosophy, ix, 13, 22–8, 51–7, 370, 379; three senses of, 20–1
logical truth, 121–3, 143–63
Lorentz, H., 260
Löwenheim, L., 10, 154
Löwenheim's Theorem, 10–11, 177–8
Lu, Hsiangshan, 359

Mach, Ernst, 12, 377, 380
Mahlo, P., 197, 203, 204
Markov, A. A., 294
Martin, D. A., xiv, 222
Marx, Karl, 143, 345
Marxism, 2, 332, 354
mathematical induction, 62–7, 175
mathematics, ix–x, 1, 13, 21, 22, 27, 34–5, 224–50; abstract history of, 243–4; as activity, 224–33; some examples of problem solving, 224–6; influence on computers, 281–3; mechanical, 228–30, 247, 283–7; philosophy of, 16, 18, 21, 30–5; and physics, 25–7, 367, 370; reduction to logic, *see* reductionism, of mathematics to logic
Matijasevicz, Ju., 297
mechanical, 15–16; intelligence. 306–9, 365; procedure, 22, 32, 37, 81–99, 174–5
mechanism, 298–303
Mendel, G., 1, 362, 384
metalogic, 166–180, *see also* logic
Mill, J. S., 91, 365
Milne, E. A., 369
Mirimanoff, D., 187, 190, 191, 213
Moore, G. E., 14, 106, 257, 270, 349, 350, 360, 376–8, 412–16

Napier, J., 243
natural number, 21, 43–5, 59–68; axiomatization of, 62–7; truth definition for, 9, 168–9
necessity, 13, 162–3, 251–79
Neurath, O., 380
Newton, I., 14, 20, 26, 162, 280, 364, 367, 368, 372
Novikov, P. S., 294

paradoxes, 41–2, 104–8, 187–8, 190–3
Pauli, W., 381

Peano, G., 43, 62, 64, 65, 75, 243, 383
Pears, David, 29
Peirce, C. S., 148
Péter, R., 98
philosophy, ix–x, 1–20, 334, 353–60. 363; on contemporary, ix–x, 3, 13, 15–16, 370–3, 374–84; and science, 4–6, 8–13, 15, 363–4, 367–74
Plato, 5, 37, 188, 377
Poincaré, H., 32, 206, 229, 240, 269, 286, 313, 352
Polya, G., 248
positivism, ix, 3, 7–13, 20, 24, 370–3, 377–84
Post, E., 148, 172, 293, 294
Prandtle, L., 366
predicate calculus, 111, 113–14, 176–9; completeness of, 8–11, 149–51, 178; as logic, 21, 143–5
Presburger, M., 175
Protagoras, 155
Ptolemy, 372
Putnam, Hilary, 162, 273
Pythagoras, 72

quantification theory, *see* predicate calculus
Quine, W. V., 3, 122, 371–3, 379, 416, 417, 421, 423

Ramanujan, S., 286
Ramsey, F. P., 54, 56, 57, 118, 120, 121, 123, 160, 377
recursive functions, 86–9
reductionism, 3–4, 298–303, 363; of mathematics to logic, 23–5, 32–3, 67, 103, 120–1, 233–9, 377, 383
Reichenbach, H., 377, 403–5
Revelle, Roger, 340
Richard, Jules, 107, 352
Riemann, G. F. B., 244, 246, 286
Rosser, J. B., 174
Russell, Bertrand, 23, 45, 56, 57, 70, 71, 74, 77, 78, 103–29, 160–1, 170, 187–8, 191, 215, 233, 235, 240, 269, 346–53, 370, 371, 377, 399, 407, 418
Ryle, Gilbert, 369

Santayana, G., 334, 351
Sartre, J. P., 347, 354
Schlick, M., 380, 382
Schönfinkel, M., 116
Schopenhauer, A., 380, 382
Schröder, E., 352

427

Index

Schrödinger, E., 13
Schütte, Kurt, 128
set, 181–223; the iterative concept of, 181–90
set theory, 22, 27, 41–2, 104–8, 181–223, 240–1; axioms of, 17, 25, 184–6, 200–4, 210–13, 246–7
Shaw, G. B., 239, 346
Skolem, Thoralf, 8–11, 66, 149–50, 168, 175, 177, 284, 351
Slote, M., 162
Smith, N. K., 264
Spengler, O., 337
Spinoza, B., 36, 331–3, 335
Stebbings, S., 228
Stein, Howard, 29
Stone, M. H., 190
Strawson, P. F., 393
substantial factualism, 1–7, 15–20, 258, 263, 384–8

Tarski, Alfred, 9, 169, 175, 379
Tharp, L. H., xiv
theory of types, 105–6
Tolstoi, L., 350
Toynbee, A., 337
Turing, A. M., 11, 81, 172, 177–9, 294, 309, 325, 326

Turing machine, 90–5, 292, 300, 302, 303, 306, 315–21

Vièta, F., 243
von Karman, T., 366
von Neumann, J., 10, 187, 190–2, 215–18, 245, 287, 291, 381

Wallas, G., 286
Weber, Max, 336–7
Weierstrass, Karl, 74, 286
Weinstein, Scott, xiv
Wessel, C., 61, 261
Weyl, H., 245, 248
Whitehead, A. N., 18, 121, 170, 269, 350, 377
Will, F. L., 409
Williams, D. C., 400–2
Windelband, W., 142, 354
Wittgenstein, L., 13, 30, 44, 54–7, 116, 118, 121, 123, 147, 158, 162, 171, 269, 270, 348, 350–2, 377–80, 382, 391

Yessenin-Volpin, A. S., 290

Zeno, 69
Zermelo, E., 12, 186–8, 190, 192, 212, 213, 352, 418–20

428

Printed in Great Britain
by Amazon

27251450R00248